THE
HISTORY OF CLEVELAND

BY
REV. JOHN GRAVES

with a new Introduction by
ROBERT WOOD

Republished by
PATRICK & SHOTTON
1972

Republished 1972 by Patrick & Shotton
17 Norton Road
Stockton-on-Tees

Printed in Great Britain by
Scolar Press Limited, Menston, Yorkshire

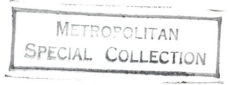

INTRODUCTION

Of all those pioneers who wrote the first histories of the districts around the Tees, the Rev. John Graves is the least known. Hutchinson published his History of Durham in 1785, the Rev. Brewster the History of Stockton-on-Tees in 1796, Graves the History of Cleveland in 1808, and Sir Cuthbert Sharp the History of Hartlepool in 1816. All these authors except Graves achieved the distinction of being included in the Dictionary of National Biography, and all except Graves have the publication of their History noted under the appropriate date in Richmond's Local Records of Stockton and the Neighbourhood'.

It is difficult to understand why. His work is as well written and as scholarly as any of the others. Indeed, even John Walker Ord in the preliminary announcement seeking subscribers for his projected History and Antiquities of Cleveland, wishing to justify the publication of a new history, had to admit grudgingly of the Rev. Graves that his work had been written with much taste and exhibited considerable industry and learning. His chief criticisms were that it was too abstruse and pedantic for general reading and its information too antiquated, being thirty-five years out of date. A queerer reason for condemning a history book I have yet to hear of!

Graves spent fifty years of his life on Teesside. Although a native of Cumberland, being born at Threkeld in 1761, he was already at Stockton by the time he was in his twenties. In 1783 he married Mary Bedford Rayner there, and it is interesting to note that it was the Rev. John Brewster who performed the ceremony, a future fellow historian he must have seen often in the subsequent fifty years, for they both spent parts of their lives at Stockton and later, when Brewster was Rector of Egglescliffe, Graves was Curate of Yarm on the other side of the river. He became the first master of the newly-established Grammar School in Stockton in 1785, and a little later the master of the Grammar School at Yarm, a post he held till within a few months of his death in 1832. In 1794 he became incumbent of Kirklevington, and later in the same year perpetual Curate of High Worsall, where he lived for a short time until he was appointed Curate of Yarm in 1797 and took up his residence there.

Little is known of any other literary activities of the Rev. Graves, but it is obvious from the contents of his History that he must have spent years compiling the information about each parish and seeking out and copying any relevant mediaeval document to which he could gain access. In his day, long before the publication of the Rolls Series and the Calendars of State Papers, accurate information about the past was hard to come by, and present-day historians can but marvel at the amount of material he succeeded in collecting before he attempted to write his book. How many documents he read through and had to cast to one side as irrelevant to his purpose, we shall never know.

Only those writers who have attempted a pioneer study in history can truly appreciate the difficulty of his task. A historian in a large scale study such as the History of Cleveland is attempting to trace the sequence of events which led to the situation at the time of his writing. He is in the position of an explorer on a mountain peak looking back over a landscape hidden beneath the clouds. Here and there he can see other peaks piercing the mist, and he knows that the road to the peak on which he stands has passed close by those other landmarks, and with their aid he seeks to penetrate the gloom and trace the unseen road. Sometimes there seem to be alternative routes and he has to decide which seems the true one, but only after vainly pursuing the others. After the outline of the road has been determined he can then examine at his leisure the portions he finds of most interest to him, and fit into their correct sequence those clearings in the mist in which everything can be distinctly observed.

The local historian in most parts of England can look back with some certainty to the Domesday Book for entries concerning his own area. He can expect to find entries and valuations arising out of the Dissolution of Monasteries and comments in any monkish chronicle concerning the national events in which his study is involved. Within the tenuous framework of these solid pieces of information he can hope to build up a complete representation of the period and the place he is interested in.

Those who follow him may do a great and valuable service in adding and enlarging on various aspects of the history of his area, but if the pioneer has done his work thoroughly and well, then every succeeding historical study simply adds weight and bulk to his original outline. We therefore have every reason to be grateful to the Rev. John Graves, and other circumstances have arisen to make his History of more than ordinary value. He wrote at a time when the Industrial Revolution had scarcely touched this part of England. Stockton was still proud of building its first bridge over the Tees, as the Bridge Penny of Christopher and Jennett bears witness, the Stockton and Darlington Railway was not even dreamed of, and Middlesbrough, as Graves says himself, 'consists only of four farmhouses'.

His description conjures up a picture of eighteenth-century bucolic serenity, a landscape of prosperous farms, and the great houses of the gentry, where the chief concern of the respectable inhabitant was the fertility of the soil, the selection of suitable crops, the tracing of ancestral pedigrees, and the suitable employment of the labouring poor. John Walker Ord was right in pressing on with the publication of a new History of Cleveland, but he gave the wrong reasons for doing so. By 1843 the Cleveland of the Rev. John Graves belonged to a different age, not yet remote enough in time to be appreciated as a world apart, but far enough to be considered hopelessly old-fashioned by smart pushing young men such as Ord. The slow tranquility of the agricultural life of Cleveland had been replaced by the brisk, brash age of the railway and other mechanical marvels, in which everyone was trying to better himself and all progress was good, for no-one questioned in which direction it was heading. In Graves' Cleveland everyone knew his place and kept to the ordered tenor of his ways. Like the charming engravings in his book, everything was pleasant and static.

Graves 'History of Cleveland' displays his love of the countryside and his solicitude for the lot of the agricultural worker. Although he treats his betters with due respect, he was no sycophant, which probably accounts for his failure to gain advancement in the Church. His indomitable industry and quiet efficiency evidently left a great impression in that small portion of the North Riding to which he proved a faithful pastor. When G. M. Tweddle went seeking information concerning him forty years after his death to include in his 'Bards and Authors of Cleveland and South Durham', the impression he gathered so stirred him that on sitting down to compose a potted biography he was filled with indignation.

That probably was the cause of the rather incoherent comment he made in his book:

'From that time (i.e. 1808) to the present the work has held a respectable place among local history. It would be as easy as it would be useless to point out a few faults and many omissions in the work under consideration: but when we remember that our author was the pioneer to open out the path for all future historians of Cleveland, with comparatively few books for reference in his labours; that he had the parishes to map out for us, and the clay and stubble alike to gather for the bricks of his edifice; even some of his brother clergymen (like poor drunken Deason of Whorlton) throwing impediments in his way instead of stretching out a helping hand; and that at the time he was writing his History of Cleveland he was also teaching the Yarm Grammar School, and (with the single exception of someone to take the Sunday duty for him at Kirklevington) he faithfully discharged his pastoral duties as incumbent of the two benefices of High Worsall and Kirklevington and the curacy of Yarm; and that his income from all sources never realised THREE HUNDRED POUNDS a year, men like Graves and the learned sources never being appreciated in the Church, whilst drones not worthy to buckle their shoes rolled in luxury—one's blood boils at the thoughts.'

Very rarely does the Rev. Graves exhibit his personal feelings in the massive work he undertook, and where he had cause to criticise he made his protest calmly, as when, for instance, the Rev. Deason of Whorlton already mentioned above ignored repeated requests to supply extracts from his Parish Register. He mildly stated:

'A slight attention to the subjects of our enquiry would not, we conceive, have interfered greatly with Mr. D.'s more important studies, nor in any degree unfitted him for the serious duties of his profession'; from which comment no stranger was likely to infer that Mr. Deason spent most of his waking moments drunk.

On one occasion I suspect he allowed his personal feelings to break the neutrality of authorship. He uses the lines of Goldsmith's Deserted Village:

'Sweet smiling village, loveliest of the lawn
Thy sports are fled and all thy charms are gone;
Amidst thy bowers the tyrant's hand is seen,
And desolation saddens all thy green.'

to describe Worsall, where he and his wife had spent part of their early married life and where, a quarter of a century after he had written his book, they were both laid to rest in the churchyard.

This reprint of Graves in its original format of ruled pages and long f's conjures up in its printing and its contents an eighteenth-century world about which we know so little and should desire to know more. It is left to John Walker Ord to show us an emergent Cleveland blindly pushing forward to the twentieth century.

OCTOBER 1972 R. WOOD

Cleveland Hills, from Cliffrigg-Wood.

Drawn by J.B.

Engraved by N. Smith.

THE

History & Antiquities

of

CLEVELAND.

Designd & Engraved by Humphrey Collins Historical Chalk Engraver.

CARLISLE

Printed and Published by F. Jollie.

1808

Lambert Sculp.

THE

HISTORY

OF

CLEVELAND,

IN THE NORTH RIDING OF THE COUNTY OF YORK ;

COMPREHENDING

AN HISTORICAL AND DESCRIPTIVE VIEW

OF THE

ANCIENT AND PRESENT STATE OF EACH PARISH

WITHIN THE

WAPONTAKE OF LANGBARGH;

THE SOIL, PRODUCE, AND NATURAL CURIOSITIES ;

WITH THE ORIGIN AND GENEALOGY

Of the principal FAMILIES within the DISTRICT.

BY THE REV. JOHN GRAVES.

CARLISLE :

PRINTED BY F. JOLLIE AND SONS;

AND SOLD BY J. TODD, YORK ; CHRISTOPHER & JENNETT, STOCKTON ; AND BY VERNOR, HOOD, AND SHARPE, POULTRY; AND W. CLARKE, NEW BOND-STREET, LONDON.

1808.

TO THE VERY REVEREND

GEORGE MARKHAM, D. D.

DEAN OF YORK,

THE FOLLOWING

HISTORY OF CLEVELAND,

IS

MOST HUMBLY INSCRIBED AND DEDICATED,

AS

A GRATEFUL TRIBUTE OF RESPECT,

BY

THE AUTHOR.

ADVERTISEMENT.

ON presenting the following work to the public, the Author feels himself called upon to acknowledge his obligations to those Gentlemen, who have contributed materials to, and otherwise occasionally assisted in the undertaking ; and has only to regret that these contributions have not been more numerous, and their assistance of greater importance.

HIS grateful acknowledgements are particularly due to the Clergy resident within the District, who (with a few exceptions) readily furnished Tables of Baptisms, &c. from their respective Parish Registers, and other local information.

INTRODUCTION.

On reviewing the materials which we have been able to collect for the compilation of the following Hiſtory, we meet with but few cir-cumſtances that throw any conſiderable light on the ancient ſtate of CLEVELAND; ſuch, however, as have occurred we will preſent to our readers, before we proceed to a more detailed account of each parti-cular pariſh within the diſtrict.

ALTHOUGH, from the natural face of the country, we are induced to believe, that the Romans were never ſtationed, in any conſiderable numbers, nor for any length of time, in this diſtrict, we are, never-theleſs, confident that it was, at an early period, known to, and in the poſſeſſion of that people; its ſituation bordering on the coaſt of the German ocean, and the vicinity of Dunſley Bay, the *Dunum Sinus** mentioned by Ptolemy, as a landing place, which they frequently uſed, are arguments that tend to confirm this opinion. Here, we are told, they landed their recruits, and marched them into the interior parts of the country, as occaſion might require.

WE have no written evidence, on which we can form any certain concluſion, as to the firſt inhabitants of this part of Britain; the moſt generally received opinion is, that they derived their origin from the *Celtæ*, or Gauls, ſettled on the oppoſite ſhores, who tranſ-ported themſelves hither for the ſake of plunder or traffic; and find-

---

* It is remarked by Mr. Gough, in his edition of Cambden, that Horſley places *Dunium* at the mouth of the river *Tees*, without noticing *Dunſley*: from which a Roman road runs for ſeveral miles over the moors to York, now called *Wade's Cauſeway*: which, it ſeems, eſcaped Mr. Camb-den's obſervation, when he viſited *Wade's Grave*.

A

ing the country fertile and falubrious, and commodioufly fituated
for trade, fettled near the fhores, and introduced the practice of agriculture. This fuppofition, which is generally adopted by our beft
hiftorians, is founded on the ftriking fimilarity in their government,
religion, language, manners, and complexion. Befides, when Julius
Cæfar firft meditated the conqueft of Britain, we are informed that
the natives had confiderable intercourfe with the Gauls, and affifted
them in their wars againft Cæfar; which is alledged as the principal
caufe of the invafion of Britain by the Romans. There are many
refpectable authorities in fupport of this affertion, which it would be
impertinent and foreign to our purpofe to produce; it is fufficient to obferve, that the diftrict under our immediate confideration, was peopled
by the *Brigantes*, whofe territories were very extenfive, including the
counties of *Cumberland*, *Durham*, *Lancafhire*, *Weftmorland*, and *Yorkfhire;*
but, whether this was the original name of the inhabitants of this part
of Britain, feems uncertain. The *Brigantes* of the Alps are ftiled by Strabo, *graffatores*, *robbers*,* and it feems no improbable conjecture, that this
name was beftowed on the Britons by the Romans, as a mark of con-
tempt, in allufion to " *the mountainous tract they inhabited, and the Tar-*
" *tar-like bands in which they marauded.*" If this definition be admitted, we may obferve that this, and many other diftricts may boaft the
honour of as noble a defcent as the city of Rome, though we are ftill
uninformed of the real Britifh name of the inhabitants.

As to the internal police, and public character of the *Brigantes*,
the Roman writers afford us a very fuperficial account: all that they

---

* It is the remark of a learned etymologift, that " in feveral languages, the fame word which
" fignifies a *robber*, or one who fubfifts by rapine, alfo fignifies a foldier. In Latin, the word *latro*
" is not unfrequently ufed to denote a foldier; fee *Plaut. Amphit. act IV. fc.* 6. and *latrocinium*
" is ufed by Cicero, in the fenfe of *open war*. In like manner, the French term *Brigand* (which is
" originally a Celtic compound, denoting the men of the farther or diftant *kents* or hills, after-
" wards called *Brigantes*,) denotes both a *mountaineer*, a *foldier*, and a *robber*, all the characters,
" it is probable, having formerly been often comprifed in one."
                                    Boucher's View of the American Revolution.

relate is, that they were the moſt numerous and powerful of the native tribes of Britain; a brave and warlike race, inured to hardſhips,
and valiant in arms; and ſuch, we know, was their reſiſtance to the
Romans, that it was not till the reign of *Veſpaſian*, about the ſeventi-
eth year of the Chriſtian æra, that they ſubmitted to the victorious
arms of *Petilius Cærialis* ;—" a conqueſt," we are told, " that concur-
" red with the victories he had before obtained in Gaul, to raiſe his
character to the higheſt pinnacle of military reputation."

The province of Brigantia being ſo very extenſive, it ſeems highly
improbable that any of the events recorded by the Roman writers,
ſhould claim their locality within the narrow boundaries of this particular diſtrict. It will therefore be an uſeleſs labour to inquire farther into this dark and uncertain part of hiſtory: but, before we call
the attention of our readers to tranſactions of a more recent date, it
will not be foreign to our purpoſe to take a ſlight view of the manners, cuſtoms, religious opinions, and military character of our Britiſh anceſtors, as we find them delineated by the moſt reſpectable authors.

WHEN the Romans, by a ſuperiority of military diſcipline, firſt
got footing in this iſland, which was about the 53d year before the
birth of Chriſt, they found the civil juriſdiction and religious prin-
ciples of the Druids * univerſally prevalent.

THIS order of men poſſeſſed all the learning of the age. They
were the inſtructors of youth, and taught them the law and religion
in verſe, which they cauſed them to learn by heart; and ſome
druids, we are told, ſpent twenty years in learning to repeat thoſe ſacred and ſcientific diſtichs, which it was forbidden to commit to writ-

---

* THE Druids, according to the opinion of Major Vallancy, firſt flouriſhed in the Eaſt, and
from thence came into Britain, with the Phœnicians. He farther thinks, that they firſt ſettled in
Ireland, and from thence migrated hither; from which he infers, that inſtead of deriving the name,
either from δρυς, or the Britiſh word *derw,* ſignifying an *oak,* it clearly comes from the Iriſh *drui,*
which, as well as *daru,* in Perſian, literally ſignifies *magus* or *wiſe man.*

ing ; either becaufe the ufe of letters was not known, or rather, be-
çaufe they did not chufe to communicate their myfteries to the vulgar.   There was a chief, or *Arch-druid* in every country, who prefided
with unlimited authority, and at his death, the moft excellent perfon
among them was elected as his fucceffor, though not always without
competition.

The religious ceremonies of the druids were few, and greatly fimilar
to thofe of the ancient Hebrews.   The unity of the Supreme Being
was the foundation of their belief ; and Origen, in his Commentary
upon Ezekiel, canvaffing the reafons of the rapid progrefs of Chriftianity in Britain, fays, that " this ifland had long been predifpofed to
it, by the doctrine of the druids, which had ever been, *the unity of*
God the creator."

THE druids have been charged, by the Roman writers, with offering human victims in their facrifices, and Cæfar gives it as their mo-
tive, and as an opinion univerfally received amongft them, that " *pro*
" *vita hominis, nifi vita hominis reddatur, non poffe aliter deorum immortalium*
" *numen placari, arbitrantur.*"   We may readily admit that corruptions
might, in length of time, creep into the worfhip of the druids,
which would otherwife have continued what it originally was—
the true patriarchal religion ; but we fhould be cautious in giving credit to all that is laid to their charge by the Romans, their
profeffed enemies, who have reprefented them as practifing a multitude of ridiculous vanities, which they were neither guilty of, nor in
the leaft acquainted with.   But admitting the charge, we may conceive the practice to have originated from their belief, that fuch a fa-
crifice was one day to promote the happinefs of mankind.   Befides,
the druids were judges in all matters, civil and religious.   They were
alfo the executors of the law ; and, being the minifters of God, to
them was committed the adminiftration of juftice.   Their executions
therefore, were facrifices made to juftice, defigned at once as punifhments and examples ; and nothing, furely, could imprefs the minds

of the fpectators with deeper horror at the fufferings, or greater de-
teftation of the crimes, than the awful folemnities that preceded this
tremendous execution.

THE criminals were fhut up in an effigy of wicker work, of a
gigantic fize, in which they fuffered an ignominious death, by burning.

THE *civil government* of the Britons was fo dependent on, and fo
connected with their religion, that they could not well be divided ;
and the fuperior power and underftanding of the Druids procured
them the cognizance of all affairs, both public and private : in the
latter, they judged without appeal ; they appointed punifhments, ex-
communication or death, according to the nature of the offence. If
public affairs were difcuffed in an affembly of the ftates, nothing
could be executed, nor even moved without the Druids ; in a word,
they reigned ; and, as Dion Chryfoftom obferves, " the kings, in all
" their pomp, were no more than the minifters of the priefts."

> " Amid the oaks, which now compofe
>   " The bulwarks of the Britifh clime,
> " The Druids curs'd their country's foes,
>   " And taught their myfteries fublime ;
> " Their theme was *liberty* and *truth* :
> " Around them flock'd th' impaffion'd youth,
>   " And, when the numbers ceas'd to flow,
> " Impatient for the glorious field,
>   " In mimic fights they rais'd the fhield,
> " Impell'd the fcythe-arm'd car, and twang'd th' elaftic bow."
>   *Mrs.* WEST's *Poems.*

WITH refpect to the public revenues of the Britifh fovereigns, or
what fubfiftence they received from their fubjects, we are uninformed. The exigencies of the ftate were fupplied by a public tax on the
people at large, the Druids being the only clafs, according to Cæfar,
that claimed any exemption. Their laws, which were not reduced
to writing, but committed to memory, confifted of a few traditional

precepts, taught orally, and to their own tribe only, confequently they expired with the extinction of that people.

THE *art of war* practifed by the native Britons was fimple, confifting of few manœuvres. The arms of the infantry were a broad fword and dagger, with a light round target. They fometimes carried fhort fpears pointed with brafs, with a bell faftened to the focket; the harfh found of which, on their advance to battle, ferved to terrify and throw the enemy's cavalry into confufion. But their chief ftrength in the field was in their *war-chariots;* which were of three forts, viz. the *covinus,* the *rheda,* and the *effedum ;* the firft of which is defcribed by *Mela,* as being armed with fcythes, and large hooks faftened to the wheels, and contained only the charioteer, who drove with furious impetuofity into the ranks of the enemy, trampling and cutting them in pieces. The rheda and effedum were unarmed with hooks, and diftinguifhed folely by the number of light armed troops they each contained; who, on paffing the enemy at full fpeed, galled them on all fides with fhowers of darts, and when the ranks of the enemy's cavalry were broken, would leap from their chariots and fight on foot, till fatigued or overpowered, they refumed their feats. The Britons are defcribed by Cæfar,* as being fo expert in the management of thefe chariots, that they could ftop or turn them at full fpeed, on the declivity of a hill; fit, ftand, or run upon the beam and yoke of their horfes, and in an inftant leap in or out, as occafion required. To render themfelves ftill more terrible to their enemies in battle, they ftained their faces and parts expofed, with dyes' of various colours. They charged with a furious impetuofity, but in a tumultuous manner, and retreated without order.

OF the *architecture* of the ancient Britons, we meet with but few documents, from which we can draw any accurate or circumftantial account. Their habitations were rude and inconvenient; and, from their fimple ftructure, calculated for no long duration. Thefe were

---

* De Bell. Gall. lib. iv. c. 33.

erected in the midft of fome deep foreft, crowded irregularly together round the hut of their chief. *Strabo,* after a diligent and minute enquiry, informs us, that the woods were their towns ;—after having cut down trees, they fenced therewith a fpacious circle, where they placed their huts, and fixed ftalls and folds for their cattle. Cæfar exprefsly affures us that there were no other forts of towns in the ifland. " *Op-* " *pidum Britanni vocant quum filvas impeditas vallo atque foffa munierunt.*"

As to their *places of defence, Strutt,* in his *Chronicle of England,* fays, that " thefe were only furrounded by a ditch and vallum of earth; " and the entrance blocked up with trees cut down, and laid acrofs " them; or, inftead of a vallum, a rude wall of great loofe ftones, " without mortar or cement." † The remains of one of thefe fortifications are ftill vifible in the county of Durham, which has been defcribed, as " of a fquare form, the plain inclining to the fouth-weft, " defended by an outward ditch, and a vallum of incredible magnitude, " compofed of loofe pebbles piled up to fuch a ridge that the interior " huts have been effectually covered and concealed by it."

With refpect to the first foreign *commerce* of the Britons, the moft probable conjecture is, that it was occafioned by the refort of the Phœnicians and Greeks to their coasts; who, finding the country to abound particularly in *tin,* received that metal of the inhabitants, and gave them in exchange, *earthen-ware, falt,* and *trinkets* made of brafs. This circumftance points out the importance of Britain, in times more remote, perhaps, than thofe of which we have any record or tradition ; being, in all probability, the only country which furnifhed the metal fo neceffary to the progrefs of civilization.

Doctor Pearfon, in a paper publifhed in the philofophical tranfactions, for the year 1796, obferves, that " in the barbarous ftate of its " inhabitants, this ifland was known to the civilized nations of " Europe, Afia, and Africa; and denominated in two of the moft " ancient languages, viz. the Phœnician and Greek, by terms, which

† Vol. 1. p. 261.

" denote the *land of tin*; for fuch, according to *Bochart*, is the import
" of *Britain*,—a corruption of *Barat-anac*, or *Bratanac* *; and there is
" no doubt of the meaning of the Greek word *caffiterides*."

It is natural to conclude, that this intercourfe with civilized
nations, whofe luxuries had rendered other articles neceffary, would
foon extend their traffic; and we accordingly find, that, although *tin*
ftill continued the principal article of foreign trade, with it were afterwards alfo exported *iron, lead, corn, cattle, hides, and dogs of chace;* which
laft, we are told, became a very gainful article of traffic to the Romans; *gagates*, or *jett*, *pearls*, and various precious ftones were alfo
exported from this ifland; for which the inhabitants received nothing
but articles of luxury and magnificence in return. We may fairly
conclude, that fome of the articles exported at this period, were produced within this particular diftrict. Corn and cattle, we may eafily
conceive, would be found in fome of the more fruitful parts of *Cleveland*. *Gagates, black-amber*, or *jett*, is found in various places upon the
fhore, and within the chinks and clefts of the rocks; the rare qualities
of which will be noticed in the fequel of this work. *Iron-ftone*
abounds in the mountainous parts of this diftrict: and the heaps of
flag, found in many places, are an evidence, that iron has been wrought
here; but, at what period, it is uncertain; it is probable that the
manufactory of that article would be difcontinued when the forefts
were deftroyed. *Agates, Cornelians*, and a great variety of beautifully
veined *pebbles* are frequently found upon the *Cleveland fhores*; and the
lands about Guifbrough, and the mountainous parts of the diftrict,
abound with *allum-rock;* which, though unknown to the Romans, is
now become an article of importance to the country.

---

* It has been juftly obferved, that whenever the Romans called any place by a name, not fignificant in their own language, they muft have retained the *Britifh* appellation, fmoothing the afperity
of the word, and adding a convenient termination for the purpofes of declenfion. Thus *Batavia*
was formed from *Wat-awe, Wet-Soil; Britannia*, probably from *Bratanac, Tin Country*.

It is probable, that the Britons inherited from their earlieſt anceſ-tors, ſome of the ruder arts of navigation. *Cæſar* and *Pliny* have deſcribed their veſſels as large open boats, framed of light timbers, wound with oſiers, and covered with hides : theſe, though furniſhed with maſts and ſails, were frequently worked by the hand, the rowers ſinging to the chimes of their oars, and the muſic of the harp; Thus equipped, they navigated the ſeas between Britain and Ireland; nor was the paſſage in theſe veſſels, however rude they may now appear, ſo dangerous as has been generally repreſented. But we are led to con-clude, that the Britons, notwithſtanding their intercourſe with the Gauls, had made no very conſiderable improvement in maritime affairs, till after the invaſion of the Romans; at leaſt, it does not appear, that when Cæfar invaded Britain, he was oppoſed by any naval force. Such, however, ſeems to have been their attention to the arts of na-vigation, after the coming of the Romans, that, about the year 286, their naval force was renowned; and ſo rapidly did their commerce increaſe, that in the time of *Carauſius*, about the year 359, no leſs than 800 ſhips were employed by them to tranſport corn to the legions on the German frontier.

The *Garments* of the Britons were chiefly the ſkins of deer, wolves, and other wild beaſts, with which the country then abounded. Theſe were caſt over the ſhoulder, and faſtened round the waiſt with a lea-thern girdle. The manufacture of woolen cloth was not known, till the Germans, by their frequent intercourſe with the inhabitants, introduced the art into Britain. The poorer ſort went almoſt naked ; and, in conſequence of this want of covering, they had recourſe to the practice of painting their bodies with a ſubſtance, that ſhut up the pores of the ſkin, and defended the nerves from the inclemencies of the weather.—The following lines, from a poem, on the original

Britons, by Mr. Richards, feem fo appropriate to this part of the fub-ject, that we fhall prefent them to our readers.

> " Rude as the wilds, around his fylvan home,
> " In favage grandeur, fee the Briton roam;
> " Bare were his limbs, and ftrung with toil and cold,
> " By untam'd nature, caft in giant-mould;
> " O'er his broad, brawny shoulders loofely flung,
> " Shaggy and long, his yellow ringlets hung;
> " His waift an iron-belted falchion bore,
> " Maffy, and purpled deep with human gore;
> " His fcarr'd and rudely painted limbs around
> " Fantaftic, horror-ftriking figures frown'd,
> " Which monfter-like, e'en to the confines ran
> " Of nature's work, and left him hardly man;
> " His knitted brows, and rolling eyes impart
> " A direful image of his ruthlefs heart,
> " Where war and human flaughter brooding lie,
> " Like thunders, lowering in a gloomy fky."

It will be unneceffary to enter farther into the hiftory of our Britifh anceftors; fince their cuftoms and manners have been minutely traced by *Cæfar*, *Strabo*, *Tacitus*, and others of the ancients, as well as by fome of our modern writers, who have drawn their information from the fame fources.

Nor will we here follow the fucceffion of the Roman commanders, or detail at length the various incidents that marked the feveral periods of their authority in Britain; it will be fufficient for our pur-pofe to remark that by an artful infinuation of their maxims into the minds of the Britons, and by promoting the adoption of Roman cuf-toms, luxuries, and pleafures, the natives became fo far reconciled to their invaders, as to intermarry with them; a circumftance, which, by degrees, would naturally lead to fubdue the ferocity of the Britons, and deftroy the diftinction between the two nations. Thus accuftomed to Roman manners, and connected by matrimonial alliances, the in-habitants became fo far interefted in the profperity and fuccefs of their conquerors, as to be ready on all occafions to fupport their ambition, and to participate in all their expectations. One inftance, out of many, of the deftructive confequences of this attachment, is worthy of being here recited. About the year 380, the Britons, prefuming to fupport Maximus their governour (a Spaniard by birth) in his pretenfions to the empire, the flower of their youth were embodied in the army; with which he paffed over to, and fubdued Gaul and Spain; but, extending his views to the conqueft of Italy, he failed in the attempt, and his Britifh followers were either cut off by the fword, or becoming wanderers in a foreign country, never regained their native fhores. Britain, thus deprived of her inteftine ftrength, lay expofed fometime to the depredations of her watchful enemies; till *Theodofius*, furnamed the *Great*, on coming to the empire, fent forces to her relief. Soon after this, about the year 420, when it was found neceffary to recall the Roman legions out of Britain, to protect the falling empire, the diftracted Britons, who had not joined in the emigration, finding themfelves deferted by thofe, in whom they had long trufted for fafety and protection, looked upon their wretched country, as abandoned to mifery and defpair. This was an awful crifis to the Britons; for the *Picts* and *Scots*, finding that the Romans had finally quitted the ifland, now regarded the country as an eafy conqueft, and attacked the northern wall, which had been erected as a barrier to fecure the frontiers from their incurfions. This rampart was found but a weak defence againft thefe northern ravagers; and the affrighted Britons, deferting their ftation, gave up their country a prey to the barbarous enemy, who carried ruin and devaftation along with them; nor was their native ferocity in the leaft mitigated by the helplefs condition and fubmiffive behaviour of the inhabitants. Finding themfelves unable to repel the incurfions of thefe northern invaders, the Britons fent ambaffadors to *Ætius*, the governour of Gaul, with a letter from their countrymen, infcribed, " THE GROANS OF THE BRITONS;"—" *The barbarians, on the one hand, drive us into the fea; the* " *fea, on the other, throws us back upon the barbarians; and we have only the* " *fatal choice left us, either of perifhing by the fword, or by the waves.*"

Ætius, at that time threatened by the arms of _Attila_, the moſt powerful enemy of the Roman empire, was unable to aſſiſt, or attend to the complaint of the allies.   In this diſtreſſed condition, no longer un- der the protection of the Romans, and every day expoſed to the rapacity of the northern invaders, the unhappy Britons, about the year 449, were reduced to the neceſſity of calling in the _Saxons_ to their aſſiſtance ; who, knowing the fertility of the country, were eager to embrace the oppor- tunity of gaining a ſettlement in the iſland.   It is ſaid, that about 1600 came over at firſt, under _Hengiſt_ their leader ; and having the _Iſle of Thanet_ aſſigned them, they performed very ſignal ſervices under _Vortigern_, who had been advanced by the Britons, to the ſovereignty of the country.

THE _Scots_ and _Picts_, unable to reſiſt the valour of theſe _Saxon_ auxi- liaries, were routed with great ſlaughter ; and the Britons being reſtored by this victory to their former poſſeſſions, were encouraged to expect peace and ſecurity under the powerful protection of that warlike people. Their gratitude and joy were at firſt ſo great, that they perſuaded _Vorti- gern_ to eſpouſe _Rowena_, the daughter of _Hengist_ ; and he made her the partner of his throne.   But, it was not long before _Hengiſt_, perceiving the imbecillity of this Prince's political judgment, and the abject ſpirit of the Britiſh councils, urged the neceſſity of placing a colony of his coun- trymen in the north, in order, it was pretended, to watch the motions of the northern invaders, and to repel them on their firſt attack.   This was a plauſible argument, and concurred with the implicit confidence with which _Vortigern_ liſtened to the advice of his pretended friend, to facilitate the plan of ſeizing upon the country.   _Octa_, the brother of _Hengiſt_, was immediately ſent for, and directed to make a ſettlement in the north, which, after plundering the _Orcades_, was effected on the north of the river Tyne, in the year 454.   Soon after this, _Hengiſt_, under pretence that ſome groſs inſults had been offered to him and his coun- trymen by the Britons, commenced hoſtilities againſt them ; at which the deluded natives ſtruck with a fear bordering on deſpair, were unable at firft, to repel the attack; and fled before the Saxons, into the moft retired and uncultivated corners of the country. At length, however, roufed from their lethargy, and with *Vortimer*, (the fon of *Vortigern*,) an able and experienced General at their head, they fell upon the Saxons, and defeated them in feveral engagements; after which, *Vortimer* enjoyed the regal dignity with his father, till the difcontented Britons invited *Aurelius Ambrofius*, a Britifh prince, to come over from *Armorica* to their affiftance.

IT was under the conduct of this victorious leader, that the Saxon General, *Hengift*, after a moft bloody and obftinate engagement, met his fate. In confequence of thefe civil broils, the Britons were greatly weakened, the Saxons, in the mean time, receiving frefh fupplies from Germany, till they were overthrown by prince *Arthur*, at the famous battle of *Badon-Hill* *; which is fuppofed to have happened about the year 492. But this advantage was only temporary; and the Saxons, in fpite of all the forces which the Britons could bring to oppofe them, continued to gain ground, till at length, their government was firmly eftablifhed, and Britain became divided into feven kingdoms, called the *Heptarchy*.

IT would be an uninterefting digreffion, to enter into the Hiftory of the different nations that conftituted the *Saxon Heptarchy*; we fhall therefore briefly obferve, that the kingdom of *Northumberland*, though the laft that was eftablifhed, was by far the moft extenfive, comprehending the greateft part of *Yorkfhire, Lancafhire, Weftmoreland, Durham*, and the County of *Northumberland*; and this is afferted by the generality of our hiftorians to have been divided into two feveral

---

* IF any credit be allowed to *Polydore Virgil*, who quotes Gildas, as his authority, we have fome grounds for confidering the fpot, where this battle was fought, to be within the diftrict of *Cleveland;* though Rapin, and fome other Hiftorians, as well as the great *Camden*, place it at *Bannefdown*, near Bath. The *Saxon-camp*, ftill vifible on the fummit of *Efton-Nab*, and other remaining evidences of fuch an engagement, will be particularly noticed in the fequel of this work.

C

kingdoms of *Deira** and *Bernicia*; but writers greatly differ in their accounts of the precife limits of thefe two divifions. *Richard, prior of Hexham*, fixes the limits of *Deira* between the rivers *Humber* and *Tees*; and thofe of *Bernicia*, between *Tees* and *Twede*; while the learned editor of the *Saxon Chronicle* allots to the former all that lies between *Humber* and *Twede*; and to the latter, all between *Twede* and the Frith of Edinburgh. On this divifion, however, it is evident that the diftrict, which is now the object of our attention, conftituted a part of *Deira*; and from its fituation, would probably experience all the calamities of a continued and bloody warfare, by which the country, if not entirely depopulated, was certainly fo far enfeebled, as to leave few traces of its Aboriginal inhabitants. In proof of this affertion, it has been re-marked, that " while the map of all the other Saxon kingdoms in the " ifland is thickly ftrewed with towns and cities, *Bernicia* and *Deira* " together fupply not more than about twenty names."

THE Saxons may therefore, with fome propriety, be confidered as the firft occupants of this part of Britain; at leaft, they muft be allowed to have introduced a new æra of manners, language, and religion. As Dr. *Whitaker* elegantly obferves, " they parcelled out the " country upon their own plan, called the lands after their own names, " and tranfmitted to pofterity a local nomenclature, and a fundamental " fyftem of legal ufages, which fuftained the fhock of the Norman " conqueft, and even fubfift at prefent."

WE wifh not to detain our readers with the recital of the bloody contefts, treafons, and ftratagems under the Saxon heptarchy, which exifted till about the year 800; when the people, wearied with blood-fhed, and oppreffed by the tyranny of the petty princes, called *Egbert* to the united government of the country; under whofe prudent con-duct and powerful protection they looked for nothing but fecurity

---

* OUR learned antiquaries have agreed on the derivation of the word *Deira*, from the Saxon Deop, fignifying *wild beafts*; from which it has been concluded, that this divifion of the kingdom took its name from the extenfive woods and forefts, which gave them fhelter.

and peace.   It was not long, however, before the profperity of the
nation excited the envy of the *Danes*, who had long infefted and
plundered thefe coafts.   They made a defcent upon the *Northumbrian
territory* ; and meeting with little or no refiftance, laid wafte the country
between *York* and the river *Tyne*, and reduced the inhabitants to the
moft miferable ftate of bondage.

CLEVELAND, as well as the other parts of the North, fuffered greatly
by the repeated incurfions of thefe northern ravagers ; the lands lay
uncultivated, and the churches, which had been built and endowed
by the Saxons, on their converfion to chriftianity, were burned and
deftroyed.   *Simeon Dunelemenfis* fays, " after the devaftation of the
" Northumbrian dominions, in A. D. 867, by the Danes, who reduced
" the churches and monafteries to afhes, chriftianity was almoft extinct,
" very few churches (and thofe only built with hurdles and ftraw)
" were rebuilt.   But no monafteries were refounded for almoft two
" hundred years after.   The country people never heard of the name
" of a Monk, and were frightened at the very habit, till fome Monks
" from *Winchelcomb* brought again the monaftic way of living to Dur-
" ham, York, and Whitby."

THESE heavy calamities, under which the country then groaned,
met with no redrefs, till the reign of *Alfred*[*], a prudent, wife and valiant prince, who overthrew the Danes in various engagements, and
compelled them to retreat into the North, from whence they found
means of tranfporting themfelves into Normandy.

BUT, notwithftanding this retreat from the arms of the victorious
Alfred, the Danes did not long defift from their acts of piracy and
plunder ; but feized the earlieft opportunity of renewing their depre-

[*] IT was during the reign of this glorious prince, that England, for the better government thereof,
was diftributed into *fhires* or *counties*, and fubdivided into *trythings*, or *ridings* ; and thefe again into
tythings and hundreds, or *wapontakes*.   A diftinct account of thefe divifions will be given in the fucceeding pages of this work.

dations; and fo weak and ineffectual was the refiftance to the repeated attacks of this invading foe, that a temporary refpite from the horrors of their predatory incurfions could only be procured by contributing large fums of money, on condition they fhould withdraw their forces out of the kingdom. The tax for raifing the money thus appropriated, was called *Danegeld* *; it was firft impofed in the reign of king *Ethelred*, about the year 991, and was an annual tax of two shillings on every hide of arable land in the kingdom; but varied according to certain emergencies; and the produce of it was greatly diminifhed by the many claims of exemption from the payment of it.

FROM this brief view of the melancholy and diftrefsful ftate of the ifland *in general*, under the incurfions of barbarous and foreign enemies, we fhall now haften to the recital of fuch hiftorical events as relate more particularly to the diftrict under confideration.

FOR fome time before the *Norman conqueft*, the contentions between the crowns of England and Scotland had greatly haraffed the inhabitants of the North; nor was it, till fome ages after, that they experienced the bleffings of peace. It might have been imagined, indeed, that the Conqueror, on his acceffion to the crown, would have been induced to grant that calm to the Northumbrians, which the other parts of the kingdom enjoyed; but the event proved otherwife; *William's* acts of clemency had not yet reached fo far to the North; and the ftout Northumbrians, who had zealoufly oppofed his government, exafperated at the horrid cruelties, which he threatened to commit, became impatient under their grievances, and openly revolted. To check this infurrection, which every day affumed a more ferious afpect, he difplaced *Earl Morcar*, whom he confidered as their leader, and appointed *Robert Cumin*, a Norman lord, to the government of that earldom; whofe

---

* THIS was probably the precedent of our land-tax. Sir Henry Spelman, in his gloffary, p. 292, makes the number of hides of land in England amount to 243,600; confequently the grofs produce of this tax, at 2s. per hide, would, at that rate, amount to 24,360*l*.

See Webb's account of Danegeld.

rough and auftere temper, he conceived, was calculated to reduce thefe turbulent fpirits to fubjection. The Northumbrians, informed of his approach to the city of Durham, and regarding him as a monfter commiffioned to exercife whatever cruelties he pleafed, armed themfelves, and furrounding the city, broke open the gates, and made a moft dreadful flaughter of the Normans; infomuch, that Symeon fays, " the ftreets were filled with blood and carcafes." The King was fo incenfed at the news of this horrid maffacre, that he was heard to fwear by his ufual oath, *(by God's fplendour,)* that he would not leave a foul alive *. He accordingly difpatched a powerful army into the North, to revenge *Cumin's* death, by ravaging and deftroying the county in a mercilefs manner.

IT is recorded, that fuch havock was made in this devaftation " for 60 miles between York and Durham, that every village was de- " ferted, and fcarce a houfe left ftanding, the whole diftrict being re- " duced by fire and fword to a horrible defart, fmoaking with blood " and in afhes." † The lands lay uncultivated for nine years, and a dreadful famine enfued, which reduced the wretched inhabitants to eat the flefh of dogs, cats, horfes, and even human carcafes ‡; multitudes lay on the ground unburied; and the few that efcaped the fword perifhed in the fields, overwhelmed with want and mifery.—Thefe horrid and unheard of cruelties made fo deep an impreffion on the mind of the tyrant that committed them, that, on his death-bed, he is faid to have exclaimed, " *multis gravibufque peccatis onuftus, contremifco, et mox ad tremendum Dei judicium rapiendus, quid faciam, ignoro; nobiles et vulgares crudeliter vexavi; injuftè multos exhæreditavi; innumeros, maximè in pago Eboracenfi, fame feu ferro mortificavi.*" § *Cleveland,* no doubt,

* HOVEDEN. Rapin.

† QUOD cum audiffet Rex Willelmus, iratus eft valdè, et congregato exercitu copiofo, Northumbriam adiit, eamque per totam sequentem hiemem in tantum devaftavit, quod per IX annos fequentes lata ubique folitudo patebat, inter enim *Eboracum* et *Dunelmiam*, nulla inhabitabatur villa, nec terra aliquâ eft culta, excepto folo territorio Beati Johannis Beverlacii.

Brompton's Chronicon.

‡ *CARTE, I. p.* 409. *Symeon.—Lel. Col. II. p.* 380.   § *THORESBY's Duc. Pref. XI.*

experienced the calamities of this dreadful devaſtation, which happened in year 1069; and the year following, *Malcolm*, King of *Scotland*,
penetrated into this diſtrict, entering by way of Cumberland; and
purſuing the courſe of the river Tees, burned and deſtroyed every
thing in his march. *   The wretched and deplorable ſituation to which
the country muſt have been reduced by theſe wanton acts of cruelty
may be eaſily conceived; and our hiſtorians have aſſerted, that even
when *domeſday-book* was compiled which was ſome years after, many
of the towns were in ruins, and the lands remained uncultivated;
which is the reaſon generally aſſigned, why " **modo baſtum eſt**," ſo
frequently occurs in this diſtrict, and other parts of *Yorkſhire*.

We might here inſert, as our authorities, the accounts at length,
which have been given us, by the hiſtorians of theſe times; but as the
repetition of ſo melancholy a ſubject might ſeem tedious and unin-
tereſting, we ſhall conclude this ſhort detail with an extract from
Langtoſt's Chronicle, in old Engliſh rhyme, publiſhed by Mr. Hearn.

> Therefore William the King, did turne agayn his hoſte,
> And ſwore a grete othe, that he ſuld never ſpare
> Neither lithe nor loſe, notheren whut ſo thei were.
> William turned agayn, and held what he had ſworn,
> All mad he waſteyn, paſture, medow, and korne.
> And ſloughe both fader and ſonne, women lete thei gon,
> Hors and houndes thei ete, uncithis ſkaped non.
> Now dwells William efte, full bare was money wone,
> Of gode men er none lefte, but ſlayn er ilk one.
> Grete ſin did William, that ſwilk wo did werk,
> So grete vengeance he nam, of men of holy kirk,
> That did no wem till him, ne no treſpaſs,
> Fro York unto Durham no wonyng ſtede was;
> Nin yere, ſays my buke, laſted ſo grete ſorrow,
> The Biſhop clerkes tuke their lyves for two borrowe.

---

* A. D. 1070. Malcolmus, Rex Scottorum, cum infinita multitudine per Cumberlandiam
verſus orientem ſe divertens, univerſam *Teſedale*, et loca ejus finitima, ultra citraque feroci depopula-
tione vaſtavit. Depopulataque quadam parte *Clivelandiæ*, quaſi ex ſubito *Herceneſſe* occupavit.
                                                              Brompton's Chronicon.

AFTER this unheard of cruelty, we find nothing in history relative to this district, worth reciting, till about the 3d year of the reign of King *Stephen;* at whose usurpation, *David,* King of Scotland, was greatly incensed; and knowing that the nation was, at that time, divided, and a civil war begun between *Stephen* and the Empress *Matilda,* entered England with a powerful army, wasting and destroying all before him. Having reduced *Carlisle* and placed a garrison there, he advanced southwards, with an intent to besiege the *city of York.* In the meantime, *Thurstan,* the venerable Archbishop of York, who was at this time entrusted by the King to guard this country, with the Barons and chief men, having raised forces, marched to oppose the enemy, whom they met near *North-Allerton;* where a terrible and bloody battle was fought, in which the Scots were routed, with great slaughter. This battle is called by our historians, *the battle of the Standard *;* and the scene of action is still distinguished by the name of *Standard Hill;* about three miles to the north of *North-Allerton.*

ROBERT BRUS of *Skelton-Castle* was particularly distinguished on this occasion; who, with his son *Adam,* and all the power he could make, joined the rest of the Yorkshire Barons; and when the English army was drawn up for battle, being a man of great age, grave in his

---

* It is asserted to have been so called, from a long pole, or mast of a ship, erected upon a carriage; upon which were suspended the banners of *St. Peter, St. John of Beverley,* and *St. Wilfred of Ripon;* having on the top a silver crucifix, and above all, in a silver box, was the consecrated wafer, or supposed body of Jesus Christ. A rude drawing of this machine is preserved in *Ailredi Rievallensis historia de bello standardi, (apud X. script.)* and the same writer has left a particular account of the engagement, with the characters of the leaders, and many of their harangues at length. *Hugh de Sotevagina,* at that time Archdeacon of York, wrote the following distich upon it;

> " *Dicitur a stando standardum, quod stetit illic,*
> " *Militiæ probitas vincere sive mori.*"
> ' Standard, from stand, this fight we aptly call
> ' Our men here stood to conquer, or to fall.'

There is also a Latin poem on this battle, by *Serlo,* a monk, brother to *Ralph,* abbot of Pack, at the end of *R. Hagul. X. script.*

deportment, and of fingular elocution, he made a fpeech, in which he reprefented to them his long friendfhip with the King of Scots; and from his knowledge and experience in military affairs, confidering the dangerous and unavoidable confequences of war, he requefted and ob- tained leave of his fellow-foldiers to go to the King; in order, if pof- fible, to diffuade him from engaging, and to prevent the effufion of human blood. On coming into the King's prefence, he fet forth, that the Englifh had always been his beft friends, inftancing the particular obligations they had conferred upon him and his brothers, when they ftood moft in need of their aid. And concluded by faying, that al- though his army was more numerous, yet the Englifh were more va- liant; and refolved to conquer or to die. This fpeech made fo deep an impreffion on the King of Scots, that he burft into tears, and would have inftantly withdrawn his forces, had not his nephew *William*, who was the chief inftigator of this invafion, prevented him; and with great fury, charging *Brus* with treachery, he diffuaded the King from hearkening to him. *Brus* returned with forrow to the Englifh army; and preparation being inftantly made for battle, the Englifh obtained a glorious and complete victory.

In the year 1215, the northern Englifh Barons, revolting againft *King John*, had recourfe to *Alexander II.* King of Scotland, for protec- tion againft his oppreffive tyranny; at which the enraged Monarch made an expedition into the North, burning and deftroying every thing before him, from York northwards. This cruel devaftation drove the revolting Barons to the defperate meafure of offering the crown of England to *Lewis*, the dauphine of *France;* and *Cleveland*, with the reft of Yorkfhire, was reduced by *Robert de Roos, Peter de Brus*, and *William de Percy*, to the obedience of *Lewis;* but providence, by the death of the Englifh tyrant, put a ftop to the acceffion of *Lewis*, which might have proved fatal to the rights and liberties of Britons.

On referring to the annals of our hiftorians, it will be found, that England fuffered the moft defolating cruelties from the repeated incurfions of the Scots; and though the *border fervice* was eftablifhed at an early period after the conqueft, in order, if poffible, to remedy this public calamity, and laws and regulations had been inftituted for that purpofe; it was in the reign of Edward II. that their devaftations became moft dreadful.

In the year 1315, after the battle of *Bannock-Burn*, fo fatal to the Englifh army, the Scots entered England at the weftern march, and penetrated into *Cleveland*; which having plundered, they retreated by way of *Durham*, with a confiderable booty. About this period, the plague raged dreadfully both in England and Scotland; and the depopulation thereby occafioned was fo great, that, as Rapin fays, " hardly could the living fuffice to bury the dead;" notwithftanding this, in the year 1318, the Scots made another incurfion, under the command of *Sir James Douglas* and the *Earl of Murray*, who laid wafte the whole country with fire and fword, to the very gates of *York*.

As it is our defign in this review, to recount fuch hiftorical facts only, as relate to this particular diftrict, we fhall pafs over in filence the miferies and calamities of the *Border-wars*, which lafted, (though with decreafed violence) till the union of the two kingdoms; a particular detail of which would be painful to the feeling mind, and no otherwife ufeful, than, by impreffing on the reader an idea of the wretched ftate of this country at that period, to lead him to exult in the enjoyment of thofe bleffings which arife from the union, and that glory, acquired by the Britifh arms, fince the kingdoms were united.

During the diffentions between the two houfes of York and Lancafter, we do not find that *Cleveland* was the fcene of any memorable tranfaction; though fome of the principal families were appointed to commands, and are confpicuous characters in that long and bloody conteft.

In the reign of *Henry VIII.* feveral infurrections were excited in England by the fuppreffion of the leffer monafteries; among which there was one carried on by *Lord D'Arcy*, and others, in the North. Beacons

D

were fired in *Cleveland*, *Richmondſhire*, and other places, as a ſignal for all men capable of bearing arms to put themſelves in a poſture of defence; when upwards of 40,000 men, well furniſhed with arms, horſes, and artillery were aſſembled. This inſurrection was ſtyled, " *The Pilgrimage of Grace*"; and the leaders *, under pretence of maintaining and defending the faith of Chriſt, and promoting the welfare of the kingdom, kept together for a conſiderable time, and committed ſeveral acts of outrage; till at length, Thomas, Duke of Norfolk, the Lord Lieutenant of the county, and ſeveral other nobles in commiſſion, with a powerful army under their command, were ordered to march againſt them. The rebels had advanced as far as Doncaſter, where they lay encamped; and the Lords haſtened to give them battle; but a proclamation for a general pardon, which was offered, to prevent bloodſhed, had the deſired effect to diſperſe the multitude; and the leaders in the revolt were taken; moſt of whom, with ſix abbots, the prior of Bridlington, and ſeveral monks and eccleſiaſtics were executed for high treaſon.

IN the 31ſt year of this reign, the greater monaſteries ſhared the ſame fate; and, in order to prevent future dangers, and to keep the northern counties in peace, a preſident and council was appointed at York, with the two ſeveral powers and authorities, under one great ſeal, of *Oyer* and *Terminer*, &c. within the counties of *York*, *Durham*, *Northumberland*, *Weſtmoreland*, and *Cumberland*. This court was continued till the civil wars, in the reign of Charles I. and was, no doubt, of great advantage to the kingdom. The Earl of Strafford was the laſt preſident in this court, and his commiſſion was more ample than any of his predeceſſors.

DURING the civil broils, which diſtracted the ſtate under the unhappy reign of Charles I. *Cleveland* became the ſcene of ſome ſlight ſkirmiſhes, in which the King's troops experienced various ſucceſs. In the year 1642, the *Earl of Newcaſtle*, who had levied a conſiderable force for

---

* LORD D'Arcy, Robert Aſk, Eſq. Sir Robert Conſtable, Sir John Bulmer and his wife, Sir Thomas Piercy, brother to the Earl of Northumberland, Sir Stephen Hamilton, Nicholas Tempeſt, and William Lumley, Eſqrs.

the King in the North, began his march towards York; but was oppos-
ed, at his paſſage of the *river Tees,* by a ſmall detachment of troops under the command of *Captain Hotham;* the Earl, however, forced his
paſſage, and reached York with 6000 troops and ten pieces of ordnance.

ON the 16th January, 1642-3, about 600 of the King's troops under
the command of *Col. Slingſby* were defeated at *Guiſbro'* by *Sir Hugh
Cholmley,* who was then governour of Scarborough Caſtle.

IN the year 1643, *Yarm* was garriſoned by 400 of the Parliament-
forces; but was ſoon reſcued from them by the *Earl of Newcaſtle,* who
reduced Yorkſhire, and all the northern counties to the King, *Hull* being
the only garriſon in the hands of the enemy. The tide of affairs however, ſoon began to turn, and the King's forces were unſucceſsful in
every part of Yorkſhire; but the battle of *Marſton-Moor,* which was
fought on the 2d July, 1644, proved fatal to the royal cauſe; for York
almoſt immediately ſurrendered to the rebels, and Newcaſtle, with moſt
of the King's garriſons in the North, followed the example.

IT would be foreign to our purpoſe to enter at length into the
troubles of this unfortunate monarch, which ended only with his life;
nor do we mean at preſent to purſue any further the detail of hiſtorical
events relative to this diſtrict; but, before we proceed to a particular
view of each pariſh, it may not be improper to take a brief notice of the
ancient tenures of the country, extracted from works of known and acknowledged authenticity.

IT ſeems the unanimous opinion of the feudal writers, that the con-
quered lands were originally parcelled out by the conquering chief, to
the ſuperior officers of his army; and by them dealt out in leſs parcels
to the inferior officers, and moſt deſerving ſoldiers; and the poſſeſſions
ſo granted were denominated *feoda,* or *feuds;* for which the poſſeſſors
were bound to render certain ſervices to him from whom they were
given. Theſe ſervices were originally purely military, and the poſſeſſor
or feudatory's homage and fealty was an engagement to be faithful and
aſſiſtant to his benefactor; Spelman therefore calls a *feud, prædium militare.*

FEUDS being thus originally in the hands of military perfons, who were frequently unable to cultivate their own lands, it was found necef-fary to commit part of them to perfons, who, having no feudal poffeffions of their own, were glad to poffefs them on any terms ; to fuch perfons, fmall portions of land were let, referving fuch returns of fervice, corn, cattle, or money, as might enable the proprietors to attend, without in-terruption, to their military duty. By this means the feudal policy was confiderably extended ; as all perfons accepting a *feud*, were obliged, under an exprefs or implied fealty, to anfwer the ftipulated renders, and to promote the peace and welfare of the *feudal fociety.*

IT is not agreed upon, and it feems difficult to determine precifely, at what time *feudal tenures* were firft brought into England ; fome have thought they were planted here long before the *Norman conqueft* ; others, that they were introduced by the *Conqueror* ; it is evident, however, that in his time, they became a principal branch of the national policy ; and *Sir Martin Wright*, in his *Introduction to the Law of Tenures*, is of opinion, that the general furvey, called *Domefday-Book*, was taken upon, or foon after our anceftor's confent to tenures, in order to difcover the quantity of every man's fee, and to fix his homage.

As the Conqueror, however, did not claim the lands of England as the fpoils of war, fo neither did he arbitrarily fubmit them to a feudal dependence; but, as the *feudal* was at that time, the prevailing law of Europe, he would certainly recommend it to our anceftors, as the moft obvious and ready way to put them upon an equal footing with their neighbours: accordingly we find, among the laws of William I. a law enacting, not indeed, *eo nomine*, but in effect, the feudal law itfelf; as it requires, " *that all owners of land fhould exprefsly engage and fwear, that* " *they would become* VASSALS *or* TENANTS, *and, as fuch, be faithful to* WIL- " LIAM, *as their lord, and that they would, in confequence thereof, every where* " *faithfully maintain and defend his, their Lord's territories and title, as well* " *as perfon, and give him all poffible aid and affiftance againft his enemies,* "*foreign and domeſtic.*" The terms of this law * are certainly feudal ; and are particularly adapted to the eſtabliſhment of that policy, with all its confequences ; fo that it is become a maxim or principle of our Engliſh law of tenures, that all lands are holden either *mediately* or *immediately*, of the King. Thoſe that held under the King *immediately*, in right of his crown and dignity, were called his tenants *in capite*, which was the moſt honourable fpecies of tenure ; and when they granted out portions of their lands to inferior perſons, they became lords with refpect to thoſe inferior perſons, as they were ſtill tenants with refpect to the King ; and were called *mefne*, or middle lords.

ACCORDING to Blackſtone, there fubfiſted four principal fpecies of lay tenures, which were diſtinguiſhed by the nature of the ſervices, due to the lords from their tenants. Theſe ſervices, in refpect to their quality, were either *free*, or *baſe* ; and in refpect to their quantity, and the time of exacting them, either *certain* or *uncertain*. *Free-ſervices* were ſuch as were not unbecoming the character of a foldier or freeman to perform ; as to ſerve under his lord in the wars, to pay a fum of money, and the like. *Baſe-ſervices* were ſuch as were fit only for peaſants, or perſons of ſervile rank ; as to plough the lord's land, to make his hedges, to carry out his dung, or other mean employments. The *certain-ſervices*, whether free or baſe, were ſuch as were ſtinted in quantity ; as to pay a ſtated annual rent, or to plough ſuch a field for three days. The *uncertain* depended upon unknown contingencies, as to do military ſervice in perſon, or pay an affeffment in lieu of it, when called upon ; or to *wind a horn*, whenever the Scots invaded the realm, which are free ſervices ; or to do whatever the lord ſhould command, which is a *baſe* or *villein ſervice.*

OF theſe different kinds of ſervices, Bracton has given us the following compendious account. " Tenements," he fays, " are of two kinds,

---

* THIS law is ſtill extant, and couched in theſe remarkable words : " ſtatuimus ut omnes liberi " homines foedere et facramento affirment, quod intra et extra univerfum regnum Angliæ Wilhelmo " regi domino fuo fideles effe volunt ; terras et honores illius omni fidelitate ubique fervare cum eo, et " contra inimicos et alienigenas defendere."—Cap. 52. Wilk. 228.

"*frank-tenement*, and *villeinage*. Of *frank-tenements*, fome are held freely
" in confideration of homage and *knight-fervice*; others in *free-focage*,
" with the fervice of fealty only. Of *villeinages*, fome are *pure*, and others
" *privileged*. He that holds in *pure* villeinage, fhall do whatfoever is com-
" manded him, and always be bound to an uncertain fervice. The other
" kind of villeinage is called *villein-focage;* and thefe *villein-focmen* do vil-
" lein fervices, but fuch as are certain and determined."—*Bracton, L. 4.*
tr. I. C. 28.

OF the above extract, Blackftone remarks, that, where the fervice
was *free*, but uncertain, as military fervice with homage, that tenure was
called the tenure, *per fervitium militare*, or by knight's fervice. Where
the fervice was not only free, but alfo certain, as by fealty only, by rent
and fealty, &c. that tenure was called *liberum focagium*, or free-focage.
Thefe were the only free holdings, or tenements; the other were *villeinous*,
or fervile; as where the fervice was bafe in its nature and uncertain as
to time and quantity, the tenure was *purum villenagium*, or pure villeinage; and where the fervice was bafe in its nature, but reduced to a certainty, this was ftill *villeinage*, but diftinguifhed from the other by the
name of privileged villeinage, *villenagium privilegiatum;* or it might ftill
be called *focage*, (from the certainty of its fervices;) but degraded by its
bafenefs into the inferior title of *villein-focage*.

THE firft, and moft honourable fpecies of tenure, was that by knight's
fervice, called in latin, *fervitium militare*; and the determinate quantity
of land, neceffary to make this tenure, was called a *knight's-fee, (feodum*
militare) the value of which, at its original in the reign of the Conqueror, was probably ftated at 20*l.* per ann. and a certain number of
thefe fees were requifite to make up a barony. * He who held a *knight's-*
fee was bound to attend his lord to the wars for *forty days* in every year,
if called upon; he who held half a fee, was bound only to attend *twenty*

* BARONIES were of no determinate fize, being more or lefs, according to the grant, each of
which being held *in capite by Barony*, was accounted a complete Barony, notwithftanding the difference in number of fees contained in each.———*Chauncey's Hertf. p.* 56.

days, and fo in proportion. Sir Edward Coke fays, that this tenure, by which the greateft part of the lands in the kingdom were holden, was created for a military purpofe: viz. *for defence of the realm by the King's own principal fubjects.*

But this perfonal military duty growing troublefome and inconvenient, the tenants found means of compounding with their Lords, firft by fending others to ferve in their ftead; and afterwards by a pecuniary fatisfaction in lieu of it; which laft came in time to be levied by affefiments, at fo much for every knight's fee, and was called *fcutage* or *efcuage*, from the word *fcutum*, a well-known denomination of money, it being a pecuniary, inftead of a military fervice. By this degenerating of *knight's-fervice*, all the advantages of the feodal conftitution were deftroyed, and nothing but its hardfhips remained, which have been juftly and feelingly ftated by Judge Blackftone, *in* 2. *Com. C.* 5. *P.* 75, 76. A flavery fo complicated and extenfive called aloud for a remedy; and palliatives were from time to time, applied by fucceffive acts of Parliament, till at length, the military tenures, with all their heavy appendages, were abolifhed by the ftatute 12. *Charles II.* chap. 24. by which all tenures in general, except *frankalmoign* †, *grand-ferjeanty* ‡, and *copy-hold*, were reduced to one general fpecies, called *free* and *common focage* ‖; the grand criterion, and diftinguifhing marks of which, as we have already obferved, are the having its renders and fervices afcertained, and not left to the arbitrary calls of the Lord.

---

† Tenure in *frankalmoign, in libera eleemofyna,* or free alms, is that by which almoft all the antient monafteries and religious houfes held their lands; and by which the parochial clergy, and many ecclefiaftical and eleemofynary foundations, hold them at this day.—*Bracton, L.* 4. *tr.* 1. *C.* 28.

‡ Grand-serjeanty was a tenure, by which the tenant was bound, inftead of ferving the King *generally* in the wars, to do fome fpecial honorary fervice to the King in perfon; as to carry his banner, his fword, or the like; or to be his butler, champion, or other officer, at his coronation. Tenure by *cornage*, which was to wind a horn, when the Scots or other enemies entered the land, was a fpecies of grand-ferjeanty.

‖ Socage, in its moft general and extenfive fignification, feems to denote a tenure by any certain and determinate fervice; the word, according to Somner being derived from the Saxon appellation, *foc*, (a liberty and privilege) and being joined to a legal termination, is called *focage*, in latin *focagium*, fignifying thereby a free and privileged tenure.

FROM this brief view of the two grand fpecies of tenures, under which almoft all the free lands of the kingdom were holden, till the reftoration in 1660, we fhall proceed to notice the other divifion of tenure, mentioned by Bracton, called *villeinage;* from which our prefent *copyholds* feem to have had their origin.

SIR William Temple, in his introduction to his Englifh hiftory, fays, " the Normans finding among us a fort of people, who were in a condi- " tion of downright fervitude, ufed and employed in the moft fervile " works, and belonging, both they, their children, and effects, to the lord " of the foil, like the reft of the ftock, or cattle upon it," enfranchifed fuch as fell to their fhare, by admitting them to the oath of *fealty,* which conferred a right of protection, and raifed the tenant to a kind of eftate fuperior to downright flavery, called *villeinage.* At length, the uninterrupted benevolence and good nature of many Lords, by permitting the *villeins* and their children to enjoy their poffeffions in a courfe of fucceffion, or life only, became cuftomary and binding on their fucceffors, and advanced fuch poffeffions into the legal intereft or eftate, now called *copyholds.* Judge Blackftone fays, " copyholders are in truth no other " but *villeins;* who, by a long feries of immemorial encroachments on " their Lords, have at length eftablifhed a cuftomary right to thofe eftates, " which before were held abfolutely at the Lord's will; which affords " a very fubftantial reafon for the great variety of cuftoms that prevail " in different manors, in regard both to the defcent of the eftates, and " the privileges belonging to the tenants."

THESE *villeins* were of two diftinct natures; viz. *villeins regardant,* annexed to the *manor or land;* or *in grofs,* that is, annexed to the *perfon of the Lord,* and transferable by deed, from one owner to another. However by the almoft univerfal encroachments above noticed, it has been obferved that at the time of the ftatute of King Charles II. there was hardly a *pure villein,* that is, a *villein in grofs,* in the whole kingdom. Sir Thomas Smith, who was fecretary to *King Edward VI.* fays, he never knew any *villein in grofs,* throughout the realm; and the few *villeins regardant,* that were then remaining, were fuch only as had belonged to

bifhop's monafteries, or other ecclefiaftical corporations, in the preceding times of popery.

BEFORE we conolnde, it may be neceffary to ftate fomewhat more
particularly, the declarations in the ftatute of Charles II. by which the
military tenures were extinguifhed. *Section 4th* declares, " that all
" fines for alienations, &c. and all charges incident and arifing, for or
" by reafon of wardfhip, &c. or tenure of knight's fervice, and
" other charges incident thereto, are taken away and difcharged, any
" law, ftatute, or ufage, to the contrary notwithftanding." *Section 5th*
declares, that " all tenures by knight's fervice of the king, or of any
" other perfon, and the fruits and confequences thereof, be taken away
" and difcharged, any law, &c. to the contrary notwithftanding; and
" all tenures of any honours, manors, lands, tenements, or heredita-
" ments, or an eftate of any inheritance at the common law, held either
" of the king, or of any other perfon or perfons, are turned into free
" and common focage."

JUDGE Blackftone hefitates not to declare, that this ftatute was a
greater acquifition to the civil property of this kingdom than even
magna charta itfelf; fince that only pruned the luxuriences that had
grown out of the military tenures, and thereby preferved them in
vigour; but the ftatute of *King Charles* extirpated the whole, and demolifhed both root and branches. Upon the whole it appears, that
whatever changes and alterations, the tenures in progrefs of time, underwent, from the *Saxon æra*, to the reign of Charles II. all lay-tenures
are now, in effect, reduced to two fpecies: viz. *free-tenure in common-
focage*, and *bafe tenure by copy of court-roll.*

E

CLEVELAND IN GENERAL.

IN the introduction we have briefly recounted such historical circumstances, as may serve to throw some light on the ancient state of the
district at large. But, before we proceed to a more minute account of
each parish, it may not be improper to observe, that the wapontake of
Langbargh, which comprehends all that is properly termed *Cleveland*,
and to which our observations in this work will be chiefly confined,
is situated in the northern extremity of Yorkshire, and constitutes no
inconsiderable part of the *North Riding* * of that county. Its greatest

---

* THE word *riding*, though it was anciently common to some other counties, as appears from
the law of Edward the Confessor, is now peculiar to the county of York. It is only a corruption of
the Saxon word Ðrihing, which, in that law, is said to be a third part of the province. Sir H. Spelman, *(sub voce hundredum,)* speaks of it thus: England, he says, was distributed by *King Alfred*,
into *counties*, which were subdivided into *trithings*, *rapes*, and *lathes*; and they again into *hundreds*
or *wapontakes*, and these again into *tythings*; but the quantities are never said to be equal in any of
them. Mr. *Thoresby*, *(in his history of Leeds, p. 84.)* has given so distinct and well-grounded an account of these *ridings*, and their subdivisions, that we cannot but particularly notice it.

He says, that in the division of England by the Saxons, there were these parts; vix. *tythings*,
hundreds or *wapontakes*, and *trythings* or *ridings*, which differ thus: *tythings* consisted of ten families,
subjected to the care of the *decurio*, or *tything-man*, who was answerable for the behaviour of the
masters of those families, as they were for their children and servants. Ten of these tythings made
an hundred or wapontake; which last, was so called, because the governor of it was put into his
place, and held up a *weapon*, (I. E.) a spear; and the elders of the *tythings* admitted him, by *tack-
ing*, † or touching their spears with his, as a token of their subjection. *Ridings*, or *trythings*, were
the third part of a county, be it greater or less; and to them were appeals made, not determinable
in the wapontakes. The North Riding is so called, because it extends itself farthest northwards,
above the city of York.

---

† HOVEDEN derives the word wapontake, *a tactu armorum*, and describes the ceremony thus:—" Cum
" quis accipiebat præfecturam wapentachii, die statuto, in loco ubi consueverant congregari, omnes ma-
" jores contra eum conveniebant, et descendente de equo suo omnes assurgebant ei. Ipsa verò, erecta
" lanceâ suâ, ab omnibus secundùm morem fædus accipiebat; omnes enim, quotquot venissent cum lanceis
" suis ipsius hastam tangebant, et ita confirmabant per *contactum armorum*, pace palàm concessâ," &c.

E 2

extent from eaſt to weſt is nearly 40 miles, and about 18 miles broad; and is bounded on the eaſt, north and north-eaſt, by the *German ocean;* on the weſt by *Allertonſhire,* and on the north-weſt, by the *river Tees,* which divides it from the county of Durham; while the ſouthern limits of the diſtrict are ſhut in by the wapontakes of Birdforth, Rye-dale, and Whitby-Strand. Theſe limits, however, require to be more particularly defined.

ON the eaſt, the boundary aſcends a ſmall rivulet, anciently called *Thordiſa* ‡-(now *Eaſt-Row)-Beck,* which takes its riſe in Mulgrave Park, and empties itſelf here into the ſea. It purſues the courſe of this rivulet, till it reaches the vicinity of Mulgrave-Caſtle, (now in ruins,) when making a turn, ſouthwards, it paſſes *Swarth-how-Croſs;* and from thence down *Brock-hole-Beck,* till it empties itſelf into the river Eſk. The boundary then aſcends the Eſk, as far as *Groſmont-Bridge,* where it receives the waters of *Goadland-Beck,* which now be-comes the boundary, in a more ſouthern direction, to the head-ſpring thereof, having *Hazle-Head* on the right, and *Goadland-Chapel* on the left; then paſſing the northern edge of *Wheledale-moor,* it runs weſt-wards, in nearly a direct line to *Shunner-Howe,* and *Rolte's-Croſs;* from thence it paſſes the head of *Weſterdale* and *Baſedale-Moors,* and con-tinues, in a ſouth-weſtern direction, along the ſummit of *Ingleby, Broughton,* and *Carleton Banks,* to the weſtern extremity of Arncliffe; when turning northwards, and paſſing *Mount-Grace* on the weſt, it falls into the river *Wiſk* near *Staddle-Bridge.* The boundary, (with a ſlight deviation to the north at *Weſt-Rounton)* purſues the courſe of the Wiſk as far as *Appleton;* from whence it runs, in nearly a direct line north-wards, to the river Tees at Low-Worſall, being bounded by *Allerton-*

---

‡ So called from an heathen temple erected here, by our pagan anceſtors, in which was an idol, repreſenting their great god *Thor.* This temple was afterwards converted into an hermitage, the ruins of which are ſtill viſible; and the village retained the name of *Thordiſa,* till about the year 1620, when being occupied by men employed in an *allum work,* that was begun there, it took the name of *Eaſt-Row,* from its eaſtern ſituation from that work.——See Charlton.

fhire on the weft. From Worfall it defcends the river Tees, in a ferpentine courfe, for about 20 miles, till that river empties itfelf into the
fea. From the mouth of the Tees, *Cleveland* bends along the coaft eaftwards, till it reaches the foot of *Thordifa*, or *Eaft-Row Beck*.

CAMDEN's defcription, which is very concife, is to the following
effect :—" From Whitby the fhore winds back to the weftwards, and
" near it ftands *Cleveland*, fo called, as it fhould feem, from precipices,
" which we call *cliffs*; for it is fituated by the fide of feveral fteep hills,
" from the foot of which, the country fall into a plain, even, fertile
" ground."

FROM the above extract it appears evident, that Camden derives
the name of *Cleveland* from the high rocks and precipices, with which
this tract abounds; though we more readily adopt the opinion of
Baxter and other authors; from which it feems, that the primary and
leading idea of the name is undoubtedly not *Cliff*, but *Clay*, as defcriptive of its foil.—The following extract from Baxter, as illuftrative of
the etymology of the name, we prefume will not be uninterefting to
the curious reader.

" *CALUVIUM.*—Ita reponendum duxi in anonymo; cum in libro,
geminato errore legeretur, fexto etiam cafu, *Calunio* et *Gallunio*, de eo
quod procul omni dubio in Græco fuerat exemplari Καλουσον, nam et in
Vaticano M. S. *Caluvio* eft atque *Galluvio*; hoc vel nomen dediffe videtur dynaftiæ cuidam, hodie dictæ CLEVELAND, five *Terra Caluviana*,
quæ in illa parte Deirorum eft, quæ Borealis Brigantum Triarchis dicitur; videtur etiam urbs *Caluvium* hodie dici *Gifborough*, five potiùs
Gheftborough, quafi dicas *fpiritualis Burgus*. Satis vetuftum hoc oppidum eft antiquo monafterio celebre, unde et Saxonicum nomen tractum videtur.

BRITANNICUM autem nomen fortitur, ut fupra, *Caleva*, de *lutofa
unda*; ac si folutò fcribatur *Calai-iii.* Quo fpectat et popularis nænia
ab erudito Camdeni interprete, huc adducta eft,

——————— *CLEVELAND* in the clay
Brings in two foles, and carries one away."
Baxter's Glofs. Antiq. Brit. P. 61.

DRAYTON, in his poetical progrefs through Yorkfhire, after noticing

" PICKERING, whom the fawnes beyond them all adore
" By whom not far away lies large fpread *Blackamore*," *

proceeds thus in his defcription of our diſtrict:

" THEN *Cleveland* north from thefe, a ftate that doth maintain,
" Leaning her lufty fide to the great germain main,
" Which, if fhe were not here confined thus in me,
" A fhire even of herfelf might well be faid to be."

Drayton's Poly-olbion.

To the above extracts we fhall fubjoin Speed's defcription of the North-Riding in general; with fome brief remarks on the climate, foil, and general appearance of the diſtrict more immediately under confideration.

" THE *aire*," according to Speed, " is fubtile and peircing, and not inclined naturally to contagious infections, which caufeth the people to live long and healthfully; and are not fubject to agues, fluxes, or other imperfections, as thofe counties be that are more troubled with mifts and vapours.

" THE *foyle* is generally indifferently fruitful; for though fome part be craggie, mountainous, and full of hills, yet fome others exceeding good for the gifts of nature in her delightfome varieties, as of corne, cattle, and pafturage; with veines of mettall and iron, befides an allum-earth of fundry colours, out of which fome have lately begunne to trie very good allum and coperaffe."

---

* IN an ancient manufcript in the *Cott. Library* (marked Julius F. C. fol. 455) defcriptive of the lordfhip of Guifborough, and the adjacent coaft, we find *Blackamore* thus noticed. " Alonge " Cleveland lyeth *Blackamoore* antyently fuppofed to be called Barton-Hyll, which by the ploughed " land and ruynes of houfes in many places feeme to have been well inhabyted, but now in fix or " feven myles together, you fhall fcarcely fynde a houfe except in a dale, the refte is heathe, and a " roufte for heathecocks."——In the further progrefs of this work, we fhall occafionally recur to this curious M. S. for the defcription of fuch parts of our diſtrict, as fhall be found to be therein noticed.

THE *climate*, † though colder than the more fouthern parts of the county, from its vicinity to the fea, is neverthelefs healthy and invigorating. The foil is various; in the vale of Cleveland, a fertile clay generally prevails, with fome rich and gravelly loam, particularly near the banks of rivers, which produce abundant crops of corn and grafs. In the eaftern part of the diftrict, which is more mountainous, and towards the coaft, the foil is barren, being chiefly a ftiff red clay, upon an *allum-fhale;* which, as we approach the moors, inclines to black, and at laft terminates in a rotten peat-mofs-earth. The vale, bordering the river Efk, is of a light fandy foil; which, however, does not extend far, before it degenerates into a cold and barren clay.*

THE *furface*, on the eaftern part of *Cleveland*, and near the coaft, is bold and hilly; but inclofing fome rich and fertile vales, well watered, and ornamented with pieces of wood-land.

BETWEEN *Guifborough* and *Whitby*, as the traveller purfues his road,

——————————" A dreary wafte
" Of lands uncultivated,"

prefents itfelf, covered with heath and fern, and " abounding in rug-
" ged hills and deep moraffes, which feem never to have been made
" fubfervient to the ufes of fociety."

---

† MR. TUKE, in his agricultural furvey of the North Riding, obferves that " Cleveland, having " a range of mountains on the fouth, the fea to the north and eaft, and lying open on the weft to the " winds from an extenfive, uncultivated, and mountainous country, ‡ is of courfe fubject to a chill " and fevere climate; but the foil, become dry and very ftiff by a long ftate of aration, and frequent " ufe of lime bakes with the fun, and haftens harveft to the time of warmer climates."

* " THE level land, at the bottom of the vales, is feldom more than 200 or 300 yards in breadth; but the land is cultivated generally from half a mile to a mile and a half up the hills, though the furface is, in many places, very irregular."

" MOST of the dales partake more or lefs of the following foils: viz. a black moory earth upon a clay,—a fandy foil, in fome places intermixed with large gritftones, upon a *fhale*,—and a light loam upon a girt rock."

Tuke's Agricult. Survey. p. 16.

‡ RICHMONDSHIRE;

On the weſt, a range of hills, of conſiderable elevation, ſtretches along the ſouthern confines of the diſtrict, in an undulating manner; in front of which, the country ſpreads out, for many miles, into an extenſive plain, interſperſed with ſome gently riſing grounds and pleaſant vales. †

THE fields are invariably divided by quick-ſet hedges, which, with the trees planted in hedge-rows, and pieces of woodland ſcattered on the banks of the rivers, and the thriving plantations around the gentlemen's houſes, conſpire to give the country a rich, pleaſing and chearful aſpect.

THE coaſt, from the mouth of the river Tees, lies open, as far as *Huntcliffe*, ‡ when the cliffs eaſtwards riſe to a conſiderable height, ſteep,

---

† SEE the engraving, as a frontiſpiece to the work.

‡ THE following lines, deſcriptive of this part of *Cleveland*, and addreſſed to the gentlemen in the neighbourhood, were written by the *late John Hall*, *Eſq. of Skelton-Caſtle*. The original is in Greek, and the tranſlation was made for the uſe of the mere Engliſh reader.—The ſubject being local, we cannot omit their inſertion here.

A CLEVELAND PROSPECT.

" I am the firſt, that with advent'rous hand
In Grecian colours, draw my native land,
Hold the fair landſcape up to public view,
And point out beauties, known to none but you.

   See! haughty *Lofthouſe* there, with allum ſtor'd,
Lofthouſe ſtill weeping for her *hapleſs Lord.* *
Kilton's deep vales, white rill, and ſylvan gloom;
Freebro's huge mount, immortal Arthur's tomb;
And *Huntly,* ſcowling o'er the diſtant main,
With cloudy head involv'd in murky rain;
Skelton beneath, the jocund muſe's bow'r,
Smiles on the bard, an ancient humble tow'r;
Where *feeling Triſtram* † dwelt in days of yore,
Where joyful *Panty* ‡ makes the table roar.

---

* THE late Zachary Moore, Eſq.   † STERNE was a frequent viſiter of Skelton-Caſtle.

‡ A familiar name, for a facetious friend, the late Rev. *Robert Laſſells*, A. M. vicar of Gilling, near Richmond.

and rocky; the feet of which are wafhed by the fea. Of this part of the coaft, the *Cott. MS.* affords us the following quaint defcription.

" ALONGE the fhoare the fandes lye fayre and levell, till you arrive " at a high hill, called *Huntly Nabb;* there the coafte begins to rife " high, full of craggs and fteepe rocks, wherein meawes, pidgeons, and " feafowle breade plentifully. Here, the fea caftinge up peble ftones " maketh the coafte troublefome to paffe."

To the foregoing remarks on the foil, and general appearance of the diftrict, we may add fome brief obfervations on the

Behold *Upleatham* § flop'd with graceful eafe,
Hanging enraptur'd o'er the *winding Tees :*
Whole provinces extended at her feet,
And crowded fhips, that feem an endlefs fleet :
No favage beauties here with awe furprize ;
Sweet, heart-felt charms, like *Lady Charlotte's* eyes.

Mark *Tockets*, || —nurfe and cradle of the loves,
Where *Venus* keeps her children, and her doves.
Thro' yon tremendous arch, like heaven's vaft bow,
See! like Palmyra, *Guifbrough* great in woe ;
Thofe tow'ring rocks, green hills, and fpacious plains,
Circled with woods, are *Chaloner's* domains,
A generous race, from *Cambro-Griffin* ¶ trac'd,
Fam'd for fair maids and matrons wife and chafte.

Obferve,—nor let thofe ftately piles below,
Nor *Turner's* princely realms unnoticed go ;
Forc'd, like Rome's conful, with reluctant brow,
To leave his oxen, cabbages, and plough ;
His all that coaft,—and *his* that wave-wafh'd feat,
Cotham, where *Cleveland* nymphs and naïds meet ;
Next fifhy *Redcar ;* view *Marfk's* funny lands,
And fands, beyond *Pactolus'* golden fands ;
'Till *fhelvy Saltburn*, cloth'd with fea-weed green,
And *Giant-Huntcliffe*, clofe the pleafing fcene."

§ THE feat of the Right Hon, Lord Dundas. || Now called *the Plantation;* the feat of General Hale.
¶ THE *Chaloners* are paternally defcended from *Trahayrne the Great*, fon of *Mayloc Krwme* (alias *Chaloner*) one of the 15 Peers or Tribes of North-Wales, by marriage with *Gwenllyan*, daughter of *Howell Koedmore*, who was lineally defcended from *Griffith*, fon of *Llyllyan ap Jerworth*, prince of Wales,—The pedigree of this ancient family will be given at length in the fequel of this work.

F

Population, and general character of its Inhabitants.

CLEVELAND being chiefly an agricultural diſtrict, and as little connected perhaps with *manufactures*,* as any part of the kingdom, of
equal extent, its population, as might be expected, is by no means large.
From the returns † made to government in the year 1801, according
to act of Parliament, the total number of inhabitants was 26,358; and
confidering, that the property within the diſtrict is ſtationary in its
nature, no material alteration, in point of number, is ſince that time
likely to have taken place.

IN reſpect to the general character of the inhabitants, the following
obſervations, by an impartial and judicious writer, ‡ will not, we prefume be unacceptable to our readers; which, although intended as a
delineation of the character of the farmers in general within the *North
Riding*, will be found to be highly applicable to thoſe within this particular diſtrict.

" IN thoſe parts of the North Riding which are beſt cultivated,"
(under which character *Cleveland* muſt certainly be included,) " the

---

* THE manufacture of coarſe linens, which is the principal one within the diſtrict, has, in its preſent ſtate, been ſo far from proving prejudicial either to the health or morals of the individuals concerned in it, that it may fairly be confidered, not only as the cauſe of an increaſe in population, but
alſo prove advantageous to the ſtate of agriculture, by increaſing the profits of ſome of the lower
claſſes, and conſequently advancing the value of the produce of the land.

† STATE of population within the eaſt and weſt diviſion of the Wapontake of Langbargh;
March 10, 1801.

	HOUSES.			PERSONS.			OCCUPATIONS.			
	Inha-bited houſes.	Fami-lies.	Unin-habit-ed.	Males.	Females.	Total.	Agricul-ture.	Trade, Manuf. &c.	Reſidue.	Total.
Eaſt Diviſion	3162	3324	143	6961	7939	14900	3766	2803	8331	14900
Weſt Diviſion	2517	2581	102	5565	5893	11458	3352	2625	5481	11458
Total.	5679	5905	245	12526	13832	26358	7118	5428	13812	26358

THE return of each townſhip within the diſtrict will be given under the head of their reſpective
pariſhes.

‡ *TUKE, in his Agricultural Survey, pp.* 48, 49.

" farmers form a very refpectable clafs of fociety, and defervedly rank
" high among their fellows in any part of England; they are generally
" fober, induftrious and orderly; moft of the younger part of them
" have enjoyed a proper education, and give a fuitable one to their
" children, who, of both fexes, are brought up in habits of induftry and
" economy. Such conduct rarely fails meeting its reward; they who
" merit, and feek it, obtain independence, and every generation, or
" part of every generation, may be feen ftepping forward to a fcale in
" fociety fomewhat beyond the laft. Fortunately, this country is pure-
" ly agricultural, and the inhabitants, folely cultivators of the earth,
" are endowed with the virtues of their profeffion, uncontaminated by
" the neighbourhood, or vices of manufactures."

To this character of the farmers, we may add, that the lower and
labouring claffes of inhabitants are generally fober and orderly in their
conduct, decent in their demeanour and appearance, and deferving of
every indulgence from their fuperiors, that may render their fituation
comfortable and eafy.

But the circumftances moft favourable to the general intereft of
the diftrict, is the almoft conftant refidence of many of the principal
proprietors of eftates, who, by their example, give encouragement to
the improved modes of agriculture; and by whofe influence and authority, the roads * are kept in a very fuperior ftate of repair; juftice
is impartially adminiftered; and thereby the good order and comfort
of individuals, and the general happinefs and profperity of the country
are invariably confulted and promoted.

---

* CLEVELAND had long to boaft of what no other diftrict, perhaps in England, of equal extent,
could do: viz. excellent roads extending in different directions for near 60 miles in length, without
any tolls, being maintained by voluntary fubfcriptions, and the ftatute-duty of the inhabitants. This
circumftance, fo creditable to the diftrict, can now be no longer boafted of; as two *toll-gates* have
been lately erected upon a piece of road, made by act of Parliament, in the year 1803, between *Yarm*
and *Thirfk*; but as this line of road leads through a pleafant and fertile part of the country, by which
not only the diftance between thofe places will be confiderably fhortened, but the road itfelf rendered
more eafy and commodious, the advantages arifing from this improvement will be an ample compenfation for the expence that will thereby be laid upon the public.

LANGBARGH WAPONTAKE

HAS the next claim to our attention; the name of which, in old records, is written *Langberge*, and fometimes *Langbergh*, and is evidently compounded of Lang, *(Longus)* and Bȳɲiꝝ, two words in the Saxon language, fignifying a *large mountain* or *tumulus;* and perhaps it might be fo called from a chain of circular entrenchments, which feem to have formed part of fome general plan of defence, by fmall pofts, the remains of which are ftill vifible on the fides, and near the fummit of many of the hills within the diftrict.

WE have been led to this conjecture from the confideration that the word *Bargh*, or *Bergh*, (the theme of which is evidently the Saxon Bȳɲiꝝ, or rather Beoɲꝝ, which *Skinner* calls *Collis*, feu *Munimentum)* includes in its fignification, according to Camden, *a rifing ground*, fuch as forts are generally built upon.

IN order, however, to indulge the curiofity of our readers with another conjecture as to the etymology of the name, we may obferve, that the word *Bargh* is merely a Yorkfhire *provincialifm*, denoting, according to *Ray*, " *a horfe-way, up a fteep hill.*" It is ufed chiefly in the compofition of local names, though frequently corrupted into *Baurgh*, or *Barff*, as *Brayton-Barff*, a hill near Selby in this county, with a road leading up to its fummit; and fometimes into *Barr*, as *Bergholt* in Effex is now called *Barfield*. How far thefe conjectures may ferve to elucidate the etymology of the name, we leave it to the judgment of our readers, obferving only that the word is fometimes written *Langbaurgh*, and generally pronounced by the inhabitants *Langbarff;* and that the concluding fyllable, with fome modification, enters into the compofition of many local names within the diftrict.

WE have no certain evidence of the proprietors of this Wapontake till after the Conqueft; the fee of which remained in the crown till the eighth year of the reign of King John, when it was granted by letters patent* to *Peter de Brus*, Lord of Skelton, to hold to him and his heirs, of the faid King and his heirs, on payment of 400 marks †, and rendering yearly at the Exchequer the due and ancient rent, and alfo an increafe of 20*l. pro omni fervitio.* But Peter, his fon and fucceffor (17 John) being found in arms, with the rebellious barons againft that king, at *Brackley*, in affiftance of Lewis, the Dauphine of France, his

---

* Charta Wapentach. ⎰
  v. Feb. viii. Johan. ⎰ JOHANNES, Dei Gratia, Rex Angliæ, Dominus Hiberniæ, Dux Normaniæ et Aquitaniæ, Comes Andeg. Archiepifcopis, Epifcopis, Abbatibus, Comitibus, Baronibus, Jufticiariis, Vicecomitibus, Prepofitis, et omnibus Ballivis, et fidelibus fuis, Salutem. Sciatis nos dediffe, conceffiffe, et prefenti charta noftra confirmaffe, *Petro de Brus*, Wapentach. de Langbergh cum pertinent. fuis in Com. Ebor. habend. et tenend. ei et Heredibus fuis de nobis, et Heredibus noftris, reddendo inde annuatim ad Scaccarium noftrum debitam et antiquam Firmam, et pretærea de Cremento xx. Libras pro omni fervitio. Ita tamen, quod de placitis quæ pertinent ad coronam noftram refpondebunt coram Jufticiariis noftris itinerantibus in partibus illis. Attachiamenta autem eorundem Placitorum fient per Vice Comitem et Coronatores. De aliis vero placitis, quæ pertinent ad Vice Com. refpondebunt coram Vic. Prædictus Petrus et Hæredes fui habeant et teneant de nobis et Hæredibus noftris prædictum Wapentach. per predictum fervitium benè et in pace, liberè et quietè, integre et honorificè cum omnibus pertinentiis et Libertatibus, et liberis confuetudinibus fuis, ficut predictum eft. Teftibus, Dno. G. Ebor. Archiepo. Dnis. J. Norwycens. P. Wynton. J. Bathon. Epif. G. Filio Petri, Com. Effex. R. Com. Ceft. Willo Breiverr. Sim. de Pateshill ; Jacobo de Paterna. Dat. per Manum Hug. de Well, Archidiaconi Wellens. Apud Oxon. v°. Die Februarii, Anno Regni noftri octavo.

Univerfis, quibus hæc charta vifura vel auditura fit, *Petrus de Brus*, Salutem in Domino. Noveritis me conceffiffe, et hac prefenti charta mea confirmaffe *Milit.* et *libere Tenent. Cleveland.* et *Wapentag. de Langberge*, et omnibus eorum, quod nullus fummoneatur nec implacitat. ad Wapentagium de Lanberge, nec per confiderationem Wapentag. vel per Rationabil. nec aliquis eorum confuatur.

Et fi aliquis eorum in Forisfact. ceciderit, amenfurabit fecundum Ætatem fuam, et fecundum Delict. per quod ceciderit ; præterea conceffi eis quam fumus.

† Petrus de Brus debet CCCC marcas pro habendo *Wapentach. de Lanbergh* cum pertinentiis fuis in Com. Ebor. tenendum fibi et Heredibus fuis de Rege et Heredibus fuis, reddendo inde annuatim ad Scaccarium, *debitam* et *antiq. Firmam‡*, et præterea de Cremento xx lb. pro omni Servitio. Ita, &c.

                                 Magn. Rot. Pip. in Scacc. Anno ix°. *Reg. Johannes, Rot.* 7. *a.*
‡ 17*l.* 11*s.* 11*d.*

eftates became forfeited, and this Wapontake came again into the
hands of the crown; but thofe differences being foon after compofed,
his fon Peter, on the death of his father, (6 Henry III.) giving one
hundred pounds for the relief of his barony, had livery thereof; and
alfo of this Wapontake, on paying *forty marks* more for the recovery
of that inheritance *. On the death of Peter his fon, the fourth of
that name, who died without iffue, his lands became divided among
his four fifters, when this Wapontake, with other eftates in Cleveland,
defcended to Walter de Fauconberg, by marriage with Agnes the eldeft; from whom, after three defcents, it came to John de Fauconberg,
fon and heir of Walter, the fourth of that name; and afterwards to
Walter, fon and heir of John. To this Walter, King Edward III. by
letters patent under the great feal of England, bearing date the eighth
day of April, in the 24th year of his reign, confirmed the faid Wapontake of Langbargh, and the liberties, privileges and franchifes, with
all the rights, members and appurtenances thereof; to him and his
heirs for ever: after whofe death it defcended to Thomas, his fon and
heir, who died without iffue male, leaving Joan, his daughter, who
married Sir William Nevill, knight; afterwards Lord Fauconberge,
and Earl of Kent. But male iffue again failing, the inheritance defcended to Joan, Alice and Elizabeth, as fifters and coheireffes. Joan

---

* *Ex Rotulo Finium de Anno fexto Henrici tertii, m. 6. Anno* 1222.

Ebor. Rex Vic. Ebor. Salutem. Scias quod *Peter de Brus*, filius et hæres *Petri de Brus* finem
fecit nobifcum per Clb. pro relievio fuo de Baronia quæ fuit ipfius Petri, patris fui, quam de nobis
tenuit in capite, et per 40 marcas pro habendo Wapentach. de Langberge, quod ipfi jure hæredit-
ario contingit; finem etiam fecit nobifcum de ij libr. 6s. et 7d. de debito quod pater ejus nobis debuit. Ita fcilicet quod de illis C. libr. de relevio fuo folvit nobis ad fcaccar. noftrum per manum
fuam L. libr. in fefto beati Johannis Baptiftæ, et anno 6to et L. lib. in fefto Sancti Andreæ prox, fequenti, anno et 7mo, et ad Pafch. fequent. Anno eodem fatisfac. nobis de predictus ij lib. 6s. et 7d.
et in fefto Sancti Michielis fequenti anno eodem folvet nobis XL. marc. Et ideo tibi percipimus
quod ipfi Petro de prædicta Baronia et prædicto Wapentach. cum pertinent quæ ipfi jure hereditario
contingunt in ballia tua plenam ei Seizinam fine delatione habere fac et fac ei interim pacem noftram habere de prædictis 2 lib. 6s. et 7d. de debito noftro. Tefte, Hubert de Burgo, jufticiario noftro, apud Weftm. tertio die Februarii.

died without iffue ; and partition being made between the furviving
fifters, this Wapontake, with the manor of Yarm, and other eftates,
was allotted to Alice, the wife of John Conyers ; in which family it
continued till the death of John Lord Conyers, (3. and 4. Philip and
Mary,) when it defcended to his two daughters, coheireffes ; viz.
Elizabeth the wife of Thomas Darcy, and Catherine the wife of John
Atherton, efq. from whofe defcendants, after divers grants and alienations *, it was conveyed to, and, about the year 1666, became folely
vefted in Sir George Marwood, of Little Bufby, bart.

---

* JOHN Atherton, efq. granted his moiety of the Wapontake to Sir Henry Ballafis, bart. †, the
grant bearing date, June 26. (12 James I.) : it afterwards defcended to Thomas Lord Fauconberg
his fon, by whom it was affigned, in 1631, to James Mauleverer, efq. whofe fon Timothy, in 1666,
conveyed it to the Marwoods. Conyers Lord Darcy, who was heir at law as well to Sir Conyers
Darcy, knight, as to Catherine, wife of John Atherton, efquire, and Ann her daughter, (who married Sir William Pennyman, bart. and died without iffue,) granted and confirmed the other moiety
to Sir George Marwood, bart. about the year 1660.

AN information being exhibited by the Attorney-General, in the Court of Exchequer, in the nature
of a *quo warranto*, (*in Hilar. Term*, 14. *James I.*) againft *Sir Henry Bellafis, bart.* for the faid Wapontake,
judgment was given for Sir Henry, that he fhould hold the faid Wapontake, with the *liberties, privileges*
and *franchifes*; which he claimed in his plea ; viz. " to have, hold and enjoy the *knight's fees* and *rents*
" of *affize*, of all and fingular the tenants and other fervices, within the faid Wapontake ; and alfo the
" *office of bailiff* and *bailiwick* aforefaid, and fines of the Wapontake aforefaid, commonly called *Wapon-*
" *take fines*, or *Blanch-Farms* ; and alfo the *execution* and *return* of all and fingular warrants, writs, and
" precepts of our faid Lord the King, his heirs and fucceffors, in or within the Wapontake aforefaid, to
" be executed, returning or happening ; and alfo to have and hold within the faid Wapontake court leet
" and view of frank-pledge of all and fingular the tenants, inhabitants and refidents within the faid Wa-
" pentake, and the Sheriff's Turn and other courts within the Wapontake aforefaid ; and to have the
" fines, iffues, amerciaments and profits of the courts aforefaid. And to have the correction and exa-
" mination of the affize of bread, wine and ale, and other victuals ; the fearch of weights and meafures ;
" pillory, tumbrel and gallows, for malefactors ; the choofing of conftables, and other officers within the
" faid Wapontake, and all that which belongeth to the view of frank-pledge : and to have all goods and
" chattells waived, called Waives ; and all goods and chattells eftrayed, called Strays ; goods and chat-
" tells of felons, fugitives, outlawed perfons,—felons of themfelves, and thofe that fly away ; goods con-
" fifcate, and to be confifcated, or in any manner of way forfeited ; deodands within the Wapontake
" aforefaid. And to have within the faid Wapontake one market every week, on Thurfday, in Yarum,
" within the faid Wapontake ; and two fairs every year, there to endure by one day refpectively,—that
" is to fay, in *the feaft of the afcenfion of our Lord*, and of *St. Mary Magdalene* ; and alfo a court there
" likewife to be held, commonly called *a Court of Piepowder*, or a Court of the Market ; and by reafon
" of the markets and fairs aforefaid, to take and have there the *tolls* of all and fingular the fubjects of
" our faid Lord the King, of all and fingular the *cattle, grains*, and *goods* and *chattells*, by them to the
" markets and fairs aforefaid brought or carried, and in the fame, or any of them fold, and the *ftallage*

Sir Henry Marwood, his fon, fucceeded him, on whofe death, in the year 1725, it defcended to his grand-daughter, Jane, wife of Chomley Turner, efq. of Kirkleatham, whom fhe furvived; but dying without male iffue, fhe devifed the faid Wapontake to her nephew, William Marwood, efq. who is now feized in fee of the fame, with its appurtenances, liberties and free cuftoms.

By virtue of the original grant from King John, the Lords of the Wapontake became entitled to the execution and return of all writs*,

---

* The Seal of the Court of Langbargh Wapontake.

It is probable that the above Seal may be a Reprefentation of the Gate of Langbargh, which, ftood formerly near the quarry, upon the road leading from *Stokesley* to *Guifborough*, where the steward ftill holds his court, *pro forma.* There was anciently a prifon belonging to the Lords of the Wapontake, for the confinement of malefactors, which, it is conjectured, was a part of the building reprefented in the Seal; as alfo a room, in which the Wapontake Courts were ufually holden.

" and *pickage* there, with all and fingular other profits, commodities and emoluments, to the fame mar-
" kets, fairs, and courts aforefaid belonging, and the profits coming thereof, to his own ufe to convert
" and difpofe; and alfo to name, elect, conftitute and admit a clerk of the market aforefaid, to do there
" all that which belongeth to the office of a clerk of the market of our Lord the King, within the mar-
" ket aforefaid; and alfo to have within the Wapontake of Langbargh aforefaid, *one court baron* from
" three weeks to three weeks, or otherwife at the liking of the faid Henry, within the Wapontake afore-
" faid, commonly called *the Wapontake Court*, to be held before his fteward for the time being; and before
" his fteward of the faid court, for the time being to have and to hold in that court, *cognizance of all*
" *pleas, fuits, plaints* and *demands* whatfoever: and alfo all manner of actions, real, perfonal, and mixed
" whatfoever, within the Wapontake aforefaid and precincts thereof, moved or to be moved, (treafons
" and felonies only excepted,) and to have *cognizance of all pleas of debts, accounts covenant, contracts,*
" *trefpaffes with force and arms,* or otherwife, and other actions and trefpaffes within the Wapontake of
" Langbargh aforefaid and precincts thereof, made or to be made, *deceipt, detinue,* and of all other pleas
" and contracts whatfoever, not amounting to the fum of forty fhillings, happening or arifing within the
" Wapontake of Langbargh aforefaid, and precincts thereof, (treafons and felonies only excepted).——
" And alfo to have one goal, called *Toll-Booth,* in Yarm, within the Wapontake aforefaid, for malefac-

iffuing againft defendants refiding within the liberty, which privilege was confirmed by a judicial determination upon a *quo warranto*, in the 20. Charles II. and has ever fince been exercifed by them. They have alfo, as Lords of the Leet, taken the benefit of felons' goods, and other forfeitures; and have received certain fmall rents, called Wapontake fines, or *Blanch-Farms*, from the feveral townfhips*, which lie within this Wapontake, amounting to 16*l*. 8*s*. 8½*d*. paid yearly at the feaft of St. Cuthbert.

---

* In *Rawlinfon's MSS*. (vol. 448, fol. 84.) preferved in the *Bodleian Library*, Oxford, there is the copy of an Inquifition, taken in the 13th year of the reign of King Edward I. before *John de Kirkeby*, the King's Treafurer; from which it appears that there were *ninety-feven townfhips* within this Wapontake; the names of which, with the quantities of land they held, and the rents payable for them, are therein particularly mentioned. The following extract from the Inquifition is all that relates to this part of the fubject; but the remaining parts of this valuable record will be parcelled out under the head of each townfhip, in the fucceeding pages of this work.

Wapentag.
de
LANGBERGHE.

INQUISITIO facta apud Ormesby, coram *Domino Johanne de Kirkeby*, Thefaur. Domini Regis, die fabbati proximo ante paffionem Domini, anno regni Regis EDWARDI tertio decimo, per hos viros; (viz.) Dominum *Ricardum de Skolerscelf Dominum de Rofelle, Gilbertum de Cambra, Walter de Hurwath, Walt. Thorpe, Petrum Bagotte, Johannem de Redmerfhall, Johan. de Kirkeby, Thomam Gower, Robertum Colby, Ricardum de Thorme, R. de Marton, Thomam Waxander,* et *Rad. de Batherfby.*

QUI dicunt fuper facramentum, quod $\overline{\text{XX}}_{\text{IIII.}}$ et XVII. villæ funt in Wapentag. de Langberghe; fcilicet; *Marfke* cum *Uplethum* cum *Weft-Cotum, Tocotts, Lafingby, Lakingby, Efton, Northmanby, Ormefby, Marton, Tollefby, Newham, Middlefburghe, Acclum, Arfum* cum *Levingthorpe, Staynfby, Hemlington, Stayntum* cum *Thorneton, Maltby, Thormonby, Barwick, Ingleby-Loring, Yarom, Wirlefdaill* cum *Stayndalbrig, Kirkelenton, Caftle-Lenington, Crathorne* cum *Foxton, Roughton, Engilby* juxta *Arnecliffe, Faceby* cum *Sexhowe, Karleton,* Magna *Bufkeby, Dromonby,* Parva *Bufkeby,* Parva *Broxton,* Magna *Broxton, Grenehowe, Engilby* juxta *Grenehowe, Baderfby, Ayton, Newton, Pinchingthorpe, Efbye,*

" tors; and to have quarries, and other mines of ftone and coals whatfoever, in the Wapontake afore-
" faid; and alfo to have free *foldage, turbary, eftovers, commons, places wafted,* free *pifcary* and *fifhings,*
" within the faid Wapontake; and alfo *wreck of fea,* and *anchorage* within the Wapontake aforefaid,
" from *Runfwick* to *Yarm* aforefaid; and *fifhes-royal* and great fifhes within the fame, from *Runfwick* to
" *Yarm* aforefaid; and alfo things left, *plankage, lagon* and *jotage,* and other franchifes of the fea, within
" the aforefaid Wapontake."

THE following TABLE OF DESCENTS will give the reader a clear idea of the fucceffion of the Lords of this Wapontake, down to the period of its firft alienation by the Lord Darcy.

Kildayll, Hoton, Gifburne, Upfall, Murton, Nunthorpe, Tonefdaylle, Seymor, Tanton cum *Newby, Hilton, Querelton* cum *Traneholme, Pottowe, Hoton* juxta *Rudby, Myddelton* cum *Thorpe, Skelton, Bretton, Skyningrave, Morefom* cum *Stayneleve, Grenerig, Danby, Wefterdaill, Leverton* cum *Wapillowe, Loftous, Boleby, Ceton, Rouefby, Hilderwell, Newton, Barntby* alias *Barneby, Lithe, Egton, Rudby, Pickton* et *Worftingby.*

Et quæ villæ funt gildabiles, et quæ non.——Dicunt, &c. &c.

AT the conclufion of this Inqueft we find the following entry: " Summa Feod. iftius Wapentag. " XXXII. Feod. et Dimid. V.ta pars unius Feod. et una Bovat. Terr."

Robert de Brus the founder of the Priory at Guisbro' came into England with the Conqueror. (ob. 1141.) = Agnes, dau. of Faulke Paynell

William de Brus was the first Prior of Guisbro'; died A.D. 1155, and buried in the Chapterhouse there.

Adam de Brus, eldest son; ob. 13. Kal. April, A.D. 1167. = Jvetta, dau. of Wm. de Arches widow of R. de Flamville.

Adam de Brus died A.D. 1180.

Robert de Brus, the 2d son; from whom the kings of Scotland of that name were descended.

Peter de Brus to whom King John granted the wapontake of Langburg. ob. 16. Kal. Feb. 1217. = Agnes, dau. of Stephen Earl of Albemarle, widow of Wm. de Romara, Earl of Lincoln.

Isabella = Sir Henry de Percy from de Brus. whom the Percies Earls of Northumberland descended.

Peter de Brus the second of that name, died at Marseiles, A.D. 1240. = Helewise, dau. of Gilbert de Lancaster, Baron of Kendal.

Peter de Brus, the 3d = Hillaria, dau. of Lord Malo-lacu, or Mauley.

Peter de Brus, the 4th died unmarried 1271; leaving his four sisters his heirs.

Agnes de Brus the eldest. = Walter de Fauconberge, Lord of Rise in Holderness, ob. A. D. 1304. (a)

2d. Lucy = Marmaduke de Thweng;
3d. Margaret = Sir Robert Rosse, Lord of Werke.
4th. Ladarina = Sir John de Bella-aqua, or Bellew.

(a) THIS Walter, on the death of Peter de Brus, performing his fealty, had livery of the purparty of his inheritance; viz. the Castle of Skelton, with its members; the manors of Marsk, Redkar, and Upleytham; the towns of Stanghow and Grenerigg, with the forrein of Skelton, (viz. the Hay and Great Park) with the hasdale and chase of Westwyt and forrein; as it is bounded with the highway betwixt Stangho and Kadriding.

Dugd. Bar. vol. 2. p. 3.

Peter 1ft fon died young.

Walter, Lord Fauconberge, 2d fon. (b) == Ifabella, dau. of Robert Lord Roos of Hamlake.

Walter, Lord Fauconberge, ob. 1318. == Anaftafia, daughter of Ralph Neville.

Walter, Lord Fauconberge.

John, Lord Fauconberge, ob. 1349. (c) == Eva de Bulmer.

Maud, dau. of John Patefhull, 1ft wife. == Walter, Lord Fauconberge, ob. 1362. == Ifabella, fifter of John Bigott, 2d wife.

Conftantia, fifter of Wm. de Felton living 1376. 1ft wife. == Thomas Fauconberge, Knt. == Sifter of Sir Thomas Bromflett, Knt. 2d wife.

John rebelled, and was beheaded at Durham.

Walter died in Spain.

Sir William Neville, Knt. afterwards Lord Fauconberge and Earl of Kent. == Johanna Fauconberge.

John died young.

John Conyers. == Alicia, the 3d daughter.

Johanna. == Sir Edward Bedhowing, Knt.

Elizabeth. == Sir Richard Strangways, Knt.

William Conyers, Knt. the first Lord Conyers. (d) == Ann, dau. of Ralph Neville the 3d Earl of Westmorland.

(b) He was made Knight, with Prince Edward, and other eminent perfons (34. Edw. I.) by bathing and other sacred ceremonies; and was summoned to Parliament from 32. Edw. I. till 12. Edw. II.

(c) THIS John (13. Edw. II.) obtained a licence from the King, for changing the weekly market-day at Skelton, from Sunday to Saturday; and for a fair there every year upon Monday in whitfun-week, and two days following (Carr. 13. Edw. II. n. 31.) and having been in the Expeditions made into Flanders, had an allowance of 270l. 7s. 5d. for wages in thofe wars, to be paid out of the fubfidy of fheaf, lamb, and wool, about that time granted in Parliament to the King. In 15. Edw. III. he was confituted Sheriff of Yorkfhire, and Governour of the Caftle of York; and died 23. Edw. III.

(d) IN 8. Henry VII. he accompanied Ralph, Earl of Weftmorland, and other northern lords, to raife the feige of Norham Castle; and in the 22d year of that King's reign bore the title of Lord Conyers. He had fummons to Parliament 1. Henry VIII. and was made conftable of the Castles of Richmond and Middleham: and marching with the Earl of Surrey againft the Scots, was at the battle of Flodden Field, where King James IV. loft his life.

Christopher Lord Conyers,=Ann, dau. of William
ob. 30. Henry 8. Lord Dacres of Gilland.

John, Lord Conyers,=Matilda, daughter of Henry Clifford
(ob. 3 & 4. Phil. and Earl of Cumberland.
Mary.) (e)

Thomas Darcy, Esq.=Elizabeth Conyers, John Atherton, Esq.=Katherine Conyers. ob. *fine prole.* Anne=Anth. Kempe, Esq. Conyers, of .... Co. Kent. (ob. *S. P.*)
ob. A. D. 1605.

John.

Ann.=Sir Wm. Pennyman of Mark, Bart. (ob. *S. P.*)

Conyers, Lord Darcy and Conyers,=Dorothy, dau. of Sir Henry Bellasis, Knt. and Bart.
ob. A. D. 1653. (*f*)

Conyers, Lord Darcy, and=Grace, dau. and heir of Sir Thomas Rokeby of Skiers, Knt.
Conyers, created Earl of
Holderness in 1682.
Died 1688. (*g*)

Conyers, Lord Darcy,=Frances, dau. of Thomas Earl of Berkshire.
Earl of Holderness.

Margaret.=Henry Marwood, Esq.=Dorothy, dau. of Alan Bellingham, of Levens,
(ob. *S.P.*) of Little Buby, died Co. Westmorland. 2 wife.
1725.

(e) THIS *John Lord Conyers* was with the Earl of Hertford, when Leith was taken by the English, and knighted there 26. Henry VIII. and 5. Edw. VI. was warden of the West-Marches, and governour of the Castle at Carlisle; and in the first year of the reign of Queen Mary, was warden of the East-Marches, and governour of Berwick.

(*f*) HE was great-grandson to Thomas Lord Darcy, who, upon that insurrection of the Yorkshiremen, called *the Pilgrimage of Grace*, was found guilty of high treason, and beheaded on *Tower-Hill*, 30. Henry VIII. After the death of John, Lord Darcy of Aston, without issue male, this *Sir Conyers Darcy*, in his petition to King Charles I. set forth, that, being the principal male branch of that ancient and noble family; and likewise son and heir of Elizabeth, daughter and coheir of John Lord Conyers; lineal heir to Margery, daughter and coheir to Philip Lord Darcy, son of John, Lord Darcy, one of the Barons of this realm, in the time of King Henry the fourth;—did humbly desire, that his Majesty would be pleased to declare, restore and confirm to him, the said *Sir Conyers Darcy*, and to the heirs-male of his body, the title and dignity of *Lord Darcy*;—whereunto his Majesty condescending, he did, by letters patent, bearing date, at Westminster, 10th August, in the 17th year of his reign, declare, restore and confirm unto him, and the heirs-male of his body lawfully begotten, the title, title and dignity of *Lord Darcy*, as enjoyed by his ancestors; whereupon he had summons to Parliament accordingly.

(*g*) THIS Conyers, Lord Darcy, conveyed the wapontake of Langbargh to the Marwood family.

CLEVELAND hath not only given name to one of the three *Arch Deaconries* into which the county is divided; but alfo the title of *Earl* to the family of Wentworth; and of *Duke* to the natural iffue of King Charles II. Thomas, Lord Wentworth of Nettlefted, in this county, having been made knight of the Bath, at the creation of Henry Prince of Wales (8. James I. 1610,) was created *Earl of Cleveland*, February 5th, 1. Charles I. He was foon after made Captain of the guards by the fame Prince, to whom, in his diftrefs, he gave the moft evident proofs of fidelity and loyalty, for which he fuffered imprifonment in the tower of London, during the greateft part of the ufurpation; yet, he lived till King Charles II. was reftored to the crown, and himfelf to his command in the guards, which he enjoyed till his death, when he left his honour and his eftates to Thomas, his fon and heir; but he dying without iffue-male, his honour became extinct; but the title of *Duchefs* was conferred, by King Charles II. in the 22d year of his reign, on Barbara Villiers, (fole daughter and heir of William, Lord Villiers, Vifcount Grandifon, who was flain in the firft battle for the King againft the Parliament,) Baronefs of Nonfuch, in the county of Surry, and Countefs of Southampton, to enjoy for life, with remainder to *Charles Fitz-Roy*, his Majefty's natural fon by her, and to the heirs-male of his body; and, for lack of fuch iffue, to his brother *George*, another of that King's natural fons.—Charles, upon his mother's death, fucceded to the title of *Duke of Cleveland* in 1709: he married Anne, daughter of Sir William Pulteney of Mifterton, in Leicefterfhire, by whom he had two fons, William and Charles; and three daughters, Barbara, Grace, and Anne. William, his fon, fucceeded him, and was fucceeded by his fon William in 1730; who dying in 1774, without male-iffue, the title became extinct.

BIOGRAPHY.

T O no part of his allotted labour does the Topographer, or *County-Hiſtorian* betake himſelf with more ſatisfaction, than to that, which calls upon him to record men of diſtinguiſhed and eminent characters; yet, we are not inſenſible to the objections that have been brought againſt this particular department of local hiſtories.

OF the compilers of ſuch works, it is expected by thoſe, who are moſt intereſted in them, and beſt able to appreciate their merits, that no perſon of any note, who was born, or reſided long, in the diſtrict, of which an hiſtory is undertaken, ſhould be paſſed over wholly un-noticed. It is owing, however, in all probability, to this cuſtom of tracing the riſe and progreſs of families *almoſt indiſcriminately*, and of examining whether they have performed any very extraordinary and memorable ſervices, that the biography of county-hiſtory has, *no leſs indiſcriminately*, been ſtigmatized as dull, unimportant, and unintereſt-ing. Far from denying that the charge is ſometimes, perhaps often, well-founded, we truſt it is not always ſo, and that the offence it gives, is neither ſo general, nor ſo important, as to juſtify its being brought into diſcredit, and abandoned. Even family genealogies, the loweſt department of biography, ſhould not, we think, be wholly driven from local hiſtories, as being, in our eſtimation, neither unneceſſary, nor without their uſe. It is not expected, nor indeed proper, that every man, whatever be his ſtation and circumſtances in life, ſhould ſeek to perpetuate his name, by the performance of great and memorable ac-tions; the ſtate of ſociety, and the condition of the world, neither re-quire, nor admit of ſuch general exertions; it is, therefore, of no or-dinary moment to mankind in general, to be ſhewn, and more eſpecially in this age of adventure and enterprize, that he does not act his part ill, in the drama of life, who is quiet and unambitious in an humble fphere; purfuing " *the noifelefs tenour of his way*," with the good-will of his cotemporaries, and contented, when he quits the fcene, to leave behind him a fair, though not a brilliant fame.

THE pride and pleafure we might have taken, in having fuch a life, as that of Dr. BRIAN WALTON, to record in our hiftory, is much diminifhed by the confcioufnefs, that though the diftrict of which we have prefumed to compile the hiftory, has undoubtedly the honour of having given him birth, we have, neverthelefs, after the moft diligent refearch, been fo unfortunate, as not to difcover the particular place of his nativity; and confequently unable to recover any unpublifhed memorials of his family, of fufficient importance to claim the notice of the public. As a native of *Cleveland* however, we have only to remark, on the authority of preceding biographers, that *Dr. Brian Walton*, after receiving the rudiments of grammar learning, was fent to *Magdalen-College, Cambridge*, in the ftation of *a Sizer;* from whence he removed to *Peter-Houfe*, and took his mafter's degree there. We are led to conclude, that he was born of honeft and induftrious parents, in the lower walks of fociety; it being recorded of him, that he entered the world meanly, teaching a fchool, and performing the office of a curate, in Suffolk; in which fituation he removed to London, where he undertook the curacy of *All-Hallows*, in Bread-Street, under the Rev. Mr. Stoke. He afterwards obtained the rectory of *Sandon* in Effex, and *St. Martin, Ogar's*, in London, where he was much efteemed by the orthodox, for his learning and religion.

ON the breaking out of the rebellion, in the reign of King Charles I. he was a faithful adherent to the royal caufe; which occafioned him to be ejected out of his livings, and forced to fly to Oxford; where having leifure, he firft laid the foundation of his defign, of publifhing the

Polyglott Bible, *which, by the help of divers learned men, he lived to effect, in the year 1657. On the reftoration of King Charles II. he prefented that great work, in fix volumes, to his Majefty, who thereupon promoted him to the bifhoprick of Chefter, which he did not however long enjoy; for he died November 29th, 1661.

* " This Bible, which is beautifully printed in 6 vols. folio, is in the *Hebrew, Greek, Vulgate,* " *Latin, Syriac, Chaldee, Samaritan, Arabic, Æthiopic,* and *Perfic* languages. In the life of Dr. " Edward Pocock, prefixed to his " *theological works,*" are fome curious particulars, relative to the " *London Polyglott.* Befides this great work, Granger fays, it is fcarce known, that an Englifh piece " of his was firft printed in the *Collectanea Ecclefiaftica* of Sam. Brewfter, Efq. London, 1752, quarto. " It is called " *a treatife concerning the payment of tythes in London.*"

Granger's biograph. hift. of England, vol. 3, p. 29.

H

THE PARISH OF YARM.

THIS parish is not extensive, stretching in length from east to west about three miles, and scarcely one mile broad. It is bounded on the east by the river Leven, till its confluence with the Tees; on the west and south by the parish of Kirklevington, and on the north wholly by the river Tees.

THE name of the town, which also gives name to the parish, is so variously written, as almost to exceed the ordinary laxity of the old English orthography. In Domesday-book, we find it written **Larun**; and in various charters and grants soon after the conquest, the place is thus differently noted; viz. *Yareham, Yareholm, Yarome, Yarum,* and sometimes *Jarum;* in which last, the J before a vowel according to the *Teutonic,* is sounded like Y. The name is thought to imply a sheltered haven and domain, with some reference to the occupation of its primary inhabitants, mariners; or if we may hazard a more probable conjecture, the etymology may be derived, with some variation, corruption, or harsh pronunciation, from the British word *ea* which signifies *water,* and *ham, a dwelling.* (*q. d. habitatio super rivum.*) This is an etymology, descriptive at least, of its situation; for the town stands low, seated on a narrow neck of land, and washed on three of its sides by the river Tees.

IN the record of *Domesday,* which was begun by order of the Conqueror, with the advice of his parliament, about the year of our Lord 1080, and completed in the year 1086, *Yarm,* according to the orthography of the survey is thus noticed, under the title

"" Terra Regis.
"" Manerium in Larun. Pauuard III. Carucatas ad Geldum, Terra
"" ad I. Car, IIII Solidos.""

Domesday-Book.

FROM which it appears, that Yarm was ancient demesne of the crown, and contained three carucates of land, rated *(ad geldum)* besides which, there was land sufficient for one plough, valued at four shillings.

YARM continued in the crown, till it was given by the Conqueror to *Robert de Brus,* or *le Brus* (from whom the Kings of Scotland of that name, and the noble family of Bruce, Earl of Aylesbury, are descended;) a person of so much note, and so much confided in by the Conqueror, that he rewarded him with no less than forty-three lordships in the east and west ridings, and fifty-one in the north-riding of Yorkshire; whereof the manor and castle of Skelton was the capital of his barony. He lived to an extreme old age, and died in the sixth year of King Stephen, leaving this and his other estates in England to Adam, his son and heir; whose descendants enjoyed this lordship for many successions; till Peter de Brus dying without issue (55. Henry III.) his four sisters became his heirs; of whom, Lucia, the second, marrying Marmaduke de Thweng, had Yarm and some other estates for her share, upon the division.—From the Thwengs this lordship passed by marriage to the Hiltons of Hilton in Cleveland, and from them to the *Meinills* of Whorlton-Castle; which last family enjoyed it, till male-issue failing, Elizabeth the daughter of Nicholas de Meinill, marrying John, Lord D'arcy; and having children by him (though she afterwards married *Peter de Malo-lacu,* or *Mauly 6th,*) when she died in the forty-second year of Edward III. left this, and her other estates to Philip, Lord D'arcy, her son, then fifteen years of age. This Philip had livery of his lands in the 47. Edward III. and was succeeded by John, his son and heir, who married Margaret, daughter of Henry,

H 2

Lord Grey de Wilton, and died 13. Henry IV. Philip his fon fucceeded, and died 6. Henry V. without male-iffue, leaving two daughters, his heirs; viz. Elizabeth and Margaret; the latter of whom, marrying Sir John Conyers, Knight, had Yarm, and divers other lands allotted to her, upon the partition. Yarm continued in the poffeffion of the Conyers' family for feveral generations; till the 3d and 4th of Philip and Mary, when John, Lord Conyers, dying without male-iffue, his three daughters became his heirs; viz. Anne, married to Anthony Kemp, Efq. and died *fine prole;* Catherine was married to John Atherton, Efq.; and Elizabeth, to Thomas D'arcy, Efq. whofe fon, Conyers D'arcy, Knight, and the faid John Atherton fold this manor and eftate in the year 1614 to Sir Henry Bellafife of Newborough, Bart. anceftor to the Earls of Fauconberg; in which family they continued till the death of Henry, the laft Earl, who, on failure of iffue-male, divided his eftates among his four daughters, when Yarm became the property of Sir George Wombwell, Bart. by marriage with Ann, fecond daughter of the faid Earl.

A Pedigree of the family of Bellasise, Viscount Fauconberg, Baron of Yarm, &c.

The name of this family, in old deeds and records, has been varioufly written Bellafife, Bellafyfe, Bellafyfe, &c. from the town of Bellafyfe, in the Bifhoprick of Durham, of which they were owners foon after the conqueft.

Rowland de Bellafyfe===Mary, daughter and heir of
knighted at Lewis, in | Sir Henry Spring, Knt.
Suffex, 48. Henry III. |

Roger de Bellafife===Joan, daughter of Sir Robert Harbottle, Knt.

Sir Robert de Bellafife, Knt.===Anne, daughter of Sir Wm. Gouldbourne, Knt.

Sir John de Bellafife===Ofward, daughter of Sir Wm. Tailbois, Knt.

Thomas.   John de Bellafife===Alice, daughter of John de la Hay.   Dionife===Sir Gerard Sallveyn.

John.   William de Bellafife===Maud, daughter and coheir of Wm. Billingham   Joan===John Buffy, Efq.
fon and heir. | of Billingham, Efq.

* John de Bellafife===Alice, daughter of Sir Robert Hanfard   1 Elizabeth===Sir John Waddome, Knt.
fon and heir. | of Walworth, Knt.   2 Julian===Sir John Carlington, Knt.

Robert de Bellafife===Alice, daughter of   William de Bellafife===Cecily, daughter and heir of   Robert de Bellafife.
fon and heir. | Wm. de Lambton.   fucceeded his brother. | Wm. Hoton of Butterwyke.

John de Bellafife
died without male-
iffue, 18. Henry VI.

* He gave to the Prior and Convent of Durham all his lands, tenements, &c. within the manor of Wolviton, and lordfhip of Bellafife, in exchange for the manor of Henknowle; upon which this proverb had its rife; viz.

" Bellafifer Bellafife, daft was thy *nowle*
" When thou gave Bellafife for Henknowle."

Thomas Bellasse,=Margaret, daughter of Sir
son and heir. | Lancelot Threlkeld, Knt.

Richard Bellasse, con-=Margery, daughter and heir of
stable of the Castle of | Richard Erfington of Morton,
Durham. | Esq. obiit 31. Henry VIII.

Anthony Bellasse, doctor of
civil laws, and master in
Chancery; to whom New-
brough-Abbey was granted
by King Henry VIII.
ob. S. P.

|| William Bellasse of New-=Margaret, daughter of Sir
brough, Knt. heir to his | Nicholas Fairfax of Multon
uncle. ob. 1604, aged 81. | and Gilling. Com. Ebor.

2. Brian born 1599, had Morton.
3. Nicholas.
4. Charles.
5. Richard, four daughters died young.
Cath.=Tho. Metham, Esq.

§ 1. Sir Henry Bellasse, Knt.=Ursula, daughter of Sir
created a Bart. 9. James I. | Tho. Fairfax of Denton,
Com. Ebor. Knt.

Thomas, created Lord Fauconberg and=Barbara, daughter of Sir
Baron of Yarm, 3. Charles I. after-| Henry Chalmondley of
wardsVisc.Fauconberg,of Henknowle, | Roxby, Com. Ebor. Bart.
18. Charles I. ob. 1652.

Dorothy=Sir Conyers D'arcy, Knt.
Mary=Sir Wm. Litter, of Thornton, Knt.

|| This William was a justice of the peace for 60 years, and a knight 50; and saw his son and grandson knighted before his death.

§ He erected a monument, in his life-time, in the cathedral of York, with the effigies of himself and his lady, his son and two daughters, with the following inscription:

Henricus Bellasis, Miles et Baronettus, Filius
Gulielmi Bellasis, Militis, ex Margaretta
Filia primogenita Nicholai Fairfax de Gilling
Militis; mortalitatis memor hunc Tumulum
Sibi et Ursulæ Conjugi charissimæ Filiæ primo-
genitæ Thomæ Fairfax de Denton Milit. posuit;
Sub quo simul requiescunt et gloriosum Christi
Adventum expectant.

Mors certa est, in certa Dies, nec certa sequentum
Cura sibi Tumulum qui parat, ille sapit;
Frequens Mortis et novissimi Judicii Recordatio
A peccato revocat.

Sir Henry Bellasse, died in his father's life-time. == Grace, daughter and heiress of Smithells, county Lancaster, Esq.

John Bellasse, cr. by Char. I. Lord Bellasse of Worlaby. ob. 1689. == Jane, dau. of T. Barton of Woodhall, Hertfordshire. 1st wife. == Lady Anne, dau. of the Marquis of Winchester. 2d wife.

Margaret == Sir Ed. Osborne, Bart.
Mary == John, Lord D'arcy.
Barbara == Sir H. Slingsby, Bart.
Ursula == Sir Wm. Vavasour, Knt.
Frances == Thomas Ingram, Esq.

Henry Bellasse, ob. 1658. == Rogersa Rogers, dau. and coh. to F. Rogers of Brianston, Dorset. 1st wife. ob. Sine Prole. == Susan, dau. and coh. to Sir Wm. Armine of Osgodby, co. Line, Bart. 2d wife.

Mary == R. Visc. Dunbar. Frances.

1 Honora == Geo. Lord Bergavenny.
2 Barbara == Sir Jno. Webb, Cranford, Dorset.
3 Catherine == Hon. J. Talbot, Langford, Salop.
4 Isabella == Tho. Stoner, of Stoner, Oxf. Esq.
three sons & five other daughters died infants.

Henry, only son.

Mildred, dau. of Nicholas, Visc. Castleton, of Ireland. 1st wife. (ob. S. P.) == Thomas, the 2d Viscount, succeeded his grandfather, was Capt. of the band of Pensioners to King Char. II. created Earl Fauconberg by King William III. ob. 31. Dec. 1700. æt. 72. S. P. buried at Coxwold, where a monument is erected to his memory. == † Mary, dau. of Oliver Cromwell, the Usurper, his 2d wife. ob. 1712.

2 Henry. 3 John died young.

3 Sir Rowland Knt. of Bath, died in the life-time of his brother Thomas, 1699. == Anne, dau. & heir of James Davenport, of Sutton, county Chester.

Grace == Geo. Visc. Castleton.
Frances == Sir H. Jones, Knt. Afton, Oxford.
Arabella == Sir W. Frankland, Thirkleby.
Barbara == Walter Strickland, Sizergh, Esq.

Thomas Bellasse, Visc. Fauconberg, succeeded his uncle; ob. 1718. == Bridget, daughter of Sir John Gage, of Firle, Sussex, Bart. ob. 1732.

Henry died unmarried. John died Sine Prole. Rowland == Frances, dau. of Christ. Roper, Lord Teynham. Two daughters.

Henry. Anthony. Bridget. Frances. Brabara. Anne.

† BISHOP Burnet says, that Cromwell's daughter, married to the Lord Fauconberge, was a wife and worthy woman, more likely to have maintained the post of protector, than either of her brothers; according to a saying that went of her, "that those who wore breeches deserved petticoats better; but, if those in petticoats had been in breeches, they would have held faster." It may be presumed that she was influenced by her lord her husband; and, (from what has been said) concurred with him in the restoration.

Thomas, created Earl Fauconberg by King George II. June 5, 1756. obiit Feb. 4. 1774. = Catherine, daughter of John Betham, Esq. coh. to Wm. Fowler of St. Thomas, Staff. Esq.

Thomas died young.

Charlotte, only dau. = Sir Matthew Lamb, Bart. ob. 2d April, 1790. 1st wife.

Henry, succeeded his father, and died March 23, 1802. The title of Earl extinct. = ..., daughter of John Cheshyre, Esq. 2d wife.

Rowland.

Henry died an infant.

John died an infant.

Mary = John Pitt, 3d son of T. Pitt, Esq. Governour of Fort St. George.

Anne
Penelope } died unmarried.

Barbara = Hon. G. Barnwell, brother to Lord Vis. Kingsland.

Catherine

Mary = Thomas Eyres, Esq. Derbyshire.

Anne = Francis Talbot, Esq. brother to the Earl of Shrewsbury.

1 Charlotte, born Jan. 10, 1767.

2 Anne, born = Sir Geo. Wombwell, Bart. Dec. 27, 1767.

3 Elizabeth, born = Lord Lucan. Jan. 17, 1769.

4 Henrietta, born 1776.

From Kirby's inqueſt, which was taken in the 13th Edward I. it appears that Yarm was held by the heir of Marmaduke de Thweng, *ſicut liberum burgum.* ‖ The lands here, at an early period, ſeem to have fallen into the hands of different proprietors; for in the ſaid inqueſt we find that the heir of Stephen Kellet held two oxgangs of land here, for which he paid a fine of ſeven-pence farthing. * Adam Stainſby likewiſe held lands here, for which he paid to the king's bailiff, a fine of four-pence farthing. ‡

By an inquiſition *poſt mortem*, taken in the 30th Edward III. on the death of John Lord D'arcy, we find that the manor of Yarm was held of the King *in capite* by military ſervice, and valued at twenty marks. §

A second inquiſition was taken here, in the forty-ſecond year of the ſame King's reign, before *John de Scotherſcelf*, eſcheator for the county of York, from which it appears that the manor and town of Yarm, with the appurtenances, mills, tolls, fairs, markets, perquiſites of court, and all other profits pertaining to the ſaid manor and town of Yarm, were then in the hands of tenants at will, and paid the ſum of 16*l.* per ann. at the terms of St. Peter and St. Martin, by juſt and equal portions. †

‖ Hæres Marmaduc. de Thweng, qui eſt in cuſtodia Domini Regis, tenet VIII. feod. milit. et dimid. (et Danby pro uno feod.) de Domino Rege in capite, et Vill. de *Jarom ſicut liberum Burgum*, &c.

* Hæres Stephani Kellet tenet duas Bovatas terræ *de dicta hæredetat.* in Yarom, unde XII ca-rucat. terr. faciunt feod. milit. et reddit Ballia pro fine VII^d. ob.

‡ Adam Stainsby tenet de dict. hæreditat. in Yarome, unde XII car. terr. faciunt feod. et red-dit Ballio, Domini Regis pro fine IIII^d. ob. *Kirby's Inqueſt.*

§ " Et dicunt quod Maner. de Yarum tenetur de Rege in capite pro fine militar. et valet per ann, XX marcas." *Inquiſitio poſt mortem* 30. Edw. III.

† " Et dicunt, quod predict. Maner. Villa de Yarom, cum pertinent. Molendinum, Tolnet. Fer. " Mercat. Perquis. Cur. et omnia alia proficua dict. Maner. et Villæ de Yarome pertinent. ſunt in " manibus tenent. ad voluntat. et reddunt per ann. XVI^lb. ad terminos Petri et ſancti Martini, per equales portiones." *Inquis. p. m.* 42. Edw. III.

L.

In the reign of Queen Elizabeth, Robert Pawle died feized of eight burgages, which were held of the heirs of the lord Conyers, in free or common burgage; together with ten oxgangs of land, which, with their appurtenances, were held of the faid heirs, as of their manor of Yarm, by military fervice, and of the yearly value of three pounds: for which he did fuit at the court held here, as alfo at the wapontake court. *

Here is a market weekly on Thurfday, and four fairs annually; ‖ viz. on the Thurfday before the 6th of April; on afcenfion day; on the 2d of Auguft; and on the 19th and 20th days of October, for fheep, cattle, horfes, and cheefes. The markets have greatly decreafed within the laft forty years, and particularly fince the erection of the bridge at Stockton, which opened an eafy communication with Cleveland. The inhabitants are, however, plentifully fupplied with provifions, and generally at reafonable prices. The fairs, which have been long eftablifhed, are much frequented, particularly that held in the month of October, which occafions a great influx of money to the adjacent country, and may juftly be confidered among the firft in the north of England.

There are no manufactories carried on here, of any confequence; corn, butter, hams, bacon, and pork, fent coaftwife to London, conftitute the moft confiderable branch of commerce. The exportation of

---

* Dicunt quod *Robertus Pawle* obiit fefitus 26. die Augufti, Anno Regni Reginæ Elizabethæ, &c. 34¹⁰· de et in VIII Burgagia et X Bovat. terræ in Yarom. Et quod Burgagia prædict. tenentur de hæredibus Domini Conyers, ut de Manerio five Burgagio fuo de Yarom, in libero five communi Burgagio, et valent per ann.—Sect. Cur. ibid. tenend. et annual. libere reddit.—Et hæ Bovat. ter. cum fuis pertinent. tenentur de dict. Dominis ut de Manerio fuo prædict. per fervitium militare, per Sect. Cur. ibidem tenend. et Sect. Wapentag. Et quod valent per ann. in omnibus, exitibus 3¹ᵇ. Et quod *Francifcus Pawle* eft ejus filius et hæres, et etatis tempore mortis patris ejus fex annorum et amplius.   *Inq. p. m. Rob. de Pawle,* 34. *Eliz. reg.*

‖ Hæres Marmaduci de Thweng clamat habere mercatum et feriam in Yarom, et Villam de Yarom *liberum Burgum* et pertinent. Scilicet, qualiter et a tempore quod non poteft inquiri.

         Kirby's Inqueft.

A View of Yarm Bridge, from the West

Drawn by I.B.

Eng.d by E. Scott

corn feems however to have greatly decreafed; as many granaries here, which have been erected at a great expence for that particular branch of trade, are now, and have for fome time, been almoft ufelefs and unoccupied.

THE traveller, on his approach to the town, is ftruck with its fin-gularly low fituation, particularly in defcending the hill from the north; which is fo much fuperior, as to afford no other profpect of the place, than the roofs of the houfes, with the river winding round in the form of a crefcent.

IT confifts chiefly of one main ftreet, running north and fouth, which is fpacious and open; but its beauty is greatly injured by the *fhambles* and *toll-both*, which ftand in the centre of the town, and have a ruinous and difgufting appearance. A covered market-crofs, in the form of a fquare with arched entrances on each fide, ftands in the centre of the market place; it was built in the year 1710, for the con-venience of the market-people, with a fpacious room above, where the fteward of the manor holds his court, and other public bufinefs is tranfacted.

THE entrance into the town from the county of Durham, on the north, is over a bridge of five arches, ‡ built about the year 1400, by Walter Skirlaw, bifhop of Durham. The arches, according to the ftyle of architecture at that period, are pointed, and the ftructure re-tained its original, and uniform appearance, till about 20 years ago, when the arch on the north was widened, and rebuilt in a femicircular form, in order, by giving a freer paffage to the current of the river, to prevent if poffible, or, at leaft, to abate the injury and inconvenience, which the inhabitants had experienced from frequent inundations.—The annexed engraving, which comprehends a view of the church, and

---

‡ LELAND, in his Itinerary (vol 1. p. 60.) fays, "Notable bridges on Tefe; Yareham bridg " of ftone, a three miles above Stoketon, made, as I hard by Bifchop Skerlaw."

2

part of the village of Egglefcliffe, in the county of Durham, will give
the reader fome idea of this ancient ftructure, and render any further
defcription of it unneceffary.

IN a note to our introductory obfervations on *Cleveland in general*,
(p. 39.) we noticed the opening of a new line of road through the
weftern point of Cleveland; a more particular account of which, as
being originally connected with the plan of erecting a new *iron bridge*
over the river Tees, at Yarm, and other improvements within the diftrict, we now readily fubmit to the attention of our readers.

THE important advantages, which the inhabitants of the maritime
diftrict of the county of Durham had acquired, from the facility of
intercourfe between the feaports and market-towns of Stockton, Sunderland, Shields, and Newcaftle, by means of the new turnpike roads,
and the novel and ftupendous *iron-arch* acrofs the *Wear* (invented and
erected by Rowland Burdon, Efq. member for that county), induced
the inhabitants of Stockton and Cleveland to wifh for a more direct
and eafy communication between *Yarm* and *Thirfk*, and confequently
a more fpeedy intercourfe with the metropolis.   Towards the attain-
ment of thefe objects, a public meeting was held at Yarm, on the 15th
of November, 1802, when it was unanimoufly refolved to petition
Parliament for an act, to fhorten and improve the road from Yarm to
Thirfk. *   A petition was immediately figned, and the members in

---

* AMONG other advantages, it has been ftated, in a provincial newfpaper, that this line of road,
by avoiding *Borrowby Bank*, and being much fhortened between *Ingleby* and *Crathorne*, will make
the diftance from London, (by Borough bridge, Thirfk, Yarm, Stockton, &c.) to Newcaftle, five
miles lefs than by York, North-Allerton, Darlington, &c.   It was alfo in the view of the promoters
of this road, and they feem to confider it a very defireable object, that one line of communication
fhould embrace all the prefent ftations of the *coal-trade*, fo as to afford them the moft fpeedy intercourfe by poft, with London, and other parts of the Ifland.   This object will be completely accomplifhed by the much wifhed for, and intended eftablifhment of a *mail* from *the general poft-office ;*
which, by reaching Newcaftle from the fouth, at ten o'clock in the morning, and returning about
three o'clock in the afternoon of the fame day, will give an opportunity to all the *coal-trade*, of correfponding with London, and other places in the fouth, *twenty-four hours* fooner than at prefent, dur-

Parliament for the counties of York and Durham were requefted to fupport the meafure; and particularly Mr. Burdon, who attended the meeting, and whofe promptitude of exertion for the benefit of the public, was, on this occafion, crowned with the moft fpeedy fuccefs. The bill was brought into the Houfe of Commons a few days afterwards, and was forwarded through its different ftages with fuch difpatch, that the royal affent was obtained on the 17th of the following month.

THIS act took effect from the 4th of January, 1803; in which there was given a fpecial power to take down certain houfes at the north-end of the town of Yarm, with a view to the improvement of the bridge, which had been found incommodious to travellers; and, from the increafing traffic on the road, was expected to become ftill more fo.

A MEMORIAL, therefore, figned by the principal inhabitants of Yarm, was in the month of January, 1803, prefented to the juftices affembled at the quarter feffions for the north-riding of Yorkfhire, and the county of Durham, refpectively, fetting forth, that the bridge acrofs the river Tees at Yarm (which was repaired and maintained at the equal and joint expence of the faid county and north-riding,) was too narrow, (being in fome places lefs than twelve feet between the parapets,) to admit of carriages paffing each other with fafety, and extremely dangerous to paffengers in general; that, in confequence of the act of Parliament recently obtained, for fhortening and improving the road between Yarm and Thirfk, the number of carriages and paffengers might be expected confiderably to increafe, and accidents more frequently to occur; that the obftruction, given by the piers of the bridge to the courfe of the river, occafioned the latter to be choaked

ing *five days* in the week, and *forty-eight* hours fooner on *the fixth*. This confideration alone, independent of the accommodation that will be afforded to Stockton, the diftrict of Cleveland, and all the intermediate parts of the road, is fufficient to counterbalance any temporary inconveniences, and muft ultimately remove all interefted objections and unfounded prejudices againft the undertaking.

up with beds of fand, fo as greatly to injure the navigation; and that
in floods, efpecially on the breaking up of frofts, the current was fo
much impeded by the ice filling up the cavities of the arches, that the
water overflowed, not only the town of Yarm, but alfo the public road
and lands adjoining, to the great injury of individuals, and danger of
the public; that the moft eligible mode of preventing accidents and
dangers, and of removing the inconveniences above ftated, would be,
to take down *the old-bridge* of five arches entirely, and to erect upon,
or near to its fite, an *iron-bridge* of one arch only, and of fufficient
breadth for public paffage.

THIS memorial was referred by the courts of feffions, to a joint
committee of acting magiftrates for the faid county and riding; to
whom it appeared (after having viewed the bridge, and confidered the
reports of Mr. Ebdon and Mr. Peacock, furveyors of bridges for the
faid county and riding, as to the imperfect ftate of the bridge at Yarm)
that the expence of widening the fame would amount to the fum of
7000*l.* and upwards; and by enlarging the piers, the obftructions
complained of would be increafed rather than diminifhed; and that
the coft of building a new bridge of ftone would exceed the fum of
14000*l.*; whilft the erection of an *iron-bridge* (according to the eftimation of Mr. Wilfon, engineer of Wearmouth bridge,) might be effected
at an expence of about 8000*l.*

THE committee, therefore, reported to the next courts of general
quarter feffions, their unanimous opinion, that an *iron-arch* would be
moft commodious and beneficial to the public, and moft effectually
remove the evils complained of in the memorial; and it was agreed
by the faid courts (April 1803,) the old bridge having been previoufly
indicted, that the north-riding and county of Durham would join in
erecting an *iron-bridge*, and ordered the fum of 8000*l.* to be applied for
that purpofe. And, for taking into confideration the beft mode of
carrying the work into execution, another committee of juftices was
appointed; who being authorifed to call to their affiftance the above-

named furveyors of bridges, and fuch other perfons as they might think neceffary, requefted the faid furveyors, together with Mr. Wilfon and Mr. Scarth, patentees for *iron-arches*, to report their joint opinion of the beft fituation for erecting the intended bridge, and of the dimenfions of the arch, abutments and materials which ought to be adopted ; and in confequence of their report, the work was lett by propofal.: viz. the ftone abutments to *Mr. Thomas Wheldon*, for the fum of 2440*l.* ; and the iron-arch to *Mr. Wilfon*, for 5560*l.* ; the whole to be completed in the fpring of 1805.

THE foundation of the north abutment was laid on the 3d day of September, 1803. The iron-work was begun to be laid acrofs the river on the 3d of September, 1804, and the ribs forming the arch, were completed in eight days. The abutments * are of folid mafonry, each thirty feet in breadth ; the flank-walls about fifty feet in length from the back of the folid abutment, and feven feet thick, diminifhing upwards by offsets of fix inches to four feet ; the parapet walls four feet and half, including the *facia.*

THE arch is of caft iron, from the foundry of *Meffrs. Walkers, of Rotherham*, and forms a circular fegment of 180 feet fpan, and twenty-feven feet in breadth within the baluftrades : viz. twenty-one feet for carriage-road, and fix feet for two foot-paths ; and is compofed of fix ribs, each confifting of thirty-nine blocks, each four feet in depth, and four inches in thicknefs. The whole weight of the arch, including the

---

* IN digging for the foundation of the fouth-abutment in the year 1804, at a confiderable depth below the foundation of the pier of the old bridge, the workmen difcovered the trunk of a large oak ; and at fome feet below, near to the rock, were found the horns, fkull, and other remains of a ftag ; a horfe-fhoe of great fize and uncommon thicknefs ; and alfo the *core* of an ox's horn, meafuring 13¼ inches in its greateft circumference, and upwards of 26 inches in length. We have no evidence to fhew, by what means, or at what period, thefe remains (which were in good prefervation) had been depofited here ; but, the circumftance of the fact clearly proves, that from their fituation, they had been lodged there fome time before the erection of the old bridge ; and at a period, when the bed of the river was at leaft twelve feet lower than it is at prefent.

crofs-ftays, pilafters, covering plates, baluftrades, &c. is 250 tons, of which the bolts or wedges only are of malleable iron.

THE erection of this beautiful arch was under the immediate fuper-intendence of Mr. Wilfon, † and is of the fame conftruction, and nearly of the fame dimenfions as the bridge erected by that gentleman, acrofs the *river Thames near Staines;* for which he obtained his majefty's *letters patent,* as being an improvement on the principle of *Wearmouth bridge.*

THERE are no remains, nor is it now certainly known, in what part of the town the ancient hofpital of St. Nicholas ftood, which is noticed by Tanner, in his Notitia, thus :—" Here was an ancient hofpital, de-" dicated to Saint Nicholas, founded by fome of the family of Brus, " before the year 1185 ;* which was afterwards granted by Alan de " Wilton, to the Canons of Helagh-Park. It continued till the time of " King Henry VIII. when it was valued at 5*l.* per annum."

FROM the charters in the Monafticon, it feems that this Alan de Wilton was a great benefactor to this hofpital, granting divers lands in Hoton juxta Rudby, to hold at the yearly rent of two marks ; alfo lands at Upleatham and Middleton juxta Leven, for the maintenance of three chaplains, and thirteen poor people. His charter is to the following effect :—

" OMNIBUS Chrifti fidelibus, ad quos prefens fcriptum pervenerit, " *Alan de Wilton,* falutem. Noveritis me &c. dediffe et conceffiffe et hac " prefenti charta mea confirmaffe Deo, et beatæ Mariæ, beato Nicholao " hofpitale *de Yarem,* et fratribus ibidem Deo fervientibus duodecem " bovatas terræ, habendum in Dominico in Hotona juxta Rudby, &c.

---

† THE joint patentees for iron-arches are Rowland Burdon, Efq. Mr. Wilfon, and Mr. Scarth ; to whom we owe our grateful acknowledgments for the annexed plate of this novel piece of archi-tecture.

IN the prefent inftance, Mr Burdon, actuated by that fpirit of difinterefted patriotifm, which fo eminently diftinguifhes his character, generoufly relinquifhed his fhare of the premium amounting to 200*l.*

* " IN which year, Adam Brus, who had been a great benefactor to the houfe, died."
Tanner's Notitia.

Drawn by J. Bird.

Engd by R. Scott.

The New CAST IRON BRIDGE *over the* RIVER TEES *at Yarm.*

" in liberam, puram et perpetuam eleemosinam, reddendo inde annuatim
" mihi et hæredibus meis duas marcas argenti pro omni servicio et con-
" suetudine præter Danegeldum cum evenerit per totam terram, quan-
" tum pertinet ad duodecim bovatas terræ, &c.

" CONCESSI etiam eisdem unam carucatam terræ in Uplium, cum
" Toftis, &c. Concessi iterum eisdem sex bovatas terræ in *Myddilton*
" juxta Leven, &c. &c. ad sustentandum tres capellanos in eodem hos-
" pitali missam celebrantes, et tredecem pauperes in victu et vestitu, ad
" inveniendum illis lectum imperpetuum. Ego verò, et hæredes mei
" has prædictas terras prædicto hospitali, et fratribus ibidem Deo ser-
" vientibus contra omnes homines imperpetuum warrantizabimus. His
" festibus, Willmo. de Tampton, Roberto de Acclum, Gregorio de
" Leventhorpe, Ada Buck, et multis aliis." *Dugd. Mon. vol. 2, p. 401.*

THIS same Alan did afterwards grant this hospital to the canons
of Helagh-Park; and the like grant was also made to the said canons
by *Peter de Brus;* who not only confirmed the grants of divers persons
to this hospital, but gave them himself certain lands here, with free
grinding in all his mills, and free pasture for all their own cattle in his
lands. ||

HERE was also an house of *Black-Friars*, * said to have been founded by *Peter de Brus* the second, who died A. D. 1240. It was surren-

---

|| THERE was a chantry founded at *Tarum Spittle ;* but neither the date of its foundation, nor
the name of the founder, have been recorded, *Francis Yowarde* occurs Cantarist May 8th, 1540.
Torr's MS.

* THIS *Dominican friery* had a church or chapel of their own, which had right of sepulture ; and
among the testamentary burials in Torr's manuscript, we find that " Dame Jane Boynton of *Yarum*
" made her will (proved 7th Feb. 1488,) giving her soul to God Almighty, Saint Mary, and All-
" Saints, and her body to be buried in the *quere of the friers* at Yarum." *Torr's MS.*

OF this house we find the following notice in *Torr's MS.* † " There was a friery in Yarum
" of Dominicans, who had a church or chapel of their own, which had right of sepulture." And

---

† WE acknowledge our obligations to the very Rev. the Dean of York, for a copy of *Torr's MSS.* and
other valuable records, from the Dean and Chapter's library in York Minster, &c,

K

dered by Miles Wilcock the prior, with five friars and six novices, in December 1539. *Willis's Abbies, vol. II. p.* 287.

A COMMODIOUS mansion has been erected upon the site of this house, now the property of Edward Meynell, Esq. which is still distinguished by the name of *the Friarage.*† The grounds to the south, upon

---

† *Pedigree of Meynells of Yarum and North-Kilvington.*

From an ancient roll in the possession of Edw. Meynell of Yarm, Esq.

Stephen de Menell—Sibilla Uxor ejus.
de Stainton.

⎰ ARMS. *Az.* 3 barrs gemmells on a
⎱ chief, *or.*
⎰ CREST. A blackamore's head couped
⎱ proper banded *arg.* and *az.*

Robert de Meinell—

| William de Meinell, lived 1203. | Stephen de Meinell—Sibilla. from whom the Meinells of *Whorlton,* &c. were descended. | Hugo de Meinell—Agnes, sister & of Hilton in Cleveland. | Nicholas de Meinell, vixit 3. Hen. 3. & 9. Edw. 1. |

the following " *copy of an auncient noate from the prior of Yarum of burials there,*" is extracted from Dodsworth's MSS. in the Bodl. library, Oxford.

DOMINA Eva, quondam ux. Domini Henrici filii Hugonis, sepulta fuit coram altari, in medio gradu. (N. B. *Filia Johannis Bulmer.*)
Hugo, filius Dominæ Evæ ad caput Domini in inferiori gradu.
Thomas, filius ejusdem juxta eum versus aquilonem
Robts de Hilton, in eodem gradu, versus australem.
(And all yese was of the progeny of the Hiltons.)
Domina Maria, quæ fuit ux. Domini Nicholai de Menell, in capitulo beat. Katerinæ.
Hugo de Menell, quondam Dominus de Hilton, in cimiterio
Alicia, quondam ux. ejusdem Hugonis, juxta eum.
Robts de Menell, juxta dictam Aliciam.
Johannes de Menell juxta dictum Robertum.
Sibilla, quondam ux. juxta dictum Johannem.
Nicholus de Hilton, et Dominus de Hilton, in cimiterio.
Cicilia ux. ejus juxta eum.
Johannes de Hilton, Dominus de Hilton jacet in capitulo beat. Katerinæ.
Isabella, ux. ejus juxta eum.
And all yese gentilmen be in the freers of Yarum.
Lord John Menell of Myddleton was one of the foundacioners of this plaice of Yarum."
Dodsworth's MSS. vol. 45. *p.* 76.

the banks of the river Tees, are cloathed with thriving plantations; a
fhaded walk winds through the wood, till we reach a terrace, running
eaft and weft; from whence there is a pleafing and extenfive profpect

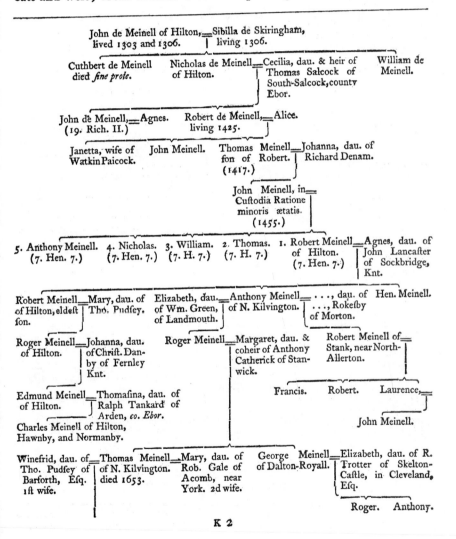

into the county of Durham on the north, with the town of Yarm on the left, and the river winding at our feet.

2. Rich. Meinell——Elizabeth, dau.   1. Anthony Meinell——Mary, dau. of   Mary——Geo. Pole of
of Broughton, co. | of J. Talbot of   of N. Kilvington, | James Thwaites | Spink-hill.
York. died 1663. | Thornton le   Efq. aged 74. | of Longmar-   Ann——Tho. Grange of
┌──────────────┘ Street, county   1665. | fton, co. York,   Harlfay, co.
John Meinell.   York. | Efq.   York.

    6. James.   5. Anthony   4. William.   3. Hugh   2. John
                     died unmarried.   died unmarried.

Winefrid, wife of   2. Clare, wife of   Mary, wife of   Collet,   ⎞
Tho. Killingbeck   Sir Rich. Forfter,   J. Danby of   Julian,   ⎬ died unmarried.
of Allerton-Grange. of Stokefley, co.   Leek, co. York. Catherine, |
                     York.   Frances,   ⎠

Richard St. George, ⎞   Thomas Meynell——Gerrard, daughter of Wm.
Norroy King of Arms. ⎬   eldeft fon and heir | Ireland of Noftell-Abbey,
(Nov. 19, 1619.)   ⎠   of Anthony. | in co. York.

4. John,   3. William,   Roger Meynell of——Mary, dau. of John   Anthony   Mary,   Elizabeth,
died young.   N. Kilvington, fon | Middleton of Thurn- eldeft fon died unmarried.
                       & heir of Thomas. | tofft, co. York, Knt. died young. Dugdale's Vifitation,
                                                                            A. D. 1665.

Thomas Meynell——Urfula, dau. of   Roger Meynell——Ann, dau. of   Ann, wife of Peter
eldeft fon. | T. Markham of   2d fon. | Edw. Charlton,   Middleton of Stoc-
(ob. S. P.) | Ollerton, Efq. | Efq.   keld, Efq.

                                                 Jane, wife of Marm.   Terefa died
                                                 Palmes of Naburne, Efq. unmarried.

Edward Meynell,   George.   Roger Meynell——Barbara Ann, dau. of Tho. Wm. Felby
M. D. died S. P.   (S. P.)   J of Biddlefton, co. Northumberland, Efq.

            ┌─────────────────┐ Margaret and Ann,   Mary——Thos. Selby of Biddlefton Efq.
                                 religious at Dunkirk. |
                                                           Eliza——Jas. Thornton of Nether-Witton.

George Meyne'l   Thomas, a Roman   Roger died   Edward Meynell——Dorothy, dau. of . . . . .
died S. P.   Catholic clergyman, S. P.   of Yarm, Efq. | Carey of Torr-Abbey, in
                  died 1804.   living 1804. | Devonfhire, Efq. died
                                                                  | 1802.

3. George living 1804,   2. Thomas Meynell——Terefa, dau. of J. Wright   Edward died
   unmarried.   born 1775, mar- | of Kelvedon, in co. Effex,   young.
                          ried 1804.   Efq.

Catherine Dorothy——Thos. Simon Scroop   Anna Maria born 1770,   Barbara died
born at York, 1768. of Danby, Efq.   living unmarried 1804.   young.

THE road, leading to the town from the south, is called the *Spital*, ‡ and the fields adjoining, *Spital-Flatts;* from which we are led to conjecture, that the ancient hospital above noticed was situated in this part of the town.

DURING the civil dissentions between King Charles I. and his Parliament, Yarm was garrisoned by the Parliament's forces; but Sir Wm. Cavendish (afterwards created Marquis of Newcastle,) having raised a considerable force for the King, routed the rebels in these parts, and taking many of their strong holds, rescued Yarm also from their possession. *

INTRENCHMENTS thrown up by the rebel forces, are still visible in the neighbourhood of the town; but they afford nothing worthy of notice; nor have the historians of those times recorded any transactions here, that demand our further attention.

YARM, from its low situation, and, as has already been observed, nearly surrounded by the river Tees, is unfortunately subject to frequent inundations. The first, from which the inhabitants suffered any considerable injury or inconvenience, happened on the 17th day of February, 1753; when many of the houses, in the lower parts of the town, were almost entirely under water; and the wretched inhabitants, at the danger of their lives, compelled to take shelter with their less unfortunate neighbours. The damage sustained in shop-goods, furniture, &c. was very considerable; and the alarming situation of the inhabitants such, as may be more easily conceived than described.—The following brief relation, extracted from a provincial news-paper, may be worthy of insertion, as it bears evident marks of authenticity.

‡ SPITAL, is a contraction of *hospital.* Hospitals were usually placed at the conjunction of several roads, for the relief of poor distressed travellers; and it is probable that this was situated here, where two roads meet.

* " FEBRUARY 1st, 1643—4. Lieutenant General King, and Lieut. General Goring, coming " from Newcastle with a great convy of much arms and ammunition, and being faced at Yarum " with 400 foot, three troops of horse, and two pieces of ordnance of the rebels, fell upon them, slew " many, took the rest of the foot, and most of the horse prisoners, with their ordnance and baggage."

Mercurius Rusticus.

" Yarm, Yorkſhire, February 17th, 1753.

" At four this morning, the banks of our river were broken, and
" the water ran through the town; the water continued riſing till noon,
" and it was, with great difficulty, we got the horſes out of the town,
" to ſome higher grounds.   When the flood was higheſt, we had ſeven
" feet of water in the higheſt part of the town; all the loweſt part was
" under water; and the current through the town ſo rapid, that many
" houſes were waſhed away; horſes, cows, pigs, dogs, and all ſorts of
" houſehold furniture were floating, and no one able to ſave them; ſome
" horſes, indeed, were ſaved in chambers.   Moſt of the bridges are
" broken down, and many lives loſt.   It was occaſioned by a ſudden
" rain melting the ſnow on the neighbouring hills." *

---

* In addition to the above, we will preſent our readers, with the following extract of a letter
(publiſhed in the *Bibliotheca Topographia Britan.*) from Mr. Johnſon of Magdalen college, Oxford;
who was at Redmarſhall near Stockton, when this dreadful inundation happened.

Extract of a letter from Mr. Johnſon to Dr. Birch.

Redmarſhall, 9th March, 1753.

We have had prodigious floods about us, to the great loſs of the public.   I fancy you may have
ſeen an account of Yarm; but as it is ſo very uncommon, I will give a particular detail of it.

The ſituation of Yarm is exceſſive low, ſurrounded with mountains on every ſide. *   A vaſt
quantity of ſnow had laid on the hills on the weſt ſide, which being ſucceeded by as great a downfall
of rain, the whole maſs of water came down upon the town in the night, ſweeping with it herds of
cattle, hay-ſtacks, farm houſes, and many other things in its paſſage; it drowned almoſt entirely the
village of *Neeſham,* having deſtroyed every houſe in the town except one; to which all the people
reſorted, and by good luck, ſaved their lives, though with the loſs of all their cattle, and ſtacks of
hay and corn.   About one in the morning it came into Yarm, throwing down all the garden and
orchard-walls, that obſtructed its paſſage, and forcing its way through the windows of the houſes in
the middle of the ſtreet, which the people, who were aware of it, readily encouraged, leſt otherwiſe
the whole houſe might fall; thoſe who perceived it coming, immediately got boats, and took the
people, whoſe houſes were low, out of their windows, and waked all the town.   The alarm preſently
made them ſenſible of their danger, and ſome had the good fortune to ſave their horſes, (which
would have otherwiſe been drowned in the ſtables) by bringing them *up-ſtairs* into their houſes.   The
flood continued riſing till *eleven o'clock* next morning, at which time the water was five feet and a

---

* What Mr. Johnſon here calls mountains, we conceive to be the banks of the river, and the riſing
grounds near the town:—the " *hills to the weſt,*" are at a very conſiderable diſtance.

YARM, however, did not again suffer from any similar calamity till the year 1771; when, as was observed by a writer in the *Annual-Register* for that year, " in the night between the 16th and 17th days of Novem- " ber, there happened the greatest land-flood ever remembered in the " north of England, which did incredible damage on the three rivers of " *Tyne*, *Wear*, and *Tees*. By the incessant, though not heavy rain, which " fell from Friday-morning, till Saturday night, the river Tees swelled " to such a degree, as to rise twenty feet perpendicular higher than the " oldest man living could remember."

THIS town, from its situation, suffered more perhaps, than any other place on the river Tees. The water, in some parts of the town rose up-wards of twenty feet in perpendicular height, and many houses were deserted, the inhabitants of which were taken into boats from the roofs. Some lives were lost; and many more must have inevitably perished, but for the active humanity and timely assistance of their neighbours from Stockton and the neighbouring villages; who, besides bodily ex-ertions to rescue the unhappy sufferers from their perilous situation, brought bread, and other necessary refreshments, which were conveyed to them by means of boats, through the windows even of the second

half deep in the lower apartments. The people got up into their uppermost rooms, where they had the melancholy prospect of a perfect sea in the street; horses, cows, sheep, hogs, and all manner of household goods floating.

THERE was one thing rather comical than otherwise happened, in the midst of this doleful spec-tacle; a sow big with young, had swam till her strength was quite exhausted; a wheel-barrow was carried by the torrent, out of some body's yard, which the sow being pretty near, laid her nose and fore-feet into, and suffered herself to be carried by the flood, till she got safe to land.

ABOUT this time there was a great cry for provisions; they got some from the neighbouring vil-lages that had not suffered, but not near sufficient.

THEY found the flood abated very fast, and in six hours it was entirely gone. I went to see the town the next day; the people of all ranks were busy in cleaning their houses, and airing them. The poor people, who had but one room *below-stairs* were entirely ruined; and those who had shops and granaries were much damaged. They made a handsome collection round about for the poor; but the loss of the merchants is computed at 3000*l.* One great happiness is, no one lost their lives.

M. JOHNSON.

ftories of many of the higheft houfes. This dreadful inundation, (which happened at the fame time that the tremendous eruption of *Solway-Mofs*, in Cumberland, covered an area of five hundred acres,) will be long remembered; for befides the lives, which were loft, and the damage done to many of the buildings, the lofs fuftained in fhop-goods, furniture, &c. &c. and the confternation naturally thereby occafioned, made fuch an impreffion on the minds of the fufferers, as can never be effaced; and their calamitous fituation will be tranfmitted by tradition to fucceeding generations.

INUNDATIONS, in an inferior degree, have fince, at different times, incommoded this place; but, with no great or ferious injury to the inhabitants; caufing them, however, from the recollection of former calamities, to remove their goods and furniture from the ground-floors to more elevated and fecure fituations.

FROM the above period (1753) in confequence of thefe alarming vifitations, with other concurrent circumftances, Yarm may certainly date its decline in trade and importance, and confequently the decreafe of its inhabitants. The following table of baptifms, marriages, and burials, extracted from the parifh regifters, will give the reader fome idea of its ftate of population.

	BAP.	MAR.	BUR.
From 1681 to 1700 inclufive	756	176	716
1781 to 1800	674	150	670
Decreafe	82	26	46

FROM an accurate furvey,* made in the year 1801, according to act of Parliament, Yarm contained 347 houfes, 360 families, and only 1300 inhabitants; which, on an average is little more than $3\frac{1}{2}$ to each family. The average number of burials in one year is $33\frac{1}{2}$; from which it appears that one in 38 nearly dies annually.

* STATE of population, taken the 10th March, 1801.

No. of houfes inhabited.	Families.	Houfes uninhabited.	Males.	Females.	Total.
347	360	16	607	693	1300

Of those laudable associations, denominated FRIENDLY SOCIE-
TIES, instituted for the mutual assistance and support of their several
members, there are two in this town. The first was established in the
year 1764, and is distinguished by the title of the *Union-Club;* it consists
of about 110 members. The anniversary festival of this society is held
on Tuesday in Easter-week; when the members assemble in the morning, at their club-room; and from thence, go in procession to church,
(preceded by the *union-flag,*) where they hear divine service, and a sermon on the occasion. From the church, they return to their club-
room, where they dine, and conclude the day in friendship and con-
viviality.

A SECOND society was formed in the year 1773, which is regulated
upon a plan, similar to the former; it consists of about 70 members,
(chiefly day-labourers, and inferior mechanics,) who hold their anniversary festival on the Tuesday in Whitsun-week, which is observed
with the like ceremony and decorum.

THE establishment of such societies, which originated from a laudable desire of providing against the possible contingencies of sickness
and infirmity, not only contributes to the relief of their respective
members, but tends greatly to the reduction of the poor's-rates; which
is a consideration that entitles them to the encouragement and support
of the public, and renders them worthy of that protection, which they
have experienced from the legislature.

THE church of Yarm, † which is dedicated to St. Mary Magdalen,

---

† YARM CURACY.

Ded. St. Mary Magdalen.   Certified val. 38*l.* 3s. 6d.   Archbishop of York, Patron.

CURATES.

Christopher Thompson,	1653	John Marsh,	1696. *post mortem* Walters.
Richard Bradley,	1658	Daniel Oughton,	1697. *post mortem* Marsh.
Thomas Smith,	1659	John Bever,	1699. *p. res.* Oughton.
Francis Ourd,	1665	Thomas Burton,	1700.
Edward Walters,	1669	Thomas Perrott, *	1712. *p. res.* Burton.

* HE was father of that eminent and learned judge, the *Honourable George Perrott,* late one of the
barons of his Majesty's Court of Exchequer at Westminster.

L

was formerly endowed with rectorial rights; but, on its appropriation
to the priory of Guifbrough, to which it had been given by Robert de
Brus, on the foundation of that monaftry, it was reduced to a perpetual
curacy; and after the diffolution, granted by King Henry VIII. to the
Archbifhop of York, who is patron and nominates the curate. The
church, the revenue of which was certified to the governours of Queen
Anne's bounty, at 38*l*. 3s. 6d. never received any augmentation; but
the Archbifhop grants a leafe of the rectorial rights to the dean and
chapter of York for 21 years, for the ufe of the curate; towards whofe
maintenance he alfo pays a penfion of 5*l*. 6s. 8d. By virtue of this
leafe, which was granted by Archbifhop Sharpe in the year 1712, the
curate becomes entitled to all the tythes within the parifh, which are
paid in their proper kinds, except a certain common-field, called the
Ings, which pays by cuftom *five pence per acre*, in lieu of tythes, and
two *fifhing-cobles*, which pay *fix fhillings* and *eight pence* a piece yearly.

THE church ftands a little to the weft from the town, upon the
banks of the Tees; and is a neat, modern ftructure, rebuilt in the year
1730. The body of the church is 74 feet in length and 56 feet wide;
neatly and uniformly feated with oak, and divided by a middle and
two fide-ailes, well lighted by fpacious windows. The altar ftands
within an angular recefs, illuminated by an elegant window of painted
glafs, erected in the year 1796, at the expence of the late William
Chaloner, Efq. a native of this place. The principal figure in this
beautiful and ornamental window, is a full-length reprefentation of
Mofes, delivering the law from Mount Sinai, executed by the late ingenious
artift Mr. Wm. Pecket, of York. The compartments are filled up with

---

Edward Abbott, 1724. *p. res.* Perrott. | Thomas Dixon, 1794. *poft mortem* Hopkinfon.
Henry Bradley, 1725. *poft mortem* Abbott. | Wm. Hall, A. M. 1797. *poft mortem* Dixon.
John Hopkinfon, 1737. *p. res.* Bradley. |

THE parifh regifter begins in the year 1642. In the firft page we find the following extract from
Ritual. Rom. p. 409. " *Si infans non fuerit ex legitimo matrimonio natus, fcribatur nomen, &c. (om-*
" *nis tamen infamiæ vitetur occafio.*")

some small appropriate paintings, the workmanship of an inferior artist.

HERE is an ancient free-school, founded by letters patent of Queen Elizabeth, bearing date July 7th, in the thirtieth year of her reign; and endowed by Thomas Conyers, of Egglescliffe, in the county of Durham, gentleman; who left by will, dated the 10th day of February, 1589, the sum of 8*l.* 6s. 8d. payable out of his lands and houses at Yarm and Darlington; and also two oxgangs of land, within the parish of Yarm, at that time of the yearly rent of *thirteen shillings* and *four pence*, together with the water and fishing belonging to the same, of the yearly rent of *four shillings.** Six of the principal inhabitants act as trustees to the school, and nominate the master. ‡ In addition to the above

---

* EXTRACT from Thomas Conyers's will.

I GIVE, grant, assign and confirm unto my wife, during her life natural, the dwelling house or tenement in Yarome, &c. now in the tenure of *Elizabeth Atkinson*, widow, late wife of John Atkinson, deceased, for to dwell in; three oxgangs and an half of arable land, three acres and an half of meadow, the Mill-close, and the water belonging to it, the Spittle-house, and Spittle-closes, with their appurtenances, &c. *Item.* I give, &c. unto *Thomas Grundy*, my servant and god-sonne, after the decease of my said wife, all the said three oxgangs, &c. to have and to hold, to the said Thomas Grundy, his heirs and assigns for ever, from and after the decease of my said wife, &c. yielding and paying yearly therefore *for ever*, towards the scholemaster at Yarome aforesaid, the *sum of seven pounds* of lawful money of England, at the feasts of Pentecost, and St. Martin's the Bishop in winter, by eaven portions. *Item.* I give, &c. for ever, my house and tenement in *Darnton*, &c. unto *Francis Nicholson*, my wife's nephew, his heirs and assigns for ever, yielding and paying therefore for ever, *twenty shillings* of lawful money, &c. at the feasts of Pentecost and St. Martins, at the schole at Yarome for ever, &c. *Item.* I give, &c. unto the said schole at Yarome, for ever, *two oxgangs* of arable land, meadow and pasture, in Yarome aforesaid, with the appurtenances, in tenure of Elizabeth Atkinson, widow, &c. being of the yearly rent of *thirteen shillings and four pence;* together with the water and fishing belonging to these two oxgangs, of the yearly rent of *four shillings. Item.* I give, &c. unto *Thomas Robinson* of Yarome, shoemaker, his heirs, &c. for ever, the house and tenement wherein he dwelleth, &c. yielding and paying to the said free-schole, &c. yearly for ever, &c. *six shillings and eight pence*, of lawful English money, &c."

THE *probate of the above will is dated* 21*st Sept. A. D.* 1590.

‡ By virtue of the letters patent, twelve governours therein named were authorized to elect a master; and with the consent of the Archbishop, to make statutes for the regulation and management of the school; but these *twelve* all dying, without electing new trustees, *the patent* is now at an end;

L 2

endowment, the late William Chaloner, Efq. left by will, to the fchool-
mafter of Yarm for ever, (after the death of Mr. Jofeph Hughes, of
Stokefley,) the fum of 400*l. three per cent. confol.* for the laudable purpofe
of educating, and inftructing in *reading*, *writing*, and *arithmetic*, eight
poor children of this parifh continually : and nominated the minifter
and churchwardens for the time being, to elect fuch children as may
be proper objects of this charity, with power to remove them for mif-
behaviour, &c.   Mr. Chaloner alfo left *thirty pounds*, in *truft*, to the
minifter and church-wardens, for the repair of the grammar-fchool;
which was expended in the year 1802, and the fchool-houfe rendered
comfortable and commodious.

FROM the tables of benefactions within the church it appears, that
the following charitable donations have been made to the poor of this
place: viz.

NICHOLAS MAYES, of Yarme, merchant, by will dated June 1ft,
1676, gave to the poor of Yarm, the fum of 2*l.* 12s. to be paid yearly
out of the grounds, called the Friarage-Garths, and his houfes at the
fouth-end of the town. §

THOMAS REED, of Yarm, merchant, by will dated April 27th, 1688,
gave to the poor of Yarm the fum of *ten pounds*.

MARGARET REED, of Yarm, fpinfter, by will dated Sept. 26th,
1706, left the fum of *twenty pounds*, the intereft of which is to be diftributed yearly upon Good-Friday, by the minifter and church-
wardens.

ROBERT BAINBRIDGE, of Yarm, cordwainer, by will, dated Oct.
26th, 1707, gave out of the rents of certain houfes in Yarm, the fum

---

and any grammar-mafter in poffeffion of the fchool, feems entitled to, and receives the endowment,
upon teaching *fix poor children*.   Since the patent ceafed, the principal inhabitants have, from time to
time, elected the mafter ; and the perfons paying the *rent-charges* have generally nominated the poor
children, with the confent and approbation of the minifter for the time being, who generally acts as
one of the truftees.

§ THE payment of this donation has been long neglected.

of *twenty pounds*, to go towards putting out such poor children apprentices, as do not receive alms of the parish.

THOMAS BARKER, of Monk-End, in the parish of Croft, left to the
poor of Yarm, the sum of *five pounds*.

WILLIAM THOMPSON, of Yarm, left *twenty shillings*, to twenty poor
widows, to be paid by the minister and church-wardens yearly, upon
St. John's day, in Christmas.

THOMAS WALDY, Esq. of Yarm, by will, dated January 17th, 1784,
left *fifty pounds*, to the minister and church-wardens upon trust, the
interest of which to be laid out in purchasing bibles, and other religious books, to be distributed by them yearly, to the poor inhabitants
of Yarm, and those of its neighbourhood, upon St. Thomas-day in
Christmas. †

THE Rev. John Hopkinson, M. A. late minister of this parish, left
by will, the sum of *fifty pounds*, to the poor of Yarm, the interest to be
distributed yearly on St. John's-day, in Christmas, by the minister and
church-wardens.

YARM, like most other market-towns in England, had a coinage of
small money, called *tokens*, for the benefit and convenience of individuals in trade; which being struck for necessary change, the figure
and device were various, and the materials of lead or tin, but more
frequently of copper or brass. One of these was lately found at Nor-

---

† EXTRACT from the will of the late Mr. Thomas Waldy, of Yarm.

" I GIVE and bequeath unto the minister and church-wardens of the parish of Yarm, the sum of
fifty pounds, to be paid by my executrix hereafter named, out of my personal estate, at the end of
twelve calendar months, next after my decease, *upon trust*, and confidence, that they shall, and from
time to time, place out the same upon good security at interest, and shall, and do, as such interest
shall come in and be received, therewith buy and purchase bibles and other religious books, and give
away, and dispose thereof, on St. Thomas-day in Christmas in every year, in such manner, to the
poor inhabitants of Yarm, and to those of its neighbourhood, as may seem most proper for the advancement of piety and true religion. And I trust, that the minister for the time being, will, on
the Sunday preceding *St. Thomas-day*, earnestly recommend, in his sermon, to his poor parishoners, a
serious reading of the scriptures; as in them are the words of eternal life."

ton, near Stockton, in the grounds belonging to, and near the houfe of the Rev. C. Anftey. It is about the fize of, and greatly fimilar to, one of the *Stockton tokens*, publifhed in Mr. Brewfter's hiftory of Stockton: viz. on one fide the head of King Charles I. and round it, *GOD SAVE THE KING*, on the reverfe, round the edge, *THOMAS PARKINSON*, with the words *IN YARM*, in the centre: *no date on either fide*. This ufeful kind of fpecie was current, as a necceffary fmall change, from and during the reign of Queen Elizabeth to the year 1672, when King Charles II. iffued a quantity of half-pence and farthings fufficient for the exigences of trade, which rendered this practice of individuals no longer neceffary. *

As a cuftom of confiderable antiquity, the *curfew-bell*, which is conftantly rung here, and in many towns in the county of Durham, is worthy of particular notice. This badge of flavery was impofed upon the Englifh by the Conqueror, when, in the exertion of his tyrannical power, he not only deprived the people of the cuftody of arms; but alfo, to prevent confpiracies and affociations, prohibited, under the heavieft penalties, the ufe of *fire and candle*, § which were to be put out immediately at the found of this bell, which might juftly be confidered by our anceftors, as the knell of their departed liberty: happily for us, under our prefent mild and equitable government, it is heard with very different fenfations, merely as a fignal of relaxation from the neceffary toils of the day.

---

* " EVERY tradefman, who iffued this kind of fpecie, was obliged to take it again, when brought to him; and in large towns, where many forts of them were current, each tradefman kept a *forting box*, into the partitions of which he put the money of the refpective tradefmen, and when he had collected a large quantity of one perfons money he fent it to him, and got it changed into filver."

§ A drawing of the inftrument called *couvre-feu*, from its ufe in extinguifhing the fire, is given in *Hutchinfon's hiftory of Durham*, (vol. 1. p. 102.) made from one in the poffeffion of the late Mr. Goftling, of Canterbury; which is there defcribed, as being made of copper, rivetted together, as folder would have been liable to melt with the heat. In applying it, the wood and embers were raked clofe to the back of the hearth, and the inftrument put over them, by which the air being excluded, the fire was immediately extinguifhed.

THIS parifh, which, as we have already obferved, is not extenfive, affords little worthy of particular remark, with refpect to its ftate of agriculture and general appearance. There are only four farms, properly fo called, within the whole parifh, the reft of the grounds being let and occupied in fmall parcels for the convenience of the tradespeople and others in the town, and are chiefly laid down to grafs. About one fourth part of the land only is in tillage. The foil, in the fouthern part of the parifh, is chiefly of a clayey nature, and produces good crops of wheat, oats, and beans. Near the town, and on the banks of the river, a rich loam prevails, which produces turnips and potatoes in great perfection, and is alfo particularly fertile both in corn and grafs. From the river, the grounds rife gently towards the fouth, ftretching eaft and weft; the fields are well fenced and divided with quickfet-hedges, which with the trees in the hedge-rows, though without any regular plantations, (except thofe of Mr. Meynell's already noticed,) give the country a rich and pleafing appearance.

ALTHOUGH the fubject of the following narrative cannot boaft the gallantry and daring heroifm of a *Nelfon*, we neverthelefs flatter ourfelves that *Capt. Chriftopher Stonehoufe*, a native of Yarm, may juftly claim the notice of the public, for a *naval exploit*, that marks at once the cool intrepidity of the Britifh character. We are well aware that the narrative of a failor's life, in the humble fituation of Capt. S. however diftinguifhed for active induftry and exertion, cannot in general, furnifh details fufficiently important to intereft or inftruct the public. It will therefore be fufficient to obferve, that after an apprenticefhip, in the hard and laborious fervice of the *coal* and *Baltic trades,* from the port of Newcaftle, by which he obtained the freedom of that town,—by his merit and good conduct, he advanced in his profeffion, and became at laft the mafter of a fhip, in the *Oporto trade;* and of which, he was the principal owner. It was in his laft homeward-bound voyage from Oporto, in the month of November, 1804, that the circumftance, which we have particularly alluded to, occurred; a brief account of which we fubmit to the attention of our readers.

CAPT. STONEHOUSE, in the fhip *Jenny* (with a convoy of about 50 fail, under the protection of his Majefty's floop of war, *La Poulette* of 20 guns,) failed from Oporto, on the 18th Nov. 1804, and continued under convoy till the 25th, when, in blowing weather, he loft the convoy; and on the 28th faw *a cruizer* at a diftance, which he foon afterwards difcovered to be a *French brig-privateer*, of 18 guns and full of men. The privateer, on coming up, run clofe under the ftern of Capt. S's fhip, hailed him, and ordered him to tack to the weftward; which, however, was not complied with by Capt. S. till compelled by a heavy fire from the enemy. After running about two miles to the westward, he was ordered to lay to; when a large boat was hoisted out from the privateer, with an intent to take possession of their prize; which Capt. S. by *setting sail* and *running*, found means, for sometime, of preventing; till his little crew, only eight in number (three of whom were Italians,) objected to give their further assistance; alledging, that by a continued resistance, they could only provoke the resentment of the enemy, and thereby subject themselves to harsher treatment. *Capt. Stonehouse* however, with a resolute, though temperate courage, at a moment of danger, when men of ordinary minds are apt to despond, and give up every thing for lost, was determined to use his utmost efforts, in order, if possible, to effect his escape; and perceiving the privateer to gain fast upon him, he ordered his crew (whose assistance was now trifling,) to go below, while he alone remained at the helm. The privateer, in passing, opened a heavy fire, but without much serious damage; and from her great rate of sailing, ran considerably *a-head*, with her boat towing after her. It was at this moment of danger that an expedient occurred to Capt. S. which (though without the assistance of his ship's company) he was determined to attempt, though certainly with no small degree of risk for his own safety; in this, it was his design to *dash* his own ship between the enemy's stern and their boat, so that by cutting off, and destroying the latter, they might not easily find means of taking possession of his ship; but, instead of running clear of the privateer, which Capt. S. no doubt, intended, from the violence of the gale he run directly on board of her, a little abaft the main-rigging, carrying away her *main-boom*, and striking her so violently in her quarter, as to throw both the ship and crew, into the greatest difficulty and confusion.

THE damage sustained by Capt. S. was fortunately very trifling; and perceiving the crippled and confused state of the enemy, he made all the sail possible; and in less than half an hour, was out of sight.

AFTER experiencing some severe gales, with further damage he arrived at Portsmouth on the 13th of December, when the *Underwriters at Lloyd's*, as a mark of approbation, and in reward of his undaunted perseverance, and ultimate success, in effecting his escape, unanimously voted him a present of 2 *per cent.* upon his ship's cargo, which consisted principally of wine, and was valued at 14,000*l*.

ON quitting his profession, in every situation of which, he was doomed to experience more than a common share of difficulties and misfortunes, Capt. S. retired with a numerous family, to the place of his nativity, where he now resides, in a laudable, and less precarious exertion of his abilities for their support.

THE PARISH OF KIRKLEVINGTON.

KIRKLEVINGTON, which is the next adjoining parifh to the fouth, lies about two miles diftant from the market-town of Yarm. The parifh is divided into the following quarters, called townfhips : viz. *Kirklevington*, *Caftle-Levington*, *Low-Worfall*, and *Pickton;* and is bounded on the eaft by the river Leven, which divides it from the chapelries of Hilton and Middleton ; on the weft by the parifh of Appleton, and the chapelry of High-Worfall ; on the north by the parifh of Yarm and the river Tees ; and by Crathorne on the fouth. Its greateft extent from eaft to weft is about five miles, and upwards of four miles broad.

IN looking for the etymology of local names, we are naturally led to confider how far the compofition of the word is fignificant or defcriptive of any ftriking circumftance or appearance about the place ; from which, though fometimes unintelligible by length of time, we fhall find the etymology frequently to arife. The general name of this parifh appears from ancient records, to have been formerly written *Leventon*, (in Domefday-book, **Lentune**), a name defcriptive of its fituation ; q. d. *a town upon the river Leven.*

THE village of *Kirklevington* was probably fo called, as being the town with the parifh-church ; for the fite of which it is particularly commodious, being nearly in the centre of the parifh. It ftands on a gently rifing eminence, running eaft and weft ; and confifts chiefly of farm-houfes, which are decent and commodious ; with a few cottages, the mean appearance of which impreffes on the traveller, an idea of poverty and wretchednefs.

M

In Domesday-book, the earliest and most authentic record, in which the name of this place occurs, *Leventon* is thus mentioned under the title of   " 𝕮𝖊𝖗𝖗𝖆 𝕽𝖊𝖌𝖎𝖘 : "
" 𝕸𝖆𝖓𝖊𝖗𝖎𝖚𝖒 𝖎𝖓 𝕷𝖊𝖓𝖙𝖚𝖓𝖊.   𝕳𝖆𝖚𝖚𝖆𝖗𝖉 VI 𝕮𝖆𝖗𝖚𝖈𝖆𝖙𝖆𝖘 𝖆𝖉 𝕲𝖊𝖑𝖉𝖚𝖒.
" 𝕮𝖊𝖗𝖗𝖆 𝖆𝖉 III 𝕮𝖆𝖗. XL 𝕾𝖔𝖑𝖎𝖉𝖔𝖘."   *Domesday-book.*

FROM which it appears, that *Kirk-Levington* was the ancient inheritance of the crown; and, at the time of making the survey, contained six carucates (about 720 acres) of land, rated, or taxed *(ad geldum)*; besides which there was land sufficient for three ploughs, valued at *forty shillings.* Who the Saxon possessors were, or of what rank and condition this *Hauuard* was, we are uninformed; but from Domesday-book, he appears to have had large possessions in this part of the district. After the conquest, it was one of those manors granted by the Conqueror, to *Robert de Brus,* of Skelton-Castle, who held it of the King *in capite* by military service. The Bruces continued possessors, till the reign of *Richard I.* or *King John;* when it was given by *Adam de Brus* then Lord of Skelton, in marriage with his daughter *Isabel* to Henry de Percy, youngest son of *Joceline Lovaine,* ancestor to the Percies, Dukes of Northumberland; for which gift (as appears from the *great Percy Chartulary, folio* 60,) " *the said Henry and his heirs were to repair to* " *Skelton-Castle every Christmas day, and lead the lady of that Castle from her* " *chamber to the chapel to mass; and from thence to her chamber again; and* " *after dining with her, to depart.*"

THE Percies held this manor and estate till the attainder of Henry, surnamed *Hotspur;* who joining with his father, in rebellion against King Henry IV. their estates became forfeited to the crown; and Kirk-Levington, with their other large possessions, was granted by that King to *John, Duke of Bedford,* his third son, who died * seized thereof (14. Henry VI.) without issue, leaving that King, his nephew, his heir. It

---

* HE died at the castle of Roan, in Normandy, and was buried in the church of *Notre-Dame,* September 14th, 1435.

feems however, not to have continued long in the crown; for, we find that Henry, the fon of Hotfpur (who had been kindly treated by King Henry V.) was, foon after reftored in blood, and to the inheritance of his father; and died feized of this manor, (33. Henry VI.) being flain in the battle of St. Albans, a ftout affertor of the Lancaftrian intereft.

KIRK-LEVINGTON, after this, continued in the Percy family, till Henry, the fixth Earl of Northumberland; who, upon the attainder of his younger brother, Sir Thomas Percy, Knight, (29. Henry VIII.) gave this, and a great part of his other eftates, to *King Henry VIII.* It afterwards became the poffeffion of Sir George Bowes, of Streatlam-Caftle, Bart. in which family it continued till male-iffue failing, it was carried by marriage with *Mary-Eleanor*, daughter of George Bowes, Efq. to the late Earl of Strathmore; whofe fon, the prefent Earl, fold the manor and eftate to John Waldy, and Henry Hutchinfon, Efqrs. the prefent proprietors.

KIRKBY, in his inqueft, fays, there were four carucates of land in Kirklevington (where ten made one knight's fee) held by Henry de Percy; who paid nothing, as being *liberum maritagium.* † From the fame inqueft it appears, that *William de Levington* held eleven oxgangs here and paid eighteen pence. ‡

THIS William de Levington, we prefume, was a younger branch of the Percy family; and on his quitting the place of his paternal refidence, and fettling here, affumed the local name, according to the cuftom of thofe times, when men, being rarely dignified with furnames, were ufually denominated from the eftates, to which they removed. The defcendants of this William flourifhed, and continued

---

† HENRICUS DE PERCY tenet quatuor Carucat. Terr. in Kirk-Levynton, unde X faciunt unum feod. milit. Et non reddit Ballivo Domini Regis finem; et eft liberum Maritagium.

Kirkby's Inqueft.

‡ WILLIMUS DE LEVYNGTON tenet XI Bovat. Ter. in Kirk-Levyngton unde X Car. Ter. faciunt Feodum; et reddit Ballivo Domini Regis pro fine 18d.   *Kirkby's Inqueft.*

to hold lands here for feveral generations; § for we find that Richard
de Levington gave ten acres of land in this townfhip to the priory of
Guifbrough; which was confirmed by Peter, fon of *Peter de Brus.* ‖

KIRK-LEVINGTON, notwithftanding its prefent apparent infignifi-
cance, did not efcape the depredations of warfare; for we find that
King Edward II. in the 13th year of his reign, iffued a mandate to the
collectors of his taxes in the north-riding of the county of York, for
exempting this town, with feveral others from the payment thereof, in
confideration that the inhabitants had been plundered, and their
houfes and property burnt and deftroyed by the rebellious Scots, in an
incurfion, which they made, the year preceding, under the command
of Sir James Douglas, and the Earl of Murray, to the very gates of the
city of York.

FROM the mandate,* which we have fet forth in the notes, it appears, that Kirk-Levington was, at that time, in the cuftody of Eleanor,
widow of Henry de Percy, who was daughter of Richard, Earl of
Arundel, during the minority of her fon.

THE church, which is an humble ftructure, but kept in decent repair, ftands a little to the fouth, near the centre of the village, on
ground, which is the moft elevated; and commands an extenfive and

---

§ STEPHEN DE LEVINGTON occurs Prior of Helagh in 1333; and was fucceeded by Richard de
Levington in 1352.   *Burton's Mon. Ebor.*

‖ DUGD. MON. vol. 11. p. 151.

* " REX taxatoribus et collectoribus decimæ octavæ in Northtrithingo in Com. Ebor. *falutem.*
Quia Alianora, quæ fuit uxor Henrici de Percy nobis dedit intelligi, pro fe, hominibus et tenentibus
villarum de Topclif, Newby, Carleton, Criftwayt, Aftenby, Kirk-Levington, Dyfford, et Renyngton,
quod predictæ villæ per Scotos inimicos et rebelles noftros funt combuftæ, et bona et catalla hominum
de prædictis villis per eofdem inimicos in parte deftructa, et in parte deprædata, per quod iidem Alianora, homines et tenentes de bonis illis taxationem dictæ decimæ octavæ nobis folvere non poffunt.
Nos ad eorum deftructionem confiderationem habentes, vobis mandamus, quod facta taxatione decimæ octavæ prædictæ de bonis fuis ibidem remanentibus juxta formam commiffionis, vobis nuper inde
factæ, levationi ejufdem fuperfedeatis omnino, quoufque aliud a nobis inde habueritis in mandatis.
Tefte Rege apud Ebor. 25. Nov. per ipfum regem et confilium."

Rymer. Tom. III. p. 801.   *Claus.* 13. *Edw. II. m.* 13.

pleafing profpect into the county of Durham on the north. The hills above Richmond terminate the view to the weft; as do the range of the Cleveland hills, and the hanging woods of Arncliff that to the fouth.

We are in poffeffion of no evidence, that points out with certainty, at what time, or by whom this church was originally built or endowed; but its ftyle of architecture difcovers confiderable antiquity. The circular form of the arch, leading to the chancel, which is fupported by round pillars, with fquare or faxon capitals, and ornamented with zig-zag mouldings of tolerable workmanfhip, induces us to conclude it of Saxon-origin; while the eaftern-window, as alfo one to the fouth, under pointed arches curioufly embellifhed, are proofs that the principal parts of the prefent ftructure cannot claim a date earlier than the reign of Henry III. when pointed arches and lancet-windows, as they are called, were firft introduced. It is hardly to be conceived, that the church would efcape the fury of the rebellious Scots in their prædatory incurfion above-mentioned; and this circumftance may ferve perhaps to account for the appearance of the different ftyles of architecture in the prefent building.

This church was anciently rectorial; and is dedicated to St. Martin. Upon the foundation of the priory at Guilbrough, it was given by Robert de Brus, the founder, to that monaftry;* and being appropriated thereto, without any refervation of a vicarage, is now only a per-

* From a confirmatory deed of King Richard I. bearing date 1189, reciting the grants of divers benefactors, to the Canons of Thornton upon Humber, in the county of Lincoln, it appears that the churches of *Leventon* and *Yarm*, were given to that monaftry by *Adam de Brus;* but from a previous grant of thefe churches to the priory of Guilbrough, by *Robert de Brus,* father of the faid *Adam,* a conteft arofe between the two houfes; which was amicably fettled in the year 1192, before *H——,* abbot of *Melfa,* Hugh, prior of *Bridlington,* and *Ivo, prior of Wartre;* to whom a commiffion was granted by Pope Celeftine III. for that purpofe; when the Canons of Thornton relinquifhed all claim to this church, and the chapel of Yarm; and, in return, the Canons of Guilbrough gave the church of *Kelerfterne* to the priory of Thornton, together with fix oxgangs of land in the fame town. *Burton's Mon. Ebor. p. 345.*

petual curacy. Upon the diffolution of the priory, it was granted by
King Henry VIII. to the Archbifhop of York, who nominates the curate.
The rectorial rights † are leafed out for three lives, under the Archbifhop, to the lord of the manor; and the leffee is bound to pay a referved rent or ftipend of 20*l.* *per annum,* to the curate.

THE church was certified to the governours of Queen Anne's bounty at 21*l.* 5s. od. ; ‡ and has received one allotment of 200*l.* laid out in
lands at Trenholme, in the parifh of Whorlton. We find no fepulchral
monuments about the church, worth notice ; a large flat tomb-ftone of
blue or Dutch marble, lies in the floor of the chancel; but the infcription is quite obliterated.

THE poor within this townfhip are fupported by a rate, which has
been confiderably increafed within the laft ten years; and now amounts
annually to about three fhillings in the pound. §

THERE is a fmall field, on the fouth-fide of the village, called the
Poor-Garth, which was left by will, by one Hall, to the minifter and
church-wardens, in truft, for the ufe of fuch poor widows, refident with-

---

† THE rectory appears to confift of the tythes in kind of every defcription of all the lands in
Kirk-Levington, Pickton, and *Low-Worfall,* and of one farm at *Caftle-Levington,* called *Howden-field ;*
with a prefcriptive payment of 3*l.* 13s. od. in lieu of the tythes of corn and hay from the other lands
in *Caftle-Levington.*

‡ KIRK-LEVINGTON CURACY.

Ded.   Saint Martin.   Certified val. 21*l.* 5s. od.   Augmented with 200*l.*

CURATES.

Edward Walters,	1669.		
John Marfh,	1696. *poft mortem* Walters.	Thomas Perrott,	1715. *p. res.* Burton.
John Oughton,	1697. *poft mortem* Marfh.	Robert Dent,	1727. *p. res.* Perrott.
John Bever,	1699. *poft mortem* Oughton.	John Hopkinfon,	1737. *p. res.* Dent.
Thomas Burton,	1700. *p. res.* Bever.	John Graves,	1794. *poft mortem* Hopkinfon.

§ IT has been with juftice remarked, that the rapid increafe of parifh paupers has arifen from the
want of timely attention in regulating the hufbandmen's wages, and the various effects of licentiouf-
nefs ; and that they, from thefe two adventitious caufes, exceed in number and confequent expence,
all thofe impotent and indigent poor, that arife from age, ficknefs, and infirmity, fuch only, who were
defigned to be fupported by the poor rate.

Hill's means of reforming the morals of the poor,
by the prevention of poverty.

in the place, as receive no alms, nor parochial relief. The rent of this field, which produces five pounds *per annum*, is diftributed, according to the directions given in the benefactor's will, twice a year: viz. at Chriftmas, and on Trinity-Sunday.

THE townfhip of

CASTLE-LEVINGTON

lies on the eaftern extremity of the parifh; it was ancient demefne of the crown, and is entered in *Domefday-Book*, under the title of

" Terra Regis.
" Manerium in alia Lentune; Hauuard IIII Carucatas ad Geldum.
" Terra ad duas Car. V Solidos."

THIS manor and eftate continued in the crown, till the reign of King Edward I. when it was granted by that King to *Nicholas de Meinill*, ‖ with free-warren in all his demefne lands. According to Kirkby's Inqueft, * this Nicholas de Meinill held half a knight's fee in Caftle-Levington, of the King *in capite*, where ten carucates made one knight's fee; and paid, as a fine, the fum of eight fhillings.

THE Meinills continued lords here, till the 23d year of Edward III. when John de Meinill, being feized of this manor and other lands, which defcended to him from John his grandfather, died unmarried, leaving his fifter Alice his heir, then married to John de Boulton.

THIS eftate, after paffing through feveral families, was at length parcelled out to different purchafers. The manorial rights have been long difufed; nor does it now evidently appear to whom thofe rights belong.

‖ Cart. 13. Edw. I. n. 20. Dugd. Baron. vol. 2. p. 110.
* " NICHOLAS DE MEINILL tenet dimid. feod. in Caftle-Leventon de Domino Rege in capite,
" unde X Carucat. terræ faciunt feod. et reddit Ballivo Domini Regis pro fine 8s."
Kirkby's Inqueft.

RED-HALL, (now a farm houfe,) fituated on the banks of the river
Leven, was the refidence of the family of *Meryton*; † who defcended
from George Meryton, D. D. Dean of Peterborough, and afterwards
Dean of York. An undivided moiety of their eftate defcended to the
Pennymans of Ormfby, which was fold in the year 1802 by Sir James
Pennyman, Bart. to Mr. Robert Caris.

WILLIAM BECKWITH of Herrington, in the county of Durham, Efq.
a defcendant from the ancient family of Beckwiths, near Doncafter, who
claim their defcent from *Sir Hercules Malbiffe, Knight*, ‡ poffeffes a confiderable eftate here; upon which, there is a circular eminence, called

---

† *MERYTONS of Caftle-Levington.*

George Meryton, D. D. chaplain to Queen Anne,—Mary, daughter of . . . . Rande, of . . . .,
(wife of King James,) Dean of Peterborough, and | county of Lincoln, fon to . . . . Rande,
afterwards of York. ob. 1624. | Bifhop of Lincoln.

| 4 John. | 3 Robert, ob. S. P. | 2 Thomas Meryton,—Grace, dau. of F. of Caftle-Levington, | Wright, of Bolton ob. 1652. | on Swale, Efq. | 1 George, ob. S. P. | Mary,—T. Moyfer. |
| | | | | | | Ann,—F. Wright. |

| 5 John. | 4 Richard. | 3 Paul. | 2 Thomas. | 1 George M. of—Mary, dau. of Caftle-Levington. | T. Pallifer, of | Kirby-Wifke. | Grace—F. Pallifer. |
| | | | | | | | Ann,—T. Pallifer. |

3 John.   2 George.   1 Thomas æt. 8. Ann. et 10 Mens. 25 Aug. 1665.

Dugdale's Vifitation, 1665.

‡ THERE is a monument in Pickering church yard, of *Sir William de Bruce*, owner of certain
lands in Pickering; whofe daughter, *Dame Beckwith Bruce* was married to *Sir Hercules Malbiffe*,
Knight; who was obliged by marriage covenant, dated 1226, to affume the name of *Beckwith*; and
from whom the family of *Beckwiths* is defcended.

THE CASTLE-HILL,

which is worth the attention of the curious; and from which we prefume the name of *Caftle-Levington* to be derived.

THE annexed fketch will give the reader fome idea of this monument
of antiquity; which is fituated on the weftern bank of the river Leven,
to which the defcent is fteep; and commands a pleafing profpect of the
windings and wooded banks of the river, and the country adjacent.

THE hill, on the weft, fouth, and fouth-weft, is nearly upon a level
with the fields adjoining, from which it is guarded by a deep trench.
The fides on the eaft, fouth-eaft, and north, are almoft perpendicular;
and rife from the bottom to the fummit, to the height of about two
hundred yards above the river. The crown of the hill is a plain of forty
paces in diameter, defended by a breaft-work of earth of confiderable
height, forming a circle of two hundred paces in circumference; with

N

an opening or entrance on the fouth. *   There are no remains of any
buildings near; but the place bears evident marks of a perfect fortification; and its circular form is highly characteriftic of a *Danifh-camp*.

THE Danes are generally fuppofed to have made ufe of this mode
of defence, upon the crown of fome eminence, encompaffed with intrenchments, and defended by a breaft-work; which might, indeed, be
afterwards followed by the inhabitants, either as a ftrong-hold, for the
fecurity of their valuables, or as a refort of fighting men, when they
had to oppofe the attacks of an enemy; for which purpofe, this hill
feems well adapted, confidering the mode of warfare, and the military
weapons of that age;—the fides of which are fo fteep, that a fmall body
of men occupying the fummit, might defend themfelves againft a numerous enemy, who attacked only with miffile weapons, or charged
fword in hand.

IT has been fuggefted to us, by an ingenious and learned correfpondent, that this place might have been appropriated to civil, or *judicial
purpofes*; like the *mons placiti*, which is defcribed by *Du Cange*, as being
a hill, where the people affemble at a court, like our affizes; by the
Scotch and Irifh, called *Parley-Hills*.—Spelman alfo obferves, " Collis
" vallo plerumque munitus in loco campeftri, ne infidiis exponatur, ubi
" convenire olim folebant centurae aut vicinae incolae ad lites inter fefe
" tractandas et terminandas.   Scotis reorque *Grith-Hail*, mons pacifica-
" tionis, cui afyli privilegia concedebantur."

---

* THIS opening has, of late years, been confiderably enlarged, by digging and leading off the foil,
of which the breaft-work is compofed; and which being of the richeft quality, has been found highly
ufeful and beneficial as a manure, particularly in the culture of turnips.   In digging into the fide of
the hill, bones, fuppofed to be human, are fometimes found, with pieces of corroded iron, and fragments of coarfe pottery, which appear to have been ufed for domeftic purpofes.

THE manor, township, and village of

WORSALL PARVA, EAST, OR LOW-WORSALL, †

lie to the weſt of Kirklevington, adjoining the river Tees on the North. It was probably ſo called in contradiſtinction to *High-Worſall*, or *Great-Worſall*, ‡ an adjoining chapelry on the weſt, which ſtands in a more elevated ſituation.

FROM Domeſday-Book, in which this place is entered under the title, " 𝕮𝖊𝖗𝖗𝖆 𝕽𝖊𝖌𝖎𝖘," it appears that Worſall was likewiſe ancient demeſne of the crown; and contained three carucates of land, rated, or taxed *(ad geldum)* beſides which there was land ſufficient for two ploughs; as will appear from the following extract from the ſurvey.

---

† WE find the name of this place thus variouſly written in ancient evidences: viz. *Werkeſell*, *Wirkſail*, *Wirleſdail*, and in Domeſday Book, *Werceſel*; the etymology of which, though dark and myſterious, we conjecture to be derived from the Teutonic, *werck*, (opus,) and *hale* (cavitas,) *quaſi dicas, a building in a low and hollow vale.*

‡ As this chapelry lies within *Allertonſhire*, and conſequently beyond the preſcribed limits of our diſtrict, we ſhall here only briefly obſerve that though there is no village at preſent remaining, to entitle it to the diſtinguiſhing appellation of *Great-Worſall*, as it was ſometimes anciently called, * we have reaſon nevertheleſs to believe, from the numerous foundations of houſes ſtill viſible in the grounds adjoining the preſent chapel, that *High-Worſall* was, at a more early period, a place of greater importance. The chapel here, it ſeems, ſhared a ſimilar fate with the village, and continued in ruins till about the year 1719, when the preſent humble ſtructure was erected out of the remains of the former. This was anciently a *chapel of eaſe*, within the pariſh of North-Allerton; but on rebuilding the chapel, which was augmented by Queen Anne's bounty in the year 1720, it was made parochial, and is now a perpetual curacy, under the patronage of the vicar of North-Allerton, who nominates the curate—The Rev. John Graves is the preſent incumbent.

THE lands within the chapelry are tythe-free, with a cuſtomary, or preſcriptive payment of 1l. 6s. 8d. (the certified value of the chapel,) to the vicar of North-Allerton. High-Worſall was part of the large poſſeſſions of George Bowes, of Streatlam-Caſtle, Eſq. and deſcended, by marriage to the late Earl of Strathmore; whoſe ſon, the preſent Earl, ſold it to Thomas Wayne, of Anngrove-Hall, Eſq. the preſent proprietor, and lord of the manor.

---

* IT is worthy of particular remark, that there is neither *inn-keeper*, *blackſmith*, *ſhoemaker*, *tailor*, nor any other mechanic, within this chapelry; which at preſent conſiſts only of *nine farm houſes*, and two cottages, and contains about 40 inhabitants.

" **Terra Regis.**
" **Manerium in alia Wercesel; Hauuard III Carucatas ad Geldum.**
" **Terra ad II Car.**"

THIS manor was granted by the Conqueror to *Robert de Brus*, lord
of Skelton; in whofe defcendants it continued till the reign of Henry
III. when Peter de Brus, dying without iffue, his four fifters became his
heirs; and Margaret had, for her fhare this and fome other eftates in
this neighbourhood, together with the barony of Kendal, in Weftmorland, which fhe held of the King *in capite*, by the fervice of one knight's
fee. *

THIS Margaret married Robert de Roos, (fon of Robert, Baron of
Werke, fecond fon of Robert de Roos, of Helmfley,) and had by him a
fon called William, to whom fhe gave the caftle of Kendal; and from
whom the *Parrs* of Kendal are maternally defcended. But the eftates
in Cleveland, which fell to her fhare, feem not to have been carried to
this family; for, in Kirkby's Inqueft, they are entered as the fee of
Marmaduke de Thweng, by gift of the faid Margaret; of whom, Robert
de Scoterfkelf and others held two knight's fees, where ten carucates
made one knight's fee. †

WE have no evidence to fhew, at what period this eftate was, at firft
parcelled out, which is now in the hands of different proprietors; and
the fucceffion of the lords of the manor is equally obfcure, till the beginning of the reign of King Charles the firft; when we find it the
property of Thomas Middleton, Efq.; from whofe defcendants it paffed

---

* MARGARETA DE ROOS (vel Rofa) tenet de Domino Rege in capite, tria feoda et dimid. pro
fervicio unius feod. unde Robertus de Scoterfkelf, Richard. Gower, et Willimus Sturmey tenent II
feod. in Faceby cum Sexhowe, Wirkefaill cum Staindale-Rigg, Acclam, Marton et parva Bufkeby
unde X Car. ter. faciunt feod. et Robertus de Scoterfkelf reddit pro parte fua pro fine VIII^d. Willimus Sturmey pro parte fua pro fine III^s. et VIII^d. et Richardus Gower pro parte fua de fine IIII^s.
et VIII^d.

† DE feod Marmaducis de Thweng, ex dono Margaretæ Roos. Dominus Robertus de Scoterfkelf, Richardus Gower, et Willimus Sturmey tenent in Faceby cum Sexhow, Wirkefaill cum Staindale-Rigg, &c. II feod. unde X Car. terr. faciunt feodum.   *Kirkby's Inqueft.*

by purchafe, about the year 1680 to Sir John Lowther, of Lowther, in the county of Weftmorland, Bart. It was afterwards fold to the Allans, and is now the property of George Allan, of Blackwell-Grange, near Darlington, Efq. who poffeffes a confiderable eftate within this townfhip.

WORSALL-HALL, a pleafant, retired fituation on the banks of the river Tees, was formerly the refidence of the late *Thomas Peirfe, Efq.*; a part of whofe eftate, with the manfion houfe and village adjoining is now the property of Mr. James Ward. During the refidence of the *Peirfe family, Worfall* (then called *Peirfburg,*) had to boaft of fome beauties; and the villagers enjoyed many comforts and advantages, while

> " Health and plenty cheer'd the labouring fwain;

but now, we may, with too much propriety, adopt the pathetic language of the fame Poet;

> " Sweet fmiling village! lovlieft of the lawn
> " Thy fports are fled, and all thy charms are gone;
> " Amidft thy bowers the tyrant's hand is feen,
> " And defolation faddens all thy green."
> *Goldfmith's deferted village.*

To account for this change, we have only to obferve, that this village, from its advantageous fituation on the banks of the Tees, formerly enjoyed fome fhare of trade, particularly in the exportation of lead, corn, and other produce of the country; for the reception of which large and commodious granaries, &c. were erected at a confiderable expence, upon the banks of the river, which is navigable hither for fmall craft. The imports were timber and merchant goods, for Richmond, Bedale, and other markets in the weft. During the flourifhing ftate of this trade, the villagers, from a conftant employment and good wages, were enabled to earn an honeft livelihood by their induftry, and to live with decency and comfort; but the premifes coming by purchafe into the poffeffion of a family deftitute of mercantile fpirit and abilities, the trade is now loft; in confequence of which, the population is much decreafed, the villagers impoverifhed, and many of the houfes uninhabited, and falling to decay.

HERE was an ancient fishery on the river Tees, which was given by *Gilbert Hanfard* to the Abbey of *Rievaux;* this fishery with a cottage and parcel of ground adjoining, called *Batt-Ings* came afterwards into the possession of Major Norton, who sold the same (33. Charles II.) to George Marwood, Efq. The ground and fishery have since passed by purchase to the lord of the manor.

THE fishery is for salmon, which are chiefly taken with a boat and net, and sent to *Leeds, Manchester,* and other populous towns at a diftance. *Smelts* or *Sparlings* are also taken here with nets in great quantities, in the months of March, April, and May, when they frequent this part of the river for the sake of depositing their spawn.

THE streams here, and about *Middleton Saint George,* abound also with *salmon-fry* and *branlins,* † which afford excellent diversion for the angler, during the summer months.

THAT part of this township, called *Staindale-Rigg,* lies to the south, and about two miles distant from the village of *Low-Worsall.* Of this place we find nothing remarkable at present, except the name, which may be considered as descriptive of its situation; being an extensive

---

† THE *branlin* succeed the *salmon smelts,* and are frequent in the rivers of Scotland, where they are called *pars* : they are also common in the *Wye,* where they are known by the name of *skirlings,* or *lasprings* ; and are the *rack-rider* of the county of Durham, and the *samlet, fingerin* or *pink-trout,* of other places.

DESCRIPTION.—Head green and ash-colour. Gill-covers tinged with a pale variable green and purple, and marked with a round dark coloured spot. Back and sides down to the lateral line, dusky, and marked with numerous dark coloured spots. Belly white. Along the lateral line, there are from sixteen to thirty bright vermilion-coloured spots. The sides are marked with nine or ten oval bars, of a dusky bluish colour. *Dorsal fin* has twelve rays marked with a few dusky spots. *Pectoral fin* has thirteen rays ; *ventral fin* nine ; and the *anal fin* eight rays, which incline to a yellow colour; tail much forked. The larger branlins never exceed 8¼ inches in length ; generally about six inches long, and three inches in circumference.

As the *branlin* has been considered by fishermen in general, to be a species of salmon of a later spawn, we beg leave to refer our readers to Mr. Pennant's observations on the subject, and his reasons for considering them of the *trout species.* See also Dr. *Heysham's* observations, in his catalogue of Cumberland animals, published in the 2d vol. of *Hutchinson's History of Cumberland.*

ridge of land, running eaſt and weſt; which, before it became incloſed and cultivated, might probably abound with ſtones, more than the ſurrounding lands; and from this circumſtance, the name is probably derived.

THE townſhip of

PICKTON,

or, as it is ſometimes written, PYKETON (q. d. PEAK-TOWN) lies to the ſouth from Worſall, and to the ſouth-weſt from Kirk-Levington. The village conſiſts of a few houſes (ſome of which are ill-built,) ſcattered irregularly on a gently riſing eminence, and commands a pleaſing proſpect to the ſouth. As this place is not ſpecified in *Domeſday-Book,* we are led to conclude, that it never claimed the title or privilege of a manor. By an inquiſition * taken in the ſeventh year of the reign of King Edward I. it appears, that Pickton contained a fourth part of a knight's fee (where twelve carucates made one knight's fee,) which was held by William de Pyckton, of Peter de Brus, lord of Skelton, who held the ſame of the King *in capite.* On the death of this Peter, Pickton deſcended to Marmaduke de Thweng, by marriage with Lucia, one of his ſiſters and coheireſſes; and according to Kirkby's Inqueſt, was held of the ſaid Marmaduke, the chief Lord of the fee, by Galfrid, ſon of William de Pyckton, who paid as a fine, the ſum of three ſhillings. § It would be no way intereſting to the reader, to trace out the ſucceſſion of proprietors here. The lands have been long parcelled out, and are now in the hands of different freeholders.

WITH reſpect to the *ſoil, produce,* and *general appearance,* we may remark, that there are no waſte † or uncultivated lands of any conſe-

---

* Eſceat. 7. Edward I. m. 32.

§ GALFRIDUS DE PYCKTON tenet quartam partem unius feodi, de dicta hæriditat. in Pycton, unde XII Carucat. terr. faciunt feod. milit. et reddit pro fine III⁵. *Kirkby's Inqueſt.*

† THERE is a tract of land, in the townſhip of Kirklevington, a little to the weſt from that village, called the *Foreſt;* which is of a rather barren unproductive ſoil. The name and other appa-

quence, within the parifh; which contains, in the whole, upwards of
5000 acres; about one half of which is in tillage.

The *foil* is chiefly a ftrong, but fertile clay, and in general, more
favourable for corn than grafs. Wheat, oats, and beans are the principal crops, with a few turnips, the cultivation of which, fince the introduction of the *Scotch-drill*, has been confiderably increafed. The level
lands, near the *Tees*, at *Worfall*, and on the border of the Leven at *Caftle-
Levington*, called *Holmes*, ‡ confift of a deep, rich loam, chiefly in grafs.
About *Pickton*, the foil is of an inferior quality, except fome fmall inclofures, near the village; the farms here are fmall, none exceeding
100*l.* a year, generally from 30*l.* to 60*l.*: in other parts of the parifh,
they are larger: viz. from 100*l.* to 200*l.* a year and upwards. The
rents arife chiefly from the fale of corn; the dairy being lefs attended
to than the plough; though the making of butter and cheefe occupies
the attention of the miftrefs of almoft every farm.

The general appearance is pleafing; the lands are nearly level, except
fome gentle flopes and fwelling ridges, chiefly inclining north and fouth.
The banks of the Leven are fteep and woody; and from the number of
trees, which are regulary difpofed in hedge-rows, the country has a
pleafing and cheerful afpect.

WE have already obferved, that this parifh is watered by the *Tees*
and the *Leven*, which conftitute the boundaries on the eaft and north;
befides thefe rivers, there are a variety of fmall brooks in different parts
of the parifh; but one only is worth particular notice, as being remark-

---

rent circumftances, lead us to conclude, that this tract remained *wafte*, (lying out, *foras*, that is, re-
jected as of no value) longer than the other lands within the parifh; though we have no evidence to
point out the exact period of its firft inclofure, cultivation, and improvement.

---

‡ " COKE on Littleton defines *Holme*, or *Hulmus*, an ifle, or fenny ground; but the prefent ac-
" ceptation of the word is, to denote a low fituation, plain, or valley." Spelman fays, " *Hulmus-*
" Anglis, Danis, Germanis, *Holme,*-locus infularis; infula amnica, etiam marina; *Holmes* etiam dici
" animadverto depreffiores humi planicies, plurimis rivulis et aquarum divortiis irriguas."

Spelman's Glofs. p. 302.

able for the different names it affumes in its courfe. In the fouthern extremity of the parifh, where this rivulet has its fource, it is called a *Stell*, (a provincial name for a fmall and fluggifh brook, and probably a corruption of the word *Skell*, which fignifies a rivulet;) it retains this name, till paffing the village of Kirklevington on the north, and taking a more weftern direction, it enters that tract of land, called the Foreft, with deep and naked banks, when it affumes the name of *Salter-Gill-Beck*, a name defcriptive of, and derived from, the nature of the lands through which it paffes. *Salter* we conceive to be merely an abbreviation of the words *faltûs terra*, (foreft land,) which if written contractedly, according to ancient cuftom, will bring us literally and directly to the word *fal-ter;* and the bottom, wherein the *beck* runs, is called the *Gill*. As foon as this beck has paffed the boundaries of the foreft, in its courfe towards *Worfall*, where it empties itfelf into the Tees, it again affumes a new name, equally fignificant: viz. *Hole-Beck*, from the Saxon word *hol* (*cavus*) and *beck;* from its deep and hollow channel.

As there are no manufactories within the parifh, (the inhabitants being chiefly occupied in the various branches of agriculture,) the population, as may be expected, is not great; and, we believe, has lately decreafed, owing to the too prevalent, but pernicious practice of confolidating two or more fmall farms; and fuffering the houfes to fall to decay.

THE following return made to Government, in the year 1801, for the different townfhips within the parifh, according to act of Parliament, will give the reader fome idea of the prefent number of inhabitants.

	Houfes	Families	Uninhabited houfes	Males	Females	Total.
Kirklevington	49	49	2	117	122	239
Caftle-Levington	9	9	0	27	20	47
Worfall	40	40	6	76	89	165
Pickton	18	18	4	42	49	91
Totals	116	116	12	262	280	542

Q

THE number of *baptifms*, *marriages*, and *burials*, according to the parifh regifter, from the year 1781 to the year 1800 inclufive, will appear from the following table:

	Males.	Females.	Total.
Baptifms	151	171	322
Burials	76	81	157
Increafe	75	90	175

Marriages within the above period 84.

A REVIEW of the above tables will naturally fuggeft to us the following obfervations. In the former we may remark, that the number of males and females within the parifh, is nearly equal; and that upon comparing the number of houfes or families, with the total number of inhabitants, there are, on an average, $4\frac{1}{2}$ nearly to each family.

THE comparative ftatement, in the fecond table, points out the difference (about two to one,) between the number of baptifms and that of burials, within the period above-ftated, as the caufe of a great apparent increafe; and the average number of burials, in one year, which is 8, out of a population of 542, fhews that one only, out of 68 nearly, dies annually. This is a circumftance, that muft be confidered as a ftriking proof of a falubrious air, and the general health of the inhabitants.

THE PARISH OF CRATHORNE

Lies to the fouth of Kirklevington, and about four miles diftant from the market-town of Yarm. The village is pleafantly feated on the weftern bank of the river Leven, which runs in a ferpentine courfe, and divides the parifh nearly into two equal parts.

THE banks of the river are cloathed with wood, and afford a variety of beautiful and picturefque views. In the language of Milton,

———————— " Their hairy fides
" With thickets overgrown, grotefque and wild
" Shade above fhade, a woody theatre
" Of ftatelieft view."

THE parifh, which is about three miles in extent, from eaft to weft, and two miles broad, is bounded on the eaft, weft, and fouth, by the parifh of Rudby, and its two dependent chapelries of Middleton and Eaft-Rounton, and by the parifh of Kirklevington on the north. Although the compofition of the word *Crathorne* bears little or no affinity to any circumftance or prefent appearance, to direct us in our etymological enquiries, we are neverthelefs induced to conclude from the ancient orthography of the word, and particularly from Domefday-book, where we find it written **Crathorne**, that the name is derived fimply from the Anglo-Saxon, *crake*, a crow,* and *thorne;* which would be eafily and naturally foftened down in pronunciation to the prefent name.

---

* THE ancient family of *Crathornes*, who were fettled here as early as the conqueft, give for their creft, a *crake*, or *crow*, which is a circumftance that may be confidered, in fome degree, to ftrengthen our conjectures, with regard to the etymology of the name.

THERE were two ancient manors within the parifh; of which in
Domefday-Book, we find the following mention:

" Terra Regis.
" Duo Maneria in Crathorne. Ulf V. Carucatas ad Geldum. Terra
" ad III. Car. XL. Solidos.*"*   *Domefday-book.*

FROM the above extract it is evident, that thefe lands, at the time
of the general furvey, were in the hands of the crown; but were foon
after granted to the Crathornes; for, in a note to an ancient pedigree
of that family, drawn out in the reign of Queen Elizabeth, and now
in the poffeffion of Thomas Crathorne, Efq. the prefent proprietor, it
is faid, that " Humphrey de Crathorne held divers hydes of land in
" the lordfhipp and towne of Baynarde (now called Craythorne, and
" lyinge on the water of Levene,) of Waltheof, Earl of Northumber-
" land; and that he mightelie refifted King William the Conqueror;
" but through the great friendfhipp of Remigius, Bifhop of Dorchefter,
" he the faid Humphrey afterwards won the King's favour, and had
" his landes reftored unto him: and he then named the faid towne,
" Craythorne."

FROM the remarkable circumftance of the Crathornes continuing
in the male-line, and proprietors here, for fo many generations, we find
little on record, touching this manor, worthy of the reader's particular
attention. By an inquifition *poft mortem*, taken in the 36th year of the
reign of King Henry VIII. it was found that James Crathorne, Efq.
died feized of this manor, † which was holden of the King, as of his
manor of Whorlton, by military fervice.

---

† JACOBUS CRATHORNE tenuit manerium de Crathorne, cum fuis pertinentiis de Domino Rege,
ut de manerio fuo de Wherlton per fervitium militare; et maneria de Eaft-Nefs et Stillingfleet de
comite Weftmorland, ut de manerio fuo de Buttercrambe per fervitium militare. Thomas Crathorne
eft ejus filius et heres.

                    Rot. Efch. 36. *Hen. VIII.* (*A.* 8. *p.* 526. *in Coll. Arm.*)

Crathornes of Crathorne.

The following pedigree of the ancient family of Crathorne of Crathorne, and Nefs, in the north-riding of the county of York, was compiled from various MSS. in their poffeffion, the records of the College of Arms, and other authentic evidences; and deduced to Henry Crathorne, Efq. by J. C. Brooke, *Somerfet-Herald.* Anao Domini 1780.

ARMS.—Argent, on a faltier, gules five croffes patonce, or.

CREST.—A crake or crow.

Humphrey de Crathorne, Lord of Crathorne; lived in the time of William the Conqueror.

Robert de Crathorne, Lord of Crathorne. = ..., daughter of Sir William Damville, Knt.

John de Crathorne, Lord of Crathorne. = Ancareta, daughter of Sir John Spencer, Knt.

Sir Robert de Crathorne, Knt., Lord of Crathorne. = ..., daughter of Godfrey Gore, of the county of Durham.

Robert de Crathorne, Lord of Crathorne, heir to his brother. = ..., daughter of John de Hilton, of Hilton in Cleveland.

Anne, wife of Thomas de Boynton of Acclam, in Cleveland.

Sir Ralph de Crathorne, Knt. Lord of Crathorne. = ..., daughter of Sir John Blundeville, Knt.

Richard de Crathorne, Lord of Crathorne. = ..., daughter of ...... Plumley, of Plumley.

Sir Ralph de Crathorne, Knt. Lord of Crathorne, died S. P.

Robert de Crathorne, Lord of Crathorne. = ..., daughter of Richard Conyers, of Sockburne, county Durham.

Sir William de Crathorne, of Crathorne, Knt. living A. D. 1322. = Ifabel, daughter of Sir John Clervaulx, Knt. *first wife.* = Margaret, daughter of John Ruffell, of Roulley, *second wife.*

John Crathorne, second fon. = ..., daughter of John Ratcliffe.

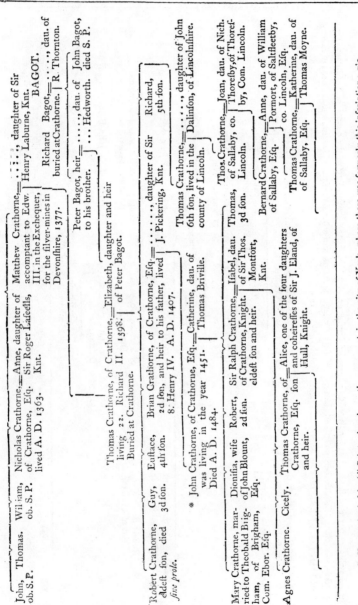

John, Thomas. ob. S.P. William. ob. S.P.

Nicholas Crathorne, of Crathorne, Efq. lived A.D. 1363. = Anne, daughter of Sir Roger Laſcells, Knt.

Matthew Crathorne, accomptant to Edw. III. in the Exchequer, for the ſilver-mines in Devonſhire, 1377. = ...:..., daughter of Sir Henry Laburne, Knt.

BAGOT. Richard Bagot, = ..., dau. of buried at Crathorne. R. Thornton.

Peter Bagot, heir = ..., dau. of John Bagot, to his brother. Hedworth. died S.P.

Thomas Crathorne, of Crathorne, living 22. Richard II. 1398. Buried at Crathorne. = Elizabeth, daughter and heir of Peter Bagot.

Robert Crathorne, eldeſt ſon, died fine prole. Guy, 3d ſon. Euſtace, 4th ſon.

Brian Crathorne, of Crathorne, Efq., 2d ſon, and heir to his father, lived 8. Henry IV. A.D. 1407. = ..., daughter of Sir J. Pickering, Knt. Richard, 5th ſon.

Thomas Crathorne, 6th ſon, lived in the county of Lincoln. = ..., daughter of John Dalinſon, of Lincolnſhire.

* John Crathorne, of Crathorne, Efq. was living in the year 1451. Died A.D. 1484. = Catherine, dau. of Thomas Briville.

Thos. Crathorne, of Sallaby, co. Lincoln. = Joan, dau. of Nich. Thorelby, of Thorelby, by, Com. Lincoln. Thomas, 3d ſon.

Bernard Crathorne, of Sallaby, Efq. = Anne, dau. of William Pormort, of Saltfleetby, co. Lincoln, Efq.

Thomas Crathorne, of Sallaby, Efq. = Katherine, dau. of Thomas Moyne.

Mary Crathorne, married to Theobald Birgham, of Brigham, Com. Ebor. Efq. Dioniſia, wife of John Blount, Efq. Robert, 2d ſon.

Sir Ralph Crathorne, Knight, of Crathorne, eldeſt ſon and heir. = Iſabel, dau. of Sir Thos. Montfort, Knt.

Agnes Crathorne. Cicely.

Thomas Crathorne, Efq. ſon and heir. = Alice, one of the four daughters and coheireſſes of Sir J. Eland, of Hull, Knight.

* HE was buried in All-Saints church, on the pavement, in the city of York, where there was formerly this inſcription : viz.

Hic iacet Johannes Crathorn armiger, qui obiit
... die menſis martii. anno Dom. M.CCCC.LXX.IIII.

Ralph Crathorne, of | James Crathorne, of = Elizabeth, daughter of | John Crathorne, of = Anne, dau. of John Littlebury,
Crathorne, Efq. eldeft | Crathorne, Efq. heir | John Sayer, of Worfall, | Sallaby, Efq. living | of Hagworthingham, Com.
fon & heir; died S.P. | to his brother Ralph. | Com. Ebor. | A.D. 1562. | Lincoln. Efq.
Died 36. Henry VIII.

Eleanor, = John Vincent, of | Anne, = Wm. Aflaby, of | Agnes, = J. Bulmer, of Pinchinthorpe, | Alice, = ... Parkinfon, of
Smeaton, Efq. | Aflaby, co. Durh. | in Cleveland. | Beaumond Hill.

2. George.
3 John.
4. Peter.
5. Fraucis.

Thomas Crathorne, of = Everilda, daughter of Sir
Crathorne and Nefs, | Rob. Conftable, of Ever-
eldeft fon and heir. | ingham, Knt.

Matthew, = Margery, dau. of | Thomas, | Robert, | Jane, dau. and heir = Ralph Crathorne, of Crathorne = Bridget, dau. of Rich.
4th fon. Anth. Hutton, of | 5th fon. | 2d fon. | of Jas. Strangeways, and Nefs, eldeft fon and heir. | Yaxley, of Yaxley, co.
Bifhop Aukland, | of Ormefby, Efq. | Living A.D. 1584. | Suffolk, Efq. fecond
Com. Durham. | firft wife. | wife.

Margaret. Thomas. Four other children.

Francis Crathorne, only
fon, by the first wife,
died a minor.

William, | Catherine, = Ralph Crake.
3d fon.
Mary, = Jos. Conftable, of Upfall, 2d fon
of Sir John Conftable, of Burton-
Conftable, Knt.

Thomas Crathorne, of Crathorne = Catherine, daughter and coheir
and Nefs, Efq. died 1637. | of Edm. Richers, of Swymming-
ton, co. Norfolk, Efq.

Thomas and James,
Margaret and Mary,
all died young.

Edmund Crathorne, = ..., dau. of | Mary, dau. and fole heir of = Ralph Crathorne, = Margaret, 2d dau. of Rob.
of Hollings, in Black- | .... Cockerell | Rob. Wright, of Plewland, of Crathorne and | Thornton, of Eaft-Newton,
amore; fecond fon. | in Holdernefs, Efq. firft | Nefs, Efq. Aged | Com. Ebor. Efq. by Dorothy
wife. | 61, 1665. | his firft wife, dau. of Thos.
Metham, of Metham, Efq.

Four children
died without
iffue.

Ann Crathorne, | Thomas Crathorne, of = Frances, dau. of Charles Thimelby,
wife of Gregory | Crathorne and Nefs, | of Snydal, Com. Ebor. Efq. by Anne,
Grange, of Eaft- | Efq. eldeft fon and heir. | his wife, dau. of John Poulton, of Def-
Harlefey. | Aged 42, Sept. 5, 1665. | borough, co. Northampton, Efq.

George, | Bridget, | Catherine,
3d fon | died un- | 2d dau.
died young. | married.

Four children
died young.

Ralph Crathorne, = Ann, dau. of Wm. Tunftall, | Francis, | John.
aged 31 years, | of Scargill & Wycliffe, Com.
Sept. 5, 1665. | Ebor. by Mary, fifter of Sir.

Dorothy, married to Henry Swale, Efq.
eldeft fon of Sir Solomon Swale, of Swale-
Hall, and South-Stainley, Com. Ebor.

F. Ratcliffe, Bart.

Bart. (afterwards Sir Henry Swale, Bart. He died 19th Jan. 1682–3).

1. Ralph.   2. Francis.   3. William.   Three other children.

Thomas Crathorne of Crathorne and Nefs, Efq. fon and heir; aged 8 years, Sept. 5, 1665.

Elizabeth, dau. of Charles Cockayne, Vifcount Cullen, by Mary, dau. of Henry O'Brien, the 5 Earl of Thomond in Ireland.

Catherine, 3d dau. wife of Thomas Pulleyne, of Carleton, Com. Ebor. Efq.

Everilda, 2d dau a nun at Louvain.

Mary, eldeft dau. a nun at Louvain.

2. Mary C. a religiousof the order of St. Auguftine at Louvain.

3. Thomas C. a religiousof the order of St. Bene- dict at Lambfpring, in Germany.

4. George C. of Nefs, Com. Ebor. 4th fon.

Margaret, dau. and coheir of F. Trapps, of Nidd, co. Ebor. Efq.

5. Francis.

1. Ralph Crathorne, of Crathorne & Nefs, Efq. fon and heir; died 17th April, 1755; buried at Crathorne.

Catherine, dau. and heir of J. Killingbeck, of Chapelallerton, co. Ebor. Efq.

6. William, ob. unmar.

7. Catherine, mar. to Major Wanf- brough.

8. James.   9. John, diedyoung.

10. James, 11. Charles, & 12. Elizabeth, were buried at Hovingham.

Ralph Crathorne, onlyfon,died aged 10 years.

Elizabeth Crathorne, only daughter, died unmarried.

Elizabeth Crathorne, only daughter; died unmarried.

Thomas Crathorne, of Crathorne and Nefs, Efq. fucceeded his uncle Ralph, in the eftate. Married at Hovingham, 1755 Died Feb. 2, 1764. Buried at Crathorne.

Ifabel, dau. of Sir John Swinburne, of Capheaton, Northumberland, Bart. by Mary his wife. dau. of Edward, third fon of Sir Henry Bedingfield of Ox- borough, in Norfolk, Bart. Living a widow 1780.

Henry Crathorne, of Crathorne and Nefs, Efq. eldeft fon and heir, born 1ft January, 1757 Lord of the ma- nors of Crathorne & Eaft-Nefs, in the North-Riding; and of Plewland, Wellwick, and Wellwickthorpe, in the Eaft-Riding of the county of York.

Ifabel Crathorne, only dau. and twin with George; died Feb. 20, 1770. Buried in the church of St. Mary, Caftle-gate, York.

George, a twin with Ifabel, born April 23, 1761.

Thomas, 3d fon, born March 7, 1760. Living 1804, unmarried.

Francis, 2d fon, born May 20, 1758.

By Kirkby's Inqueft, * the Percies held lands here, in the reign of Edward I. William de Percy, Lord of Kildale gave eight oxgangs, with a toft and croft in this territory, to the Priory of Helagh-Park ; and Sir Ernald de Percy, Knight, afterwards agreed with the Prior and Convent, that if they neglected to appoint a chaplain at Yarm, on the death or ceffion of the former one, that then the faid Ernald fhould have a right to diftrain upon their premifes at Crathorne. †

WE are in poffeffion of no evidence to point out the particular lands held by the Percy family ; the Crathornes have been fole proprietors here for feveral generations.

FOXTON, which confifts of a few farm-holds, lies to the eaft, and adjoins upon the chapelry of Middleton. This manor was given by William de Grey, to the monks of Rievaux; and the grant was confirmed in the reign of Edward I. by William, ‡ fon of Walter de Percy, faving his free-warren within the manor. By an inquifition *poſt mortem*, taken at Stokefley, in the 43d year of the reign of Queen Elizabeth, we find that Francis Fulthorpe died feized of a free tenement here, which he held of the heirs of the Lord Conyers as of his manor of Skelton, by the fervice of rendering a red rofe and fuit at the Wapontake court. §

THE Crathornes have fince purchafed, and are now proprietors of all the lands here, except one farm at *High-Foxton*, belonging to the hofpital at Kirkleatham.

---

* WILLLIMUS DE PERCY, de Kildale, tenet III feod. milit. (de dict. hæreditat.) In Kildale, *Crathorne*, Barwick et Thormanby unum feod. unde XII carucat. faciunt feod. un. milit. &c.

Kirkby's Inqueſt.

† DODSWORTH's *MSS. A. p.* 84.

‡ THIS William de Percy fucceeded his father Walter, (who was left in poffeffion of Kildale, and the feveral manors adjoining thereto ;) and as appears from *Rymer's Fædera*, attended King Edward I. in his Welch expedition, A. D. 1282.

§ FRANCIS FULTHORPE fuit fefitus de libero tenemento de Foxton, quod tenebatur de heredibus domini Conyers, ut de manerio fuo de Skelton, per fervitium *Rubræ Rofæ*, et fect. wapent.

Inq. p. m. 43. *Eliz. reg.*

THE church of Crathorne is rectorial, and dedicated to All-Saints. ‖
It was given by William de Percy to the Priory of Guifbrough; and
the grant was afterwards confirmed by Peter, fon of Peter de Brus;
but the church was never appropriated to that monaftry. The rectory
ftands valued in the King's books at 10l. 11s. 10½d. with a glebe of
about 146 acres, given thereto by James Crathorne, Efq. about the
year 1540. The right of prefentation, after the diffolution of the
priory, was granted to the Crathorne family; and was transferred by
them to the prefent Lord Cullen's anceftors, before the paffing of the
act of Parliament, which debarred *Catholics* from prefenting to ecclefiaftical livings. Lord Vifcount Cullen the prefent patron. *

‖ CRATHORNE RECTORY.

DEDICATION, All-Saints.   Lord Vifcount Cullen, patron.

FIRST Fruits 10l. 11s. 10½d.   Tenths 1l. 1s. 2¼d.   Procur. 7s. 6d.   Syn. 18s.

INCUMBENTS.—1226, John de Wyfebeck, *pres. prior and convent, Guifbrough*. 1233, Peter de
Vallibus. 1288, Reginaldus de Sancto Albans. 1293, Roger de Ellefey. ——, Richard de Wynnington. 1331, Hugh de Newton, *poft refig.* Wynnington. ——, William de Skypwith. 1343,
Robert Hafelbeck. ——, William de Frithby, *poft res.* Hafelbeck. 1348, Adam de Darlington,
p. m. Frithby. 1357, John de Neyranyt de Wetwang, *p. res.* Darlington. ——, John Gretham.
——, Robert Crathorne, *p. m* Gretham. 1431, Richard Blome, *p. m.* Crathorne. 1445, John
Driffeld, *p. r.* Blome. 1459, Rich. Corbrigge, *p. r.* Driffeld. 1479, John Wynnall, *p. m.* Corbrigge.
1480, Thomas Crathorne, *p. r.* Wynnall. 1491, John Dent, *p. m.* Crathorne. 1500, Henry Davy,
p. res. Dent. 1510, John Cailey, *p. r.* Davy. 1512, Laurence Wright, *p. r.* Cailey. 1547, Thos.
Smithfon, *p. r.* Wright, *pres. affign. prior. et conv. Guifbrough.* 1574, John Scarthe, *pres.* Richard
Crathorne, Efq. 1606, David Jaire, S. T. P. *pres.* Thos. Crathorne. 1608, David Jacye, S. T. P.
p. m. Jaire, *pres.* the King per Lapfum. 1623, Roger Belwood, M. A. *pres.* Thomas Crathorne.
——, Robert Hume. 1674, James Pearfon, *pres.* Sir James Pennyman, Bart. 1715, James Pearfon,
p. m. Pearfon, *pres.* Mr. Cockayne. 1744, James Pearfon, *p. m.* Pearfon, *pres.* Mrs. Ann Ingram.
1751, William Prefton, *p. m.* Pearfon, *pres.* Jofeph Prefton, of Stockton upon Tees, gent. 1768,
John Grenfide, *p. m.* Prefton, *pres.* Charles Cockayne, Vifcount Cullen of the Kingdom of Ireland.
1781, Rev. Ralph Grenfide, A. M. *poft res.* Grenfide, *pres.* Lord Vifcount Cullen.

* ON Lord Cullen's prefentation of the Rev. John Grenfide, in the year 1768, a caveat was iffued by the Univerfity of Cambridge, who prefented the Rev. Mr. Fairclough, M. A. Fellow of St.
John's College; the caufe was tried at York, in the Summer affizes of that year, and finally decided
in favour of Lord Cullen's right of prefentation.

THE church, which is an ancient but humble ftructure, ftands on the eaftern extremity of the village, and commands a pleafing view of the ferpentine courfe, and wooded banks of the river Leven. Within the chancel, there is an effigy of a knight, cumbent in armour, crofs-legged; † and upon the fhield, the arms of Crathorne; viz. *Argent, on a faltier, gules, five croffes patonce, or.* This, it is conjectured, is the monument of Sir William Crathorne, Knight, who lived A. D. 1322.— There is alfo, within the church, an ancient tomb, with the arms of Bagot carved thereon: viz. *on a fefs, three birds between* 14 *crofs-crofslets;* which, it is fuppofed, was erected for *Richard Bagot*; and in the floor of the chancel, there is a flat ftone, which feems to have been placed over Thomas Crathorne, ‡ and Elizabeth Bagot his wife, with the following infcription:

" 𝔥𝔦𝔠 𝔧𝔞𝔠𝔢𝔱 𝔗𝔥𝔬𝔪𝔞𝔰 𝔠𝔯𝔞𝔱𝔥𝔬𝔯𝔫𝔢, 𝔢𝔱 𝔢𝔩𝔦𝔷𝔞𝔟𝔢𝔱𝔥𝔞, 𝔲𝔯𝔬𝔯 𝔢𝔧𝔲𝔰;

" 𝔮𝔲𝔬𝔯𝔲𝔪 𝔞𝔫𝔦𝔪𝔞𝔟𝔲𝔰 𝔭𝔯𝔬𝔭𝔦𝔱𝔦𝔢𝔱𝔲𝔯 𝔇𝔢𝔲𝔰. 𝔞𝔪𝔢𝔫."

THERE is likewife, within the chancel, a mural monument, with the following infcription:

" UNDERNEATH LIETH THE BODY OF THE HON. RALPH
" CRATHORNE, LORD OF CRATHORNE, OF NESS, OF PLEW-
" LAND, OF WELWICK, AND THORP JUXTA WELWICK."

THE village confifts of about 50 houfes, with the manfion houfe of the Lord of the manor, which is fituate on the eaftern extremity, clofe upon the bank of the river Leven, and fheltered on the north and weft by thriving plantations. The profpect, from the grounds adjoining, though not extenfive, is pleafing and romantic, and prefents, in its general afpect, a fcene of tranquillity and retirement. The houfe, which

---

† SIR WILLIAM DUGDALE, in his ancient ufage in bearing arms (p. 43.) has thefe words:— " *Such as lie crofs-legged are thofe, who were in the wars of the Holy Land, or vowed to go, and were* " *prevented by death.*"

‡ THIS Thomas Crathorne, of Crathorne, lived 22. Richard II. A. D. 1398.

was the ancient refidence of the Crathorne family, § is plain and modern, having been lately fitted up and repaired by the prefent proprietor, who now refides and is making confiderable improvements
upon his eftate here. ||

As a proof of the thriving condition of this village, and the comfortable fituation of its inhabitants, fo creditable at the fame time to
the character and humane difpofition of Mr. Crathorne, we are induced
to remark, that upwards of feventeen cottagers, at rents, not exceeding
12l. *per ann.* keep cows here; among whom there are feveral weavers,
who are employed in the manufacture of linen cloth for fale.

THERE is an extenfive *bleach-ground* here, with a bleach-houfe, fituate
on the eaftern brink of the Leven, (over a ftone bridge of one arch,)
at a little diftance from, and nearly oppofite to the village; which confifts of two beetling mills, and a variety of other machinery, where
linens are made up fimilar to the Irifh.   Here is alfo a flour-mill,
which is worked by the fame ftream, that fupplies the bleaching ma-

---

§ WHEN *Robert Glover, Efq. Somerfet Herald,* made his vifitation of the county of York, A. D.
1584, as deputy of *Wm. Flower, Efq. Norroy King of Arms,* the arms of Crathorne, quartered with
thofe of Bagot, were in the windows of the houfe here; as appears from the following entry:

" IN feneftra vitrea in aula Radulphi Craythorne, ar. funt arma, quæ afcribuntur Bagoto, fed
" potius funt arma ejufdem Craythorne, ut apparet in figillis.   Et funt quarteriatim pofita cum ar·
" mis de Craythorne, et funt *de Sabulo, cum crucibus cruciatis argenteis*; *et fuper fecem de B. Azure;*
" 3 *Aves arg.* fed cujus generis ignoratur."   *Glover's Vifitation.*

|| FOR the information of the curious, we may remark, that a large collection of Chinefe curi-
ofities is now in the poffeffion of Thomas Crathorne, Efq. (made in the year 1796 by his brother,
the late Henry Crathorne, Efq.) confifting of various articles of drefs, a number of drawings, taken
upon the fpot, defcriptive of the *dreffes modes of travelling, &c.* ufed in China, together with a *Chinefe
gong,* the found of which may be diftinctly heard at the diftance of three miles and upwards.

SIR GEORGE STAUNTON, in his account of the embaffy to China, obferves that " no guns are
" fired in China by way of fignal; but circular rimmed plates of copper, mixed with tin or *zinc,* to
" render it more fonorous, are ftruck with wooden mallets, and emit a noife, almoft deafening to thofe
who are near it, and which is heard at a great diftance."

THIS inftrument, which the Chinefe call *loo,* and the Europeans in China *gong,* from the name it
bears in other parts of the eaft, is generally ufed upon the water.

chinery; and at which a confiderable quantity of flour is manufactured for the London and other markets.

CRATHORNE is worthy of particular notice for the falubrity of the
air, and the excellence of its waters; * and as a proof of the good effects
of thefe on the general health of its inhabitants, we may remark, that
the average number of burials in one year is only four, † out of a population of upwards of 300 inhabitants, from which it appears that
one in 75 dies annually; to this we may add the following inftance of
longevity, collected from the parifh regifter, from which it appears,
that within the laft 20 years, fixteen perfons have died here, whofe ages
together amount to 1369 years, giving an average of 85 years and upwards to each individual; the youngeft attained to the age of 76, and
the oldeft to that of 100 years and upwards.

THE population of the parifh has been ftated to us, to be confiderably upon the increafe; but owing to the number of diffenters of different denominations, ‡ no accurate ftatement could be obtained from
the parifh regifters; as feveral children are born every year, but not
regiftered.   From the return, made to government, in the year 1801,
which is given in the notes, § we find that there were then within the

---

* IN a wood, on the weftern bank of the Leven, at a fmall diftance from the village, there is a
fpring, the water of which is of an extremely petrifying quality: the pipes which formerly conveyed
the water acrofs the river to the bleach grounds, where it is made much ufe of in the procefs of
bleaching, became in a few years, fo incrufted, as to be rendered totally ufelefs.

† WITHIN the laft 20 years, there have been 50 marriages, 119 baptifms, and 76 burials.

‡ THE Roman Catholics, who are the moft numerous, have a chapel, with a falary of 30l. per
ann. paid to the Catholic clergyman officiating here; being the intereft of a fum of money left by
the late Ralph Crathorne, Efq. and depofited in the hands of the Catholic Bifhop of York.

§ STATE of population, 10th March, 1801.

	Inha-bited houfes.	Fami-lies.	Uninha-bited houfes.	Males.	Females.	Total.	Agri-cul-ture.	Trade.	Refi-due.	Total.
Crathorne.	59	65	1	160	147	307	52	45	210	307

WE owe our acknowledgments to the Rev. Ralph Grenfide, M. A. for much valuable information
touching this parifh.

parifh 59 inhabited houfes, occupied by 65 families, containing in the whole 307 inhabitants; which, on an average is 5⅓ nearly to each houfe. Of thefe, it may be remarked that the number of males exceeds that of females, which is found to be the cafe only in few parifhes within the diftrict; and that the number of perfons employed in trade or manufactures is nearly equal to thofe occupied in agriculture.

The lands within the parifh confift of a mixture of arable, and pafture; and the foil, like the reft of Cleveland, chiefly of a clayey nature, with fome rich and fertile meadows on the banks of the Leven, which are employed as bleach-grounds. A part of the parifh was in open fields about 80 years ago, but the whole is now inclofed; the principal crops are wheat, oats, and beans, with fome fmall patches of turnips; the lands near the village, upon the banks of the river, produce abundant crops of grafs.

We have been favoured by a correfpondent with notes on the *Natural Hiftory* of feveral animals that frequent this parifh and neighbourhood; but we forbear to infert them from the confideration that a general catalogue of *Cleveland animals* is intended to be given, as an appendix to the work. We fhall, therefore, clofe this account of Crathorne, with remarking, that game is abundant within the parifh, particularly hares and partridges. The woods here alfo furnifh woodcocks and pheafants; which laft, by being preferved from poachers, are becoming more numerous. Foxes are likewife frequently found in the covers, on the banks of the Leven, the breed being encouraged by the neighbouring gentlemen, for the pleafures of the chace; and to complete the character of the parifh, as an excellent fporting-country, we may finally add, that there are few ftreams, in which a *brother angler* can meet with more diverfion, than in this part of the Leven.

THE PARISH OF APPLETON UPON WISK.*

APPLETON is the extreme parish in that part of Cleveland, which runs out into a narrow point towards the weft; and is diftant about 7 miles from the market town of Yarm, eight from North-Allerton, and ten from Stokefley.   It is bounded on the eaft by the parifhes of Kirklevington and Weft-Rounton; on the weft, by the parifh of Smeaton; on the north by the chapelry of High-Worfall; and on the fouth by the river Wifk, which runs in an eafy and fluggifh current towards the weft, at a little diftance from the village, and feparates this parifh from the chapelry of Deighton in Allertonfhire, and the parifh of Welbury, within the wapontake of Burdforth.   Its greateft extent from eaft to weft is not more than two miles, and about a mile and a half broad.

THE etymology of the name is confefledly difficult; it has been confidered by fome, at leaft, to be fo dark and uncertain, that we cannot with confidence, conneft it with the word *apple;* the derivation, however, is probably the fame with that of *Appleby* in Weftmorland; and confidering the great number of *Appletons* within the north-riding

* THE moft obvious derivation is certainly from the Saxon Æpple, *pomum,* and tun; q. d. *Villa pomaria:* although there is nothing about the prefent village, or any part of the parifh to corroborate this conjefture, we may, neverthelefs, conclude, that it was at an early period, remarkable for the growth of that particular fruit; " Nothing," as Mr. Thorefby obferves, " being more common, in " former ages, than for towns and territories to receive names from the fort of trees, with which they " abounded.

Wisk, (which is a fynonymous term with *Ifk, Ifis,* or *Ouse,)* is derived from the *Gaelic* word, *ui, uis,* or *uifk,* which fignifies *water* in general.

of this county, we may reasonably conclude, that the name is merely incident to the situation, or owing to some circumstance common to all.

THE manor of Appleton, at the time of the general survey, was in the hands of the Conqueror; in *Domesday-book* we find it thus mentioned.

" **Terra Regis.**

" **Manerium in Apeltune. Orme VI. Carucatas ad Geldum, Terra**
" **ad III Car. XX Solidos.**"

FROM the above extract it appears that Appleton then contained six carucates, besides land sufficient for three ploughs, valued at twenty shillings. It was afterwards granted by the Conqueror to Robert de Brus, Lord of Skelton, who gave the same " to the Abbey of St. Mary's, " at York, together with the lordship of Horneby, and all the lands " lying between that, and the great road-way leading from York to " Durham, which was parcel of his lordship of Middleton." †

IT continued part of the possessions of that rich monastry, to the time of the general dissolution, when it was granted by King Henry VIII. to Charles Brandon, Knight. and the heirs male of his body lawfully begotten: but male-issue failing of this family, the manor and estate were granted in the year 1551, by letters patent of King Edward VI. to Charles Vincent, Esq.; from whom they descended to Theodore Godwyn, of Little Stoneham, in the county of Suffolk, Esq. who, in the 36th year of the reign of Queen Elizabeth, granted a lease of the same, to John Grange, ‡ of Swafham Bulbeck, in the county of Cambridge, for the term of *two thousand* years, at the yearly rent of 20*l.* 11*s.* to be paid at the two usual feasts of the year, viz. the feast of the Annunciation of the blessed Virgin, and St. Michael the Archangel, by

---

† *DUGDALE's Baron. vol* 1. *p* 448: *Mon. Ang. vol.* 1. 388 *b. n.* 50 *and* 60.

‡ IN Godwyn's Deed of Conveyance to Grange, it was stipulated, that in default of payment of the annual rent, the said Grange was to forfeit the sum of three pounds *(nomine pænæ)* to be distrained for the same, as well as the arrearages of rent.

even and equal portions.   After divers alienations, Appleton came into
the poffeffion of Jofeph Hall and Robert Wharton, Efqrs. aldermen of
the city of Durham, who, in the year 1732, fold to the Rev. George
Walker, of Stockton upon Tees, from whom it defcended by marriage
to —— Ferrand, Efq.   The eftate foon after was parcelled out to different purchafers; a part of which, with the manor, was fold to Mrs.
Allan, of Grange, near Darlington, whofe fucceffor, George Allan, Efq.
is the prefent proprietor, and lord of the manor.

APPLETON is a chapelry under Smeaton; which, being a rectory
within the diocefe of Chefter, and Archdeaconry of Richmond, and
confequently beyond the prefcribed limits of our diftrict, will not require our further notice, than that it was given, by *Hardewyne des*
Efcalliors, to the Abbey of St. Mary's, at York; and is valued in the
King's books, at 13*l*. 13s. 4d.   The chapel of Appleton was not certified to the governours of Queen Anne's bounty.   Bifhop Gafterel, in
his MS. account of livings within the diocefe of Chefter, fpeaking of
Smeaton, alias *Smitheton magna*,* obferves, that " Appleton upon Wifk
" is a chapel under this rectory, value 50*l*. per ann. but in the diocefe
" of York."

THE chapel, which ftands on the weftern part of the village, is
fmall; but by fome neceffary modern repairs, is rendered decent and
commodious.   The ftyle of architecture difcovers nothing of great
antiquity; nor are there any monuments worthy of notice, except that
within the chancel of the chapel there is a tomb-ftone with an infcription; but fo much obliterated, as to afford no other information, than

---

* *SMEATON*, in ancient records written *Smithyton*, and *Smitheton*, is fituate on the great north-
road leading from London to Edinburgh, and is conjectured to derive its name from a *forge*, under
the tutelage of Saint *Elegius*, *Eloy*, or *Loy*, the great patron of farriers and travellers, where a daily
mafs and benediction were celebrated for the fafety of fojourners and their cattle.   Chapels for this
purpofe were erected at various places, and *wells* dedicated to this faint, famous for their fanative
qualities.

R2

that the perfon buried under it was named *Rokeby*, and an *alderman of London;* who is fuppofed to have poffeffed confiderable property here.

THE village ftands on the fouthern extremity of the parifh, which receives its diftinguifhing denomination from its fituation on the border of the river *Wifk.*† Two Roads interfect each other at right angles, at the north end of the village, the one running eaft and weft between Stokefley and Richmond; and the other north and fouth between North-Allerton and Yarm. The number of inhabitants, according to the return made to government in the year 1801 was 451, principally employed in the manufactory of linen cloth in its different branches. On a review of the table, fet forth in the notes; ‡ it will be feen, that there are 96 inhabited houfes, and 100 families, which is about $4\frac{1}{2}$ to each family; and like Crathorne, that the number of males exceeds that of females, which is a circumftance that can be accounted for, perhaps, only, by the introduction of, and the encouragement given to manufacturers.

---

† *THE Wifk* is a fmall rivulet, which rifes on the breaft of the hills near the town of *Ofmotherley*, and at firft-takes a northern direction as far as *Staddle-Bridge*, leaving the monaftry of *Mount-Grace* on the left; from thence it becomes the boundary of the wapontake, and dozes over a muddy channel, in a more weftern courfe, till paffing *Appleton* and *Smeaton* on the fouth, it turns fouthwards, and runs for feveral miles in that direction, giving a diftinguifhing name to fome villages in its courfe when it empties itfelf into the *river Swale*, below *Kirkby-Wifk*. The name of this river, though written with an *afperate w*, is generally confidered to be fynonymous with *Efk, Ifis,* and *Oufe,* the etymology of which is probably from the Gaelic word *üi, üis,* or *üifk,* which, like *Avon* (from whence we conjecture the *Leven* to be derived) merely fignifies water in general. Skinner, *(fub voce Oufe)* fays, " *Oufe, Lat. ISIS, fluvius. Idcirco fere aufim affirmare OUSE et AVON, olim Brit. fluvium in* " *genere, feu aquam fignificaffe.*"

‡ STATE of population, 10th March, 1801.

	Inhabited houfes.	Families.	Uninhabited houfes.	Males.	Females.	Total.	Agriculture.	Trade, &c.	Refidue.	Total.
Appleton.	96	100	7	242	209	451	174	224	53	451

The number of baptifms for the laft year 20.   Burials 6.   Marriages 2.

FROM the parifh regifters it appears, that within the laft twenty years, there have been 314 baptifms, 156 burials, and 53 marriages. On comparing the number of baptifms with that of burials within the above period, we are led to conclude that the population of the parifh is confiderably on the increafe; and from the average number of burials in one year, it will be feen, that one out of 56 nearly dies annually.

WE find nothing worthy of particular remark, in regard to the ftate of agriculture within the parifh; the foil, produce, &c. being greatly fimilar to thofe in the adjoining parifhes, already noticed.   About one half of the land is in tillage; the fields near the village, and adjoining the river Wifk, lie low, and are fubject to be frequently inundated. From the river, the grounds rife by an eafy and gradual afcent towards the north.

THE PARISH OF ARNECLIFFE ;

Or, as it is sometimes called, INGLEBY-ARNECLIFFE, is the next that claims our attention.   It is situated about six miles west from the market town of Stokesley; and is bounded on the east by the parish of Whorlton; on the south and west, by the parish of Osmotherley and by Rounton on the north.   Its greatest extent from east to west three miles, and about two miles broad.

The name of this parish has been explained, by some officious etymologists, by *Greencliffe;* which we find, however, to be no way particularly descriptive of any local appearance; and we submit to our readers, whether a more probable interpretation may not be obtained from the old and vulgar word *erne*, which signifies a *cottage;* or perhaps it may be still more appropriately derived from *erne*, a Scottish appellation of the *cinereous eagle;* or the English *heron:* nothing, at least, can be more apposite than this idea of the name; *cliffs*, or *hills*, such as those on the southern boundary of the parish being the usual resort of these birds.

From Domesday-book it appears that there were anciently two manors within the limits of this parish: viz. *Ingleby* and *Arnecliffe;* which, before the conquest, were held by *Malgrin;* and were afterwards in the hands of the Conqueror; being thus entered in the general survey, under the title

" Terra Regis.
" Manerium in Engelebi.   Malgrin VI.   Carucatas ad Geldum.
" Terra ad III. Car. XX. Solidos.
" Manerium in Erneclive.   Malgrin II.   Carucatas ad Geldum,
" Terra ad Dimid. Car."   *Domesday-Book.*

THESE manors were afterwards given by the Conqueror to Robert
de Brus, as parcel of the barony of Skelton, to hold of the King *in capite:*
but we have no certain evidence, to whom they were at first granted
out by the Bruces. In the reign of Edward I. as appears from Kirkby's
Inqueft, William de Colville held half a knight's fee in *Engleby juxta
Arnecliffe* (where twelve carucates made one knight's fee,) of Walter de
Fauconberge, Lord of Skelton.* Arnecliffe, at an early period, was the
property of the *Ingelrams*; and in the reign of Edward first, was held
by Robert Ingelram; † whofe daughter Ingalis, marrying Philip, fon
and heir of the faid William de Colville, carried it into that family.
By this marriage, the two manors became united in the Colvilles; and
in the reign of King Edward the fecond, we find that Robert de Colville
obtained a licence of that King, to inclofe 2200 acres, for a park at
Arnecliffe. ‡ The defcendants of this family continued in poffeffion
for feveral generations, till male iffue failing in the reign of Edward
IV. their inheritance defcended by marriage with Joan, daughter and
coheir of Sir John Colville, to Sir William Mauleverer, of Wotherfome,
Knight, anceftor to the prefent family of Mauleverers, who are lords
here, and have been long refident at Arnecliffe.

---

* " DICUNT etiam quod Dominus Walterus de Fauconberge tenet de Domino Rege in capite,
quinque feoda milit. una cum Caftro de Skelton cum pertinenteis, unde Willimus de Colville tenet
dimid. feodi in Engleby juxta Arncliffe, unde XII. Carucat. terræ faciunt feod. unius milit. et reddit balliorum Domini Regis de fine cum wapentag. Vs. Xd. "   *Kirkby's Inqueft.*

† ROBERTUS INGELRAM tenet tria foeda milit. in Erneclive, Heflerton, Dale et alibi de Petro de
Brus, qui ob.   *Efc.* 7 *Edw. I. Lib. F. fo.* 2. *Dodfworth's MSS.*

‡ ROBERTUS DE COLVILLE habet licentiam claudere 2200 acras in Einecliffe, et inde parcum
facere.   *Lib. U. Edw. II. Ibid.*

Mauleverer of Arncliffe.

THE name of this family, in ancient writings, is called *Malus-Leporarius* (*Mal-levorer*) the bad *hare-hunter*; and tradition fays, that a gentleman of Yorkfhire, being to let flip a brace of grey-hounds, to run for a great wager, fo held them in the fwing, that they were more likely to ftrangle themfelves, than kill the hare; whereupon this furname was fixed on the family.

BUT *Peter le Neve*, Efq. Norroy, in his MS. hiftory of Baronets (vol. 1. p. 131.) fuppofes it to be *Malus-Operarius*, or the *bad worker*; becaufe that in Domefday-book, (*title Effex, p. 94.*) is this title, terra Ranulfi, filii Durandi de Malis Operibus, in French *Mal-ouverrer*, which is eafily varied to *Mauleverer*.

ARMS.—Sable, three grey-hounds, current in pale argent; collared, or.

CREST.—A maple branch arifing out of the trunk of a tree.

MOTTO.—En Dieu ma Foy.

Sir Richard Mauleverer, Knt. came into England, with William the Conqueror, who made him mafter of the forefts, chafes, and parks north of Trent.

Sir John Mauleverer, Knt.==Bendreda, daughter of Sir Henry Hirft, Knt.

Nicholas Mauleverer,==Alice, dau. of Sir Thos. Grofvenor, Knight.

John Mauleverer,==Caffandra, dau. of Mr. Bridgaile.

Robert,==Dionifia, dau. of Sir Geo. Pierpoint, Knt.

Sir Rob. Mauleverer, Knt.==Amifia, dau. of Sir John Truffel, Knt.

Anne, married Sir Rich. Yorke, Knt.

Mary, married Mr. Clapham.

Margaret, married Mr. Strangwayes.

Julian, married Mr. Dove, *alias* Deane.

John Mauleverer, Efq.==Dorothy, dau. of Sir Ninian Markinfield, Knight

Richard Mauleverer. Thorefby fays, he mar. Frances, dau. of Mr. Dynely,

Thomas Mauleverer. and that Thomas mar. Jane, dau. of Sir Gerard Salvin.

Mary, married John Dynely, Efq.

Anne, married Sir Gerard Salvin, Knt.

John Mauleverer,==Margaret, dau. of Sir Hugh Norton, Knt.
living 13. Edw. I.

Richard,==...., dau. of Sir John Sturley, Knt. From this match the Mauleverers of Bramley are defended.

Thomas, ob. S. P.

Ifabell, mar. Sir T. Pigott, Knt.

Jane, mar. 1ft, Sir Geo. Grey, Knt. 2dly, to Sir Geo. Pen-bruge, Knt.

Henry Mauleverer, Efq.==Margaret, dau. of Sir Tho. Lowther, Knt.

John Mauleverer,==Edith, dau. of Mr. Daville.

Thomas,==Catherine, dau. of Rob. Mennil, Efq.

Margaret, married John Crathorne, Efq.

Sir W. Mauleverer,==Mary, dau. of Sir   John Mauleverer, of Allerton-Mauleverer, Efq. from whom
Knt.　　　　　　 | Rich. Hanfard, Knt.　　 that family is defcended.　Living 10. Henry III.

Thomas Mauleverer, Efq.==Ellen, dau. of Sir Thos.　　Margaret, married Sir　　Anne, married Henry
　　　　　　　　　　　 | l'empeſt, Knt.　　　　 Richard Conyers, Knt.　　Witherington, Efq.

Sir William Mauleverer,==Anne, daughter of Sir John　Robert,==. . . . ., dau. of Sir Hugh Willoughby,　Jane, mar. John Hopton,
Knt.　　　　　　　　 | Neville, of Liverfage, Knt.　　 | of Wollerton, in co. Notts. Knt.　　Efq. of Ormley.

Sir W. Mauleverer,==Margaret, dau. of Sir Ralph　John,==. . . . ., dau. of　Richard,==Ann, dau. of　Margaret,==J. Mufgrave,
Knt.　　　　　　 | Bygod, of Settrington, Knt.　　 | Mr. Woodruffe.　　　 | T. Clifford, Efq.　Ann,==Mr. Vavafour.
　　 COLVILLES.

Sir Wm. Mauleverer,==Ifabel, dau. of Sir　John,==Mary, dau. of　Mary, mar. J.　Anne.　　　Philip Colville, Efq.==
Knight.　　　　　 | H. Oughtred, Knt.　　 | John Afke, Efq.　Vavafour.
　　　 Wm. Colville, Efq.==

Wm. Mauleverer, of==Catherine, dau. of Sir　Jane, mar. Wm.
Potter-Newton, Efq. | Ra. Bofiville, of Ar-　Skargill, Efq.　　Philip Colville, Efq.==Ingalis, dau. and heir of Rob. Ingram, Efq.
living 19. Edw. III.　 gelly, Knt.　　　　　　　　　　　　　　　　　　　 | in whofe right he was lord of Arncliffe Dale.

Wm. Mauleverer,　　Robert Mauleverer,==Elizabeth, dau. and heir　　William Colville, Efq.==
35. Edw. III. ob.　　living 1364.　In his | of John Barlow, of Wo-
S. P.　　　　　　　wife s right he was　 therfome, Efq.　　　　Robert Colville, Efq.==
　　　　　　　　　feized of the lord-
　　　　　　　　　fhip of Wotherfome.　　　　　　　　Rob. Colville==Eliz. dau. and heir of Sir John Conyers.

　　　　　　　　　　　　　　　　　　　　 Rob. Colville, ob. infans.　　Wm. Colville, Efq.==. . . . ., dau. of John Lord Fauconberg.　　Philip.

　　　　　　　　　　　　　　　　　　　　　　　　　　　　　　　 John Colville, Efq.==. . . . ., dau. of John Lord Darcy.

Sir Wm. Mauleverer,==Joan, dau. and coheir of Sir　The other coheir　　Robert Colville, Efq.==Elizabeth, dau. and heir of Sir
of Wotherfome, Knt. | John Colville, Knt.; by whom　married Sir John　　　　　　　　　　 | Wm. Fowthroppe, Knt.
living 3. Edw. IV.　 came the lordfhip of Arncliffe.　Wandfworth, Knt.

　　　　　　　　　　　　　　　　　　　　　　　　　　　　　　 John Colville, Efq.==. . . . ., dau. of Sir Pearce
Edmond Mauleverer, of Arncliffe, Efq.==Elinor, dau of . . . Vavafour, Efq.　　 ob. fine prole　　　 | Tylioff, Knt.

Sir Wm. Mauleverer,==Jane, dau. of Sir John Conyers, of Sockburne, Knt.　　John.　　　Henry.

James Mauleverer,==Anne, dau. and coheir of　Robert,==Alice, dau. of Sir　William,　　Henry,　　Anne, mar.　Catherine, mar. W.
　　　　　　　 | Ralph Wycliffe, of Wy-　　　　 | Tho. Markinfield,　ob. S. P.　　a prieft.　　J. Rowcliffe,　Womlwell, Efq.
　　　　　　　　 cliffe, Efq.　　　　　　　　　　 Knt.　　　　　　　　　　　　　　　 Efq.

PARISH OF ARNECLIFFE.

Sir Edmond ═ Mary, dau. of Sir   William,   Thomas,   Dorothy, ═ John Kay, of
Mauleverer,   Chriſt. Danby, of   ob. S. P.   ob. S. P.   Wotherſome.
Knight.   Thorp, Knt.   Anne, ═ Tho. Leigh, of
                                                                  Middleton, Eſq.
                                                                  38. Hen. VIII.

John,   Elizabeth, mar. Ra. Gower,   Catherine, died   Alice, married
ob. S. P.   of Stitnam, Eſq.   unmarried.   Anth. Garforth.

Elizabeth, ═ ... dau. of Sir Alice, mar. Anne. Martha, mar. Dorothy. Mary. Lancelot. Chriſt. Cath. Eliz. Edmund.
           Tim. Hutton, of Mr. Rich.
           Marſke, Knt. Tempeſt.

William, Matthew, John, Mary. Elinor, mar. Beatrice, mar. Timothy, ═ Eliz. dau. of Geo. Jas. & Henry
ob. S. P. ob. S. P.   Anth. Novell. Geo. Wright.   Metcalfe, of North- died without
                                                                    allerton, Eſq.   iſſue.

Elizabeth, dau. of James Bellingham,   Elizabeth.
of Levens, in Weſtmorland, Eſq.

Jane, dau. of Tho. Hodginſon, of   William.   Thomas.   Bellingham.   Allan.
Preſton, co. Lancaſter, a coheireſs;
buried at Arnecliffe.

T. Mauleverer, Eſq. ═ Sarah Pawſon, dau. of John Wil-   Henry. Mary. Timothy.
ob. 1784. Buried at   berſols, of Gainbrough, co. Line.
Arnecliffe.   Eſq. a coheireſs; living 1804.   Catherine.   Dorothy.

Anne, mar. Clotworthy   Thomas & John,   Frances, liv-   Mary, liv-   Richard & Elizabeth,
Gowan, of Beſſingby,   ob. infantes.   ing unmar.   ing unmar.   ob. infantes.
near Doncaſ- near Bridlington, Eſq.   1804.   1804.

Jane, mar. Rich.   Ann, mar. Tho.   Catherine, mar.
Aldburgh, of   Gower, of Stit-   Wm. Conyers,
Aldburgh, Eſq.   nam, Eſq. ob.   of Marſke, Eſq.
                  S. P.

Wm. Mauleverer, Eſq. ═ Elinor, dau. of Rich. Ald-
living 1584.   burgh, of Aldburgh, Eſq.

William, Jas. Mauleverer, ═ ... dau. of Sir
ob. S. P. Eſq.

Timothy, Elizabeth, mar. William,
ob. S. P. John Blaketon.

Beatrice. Timothy Mauleverer, Eſq. ═
          Thoreſby ſays, he was gover-
          nor of the poor Knights at
          Windſor in 1694.

James. Dorothy. Elizabeth. Timothy Mauleverer ;
ob. S. P.   buried at Arnecliffe.

Elizabeth, Jane, married William & Timothy,
died unmar. ... Marſingale; ob. fine prole.
            had iſſue.

Jane, mar. Rob. Lindſay, Sarah, mar. J. Arthur
of Lavighry, in co. Ty- Worfop, of Alverly-
rone, in Ireland, Eſq. Grange, near Doncaſ-
                       ter, Eſq.

THE lands at Ingleby, after divers alienations, came into the hands of the Pennymans of Ormefby; and have been fince parcelled out, by Sir James Pennyman, the prefent Baronet.

THE village of Ingleby, which is the only one within the parifh, is fmall, and confifts chiefly of farm-houfes, neatly built. It ftands in a retired fituation, on the fummit of a gentle ridge, at a little diftance from the road, leading between Stokefley and Thirfk. The lands adjoining, particularly on the fouth, are divided into fmall inclofures, and are chiefly laid down to grafs.

ARNECLIFFE-HALL,

The feat of Mrs. Mauleverer, ftands to the fouth. The houfe is a handfome modern ftone building, fheltered on the eaft by a noble and extenfive wood, which hangs on the declivity of a hill; the majeftic appearance of which (being cloathed with ftately oaks to the very fummit,) brought to our recollection, the following beautiful and appropriate lines of Thompfon :

> " Still let me pierce into the mid-night depth
> " Of yonder grove, of wildeft, largeft growth,
> " That forming high in air, a woodland quire,
> " Nods o'er the mount beneath. At every ftep,
> " Solemn and flow, the fhadows blacker fall,
> " And all is awful, lift'ning gloom around."

ON contemplating the grandeur of this wood-land fcene (the uniformity of which is fometimes broken by white and rugged rocks peeping through the foliage, which give relief to the eye, and add variety to the landfcape,) the feeling traveller is led to regret the ravages of the woodman's axe, which occafionally prefent themfelves to his view. With a figh he turns away, his imagination being impreffed with the reflection, that *now* perhaps for the laft time, he beholds thofe objects, fo richly ornamental to the " *dark hill, fteep and high,*" which in a few years, may poffibly be robbed of its verdure, and prefent to the eye, nothing but a chain of barren and naked rocks.

R

BETWEEN Arnecliffe-Hall, and the village of Ingleby, there is a small hamlet, with a commodious inn, called *Ingleby-cross;* which is probably fo named, from its fituation upon the point where two roads crofs each other at right-angles. The road from thence to Arnecliffe-Hall, leads over a fmall bridge, that croffes a rivulet called *Carr-Beck;* * which takes its rife in the parifh of Whorlton, and runs in a fouthern direction, till it empties itfelf into *the Wifk,* near *Staddle bridge,* about a mile from the above hamlet, upon the road leading from thence to Thirfk.

IN our account of the parifh of Yarm, we briefly noticed fome advantages and accommodation of a *new turnpike road,* through this part of Cleveland, which runs from *Crathorne,* in a direct line fouthwards, till it joins the Stokefley road, at the weftern extremity of this parifh. At the junction of thefe roads, for the convenience of travellers, and for accelerating a daily *coach-conveyance* to and from the fouth, a large and commodious *INN* has been erected by fubfcription, in the nature of a *TONTINE,* called the CLEVELAND-TONTINE-INN.

THE fubfcription was opened on the 1ft of February, 1804, and fo liberally fupported by the gentlemen in *Cleveland* and its vicinity, that in a fhort time it amounted to the fum of 2500*l.*

THE foundation of the *inn,* which was defigned on an extenfive and elegant plan, † was laid on the 13th of July, 1804; on which day, a memorial to the poft-mafter-general was figned by the principal inhabitants of *Cleveland,* reprefenting the inconvenient and imperfect mode of conveying letters through that diftrict, and praying that a daily poft might be eftablifhed between *Thirfk and Guifborough,* which commenced on the 5th day of September following.

---

* FROM *Kar, palus five marifcus,* a *fen* or *bog;* a name highly characteriftic of the nature of the grounds through which it runs.

† THE work was under the fuperintendence of *Mr. Hickfon,* of Guifborough, *Mr. Wadefon,* of Stockton, and of *Mr. Scarth,* of Caftle-Eden, under whofe more immediate direction the plan was defigned and executed.

THE fituation of this elegant ftructure is romantic and retired, being
fheltered on the eaft by the hanging woods of Arnecliffe, already noticed, and commanding a pleafing view of the ruins of *Mount-Grace-
Priory*, whofe ancient tower, and broken arches are feen, at no great
diftance towards the fouth, peeping through the thick foliage of " lofty
elms and venerable oaks."

NEAR to the feat of Mrs. Mauleverer, ftands the church or chapel
of Arnecliffe ; which is an ancient ftructure, of a fimple form and fmall
dimenfions ; but we have no evidence of its original foundation ; nor
does it appear to what Saint it is dedicated.   It was given by Walter
Ingelram, to the priory of Guifbrough, together with two oxgangs of
land, and a manfe or dwelling in this townfhip : the grant was confirmed by Peter, fon of Peter de Brus ; as alfo by Henry Murdoc, Archbifhop of York ; it was afterwards appropriated to that monaftry, and
at the diffolution, became a perpetual curacy, certified to the governours
of Queen Anne's bounty at 6*l. per ann.*   It has fince received fome
augmentions, by which the revenues at prefent amount to about 30*l. per
ann.*   The Mauleverers were anciently in poffeffion of the rectorial
rights ; which were fold about the beginning of the laft century to Wm.
Cooper, Efq. whofe defcendant Brian Abbs, Efq. is the prefent proprietor, and nominates the curate.

THERE are no monumental infcriptions here worthy of notice.
Within the quire of the church, on the north, there is an effigy of a
Knight in armour, with his legs croffed, cut in freeftone ; but the arms
upon the fhield are defaced, and the whole figure fo mutilated, and over-

---

ARNECLIFFE CURACY.

Certified value 6*l.*   Brian Abbs, Efq. patron.

CURATES.

1708, Peter Alcock, on the nomination of Sir   1736, John Hudfon, on the nomination of Wm.
    Wm. Foulis, Bart.   Cooper, Efq.
1715, John Nicholfon.   1782, Jonathan Steel, nominated by Cooper
1722, Philip Kitchen.   Abbs, clerk.

R 2

run with duft, and filthinefs as to render it difficult to afcertain to whom it might belong. We conjecture it, however, to be the monument of fome of the Ingelrams.

In a parifh of fo fmall extent, which contains only one fmall village, and chiefly occupied by farmers, the population, as may be naturally conceived, is not large. In the year 1801, when an exact account was taken, and a return made according to Act of Parliament, * there were 58 inhabited houfes or families, containing 253 inhabitants, which gives $4\frac{1}{2}$ nearly to each family. The number of baptifms, &c. for the laft twenty years, will appear from the following table, extracted from the parifh regifter :

	Males.	Females.	Total.
Baptifms	67	76	143
Burials	36	43	79
Increafe	31	33	64

The number of marriages within the above period 37.

THE average number of burials in a year is 4 nearly; from which it appears, from a population of 253, that one only out of $63\frac{1}{4}$ dies annually.

MOUNT-GRACE PRIORY.

In order to render our publication more interefting to the general reader, we were induced to vifit the remains of *Mount-Grace Priory*; which, though ftrictly fpeaking, not within the boundary of our diftrict, lies fo contiguous to, and appears to have been always fo much connected with this parifh, that our account of it might certainly be

---

* STATE of population, 10th March, 1801.

	Inhabited houfes.	Families.	Males.	Females.	Total.	Agriculture.	Trade.	Refidue.	Total.
Arnecliffe.	58	58	124	129	253	152	87	14	253

N. B. THE Number of baptifms for the laft year 9. Burials 7. Marriages 2.

confidered imperfect, without fome particular defcription of this venerable ruin.

THIS was a Carthufian priory, dedicated to the bleffed Virgin Mary,
and St. Nicholas, and founded (21. Richard II.) by Thomas de Holland,
Duke of Surrey, Earl of Kent, and Lord Wake, who endowed it with his
manor of BORDELBY, (*near* CLEVELAND,) which he willed, fhould
for the future be called *the houfe of Mount-Grace, of Ingleby;* and by the
affent of the prior of the grand Carthufians, made *Robert de Tredway*
the firft prior; to whom and his fucceffors, &c. he granted and confirmed in pure alms, his faid manor of *Bordelby*, to be an habitation for

the faid prior and monks, and their fucceffors; for them efpecially to recommend in their maffes, prayers, and divine fervices, the good eftates of King Richard II. and Queen Ifabella his confort; and of himfelf, the faid Thomas, Duke of Surrey, and Joan his wife, &c. &c. †

In the 22. Richard II. at the fpecial inftance of the fame Thomas Duke of Surrey, the King granted to Edmund, prior of the houfe of Mount-Grace, and the monks thereof, and their fucceffors, the lands and poffeffions of the religious at *Hinkley*, in the county Leicefter, of *Wharham* in Dorfetfhire, and of *Carefbrooke*, in Southamptonfhire, three alien priories, belonging to the Abbey of St. Mary *in Lyra*, (in Normandy,) to hold the fame as long as the war between England and France fhould continue. But he dying foon after in arms againft King

† CARTA FUNDATIONIS.

Universis fanctæ matris ecclefiæ prefentes literas vifuris, vel audituris, *Thomas de Holland*, dux Surriæ, &c. Salutem in Domino fempiternam. Cum pium et meritorium fit pro parentibus, cunctifque dei fidelibus opera caritatis adminiftrare; et jam a primæva ætate, in mente habuimus, & defideravimus, deo infpirante, cultum divinum augmentare; et quia credimus et veraciter fcimus, quod omnes ftatus et ordines fanctæ ecclefiæ boni fint et devoti; tamen infpirante Deo, fpecialem devotionem, et potiffimam affectionem gerimus ad fanctiffimam ordinem *Carthufienfem*, cujus obfervantias fanctas & fingulares, atque perfonas in eodem ordine degentes, non folum diligimus, fed valde miramur: quorum numerum, gratia divina cooperante, augere cordialiter peroptamus. Idcirco fciatis quod, ob reverentiam & honorem Dei, et fuæ fanctiffimæ matris, et virginis *Mariæ* et fancti *Nicholai*; et ob affectionem quam habemus ad fefta affumptionis ejufdem gloriofæ virginis, et beati *Nicholai*; et ob affectionem quam gerimus ad fanctam religionem fupradictam, nos prædictus *Thomas* dux, de licentia Regia, per prefentem chartam noftram fundamus & facimus unam Domum Monachorum ejufdem ordinis *Carthufienfis* infra manerium noftrum de BORDELBY *prope* CLEVELAND, in Com Eboracenfi, quam vocamus et vocare volumus, infuturum, Domum MONTIS-GRATIÆ de INGELBY, in honorem & perpetuam memoriam benedictorum feftorum præfcriptorum. Volumus etiam, quod unus monachorum dictorum vocetur *Prior*; & per affenfum Prioris Carthufienfis majoris ordinis prædicti facimus Dominum *Robertum Tredewy*, priorem nominatum domus noftræ prædictæ, &c. Volumus infuper & ordinamus quod prædictus prior, &c. habeant fpecialiter in miffis, orationibus, & aliis divinis ferviciis recommendatum ftatum illuftriffimi Regis noftri, Domini *Ricardi fecundi*, & *Ifabellæ*, illuftriffimæ reginæ & confortis ejufdem regis, & ftatum noftrum & *Johannæ* confortis noftræ, &c. &c. Et nos prædictus *Thomas* dux, & hæredes noftri totum prædictum manerium cum fuis pertinentiis prædicto *Roberto* priori, &c. contra omnes gentes warrantizabimus, acquietabimus, & defendemus imperpetuum.   *Dugd. Mon. Tom. I. p.* 968.

Hénry IV. befote all the buildings were finifhed, the work was at a ftand, and the right of the monks to their poffeffions was queftioned, till King Henry VI. about the year 1440, confirmed in Parliament, all the Duke's grants to them. * The buildings, after this, were foon completed, and the monaftry flourifhed, till the general diffolution when the revenues were valued at 382*l*. 5s. 11d. per ann. according to Speed ; and at 323*l*. 2s. 10d. as reported by Dugdale.

THE furrender of this priory was inrolled, on the 18th December, (31. Hen. VIII.) and the fite was granted (32. Hen. VIII.) to James Strangwaies, Knt. to hold the fame of the King *in capite*, by military fervice. ‡ From the Strangwaies, it defcended to the Lafcells, and was

---

* *RATIFICATIO fundationis per Regem Henricum VI.*

REX omnibus, &c. Salutem. Sciatis quod cum dilecti nobis in Chrifto, prior & conventus monafterii domus *affumptionis beatæ Mariæ*, de MOUNTGRACE, ordinis Carthufienfis, in Com. Ebor. per quandam petitionem fuam nobis in ultimo Parliamento noftro exhibitam, nobis monftraverunt, qualiter monafterium fuum prædictum, tempore Domini *Ricardi*, nuper Regis Angliæ fecundi poft conqueftum, Anno Regni fui vicefimo, per licentiam fuam, in villa de BORDELBY, per venerabilem Dominum *Thomam*, ducem *Surregiæ*, fundatum extitit; idemque dux, tempore fundationis illius, eandem villam, quæ facit manerium de BORDELBY, et quæ valoris annui decem marcarum, vel circiter, exiftit, prædecefforibus prædictorum prioris & conventus, & fuccefforibus fuis donavit imperpetuum. Ac non diu poft quod ipfe monafterium prædictum inceperat edificare, obiit ; qua de caufa monafterium illud in magna fua parte edificandum exiftit, ad ipforum prioris & conventus, &c. non modicum nocumentum & dampnum: idemque prior & conventus ulterius procedere in edificatione monafterii fui prædicti pro malignitate, & indifpofitione temporis, prefertim ipforum qui fingere titulos & querelas, et gentes fimplices abfque jure feu caufa turbare non curant, aufi non exiftunt: unde nobis humiliter fupplicarunt ut, præmiffis confideratis, ad ipfum priorem, et conventum & fucceffores fuos, ab omnibus perplexitatibus et dubiis ponendis vellemus, ex certis confiderationibus eadem petitione fpecificatis, per affenfum Dominorum fpiritualium et temporalium, ac communitatis regni noftri *Angliæ* in dicto Parliamento exiftentium; donationem et conceffionem prædictas per dictum fundatorem factas (&c.) ratificare, approbare (&c.)

Dugd. Mon. Tom. I. p. 969.
Cart. 19. Hen. VI. m. 22.

‡ REX conceffit Jacobo Strangwaies, militi, fcitum pricratus de MOUNT-GRACE, in Com. Ebor. ac eccles. campan. & cœmiterium ejufdem monafterii ; ac duo mef. in fimul jacentia, vocata *Calf-Clofes*; ac pratum vocatum *Broadings*; ac maner. *de Moreton* juxta *Eaft-Harlfey*, in dict. Com. Ebor. nuper monaft. *de Rievalx* fpectant. tenend. de rege in capite per fervitium militare.

Efc. 32. Hen. VIII. pt. 4 ta.

fold by the late Rev. Robert Lafcells, to the Mauleverers, the prefent
proprietors.

THE fecluded fituation and romantic gloom of this monaftry feem
to have been particularly adapted to the aufterjties of the rigid order of
Carthufians placed here; and of which there were only nine houfes in
England. * The vale, in which thefe venerable remains are fituated, is
fhut in on the fouth-eaft, by a lofty hill, cloathed with wood, which
adds a folemn grandeur to the fcene; and the ruins of the monaftry,
though at no great diftance from the road, being fheltered from public
view,—" *embofom'd high in tufted trees*,"—efcape the general notice of
ftrangers.

WE approached the buildings on the weft, by a narrow lane leading
from the main road; and entered, by a gothic gateway, into the quadrangle of the monaftry; the outer-walls of which inclofe about three
acres of ground, and are ftill ftanding, fantaftically covered with ivy,

---

* THE order of *Carthufians* was firft eftablifhed in the year 1080, in the defert of *Chartreaux* in
Grenoble, by one Bruno, who is faid to have been moved thereto, by hearing a dead man's voice cry
out three times, " *that he was condemned by the juft judgment of God;*" which induced him to declare
that man had no chance for falvation, unlefs they renounced the world, and retired to live in deferts.
Accordingly to fet the example, he and fix others withdrew themfelves to the defert of *Chartreaux*,
fituate among the high mountains. They profeffed to follow the rule of *St. Bennett*, adding thereto
many great aufterities, by way of reformation; amongft others, that they ought to be fatisfied with
a very little fpace of ground about their cells, and confine themfelves within the walls of their monaftry, fo as not even to walk about their own grounds above once a week, and to keep an almoft
perpetual filence; they were to fubfift one day in the week, on bread and water; and the eating of
flefh was originally forbidden at all times, even in cafes of extreme ficknefs; but this was afterwards
difpenfed with; yet, as Stevens fays, " he who accepted it, was deemed an infamous man who had
" preferred a morfel of meat, to a precious death before God."

THE rule was confirmed by Pope Alexander III. in the year 1174, and the order firft introduced
into England in the year 1180.

THEIR habit was white, a plaited black cloak excepted, and they wore a hair fhirt next their
fkin.

NOTWITHSTANDING thefe great aufterities, in which they feem to have far miftaken the benevolent plan of providence, we find, that in a fhort time after their eftablifhment in England, their cells
became ftately palaces, and their little plots of ground ftretched themfelves into large tracts of land.

Mount Grace Priory

which has acquired fuch a degree of ftrength and beauty, as to realize
the obfervation of the poet:

> " Whofe ragged walls with ivy creeps
> " And with her arms from falling keeps;
> " So both a fafety from the wind
> " In mutual dependance find."
>
> *Grongar-Hill.*

A PART of the buildings on the weft, near the gateway, has been
converted into a farm-houfe, of a caftellated form, with fpacious apartments, which appear to have been cotemporary with the priory. This,
it has been conjectured by fome vifitors, was the prior's lodging, but
from its vicinity to the kitchen offices, ftill remaining, we are induced
to think, it was probably occupied by the fecular fervants of the monaftry. Over the door is the date (1654) which points out the time
of the repairs, with the initials (J. L.) of the name of one of the family
of *Lafcells,* who were then proprietors.

THE church, which ftood on the north fide of the firft court, and
is now in ruins, was in the form of a crofs, with the tower which is
ftill perfect,* rifing in the centre, fupported by four light gothic
arches. Befides the eaftern window, which, as well as the walls of the
chancel, is now levelled with the ground, the church was lighted on
the weft, north, and fouth, by mullioned windows, under pointed arches. The principal entrance was on the weft, by a door under a
pointed arch; and from the nave on the north, was an arched door-
way, for the admittance of the religious from the cloifters: the entrance into the chancel was through the arches fupporting the tower.

---

* THERE are fome lines in Bifhop Hall's Satire, fo appofite to the circumftance of deftroying
monaftic edifices, that we cannot forbear prefenting them to the reader:

> " Yet pure devotion lets the fteeple ftand
> " And idle battlements on either hand;
> " Left that, were all thofe holy relics gone,
> " *Furius's* facrilege could not be known."
>
> *Bifhop Hall's Sat.*

S

The veſtry room appears to have been on the north ſide of the chancel, which, like every other part of the building, is now entirely roofleſs.

THE ſecond or inner court is ſurrounded by double walls, and contained the cells of theſe ſolitary monks; the doors of which though now walled up, may be diſtinctly traced; there being four on the eaſt, five on the weſt, and five on the north. On the ſide of each door there is a ſmall zig-zag opening in the wall, to communicate with the apartments; and ſo contrived, that victuals, &c. might be conveyed into the cell, without the perſon being ſeen. Around this court, which meaſures 8o paces from north to ſouth, and 73 paces from eaſt to weſt, there appears to have been a ſhade or covering, to ſhelter the religious in their proceſſions; and in the weſt wall, under an arched receſs, is the *piſcena*, or ciſtern, where a pump ſeems to have been fixed, and reſembles one in a vaulted veſtry, at York Minſter: this was probably for the prieſts to waſh in, before the performance of divine ſervices.

FROM the north-eaſt corner of this court, there is a ſmall ſtream of clear water, which, at preſent, runs in an open channel, till it reaches the centre of the court; from whence, it is arched over, and conveyed beneath the buildings, till it comes in front of the farm houſe, where it breaks out, and terminates in a fine flowing well.

ON the ſouth of the firſt court or quadrangle, the faint veſtiges of many buildings appear, which we are led to conjecture might have been the barns, kilns, and other out-offices, that once ſupplied the monaſtry.

SUCH are the moſt prominent features of this venerable ruin; every part of which, even the looſe fragments that lie ſcattered around, are luxuriantly covered with ivy, and conſpire with the ſurrounding ſcenery, to impreſs the mind with that calm compoſure and pleaſing melancholy, which ariſes from viſiting the ſacred ruins of time.

AT ſome diſtance, on the ſummit of the mountain that ſhelters the monaſtry, on the eaſt, are the ruins of an ancient building, called the

LADY-CHAPEL,

which was founded in the year 1515. † The edifice has been but of
fmall dimenfions; and from the prefent remains, appears to have contained nothing remarkable, in point of architecture. The road from
the monaftry to this chapel, which leads up the fteep brow of a lofty
mountain, is rugged; and by the growth of trees, rendered at prefent,
a painful and difficult afcent.

NUMEROUS miracles are reported to have been performed at this
chapel, by our lady's help; fuch as the fudden recovery of a child
that feemed dead, and the cure of many from the *fweating ficknefs*, and
other afflicting maladies; but thefe carry with them fo much the appearance of fuperftition, that we, at prefent, forbear any further repetition.

---

† IF we may be allowed to hazard a conjecture, as to the motives for fuch erections, which were
fometimes contiguous to the prior-church, it will be found, perhaps, that this chapel was placed at
a diftance from the monaftry, not only to fignify that thofe who would rightly reverence the Holy
Virgin's contemplation, fhould fometimes lay afide and forget the troublefome noife of towns and
cities; and *go as it were with Mofes to the mount*; but alfo, that thofe, who came for devotion to
the chapel of our lady, might receive encouragement from the example of the *religious*, whofe life
they might, by enquiring, know; while the *religious themfelves* might remain quiet and undifturbed
by the frequent vifits of ftrangers.

S 2

THE PARISH OF WHORLTON;

OR, as it is fometimes written, *Wherevelton, Querelton, Quarlton, Ferwel-thun;* and in Domefday-book, **Wereltun,** appears to have been fo named from a detached and conical formed mountain within the pa-rifh, of no great elevation, called *Wharl,* or *Whorl-Hill,* which, accord-ing to *Minfhew,* is conjectured to be derived from the Belgic word, WERVELEN, *in Orbem vertere;* or rather perhaps, according to *Somner,* from the Saxon Ƿpeoɲɼa, *verticulum;* an etymology that points out the remains of our aboriginal language, which have furvived the lapfe of fo many centuries, and the fhock of fo many revolutions.

THE parifh is about five miles in extent from north to fouth, and four miles broad; being bounded by the parifhes of Rudby and Face-by on the eaft; by Arncliffe and Rudby on the weft; by Rudby on the north; and by a range of hills, running eaftwards, which divide it from Ofmotherly and Bilfdale on the fouth. It is divided into the townfhips of *Whorlton* and *Pottowe;* and befides thefe, comprehends the village of *Swainby;* and the feveral hamlets of *Huthwaite, Scarthe-wood, Trenholme,* and a part of *Faceby.* *

WHORLTON, in the Conqueror's time, was ancient demefne of the crown, it being entered in Domefday-book, under the title of

---

* GREAT confufion is fometimes met with, in the boundaries of parifhes; of which Whorlton affords a particular inftance, being intermixed with *Faceby,* a part of which lies within this parifh; as appears from a petition prefented to Archbifhop Sharpe, in the year 1706, (wherein the parifh-oners defired a minifter that might refide among them,) fetting forth, " that the parifh of Whorlton " confifts of fix towns: viz. *Whorlton, Huthwaite, Scarthwood, Swainby, Pottoe,* and the *greateft part of Faceby.*"   *Archbifhop Sharpe's MSS.*

Terra Regis.

Manerium in Wereltun. Gofpatric I. Car. et dimid. ad geldum. Terra ad I. Car. Nunc eft ibi in Dominio I. Car. et VII. Uillani cum II. Car. et IIII. Acris prati. Silva paft. III. Quarent. Totum manerium I. Leuca long. et III. Quarent. lat. T. R. E. valebat X. Solid. modo VI. Solid. et VIII. Denar.

FROM the above furvey it appears that before the conqueft, this manor was held by Gofpatric, probably the fame who was Earl of Northumberland, and forfeited his eftates for treafon, in taking part with the rebels at York againft the Conqueror; it contained at that time only one carucate and a half of land, charged with the tax of *Danegeld;* with arable land fufficient for one plough. There was then in *Demefne* one carucate, and feven villeins † with two ploughs, and four acres of meadow. There was alfo a wood with pafturage for cattle or deer, containing three *quarentens.* The manor was one mile long, * and three quarentens broad; and in the time of Edward the Confeffor was valued at ten fhillings; but at the time of the furvey, was worth no more than fix fhillings and eight pence. It alfo appears from another part of the furvey that there were twenty villeins with eight ploughs here, which were within the foke or liberty of the manor of Hutton, at that time held by Robert, Earl of Mortain in Normandy, who was half-brother to the Conqueror.

THE Meinills, at an early period after the conqueft, became lords here; of which family we find mention made of Stephen, fon of Robert de Meinill, who, in the time of King Henry I. founded a religious houfe at Scarthe, in this parifh. This Stephen was fucceeded by Robert his fon, who married Emma, daughter of Richard de Malbiffe,

---

† THE *Villani,* or *Villeins,* were tenants of fuperior degree to *Servi,* and held fome cottage and lands; for which they were burthened with fuch fervile works, as their lords had annexed to them.

* THE word *leuca* fignifies a mile, which in Domefday-book is 1000 paces. *Quarenta* was the ufual menfuration of woodlands. *Kennet's Paroch. Antiquities.*

Knight; he died in the 8th year of King John's reign, Emma his wife
furviving; the benefit of whofe fecond marriage was granted to her
father, on the payment of three hundred marks to the King.* He
was fucceeded by his fon Stephen, who being under age at his father's
death, Robert de Turnham had a grant of his wardfhip, and marriage
(9. John,) for the fum of one thoufand marks. † In the fecond year
of Henry III. the cuftody of his whole barony within the county of
York was given to the Archbifhop of Canterbury, it being of his fee. ‡
Nicholas de Meinill, his fon, fucceeded; to whom, for his great fervices
in the wars againft the Welch, § King Edward I. remitted a debt of
one hundred marks; and granted to him free warren throughout his
manors of Whorlton, Grenehowe, Seamer and Efton; as alfo free-chace
in all his woods within the faid lordfhip. ‖ He died 28. Edw. I. and
was fucceeded by his fon Nicholas, then 24 years of age; who, doing
his homage, had livery of his lands, except the manor of Efton, and
certain lands in Pottowe, which were affigned as the dower of his mother Chriftian then furviving. This Nicholas died 15. Edward II.
without lawful iffue; John, his brother being found his next heir; but
left a natural fon, named Nicholas, by Lucia, daughter and heir of
Robert de Thweng, his concubine.

---

* CLAUS. 8. John. m. 3.   † ROT. Pip. 9. John. Ebor.

‡ REX dedit feizinam totius Baroniæ Roberti de Menill, Archiepifcopo Cantuar.

Claus. 2. Hen. III. m. 6.

§ NICHOLAS, fil. Domini Steph. de Menill, pro bono fervitio fuo nuper in exercitu Regis in
Wallia, perdonatur debit. 100 marcis, quibus jufte tenebatur.

Com. Term. Michus. A°. 9. Edward I.

‖ THIS Nicholas brought a charge againft Chriftian his wife (18. Edw. I.), that fhe had an intent to poifon him, and accufed her before the Archbifhop of York; where, though fhe manifefted
her innocence, yet would he not be reconciled to her; fo that fhe was obliged to complain for ali,
mony, not daring to live with him without good fecurity, that fhe might be treated as a wife.

Dugd. Baron. vol. 2. p. 110.

THERE is fome confufion in Sir Wm. Dugdale's account of this family; from the annexed pedigree,* it appears that the defcendants of John the lawful heir, ending in female iffue, this Nicholas, (by Lucia de Thweng,) became the chief of the family, and was fummon-

---

* THE *Pedigree of the ancient family of* MEINELLS *of Whorlton-Caftle*, fometime Barons of this realm; from whom defcended many branches of Knight's families; as the Meinells of Ingleton, Hilton, and North-Kilvington. Extracted from the Herald's office, by Ralph Bigland, Efq. *Norroy-King at Arms.*

Stephanus de Maifnill de Stainton, dedit___Sibilla, uxor ejus.
terras in Stainton, *Abbatiæ de Rievaulx.*
(*Monaft. Angl.*)

Henricus. Emma, filia___Robertus de Menill, tenuit___Agnes, filia Johanna, foror Roberti nupta
Richard de | Baroniam de Dynelfton, in ... de Rotefe. Willimo, fil. Roberti de
Malbiffe. | Comitat. Northumb. Grymfthorpe.

Dominus Willimus Hugo de Menill de Stephanus de Menill___Sibilla, uxor Nicholus de Menill,
Meinill, vixit 1203. Hilton; a quofamilia miles, infra ætat. et | ejus. vixit 3. Hen. III.
de Hilton & *Kilvington.* in cuftodia Roberti de et 9 Edw. I.
(See pedigree, page 70.) Turnham. (9. Joh.)

John de Mennill de Rungeton, Nicholaus de Menyll, miles, Dominus de___Chriftiana, Petrus filius
ten. de fil. de Anne de Menill, Wherelton, in com. ebor. fumonitus ad | uxor ejus. Stephani.
28. Edw. I. Parl. temp. Edw. I. et ob. 28. Edw. I.
Efceat. n. 38. *ebor.*

Willimus Latimer,___Lucia, fil. & coheir.___Nicholaus de Menill de Johannes de Meynill,___Catherina,
junior; primus ma- R. de Thweng de Whereleton; fil. et hæ- frater et hæres Nichi. | uxor ejus,
ritus. Danby, miles; fe- res, ætat. 24. Annos: et ætat. 40. Annos. obiit 19.
cundè nupta Rob. | fumon. ad Parl. temp. Obiit 23. Edw. III. | Edw. III.
de Everingham, | Edw. II. et obiit 15. fuit de Caftle-Leving-
militi. | Edw. II ton.
Willimus Latimer de Danby, miles.___

Johannes de Meynill___.....
obiit ante patrem. | ..... Chriftiana, nupfit Roberto
de Sproxton, de com. ebor.

Johannes de Menill, confang. Walterus de___Alicia, foror et hær.___Willimus Percy,
et hæres Johannis; ætat 3 An- Boynton, mi- | Johannis, uxor Rob. | *primus maritus.*
nos. 2. Edw. III. ob. 23. Edw. les. de Boulton.
III. *fine prole.*

Walterus Boynton. Willimus Percy Margareta, foror et___
Nicholaus de Menill, miles;___Alicia, filia W. Baronis defunctus 15. hæres; uxor Thomæ
fumonitus ad Parl. 9, 10, 12, | Roos de Hamlake, quæ Richard II. Blanfront. *Claus.*
13, 14. Edw. III. inter Ba- | fupervixt maritum 16. *ant.* 1. *Hen IV.*
rones. Obiit 16. Edw. III. | Edw. III.

Johannes Blanfront.

ed to Parliament among the Barons, from the 9th to the 16th Edw. III.
He married Alice, daughter of William-Lord Roos, of Helmsley, and
died 16. Edward III. being seized of the manors of Whorlton, Hutton
juxta Rudby, Seamer, and Middleton, with the hamlets of Carleton,
Pottowe, and Trenholme, which were held of the Archbishop of Canterbury, by the tenure of serving the said Archbishop with the cup, in
which he should drink, on the day of his consecration. †

HE left issue, a daughter, named Elizabeth, who was first married
to John Lord D'arcy, whom she survived; and afterwards to Peter de
Mauley, the 6th. She died 42. Edw. III. leaving Philip, Lord D'arcy
and Meinill, her son and heir, then fifteen years of age.

WHORLTON remained in the D'arcy family for several successions,
till Philip, Lord D'arcy and Meinill, who married Eleanor, daughter
of Henry Fitz-Hugh, died without male-issue, (6. Hen. V.) leaving

---

Johannes D'arcy de—Elizabetha,* filia et hæres—Petrus de Malolacu, sextus ejusdem
Knayth, miles, *pri-* | unica, probavit ætatem ant. nominis, Baro. de Mulgrave; *mari-*
mus maritus. | 22. Edw. III. ob. 42. Edw. *tus secundus.*
| III.

* Ista Elizabetha nata fuit apud Wherlton in
com. ebor. 15. Die Octobris, 5. Edw. III. et
Philippus D'arcy, hæres—Elizabetha, fil. Thomæ   in ecclesia sanctæ crucis in eadem villa bap-
matris, ætatis 15. Annos. | Gray, de Heton, miles,   tizata; et fuit ætatis 16 Annor. Anno 21.
ob. 22. Richard II. | ob. 13. Hen. IV.   Edw. III.

John, Lord D'arcy and—Margaret, daughter of Henry,
Meinell; ob. 13. Hen. IV. | Lord Gray de Wilton.

Philip D'Arcy, ob. infra—Eleanor, dau. of Henry,   John D'arcy, brother and—Johanna, daughter
ætatem; 6. Hen. V. | Lord Fitzhugh.   heir from whom sprung   of John Baron
the Lords D'arcy, and   Greystoke.
Elizabeth, wife of James   Margery, wife of John   Earls of Holdernesse.
Strangeways, Knight.   Conyers, Knight.

---

† NICHOLAUS DE MENYLL tenuit manerium de Whorlton, &c. de Archiepiscopo Cantuariensi,
serviendo dict. Archiepiscopum die consecrationis suæ de coupâ, quá idem Archiepiscopus bibere
debet eodem die.   *Esceat.* 16. *Edw. III. No.* 37.

CAMDEN remarks, that "the Baron Menill held certain lands in this county (York) of the Arch-
"bishop of Canterbury; and that the Coniers and Strangwaies, with some others descended from
"them are obliged to be attendant, and pay certain military services to the Archbishop for the
"same."

two infant daughters his coheirs; viz. Elizabeth and Margaret. Elizabeth married James Strangways, Knight; and had Whorlton and other lands, for her fhare, upon the divifion. Leland fays, " Whorlton in " Cleveland was the principal houfe of the Lord Menell; which fence " came to Mafter Strangwayes in particion."

Lel. Itin. vol. 9. p. 177.

WE have met with no certain evidence to point out, to whom Whorlton defcended after the Strangways. By an inquifition *poft mortem* taken at Topcliffe, *(2d October, 27. Eliz.)* it was found, that Henry, Earl of Northumberland, who fhot himfelf in the Tower, was feized (among others) of the Caftle and manor of Whorlton, with the appurtenances, which by letters patent, (dated July 12th, 36. Henry VIII.) had been granted to Matthew, Earl of Lennox; on whom that King had beftowed his fifter's daughter in marriage, with a large eftate. From hence it would appear, that from the Strangways, in the reign of Henry VIII. it came into the hands of the crown; and was granted, on his marriage to Matthew Stewart, Earl of Lennox,* and Margaret his wife. But, how long this Earl continued in poffeffion, we are not informed; nor have we evidence to fhew, at what period it came to the Percy family; from whom, on the death of Henry, as above noticed, we are led to conclude, that it came by forfeiture again to the crown. It was afterwards granted to Edward Bruce, of Kinlos; whofe fon Thomas was advanced by King Charles I. to the honour of Lord Bruce of Whorlton (17. Charles I.). Robert, his fon, was created Earl of Aylefbury by King Charles II. in whofe pofterity the title and eftate continued till Charles, who dying without iffue-male, the title became

---

* MATTHEW, Earl of Lennox, married Margaret, daughter of Archibald, the fixth Earl of Angus, by Margaret, the daughter of King Henry VII. (fifter of Henry VIII.) and mother to James V. King of Scotland. Camden fays, " the iffue of this happy match were Henry and Charles; the " former of whom by Mary, Queen of Scots, had James VI. monarch of Great Britain, happily born " for the general good of thefe nations."

T

extinct; but was renewed in Thomas Bruce Brudenell, the youngeft
fon of George Brudenell, third Earl of Cardigan, by Elizabeth, eldeft
daughter of Thomas Bruce, Earl of Aylefbury, who was created Lord
Bruce, April 17, 1746, with remainder of that barony to the prefent
Earl. He died without male-iffue, Feb. 10, 1747, and was fucceeded
by the prefent Earl, his nephew; who, by act of Parliament 1767, took
the name and arms of Bruce, and was created Earl of Aylefbury, June
8, 1776. †

BEFORE we proceed to a more minute defcription of the parifh, it
will be neceffary to advert to the ancient ftate of the manor, as it appears from the moft authentic records. From Kirkby's Inqueft we
find that all the lands belonging to the Meinills were exempt from
the payment of danegeld; and that Nicholas de Meinill, in the reign
of Edward I. obtained a charter for keeping a fair here; and alfo had
a grant of free-warren, free-chace, and divers other privileges within
the manor. From the fame Inqueft it alfo appears, that he paid the
fum of thirty fhillings for his lands at Whorlton, &c. &c. which were
held of the fee of Canterbury. ‡

---

† His lordfhip was born 1730, and married firft Sufannah, daughter of Henry Hoare, Efq.
and widow of Charles Boyle, Vifcount Dungarvon, by whom he had iffue George Lord Bruce (born
1762, died 1783), Caroline-Anne, Frances-Elizabeth, Charles (died an infant), Charles Lord Bruce
born 1773, married 1793 Mifs Hill, daughter of Lady Barwick. His lordfhip married, 2dly, Feb.
14, 1788, Anne, eldeft daughter of the late, and fifter to the prefent Earl of Moira, by whom he has
a daughter, born Feb. 22, 1790.

‡ DICUNT quod omnes terr. Nicholai de Meynill, funt de libertate ecclefiæ Cantuar. quare dicunt
quod *non funt gildabilis*, ut intelligunt. Dicunt etiam, quod ftatus villar. de *Querelton, Seamer, Hilton, Middleton, Eflton, Grenehow, Hoton, Pottowe, Goweton, Rymekton, Kerlton*, et duar. car. terr. de
Newby, et VI bovat. in *Scoterfkelf, et cæt.* quæ funt de tenura ecclefiæ Cantuar. quas Nicholaus de
Meynell tenuit, mutat. eft per Stephanum de Menel, patrem prædicti Nicholai in hoc, quod ubi dare
confueverunt commun. amerciam, eas dare defendit a tempore viginti annorum. Dicunt etiam, quod
Dominus Nicholaus de Meinell non permittet ballivo Domini Regis tenere wapontag. infra libertat.
ecclefiæ Cantuar. de feod. milit. quia tenetur de Domino *Rege in capite.*

NICHOLAUS DE MEYNELL clamat habere feriam in Whorlton, per chartam Domini Edwardi Regis; et Warrenam, Parcum et Furtam, fcilicet qualiter, et a quo tempore non poteft inquiri.

By an inquisition *post mortem*, taken 30. Edw. III. on the death of John Lord D'arcy, it was found that the castle and manor of Whorlton, with other lands, which descended to him by marriage with Elizabeth, the sole daughter and heir of Nicholas de Meinell, had been granted to Thomas Swinford and John Charteray in trust *pro fine*; that in case the said Lord D'arcy, and Elizabeth his wife (who survived him,) should die without issue, the said castle and manor of Whorlton, &c. should remain in the hands of the King. A second inquisition § was taken at Yarm, (42. Edw. III.) by which it was found that

DICUNT etiam, quod Nicholaus de Menell reddit ballivo Domini Regis pro *Whorlton, Seamer cum Braithwaite, Eston, Grenehow, Hilton* (excepta portione Willi. de Pottowe), *Middleton, Rudby, Hoton, Pottowe cum Goweton* (excepta una carucat. terr. quæ est de feod. hæred. Marmaduci de Thweng), *Carleton, Rungbton*; et pro una carucat. in *Newby*, et una carucat. terr. in Trenholme; quæ sunt de libertate ecclesiæ Cantuar. pro finibus XXX^s. &c. &c.   *Kirkby's Inquest.*

§ 42, EDW. III.

INQISITIO capta apud Yarom in Cleveland coram *Johannem de Scotherscelf*, estaetorem Domini Regis in com. ebor. XVI^{to.} die Octob. Anno Edw. tertii post conquest. XLII^{do.} virtute brevii Domini, &c. de die exclam. eidem estaetor. direct. per sacramentum *Ric. de Aiselby, Johannis Russell* de eadem; *Matthei de Rughton* de Quarlton, *Johannis filii-Walteri* de eadem; *Ric. de Preston* de Jarum; *Walteri de Erghowe* de eadem; *Johannis filii* de eadem; *Willmi. filii Johannis* de Eston; *Johannis filii-Henrici* de eadem; *Johannis filii Nicholai* de Semer; *Willmi. Gill* de Hoton juxta Rudby; *Alex. de Wadborne* de Aldwerke, et *Robti. Westby*, de Boynton, juratorum. Qui dicunt super sacrament. sua quod Elizabetha, quæ fuit uxor *Petri de Malo-lacu*, tenuit, die quo obiit, convictum cum Johanne D'arcy, defunct. nuper viro suo, in dominio suo, ut de feodo, castrum *de Querlton*, et villas *de Querlton* et *Swainby* cum membris et pertinent. suis, et vill. de *Hoton juxta Rudby*, &c. de hæreditate sua, ut filia et hæres Nicholai Meynell, *Chiv.* defunct. patris sui, cujus hæres ipsa fuit. Et dicunt, quod est unum castrum, quod nihil valet *per ann.* ultra reprisas. Et est ibid. unus parcus cum feris inclusis qui valet *per ann.* ultra sustentationem ferarum XL solid. Et sunt ibid. duæ vinar. quæ nihil valent *per ann.* Et est ibid. in dominico, una placea vocata *West-Lathes*, cujus situs nihil valet *per ann.* Et sunt ibid. in dominico CCCCVII acr. terr. diverse arabil. quæ nondum sunt arentat. quæ valent *per ann.* LVII solid. Et sunt ibid. IX. tofta et IIII bovat. terr. jacent. prædict in dominico, quæ solebant valere *per ann.* XX solid. Et est ibid. unus boscus vocat. *Scougdale*, cujus herbag. valet *per ann.* XL solid. Et est ibid. unum molendinum aquaticum, et reddit *per ann.* IIII lib. Et est ibid. quædam placea terr. et pratum vocat. *Pilster*, continens XXX acr. et reddit *per ann.* VI^s. VIII^d. Et sunt apud *Pottowe* et *Trenholme* diversi tenent. ad voluntat. Et dicunt quod perquis. cur. in dict. manerio de *Querlton* valent *per ann.* XL solid. Et dicunt quod prædict. castr. *de Querlton*, et villæ de *Querlton et Swainby* cum membris et pertinentiis suis, simul cum aliis villis prædict. tenentur de Archiepiscopo Cantuar. per servitium militare.

Elizabeth the daughter and heiref of Nicholas de Meynill, held at the
time of her death, the caftle and manor of Whorlton in demefne, as of
fee, together with the villages of Whorlton and Swainby, with their
members and appurtenances, &c. that the caftle at that time was of no
annual value, *ultra reprifas;* that there was a park, which befides fupporting the inclofed deer, was valued at forty fhillings *per annum;* that
there were two orchards within the manor, and a place called *Weft-
Lathes,* the fite of which was nothing worth by the year; that there
were four hundred and feven acres of land in demefne, part of which
was arable, of the yearly value of two pounds, feventeen fhillings and
ninepence; with nine tofts, and four oxgangs of land, of the yearly
value of twenty fhillings; and the herbage of a certain wood called
Scugdale, of the yearly value of two pounds; one water-corn-mill of
four pounds yearly rent, and a certain place, with a meadow called
Pilfter, containing thirty acres, of the yearly rent of fix fhillings and
eight-pence.   By the fame record, as fet forth in the notes, it alfo appears, that the faid caftle and manor of Whorlton, with the villages of
Whorlton and Swainby, and their appurtenances, were held of the
Archbifhop of Canterbury, by military fervice; and that the perqui-
fites and profits of the court within the faid manor were valued at
forty fhillings yearly.
    The remains of

Whorlton-Castle

are but faintly vifible to the traveller, though at no great diftance to the left from the road leading from Stokefley to Thirfk. We approached the ruins on the eaft, which ftand on the weftern bafe of Whorl-hill, on the fummit of a natural eminence, not fufficiently extenfive to admit of a very fpacious building, which appears to have been of a circular form defended by a deep foffe. Nothing of the caftle, in its priftine ftate, is now left, except the gateway-tower, of a fquare form, which feems to have been the principal entrance, and was probably kept by a draw-bridge. The out-works are principally deftroyed; a part of the building is converted into a farm-houfe; and "*the ragged remnants*," confifting chiefly of dark and dreary vaults, are occupied by the farmer, as ftalls for his cattle.

We have no authentic evidence of the precife æra of the original foundation of this fortrefs. From the hiftorical circumftances already noticed, it is evident that Whorlton became the baronial feat of the Meinells foon after the Conqueft; about which period we are inclined to think that the caftle had its rife; and that it was firft erected by that family. But it appears probable, that it received fome additional ornaments, or at leaft underwent fome confiderable repairs by fucceeding proprietors.

The gateway-tower is ornamented with the arms of Meinell, D'arcy, and Gray; which point out to us, that this part of the edifice was erected or repaired about the latter part of the reign of Richard II. Philip, Lord D'arcy and Meinell, (who was fecond fon of John Lord D'arcy, by Elizabeth, the daughter and heirefs of Nicholas de Meinell,) having married Elizabeth, the daughter of Sir Thomas Gray, of Heton. The fhield in the centre bears the arms of D'arcy: viz. *a femi of crofslets, three cinque-foils, arg.* that on the dexter fide, the arms of Meinell: viz. *az. three bars gemmels, on a chief, or.* The finifter fhield bears the arms of Gray: viz. *gules, a bordure engrailed arg. a lion rampant.*

OVER thefe, in the centre there is a fhield, impaling the arms of D'arcy and Meinell.

WE have no means of afcertaining at what period this fortrefs was difmantled and rendered untenable. In Camden's time, it was ftated to be "*old and ruinous :*"

——————— " The tower that long had ftood
" The crufh of thunder, and the warring winds,
" Shook by the flow but fure deftroyer—*time,*
" Now hangs in doubtful ruins o'er its bafe."

THE church of Whorlton, dedicated to Holy-Crofs, was given by Robert, fon of Stephen de Meinell, to the Priory of Guifbrough; and being appropriated, was reduced at the diffolution of that monaftry, to a perpetual curacy. It was certified to the governours of the bounty of Queen Anne, at 13*l.* 10s.; and has received three augmentations, laid out in lands, which, with other dues, produce an income of about fifty pounds *per annum.*

THE rectorial rights were granted to the Ingrams of Temple-New-fom, and were in the poffeffion of Arthur Ingram, Efq. who, dying with-out iffue in the year 1708, was fucceeded by Arthur Ingram, Efq. of Barrowby, his uncle; from whom they defcended by marriage with Ifabella, daughter of the faid Arthur, to the Honourable General Cary, brother of Lord Vifcount Falkland; by whofe defcendants they have been lately fold to Edward Wolley, Efq. of York, who is the prefent proprietor, and nominates the curate.

WHORLTON CURACY.

Certified value 13*l.* 10s. Ded. Holy-Crofs. Augmented with 600*l.*

CURATES.

1700 Thomas Morley, nominated by Arthur Ingram, Efq.
1715 Michael Lythe, · · · · · · · Arthur Ingram, Efq.
1717 Donald Grant, · · · · · · · Hon. General Cary.
1767 William Robinfon, *poft res.* Grant,   idem.
1779 Thomas Deafon, *poft mortem* Robinfon, idem.
1797 William Deafon, *poft res.* Deafon, by the Hon. Ifabella Carey.

THIS church has been- fuppofed by fome to be a chapel under Rud-by; but it being called in the Archbifhop's books fometimes a free-chapel in the caftle of Whorlton, where there was a chauntry, and fometimes a parifh church, it is now confidered to have no dependence thereon.

THE chauntry here, above mentioned, was called D'arcy's chauntry, founded according to Torr, " *in the free chapel of St. ——, within the caftle;*" but the nature of the endowment is not ftated : a catalogue of cantarifts or wardens, as they occur in Torr's MS. is given in the notes. †

THE church, which ftands at a little diftance to the eaft from the caftle, is a plain and humble ftructure, with a fquare tower placed at the fide. It feems to have undergone little or no alteration fince the Æra of reformation, and exhibits traces of the Roman Catholic worfhip in the niches for Saints, &c.

THERE are no monumental infcriptions worthy of particular notice. ‡ Within the church, on the north fide of the chancel, in an arch of the

---

† CATALOGUE OF CANTARISTS.

—— Robert de Wyclyffe.
1413 Thomas Chickeles, cl. *Archbifh. of Cant. ut guardianus hæred. Domini Philip D'arcy.*
1438 William Boynton, cl. *Jac. Strangwayes & Eliz. uxor.*
1454 Thomas Claghton, pbr.   *idem.   P. M.*
1472 Rad. Surteys,   cap.   *idem.   P. M.*
1475 Geo. Strangways,   *idem.   P. M.*
1504 John Sutton,   cap.   *idem.*
—— - - - - - - - - - - - - - - - - - -   *P. M.*
1544 Carolus Smyth,   cap. *Matt. Lennox et Margareta, uxor.*

‡ OVER a window near the door of the quire there is a fhield, bearing the arms of Bate ; viz. *fable, a bar engrailed arg. between three dexter hands, or :* and on a fhield adjoining is the following infcription : viz.

ORA
TEƧNO
BIS. *A. D.* 1621.

THIS, we imagine, has been erected in memory of William Bate of Efton who married Elizabeth, daughter of Marmaduke Harperly of Whorlton, and died 13th October, 1621.

wall which divides the chancel from what we fuppofe to have been the chauntry-chapel, there is an ancient monument of Sir Nicholas de Meynill. The effigy is of excavated oak, painted white, and habited as a Crufader, crofs-legged, with his hands elevated and a dog at his feet; much mutilated, and executed in a bad ftyle, and ill proportioned.

THE monument is of that fpecies of free-ftone, which is found in great abundance, in the quarries on the moor within the parifh. The fuperior terminations of the buttreffes, which are beautifully carved, appear to have confifted of fpiracles, which, as well as the rich *finiale* that terminated the pediment, are now broken off and loft.

As the arms upon the tomb or bafe are not blazoned in their proper colours, it is difficult perhaps to ftate with precifion, to whom they belong; but the names of thofe families, with whom the defcendants of Sir Nicholas de Meynell intermarried, as they ftand in the foregoing pedigree, lead us to conclude, that the fhield in the centre of the tomb bears the arms of *Roos*, viz. *three water bougets,*—Sir Nicholas de Meynill having married Alice, daughter of William Lord Roos, of Hamlake. The fhield on the dexter fide bears the arms of *Latimer*; viz. *gules, a crofs flurte, or.* and that on the finifter fide the arms of *D'arcy*; the fecond fhields from the centre, both on the dexter and finifter fides appear to bear the fame, and are probably the arms of *Gray*; the laft on the dexter fide bears the arms of *Neville*; and that on the finifter fide the arms of *Fitz-hugh*. The oppofite fide of the tomb contains an equal number of fhields; fome of which bear arms, the fame as thofe already noticed, with others not fo eafily afcertained.

THE annexed plate, * from an accurate architectural drawing taken in the year 1802, will give the reader a juft idea of the curious workmanfhip of this richly ornamented monument; and render a more minute defcription of it unneceffary.

---

* THE plate of the *Whorlton-monument* was prefented to the Editor by the late Sir George Ruffell, of Leven-Grove, Bart. to whofe memory for this, and many valuable and friendly communications he owes this acknowledgment, as a grateful tribute of refpect.

Henry Rhodes Architect del.   J.ᵖBasire sculpᵗ

The Monument of Sir Nicholas De Meynil in Whorlton Church

Scale of Feet

THE village of Whorlton, which is about fix miles diftant from the market town of Stokefley, is fmall, confifting of a few houfes irregularly built, and feated on the weftern declivity of Whorl-Hill. At a little diftance towards the fouth lies the vale of *Scuggdale*, * which is a narrow but extenfive and fequeftered dell, winding with a gentle afcent eaftwards, and fhut in on the north and fouth between two parallel ranges of mountains. The bottom of the vale is cultivated, with inclofures running up the fides of the mountains; fome of which are covered with brufh-wood, and a few ftraggling trees interfperfed. A fmall brook, after collecting its ftream from a variety of fprings on the furrounding eminences, winds northwards in a rapid current through the bottom of the vale; towards the weftern extremity of which there are bleach-grounds of confiderable extent, carried on with great fuccefs, by Mr. William Boville, a native of the parifh. The brook which now affumes the name of *Cold-Beck*, (probably from the coldnefs of its water,) runs in a more direct courfe through the parifh to the north; and after paffing the villages of Swainby and Pottowe, empties itfelf into the river Leven between Sexhowe and Hutton-Rudby.

BURTON, (in his *Monafticon Ebor. p.* 352.) fays, that " the Canons of " Guifbro' held 14 acres and three roods of land in Scuggdale, by gift " of William, fon of Robert de Gifeburn; who afterwards, viz. in the " year 1222, for a fum of money, demifed to the faid Canons for the " term of twenty-four years, all the moor, wood, pafture, and that part " of Scuggdale, which he held of Gregory de Bernaldby, faving right of " common for his own cattle, except his goats and hogs. Gregory de " Newton gave all his fhare of this culture; and quit-claimed all his " right in the wood and moor and cliff of Scuggdale."

---

* THE name of *Scuggdale*, we conceive to be derived from the word *fcough* or *fkeugh*, which is fynonymous with *fkaw* and *fhaw*, and always imports the fame thing; viz. *a wood ground ftanding on a hill.*

Ð

SWAINBY, a small village within the manor and township of Whorlton, lies low, at a little distance to the west from Whorlton-castle. From the etymology of the name, which, according to Spelman, seems to be derived from the Saxon Spang, which signifies a *husbandman*, or *country swain*, and the common termination *by*, a *dwelling*, we are led to conjecture, that this was probably, at an early period of the Heptarchy, the residence of some Saxon leader; who surrounded by the huts of his shepherds and husbandmen, lived here, in the peaceful occupation of husbandry and pasturage.

SCARTHE, or SCARTH-WOOD, about half a mile to the south-west from Swainby, is situated on a rising ground, and stands high in comparison with the country towards the north, but is shut in on the south by an elevated hill, with inclosures to its summit, succeeded by a gradual range of hills still higher, as far as Black-Hambleton.

THERE was anciently a religious house here, founded in the reign of Henry I. by Stephen de Meinill; which he afterwards annexed to the priory of Guisbrough, and made it a cell of canons, of the order of St. Austin, to that monastry.

BURTON says, " Stephen de Meinill, senior, Robert his son, and " Stephen, son of Robert, gave the place of *Scarthe*, (to which Robert de " Meinill gave the church of Rudby, and also the church of Whorlton, " with the chapelry of his own house) to the priory of Guisborough; " for that house to place some canons of their own order in that cell."

Mon. Ebor. p. 357.

THIS, it is remarked by Tanner, is agreeable to the charter printed by Dugdale in his *Monast. Anglicanum;* but, as there is no mention of Scarthe or Rudby in the deeds of Guisbrough, nor in the valuation of that priory, taken 26. Henry VIII. it is much doubted whether the grant ever took effect. There are no remains of the building, nor any traces left, to give an idea of its extent. " The banks of earth," which Burton says were " thrown up, when the foundation stones were removed about the year 1746," are now levelled with the plough; and the stone-coffin which was then difcovered, is now placed in a field, adjoining to the clofe, called the chapel-garth, and is ufed by the farmer, for his cattle to drink out of.

THE road, leading from Yarm, over Hambleton to Helmfly, &c. winds with a fteep and contracted afcent up the fide of the mountain to *Scarthe-Nich*; † a pafs that feems to have been formed by fome great convulfion of nature, which has rended afunder the ftrata of the earth to a confiderable depth. The profpect from an elevated point, a little to the weft of the road, is beautiful and extenfive, commanding a view of the weftern part of Cleveland richly cultivated, and interfperfed with villages and farm-houfes, which diverfify the landfcape, and give to the whole an air of chearfulnefs and repofe. Whorl-Hill appears to the right, in a picturefque point of view, interfected with hedges, and cultivated to the fummit; beyond which, to the north-eaft, Rofeberry-Topping

" ———— Steep and high
" Holds and charms the wand'ring eye."

At the foot of the broad promontory of Efton-Nab, the mouth of the river Tees, and the fhore bending towards a femicircle, forms a fine eftuary or bay; while the church and buildings of Hartlepool, ftanding on a peninfula, are feen jutting into the fea. An extenfive tract of cultivated country is feen to the weft, bounded by a chain of mountains above Richmond; while the higher grounds in the county of Durham, finking in the horizon, terminate the profpect to the north.

THE townfhip or manor of POTTOWE, fituated in the northern part of the parifh, was anciently held by the Meinills, Lords of Whorlton; from whom it defcended by marriage to the D'arcies, and afterwards to

† IT feems a very probable conjecture of the learned naturalift *(Pallas)*, that " many extenfive " devaftations" (fuch as are found in the mountainous parts of Cleveland) " have been occafioned " merely by fprings undermining the fide or bottom of fteep eminences; and that fuch fiffures are " not, as others have fuppofed, the effects of volcanos."

the Strangwayes. The village gave name to a refident family in the
reign of Edward I. Robert de Pottowe, according to Kirkby's Inqueft, ‡
held lands here of the fee of Canterbury, for which he paid two fhillings
as a fine to the King's bailiff. Edward Wolley, Efq. of York, is the
principal proprietor, and lord of the manor.—Within this townfhip,
towards the north-weft, lies the hamlet of *Trenholme;* where, according
to Kirkby's Inqueft, Nicholas de Meinill, Lord of Whorlton, held one
carucate of land of the Archbifhop of Canterbury, by military fervice.
We find nothing worthy of particular notice, touching Pottowe and
Trenholme in their prefent ftate; the lands which are freehold have
been long parcelled out, and are now in the hands of different proprietors.

THE foil within the parifh is found to vary according to its fituation;
to the fouth, there is a confiderable extent of mountainous common,
chiefly of a black peat-mofs earth, covered with heath, and depaftured
with fheep of a fmall but hardy breed; the inclofed grounds, running
up the fides of the hills, are cold and unfruitful; but more immediately
around the villages of Whorlton and Swainby, and in the lower part of
the vale of Scuggdale, a gravelly loam prevails, and the lands, under a
fkilful management, produce abundant crops of corn and grafs. The
foil, in the northern parts of the parifh, is of a more clayey nature.

THE furface of the parifh towards the fouth is rather uneven, with
a general inclination towards the north; and being greatly fhaded from
the fun, by a range of hills on the fouth, the climate is cold, but healthy
and invigorating; and the parifh affords fome remarkable inftances of
longevity. The northern part of the parifh is more even, the lands

---

‡ ROBERTUS DE POTHOWE reddere tenetur II^{s.} ballivo regis pro titulo fuo in Pothowe, quia eft
de libertat. ecclefiæ Cantuar. Et Johannes de Pothowe reddit pro parte fua XII^{d.} quos dict. Robertus et Johannes de toto tempore fuo non reddiderunt; et a tempore Roberti X annor. a tempore dicti
Johannis XII annor.   *Kirkby's Inqueft.*

floping gently to the fouth, which form a pleafing vale, through which
the road leads between Stokefley and Thirfk.

UPON the moor at *Scarthe-Nich* there are fome valuable and extenfive quarries of freeftone of a fine quality, which is much ufed for buildings in the parifh and neighbourhood.

THERE being no manufactures of any confiderable extent within the
parifh, except a few linen weavers at Swainby, and the men employed
in the bleach-grounds above-mentioned, the inhabitants may be faid to
be occupied chiefly in agriculture.   From the return made to Government in the year 1801, according to act of Parliament, it appears that
there were at that time, 157 inhabited houfes, 160 families, and 718 inhabitants within the parifh, making about 4½ to each family.   Of thefe
the males and females are nearly of an equal number. *

* STATE of population, taken 10th March, 1801.

Townfhips.	Inhabited houfes.	Fami- lies.	Uninhabit- ed houfes.	Males.	Females.	Total.
Whorlton.	121	124	2	273	271	544
Pottowe.	36	36	4	92	82	174
Totals.	157	160	6	365	353	718

WE regret that we cannot give any ftatement of the probable increafe or decreafe of the inhabitants within the parifh; as, notwithftanding our repeated and moft folicitous application to *the Rev.
Wm. Deafon,* for the neceffary extracts from the parifh regifters, our humble efforts have been treated
only with contumely and filent neglect.   A flight attention to the fubjects of our enquiry would not,
we conceive, have interfered greatly with Mr. D's *more important ftudies,* nor in any degree unfitted
him for the ferious duties of his profeffion.

THE PARISH OF FACEBY,

LIES on the eaftern fide of Whorl-Hill, and is of no great extent, be-ing bounded on the eaft, weft, and north by the feveral parifhes of Carleton, Whorlton, and Rudby, and fhut in by the mountains on the fouth.

FACEBY appears from Domefday-book, to have been ancient inhe-ritance of the crown; and is thus noted in the general furvey under the title

" Terra Regis.

" Manerium in Fezbi. Archil et Lefing VIII. Carucatas ad Geldam,
" Terra ad III. Car. Ibi eft modo un. vill. et III. Bord. habent. I.
" Car et X. Acr. prati. Duas leucas longas, et dim. lat. T. R. E.
" XXX. Sol. modo V. Sol."

FROM which it appears, that before the conqueft, *Archil* and *Lefing* held this manor, which contained eight carucates of land rated *(ad geldum;)* befides land fufficient for three ploughs. At the time of the furvey there was one *villein*, and three *bordars*, * who had one plough and ten acres of meadow. The manor was two miles long, and half a mile broad; and in the Confeffor's time, was valued at thirty fhil-lings, but at the time of the furvey only at five fhillings.

FACEBY, foon after the conqueft, was granted by the Conqueror, to *Robert de Brus*, who held the fame of the King *in capite;* and his

---

* THE *bordarii,* or *bordars,* were diftinct from the *fervi* and *villani,* and feem to be thofe of a lefs fervile condition, who had a *bord* or cottage with a fmall parcel of land allowed to them.

Cowel.

defcendants continued Lords here till male iffue failing in Peter, the fourth of that name, his four fifters became his heirs; and this, with other eftates in Cleveland, fell to the fhare of Margaret, wife of Robert de Roos; who, on the death of her hufband, granted the fame to Marmaduke de Thweng, of whom, as appears from Kirkby's Inqueft already noted *(p.* 96*)*, Robert de Scoterfkelf, Richard Gower, and William Stormey, held two knight's fees in Faceby, &c. where ten carucates made one knight's fee. From the Thwengs the manor came by marriage with Margery, daughter of Marmaduke de Thweng, to Ralph de Neville, Lord of Raby; in whofe defcendants it continued till the attainder of John Neville, † Marquis of Montague, when it was granted to Richard, Duke of Gloucefter (afterwards King Richard III.), who, by a fpecial act of Parliament *(6th October*, 12. *Edward IV.)* was enabled to hold the fame, with Carleton and divers other lordfhips and eftates, to himfelf, and the heirs male of his body lawfully begotten, fo long as any heir male of the body of the faid John Neville, Marquis of Montague, fhould continue.

How long this manor continued in the poffeffion of Richard, Duke of Gloucefter; or, to whom it afterwards immediately defcended, we find not on record. In the latter part of the reign of Queen Elizabeth, ―― Mann, Efq. died feized thereof: from whofe defcendants, after divers grants and alienations, it came, with a confiderable eftate, into the poffeffion of the Prifficks, who fold the fame to Edmund Bunting and William Sutton, Efqrs.; and is now the property of George Sutton, Efq. of Stockton, in the county of Durham.

---

† John Neville, Marquis of Montague, was flain at Barnet, leaving iffue two fons; viz. John, the younger, who died unmarried, and was buried at Salfton, in Cambridgfhire; and George, created Duke of Bedford, (9. Edw. IV.) but, on his father's attainder, being degraded from his titles of dignity and honour, (17. Edw. IV.) died without iffue, and was buried at Sheriff-Hutton, May 4th, 1483. *Dug. Bar. vol. I. p.* 308.

THE lands, which according to Kirkby's Inqueft, were held by the Stormeys, defcended by marriage with Alice, daughter and fole heirefs of John Stormey, to Robert Conftable, of Dromonby; which family, ending in female iffue, in the reign of Charles I. their eftate was fold to feveral purchafers.

THE village of Faceby is fmall, confifting chiefly of farm houfes irregularly built, and fituated on the eaftern declivity of Whorl-Hill, about four miles from the market town of Stokefley. A confiderable part of the parifh was in open, undivided common-fields, till about the year 1749, when it was inclofed under an act of Parliament; in which it was provided, that a certain yearly rent fhould be paid to, and accepted by the impropriators in lieu of all tithes great and fmall, that might be claimed for the faid allotments.

THE new inclofures, in general with the reft of the grounds within the parifh, are divided with quickfet hedges in a thriving condition; the lands incline gently towards the north, about one half of which is in tillage. The foil is chiefly a clayey loam; which (notwithftanding the unfavourable afpect, and the proximity of the mountains on the fouth,) is rendered, by a fkilful management, tolerably productive.

THE church of Faceby, dedicated to *St. Mary Magdalen*, is a plain and humble edifice of fmall dimenfions, and contains no monuments, or monumental infcriptions worthy of notice. ‡ It was certified to the governours of the bounty of Queen Ann at 19*l.* 5s.; and is ftated in Ecton to be a chapel under Carleton; but we are induced to confider the ftatement to be erroneous; in the act of Parliament already allud-

---

‡ THERE was formerly within the church an ancient monument, with an infcription engraven on brafs, to the memory of *Sir Lewis Goulton, Knight,* who came into England with the Conqueror, and performed great acts of valour at the battle of Haftings, where he was knighted, and had the manor of Goulton, and other eftates given him by the King. The infcription has een ftated to us to be curious, and is now in the poffeffion of *Chriftopher Goulton, Efq of Highthorne, near Eafingwold;* a copy of which, for the gratification of the public, notwithftanding our moft folicitous application, we have not been able to procure.

ed to, a short abstract of which we have given in the notes,* it is called a vicarage, and a parish church, under the patronage of the lords of the manor; and being *a donative benefice*, was consequently exempt from ecclesiastical jurisdiction, till, by the consent of the patrons, it was augmented by the governours of the said bounty; when it became presentable, and is now subject to the visitation and jurisdiction of the diocesan, under the denomination of a curacy. †

THE poor within the parish, which are not numerous, are supported by a moderate rate upon the old rentals. Anthony Lazenby, merchant

---

* THE act of Parliament (21. Geo. II.) intitled "a bill for inclosing, dividing, and exchanging the common fields, common pastures, common meadows, and other grounds in the manor and township of Faceby, in Cleveland, in the north-riding of the county of York; and for providing certain recompences to the rector and vicar of Faceby, in lieu of tithes,"—*recites*,—"that there were several common fields, &c. consisting of 12 large oxgangs of land, and 36 small oxgangs of arable and meadow lands, containing 700 acres or thereabouts; and a common pasture, &c. containing 400 acres, and a common or waste containing 500 acres; that William Sutton and Edmund Bunting were lords of the said manor of Faceby, and were also owners of the impropriate rectory, and patrons of the parish church of St. Mary Magdalen in Faceby aforesaid, which was a *donative benefice*; and were also entitled to the tithes of calves, wool, lambs, geese, and hens; and to the greatest part of the tithes of corn and hay, arising within the said township of Faceby, &c. That William Deason, clerk, was vicar of the said parish church, and was, in right of his church, entitled to the rest of the tithes of corn, hay, &c. and also to two small tenements and common of pasture for two beasts, in the common pasture of Faceby, &c."

By the said bill it was further enacted, "that a certain yearly rent therein provided to be paid to the said William Sutton and Edmund Bunting, their heirs and assigns, should be by them accepted in lieu of tithes, both great and small, payable, or that might be claimed by them, for and in respect of all or any messuages, farms, grounds, tenements, and hereditaments within the said manor, or parish of St. Mary Magdalen, in Faceby aforesaid, &c."

† FACEBY CURACY, or CHAPEL.

Ded. St. Mary Magdalen. Cert. val. 19*l.* 5s. Geo. Sutton, Esq. patron.

CURATES.

1715 Robert Warton, curate.
1730 John Hudson, nominated by Sarah Priffick.
1736 William Deason, nominated by Cotherington Priffick.
1792 Thomas Deason, nominated by George Sutton, Esq.

X

taylor and citizen of London, a native of this parifh, devifed by will, bearing date 20th September, 1634, the fum of 50*l.* to the minifter, church wardens and overfeers of the poor of Faceby, for the purchaf- ing of lands *in fee fimple*, the rents and profits of which to be laid out in bread, and diftributed weekly among twelve poor people inhabit- ing within the faid parifh, to be elected by the faid feoffees; that is to fay, to every one of the faid twelve poor people, *one penny loaf* upon every Sunday or Sabbath day for ever. The overplus (if any) arifing from the yearly rent of the faid lands to be given and parted between the minifter, church-wardens, and parifh-clarke of the faid parifh for their trouble in diftributing the faid bread weekly for ever.

As we have not been favoured with the neceffary documents from the parifh regifters, we are unable to ftate the probable increafe or de- creafe of the inhabitants: from the nature of the property, however, within the parifh, and the total abfence of manufacturers, we are in- duced to confider the number to be nearly ftationary.

From the enumeration of inhabitants, taken in the year 1801, un- der the population act, ‡ it appears that there were then 26 houfes, 30 families, and 127 inhabitants, which gives upon an average, $4\frac{7}{30}$ to each family.

‡ STATE of population, taken 10th March, 1801.

Inha- bited houfes.	Fami- lies.	Uninha- bited houfes.	Males.	Females.	Total.	Agri- cul- ture.	Trade, &c.	Refi- due.	Total.
26	30	3	54	73	127	21	7	99	127

THE PARISH OF CARLETON,

Was probably fo named, as being when firft inhabited, *villa ruftica*, a town of hufbandmen; and therefore called *Carle's Town*.

The parifh is about three miles in extent from north to fouth, and two miles broad; and adjoins to Stokefley on the eaft, Faceby on the weft, Rudby on the north, and to Bilfdale on the fouth.

It appears from Domefday-book, that Carleton, in the Conqueror's time, contained eight carucates of land, *(ad geldum)* within the foke or liberty of the manor of Seamer, which was held, at the time of the furvey, by Robert, Earl of Mortain, in Normandy; but which had been before in the poffeffion of Gofpatric, Earl of Northumberland; and, from the expreffion in the furvey *(wafta funt)* we are led to conclude, was deftroyed, when the Conqueror, enraged at the rebellion againft him, laid wafte the country between York and Durham.

We have no clear evidence to prove at what period Carleton was firft granted out as a manor; it was anciently in the poffeffion of the Meinills, Lords of Whorlton, on which it was dependent; Nicholas de Meinill died feized thereof (15. Edw. II.) and left it with his other eftates to John his fon and heir; whofe fon and grandfon of the fame name dying in his father's life-time, moft of his eftates defcended to Alice, his grand-daughter, then the wife of John de Boulton; but this, with fome others, it feems was entailed on the heir-male; for we find, that Nicholas, fon of Nicholas, the brother of the faid John, died feized thereof (16. Edw. III.), from whom it defcended by marriage to the Darcies; and from them to the Strangwayes. We afterwards find it

X 2

in the poffeffion of the Nevilles, of Raby; in whofe defcendants it continued till the attainder of John Neville, Marquis of Montague, when it was granted, by fpecial act of Parliament, to Richard, Duke of Gloucefter. Who the fucceeding proprietors were, we are not informed; in the reign of James I. it was granted to Charles Bruce, of Kinlos, anceftor to the Earls of Aylefbury; from whom it came by purchafe to the Priflicks, and was carried by marriage with the coheirefs of that family, to the late John Healey, Efq. The lands here, which are freehold, had been granted, and cantoned out in parcels at an early period, and are now in the hands of different proprietors.

THE village of Carleton is pleafantly fituated, at the foot of a confiderable eminence, about three miles from the market town of Stokefley, and ten from Yarm; and at a fhort diftance towards the foutheaft, from the main road leading between Stokefley and Thirfk. The houfes are fcattered irregularly on the banks of a fmall mountain rivulet, that runs through the village towards the north, and empties itfelf into the Leven between Rudby and Stokefley.

THE manfion houfe of the lord of the manor ftands on the weft, and is built of freeftone, with good gardens, and convenient offices; forming a neat and defirable country refidence for a genteel family.

AT a little diftance from the village, towards the fouth, there is an extenfive mountainous common; on the elevated fummit of which, a large allum work was for fometime fuccefsfully carried on by the lord of the manor; but on the difcovery of this mineral in the parts of Cleveland more contiguous to the fea, and more advantageoufly fituated for exportation, the works were difcontinued. The excavation in the allum-rock is very extenfive; and, when viewed from its fummit, prefents a fpectacle at once awful, magnificent, and interefting. Petrified fhells of the *bivalve* kind, and other marine productions, are found in great abundance, in the allum-rocks here, and in different parts of the diftrict; which we fhall have occafion to notice in the further progrefs of this work: it will be fufficient at prefent, to remark that the ſtrata, in which theſe petrifactions of marine animals are thus found, atteſt beyond contradiction, the revolutions, which the ſurface of this globe muſt have experienced; and ſuggeſt the probability, that the ſea muſt once have covered thoſe regions, (however elevated) which are now dry land, and which have been in this ſtate, as long as hiſtory affords any record.

THE church of Carleton is a ſmall modern-built ſtructure, and ſtands in a retired ſituation, adjoining upon the farm-yard of the man-ſion houſe, towards the weſt.

IT was. probably, on its firſt foundation, endowed with rectorial rights; but being given to the monaſtry at Whitby to which it was made appropriate, it was reduced at the diſſolution, to a perpetual curacy; which was certified to the governours of Queen Anne's bounty at 7l. 7s. 4d. It has received ſeveral augmentations. * The rectorial rights have been long in the poſſeſſion of the lord of the manor; who has alſo the right of nomination to the curacy.

WITH regard to the population, and the probable increaſe or de-creaſe of the inhabitants within this, and the two preceding pariſhes, our accounts, for the reaſon already mentioned, muſt be greatly defec-tive. In the year 1801, a return was made to government, according to act of Parliament; † when there were then 66 houſes or families, and 275 inhabitants, giving upon an average, 4⅙ to each family; and as theſe are chiefly occupied in huſbandry, except a few within the

---

* CARLETON is not noticed in *Torr's MSS.*; but in Archbiſhop Sharpe's it is called a chapel un-der Rudby; on which, however, we conceive it has at preſent, no dependence. The Rev. Thomas Deaſon is the preſent incumbent.

† STATE of population, taken 10th March, 1801.

Inha-bited houſes.	Fami-lies.	Uninha-bited houſes.	Males.	Females.	Total.	Agri-cul-ture.	Trade.	Reſi-due.	Total.
66	66	3	127	148	275	59	28	188	275

village who are employed in the manufacture of coarse linens for sale, no very material increase since that period can be expected.

THE inclosed lands ‡ within the parish incline gently towards the north; and being chiefly of a gravelly loam, are in general fertile, and yield abundant crops of corn and grass, with some turnips, and potatoes of an excellent quality. The fields are well fenced, and divided with quickset-hedges in a thriving condition; and, though there are no plantations of any considerable extent, yet the general practice of rearing trees near the houses, and in hedge-rows, contributes to give the country a rich and pleasing appearance.

---

‡ THE uninclosed common contains about 1000 acres, and belongs to the several freeholders within the parish.

THE PARISH OF RUDBY.

FROM Carleton we proceed northwards to Rudby; the etymology of which is probably from the Saxon word Rod, a crofs; and *by* or *bya;* which laft, although in its general acceptation, it fignifies *to live,* frequently denotes merely *juxta* pofition, and is fynonymous with the prepofition *nigh,* or *near;* hence the name of Rudby fignifies merely a place near a crofs, which we may conclude formerly ftood here; " it being cuftomary, on the eftablifhment of chriftianity in this ifland, " and before the foundation of churches became common, to erect " croffes in places of public concourfe, to remind the people of the be- " nefits vouchfafed to them by the crofs of Chrift."

THE parifh of Rudby, including its two dependent chapelries, is in its greateft extent from eaft to weft about feven miles, and nearly five miles broad; and is bounded by the parifhes of Seamer, Stokefley, Carleton, and Faceby on the eaft; by Weft-Rounton, Crathorne, and Kirklevington on the weft; by Hilton and Seamer on the north; and by Whorlton and the river Wifk, dividing it from Eaft-Harlefey on the fouth. Befides fome fcattered farm-holds, it contains the following divifions called townfhips: viz. Rudby, Hutton *juxta* Rudby, Sex-how, Skutterfkelfe, Eaft-Rounton, and Middleton.

THE townfhip of RUDBY, which gives name to the parifh, and in which the parifh church ftands, is fituated on the northern bank of the river Leven, and nearly in the centre of the parifh. The village, about four miles from the market town of Stokefley, and fix from

Yarm, is at prefent fmall, confifting of about a dozen inhabited houfes; but, from the numerous foundations of buildings ftill vifible in the grounds adjoining on the weft, we are induced to conclude, that it was anciently a place of much greater extent and importance.

From Domefday-book, it appears, that at the time of the furvey the lands here were within the foke of Hutton; but the number of carucates is not particularly mentioned. It was foon after granted out as an independent manor to the Meinells, lords of Whorlton; from whom it defcended by marriage to the Darcies, and from them to the Conyers. In the reign of James I. it was fold to Sir Arthur Ingram, of Temple-Newfom; from whom it came by marriage, with the heirefs of that family, to the late Honourable General Cary, brother to Lord Vifcount Falkland; whofe only furviving daughter, the Right Hon. Elizabeth, Lady Amherft, relict of Field Marfhall Jeffery, Lord Amherft, late commander in chief of the Britifh forces, is now the fole proprietor.

INGRAM, of TEMPLE-NEWSOM.

Arms.—*Ermine*, on a fefs, *gules*, three efcallop-fhells, *or*.

Hugh Ingram, a merchant in London, died 1612.—Anne, daughter of . . . .

Sir Arthur Ingram, of Temple-Newfom. in county York, Knt.—Catherine, 2d daughter of Thomas, Lord Fairfax Vifcount Emuly.

Sir Wm. Ingram, of the city of York, Knt. doctor of the civil law. ob. 1623.—Catherine, dau. of John Edmonds, of Cambridge, Efq.

From the above Sir William defcended the Ingrams of *Cattall*, and *Thorp*.

Arthur Ingram, Efq. 3d fon. purchafed the manor of Barrowby, of Mr. Layton.—He—Jane, dau. of Sir John Mallory, of Studley, Knt.

Thomas, ob. 1703.—Frances, dau. and heir of Dr. John Nicholfon, late of York.

Arthur Ingram, of Barrowby, Efq. heir to his nephew.—Elizabeth, dau. of . . . . . Barns, Efq.

1. Mary.
2. Catherine.
3. Elizabet.

Arthur, ob. 1708.*

Frances.

Thomas, a pofthumous fon, died an infant.

Ifabella, only dau. and heir, died 1799, aged 81. Buried at Rudby.—The Hon. General Cary, bro. to Lord Vis. Falkland, died 1792, aged 81. Buried at Rudby.

Elizabeth, living 1805.—Jeffery, Lord Amherft. ob. S. P.

Catherine, died 178—.—Sir John Ruffell, of Checkers, Bart. ob. 1783.

* This Arthur dying young, the eftates went to Arthur, his uncle; who left a fole daughter and heir.

1. Sir John Ruffell, of Checkers, Bart. died unmarried, 1802.

2. Sir G. Ruffell, of Leven-Grove, Bart. died unmarried, 1804.

THE church of Rudby is dedicated to All-Saints; and was an ancient rectory in the patronage of the Lords Meinells, of Whorlton-Castle. According to the charters printed in Dugdale, it was given by Robert de Meinell, to the priory of Guisbrough, for that house to place canons of their own order at Scarthe, a religious house founded by Stephen, his ancestor; but the grant, we conclude, never took effect; for it continued a rectory under the patronage of the Meinells and their descendants, till the reign of Henry VIII. when it was given to the Dean and College of Thomas Wolsey, in the university of Oxford; to which it was, as it seems, appropriated, and a vicarage ordained out of it, valued in the

RUDBY VICARAGE.

DEDICATED to All-Saints. The Right Hon. Dowager Lady Amherst, patron. First-fruits 30*l.* Tenths 3*l.* Procur. 7s. 6d. Syn. 1*l.* 4*s.*

RECTORS.—1229. Walter de Kirkham, *pr. Steph. de Menill.* 1230. Dominus John de Bruyell, cl. *idem.* 1235. Ranulf, Fitz-Ranulf, cl. *idem.* ——. Thos. de Werlington. 1329. William de Boulton, *pr. Nich. de Meinill, miles.* 1336. John de Wodehouse, *idem.* 1355. Thomas de Burton, *pr. John Darcy, miles.* 1366. Robert de Malolacu, cl. *pr. Peter de Malolacu, or Mauley.* 1369. Henry de Wakefield, * pbr. *pr. Will. Lord Latimer.* 1375. Rob. de Crull, cl. *pr. Philip Darcy, miles.* 1377. Rob. de Wycliff, † *idem.* 1423. John Castell, pbr. *pr. Henry, Archbishop of Canterbury, ut custos duar. filiar. Domini P. Darcy.* 1456. Christ. Conyers, cap. *pr. J. Conyers.* 1483. Cuthbert Lightfoot, cap. *idem.* 1498. Cuthbert Place, cl. *pr. Wm. Conyers, miles.* 1513. Cuthbert Conyers, dec. *idem.*

VICARS.—1529. William Mountford, pbr. *pr. Dec. & Coll. Xt. Ch. Oxford.* ——. George Conyers. 1582. William Lawson, cl. *pr. John Ingleby, Armiger.* 1617. Robert Clay, cl. S. T. P. unus cap. regis. *pr. King James.* ——. William Lawson, cl. *p. m. Cloye.* 1636. Henry Ogle, A. M *p. m. Lawson; pr. Sir Arthur Ingram.* 1679. Joseph Cragg, *pr. Lady Frances Ingram.* 1700. Michael Lythe, *pr. Arthur Ingram, Esq.* 1735. Geo. Stainthorpe, *pr. John Lumley, of Dalby, Gent.* 1767. Donald Grant, *pr. Hon. Gen. Cary; p. m. Stainthorpe.* 1774. Francis Blackburne, A. M. *idem. p. res. Grant.* 1781. Jeremiah Grice, A. M. *pr. Hon. Gen. Cary; p. res. Blackburne.*

* HE was consecrated the 57 Bishop of Worcester, and appointed Lord Treasurer in the year 1373.

† HE was temporal chancellor to the Bishop of Durham in 1390, and occurs again in 1391, and all the time of Bishop Skirlaw's life; he was appointed master of Kepier-Hospital; was temporal chancellor, constable of the castle, and receiver general; also one of Bishop Skirlaw's executors; and died at Kepier, 1423.

King's books, at 30*l. per ann.* Lady Amherſt is the preſent patron and impropriator, and pays to the vicar a yearly ſtipend of 40*l.* which is the real value of the vicarage.

THE church, which ſtands cloſe to the northern bank of the Leven, is neat and commodious, having undergone ſome modern repairs; †
and conſiſts of a nave and chancel, with a ſquare tower placed at the ſide, through which, under a pointed arch, is the door or principal en-

---

† By an ancient cuſtom, the expences and diſburſements occaſioned by the repairs of the church are collected and levied out of the different townſhips within the pariſh, which are rated proportion-ably according to the following ancient annual rentals: viz. *Hutton* 576*l.*; *Rudby* 288*l.*; *Eaſt-Roun-ton* 224*l.*; *Sexhow* 216*l.*; *Middleton* 192*l.*; *Hilton* 192*l.*; *Braworth* 80*l.*; *Skutterſkelfe* 72*l.*

MONUMENTAL INSCRIPTIONS.

IN the ſouth wall of the chancel, on a circular tablet of white marble, with the arms of Cary: (viz. *argent on a bend ſable,* 3 *roſes of the field*; *in chief a creſcent for difference*; with an ineſcutcheon bearing *ermine on a feſt, gules, three eſcallop ſhells, or*; the arms of Ingram,) is the following inſcrip-tion.

HERE
LIES THE BODY OF
THE HON^{ble.} GEORGE CARY,
SON OF LUCIUS HENRY
VISCOUNT FALKLAND,
GENERAL OF HIS
BRITTANNIC MAJESTY'S FORCES,
AND COLONEL OF THE 43^d
REGIMENT OF INFANTRY.
HE DIED APRIL 11th, 1792, AGED 81,
AFTER HAVING SERVED HIS COUNTRY
MANY YEARS,
WITH COURAGE, FIDELITY, AND HONOUR.
HE WAS IN PRIVATE LIFE AN HONEST
AND CHARITABLE MAN
AND A GENEROUS FRIEND.
HIS AFFLICTED WIDOW,
ISABELLA,
DAUGHTER OF ARTHUR INGRAM,
OF BARROWBY, ESQ.
INSCRIBES THIS TRIBUTE
TO HIS MEMORY.

trance. In a window that lights the nave from the eaft, there is a fhield in painted glafs, bearing quarterly the arms of *Conyers, Darcy,* and *Meinell;* beneath which in an arch, or niche in the wall within the church, is an effigy of an ecclefiaftic cut in ftone, probably the monument of Cuthbert Conyers, who was Archdeacon of Carlifle, and the laft rector of this parifh; and as appears from Torr's MSS. " *was buried in the high-kirke of All-Hallows, in Rudby, before the high altar.*"

ADJOINING to the church yard on the weft, there is a fchool-houfe, which was erected about the year 1740, at the expence of Charles Bathurft, Efq. and the principal inhabitants, upon a parcel of ground de-

---

NEAR to the above, in the fouth wall of the chancel, upon a monument of white marble, is the following infcription:

NEAR THIS MARBLE IS LAID WHAT
REMAINS ON EARTH OF ISABELLA CARY:
A WOMAN MEEKLY WISE & INNOCENTLY
CHEARFUL: WHOSE CHARITY WAS THE REFUGE OF
THE POOR: WHOSE BENIGNITY WAS THE DELIGHT
OF THE GOOD: WHOSE ATTACHMENT THROUGH THE LONG
PERIOD OF THEIR UNION WAS THE HAPPINESS OF HER
HUSBAND: WHOSE TENDERNESS TO HER CHILDREN CEASED
ONLY WITH THEIR LIFE, OR HER OWN: IN EVERY VICISSITUDE, IN
YOUTH, IN AGE, AND IN THE LAST AWFUL CHANGE
THE GOSPEL WAS HER STAY AND SUPPORT.
HER DEATH WAS LIKE HER LIFE, CALM AND SERENE; SUDDEN, YET
NOT UNEXPECTED; AFTER MANY INFLICTIONS OF PAIN FROM A
CHRONICAL DISEASE, IN ITS LAST ACCESS THIS GOOD AND PIOUS
WOMAN CLOSED HER EYES, AND FELL A SLEEP IN DEATH.
SHE WAS THE DAUGHTER AND HEIRESS OF ARTHUR
INGRAM, ESQ. OF BARRABY, IN THE COUNTY OF YORK,
AND HIS WIFE ELIZABETH BARNS:
SHE WAS MARRIED TO THE HONOURABLE
GEORGE CARY, THIRD SON OF LUCIUS HENRY
VISCOUNT FALKLAND;
SHE DIED ON
THE 12th DAY OF APRIL 1799,
AGED 81 YEARS.

Y 2

mifed to them for that purpofe, by the deed of Arthur Ingram, of Barrowby, Efq. for the term of 999 years, at the yearly rent of *two pence* if demanded.

On the erection of the fchool-houfe, in order to carry the laudable intention of the original founder into effect, it was endowed by Charles Bathurft, Efq. of Skutterfkelf; ‡ who, for the purpofe of eftablifhing a fchool-mafter for the inftruction and education of the children of poor perfons within the parifh, gave by deed, dated March 13th, 1740, a rent-charge of 10l. *per annum*, payable out of his lands at Skutterfkelf; and alfo a donation of 100l. to be paid within fix months next after his deceafe (1743) to the grantees by deed appointed, *in truft*, that the faid fum of 100l. fhould be by them laid out in lands, or put out to intereft; the rent or intereft of which, together with the faid rent-charge of 10l. *per annum*, to be paid to the fchool-mafter for the time being, who fhould be duly nominated by the faid grantees, and licenfed by the Archbifhop of York. It is greatly to be regretted, that for the want of regularly appointed truftees, a part of the original endowment is likely to be irrecoverably loft.

From Rudby, over a ftone bridge of two arches, we entered the village and townfhip of Hutton; or, as it is called emphatically, and by way of diftinction, Hutton-Rudby, or Hutton *juxta* Rudby. The vil-

---

‡ To record the merits, and at the same time difcharge the office of panegyric, we fhall tranfcribe the following lines, which we found written on a blank leaf of an early edition of Ainfworth's Dictionary, belonging to this fchool.

Ex Dono

Caroli Bathurft, armigeri illuftriffimi,

Scholæ Hutton-Rudby;

Quam ipfe prius erexerat, (bonis quibufdam adjutus)

Et largo ftipendio donaverat;

Literarum bonarum amans, literatus ipfe

Boni ftudiofus publici, fui fecurus,

Doctis honoratiffimus, omnibus amabilis,

Et per omne Ævum memorandus.

lage is advantageously fituated on the elevated bank of the river Leven, which rifes abruptly, and nearly perpendicular from the water's edge; and was probably fo named, as being originally *a town of huts*, or inferior dwellings; Rudby, at that period, being the principal place of refidence within the parifh. The houfes, fome of which are neat and modern, form a wide and irregular ftreet of confiderable extent, occupied chiefly by weavers, employed in the manufacture of linen cloth, and other mechanics.

HUTTON, the principal and moft extenfive divifion within the parifh, was an ancient manor; of which we find the following mention in Domefday, under the title

" **Terra Comitis Moretonienfis**.

" **In Hotun ad geldum VI. carucatae, et III. car. poffunt effe. Ibi**
" **habuit Gofpatric I. manerium. Uunc habet Robertus Comes. Ibi**
" **eft aecclefia et presbiter. Tot. manerium I. leuca et dim. longum,**
" **et I. leuca latum. T. R. E. bal. XXIII. lib. modo XXVI. fol. et**
" **VIII denar.**".

" **Ad Hotun jacet foca haec. Rodebi, Codrefchef, Blatun, Wiruel-**
" **tune, Gouton, Gratorn. Inter omnes XX. carucatae ad geldum, et**
" **XII. car. poffunt effe. Omnes funt waftae, excepto Wirueltune, in**
" **qua funt XX. billani cum VIII. car.**"   *Domefday-book.*

FROM the above extract we learn that this manor was firft held by Gofpatric, Earl of Northumberland; but, on his rebellion againft the Conqueror, was forfeited, and afterwards given to Robert, Earl of Mortain. It contained fix carucates, befides land fufficient for three ploughs, with a church and minifter. The whole manor was one mile and a half in length, and half a mile broad; and in the time of the Confeffor was worth 24*l.* but in the Conqueror's time, valued only at twenty-fix fhillings and eight-pence. From the fame record it appears, that to this manor there was a foke or liberty within the following places, viz. Rudby, Skutterfkelf, *Blatun*, Whorlton, Goulton, and Crathorne, making in the whole twenty carucates *ad geldum*, and twelve more that

might be rendered arable; all of which had been laid waste by the Conqueror, except Whorlton, where there were twenty villeins, who had
eight ploughs.

THE manor of Hutton became, at an early period the property of
the Meinells; who, in the reign of Edward I. held this, and other estates,
of the Archbishop of Canterbury, by military service. Nicholas de
Meinell, having obtained a charter of free-warren in all his demesne
lands, died seized of this lordship 16. Edw. III. and left it to Elizabeth,
his only daughter and heir; by whom this and other large possessions
descended by marriage, to the Darcies, and afterwards to the Conyers.
We have met with no evidence that points out the succeeding proprietors of this manor. The lands have been long granted out into tenan-
cies, and are in the possession of different freeholders.

THE manor, with a small estate, is now the property of Thomas
Wayne, of Ann-Grove-Hall, Esq. whose ancestor purchased of the Turners of Kirkleatham.

THE township of SEXHOW, or, as it is sometimes written, SAXHOE,
(q. d. *Collis saxosus,*) lies to the south-east; and is of a small extent,
consisting only of six farm-houses and 44 inhabitants. We have no
account of Sexhow in Domesday-book, nor have we met with any record touching the lands here, of an earlier date, than the reign of Edw.
I. when by an inquisition, taken in the 7th year of that King's reign, it
was found that Peter de Brus held this and other estates of the King *in
capite;* on whose death, partition being made of his lands, Sexhow came
to his sister Margaret, the wife of Robert de Roos; and after his death,
by the gift of the said Margaret, to Marmaduke de Thweng; of whom,
according to Kirkby's Inquest, Richard Gower held the lands here; for
which he paid to the fine of the Wapontake the sum of four shillings
and eight-pence. From the Gowers, (ancestors to the Gowers of Stitnam,) Sexow descended by marriage in the reign of Richard II. to the
Laytons, of East-Layton, whose descendants continued resident here for
several generations; and from whom the manor and estate came by

purchafe, in the year 1717, to the family of Foulis, of Ingleby-Manor; and are now the property of Sir William Foulis, the prefent Baronet, who is a minor.

The manor-houfe, which was the ancient refidence of the Laytons, ftands on the fouthern bank of the Leven, and ftill bears evident marks of antiquity, notwithftanding the alterations which have been made, in order to render it more commodious as a farm-houfe.

LAYTONS of SEXHOWE.

Extracted from the Herald's office, by *Wm. Radclyffe, rouge croix, pourfurvant.*

Arms; Entered at the Herald's office, c. 13. fol. 135.
Quarterly of four.
1. Arg. a fefs between fix crofs-crofslets, fable.
2. Arg. on a chief, fable, 3 griffin heads erafed of the firft.
3. Azure, a cheveron, between 3 talbot dogs paffant arg.
4. As the firft.
No creft.

Thomas Laton, miles, had — Matildis, land &c. in Eaft-Laton.

Robertus Laton, miles — Johanna, vixit 43. *Edw. III.* vixit 43. *Edw. III.*

John Laton, — Elena.

John Laton, — H . . . . .

Robertus Laton, —

Elizabeth, uxor, Henrici Pudfey.

Thomas Layton, — Elizabeth, filia, of Sexhowe, ... Gower, de Rich. II. et 9. Sexhowe; 9. *Hen. VI.* *Hen. VI.*

Robert Layton, —

John Layton — . . . . ., dau. and heir of Henry Newfam.

John Layton, of Sex- — how, Efq. *vixit* 37. *Hen. VI.*

Robert Layton, 2d fon.

John Layton, ob. S. P.

William, *ob.* — Margery, dau. of 6. *Hen. VIII.* Thos. Montfort.

John Layton, — . . . ., filia Doddefworth de Watlons.

Robert Layton, of — Eleanora. Melfonby, Efq. *vixit* 37. *Hen. VI.*

John Layton, de Siddal, ob. S. P

Chriftopher, ob. S. P.

George, ob. S. P.

Henry, ob. S. P.

Anna, filia Roberti — Thomas Layton, eldeft fon — Margaret, filia Richardi Mauleverer; 2d *uxor.* and heir, 37. *Hen. VI.* Clervaux. 1. *Uxor.*

Lancelot — Anna, filia Radi. Layton, Bulmer, militis

Gawinus Layton, 2d fon.

Anna, uxor Edw. Warcup.

Robert Layton, of — Ann, dau. of Ralph Sexhowe, Efq. Rookeby, of Marfk.

THE townſhip of SKUTTERSKELF lies on the northern bank of
the Leven, and adjoins to Rudby on the eaſt.   The manor, according
to Domeſday-book, contained two bovates of land *(ad geldum)*, at that
time demeſne of the crown ; entered under the title

" 𝕿erra 𝕽egis.

" 𝕸anerium in 𝕲odreſchelf. 𝕮amel II. bob. terrae ad geldum."

THERE were alſo lands here within the ſoke of Hutton ; and two
carucates and two oxgangs within the ſoke of Stokeſley.

THORALDBY, another ſmall manor within this townſhip, lies to
the eaſt : it was alſo ancient demeſne of the crown ; and at the time of
the ſurvey, contained one carucate *(ad geldum)*, beſides half a ploughland valued at ſixteen pence.

" 𝕸anerium in 𝕮oroldesbi. 𝕬rchel I. car. ad geldum. 𝕿erra ad
" dim. car. XVI[d.]"

IT appears from Kirkby's Inqueſt, that the lands here in demeſne,
and thoſe at Skutterſkelf within the ſoke of Hutton, were held of the
Meinells, Lords of Whorlton; thoſe within the ſoke or liberty of Stokeſley, were held under the Baliols, Lords of Stokeſley, by *Robert de Skutterſkelfe ;* who paid as a fine to the King's bailiff, the ſum of two ſhillings.

Thomas Layton, of Sexhowe,⎯Muriel, dau. and coheir of Thos.
Eſq. *ob.* 27. *Hen. VIII.* | Linley, of Skutterſkelf.

Thomas Layton, of Sexhowe,⎯Elizabeth, dau. of Sir James
Eſq. *ob.* 26. *Eliz.* | Metcalfe, of Nappa, Knight.

Ann, dau. of Chriſt.⎯Charles Layton, of⎯Maria, only dau. and   Thos. Layton,⎯ . . . . ., dau. of
Preſton, of Holcar. Sexhow, Eſq. liv- | heir of T. Milner, of   Chriſt. Thwaites,
1ſt wife; ob. S. P. ing 1612. | Skutterſkelf. 2dwife.   of Marton.

3. Brian⎯Alice, dau. of J. Turner, Eſq.   2. Robert   1. Thos. Layton, ſon⎯ . . . . ., dau. of Sir
Layton, widow of Richard Seaton, of   Layton.   and heir; *Ætat.* 15. Thomas Fairfax, of
         Skinnergrove.   1612.   Walton, Knt.

J. Bird Delin.

Eng.d by R. Scott.

LEVEN GROVE

The Seat of the Rt. Hon.ble Dowager Lady Amherst.

To whom this plate is most respectfully Dedicated by

The Editor.

WHEN the eftates came afterwards to unity of poffeffion, we find the Linleys of Skutterfkelfe, owners thereof.* Thomas Linley died feized of thefe manors in the year 1530, leaving three daughters coheireffes; the eldeft of whom married Thomas Layton, of Sexhow; whofe defcendants, becoming at length fole proprietors, fold the fame in the reign of Charles II. to John Bathurft, of the city of London, doctor of phyfic. From the Bathurfts the eftate defcended by marriage to the Turners of Kirkleatham, and was fold by the late Sir Charles Turner, Bart. to the Honourable General Cary; whofe only furviving daughter, the Right Hon. the Dowager Lady Amherft, on the death of Sir George Ruffell, Bart. her nephew, became the fole proprietor. Within this townfhip about a mile to the eaft from Rudby, we approach

LEVEN-GROVE,

the feat of the Right Hon. Lady Amherft; which ftands on the northern bank of the river Leven, on rifing ground, and commands a

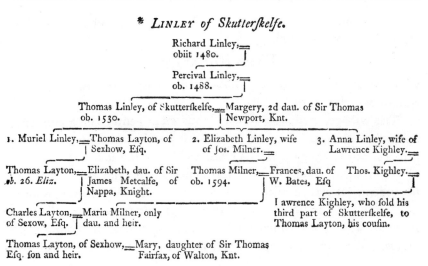

* *LINLEY of Skutterfkelfe.*

Richard Linley,
obiit 1480.

Percival Linley,
ob. 1488.

Thomas Linley, of Skutterfkelfe,—Margery, 2d dau. of Sir Thomas
ob. 1530. | Newport, Knt.

1. Muriel Linley,—Thomas Layton, of | Sexhow, Efq.

2. Elizabeth Linley, wife of Jos. Milner.

3. Anna Linley, wife of Lawrence Kighley.

Thomas Layton,—Elizabeth, dau. of Sir
ob. 26. *Eliz.* | James Metcalfe, of | Nappa, Knight.

Thomas Milner,—Frances, dau. of ob. 1594. | W. Bates, Efq

Thos. Kighley.

Lawrence Kighley, who fold his third part of Skutterfkelfe, to Thomas Layton, his coufin.

Charles Layton,—Maria Milner, only of Sexow, Efq. | dau. and heir.

Thomas Layton, of Sexhow,—Mary, daughter of Sir Thomas
Efq. fon and heir. Fairfax, of Walton, Knt.

Z

pleafing profpect over a fertile and richly cultivated country. The houfe is a modern edifice, erected by the Bathurfts, after they became owners of the eftate; but has fince received confiderable improvements from fucceeding proprietors. It is fheltered on the north and eaft by thriving plantations. The winding river gliding peacefully down its courfe, with its floping banks richly ornamented, appears immediately in front; while the verdure of fertile meadows, the fcattered trees and rich inclofures all confpire to give variety to the fcene, and im-pofe an afpect of dignified retirement on the whole. Whorl-Hill, and a range of mountains on the fouth, with the rifing grounds of Bufby, and Arnecliffe cloathed with wood, form a pleafing contraft to the cul-tivated lands, and terminate the view.

> " Say, can the pencil's warmeft touch convey
> " The varied richnefs of the glowing fcene?
> " How fweetly doth the chryftal ftream pour forth
> " Its dimpled current o'er the velvet coats
> " Of moffy pebbles;—foft the tinkling found
> " Where 'twixt the rocks it bubbles,—whilft the dove
> " Coos to her diftant mate the plaintive ftrain."

IN our tour from Appleton upon Wifk to the parifh of Arnecliffe, we paffed through the chapelry of

EAST-ROUNTON;

which we however omitted to notice, till we came to treat of this pa-rifh, of which it forms a part.

THE village, which is fmall, ftands on a gently rifing eminence upon the eaftern brink of the river Wifk, and commands a pleafing profpect of the hanging woods of Arnecliffe on the fouth.

THIS was an ancient chapelry under Rudby, on which it is ftill dependent. It was certified to the governours of Queen Anne's bounty at 5l. 2s.; and has fince received three augmentations by lot, laid out in lands, which, with other dues, produce an income of about 35l. *per annum.* The rectorial rights here, and thofe within the townfhip of

Hutton-Rudby, are now in the poffeffion of Meffrs. Drinkrow and Kendal, who purchafed the fame of Lady Amherft, and the late Sir John Ruffell, Bart.

Of the manor of Rounton we find the following mention in Domef-day-book, under the title

" Terra Regis.

" Manerium in Rantune Tor et Carle VIII. car. ad geldum. Terra
" ad IIII. car. XL. fol."

From which it appears that, at the time of the furvey, it was de-mefne of the crown ; but before the conqueft, was held by *Tor* and *Carle* ; and contained eight carucates, *ad geldum*, befides arable land fufficient for four ploughs, valued at forty fhillings.

We have no documents to fhew how long the manor remained in the crown : it was probably firft granted out to the Meinells, Lords of Whorlton. In the reign of Edward I. according to Kirkby's Inqueft, Nicholas de Meinell held this and other eftates of the fee of Canter-bury, by military fervice ; and his defcendants continued in poffeffion for feveral generations. It would be uninterefting to the reader to trace out the fucceffion of proprietors of the lands here ; which have been long held in parcels, and are now in the poffeffion of different freeholders.

The townfhip, or chapelry of

MIDDLETON

lies on the northern extremity of the parifh ; and is fometimes, for the fake of diftinction, called Middleton *fuper* Leven, from its fituation on the banks of that river.

The lands here, in the Conqueror's time, were within the foke of Seamer, held by Robert, Earl of Mortain ; and confifted of eight caru-cates, *ad geldum*, with three villeins who had three ploughs. The Meinells, foon after the conqueft, were Lords here, from whom the eftate defcended by marriage to the Darcies, and afterwards to the

Conyers ; but of the fucceeding proprietors we are uninformed. The manor and a confiderable eftate within the townfhip are now the property of the Earl of Egremont.

MIDDLETON is a chapelry under the church of Rudby. The chapel, dedicated to Saint Cuthbert, is a fmall modern built edifice, and ftands on the eaftern bank of the river Leven ; the revenues of which were certified to the governours of Queen Anne's bounty at 4*l.* 9s. 8d. † It has fince received three allotments, by which lands have been purchafed to increafe the income to about 40*l. per ann.* The rectorial rights in this, and the two adjoining townfhips of Skutter-fkelfe and Rudby, are the property of Lady Amherft.

AFTER this detailed account of the feveral townfhips within the parifh, we fhall proceed to fome notice of the population and probable number of inhabitants ; which will be found to be confiderable, owing chiefly to the introduction of manufactures, there being upwards of 120 linen weavers within the villages of Rudby and Hutton ; befides

---

† THE vicar of Rudby, who is alfo curate of its two dependent chapelries, is entitled to the tithe of geefe, &c. within this chapelry ; and befides an ancient cuftomary payment of 3*l. per ann.* paid by the impropriator, the curate receives the following compofition, due annually at Michaelmas, from the inhabitants : viz.

> For each houfe *four pence* ; and *three pence* in the pound from
>   every fervant out of their refpective wages.
> For every oxgang of land, *two pence.*
> For every orchard, *fix pence.*
> For lands, called Priffick's Garths, *one fhilling* and *eight pence.*
> For ditto, called Rofe's Garth, *feven pence.*
> For every other Garth, each *four pence.*
> For every cow's milk, *one half-penny.*
> For every calf, (under five), *one penny.*
> For every fwarm of bees, *one penny.*
> For each foal, *one penny.*
> For every plough, *one penny.*

WE acknowledge our obligations to the *Rev. Jeremiah Grice,* M. A. for much information relative to this parifh.

a paper-mill at Hutton, and a confiderable water corn-mill at Rudby, which, with the bleach-grounds at Middleton, employ between twenty and thirty hands.

THE following extract from the return made to government under the act of the 41. George III. will fuggeft to us an idea of its prefent ftate of population.

	Inha-bited houfes.	Fami-lies.	Uninhabited houfes	Males.	Females.	Total.	Agri-cul-ture.	Trade.	Refi-due.	Total.
Rudby - - -	13	15		42	38	80	13	17	50	80
Hutton - - -	161	161		359	348	707	97	169	441	707
Sexhow - - -	6	6		21	23	44	15	1	28	44
Skutterfkelfe	6	6		21	21	42	14	0	28	42
Eaft-Rounton	20	20		53	56	109	35	3	71	109
Middleton - -	20	20	3	61	49	110	28	11	71	110
	226	228	3	557	535	1092	202	201	689	1092

FROM the above table it will appear that there are 226 houfes, 228 families, and 1092 inhabitants, giving an average of $4\frac{1}{2}$ nearly to each houfe. The number of males and females within the parifh is nearly equal; as is alfo the number of perfons employed in trade or manu-factures, to that of thofe occupied in the different branches of agricul-ture.

IT further appears from the parifh regifter, which begins in the year 1584, that from the year 1781, to the year 1800 inclufive, there have been 602 baptifms, 375 burials, and 169 marriages; ‡ which, on comparing the number of baptifms with that of burials, ftrongly in-dicates that the population of the parifh muft be confiderably on the increafe. The average number of baptifms, in one year, is about 30, and of burials 18; which fhews, that to every 36 of the inhabitants a child is born; and that, from the population of the whole parifh, one only out of $60\frac{3}{4}$ dies annually.

‡ IN the above ftatement of the number of baptifms, &c. within the parifh we have included thofe within the chapelries of Middleton, and Eaft-Rounton; where entries of baptifms and marriages (but not of burials) are regularly kept. The inhabitants of thefe chapelries bury at the parifh church of Rudby.

In our obſervations on the ſoil, produce, and general appearance of the pariſh, we may remark, that there are no common, or uncloſed lands, which is a circumſtance of ſome advantage and conſequence to huſbandry. The ſoil is chiefly a ſtrong, but fertile clay, with ſome deep ſandy loam upon the banks of the Leven, generally laid down to graſs. About one half of the land is in tillage; and the mode of management is equal, if not ſuperior to that in moſt of the adjoining pariſhes. Wheat, oats, and beans are the crops moſt ſuccefsfully cultivated; § with ſome ſmall patches of turnips, and an occaſional field of rape; which, when ſown upon *maiden ſward*, pared and burnt, is generally found a very profitable crop. The lands are nearly level, with the exception of ſome gently ſwelling ridges, which have a pleaſing effect on the general aſpect of the country. The banks of the river Leven, which winds in a ſerpentine courſe nearly through the centre of the pariſh, in ſome parts riſe abruptly to a conſiderable height, and where cloathed with wood, have a pleaſing and picturefque appearance. ‖

§ We have been favoured with the following ſtatement of the number of acres, reaped in the townſhips of Hutton, Sexhowe, Skutterſkelfe, and Rudby, in the year 1801: viz.

Wheat - - 557¼ acres.	Peaſe - - 38 acres.
Barley - - 10 ditto.	Beans - - 78¼ ditto.
Oats - - - 412 ditto.	Turnips - 48 ditto.
Potatoes - 8 ditto.	Rape - - 15¼ ditto.

‖ To the poor of this pariſh, who are numerous, and ſupported at a proportionably greater expence, than in moſt of the adjoining pariſhes, owing probably to the introduction of manufactures, the two following charitable donations have been made: viz.

JOHN BATHURST, of the city of London, M. D. gave by will, dated the 23d day of April, 1659, an annuity or yearly rent charge of *twenty ſhillings*, out of his manors and eſtates of *Skutter-ſkelfe*, *Thoraldby*, and *Braworth*, to be paid on the 20th day of December yearly, at the pariſh church of Hutton-Rudby, to the church-wardens and overſeers of the poor for the time being for the uſe and benefit of the poor of the ſaid pariſh.

DAVID SIMPSON, late of the pariſh of Rudby, gave by will, bearing date 1783, the ſum of *twenty ſhillings*, being a yearly rent charge upon an eſtate called *Tunſtall-Ground*, ſituated in the townſhip of Hutton, to be diſtributed to the widows within the ſaid townſhip, yearly, on Saint-Thomas-day, at the diſcretion of his grandſon, Benjamin David Sugget; and after his deceaſe by the overſeer of the poor for the ſaid townſhip.

THE PARISH OF HILTON,

L IES to the north from Rudby, about four miles from the market town of Yarm, and nearly at an equal diftance from that of Stokefley. It is bounded on the eaft by the parifh of Seamer, and on the weft by the parifh of Kirklevington, from which it is feparated by the river Leven; on the north by the parifh of Stainton, and by the chapelry of Middleton in the parifh of Rudby on the fouth. The parifh is fmall, its greateft extent from eaft to weft being about two miles, and nearly two miles broad.

T HE village, which confifts of a few farm-houfes and cottages, fcattered irregularly by the fide of the road leading between Yarm and Stokefley, is fituated on a gently rifing eminence, with a profpect to the north; and was at firft perhaps fignificantly named *Hilton*, to exprefs the peculiar circumftance of its elevated fituation; q. d. *Hill-Town; villa fuper collem.*

T HE Manor here, as appears from Domefday-book, contained three carucates of land, rated *ad geldum*, which was ancient demefne of the crown, being entered in the general furvey, under the title

" Terra Begis.

" Manerium in Hiltune. Aluer III. car. ad geldum. Terra ad I. car. et dimidium."

T HERE were alfo fix carucates of land *ad geldum*, which were then within the foke or liberty of Seamer.

H ILTON, at an early period, gave name to the refident family; in the reign of Henry III. the lordfhip and eftate were the property of

Adam de Hilton; whofe fifter and heir, marrying Hugh,* the fon of Robert de Meinell, carried them to that family; a branch of which, † as appears from the foregoing pedigree, (p. 71.) became lords, and continued refident here for many generations ‡ From the Meinells, Hilton became the property of the Morleys of Normanby; and in the reign of Charles II. was fold to the Lowthers of Marſk, and from them defcended to the Cavendiſh family. Lord John Cavendiſh is at prefent the fole proprietor, and lord of the manor.

* OMNIBUS Chrifti fidelibus hoc fcriptum vifuris vel audituris Willelmus, filius Roberti de Meinell *falutem.* Noveritis me conceffiffe Hugoni de Meinell, fratri meo et hæredi, illud toftum cum crofto in villa *de Hilton in Cliveland,* quod habui ex dimiffione Alani de Malteby illas duas bovatas terræ, in villa de Malteby, quas habui ex dimiffione ejufdem Alani. Teftibus Johanne de Malteby, Stephano de Gower et aliis. *Sine dat.*

† SCIANT prefentes et futuri, quod ego Stephanus de Roffelles dedi, &c. Johanni de Hilton de Cliveland, et Sibillæ uxori ejus, totum manerium de *Hilton in Cliveland,* &c. Homag. et fervitus liberorum hominum et nativorum, &c. fimul cum reverfione iftius terræ, quam Dominus Richard de Kirkbride, et Chriftiana uxor ejus tenent ad terminum vitæ dictæ Chriftianæ. *Data apud Hilton die veneris in craftino afcentionis Domini, A. D.* 1303. 31. *Edw. I.* Tefte Johanne de Menill, de Caftle-Levington.

‡ Hæc indentura facta inter *Robertum,* fil. Nicholai de Hilton ex una parte, et *Johannem de Cotome* capell. et *Ricardum Denam* ex parte alterâ teftatur, quod predictus Kobertus dedit, conceffit, &c. præfatis Johanni et Ricardo unum meffuagium vocatum *Prefton's place,* un mefs. in tenura Ricardi Gill, un mefs. in tenura Thomæ Nicholfon, un. mefs. in tenura Johannis Hafilden, un. mefs. in ten. Elenæ Smith, un. toftum in ten. Walteri Pacock, duas bovatas terræ in ten. Roberti Shurton, duas bov. terr. in ten Johannis Brown, fenioris, duas bov. terr. vocat. *Belmſland* et quatuor bov. terr. in ten. Roberti Prefton, quatuor bov. terr. in ten. Thomæ Nicholfon, et quatuor bovatas terr. in tenura Johannis Hafilden, cum pratis eifdem annexis et fuis pertinentiis in *Hilton in Cliveland,* tenend. &c. omnia prædict. terr. et ten. &c, præfato Johanni et Ricardo, et hæredibus fuis, &c. *fub conditione,* quod Ricardus poft matrimonium inter Thomam, fil. prædicti Roberti et Johannam, filiam prædicti Ricardi folemnizatum, de exitibus dict. terr. et tenementorum provenientibus, et de fuis propriis donis, fi neceffe fuerit, præfatum Thomam & Johannam in *victu et veftitu,* et aliis neceffariis ei incumbentibus inveniet per octo annos dictum matrimonium proximè fequentes. (*viz.*) tribus primis annis prædict. Thomam ad grammaticam erudiendum, et anno quarto ad fcholas *Oxon. vel Cantab* et quatuor aliis annis in un. quatuor. Hofpitiorum curia viz. *Lincolnſyn, Grayſya, Middle-Temple,* et *Inner-Temple,* fi prædict. Thomas ad hæc confentire voluerit; et fi prædictus Ricardus hæc ex parte fuâ non obfervaverit, quod tunc bene liceat prædict. Roberto, et hæredibus fuis in prædict. terr. &c. reintrare et ea

HILTON was anciently a chapel of eafe to Rudby; but, on being augmented by the bounty of Queen Anne, it was made parochial; and is now no otherwife dependent on, or connected with that parifh, than in contributing towards the neceffary repairs of the mother-church.

THE chapel, which is a fmall edifice, ftands in the centre of the village; and by fome neceffary modern repairs is rendered a decent and commodious place of worfhip.

IT was certified to the governours of Queen Anne's bounty at 5*l.* 9s. 4d. and has fince received three allotments, laid out in lands; which, with other dues paid to the curate, produce a falary of about 40*l. per ann.* The Rev. Alexander Beane is the prefent incumbent.

THE tithes within the parifh are the property of Lord John Cavendifh, who is alfo the patron of the chapel, and nominates the curate.

The parifh being of fmall extent, and the inhabitants chiefly occupied in agriculture, we find little worthy of particular remark, as to its ftate of population; which, however, if any conclufion can be drawn from the number of baptifms compared with that of burials within a given period, will appear to be confiderably on the increafe.

	Males.	Females.	Total.
Baptifms from 1781 to 1800 inclufive	38	43	81
Burials from ditto to ditto -	11	14	25
Increafe	27	29	56
The number of marriages within the above period -			24

ufque ad finem dictorum octo annorum retinere; et dicti Johannes et Ricardus de prædict. terr. &c. præfato Roberto et hæredibus fuis annuatim pro termino vitæ Sibillæ, quæ fuit uxor Johannis, fratris prædicti Roberti, reddent quinque marcas, &c. In cujus rei teftimonium prefens indentura partes fu-pradictæ figilla fua alternatim appofuerunt. Teftibus Willmo Paule, Thoma Blawfront et aliis. *Dat. apud Hilton,* 20. *die Aprilis, anno* 5to. *Henrici* 5ti.

A a

FROM the table, given in the notes, * being an extract from the return made to government in the year 1801, according to act of Parliament, it will be found that there were then 27 houfes, 28 families, and 136 inhabitants. On comparing the number of houfes or families with the total number of inhabitants, one half of whom are females, it will appear, that there are five nearly to each houfe. The average number of baptifms in one year for the period above ftated is $4\frac{1}{2}$, and of burials $1\frac{1}{4}$; which fhews, that the mortality is only 1 in 108; while the births are as high as 1 to 30; a circumftance that indicates a rapid increafe of population.

ALTHOUGH it will not be neceffary to detail at any length, the nature of the *foil*, *produce*, &c. which will be found greatly fimilar to thofe in the adjoining parifhes, we may neverthelefs remark, that a greater proportion of the land is in tillage; and though the foil is, in general, a ftrong gravelly clay; yet, owing to its dry, elevated fituation, the crops are heavy, and the harvefts earlier than in fome of the neighbouring diftricts.

* STATE of population, taken 10th March, 1801.

	Inhabited houfes.	Families.	Uninhabited houfes.	Males.	Females.	Total.
Hilton	27	28	0	67	69	136

THE PARISH OF SEAMER.

PROCEEDING eaftwards from Hilton, we approach the village of Seamer, about two miles diftant from the market town of Stokefley. On examining into the etymology of the name, we are led to conclude, from the compofition of the word, that the parifh was at firft named *Seamer,* from two Saxon words, fimilar in their fignification, viz. SEA, *Lacus* or *Stagnum,* and MER or MAR, an old Saxon word derived from the French *mer,* or the latin, *mare,* on account of the much ftanding water in the low fenny grounds, now called *Seamer-Carrs;* or, it may perhaps mean fimply the *mere* or lake lying to the north; it being an-ciently a cuftom, which is ftill prevalent in many of the northern counties, to defcribe the north by the term *fea,* while *fun* was as gener-ally defcriptive of the fouth. In confirmation of thefe etymological conjectures, we may remark that moft of the low meadows in this pa-rifh were once probably lakes, or covered with ftagnant water at that period, as fome of them ftill are, during the rainy feafons of the year, notwithftanding the improved ftate of agriculture in the country.

THE parifh, which comprifes the townfhip and village of Seamer, and the townfhip and part of the village of Newby, is, in its greateft extent, about four miles from eaft to weft, and upwards of three miles broad; and is bounded by the parifh of Ayton on the eaft, and by Hil-ton and the chapelry of Middleton on the weft; by Stainton on the

north; and on the fouth by the parifh of Stokefley; from which it is
feparated by the *Tame*, a fmall brook or rivulet that takes its rife on
Barnaby Moor, and winds in a flow and fluggifh courfe, over a muddy
channel, in a fouth-weft direction, till it joins the Leven, about a mile
to the weft below Stokefley.

Seamer and Tameton, a fmall Hamlet, now within the parifh of
Stokefley, were anciently comprifed in one manor; which, at the time
of the Norman conqueft, was held by Gofpatric, Earl of Northumberland, till that Earl joining in rebellion againft the Conqueror, his eftates
were forfeited, and this with others in this neighbourhood already noticed, was given to Robert, Earl of Mortain in Normandy, half brother
to the Conqueror; as appears from Domefday-book, where it is entered under the title

　　　" Terra Comitis Moritonienſis.

　" In Seamer et Cametum ad geldum XIII. carucatae, et VIII. car,
" poſſunt eſſe. Ibi habuit Gofpatric unum manerium. Nunc Ricar=
" dus de Comite. In Dominio I. carucat. et V. villani cum III. car.
" Totum manerium II. leucas longum, et dimidium latum. T. R. E.
" valebat XL. ſolid. modo XX. ſol."

　　" Ad hoc manerium pertinet ſoca haec. Hiltune VI. car. Middle=
" tun VIII. car　Foſtun III. car. Carleton VII. car. id eſt ad gel-
" dum XXV. car. et XIII. car. poſſunt eſſe. Waſta ſunt preter quod
" in Middletun ſunt III. villani cum III. car."

FROM the above record it appears, that the manor contained thirteen carucates of land taxed, or rated *(ad geldum)* of which eight might
be rendered arable; and, at the time of the furvey, was in the hands
of Richard, who held the fame of Robert Earl of Mortain; that there
was one carucate in demefne and five villeins or bondmen, who had
two ploughs; that the manor was two miles in length, and half a mile
broad, and in the confeffor's time was valued at forty fhillings, but at
the time of the furvey, only twenty.

I⊤ alfo appears that this manor had a foke or liberty within the following places : viz. Hilton, Middleton, Foxton, and Carleton, which together contained twenty-five carucates of land rated *ad geldum*; thirteen of which might be ploughed ; but that they were all laid wafte by the Conqueror, except Middleton, where there were three villeins with three ploughs.

S⸺ᴇᴀᴍᴇʀ was afterwards one of the Lordfhips belonging to the Meinills of Whorlton-Caftle.   In the ninth year of the reign of Edward I. Nicholas de Meinill procured a charter of free warren in all his demefne lands here, and died feized thereof in the 28th year of that King's reign, leaving Nicholas his fon and heir, who died 15. Edward II. and was fucceeded by his natural fon Nicholas, who, in the 2. Edward III. procured a charter of free warren ; but dying without iffue-male, his only daughter Elizabeth was found his next heir ; who by marriage with John Lord D'arcy, carried this, and other large eftates into that family ; and their defcendants continued Lords here for many generations.

T⸺ʜᴇ manor, with a confiderable eftate here, and at Newby is now the property of the Earl of Egremont; whofe anceftor, in the year 1760, purchafed of Francis, Earl of Deloraine.

B⸺ʏ an inquifition *poft mortem*, taken at Yarm, in the 43. Edward III. it was found, that Elizabeth, the daughter and heir of Nicholas de Meynill, (who furvived her hufband John Lord D'arcy,) died feized of this manor, which was held of the Archbifhop of Canterbury by military fervice; and that there were divers bond-tenants, who paid the fum of 31*l.* 1s. 11d. yearly, at the feafts of Pentecoft and St. Martin, and three fhillings, as a fine of the wapontake.   By the fame inqueft it appears that there were divers free-tenants at Newby who paid as a fine to the wapontake, the fum of two fhillings and fourpence. *

---

* Eᴛ funt apud Semer diverfi tenent. in bondag. qui reddunt per ann. XXXI^l· I^s· XI^d· ad terminos pent. et fancti Martini ; et III^s· pro finibus wap. *ad feft. div. in ramis palmarum.*

Eᴛ funt apud Newbye diverfi tenentes, qui reddunt per annum II^s· IV^d· pro fine wap. ad feft. div. prædict.   *Inq. p. m. 43. Edw. III.*

THE village of Seamer, which is small and irregularly built, stands on a dry, elevated situation, and commands a pleasing and extensive prospect of the country adjacent, which is finely diversified with cultivated fields, farm-houses and neat inclosures adorned with hedge-rows, and terminated on the south by a stretch of mountains that form a beautiful back-ground to the landscape.

THE church, dedicated to Saint Martin, stands towards the northern extremity of the village; it is a low structure apparently of remote origin, and consists of a tower, a nave, and chancel. It is called, in Ecton, a chapel under Carleton; but, according to Archbishop Sharpe's manuscript list of livings, it appears to have been formerly a chapel of ease to Rudby; from which it was probably separated about the commencement of the last century, on its being augmented by Queen Anne's bounty, when it was made parochial, and is now a perpetual curacy, the annual revenues of which were certified at 7l. 17s. It has received three allotments laid out in lands, by which the salary has been increased to about 50l. per ann. The Rev. Henry Gale is the present incumbent.

THE rectorial rights within the parish descended from the Ingrams by marriage with the heiress of that family, to the late Hon. General Cary; whose only surviving daughter, the Right Hon. Elizabeth Lady Amherst, sold them in the year 1801, to her nephew, the late Sir George Russell, Bart. who bequeathed the same to Robert Greenhill, of Lincoln's Inn, Esq. who is the present proprietor, and nominates the curate.

THE township and village of NEWBY, (a part of which lies within the parish of Stokesley) are situated about two miles to the north-east from Seamer. According to Kirkby's Inquest (page 142.) the Meynells of Whorlton held two carucates of land here of the fee of Canterbury. The Earl of Egremont is the principal proprietor, and lord of the manor.

To the poor within this township the following charitable donations have been made, by Christopher Coulson, citizen and dyer of London, a native of this village. Having by virtue and fuccefsful induftry ac-quired a competent fortune, he purchafed of Sir David Foulis, of Ingle-by, Knight, the manor and an eftate at Great Ayton; two farms of which, amounting at that time to 14*l.* 10s. *per ann.* he fettled and con-veyed by deed to his fons John and William Coulfon, Henry Foulis, of Ingleby-Manor, Efq. Chriftopher Milburne, Brian Cottam, Giles Cal-vert, and William Aynflowe, their heirs and affigns, *in truft* to receive and employ the faid rents, and all the benefit, profit and gain arifing from, or which fhall hereafter be improved out of the faid lands, which he devifed by will, (dated 1640.) to the following charitable purpofes: viz. Having previoufly, in his will, provided for the building of a fit and convenient fchool-houfe at Newby, he bequeathed the fum of five pounds *per annum*, to be paid quarterly to fuch religious fchool-mafter, as fhall be duly nominated and appointed † to the faid fchool, for the teaching and inftructing of ten poor children, born within the town-fhip of Newby or Seamer; to each of the faid ten poor children, he alfo bequeathed the fum of *three fhillings yearly*, in the months of September or October, to be beftowed in *hofe and fhoes* every winter; and alfo *two fhillings* a piece to buy each of them *a fhirt*, and *twelve pence* a piece to buy every of them a *motley, or blue cap*, thereby to be diftinguifhed from the reft of the fcholars.

BESIDES the above endowment towards the maintenance of a fchool-mafter, and the provifion, at that time competent, for the comfortable fubfiftence of the fcholars; he alfo bequeathed the fum of 6*l.* 10s. year-ly, iffuing out of the faid two farms, to be paid quarterly by even por-tions, to fome godly and reverend minifter, for *thirteen fermons* to be yearly preached in the church of Seamer, on the firft Lord's day in

---

† IT is directed in Mr. Coulfon's will, that the fchoolmafter fhall be nominated and appointed by fix of the principal inhabitants of Newby, and their fucceffors, of whom the minifter and upper church-warden of Seamer were always to be two.

every month; the preacher from time to time to be nominated and appointed by his son John Coulson, or his heirs and assigns for ever; provided that one of the said sermons be always preached on Easter-day
yearly in the morning. ‡ All the profit and advantage which hereafter might be improved out of the said two farms and the lands and
tenements thereunto belonging, as a surplus over and above the said
yearly rent of 14*l.* 10s. he bequeathed to the poor of Newby, to be distributed at the discretion of the minister and church-wardens of Seamer every year, yearly for ever. §

BESIDES a great variety of small donations to the poor of several
parishes in London, he bequeathed the sum of *fifty shillings* to the poor
of the township of Newby, and *thirty shillings* to the poor of Seamer, to
be distributed by the minister and church-wardens. And as a mark of
his great regard and serious attention to the religious education of youth,
to each of his *god-children*, living at the time of his decease, he gave, by
will, the sum of *twenty shillings*, to be paid to them severally demanding
the same in their own persons, and being able and willing to rehearse
and answer readily and understandingly, according to their years and
capacities, to all the articles of the creed, all the petitions of the Lord's
prayer and ten commandments, to be examined as often as they should

‡ IT is an express clause in the founder's will, that " *if the minister of Seamer be an able man, and*
" *one that will take pains,*" he was to " *be admitted preacher of the said sermons, and to receive the*
" *salary appointed thereunto.*" We are sorry however, to observe, that this pious institution has been
prostituted to purposes different from those intended by the beneficent founder; as no curate of Seamer, however " *able and willing to take pains,*" has for many years been appointed preacher, or received any benefit from the charity. In opposition to the above clause, *the salary appointed thereunto*"
has been given to a *presbyterian minister,* whose claim under Mr. Coulson's will, however respectable
his individual character, cannot surely be superior to that of some able clergyman of the established
church.

§ IT has been justly observed, that if the Legislature should pass an act for examining into the
state of all charitable donations, and the mode in which the produce ought to be applied, numerous
abuses would be discovered. Many charities, we know, are now entirely lost, and the present is by
no means, a solitary instance within our district, where the objects intended to be relieved do not receive the full *improved* benefit of the charity.

make demand thereof, until they were found to be well inftructed in
all the faid points, by fome fufficient minifter to be called thereunto;
to whom he gave, for every time of fuch his examination *twelve pence;*
although the examined were infufficient for the time: but none of the
faid parties examined to be paid any part of their legacies until they
fhould be approved to be fufficiently inftructed, and willing to make
anfwer as aforefaid.

WITHIN this townfhip, and nearly at an equal diftance between the
villages of Seamer and Newby, there is a remarkable tumulus, fignificantly called HOW-HILL, * which is not known to have ever been
opened.   In the fields adjoining towards the fouth, on the fide of a hill,
are evident marks of an intrenchment; and in the valley or plain beneath, it is reported that armour, fwords and human bones have been
frequently turned up by the plough.

IT is difficult perhaps, at this remote period, from the imperfect accounts we have received, to afcertain to what people they could belong.
The circular camp, on the fummit of Efton-Nab, which is generally
fuppofed to be of Saxon origin, is not more than about four miles diftant; and, confidering the nature and fituation of the country, it feems
probable, that this might have been the fcene of action, when the Saxons were overthrown by Prince Arthur, at the memorable battle of *Badon-Hill;* which, according to *Holinfhed* and fome other hiftorians, is
conjectured to have been fought in this neighbourhood, about the year
492.   *Holinfhed's* account, which is almoft a literal tranflation of what
is related by *Polydore Virgil* upon the fame fubject, is to the following
effect: †

---

* GREAT and ftrongly marked objects frequently retain fome portion of their *aboriginal* names;
of which we have an inftance in the compofition of the word *How-Hill;* where the final fyllable is
added as merely explanatory of the former, which, from a change of language, had become unintelligible; *how,* in the Saxon language, fignifies a *hill.*

† AT Saxones ad fpoliandos modis omnibus Britannos poffeffione infulæ partis, quam tenebant,
excitati, cum urbes et oppida deferta, uti Gildas teftificatur, pro derelicto haberent, non multo poft

B b

" Bu r the Saxons, defirous to fpoile the Britons of the whole poffef-
" fion of that part of the ifle which they held, (whereas they accounted
" the cities and towns of fmall ftrength to be defended,) they got them
" to an high mountain called *Badon-Hill*, which Polydore fuppofeth to
" be *Blackamore*, that lieth near to the water of *Theife*, which divideth
" the Bifhoprick of Durham from Yorkfhire, having at the mouth there-
" of an haven meet to receive fuch fhips as come out of Germanie, from
" whence the Saxons looked for aid, having already fent thither for the
" fame.

" The Britons being thereof advertifed, made hafte towards the
" place, and befieged it on every fide; they alfo laie the fea coafts full
" of fouldiers, to keep fuch of the enemies from landing, as fhould come
" out of Germanie. The Saxons kept themfelves for a certaine fpace
" aloft upon the high ground; but in the end conftreined through
" want of vittels, they came down with their army in order of battle
" to the next plains, and offering to fight, the battle was anon begun,
" which continued from the morning till far in the day, with fuch
" flaughter, that the earth on every fide flowed with bloud. But the
" Saxons fuftained the greater loffe, their captains *Occa* and *Ofca* being
" both flaine, fo that the Britons might feem quite delivered of all dan-

---

montem quendam editiffimum, in ea infulæ ora, quæ contra Germaniam eft, occupant, quem id temporis *Badonicum* appellabant, quemadmodum idem Gildas ait. Hunc ego putarem effe, qui vulgo
vocatur *Blachemora*, et pertinet ad *Atkefin* flumen, quod Eboracenfem agrum a Dunelmenfi dividit,
et oftium habet, quo commodum ex Germania venientes fuas naves appellunt, id quod Saxones An-
gli in dies fingulos expectabant, nam quotidie auxilia ex patriâ arceffebant. Hæc ubi Britannis
nuntiata funt, eo concurrunt, montem circumfident, loca maritima præfidiis vinciunt, ut aditus veni-
entibus ne pateat, ad defcendendum in terram. Saxones per aliquot dies fe illis arduis locis tenuerant,
fed deinde commeatûs inopia urgente, neceffario cum inftructis copiis in proximam planitiem defcen-
derunt; factaque pugnandi poteftate ad manus venerunt; a mane ad multum diem dimicatum, tanta
edita cæde, ut paffim terra cruore manaret; fed longe majorem plagam Saxones acceperunt, amiffis
ducibus OSCA et OTHA; ita ut a Britannorum cervicibus depulfi viderentur. Cæterum omen
averti non potuit, ut infra demonftrabitur. Hujus fingularis pugnæ Gildas cum primis meminit, qui
eo illo anno, ut ipfe affirmat, natus eft, qui fuit ab adventu Anglorum *XLIIII*, et falutis humanæ
CCCCLXXXXII. *Polydori Virgilii Urbinat. Angl. Hift. lib.* 3. *p.* 80.

" ger of thofe enemies; but the fatal deftinie could not be avoided, as
" hereafter may appeare; and thus was the flaughter made of the Sax-
" ons, at *Badon-Hill*, whereof *Gyldas* maketh mention, and chanced the
" fame yeare that he was borne, which was in the 44th yeare after the
" firft coming of the Saxons into this land,—the year of grace 492."

Holinfhed's Hift. of England, book 5. p. 88.

ALTHOUGH we cannot prefume fo far, on the authority of the above
extract, or that from *Polydore Virgil* given in the notes, as to controvert
the opinion of Camden and thofe hiftorians, who have placed the *Mons
Badonicus*, or *Badon-Hill*, mentioned by *Gildas*, at Bannefdown near
Bath, we are neverthelefs led to conclude, from the proximity of the
camp at *Efton-Nab* and other concurrent circumftances, that a battle
has been undoubtedly fought in this neighbourhood, and probably
about the period already mentioned. Between the camp and the intrenchments at *How-Hill* there is a plain of confiderable extent, anfwer-
ing exactly to the defcription of the country given by the Authors
above quoted, and which was certainly a proper place for the engagement of the two armies.

WE can hardly fuppofe the *tumulus*, ‡ or the works adjoining to be
of Roman origin; as there is no tradition of any coins, or other diftinguifhing marks of that people having been ever difcovered near this
fpot.

POPULATION.—Confidering that there are no manufactories within the parifh, and no other inhabitants befides a working peafantry, occupied in the various branches of agriculture, we find little worthy of
particular remark on the ftate of population; which however, by the

‡ THE *tumulus* was not a mark of Roman fepulture only; *Skynner*, under the word *bury*, fays:
" Nec tantum *Anglo-Saxones, fed et veteres Romani lapidum moles et terræ aggeres in fepultorum memo-
" riam erexerunt.*" *Etymologicon Linguæ Anglicanæ.*

extract from the parifh regifter, § given in the notes, appears to be upon the increafe. According to the following enumeration made in the
year 1801, by order of the Legiflature, the number of inhabitants then
ftood as follows: viz.

	Inhabited houfes.	Fami-lies.	Uninhabit-ed houfes.	Males.	Females.	Total.
Seamer	49	52	1	122	127	249
Newby	30	30	4	63	64	127
Totals	79	82	5	185	191	376

ON a review of the above table we may remark, that the males and
females are nearly equal; and comparing the number of houfes or families with the total number of inhabitants, we fhall find that there are
$4\frac{1}{2}$ nearly to each family.

§ ABSTRACT of Seamer parifh regifter.

A. D.	BAPTISMS. Males.	BAPTISMS. Females	BURIALS. Males.	BURIALS. Females.
1700	2	7	0	4
1710	3	0	2	4
1720	1	2	3	5
1730	5	2	1	5
1740	4	4	2	3
1750	2	3	2	5
1760	10	2	4	4
1770	1	4	0	4
1780	4	4	4	0
Totals	32	28	18	34

A. D.	BAPTISMS. Males.	BAPTISMS. Females.	BURIALS. Males.	BURIALS. Females.	MARRIAGES.
1781	10	3	6	4	1
1782	4	3	9	2	3
1783	5	8	3	3	4
1784	4	5	3	1	0
1785	7	5	4	1	2
1786	9	5	4	5	2
1787	4	10	5	3	0
1788	5	6	1	7	1
1789	3	9	4	2	3
1790	5	2	6	8	5
1791	6	8	5	1	2
1792	5	3	1	3	2
1793	2	5	3	5	2
1794	5	5	4	2	2
1795	4	7	3	4	2
1796	5	3	4	4	3
1797	4	10	1	7	4
1798	2	5	5	1	1
1799	4	4	4	4	2
1800	7	6	2	4	1
Totals	100 / 77	112 / 71	77	71	42
Increafe	23	41			

THE average number of births in one year is 10, and that of burials 7¼; from which it will appear that, out of a population of 376, the number of children born within the parifh is as 1 to 37⅙, while the mortality of the inhabitants is nearly as 1 to 52.

SOIL, PRODUCE, and GENERAL APPEARANCE.—The foil within the parifh is found to vary, according to fituation; near the village, where the lands are dry and elevated, there is a fine black and gravelly loam, which produces all forts of grain and grafs in great abundance, and at as early a feafon as any within the diftrict. The low grounds called *Carrs* are, as the name imports, of a wet, marfhy nature; but by judicioufly carrying off the rain and furface-waters, are now in a progreffive ftate of improvement, and in a few years, may be rendered fertile meadows. The lands, at the extremities of the parifh, are more inclined to clay, but produce wheat, oats, and beans, which are the crops principally cultivated.

WE have already noticed the elevated fituation of the village and its beautiful and extenfive profpect; the general appearance of the parifh, although deftitute of woods and extenfive plantations, is rendered pleafing by the gentle inequalities of its furface, and the mixture of corn and pafture, with trees fcattered in the hedge-rows, which diverfify the fcene.

THE PARISH OF AYTON;

OR, as it is fometimes written, *Hayton*, and in Domefday-book, ATUN, lies to the eaft, and is the next that claims the reader's attention.

THE moft obvious etymology of the name is from the original Saxon Þeᵹe or Þæᵹ, fignifying a hedge, which we find frequently foftened down into the old French *haie*, or *haye;* hence the word *Ayton* may be fuppofed to mean a *town inclofed*, or, a town with a *haie*, or *hedge.* †

THE parifh, including the townfhips of *Great-Ayton, Little-Ayton,* and *Nunthorpe,* is, in its greateft extent from eaft to weft, about three miles, and nearly three miles broad; and is bounded by the parifhes of Seamer and Stokefley on the weft; by Marton and Newton on the north and north-eaft; by Stokefley on the fouth; with a tract of hills running feveral miles to the fouth and fouth-weft, which divide it from the parifhes of Guifborough and Kildale on the eaft.

IT appears, on the authority of Domefday-book, that the townfhip of *Ayton magna*, in the Conqueror's time, contained three diftinct manors; of which the firft that occurs in the furvey was antient demefne of the crown, being entered under the title

" Terra Regis.

" Manerium in Atun. Ulchil II. carucatas ad geldum. Terra ad " I. car. XVI. folid."

FROM the fame record it alfo appears, that there were fix carucates rated *ad geldum*, held formerly as one manor by Norman; but, which, at the time of the furvey, was in the hands of Nigel, and held of Robert, Earl of Moreton, being entered under the title

---

† IT is conjectured by fome that *Ayton* was fo named from a modification of the Britifh *ea*, which fignifies water; an etymology defcriptive at leaft of its fituation on the river Leven, which runs through the village.

" Terra Comitis Moritoniensis.

" In Atun ad geldum VI. carucatas, et III. car. possunt esse. Ibi habuit Norman l. manerium. Nunc habet Nigel de Comite. In Dominio l. car. et VIII. villani cum II. car."

" Aecclesia, et VI. acri prati. T. R. E. valebat XL. solid. modo XXX. sol."

FROM the above it appears, that there was one carucate in demesne, and eight villeins, with two ploughs; that there was a church and six acres of meadow; that the manor, in the Confessor's time, was valued at forty shillings, but at the time of the survey worth thirty.

THE third manor recorded in the Domesday survey, is entered under the title

" Terra Roberti Mallet.

" Manerium in Atun. Aldred, Edmund et Turorne habuerunt IIII. carucatas terrae ad geldum, ubi II. car. possunt esse. Nunc habet Robertus ibi I. car. et IX. villani, cum II. car. et III. acris prati. T. R. E. valebat. XX. solid. modo XXV. sol. et IIII. denar."

FROM which we find, that this manor contained four carucates of land *ad geldum*, two of which might be rendered arable; that at the period of the survey Robert Mallet had one carucate and nine villeins or bondmen under him, who had two ploughs and three acres of meadow. It was valued in the Confessor's time at twenty shillings; but at the time of the survey was worth twenty-five shillings and four pence.

WE are unable, at this remote period, to define the different manors, noticed in the above extracts; nor have we any documents to shew when they first became united: it appears however, from early and authentic records, that the present manor of Ayton was granted, at a very early period, to Robert de Estoteville, one of the valiant northern Barons, who in the 3d year of King Stephen's reign, fought against the Scots at the famous battle of the Standard, near North-allerton. In this family it continued till the 17. Henry III. when issue-male fail-

ing it defcended by marriage with Joan, daughter of Nicholas de Ef-
toteville, † to Hugh, fon of Baldwine de Wake; in which family it
continued till the reign of Edw. III. when John and Thomas, fons of
Baldwine, fon of Hugh de Wake, dying without iffue, Margaret their
fifter, Countefs of Kent, widow of Edmund de Woodftock, Earl of Kent,
became the next heir; from whom it afterwards defcended to Sir
Thomas Holland, Knight, by marriage with Joan, daughter of the faid
Margaret, in whofe right he became Earl of Kent. This Thomas died
feized of this manor 34. Edw. III. leaving Thomas, his fon and heir;
whofe profterity enjoyed it for divers fucceffions, till by marriage with
Elizabeth, fifter and coheir of Edmund Holland, Earl of Kent, it paffed to the Nevilles, Earls of Weftmorland, who had an occafional refidence at Ayton, and continued proprietors here till the 13. Elizabeth,
when, on the attainder of Charles, Earl of Weftmorland, it became
forfeited to the crown. The manor was afterwards granted by King
James I. to Sir David Foulis, of Ingleby-manor, Knight, who fold it,
in the reign of Charles I. to Chriftopher Coulfon, dyer, and citizen of
London. From the Coulfons it defcended by marriage to the Scot-
towes, by whofe defcendant it was fold, in the year 1801, to Mr. Henry
Richardfon, the prefent proprietor, and lord of the manor.

THE lands here have been long held in parcels; according to Kirkby's Inqueft, Nicholas de Meinell, had three carucates, which he held
of Peter de Mauley, as of the barony of Mulgrave;* and from the
fame record it appears that the heir of Baldwine de Wake, Lord of
Ayton, fo early as the reign of Edward I. certified his right to a weekly

---

† SIR WM. DUGDALE in his Baronage (vol. 1. p. 458) fays, that this Nicholas left iffue two
daughters, Joan and Margaret; Margaret, wife of Wm. Maftoc, died without iffue, 20. Henry III.
when Joan her fifter, then wife to Hugh de Wake, had livery of the whole inheritance.

* DICUNT, quod Petrus de Malo-lacu tenet quatuor feoda milit. cum Câftro de Mulgrave, de
Domino rege in capite, unde Nicholaus de Meinell tenet unum feodum in magna Ayton, magna Broughton et Tunftall, unde X. car. terræ faciunt feodum, et reddit Ballivo regis pro fine II· Xd.

market here; where he had alfo the jurifdiction of trying felons, and other privileges within the manor. *

THOUGH the market here has been long difcontinued, owing probably to its vicinity to the town of Stokefley, *Great Ayton* is neverthelefs a confiderable village, being nearly a mile in extent from eaft to weft, with fome good buildings, chiefly of freeftone, which abounds in quarries in the neighbourhood. It is pleafantly fituated, at the weftern fkirt of a conical formed mountain, called *Rofebury Topping*, about two miles to the eaft from the market town of Stokefley; and is watered by a branch of the Leven, which takes its rife near Kildale, about four miles to the eaft, and runs in a weftern direction through the middle of the village, where it is croffed by one ftone bridge of two arches, and another of one arch; befides three wooden bridges for the accommodation of the inhabitants.

THE population of the village, as we fhall ftate more particularly hereafter, is confiderable; and the inhabitants are chiefly employed in the different manufactories carried on here; there being, befides the more ordinary occupations, three tan-yards, one comb and horn-manufactory, a tallow-chandlry, a common brewery, one oil-mill, one water-corn-mill, and a brick and tile kiln.

THE CHURCH of Ayton, dedicated to All-Saints, is fituated towards the weftern extremity of the village; it is an ancient ftructure, but by fome modern repairs, is rendered a decent and commodious place of worfhip. It is difficult to ftate the precife era of its foundation; the preceding extract from Domefday-book leads us, however, to conclude, that it had its origin before the conqueft; though there is nothing about the prefent edifice, that can claim fo remote antiquity. This church was formerly endowed with rectorial rights, and in the

* HÆRES Baldwini de Wake, qui eft in cuftodia Domini regis, clamat habere *Mercatum* in magna Ayton, et *Warrenam* per cartam Domini Regis Henrici, et *Furcam*; fcilicet qualiter, et a quo tempore non poteft inquiri. *Kirkby's Inqueft.*

C C

year 1123, was given by Robert de Meynill and Gertrude his wife, together with the chapel of Newton under *Ornbach* (Rofebury) and four oxgangs of land there, and fome houfes, to the Abbey of Whitby, for a perpetual alms. This grant was confirmed by William de Eftote-ville, and King Henry II; as alfo by Stephen de Bulmer, who added 24 acres to it, out of his lands here. It was afterwards appropriated to that monaftry, † by Roger, Archbifhop of York; and at the diffo-lution, reduced to a perpetual curacy, which was certified to the gover-nours of Queen Anne's bounty, at 14*l. per annum.* It has fince receiv-ed feveral augmentations, which, with other dues, have increafed the income to about 70*l.* a year.

THE rectorial rights, upon the diffolution of the monaftry, were granted by letters patent to the Duke of Suffolk; and in the 28th year of the reign of Queen Elizabeth, came by purchafe to the Marwoods of Little Bufby. William Marwood, Efq. is the prefent impropriator and patron, and nominates the curate. *

---

† IT appears from the Regifter-office of the monaftry that an inventory of its effects was made according to canonical statutes, in the year 1394; when among other things in different places, there were found at their "*rectory of Aton in Clyffland*," as follow: viz.

Wheat and Mafceline	- -	30 quarters.
Oats	- - - - - - -	60 ditto.
Barley	- - - - -	3 ditto.
Peafe	- - - - - - -	2 ditto.
At Nunthorpe,—Wheat	- - - - - -	14 ditto.
Oats	- - - - - - -	20 ditto.

IT was found at the fame time, that Ayton required the fum of 10*l.* for repairs in buildings be-longing to the faid monaftry.

* AYTON CURACY.

DED. All-Saints. Cert. val. 14*l.* William Marwood, Efq. patron. Charged with *procurations* 7s. 6d. *Synodals* 2s. 8d.

CURATES.

——, —— Stephenfon.	1727, Ralph Jackfon, nom. by Chomley Turner, Efq.
1705, Geo. Spencer, nom. by Sir H. Marwood.	1747, Geo. Metcalfe, by Chomley Turner, Efq.
1715, Maurice Lifle, by the fame.	1761, Anth. Haftewell, by Mrs. Turner.
1718, Peter Moone, by the fame.	1794, Tho. Deafon, by Wm. Marwood, Efq.
1723, Thomas Morley, by the fame.	1795, Wm. Deafon, by the fame.

In the centre of the village, near the bridge, there is a SCHOOL-HOUSE; which, from an infcription over the door, appears to have been firft built by the late Michael Poftgate, yeoman, in the year 1704, and rebuilt in 1785; with a fmall endowment, for the inftructing of eight poor children within the townfhip, in reading, writing, and arithmetic. ‖ Adjoining to the fchool-houfe, there are three *poor-houfes;* over the doors of which is the following infcription: " THESE " HOUSES WERE BUILT BY VOLUNTARY SUBSCRIPTION; " EXCEPTING TWENTY POUNDS, THE INTEREST OF WHICH, " SIXTEEN SHILLINGS A YEAR, IS TO BE PAID FOR EVER " BY THE OVERSEERS OF THE POOR, FOR PUTTING TWO " POOR CHILDREN TO SCHOOL; BUILT 1764."

It appears that the old fchool-room and fchool-houfe, bequeathed by the late Michael Poftgate, yeoman, became in time fo ruinous, as to require a very expenfive repair; it was therefore thought expedient by the inhabitants, that the faid houfes fhould be taken down and re-built; when a poor-houfe was erected by fubfcription on their fite; appropriating one commodious apartment to the ufe and purpofe of a fchool-houfe; for the building of which the old materials were con-fidered a full and adequate compenfation. The fubfcriptions towards building the poor houfe amounted to the fum of 100*l.* 2s.; the intereft of which, together with the fixteen fhillings above mentioned, is paid out of the poor's rate, to be applied to the yearly falary of the fchool-mafter for ever.

On the north fide of the village, near the church, ftands the man-fion of Mrs. Wilfon, widow of the late William Wilfon, Efq. formerly

---

‖ It is here worthy of particular remark, that in this humble village feminary, the immortal *Capt. Cook* received his fchool-education at the expence of *Thomas Scottowe, Efq.*; under whom his father acted as hind or head fervant at his farm at *Airy-Holme,* in this parifh. A biographical me-moir of this fcientific circumnavigator will be given under the *parifh of Marton,* the birth-place of that extraordinary man.

commodore and commander in chief of the marine force of the Englifh Eaft-India Company; in which fituation " he difplayed one con-
" tinued feries of acts of difinterefted patriotifm, and diftinguifhed
" fervices." ‡   The fituation of the manfion, which is neat and com-

---

‡ WE have been favoured with the following brief memorials of the late *William Wilfon, Efq.* of
Ayton, which we here prefent to our readers, as a tribute of refpect to the memory of departed merit.

IT may, perhaps, be objected by fome, that as the fubject of this biographical fketch was not a
native of *Cleveland*, he cannot, with propriety, claim a place in the hiftory of that diftrict : but, when
it is confidered that, after the active part of life fpent in the fervice of the firft commercial company
in Europe, in which he was eminently diftinguifhed for his worth and talents, he chofe *Ayton* for his
retirement, where, during the evening of his days, his virtues fhone forth in the milder luftre of private life, we truft we fhall be excufed, if we annex to the *hiftory of this parifh*, the following brief
particulars of his life and character.

CAPT. WILSON was defcended from a very refpectable Yorkfhire family ; his father was an inhabitant of London, and proprietor of confiderable glafs-works there ; but, from fome embarraffment
in his affairs, left this, his third and only furviving fon at an early age, to promote his own intereft ;
and to form himfelf for the future fervice of his country in the fchool of adverfity, which gradually
eftablifhed his character, and afterwards enabled him to meet the moft trying circumftances with
heroic fortitude.

HE was born in the year 1715 ; and after an education that peculiarly qualified him for the profeffion of a failor, he entered at the early age of 14, from his own choice into the fea-fervice of the
Hon. Eaft India Company. After having, in the courfe of 15 years, paffed through the different
gradations of rank, with great credit to himfelf, principally under *Capt. Weftcot*, of the *Scarborough*,
and *Capt. Crompton*, of the *Duke of Loraine*, he was advanced, in the year 1744, to the command of
the *Great Britain*, a private fhip of war, of 30 guns, 12 and 18 pounders, 250 men, and three
Lieutenants ; the gentlemen, who accompanied Capt. Wilfon in this capacity, were *Meffrs. Norway,* *
Hutton, and *Curlet*, all belonging to the fervice of the Eaft-India Company.

HE failed in the *Great Britain*, from the Downs, on the 10th November ; and on the 17th fell
in with a Spanifh frigate, of fuperior force, which he obliged to fheer off, and would probably have
captured her, had not the difabled ftate of his fhip's rigging put it out of his power to prevent her
efcape.

ON the 22d of December following, he took a Spanifh floop of war, carrying difpatches, and with
ten thoufand pounds in fpecie, on board. He, foon after this, fell in with and engaged three French
Weft Indiamen, furnifhed with *letters of marque*, and mounting from 20 to 24 guns each ; two of
which he captured, after fuftaining confiderable damage in his fhip's rigging, &c.

---

* MR. NORWAY was afterwards the commander of the *Britannia*, Eaft Indiaman.

modious, is rather elevated, with some rich and fertile grounds adjoining.

On relinquishing the command of the *Great Britain*, in the beginning of the year 1746, *Captain Wilson* re-entered the service of the East India Company; and in the year following was sworn into the command of the *Suffolk*, *East Indiaman*. For some years after Capt. Wilson's appointment to this command, nothing remarkable seems to have occurred, till, in his last voyage in this ship, in the year 1756, he was overtaken, in his outward-bound passage, off the *Macclesfield Shoals*, by one of those dangerous and tremendous storms, known by the name of *tuffoons* or *tysongs*. Capt. Wilson, in describing the astonishing violence of this hurricane, has been heard to say, that " the fury of the " elements was far beyond conception, and that a faint idea only of their rage could be conveyed " perhaps by saying, that it seemed as if *heaven and earth* were coming together."

During his stay at China in the year 1757, there being every reason to conclude that a war with France had already broken out, Capt. Wilson, having taken care to have his ship furnished with the best means of defence, was ordered to proceed to England, as commanding officer, with the ships, then ready to sail. Nothing remarkable occurred, till he reached the latitude of 35. 4" south, and 6. 30" to the eastward of the Cape of Good Hope; when, on the 9th of March, being supported by the *Hon. Capt. Walpole* of the *Houghton*, and *Capt. Hutchinson* of the *Godolphin*, the only ships then in company; *Capt. Wilson* had the courage to encounter, and the skill, conduct, and good fortune, to beat off the *Compte de Provence*, a French ship of the line of 74 guns, commanded by *Monsieur de la Chaise*, together with the *Sylphide* frigate of 36 guns

In the month of June following, the *Suffolk*, *Houghton*, and *Godolphin*, arrived safe at Leith; and soon afterwards sailed for the river, with his Majesty's ship, the *Southampton*. While at Leith, Capt. Wilson received the following letter from Mr. Cleveland, Secretary of the Admiralty:

" *Admiralty-Office, 4th June*, 1757.

" Sir,
" I have received and read to my Lords Commissioners of the Admiralty, your letter of " the 24th past, giving an account of your having in company with the *Houghton* and *Godolphin*, In- " diamen, engaged two French men of war, in your passage home from the Cape of Good Hope; " and I am to acquaint you, that your behaviour with that of the other officers, has given the Lords " very great satisfaction.
" I am, Sir, your very humble servant,
J. CLEVELAND."

On this occasion *Capt. Wilson* also received the thanks of the Court of Directors of the East-India Company, who presented him with a *golden-medal*, of one hundred guineas value, in testimony of the sense the members of that Court entertained of his gallant conduct.

When *Capt. Wilson* accepted the command of the *Great Britain*, to which he was appointed in the year 1744, he had, at the same time, an offer of a ship in the East-India service; but, he made choice of the former, as being a situation that would afford him an opportunity of devoting a greater portion of his time to the acquisition of professional knowledge. The period was now arrived, when he was called upon to fill a situation, which would allow scope for the display of that ability, which,

THE township of

LITTLE AYTON,

lies at a ſhort diſtance to the ſouth eaſt, and is of ſmall extent; con‑
taining thirteen houſes, and about ſeventy inhabitants, occupied chiefly

---

from motives the moſt laudable, he had ſought and acquired with no inconſiderable ſhare of peril and
fatigue. It being judged expedient by the Court of Directors of the Eaſt-India Company, for the
better protection of their trade, to fit out a ſhip of war, *Capt. Wilſon* was ſolicited to accept the
command, as being an officer highly qualified for ſuch an appointment.

ALTHOGH the fortune he had acquired, amounted only to a very moderate competency, yet, as it
was, in ſome meaſure equal to the moderation of his deſires, he had now begun to turn his thoughts
towards the gratification of a wiſh he had long cheriſhed, of paſſing the remainder of his life in retire‑
ment, and in the boſom of his friends. But, the *amor patriæ* which glowed within his breaſt, and the
wiſh he gratefully entertained of juſtifying the deference paid to himſelf, as being the perſon, beſt
qualified to diſcharge the duties of ſo arduous a truſt, determined him to relinquiſh every private
conſideration, and to accept the appointment ; * and being conſtituted, (by a ſpecial commiſſion bear‑
ing date 23d December, 1757) *commodore and commander of all ſhips and veſſels in the ſervice of the
Engliſh Eaſt-India Company*, he took his departure the year following, in *the Pitt*, † a ſhip of war of
54 guns and 250 men ; and having received on board *Colonel Sir William Draper*, and *Major Brere‑
ton*, with ſome troops under their command, he ſailed from St. Helen's on the 7th of March, in
company with his Majeſty's ſhip, *the Grafton* of 74, and *the Sunderland* of 60 guns, having ſeven Eaſt-
Indiamen under convoy. After landing theſe officers and troops at Fort St. George, he ſailed from
thence to China by a route till then unknown; and returning by the ſame tract, proved this paſſage
to be practicable at all ſeaſons of the year.

THE ſtraits, through which he paſſed from the Indian ſeas, into the pacific Ocean, the iſlands
which form them, together with ſome of their capes and head-lands, retain, to this day, the names
they received from him.

FOR this important diſcovery, and the facility, which the ſucceſsful exertion of his bold and enter‑
priſing ſpirit thus obtained to eaſtern commerce and navigation, *Commodore Wilſon* was on his return
to England, again unanimouſly voted the thanks of the Hon. Court of Directors ; and was alſo pre‑
ſented with a *golden-medal*, commemorative of his meritorious ſervices.

---

* As a proof that the conduct of *Commodore Wilſon* did ample credit to the judgment with which this
honourable and important commiſſion was beſtowed, it is recorded that " on his arrival in the Eaſt-Indies
" he volunteered his ſhip, and his ſervices to Admiral *Sir George Pococke* ; in the Bay of Bengal he chaſ‑
" ed, and brought to action a French ſhip of the line, greatly ſuperior to his own, in *rate* and *force* ; and
" at Batavia he vindicated the rights of his country againſt the Dutch, and by his firmneſs and ſpirit com‑
" pelled the Governour-General to acknowledge, that *the Engliſh had a right to navigate, wherever it had
" pleaſed God to ſend water.*"   *See the Naval Chronical for Auguſt* 1805.

† THE *Pitt* was originally a French ſhip of 64 guns, called *the Pondicherry*; and received this new name
from *Commodore Wilſon*, as a teſtimony of reſpect to the illuſtrious *Earl of Chatham*; under whoſe auſpices
the whole naval department had proſpered, and become gloriouſly formidable.

in agriculture. The manor, at the period of the Domefday-furvey, was found to be taxed at two carucates; befides land fufficient for one plough, valued at ten fhillings.

HAVING achieved what no other officer in the fervice had ever dared to undertake, *Commodore Wilfon* refigned his commiffion in the year 1762; and uninfluenced by vain ambition, or the defire of courting empty popularity (having, in the year 1755, married Rachael, third daughter of George Jackfon, Efq. of Hill-Houfe, Richmond, Yorkfhire), he retired to the village of Ayton; where, practifing thofe virtues, which come within the reach of general imitation, he gave dignity to the walk of private life, by the purfuits of genius, the exertions of philanthropy, and the example of integrity.

SUCH was *Commodore Wilfon;* who, (having inculcated both by precept and example, that our country's intereft is the nobleft impulfe of the truly brave) departed this life on the 5th day of June, in the year 1795, and in the 8oth year of his age.—He was buried within the parifh church of Ayton, where a marble monument of elegant workmanfhip has been lately erected by his fon, William Wilfon, Efq. with the following infcription:

To the Memory of
WILLIAM WILSON, ESQ.
He derived his DESCENT from a refpectable FAMILY;
AFFLUENCE and CREDIT from his VIRTUES and ABILITIES;
How fully thefe were difplayed
With what GALLANTRY and JUDGEMENT they were exerted
The THANKS which he received on different OCCASIONS
From the COURT of DIRECTORS of the Honorable the EAST INDIA COMPANY
Were ample TESTIMONIES.
Retiring from an active Scene,
He paffed the remainder of his Life in this Village,
Where, during TWENTY-SIX Years,
PHILANTHROPY and ftrict INTEGRITY actuated his Conduct as a MAGISTRATE;
Exemplary PIETY, as a CHRISTIAN.
On this Tablet
Affection with Truth muft record,
That, in every Situation defervedly efteemed,
He poffeffed all the amiable and focial Qualities
Which muft endear the HUSBAND, the PARENT, and the FRIEND.
THE ALMIGHTY,
Whofe gracious Protection he had often experienced
And on whom alone he had ever relied,
Was pleafed to remove him from this Life
On the 5th June, 1795.
Aged 8o.

THIS was ancient demefne of the crown, entered in the furvey, under the title   𝕮𝖊𝖗𝖗𝖆 𝕽𝖊𝖌𝖎𝖘.

"𝕸𝖆𝖓𝖊𝖗𝖎𝖚𝖒 𝖎𝖓 𝖆𝖑𝖎𝖆 𝕬𝖙𝖚𝖓.   𝕳𝖆𝖚𝖚𝖆𝖗𝖉 II. 𝖈𝖆𝖗𝖚𝖈𝖆𝖙𝖆𝖘 𝖙𝖊𝖗𝖗𝖆𝖊 𝖆𝖉 𝕲𝖊𝖑: "𝖉𝖚𝖒.   𝕮𝖊𝖗𝖗𝖆 𝖆𝖉 I. 𝖈𝖆𝖗. X. 𝖘𝖔𝖑𝖎𝖉𝖔𝖘."

THERE were alfo two carucates, held before the conqueft, by *Af-chil*, valued at ten fhillings in the Confeffor's time, and held afterwards by Robert Mallet, but was then wafte.

𝕮𝖊𝖗𝖗𝖆 𝕽𝖔𝖇𝖊𝖗𝖙𝖎 𝕸𝖆𝖑𝖑𝖊𝖙.

"𝕸𝖆𝖓𝖊𝖗𝖎𝖚𝖒 𝖎𝖓 𝖆𝖑𝖎𝖆 𝕬𝖙𝖚𝖓.   𝕳𝖆𝖇𝖊𝖇𝖆𝖙 𝕬𝖘𝖈𝖍𝖎𝖑 II. 𝖈𝖆𝖗𝖚𝖈𝖆𝖙𝖆𝖘 𝖙𝖊𝖗𝖗𝖆𝖊 𝖆𝖉 "𝕲𝖊𝖑𝖉𝖚𝖒. 𝖊𝖙 I. 𝖈𝖆𝖗. 𝖕𝖔𝖙𝖊𝖘𝖙 𝖎𝖇𝖎 𝖊𝖘𝖘𝖊.   𝕽𝖔𝖇𝖊𝖗𝖙𝖚𝖘 𝖍𝖆𝖇𝖊𝖙, 𝖊𝖙 𝖜𝖆𝖘𝖙. 𝖊𝖘𝖙.   𝕮. "𝕽. 𝕰. 𝖛𝖆𝖑𝖊𝖇𝖆𝖙 X. 𝖘𝖔𝖑𝖎𝖉."

THE manor was foon afterwards granted to the ancient family of Malbiffe; and was held by the King *in capite, ut de honore;* * it was afterwards in the poffeffion of the Lords Eures of Eafby; and after divers alienations, was purchafed by Mr. Henry Richardfon, the prefent proprietor.

THERE was anciently a chapel here, built by Sir William Malbiffe, Knt. about the year 1215; but the Abbot and Monks of Whitby, jealous of their privileges, and difapproving of the building, fecurity was given, that it fhould be of no prejudice to their church of Great Ayton; but that all oblations and obventions at any time made thereto, fhould be faithfully given up to the mother church.   This chapel was afterwards ceded to the mother-church, and confequently came under the direction and management of the Abbot and Monks of Whitby.   It does not appear, at what period this chapel was deftroyed; there are no remains of the edifice now ftanding, the foundation of which is hardly vifible.

THE Townfhip of

NUNTHORP

with the hamlet of *Tunftall*, lies about two miles to the north from the village of Ayton.   It appears from Domefday-book and other authentic

---

* RADULPHUS DE MALBISSE clamat habere *furcam* in parva Ayton; et terras fuas non gildabiles in eadem, quæ funt de honore Regis.

records, to have been anciently written *Thorp*, from the Saxon Ðoppe, which fimply fignifies a village; and received its prefent diftinguifhing name from a fmall *Ciftercian Nunnery*, which was firft founded at *Hutton*, in the parifh of Guifborough, by Ralph de Neville, about the year 1162; and afterwards removed hither, when the place, from that circumftance, was called *Nun-thorp*.

The manor here, at the period of the Domefday furvey, was rated at three carucates, and was ancient demefne of the crown, valued, in the Confeffor's time, at ten fhillings.

" Terra Regis.

" Manerium in Corp. Ulchil III. carucatas terrae ad geldum.
" Terra ad I. car. XVI. folid. et dimid. Ibi IIII. acri prati. T. R. E.
" X. folid."

It was granted by the Conqueror to Robert de Brus, lord of Skelton, to be held of the King *in capite*, by military fervice, and defcended by marriage to Marmaduke de Thweng; of whom, according to Kirkby's Inqueft, William de Percy, of Kildale, in the reign of Edward firft, held one knight's fee in Nunthorp, Upfall, and Arfum, where twelve carucates made one knight's fee. *

From the Percies, as *mefne* lords, the manor defcended, in the reign of Edward III. to Robert Conyers, Knight, by marriage with Juliana, daughter and heir of William de Fercy; and in the reign of Charles I. it paffed from the Conyers, by marriage to the Conftables, and afterwards to the Bradfhaws. Conftable Bradfhaw died in the year 1702, leaving a daughter, Ann, who married William Pierfon, Efq. of the Middle Temple, London, who, in right of his wife became poffeffed of Nunthorp and other eftates in the neighbourhood. Bradfhaw Pierfon, his fon, fucceeded; but dying without iffue in the year 1746, he left this and other eftates by will, to Edward Wilfon, Efq. of Brizencourt, in the

---

* Willielmus de Percy de Kildaile tenet in Upfall, Nunthorpe, et Arfum, unum feodum, unde XII. car. terræ faciunt feod. milit. &c.   *Kirkby's Inqueft.*

D d

county of Derby, *for life*, *fans wafte*; remainder *in truft* to his iffue *in tail*; and on failure of fuch iffue, to the iffue of his coufin Winifred Langdale, wife of Victor Repinder, in *tail-male*. Upon the death of Edward Wilfon without iffue, James, the eldeft fon of Winifred Repinder, fucceeded to the eftate, and according to the tenor of the faid will, affumed the name of *Bradfhaw Pierfon*. But, in order to cut off, bar, and deftroy all *eftate tail*, and all remainders and reverfions, the faid James Bradfhaw Pierfon and his fon, in the year 1790, fuffered a common recovery; and moft of the eftates have been fince fold to different purchafers.

NUNTHORP-HALL, with the manor, and farm adjoining, was purchafed by Mr. Thomas Simpfon, the prefent proprietor, and lord of the manor. The manfion, or manor-houfe, is a ftrong ftone edifice, with fpacious apartments, which have been modernized and rendered commodious by fome judicious repairs, by the prefent owner. This was formerly a feat of the Conftables, and probably built about the time of Charles I. Over a door, on the fouth end of one of the out-buildings there is a fhield cut in ftone, bearing the arms of Conftable: vix. *quarterly gules and vair, a bend, or, charged with an orle.*

THE lands within this townfhip feem to have been held in parcels at an early period. Ralph de Neville, in the reign of Henry II. gave two carucates and one oxgang of land, with a mill in this townfhip, to the priory, which he founded for nuns here, by the licence of Arnald de Percy, and Adam de Brus. This grant, which conftituted no inconfiderable part of the original endowment, was confirmed by King Henry III. when the nuns were fettled at Bafedale, ‡ in the parifh of Stokefley.

---

‡ In the year 1231, there arofe a difpute between *Roger*, abbot and convent of Whitby, and *Sufannah*, priorefs and convent of Bafdale, about the tithes of corn for certain lands at Nunthorp called *Ingle-flatt* and *Plumtree-flatt*; and the tithes of a mill belonging to the faid nuns in Nunthorp, and the tithes of a meadow alfo belonging to them in the faid territory; which tithes the faid abbot and convent demanded as pertaining to their church at Ayton. This difpute was at length amicably fettled, in a chapter held for Cleveland before *Serlo*, the Archdeacon, and others; when it was agreed

After the fuppreffion of the priory in the 27. Henry VII. the premifes at Nunthorp, called *Nunhoufe-Grange* were leafed (31. Henry VIII.) by the King to William Snowball, for the term of twenty one years, at the yearly rent of 6*l.* 13s. 4d. and as appears from a record in the augmentation office, were afterwards granted by King Henry VIII. in *eftate tail*, to King's College, Oxford.

WITHIN a few yards to the north from the manfion, there is an ancient chapel, dedicated to St. Mary; in which there was a chauntry, founded in the time of King Edward III. John de Nunthorpe, according to Torr's MS. occurs the firft cantarift, and was fucceeded in the year 1358 by William de Marton, on the nomination of John Grethead. † This chapel appears to have been originally private, built and endowed by the lord of the manor, for the convenience of his tenants and domeftics; the patronage of which is ftill appendant to the manor: it continued *donative*, and exempt from ordinary jurifdiction, till with the confent of the patron, it was certified to the governours of Queen Anne's bounty at 10*l.* 12s.; and on its augmentation, it became prefentable as a perpetual curacy; but does not enjoy the parochial rights of baptifms, marriages, or burials.

TUNSTALL, a fmall hamlet within this townfhip, was an ancient manor; and as appears from Domefday-book, was taxed for three caru-

---

that the abbot and convent fhould give away for ever, and quit-claim to the faid nuns, the tithes of corn in *Plumtree-flatt*, as alfo the aforefaid meadow; but that the faid nuns were to pay tithe for ever for their corn in *Ingle-flatt*, and for their mill at Nunthorp, to the mother church of Ayton. In teftimony whereof, the Chapter feal of Whitby, and the priorefs' feal at Bafedale, were fet to two records, one of which was preferved in each of the aforefaid religious houfes.

---

† THIS family appears to have poffeffed confiderable property at Nunthorp. About the year 1360 Robert Grethead granted 10 meffuages and 12 ——, with an oxgang of land here, to *John Aklee*, chaplain of the church of *Saint George*, in Newcaftle-upon-Tyne, to be held of the lord of the fee by the due and accuftomed fine. Witneffes, *Lord Robert Conyers, Knight*, J. Grethead, J. de Eure, John de Maltby, Richard Waxander, William de Mowbray, Walter de Stainfby, Richard de Marton, *cum multis aliis.*

D d 2

cates, befides land fufficient for two ploughs. It was ancient inheritance of the crown, entered in the general furvey under the title

"**Terra Regis.**

"**Manerium in Connestale Lesing III. car. terrae ad geldum.
"Terra ad II. car.**"

TUNSTALL, in the reign of Edward I. was held by Nicholas de Meinell of Peter de Mauley, and he of the King *in capite*, as parcel of the
barony of Mulgrave. The hamlet gave name to a refident family; for,
according to Kirkby's Inqueft, Hugo de Tunftall held certain lands
here of the faid Nicholas; for which he paid as a fine, the fum of two
fhillings.

WE find little further worthy of particular notice, touching this
place. The Pennymans, of Ormefby, have for fome time, been principal proprietors here; but the manorial rights have been long difufed.

WITH refpect to the *foil, produce,* and *general appearance* of the parifh,
we have to remark that the village of Ayton is fituated in a low and
pleafant vale; but being fhut in by a range of mountains on the eaft,
which run for feveral miles fouthwards, does not enjoy any extenfive
profpects. The foil near the village is a rich clayey loam, and produces
abundant crops of corn and grafs, and on which clover and turnips are
occafionally cultivated. ||

TOWARDS Nunthorp, and the northern extremities of the parifh,
the grounds rife gently, with an eaftern and fouthern afpect; the foil
here is of a ftronger clay, but well adapted to the growth of wheat;
and in fome low grounds near *the Tame*, which runs through this part
of the parifh, clay, with a mixture of moorifh earth, prevails. The

---

|| AYTON has to boaft of an early introduction of experimental agriculture by the late *William
Wilfon, Efq.* about the year 1769; whofe trials were chiefly in the drill-hufbandry, by a plough of
his own invention, upon the principle of the *Perfian wheel,* which lifted up the feed, and threw it over
into tubes that conveyed it into the ground. With this machine, which fowed three rows at 14 inches afunder, or fix at 7 inches,) Mr. W. drilled wheat, barley, beans, and turnips with fuccefs.
See a fix Months' Tour through the North of England, 2d edition, 1771.

crops principally cultivated are wheat, oats, and beans. The inclofures, except thofe on the fkirts of the mountains, are divided with quickfet-hedges, which, with the trees in hedge-row, and fome fmall plantations, give the country a rich and woody appearance.

Of *natural curiofities* within the parifh, we may obferve, that at the foot of *Rofebury Topping*, there are two fmall woods, chiefly of hazel and oak, known by the name of *Cliffrigg-woods;* in one of which there is a place called the *Iron-Mine*, where iron ftone is found; but, we have no evidence, nor is there any appearance, that it has ever been much wrought. At a little diftance to the north, a rocky ridge runs eaft and weft, called *Langbargh-Ridge;* * at the end of which, on the left of the road leading to Guifborough, there is a fingular quarry of hard, blue whin-ftone, or granite; which has been found of infinite value to the public, in making and repairing the turnpike roads in this part of Cleveland. The ridge is evidently a continuation of the great blue ftone dyke, which appears on the furface, on Cockfield-Fell, in the county of Durham, and which is defcribed as running through Cockfield colliery, and from thence eaftwards through that county, and below Yarm to Ayton in Cleveland. † The dyke, which makes its appearance in different places in the county of Durham, and at Stainton in this diftrict, has been traced running in a line eaftwards over the moors, to the fea below Whitby. It is conjectured to be formed of a fpecies of Lava, fimilar to the Derbyfhire toadftone; or, what Mr. Whitehurft calls *Iceland-lava;* but does not feem to have experienced any great degree of heat in its formation. On the furface it has the appearance of iron-ftone; and by a chemical procefs, would probably be found to contain much of that metal. The working of the quarry is carried on by a large excavation of the rock, of about twenty yards in breadth, forming a long level or paffage.

---

* Probably fo called from the *wapontake courts* being anciently held here, as they ftill continue to be *pro formâ.*

† See Hutchinfon's Hiftory of Durham, vol. III. p. 505.

On the brow of a hill towards the eaftern extremity of the parifh, an *allum-work* was formerly carried on with confiderably fuccefs; but, like the other workings of that mineral in the weftern part of Cleveland, it has been for fometime difcontinued.

We muft conclude our account of this parifh with fome brief remarks on its population, which, as we have already obferved, is confiderable. From the return made to government in the year 1801, under the population act, ‡ it appears there were at that time within the parifh 236 families, and 1066 inhabitants, making 4½ nearly to each family.

The following table of marriages, baptifms, and burials, given in the notes, * will afford fome idea of its increafing ftate of population;

‡ State of population, taken 10th March, 1801.

	Inhabited houfes.	Families.	Uninhabited houfes.	Males.	Females.	Total.
Great Ayton	201	206	5	409	456	865
Little Ayton	13	13	–	34	35	69
Nunthorp	17	17	–	75	57	132
Totals	231	236	5	518	548	1066

* Abstract of Great Ayton regifter.

A. D.	Marr.	Bap.	Bur.	A. D.	Marr.	Bap.	Bur.
1680	4	7	28	1780	8	21	17
1681	5	10	22	1781	3	15	12
1682	1	15	24	1782	9	26	13
1683	4	11	13	1783	9	26	21
1684	5	12	6	1784	6	29	20
1685	1	14	6	1785	5	22	18
1686	1	15	12	1786	9	24	20
1687	1	14	8	1787	6	28	15
1688	0	8	15	1788	9	25	16
1689	4	15	4	1789	3	28	19
1690	5	16	9	1790	9	14	21
1691	2	9	9	1791	5	25	20
1692	3	12	14	1792	3	22	19
1693	2	10	18	1793	7	18	15
1694	2	17	9	1794	7	18	16
1695	4	14	12	1795	4	30	25
1696	2	14	13	1796	7	22	18
1697	5	11	4	1797	8	35	17
1698	5	19	12	1798	1	30	8
1699	5	7	7	1799	2	24	16
Total	61	250	245	Totals	120	482	346
					61	250	245
				Increafe	59	232	101

and from which it will appear that on an average of twenty years, the annual number of burials to that of baptifms is as $17\frac{1}{3}$ to $24\frac{1}{10}$, and that for every 44 of the inhabitants a child is born, while the mortality within the parifh is as one to $61\frac{1}{2}$ annually.

THE PARISH OF NEWTON

LIES to the north-eaft.   This was anciently a chapelry under Ayton; but as it now enjoys parochial rights, we have confidered and treated it as a diftinct parifh.

IT is bounded on the eaft by the parifh of Guifborough, and by Ayton on the weft; by Ormefby on the north, and Kildale on the fouth. Its greateft extent from eaft to weft is not more than one mile, and about two miles from north to fouth.   The name literally fignifies a *new town*, * or dwelling; and is one of the moft common in the kingdom, there being upwards of one hundred places of the fame name enumerated in Spelman's *Villare Anglicanum.*

HERE was an ancient manor; which, on the authority of the Domef-day furvey, was taxed for fix carucates, befides land fufficient for three ploughs, and one carucate within the foke of Ayton.   It was held before

---

* As names were undoubtedly meant to be characteriftical of the places to which they were given, we cannot greatly admire the fagacity of our anceftors in their choice of this epithet *new*, which could be fuited only to their own times; and would be, as the Roman hiftorian expreffes it, only *res unius ætatis.*

the conqueſt by *Magbanec*, which is probably a corruption of the Iriſh name *Mac-ben-og*, that is, a ſon by a ſecond wife, *filius junioris uxoris*. In the Confeſſor's time the manor was valued at ten ſhillings; and at the time of the ſurvey, was demeſne of the crown, entered under the title of

" **Terra Regis.**

" **Manerium in Neuuetun. Magbanec VI. carucatas ab geldum.**
" **Terra ad III. car. una carucata eſt ſoca in Atun. T. R. E. X. ſolidos.**

NEWTON was afterwards granted to Robert de Brus, lord of Skelton, to be held of the King *in capite*. O.1 the death of Peter de Brus, the fourth of that name, it deſcended to his ſiſter Lucy, wife of Marmaduke de Thweng; of whom, according to Kirkby's Inqueſt, † *William de Roſ-ſells* held certain lands here, in the reign of Edward I. The heir of *Gilbert de Luda* alſo held two carucates of the ſaid Marmaduke; and from the ſame record it further appears, that *Adam de Arundall* had three carucates, of the fee of Margaret de Roos, which were held of the ſaid Adam as *meſne* lord, by Roger Maliverer, who paid, as a fine, the ſum of two ſhillings and four-pence.

THE manor, with a conſiderable eſtate, came into the poſſeſſion of the family of Welbury, of Lazenby; and deſcended, about the year 1600, by marriage with Margaret, ſole daughter and heir of William Welbury, to William Norton, of Sawley, whoſe deſcendants have con-tinued lords here for ſeveral generations.

NEWTON, or, as it is ſometimes, for the ſake of diſtinction, called Newton *under Roſebury*, from its ſituation at the foot of a conical form-ed mountain of that name, (by ancient writers called *Oonſbury*, and

---

† WILLIELMUS DE ROSSELLS tenet in *Newton Othenburgh, &c.* tres partes unius feodi, unde de-cem car. faciunt feodum.

HÆRES Gilbert de Luda tenet ibidem duas carucatas terræ unde XII. car. faciunt feodum.

ADAM DE ARUNDALL tenet tres carucatas terræ in Newton Thuerburgh, de hæreditate Margaretæ Roos, unde X. car. terr. faciunt feodum. Et Rogerus Maliverer tenet eas de dicto Adamo; et idem Rogerus reddit ballivo Domini Regis pro fine, *II. ſol. et IV. denar.*

Kirkby's Inqueſt.

fometimes *Othenburgh* *), is a fmall ftraggling village, confifting chiefly of farm-houfes, and contains about 150 inhabitants.

THE chapel, which is a fmall mean ftructure, the dedication of which is unknown, appears to have been anciently connected with, and dependent on the church of Ayton, and with it was given, in the year 1123 by Robert de Meinell, to the abbot and convent of Whitby. On the diffolution of that monaftry it was made parochial, and was certified to the governours of Queen Anne's bounty at 6*l*. 4*s*. It has fince received three augmentations by lot, and the prefent income is about 35*l. per annum.* The tithes within the parifh are held under leafe from the Archbifhop of York, by the lord of the manor, who is alfo patron and nominates the curate. †

THE following ftatement will give the reader an idea of its prefent ftate of population. When an actual enumeration was made in the year 1801, according to act of Parliament, there were then 38 houfes or families, and the total number of inhabitants was 149, which gives not quite four to each family. From the parifh regifter it appears

---

* *ROSEBURY* is a word of Britifh origin, denoting a *fortified hill*; and was probably ufed as an exploratory ftation; it was fo named of the Britifh *rofs*, a heath or common, and the Saxon *bury* or *berg*, a caftrum or fortrefs. *Oonfbury* is a word of fimilar import, from *Oon*, which fignifies a hill. The word *topping*, which is frequently annexed, is evidently Danifh, from *toppen*, an apex or point, as defcriptive of the peaked fummit of the mountain, which is now ufed as a beacon, to give an alarm to the country in times of public danger. *Othenburgh*, the name which fometimes occurs in ancient records, is conjectured to be derived from *Othan*, or *Odin*, the fame as *Woden*, which fignifies *fire*, and by our Saxon anceftors efteemed and honoured for their *god of battle*, as the Romans did their god, *Mars*. But this conjecture will be confidered by fome etymologifts, perhaps, as more ingenious than conclufive.

† WE acknowledge our obligations to the Rev. J. Metcalfe, for much information relative to this parifh.

STATE of population, 10th March, 1801.

	Inhabited houfes.	Families.	Uninhabited houfes.	Males.	Females.	Total.	Agriculture.	Trade, &c.	Refidue.	Total.
Newton	38	38	0	68	81	149	35	8	106	149

that within the laft twenty years : viz. from the year 1786 to the year 1805 inclufive, there have been 18 marriages, 76 baptifms, and 52 burials ; from which we are induced to conclude, that the population of the parifh is nearly ftationary ; and from the average number of burials in one year, it will appear that the mortality of the inhabitants is as one to 60 nearly.

WE find little worthy of particular remark touching the *foil* and *produce* of the parifh, which will be found greatly fimilar to thofe of the lands in the adjoining parifhes already noticed ; but with refpect to *general appearance* we have to remark that the moft ftriking object, and what, in every point of view, particularly arrefts the traveller's attention, is the pyramidal, peaked mountain called

ROSEBURY TOPPING,

which rifes abruptly, and to a confiderable height, over the village ; from the fummit of which the country prefents an immenfe plain, which lofes itfelf in the horizon at its northern extremity.

WE have been favoured with the following defcriptive view from this remarkable promontory, written by a gentleman a few years ago, on his tour through this part of Cleveland.

THE party fet out from the village of Ayton, and the day being clear, never was expectation more amply gratified ; he then proceeds in his defcription thus :—" After a tedious labour of near an hour up " the fteep afcent, we reached the rocky fummit, from whence the " moft enchanting profpect opened to our view. Before us lay extend- " ed the beautiful vale of Cleveland, with the county of Durham ; " woods, meadows, and corn-fields interfperfed with views of rural " villages, farms, and gentlemen's feats ; fome of which by their white- " nefs, gave an animating gaiety to the fcene. The river Tees is feen " winding through the valley, with ftately veffels gliding on its bofom, " which give additional beauty and variety to the profpect. To the " eaft we had the firft view of the fea, covered with fhips, whofe glit- " tering fails, now fully-bofomed to the wind, now edying to the

Roseberry Topping, from the N.º West

J.B. del.ᵗ

R. Scott sculp.ᵗ

" breeze, formed various fhades contrafted by the fun-beams, as they
" ftood in different directions, and prefented a pleafing variety to the
" enraptured fight. To the fouth, the profpect is bounded by a chain
" of hills, rifing behind each other in towering height, which feem to
" vie in lofty majefty with that on which we ftood ; the whole com-
" pofing fuch a fcene of beauty and fublime grandeur as can feldom
" be found united in one view ; it mocks defcription, and completely
" realizes the following beautiful lines of the poet :

> " Ever charming, ever new
> " When will the landfcape tire the view ?
> " The fountain's fall, the river's flow
> " The woody vallies, warm and low
> " The windy fummit, wild and high
> " Roughly rufhing on the fky
> " The pleafant feat, the ruin'd tow'r
> " The naked rock, the fhady bow'r,
> " The town and village, dome and farm
> " Each give to each a double charm."

Dyer's Grongar-Hill.

" WE left this delightful profpect with regret, highly gratified with
" our excurfion, the impreffion of which will dwell upon our minds,
" as long as the faculty of recollection remains unimpaired."

THIS remarkable eminence has been particularly noticed, both by
Camden and Speed ; the latter of whom, it has been afferted, borrow-
ed his defcription from the former ; and the following extract from an
ancient MS. in the Cott. library *(marked Julius F. C. fol. 455,)* compared with Camden's defcription given in the notes, ‡ will fhow how

‡ *EXTRACT from Camden ; (Bifhop Gibfon's edition).*
" NEXT Ounefberry Topping, a fteep mountain, and all over green, rifeth fo high as to appear
" at a great diftance ; and it is the land-mark that directs failors, and a prognoftic of weather to the
" neighbours hereabouts ; for when its top begins to be darkened with clouds, rain generally follows.
" Near the the top of it there iffues from a huge rock, a fountain very good for fore eyes ; and from
" hence the vallies round it, the graffy hills, green meadows, rich paftures, fruitful corn fields, rivers
" full of fifh, the creeky mouth of the Tees, fhores low and open, yet free from inundation, and the
" fea with fhips under fail, rendered the profpect very agreeable and entertaining."

E e 2

far that learned antiquary has been indebted to this curious manufcript.

"Towards the weft, there ftands a highe hill, called *Rofeberrye*
"*Toppinge*, which is a marke to the feaman and an almanack to the
"vale, for they have thys oulde ryme common

"When Rofeberrye Toppinge wears a cappe

"Let Cleveland then beware a clappe:

"thoe indeede yt feldome hath a cloude on yt that fome yll weather
"fhortly followeth yt not; where not farre from thence on a moun-
"tayne's fyde there are cloudes almofte contynually fmoaking, and
"therefore called the Devil's Kettles, which notwithftanding prognof-
"ticate neither goode nor badde; there are likewife many other ra-
"ryties more excellent than that I have fcene; yt hath fometymes
"had a hermytage on yt, now a fmall fmithes forge, * cut out of the
"rocke, called Willifryds Needle, whither blynde devotyon led many
"a fyllie foul, not without hazard of a breaknecke tumblinge, while
"they attempted to put themfelves to a needleffe payne creepyinge
"through that Needle's eye. †

"Out of the toppe of a huge ftone near the toppe of the hill, drops
"a fountaine which cureth fore eyes, ‡ receaving that virtue from the
"mineral; it is wonderful to fee, with what vyolence a ftone will
"tumble from the toppe of the hyll towards a lytle towne, called New-
"ton, the noife that yt makes is foe terrible, and then boundes aloft

---

* By modern vifitants called *the Cobler's Shop.* On the fide of the rock there are many initials
of names, and dates; the oldeft of which that we could difcover, is 1527.

† This fuperftirion muft be confidered fimilar to that practifed in the church of Ripon, which
Camden fays, in the days of his anceftors, was very famous, and called alfo *St. Wilfrid's Needle;*
this "was a ftrait paffage into a room elofe and vaulted under-ground, whereby trial was made of
"any woman's chaftity; if fhe was chafte, fhe paffed with eafe: but, if otherwife, fhe was, by I know
"not what miracle, ftopped and detained there."

‡ At prefent a fmall, infignificant fpring of clear water, which oozes through the fiffures of a
rock, and lofes itfelf on the brow of the hill; its fanative qualities are no longer known. The traditionary ftory that the Northumbrian Prince, *Ofwy,* was drowned here is too ridiculous to deferve
notice.

" in the ayre foe high, that as I am informed when you cafte a ftone
" once downe that hyll, a horfe that was tethered afar off for fear
" leaped over a great gate; and one encountring a bigge ould haw-
" thorne tree which onely ftood on the fyde of the hyll, yt dafhed it
" all in pieces as a tempeft, and ran forward without ftay till it ran to
" an earthen fence of a clofe, into which yt perced as yf it had been a
" great fhott, havinge ran in a moment from the toppe whence it was
" cafte, to the wall or fence aforefaid, at leafte a longe myle. I found
" in thys hyll *geate* and other myner011s, which I have not yet thought
" good to difcover. There is a moft goodly profpecte from the toppe
" of thys hyll, though paynefully gayned by reafon of the fteepneffe of
" yt, but efpecyally from the fide of the race on Barnaby-Moore;
" there you may fee a vewe the like whereof I never faw, or thinke
" that any traveller hath fcene any comparable unto yt, albeit I have
" fhewed yt to divers that have pafte throughe a greate parte of the
" worlde, both by fea and land. The vales, rivers, great and fmall
" fwellinge hylls and mountaynes, paftures, meadows, woodes, corne-
" fields, parte of the Bifhopricke of Durham, with the newe porte of
" Teafe lately found to be fafe, and the fea replenyfhed with fhippes,
" and a moft pleafaunt flatt coafte fubjecte to noe inundation or ha-
" zarde, make that countrye happy if the people had the grace to make
" ufe of theire owne happineffe, which may be amended if it pleafe
" God to fend them trafique and good example of thrifte."

Antiquarian Repertory. vol. V. No. I.

About half way up the fide of the hill, above the village of Newton, there is a large laminated rock, which confifts of a friable, and in-
durated ferruginous, or ochrey clay, of a gritty texture; and contains
an innumerable quantity of petrified fhells, and other marine fub-
ftances, fuch as are common in the northern feas. Thefe petrifactions
are *bivalves*, chiefly of the *cockle* and *oyfter kind;* the former are in a
good ftate of prefervation with refpect to their fhape, but on breaking
them, inftead of fifh they are found to contain a fubftance fimilar to

the rock, in which they are embedded.* The fhell appears different from its contents ; and being very brittle, breaks into thin, fhining flakes. The feams and traces, which diftinguifh the growth and texture of real fhells are, in many fpecimens, very perfect, and nicely preferved.

PETRIFIED *fcallop-fhells*, and the *ammonitæ*, or fnake ftones, are alfo found in the fub-ftrata of the rock ; but thefe are more rare, and feldom perfect. Befides thefe, *jett*, and pieces of *petrified wood* are fometimes difcovered ; and alfo *trochitæ*, or thunderbolts, as they are vulgarly called, in great numbers : which are conical ftones of various fizes from two to five or fix inches long, and from half an inch to one inch and a half in diameter at the bafe ; and are found fticking in pieces of the rock in a confufed manner, and in different directions ; from which circumftance, it is prefumed, they were called *thunderbolts* by the vulgar.

THERE is nothing, perhaps, in nature more difficult to be accounted for, or, which has given rife to more curious fpeculations, than the production of fuch petrified fea fhells, as may be found in this, and many of our higheft mountains. §

SEVERAL learned men of all nations have exercifed themfelves on this wonder, to fhew by what means, animals void of all local motion, or ponderous and moftly living at the bottom of the fea, came to be on high places at a diftance from the ocean.

---

* THE bafe of *Rofebury*, as well as the other hills in Cleveland, is compofed of immenfe ftrata of *alum-rock*, which extends to a depth unexplored; and when decompofed by expofure to the atmofphere, excludes almoft all vegetation, by the ferruginous particles it contains. Iron-ore is alfo found in great quantities in this, and the other Cleveland mountains, fometimes in detached pieces; but more frequently in a regular ftratum from fix to fourteen inches thick, extending from eaft to weft, in a line parallel to the horizon; but the ftrata here are found to dip to the fouth; which is a proof that they are not in the fame pofition, in which they were originally formed, but have been thrown up by one of thofe great convulfions of nature, which caufed the uneven furface of the earth.

§ THE elevation of the fummit of Rofebury has been found by obfervation to be 1488 feet above the level of the fea.

M. ANTHONY MORO, in a treatife on marine productions found in mountains, in which he endeavours to account for the wonder of their being carried up to fuch heights, is of opinion, that the mountains, in which fhells are found, were raifed by fubterraneous fires, which, burfting out under the fea, carried every thing in earth and fea before them. *Strabo, Juftin,* and *Seneca* certify, that feveral ifles have been formed by fuch eruptions; and Pliny mentions *Delos* and *Rhodes*, with other iflands rifing out of the bottom of the fea. ‖

MORO further fuppofes, that the earth was originally environed and covered with water. According to the account given by Mofes, *God commanded the waters to be gathered together*, which formed the fea, and *the dry land to appear;* which was done partly by fire, under the agency of that hand, *who maketh the fea to boil like a pot.* The earth, he believes, had a cruft of ftone, of an equal thicknefs; and fire, which was, and is ftill copioufly diffufed through the bowels of the earth, was the inftrument of the divine will to break it; by which explofion, the mountains were produced, and the mofs thown into its prefent figure and condition; * thus was that infinite number of teftaceous creatures thrown up from the bottom of the waters, to the fummit of the mountains.

THE vaft quantity of petrified fhells of different fpecies, in fo fmall a compafs, proves that they were fuddenly brought and left here; for had the waters, at the deluge, covered thefe places, and gradually ebbed off, which is the conjecture of fome writers, the fhell-fifhes would naturally have followed the current, and made their efcape; it is there-

---

‖ A NEW ifland, ten miles in circumference fprung up in the Archipelago, on the 12th day of May 1707; which, from the flames and fmoke that were feen at its appearing, and during its increafe, is concluded to have been produced by a fubterranean fire.

* MR. PLAYFAIR fuppofes that the power of the fame fubterraneous heat, which confolidated and mineralized the ftrata at the bottom of the fea, has fince raifed them up to the height, at which they are now placed, and has given them the various inclinations to the horizon, which they are found actually to poffefs.

fore, probable, that thefe mountains were heaved up by inward fire; a vaſt volume of water ruſhing through the chaſm, and in length of time draining away, the ſhells would be left dry; their petrifaction began with that of the land, earth, and mud, in which they were inveloped, as it happens in other petrifactions; that is, if any ſolid ſubſtance lodges in a liquid, or any ſoft matrix, which in proceſs of time, by natural agency, hardens and becomes ſtone, it petrifies along with its matrix, and without any change of figure or appearance, acquires a hardneſs and weight, beyond the ſtone, in which it is lodged.

To the above conjectures, we ſhall ſubjoin the following extract from *Sullivan's View of Nature*, which will be found applicable to, and illuſtrative of the ſubject.

" THE ſtrata, in which many foſſils are thus found, prove them, I muſt believe, to be of antediluvian period,—a period beyond the records of men, and attended with ſuch circumſtances, that we might not unreaſonably conceive ſome calamitous event had deſtroyed the greateſt part of animal life from the face of the earth, and conſigned to oblivion a cauſe, the record of which muſt otherwiſe have been tranſmitted from poſterity to poſterity to the very end of time."

THESE foſſil phenomena, indeed, afford a ſufficiency of examples to incline philoſophers to the opinion, that the earth has undergone commotions, abſtracted from a deluge; and that thoſe commotions might have deſtroyed its inhabitants partially, if not generally. But, had the ſea, little by little, got over the face of the earth; had it covered, and proportionably uncovered the plains and loftieſt mountains, we ſhould, in ſuch caſe, with the ſpoils of that element, every where find innumerable veſtiges of the habitations of men. But, there are no ſuch traces to be diſcovered. In every corner, we ſee marks of the dwellings of the ſea, but none of thoſe ſubmerged monuments, which ought to be met with. The earth, then, muſt repeatedly have burſt, and the waters have ruſhed into the chaſms, and cloſed the ſcene of exiſtence.

The petrifactions, which are thus found in a foffil ftate, are various; it is worth, however, obferving, that thofe of fhells are found on, or neareft to the earth, thofe of fifh deeper, and thofe of wood deepeft.

It would be impertinent, perhaps, and uninterefting to the generality of our readers, to notice further the various conjectures of different writers relative to this curious fubject; confidering however, the prominent idea which pervades the whole, we may with propriety, felect the following appofite lines from Ovid:

"Vidi ego, quod fuerat quondam folidiffima tellus
"Effe fretum; vidi factas ex Æquore terras;
"Et procul a pelago conchæ jacuere marinæ,
"Et vetus inventa eft in montibus anchora fummis;
"Quodque fuit campus, vallem decurfus aquarum
"Fecit; et eluvie mons eft deductus in Æquor."

Ovid. Met. lib. 15.

Within this parifh, at the northern extremity of Cliffrigg-Wood, and about two hundred paces to the eaftward from Langbargh-Quarry, there is a copious fpring of clear water, called *Chapel-Well*, which had formerly a bath, &c. and was, till of late years, much reforted to on the Sundays in the Summer months by the youth of the neighbouring villages, who affembled to drink the fimple beverage, and to join in a variety of rural diverfions. But the harmleffnefs of this innocent recreation was at length deftroyed by the introduction of *fpirituous liquors*, furnifhed by the village-innkeepers; when the cuftom became difcountenanced, and was foon afterwards difcontinued.

Near the well, there were the remains of feveral buildings; the foundations of which have been lately cleared away, in order to reduce the grounds to a ftate of cultivation; when, at the fame time, the bathhoufe was demolifhed, and the water conveyed by a drain to fome diftance.

From the veftiges of the buildings, and the name, *Chapel-Well*, it is probable that there was a hermitage or cell near, inhabited by fome monk, who, in the dark days of fuperftition, difcovered and promulged

F f

the virtues of its waters; which, even in modern times, were efteemed very efficacious in curing lamenefs, particularly when originating in *rickets*, *rheumatifm*, and fimilar complaints.

THE PARISH OF STOKESLEY.

FROM Seamer we were induced to proceed eaftwards to the parifh of Ayton, and from thence to Newton; but for the fake of connection, we muft now conduct the reader weftwards to the parifh of Stokefley, which is of confiderable extent, being upwards of feven miles from eaft to weft, and nearly feven miles broad; and contains the feveral town-fhips of Stokefley, Bufby and Eafby, with the hamlet of Tameton and a part of Newby. The parifh is bounded by Ayton, Kildale, and Kirk-by on the eaft, and by Rudby and Carleton on the weft; by Seamer and Marton on the north, and by Kirkby and Bilfdale chapelry on the fouth.

THE name feems to have a reference to the times of the Saxons; and the town which gives name to the parifh, was probably denomi-nated Stokefley, from *flock* or *floke*, which fignifies wood, and *ley*, a field or place; the fite of the town being then perhaps overfpread with ftocks or trunks of trees, which had efcaped ignition after the Roman invafion.*

---

* THE country, we may prefume, for many miles in circumference, was anciently one continued foreft of oaks; and when this part of Britain was reduced by *Cerealis*, in the reign of Vefpafian, no military plans could be effectually executed till the country was denuded, from whence the Romans were fubject to the frequent and dangerous incurfions of the *Brigantes*.

Upon the authority of Domeſday-book, it appears that Stokeſley
was anciently in the poſſeſſion of one of thoſe who were denominated
Thanes; who, according to Spelman, were the Saxon nobility, and divided into *Thani Regis, mediocres,* and *inferiores.* The firſt, in the Saxon
times, were equal to the barons in the Normans; as the *Thani mediocres*
were the leſſer barons, or lords of manors; and the *inferiores* made up
the loweſt degree of freeholders.

The manor here is entered in the general ſurvey, under the title

" Terra Tainorum Regis.

" Manerium in Stocheſlage, habuit Hauuart VI. carucatas terrae
" ad Geldum. Terra ad III. car. Ibi habet Uſtred I. carucatam, et
" VIII. villanos cum IIII. car. Ibi presbiter et Aeccleſia, et I. moldi=
" num X. fol. et VIII. acr. prati. Una legua long. et dim. latum. T.
" R. E. valebat XXIIII. lib. modo VIII. lib.

" Soca in Codeſchelf II. car. et II. bov. Turoldesbi II. car. En=
" glebi VII. car. Broſtune VIII. car. Tametun I. car. et dimid. cherchbi
" III. car. Dragmalbi III. car. Buſchebi V. car. et alia Buſchebi III.
" car. Simul ad geldum XXXIIII. et dimid. car. terrae ad XVI. car.
" Ibi funt nunc IX. ſochmanni, et XVIII. villani habentes X. car."

From the above extract it appears that the manor here was taxed at
ſix carucates held by *Hauuart,* with land ſufficient for three ploughs;
that *Uſtred* had one carucate and eight villeins with four ploughs; that
there was a miniſter and church; and one mill valued at ten ſhillings,
and eight acres of meadow. The manor at that period was only one
mile long, and half a mile broad; and in the Confeſſor's time was valued at twenty four pounds; but at the time of the ſurvey was eſtimat-
ed only at eight pounds.

To this manor there was a *ſoke,* or liberty within the following
places: viz. Skutterſcelf, Thoraldby, Ingleby, Broughton, Tameton,
Kirkby, Dromonby, great Buſby, and little Buſby, containing in the
whole thirty-four carucates of land and a half, *ad geldum;* beſides lands

F f 2

fufficient for fixteen ploughs; with nine fokemen and eighteen villeins who had ten ploughs.

THE lordfhip of Stokefley was granted at an early period, to the Ba- liols; who, as appears from Kirkby's Inqueft, † held this and other lands in Cleveland, of the King *in capite.* Guy de Baliol, who came in- to England with the conqueror, was lord here in the reign of William Rufus; and gave the church of Stokefley, and one carucate of land, to the Abbey of St. Mary's in York. The Baliols continued lords till the reign of Henry II. when the manor and eftate defcended by marriage with Ada, daughter of Robert, fon of Roger de Baliol, to John de Eure, lord of Warkworth, who procured a charter (8. Henry III.) for a fair here upon the eve and day of St. Thomas the martyr, (July 7th). ‡ He died 24. Henry III. leaving Ada his wife furviving, who gave to the King a fine of two thoufand marks for the wardfhip of his two fons by a former marriage: viz. Hugh and Robert. To Hugh and his heirs lawfully begotten fhe gave her manor houfe of Stokefley, and a moiety of the barony of Stokefley, and alfo a moiety of the foreft of Bafedale; and in default of fuch iffue, to Robert his brother (her fon, as fhe calls him), and his heirs.

THE Eures, who were a family of ancient note and eminence, and defcended from the Lords Clavering and Warkworth, and by the female line from the Vefcies and Attons, continued proprietors here for feveral generations; of whom Sir William Eure, Captain of the town and caftle of Berwick upon Tweed, and lord of the eaft marches of Scotland, was advanced (35. Henry VIII.) to the dignity of a Baron of this realm,

---

† JOHANNES DE BALIOL tenet IIII. feod. *de Rege in capite,* in Stokefley, Batherfby, Ingleby juxta Greenhowe, parva Broughton, Dromondby, Kirkby, magna Bufkeby, parva Bufkeby, Skotterfkelfe, Thoraldby et Newby: and Robertus, fil. Roger tenet ea de dicto Johanne. Et Hugo de Euer tenet eadem feod. de dicto Roberto, unde XIIII. car. ter. faciunt feodum. Et idem Hugo reddit Ballivo Regis Domini pro fine XVs. *Kirkby's Inqueft.*

‡ HUGO DE EURE clamat habere feriam in Stokefley, per cartam Domini Regis Henrici, patris Domini Regis, nunc *(market town)* et furcam; fcilicet qualibet, et a quo tempore non poteft inquiri, *Kirkby's Inqueft.*

which was enjoyed by his defcendants till the year 1707, when Ralph, Lord Eure, dying without iffue, the title became extinct.

THE manor and eftate at Stokefley were fold by William Lord Eure to Sir Richard Forfter, Bart. and the premifes conveyed are defcribed to be the barony, manor, and lordfhip of Stokefley, with the caftle or manor houfe and thirty oxgangs of land, within the fields and territories of Stokefley aforefaid; a water-corn mill, with the appurtenances, a common bake-houfe within the town of Stokefley, and all that foreft, moor, or wafte, called Stokefley, or Stockdale moor.

FROM the Forfters * the eftate defcended by marriage with Mary, fifter and heir of the laft Sir Richard Forfter, Bart. to William Collingwood, of Eflington, in Northumberland, Efq. who fold the fame, about the year 1690, to William Peirfon, of the Middle-Temple, London. He married Ann, daughter of Conftable Bradfhaw, of Nunthorp, Efq. and left iffue a fon, named Bradfhaw; who dying unmarried in the year 1746, devifed his eftates to the male-iffue of Winifred, wife of Victor Repinder, an Italian, whofe fon took the name of Bradfhaw Peirfon, and fucceeded to the eftates, which have been lately fold to different purchafers.

* *FORSTER of Stokefley.—Dugdale's Vifitation 1665.*

| William Forfter, of Erdfwick, in co. York, defcended from the Forfters of . . . . ., in the county of Northumberland. | . . . . ., daughter of . . . . . Longley, of . . . . ., in the Bifhoprick of Durham. |

| Sir Richard Forfter, of Stokefley, in co. York, Knt. and Bart. treafurer to Queen Mary, and likewife to Charles II. during their abode in France before the Reftoration. Created Bart. by Charles II. by his patent bearing date at St. Germains 18th Sept. 1649. He died in France 17th January 1661. | Joan, daughter of . . . . . Middleton, of Leighton, in co. Lancafter, Efq. Seth died unmarried. |

| Sir Richard Forfter, of Stokefley, Bart. ætat. 42. 1665. | Clare, daughter of Anthony Meynell, of Kilvington, in co. York, Efq. | Henry died in his father's life time. S. P. | Martha, dau. of . . . . . Anne, of Trickley, in co. York. | Anne, Lady Abbefs, of Pontoife, in France. |

| Sir Richard Forfter, Bart. died unmarried. | 1. Mary, fifter and coheir. | Wm. Collingwood, of Eflington, in Northumberland. | 2. Clare, fifter and coneir of Sir Richard, died unmarried. |

The manor, manfion houfe, and part of the eftate at Stokefley were purchafed by Thomas Wilkinfon, Efq. who has fince fold to the Rev. —— Hillyard, the prefent proprietor.

Stokesley is a fmall market-town; the houfes being difpofed in one broad ftreet running eaft and weft, and wafhed on the fouth by a principal branch of the river Leven. The buildings are neat, chiefly of a modern ftile, and not much of the countenance of antiquity remains, except in the fhambles and toll-booth which appear ancient and unfightly. The town is furrounded with rich and fertile lands; and being in a fine fporting country, the fituation poffeffes all the advantages of rural pleafures and retirement.

There is a weekly market here on Saturday, which is plentifully fupplied with provifions at reafonable prices; and two fairs annually: viz. on *Palm-fun-eve*, and on the eve of the Holy Trinity, for horfes, fheep, cattle, and coarfe linens, manufactured within the diftrict. There are no manufactories carried on here; and the lands near the town, which are chiefly in grafs, and occupied in fmall allotments, not affording conftant employment for the inhabitants, a general languor feems to prevail; and to thofe accuftomed to the more bufy fcenes of life, where the eagernefs and anxiety of every countenance is vifible, the contraft muft appear ftriking. So ftrangely are men's lives and purfuits varied, that we fee fome born down with the anxious cares and buftle of the world, whilft others are almoft totally unemployed. *

* The following extract of a letter from Stokefley, dated December 27, 1746, (publifhed in a provincial newfpaper) may ferve to evince the ftrong attachment of the inhabitants to the eftablifhed religion, and their loyalty to the family of the reigning Monarch of thefe Kingdoms.

Last Tuefday a number of *Stokefley* boys pulled fome tiles off *Mr. Pearfon's* mafs houfe, the damage of which might amount to 11s. The Papifts could not fee their place of worfhip thus infulted without refenting it; therefore got a warrant from *Mr. Skottowe* againft one of the boys (a failor) who had been the moft active in the affair. The conftables apprehended the boy the next day; upon which his affociates were called together to the number of near 200, and being joined by fome young fellows, marched in order (with drum beating and colours flying,) to *Mr. Skottowe's,* and declared to him, that they all acknowledged themfelves equally guilty with the boy charged with

THE church of Stokefley, dedicated to St. Peter, is rectorial. We have no evidence of its original foundation; but upon the authority of Domefday-book, it may claim a remote antiquity. It was granted at an early period, by Guy de Baliol, in *frank almoigne*, to the abbot and convent of Saint Mary at York, with one carucate of land, and the tithes of his demefne here; and continued a rectory in their patronage till the diffolution of the monaftry, when it was given by King Henry VIII. to the Archbifhop of York; †

---

the fact. *Mr. Skottowe* could not forbear laughing at them; however, after giving them a gentle reprimand, he difmiffed them, recommending it to the papifts, to put up with the damage. Upon this the boys went to *Ayton* beating up for volunteers for his Majefty's fervice, and enlifted about 30 or 40 boys; then march'd to *Stoksley-crofs*, fixed their colours upon it, and made large coal fires about it, the fpectators all wondering what were their intentions to act next: when they had completed the fires, they marched in a full body to the mafs-houfe, got upon it, ftripp'd off all the tiles, and beat down the cieling; from thence they let themfelves down into the chapel, pull'd it all to pieces, and tofs'd the things out of the windows into the yard, where they had placed a guard to fecure them. When they had got every thing out, not even fparing the doors and wainfcot, they march'd with their booty to the market-crofs, and fet the things around the fires; then, one of them put on a fine veftment and cap, with a mitre in his hand, and mounted the crofs, called them all around him, and made them a fpeech, in the conclufion of which he told them, that in confideration of the great fervice they had done to their King and country, in deftroying the mafs-houfe that day, he prefum'd from the great authority he was then invefted with, to abfolve them from all their paft fins; but exhorted them for the future to lead a peaceable and godly life; upon which they gave a great huzza, —*God fave King GEORGE; and down with the mafs*; then he put off his robes, and threw them into the fire; at the fame time each hand was employed in burning the reft of the things, laid ready for the flames: after which they difperfed, and went to their respective homes.

---

† STOKESLEY RECTORY.

DEDICATED to St. Peter. Archbifhop of York, patron.

FIRST fruits 30*l.* 6s. 10¼d. Tenths 3*l.* os. 8d. Procur. 7s. 6d. Syn. 2*l.* 14s.

INCUMBENTS.—1226, Laurence de Wilton. 1230, Stephen Pape, capell. 1255, Stephen de Anigma. 1311, John de Gilling. ——, John de Cockermouth. 1335, John Burton, *p. m.* Cockermouth. 1339, Thos. de Ripplyngham, *poft res.* Burton. 1339, William de Feriby, *poft res.* Ripplyngham. 1350, Walter de Wodehoufe, *poft res.* Feriby. ——, Ralph de Langley, *poft res.* Wodehoufe. 1372, Thos. de Fenby, *poft res.* Langley. 1373, John Carper, *poft res.* Fenby. ——, Adam dé ——, *poft res.* Carper. 1376, John de Sedgefield, *poft res.* ——. 1404, Thos. Wykerfley, *poft res.* Sedgefield. 1405, Thos. de Kirkeby, *poft res.* Wykerfley. 1416, John Barton, *poft res.*

There was a chantry within the church called Middleton's chantry; which, according to Torr, was founded about the year 1363, at the altar of St. Mary the Virgin, by William de Stokesley, for the souls of John de Middleton and Cecily his wife.

The church which stands towards the eastern extremity of the town, is a plain, but neat modern structure, roofed with blue slate, the ancient tower remaining. It is divided by a middle and two side-ailes, commodiously seated, and well lighted; and has a gallery on the west, with a small but handsome well-toned barrel-organ.

The rectory-house stands at a little distance towards the south, in a rather low, but pleasant and retired situation, on the southern brink of the Leven, sheltered on the north. It was rebuilt in the year 1792, on the site of an ancient edifice; and under the improving hands of the very Reverend the Dean of York, the present incumbent, is rendered an agreeable and commodious residence; the gardens are judiciously laid out, and the grounds enriched with plantations.

Adjoining to the church-yard on the north, stands the mansion or manor house; a square stone edifice, with spacious gardens, and a rising shrubbery in front, in a thriving condition. The house had, for some time, remained in a neglected state; but after it came into the possession of Mr. Wilkinson, it underwent a complete repair, and received considerable improvements, which render it a neat and commodious residence for a genteel family.

Within this township, at a little distance towards the north, lies the hamlet of *Tameton*, so called from its situation on the bank of the

---

Kirkeby. 1423, Robert de Newton, *post res.* Barton. ——, John Appilton, *p. m.* Newton. 1454, Rich. Wetwang, L. B. *p. m.* Appilton. 1463, Thos. Hornby, *p. m.* Wetwang. 1463, Geo. Ughtred, *p. m.* Hornby. 1487, Bryan Young, *post res.* Ughtred. 1517, Bryan Higden, D. D. *post res.* Young. 1539, Thos. Watson, *p. m.* Higden. ——, Hodde. 1554, Thos. Tenaunt, *post. privat.* Hodde, *pres. Queen Mary.* 1567, Richard Barnes, S. T. P. *pres. Archbishop of York.* ——. Thos. Cole. 1614, Henry Thurscoffe, M. A. *p. m.* Cole. 1653, Thos. Pennyman, D. D. 1688, Robert Ward, *pres. King James, in the vacancy.* 1723, Henry Cooke, *pres. Archbishop of York.* 1750, Francis Wanley, *pres. ibid.* 1791, George Markham, D. D. Dean of York.

river *Tame*. Here was an ancient manor which, according to Domefday furvey, was taxed for two carucates and a half; befides land fufficient for one plough, valued at twenty fhillings. This was demefne
of the crown entered in the general furvey, under the title

" Terra Regis.

" Manerium in Tametun. Leſing II. carucatas et dimid. ad gel-
" dum. Terra ad I. car. XX. folid."

THE manor of Tameton was foon afterwards granted by the conqueror to Robert de Brus, lord of Skelton, who held of the King *in
capite*; and his defcendants continued lords here, till the death of Peter
de Brus, the fourth of that name, without iſſue, when his fifters became
his heirs; and this with other eſtates, came by marriage with Lucia,
to Marmaduke de Thweng; of whom, according to Kirkby's Inqueſt, *
Nicholas de Meinell held a fourth part of one knight's fee, and paid,
as a fine, the fum of two fhillings.

TAMETON afterwards gave name to the refident family; and in
the reign of Henry III. we find the Moubrays proprietors here. William, fon of Walter de Moubray, was lord of Tameton about the year
1228; and poffeffing certain lands within the territory of Ayton, a
difpute arofe between the abbot and convent of Whitby, rectors of the
church of Ayton, and Laurence de Wilton, rector of Stokefley, about
a moiety of the tithes of lambs, wool, milk, and pigs, arifing from
the houfe of the faid William, lord of Tameton, which the abbot and
convent then received, but were claimed by the faid Laurence, as of
common right wholly belonging to his church at Stokefley, becaufe
the houfe, from which the faid tithes came, was fituate within the limits of Stokefley parifh. A diligent inquifition was at length made,

---

* NICHOLAUS DE MENNEL tenet quartam partem unius feodi de dicta hereditate (*Marmaduke
de Thweng*) in Tameton, unde XII. carucat. faciunt feod. et reddit Ballio Domini Regis II*.

Kirkby's Inqueſt.

G g

touching the right and poffeffion of the faid abbot and convent, when it was decreed that the abbot and convent, on account of a pafture in the territory of Ayton, where the cattle of the lords of the faid houfe of Tameton grazed, were juftly and lawfully entitled to a moiety of the faid tithes, as of right belonging to their church of Ayton. †

TAMETON at prefent affords little worthy of further notice; the lands have been long parcelled out, and the manorial rights are now difufed.

THE townfhip of

BUSBY,

comprehending great and little Bufby, lies about two miles to the fouth-weft from the town of Stokefley. Befides the lands, within the foke of Stokefley granted to the Baliols, there was a manor here, which was ancient demefne of the crown, taxed, according to the Domefday fur-vey, at one carucate and a half, with land fufficient for one plough.

" Terra Regis.

" Manerium in Bufchebi. Lefing I. Carucat. et dimid. ad geldum. " Terra ad I. car."

THIS manor, as appears from the appendix to Domefday-book, was granted by the conqueror, to Robert de Brus, of Skelton-caftle; whofe defcendants continued lords, till the death of Peter de Brus, the fourth, *fans iffue*; when the lands here defcended to his fifter Margaret, wife of Robert de Roos, who held of the King *in capite*; and of whom, according to Kirkby's Inqueft, Robert de Scoterfkelf, Richard Gower, and William Sturmey held two knights fees, where ten carucates made one knight's fee.—(See p. 96.)

---

† " THE difpute about the faid tithes was afterwards renewed by the agents of Stephen, rector of Stokefley, in the times of Serlo, John, and Roger, Arch-deacons of Cleveland, (Ralph Tameton, John the phyfician, Walter de Moubray, and William his fon fucceffively poffeffing the town of Tameton) when it was proved, by the evidence on oath of the vicars and chaplains belonging to the chapter of Cleveland, that the abbot and convent of Whitby were, beyond all contradiction, entitled to a moiety of the faid tithes."   *Chorlton's Hift. of Whitby.*

WILLIAM DE MOUBRAY, junior, alſo held a certain tenement in little Buſby of the ſaid Margaret, for which he paid as a fine, the ſum of two ſhillings. ‡

WE have no regular ſucceſſion of proprietors; the lands appear to have been long held in parcels. There was one culture of land, called *Stedflat*, within the territory of great Buſby, which was given by Gaufrid de Bret, de Carleton, to the abbey of Rievaulx; and it appears by the *fin. ebor.* (14. Edw. I. n. 36.) that theſe monks had 14 oxgangs of land in little Buſby. John de Langbergh alſo gave four oxgangs of his fee here to the monks at Rievaulx, which were confirmed by Robert de Scoterſkelfe. § The monks at Fountains alſo poſſeſſed lands here; to whom William de Tameton gave a way through his lands to their grange; through which none, except the monks of Rievaulx, ſhould be allowed to paſs.

THE village of great Buſby conſiſts of a few farm-houses and cottages, neatly built, and kept in decent repair. The Marwoods * have,

---

‡ WILLIMUS MOUBRAY, junior, pro quodam tenemento, quod tenet de illo feodo, in *parva Buſkeby*, reddit pro fine II^{s.}   *Kirkby's Inqueſt.*

§ THE land at little Buſby, and Standall-Coitt, belonging to the abbot and convent of Rievaulx, was leaſed out by them to James Crathorne, of Crathorne, Eſq. for the term of *twenty-one* years, next immediately after the death of *Raufe Conyers, Eſq.* then farmer thereof, for the ſum of 26*l.* 15s. This leaſe bears date, July 10, 1535.

* *THE pedigree of MARWOOD, of Little Buſby.*

Edward Marwood, de Nunthorpe, obiit, 3d October, 1557.

Marmaduke Marwood, ſon and heir.

James Marwood, of Nunthorpe, ..., daughter of James Cleaſby, in co. York.   of Cleaſby, in co. York.

2. Henry Marwood, of Little Buſby, heir to his brother; ob. 1639. — Ann, dau of J. Conſtable, of Dromonby, in co. York.   1. William, ob. S. P.   Margary, wife of .... Ward, of Nunthorpe.   Dorothy, wife of ... Winterton, of ..., co. Warwick.

for fome time, been the principal proprietors : William Marwood, Efq.
is the prefent owner and lord of the manor ; whofe manfion at little
Bufby, fituated on the brow of a hill, and furrounded with thriving
plantations, is ftrikingly romantic ; but at too great a diftance from
the public road to afford a diftinct view to the traveller.

THE townfhip of

EASBY ;

(q. d. *Eaftby,*) was probably at firft fo named from its fituation in the
eaftern extremity of the parifh, about four miles eaft from the town of
Stokefley.   It appears from the Domefday-book, that the manor here
was ancient demefne of the crown ; and at the time of the furvey,
where it is entered under the title "𝕮𝖊𝖗𝖗𝖆 𝕽𝖊𝖌𝖎𝖘," was taxed for two
carucates ; befides land fufficient for one plough.

Barbara, wife of Jofias Matthews, grandfon to Tobias Matthewes, Archbifhop of York.

Anne, wife of Gyles Wetherall, of Stockton, in co. Pal. Durham.

1. Sir G. Marwood, of Little Bufby, Bart.__Frances, dau. of Sir Walter Bethell, of Alne, *co. Ebor. Knt.*

2. William.

3. Francis, a citizen of London.

3. Walter. 2. George, a Hambro' merchant.

Margaret, dau. of Conyers Lord Darcy and Conyers, 1ft wife ; ob. S. P.__Sir Henry Marwood, Bart. obiit. 1725.__Dorothy, dau. of Alan Bellingham, of Levens, co. Weftmorland, fecond wife.

1. Barbara, wife of Sir Tho. Hebblethwaite, of Norton, co. York, Knt.

2. Anne, wife of Wm. Metcalfe, of Northallerton, Efq. anceftors of the prefent Wm. Marwood, Efq.

3. Frances, wife of Rich. Wefton, of Gray's Inn.

Margaret, aged 4, 13th Sept. 1665 ; died in her mother's lifetime.

George Marwood, Efq. died in his father's lifetime.__Lucia, daughter of . . . . Smith, of . . . .

Jane Marwood, only dau. and heir to her grand-father. She died without male-iffue, and devifed her eftates to her nephew Wm. Metcalfe, Efq. of Northallerton, who took the name of Marwood.__Chomley Turner, of Kirkleatham, Efq.

Marwood William Turner died unmarried, and in his mother's lifetime.

A daughter married to Colonel Straubenzie.

" Manerium in Esebi. Hauuard II. carucatas ad geldum. Terra
" ad I. car."

WE have no evidence, to fhew how long Eafby continued in the
hands of the crown; it was probably firft granted out by the conqueror, together with the manor of Stokefley and other lands in this
neighbourhood to the Baliols; and from them came by marriage to
the Eures; who, being defcended from a younger branch of the Barons
of Warkworth, took their name from their lordfhip and feat of *Eure*
in Buckinghamfhire. John de Eure was lord of Eafby in the reign
of Edward I. and in the 35th year of that King's reign, obtained a
charter of free-warren in all his demefne lands here. This family
became afterwards very famous; and feveral of their defcendants
were fheriffs of Yorkfhire in the reigns of Edward II. Richard II. and
Henry VI. The Eures continued lords of Eafby for feveral generations; till male-iffue failing in Ralph, the laft Lord Eure, who died
in the year 1707, his fifters became his heirs. Elizabeth, the eldeft,
married William Kay; whofe grand-daughter Elizabeth (the daughter and heirefs of Horatio Kay) wife of William Walker, of Doncafter,
Efq. left iffue a daughter married to the late John Matthews, of Stokefley; who, in right of his wife, was poffeffed of one half of the eftate
of the Lord Eure. William Lee, of Stokefley, by marriage with Frances,
daughter of the faid John Matthews, became the principal proprietor
of Eafby, and is the prefent lord of the manor.

THE village of Eafby, which confifts chiefly of a few farm-houfes,
ftands in a pleafing wooded vale, watered by a branch of the Leven;
on the eaftern bank of which ftands EASBY-HALL, formerly a feat
of the Lords Eures. This is an ancient edifice of no very great dimenfions, now converted into a farm-houfe, which is old and ruinous, and
falling faft to decay.

PEDIGREE of EURE of Easby, Ingleby, &c. in Cleveland, in the county of York.

THORESBY (in his *Ducatus Leodiensis*) says, 'the following pedigree is transcribed from an ancient roll in the possession of the last Lord Eure; and from other writings of the family, communicated to him by the coheirs thereof. Some further additions have been communicated to us by a particular friend.

ARMS.—Quarterly *or* and *gules* upon a bend *sable*, three escallops, *argent*.

Ricardus, pater originalis hujus familiæ.——Rose, daughter of Walter Gifford, Earl of Langueville, in Normandy.

Roger, lord of Warkworth, in Nor-thumberland, by gift of Henry II.——Adeliza, dau. of Henry de Essex; who by her husband, Albert de Vere, had issue, Robert, Earl of Oxford.

Robert, lord of Warkworth and Clavering, in Essex, by gift of Henry II.——Margaret, daughter of W. de Cheney, relict of H. de Cressy.

John, lord of Warkworth, Clavering, and Eure, by gift of Henry I.——Ada de Baliol, daughter of Robert, son of Roger de Baliol.

Roger, lord of Warkworth, Clavering, and Eure; from whom the Claverings descended.

Hugh de Eure; he added 3 escallops to the bend on the arms.

......, daughter of Roger Bertram, baron of Mitford.

Robert de Eure, Knt. had Axholme, in Lincolnshire; he added 3 fleur de lis to the bend.——Isabel, dau. of Roger de Merlaco, baron of Morpeth, in Northumberland.

Robert Eure, of Axholme.=

John de Eure, Knt. 35. Edw. I.——Agnes, daughter of John de Insula, Knt.

Stephen Eure.——Margaret, daughter and heir of Sir Peter Lound, Knt.

John de Eure, Knt. obiit 30. Edw. III =

Sir Hugh de Eure, K t =....., dau. and heir of ....

John de Eure, Knt. ob. 35. Edw. III. 1362.——Margaret, dau. of .....

Robert Eure,——Catherine, dau. of .... Cheney.

Robert de Eure, æt. 26, 40. Edw. III.——Isabel, dau. of Adomar de Atholia, lord of Fenton.

Wm Eure, Knt. living Rich. II.——Catherine, dau. and coheir of Wm de Ayton, Knt. (Lord Vesey).

James Eure.——Elizabeth, dau. of Sir Richard Tempest, Knt.

Margaret.——John Pudsey.

Robert Eure, Esq.=

Ralph, Knt. ob. vitâ patris. (S. P.)

William Eure, Knt. 17. Henry IV.——Matilda, dau. of Henry Lord Fitz-Hugh, Baron of Ravensworth, co. York.

Robert Eure——....., of Leicester.

Henry Eure, ob. S. P.——.....dau. of Rob. Danby.

William was vicar of Leeds.

Ralph Eure, Knt. killed at Towton Field, 1. Edw. IV.——Eleanor, dau. of John, Baron of Grayftock.

Thomas.——Margaret, dau. of ... Danby.

John.

Robert =...; dau. of Robert Tempest.

Margaret, dau. of = Sir W. Eure, = Conftance, widow Sir Robert. Ralph. Hugh, a John, Henry. Anne. Margery a nun Joan.
Rob. Conftable, | Knt. | of Sir H. Percy. clergyman. ob. S. P. at Witton, in co. Elizabeth.
Knt. Durham.

Henry. John. Euftace.

Robert Eure, = ..., daughter William, Merriel, dau. of = Sir Ralph Eure, = Agnes, dau. of ... Margery Elizabeth. Ann.
of Bradley, of R. Tempeft, vicar of Sir Hugh Haift. | Knt. ob. 1533. | Conftable, widow of a nun.
ob. S. P. Leeds. .ings, Knt. Ralph Bagot. Agnes.

Sir Wm. Eure. = Eliz. dau. of Chriftopher Lord Hugh and John Frances married Sir G. Margaret mar. Henry Pudfey, of Jane.
Willoughby, of Ereby. died infants. Conyers, of Stockburn. Barforth; 2dly to ... Pennington.

Sir Ralph Eure, Knt. = Margery, dau. of Henry Eure, = Eleanor, dau. of Anne, married Merriel, married Sir Margery, married
killed at Peniel-beuch; Sir Ralph Bowes, of Bifhop- | John Hebborne. Anth. Thorpe. G. Bowes, of Dalden. Wm. Buckton.
vita patris. 1545. of Streatlam. Middleham.

William. Ralph. Margery. Mary.

Sir William Eure, Knt. created Lord Eure. = Margaret, dau. of Sir Edw. Dymock, Knt. Ralph. Thomas. Frances, married
1584. Buried at Ingleby 13th Feb. 1593. | Buried at Ingleby, 15th September, 1591. Rob. Lambton.

Mary, dau. of = Ralph, Lord Eure, Lord = Elizabeth, dau. of Sir Eliz. dau. of = Sir Francis. Ellen, dau. of .... Morris,
Sir G. Dawney, | Prefident of Wales; fold John Spencer, Knt. J. Lennard, | Eure; ob. | widow of John Owen.
of Seffay. Ingleby to Sir David Fou- widow of Geo. Lord 1ft wife. 1621.
lis, 1609. Hunfdon; ob. S. P. Crompton Eure.

Sir Wm. Eure. = Catherine, dau. of Sir Wm. Bowes. Charles Eure. = ..., dau. of Ingham. Merriel. Ann. Martha.

3. Henry, ob. infans. 2. Wm. Eure, of Elvet, æt. 58. 1656. = Mary, dau. of Pelir Forcer, of Harberhoufe. Thomas, of Bradby.

Peter, æt. 12, 1666. ob. unmar. 1687. Mary, æt. 15, 1666 = N. Johnfon, of Twizil, in North Bifhoprick, Efq.

Wm. Lord Eure, K. B = Lucy, daughter of Andrew Noel, Knt.

Ralph Eure, ob. = Catherine, dau. of Thos. Will. am Eure, killed = ..., dau. of Mary. Elizabeth. Margaret. Frances.
vita patris. | Lord Arundal, of War- in 1645. | Tho. Denton.
dour.

Wm. Lord Eure, died unmarried; Thomas Eure, Margaret, married Thos. Danby, Mary, married Wm. Palmes, Efq.
fucceeded his grandfather. killed 1645. Efq. firft Mayor of Leeds. of Linley, co. ebor.

Horace Eure.=Deborah, dau. and coheir of　William, ob.　Sir Sampson Eure, one=Martha, dau. of　Frances Eure.
　　　　　　　| John Brett, Esq. of Kent.　1620, S. P.　　of the Welch Judges.　　Anth. Cage, Esq.

Francis,　George, Lord Eure,　Horace & Sampson,　Ralph, the last　Elizabeth, eldest=Wm. Kay.　Deborah, the___John Pickering,
ob. S.P.　ob. 1672, S. P.　　ob. S. P.　　Lord Eure, died　sister & coheir of |　　younger sister　gent. ob. 1699,
　　　　　　　　　　　　　　　　　　　　S. P. 1707.　　Ral. Lord Eure. |　　and coheir.　　ætat. 75.

Horatio Kay.=Frances, dau. of Edward　　1. Bathia　=Joseph Sikes, of Leeds,　2. Bathshua.　John Lister, ob.　3. Mercy.=
　　　　　　| Armstrong, of Corby, Esq.　　　　　　| merchant, ob. 1709.　　　　　　S. P. 1707.

Horatio Kay.=Eliz. dau. of Wm. Gregory,
　　　　　　| of Barnby Dunn, Esq.　　　　　　John.　Caleb.　Elisha.　Hannah Hesketh, 1712.=Robert.　Elizabeth.

Elizabeth, dau.=William Walker, of Doncaster,
and heiress.　| Esq. ob. January 15, 1722.　　　　　　　　　　　　　　　　　　　　Joseph.

Ralph, ob.　Armstrong,　Ann =Rich. Hornby.　　　Susannah.=John Matthews, of Stokesley, gent. who in right of his wife, was
S. P.　　died S. P.　　　|　　　　　　　　　　　　| possessed of half the estate of the Lord Eure; as appears from a
　　　　　　　　　　　　　　|　　　　　　　　　　| partition deed of the last Lord Eure's estates; dated June 17, 1708.

Elizabeth, died Aug. 26, 1739. aged 12.　Wm Hornby, ob. S. P.

Hannah, dau. and heir.=John Matthews, Esq.=Anne, dau. of Stephen　Elizabeth.　Frances.=Wm. Lee, of　Susannah.=Zach. Hub-
of John Wilkinson, of | of Tynemouth, co. | Wright, of Dockeray　　　　　　has issue.　Stokesley,　　　　berthy, Esq.
Whitby, Esq. 1st wife. | Northumberland. | Square in the parish of　　　　　　　　　　　Esq.
　　　　　　　　　　　　　　　　　　　　| Tynemouth.

A son and three daughters.　　　　　Two sons and four daughters.

At the south end of the village, there was an ancient chapel; " for the dedication whereof, and of its chapel-yard a conceffion iffued " out on 7th Auguft, 1349." *Torr's MSS.*

There are no remains of this chapel left; the fite of which was diftinctly vifible, till within a few years; but the ground which is ftill known by the name of the *Chapel-Garth*, having been lately brought into tillage, the foundation of the building can now, with difficulty be traced.

The SOIL, PRODUCE, and GENERAL APPEARANCE of the parifh next demand the reader's attention; and thefe will be found to vary according to the different afpect and fituation. Near the town of Stokefley, the foil is in general a deep fertile loam; and the lands being chiefly in grafs, and inclofed with quickfet-hedges, the general appearance is pleafing. Towards *Tameton* and in the northern extremity of the parifh, the land inclines towards the fouth; where the foil is more of a clayey nature, but produces abundant crops of wheat, oats, and beans, which are principally cultivated.

The townfhip of *Bufby* lies towards the fkirts of the mountains, with an eafy inclination to the north; the foil here is chiefly a gravelly loam, and notwithftanding its northern afpect, tolerably fertile. The grounds of BUSBY-HALL exhibit the beautiful effects of planting; and the manfion, being placed on the brow of a confiderable eminence, commands a pleafing profpect.

The lands within the townfhip of *Eafby* afford little worthy of particular notice; the foil inclines to a clayey loam; and the inclofures being divided with quickfet-hedges, with a number of trees in the hedge-rows, the country wears a rich and woody appearance. From the bottom of the vale, Rofeberry Topping prefents its peaked fummit in a picturefque point of view.

POPULATION.—We have already noticed the almoft total abfence of manufactures, which will in fome degree account for the flow, but

H h

gradual increafe of inhabitants within the parifh. From the return made to government, under the population act, * in the year 1801, it will appear that there were then 372 houfes, 394 families, and 1628 inhabitants; giving an average of 4⅓ nearly to each family. The following table of baptifms, &c. extracted from the parifh regifters, will enable the reader to judge of its increafing ftate of population.

	Bap.	Bur.	Mar.
From the year 1680 to 1699 inclufive -	438	519	122
1780 to 1799 - - -	1042	821	231
Increafe	604	302	109

FROM the above table we may remark, that on an average of 20 years, the annual number of baptifms to that of burials is $52\frac{1}{10}$ to $41\frac{1}{2}$; and that out of the total number of inhabitants, (the males and females being nearly equal) one out of 40 nearly dies annually.

* STATE of population, taken 10th March, 1801.

Townfhips.	Inhabited houfes.	Fami-lies.	Uninhabit-ed houfes.	Males.	Females.	Total.
Stokefley	334	351	9	610	759	1369
Bufby	17	17	1	60	61	121
Eafby	21	26	–	61	77	138
Totals	372	394	10	731	897	1628

THE PARISH OF KIRKBY;

WHICH is of no great extent, lies about two miles diftant from the market town of Stokefley, towards the fouth; and is bounded by the parifhes of Ingleby and Stokefley on the eaft, weft, and north; and fhut in by the mountains, which divide it from the chapelry of Bilf-dale, on the fouth.

THE village of Kirkby is fituate at a fhort diftance from the bafe of the mountain, and contains about twenty families occupied chiefly in hufbandry. The houfes run nearly north and fouth, and are built of freeftone, dug from quarries upon the adjoining common.

FROM Domefday-book it appears that the lands here were, at the time of the Conqueror's furvey, within the foke of Stokefley, and contained three carucates rated *ad geldum.* The Baliols were anciently proprietors, from whom the manor came by marriage to the Eures, who continued lords for feveral generations, and defcended in the year 1707 to the coheireffes of the laft Lord Eure, who died without iffue; and afterwards by marriage became the property of the late John Matthews, Efq. of Stokefley, who fold the fame to Thomas Wayne, Efq. of Anngrove-Hall, the prefent proprietor, and lord of the manor.

MUCH of the lands within this parifh appear to have been granted, at an early period, to different religious houfes; and this town, like many others, gave name to a refident family here; for we find, that Simon, fon of Adam de Kirkby, gave an oxgang of land, with a toft

H h 2

and croft in this territory, to the priory of Guifborough, for fupporting a light at the great altar; and that William de Mowbray, lord of
Tameton, gave to the faid priory, the homage and fervice of John, fon
of Robert, fon of Rayner de Kirkby, and Alan his brother, with their
families, and all their cattle.   *Burton's Mon. Ebor. p.* 347.

THE monks of Rievalx had alfo lands here, and at Broughton within this parifh, for which, according to Kirkby's inqueft, † they were
exempted from doing homage by John de Eure.

THE church of Kirkby, (dedicated to St. Auguftine) ftands upon
a dry, elevated fituation, and is built in the form of a crofs, with a
low fquare tower rifing in the centre. We have no documents to
point out the era of its original foundation; nor do we find any particular traces of great antiquity in its ftyle of architecture; but the
circumftance of the church giving name to the parifh concurs with
the form of the building, to point out its original importance, there
being few, we believe, with the tower between the chancel and the
nave, except churches of more than ordinary confequence.

THIS church was given by Adam de Aengleby, fon of Viel, to the
abbey of Whitby; and, according to Torr, " confifted both of a rec-
" tory and a vicarage, which continued in the patronage of the abbot
" and convent till the diffolution of their monaftry, in the reign of
" Henry VIII. and then the King exchanged the rectory with the
" Archbifhop of York, for other lands belonging to his fee; where-
" upon the patronage thereof was the Archbifhop's and his fucceffors;
" and the patronage of the vicarage did from that time belong to the
" rector for the time being."   *Torr's MSS.*

---

† DICUNT, quod Abbas de Rievallibus clamat habere libertat. in omnibus terr. finibus in *Brough-*
ton et *Kirkby*, quas habuit ex Dono Jurdon Payne, Alani Baren, et alior. liberor. hominum de eifdem villis prædictis, tenend. eas terras quiete et folute ab eorum fervitio feculari, et ab omni opere
fervili, per cartam Richardi Regis, et Regis Henrici, patris Domini Regis nunc Anno LIVto.
                                                      Kirkby's Inqueft.

THERE are no monumental infcriptions worthy of notice; within the church-yard there are two effigies cut in ftone, reprefenting a malé

RECTORY OF KIRKBY.

DEDICATED to St. Auguftine.   Archbifhop of York, patron.

FIRST FRUITS, 21*l*. 8s. 6½d.   Tenths, 2*l*. 2s 10¼d.   Procur. 7s. 6d.   Syn. 2*l*. 8s.

INCUMBENTS.

RECTORS.	VICARS.
1305, Thomas de Eure, *cl.*	1313, John Barthum, *de Gyfburne,*
1317, Galfrid de Fulford, *pbr.*	1317, Galfrid de Fulford, *pbr.*
1318, John de Heflarton, *cl.*	1333, William de Lythum, *pbr.*
1321, Robert de Heflarton,	1348, John de Mikilby, *cap.*
1329, Edm. de Hawefworth, *acolitus,*	1349, Thomas Meaux, *pbr.*
1336, John de Carnubia, *pbr.*	1362, William Gorton, *cap.*
1340, John de Wilton, *cappellanus,*	1370, Richard Bergh, *pbr.*
1342, John de Carnubia, *pbr*	——, William de Aton,
1347, Thomas de Middleton, *cap.*	1397, John, fil. Henry Glover, *cap.*
1371, John de Ulfeby, *pbr.*	1414, John Dun, *pbr.*
——, Adam de Neffefeld,	1420, John Nikfon, *de Semer, pbr.*
1387, William Sutton de Farndon,	1437, John Neffe, *alias* Roridon,
——, William Salefbers,	1442, John Selby, *pbr.*
1401, John Fraunceys, *pbr.*	1449, Richard Mildynhall, *pbr.*
——, John Bollefer,	1501, Richard Tollerton, *pbr.*
1406, Thomas Parye,	1529, Thomas Smyth, *pbr.*
1410, Robert Darbridge Court,	1570, Richard Turner, *cl.*
1414, John Bakepar, *pbr.*	1572, Henry Rountree, *cl.*
1416, Thomas Aleby, *cl.*	1592, William Jagger, *cl.*
1457, Richard Driffeld, *pbr.*	1627, Thomas Oddie, B. A.
1462, Thomas Wright, *pbr.*	1661, Jac. Wilkynfon, *diac.*
1464, Chriftopher Brown, *cap.*	1697, Robert Carr,
1500, Robert Mafon, *pbr.*	1727, Richard Carr,
1502, Martyn Collyns,	1728, Robert Warton,
1509, Thomas Magnus, *pbr.*	1745, William Ellis,
1550, William Latymer, *pbr.*	1788, George Grenfide.
1554, William Berry, *cl.*	
——, Robert Pala, *pbr.*	
1575, Thomas Sucklemore, *cl.*	
——, Thomas Cole,	
1614, George Proctor, M. A. *cap. ordin. Regi.*	
1625, Jofias Matthew, B. A.	
1662, John Matthew, M. A.	
1673, Lucius Walker, M A.	
1691, Charles Palmer, S. T. P.	
1705, The Hon. Edward Finch,	
1737, Thomas Hayter,	
1749, Thomas Murgatroyd, *by the King.*	
1780, Pierfon Lloyd,	
1781, Cyril Jackfon, D. D.	

and female, § much mutilated, which we conjecture to have been erected for some of the family of Eure, who were anciently lords here.

Not far from the church, towards the southern extremity of the village, there is a free-school, with a house and garden for the use of the master, built in the year 1683, by Henry Edmunds, Esq. ‡ who possessed considerable property within the parish, and endowed the said school with lands here, which produce an income of about 40*l.* per annum, for which all the children within the village and township of Kirkby claim the privilege of education. The rector and vicar, and two church-wardens of Kirkby for the time being,—the rector of Stokesley, and the lord of the manor of Kirkby are trustees, appointed for the government of the said school, the nomination of the master, and other purposes.

Within this township, at a little distance to the west from the village of Kirkby, lies the hamlet of Dromonby ; which consists of a few scattered farm-houses, with the capital messuage, or mansion-house of the lord of the manor, called Dromonby-Hall, anciently the residence of the Constables.

Dromonby, at the time of the Domesday survey, was within the soke of Stokesley, and rated for three carucates. It appears from Kirkby's Inquest, and other authorities, that the Stormeys were ancient proprietors here, and held under the Baliols lords of Stokesley. From the Stormeys, the manor and estate passed by marriage to the Con-

---

§ The traditionary story, that this is the monument of one Lockey, or Lockwood, and his wife, who died through an extraordinary exertion in mowing a certain field, still known by the name of *Lockey's day's work*, is hardly worthy of attention.

‡ Over the door of the School-house, upon a square stone, is the following inscription :—

DONVM H. EDMVNDS, Ari.

A. D. 1683.

ftables, * who continued lords for feveral generations, and from them defcended by marriage with Dorothy, daughter of John Conftable, to Thomas Middleton, Efq. Of the immediate fucceeding proprietors

* CONSTABLES of Dromondby.

FROM the vifitation, A. D. 1612. Extracted from the Herald's Office, by *W. Radyclyffe, Rouge Croix, pourfurvant.*

ARMS.—Quarterly *gules* and *vair*; a bend, *or*, charged with an *orle*. Quartering *fable*, a lion rampant, *arg.* No Creft.

Sir Robert Conftable,— of Flamborough.

Stormey, fuit Dominus de Dromonby, in Cleveland.—

Sir Marmaduke Conftable.—

William Stormey.—Juiyan.

John Stormey.—Alice.

Agnes, daughter of Sir Roger Wentworth, of Nettlefted, in the county of Suffolk, Knt. 1ft *wife.*—Sir Robert Conftable.

Sir Robert—...., dau. of .... 2d wife.

Thomas Stormey.—Ifabell.

Sir Marmaduke. Sir William.

John Stormey.—Alice.

Robert Conftable.—Alice, daughter of John Stormey.

Robert Conftable.—Beatrice, daughter of .... Nesfield.

....., daughter of ....—Robert Conftable, of—Joan daughter of Thomas Gower, Roos, of Igmanthorpe. | Barnby Buffall. | of Stitnam, (2d wife).

Robert Con-—Eliz. dau. of Sir Tho. ftable. | Gower, ob. S. P.

Marmaduke—Anne, dau. of Sir Tho. Conftable | Mauleverer, of Allerton, Knt.

William, 2d fon.

Thomas, 3d fon, S. P.

John Conftable, Efq.—Margaret, dau. of Wm. Fulthorpe, of Ifelly, Efq.

Anne, wife of Tho. Pawle.

Agnes, dau. to—John Conftable, of—Ann, dau. of John William Bate, | Dromonby, in Cleve- | Conyers, of Hoton, (1ft wife). | land, Efq. 1612. | (2d wife).

Frances, wife of Laurence Sutton.

John Conftable,—Jane, daughter of fon and heir, | Chriftopher Wilde, (living 1612). | of Lazenby.

Marmaduke,—...., dau. of Marga- 2d fon. | Ralph Hurfte. ret.

Dorothy.—T. Middleton.

1. Anne. ....., 2d dau.

Charles, fon and heir, æt. 10, 1612.

Anne, wife of Henry Marwood, (had iffue).

1. Sir John—Dorothy, 3d dau. & Conftable, | coheir of Benedict Knight. | Barnham, Alderman | of London.

2. Thomas, 3. William, 4. Roger, 5. Marmaduke, (*vifitation* 1612.)

6. Charles, 7. Philip, 8. Robert.

1. Jane.—..... Ellerker. 2. Ann.—John Holmes. 3. Mary died unmarried. (*Signed John Conftable.*)

we are uninformed.　The lands are in the poffeffion of different freeholders, and the manor, with the ancient manfion and a good eftate
are now the property of —— Farrer, Efq.

THE abbot and convent of Fountains poffeffed lands in this territory, by the grants of different benefactors; which were confirmed
by Thomas, fon of John de Stormey, 25. Edw. III.

THE townfhip of

BROUGHTON

comprehending great and little Broughton, lies to the eaft.　The village of Great Broughton, which contains about 100 houfes, and upwards of 400 inhabitants, is regularly built upon a fpacious level green
or common; and the houfes running in a direction nearly north and
fouth, are built of freeftone, and are neat, and kept in good repair.

THE inhabitants, befides a few farmers and independent families,
are chiefly linen weavers, and other mechanics.

OF the manor of Great Broughton, we find the following mention
in Domefday-book, under the title

" 𝕮𝖊𝖗𝖗𝖆 𝕮𝖔𝖒𝖎𝖙𝖎𝖘 𝕸𝖔𝖗𝖎𝖙𝖔𝖓𝖎𝖊𝖓𝖘𝖘.

" 𝕴𝖓 𝖒𝖆𝖌𝖓𝖆 𝕭𝖗𝖔𝖈𝖙𝖚𝖓𝖊 𝖆𝖉 𝕲𝖊𝖑𝖉𝖚𝖒, V. 𝖈𝖆𝖗𝖚𝖈𝖆𝖙𝖆𝖊, 𝖊𝖙 III. 𝖈𝖆𝖗. 𝖕𝖔𝖋𝖋𝖚𝖓𝖙
" 𝖊𝖋𝖋𝖊.　𝕴𝖇𝖎 𝖍𝖆𝖇𝖚𝖎𝖙 𝕯𝖔𝖗𝖒𝖆𝖓 I. 𝖒𝖆𝖓𝖊𝖗𝖎𝖚𝖒; 𝖓𝖚𝖓𝖈 𝖍𝖆𝖇𝖊𝖙 𝕹𝖎𝖌𝖊𝖑 𝖉𝖊 𝕮𝖔-
" 𝖒𝖎𝖙𝖊, 𝖊𝖙 𝖜𝖆𝖋𝖙𝖚𝖒 𝖊𝖋𝖙.　𝕿. 𝕽. 𝕰. 𝖇𝖆𝖑𝖊𝖇𝖆𝖙 XXV. 𝖋𝖔𝖑.　𝕮𝖔𝖙. 𝖒𝖆𝖓𝖊𝖗𝖎𝖚𝖒
" II. 𝖑𝖊𝖚𝖈. 𝖑𝖔𝖓𝖌. 𝖊𝖙 I. 𝖑𝖆𝖙."

Margaret, dau. of William, Lord Howard, of Naworth Caftle, Cumberland, (1ft wife.)	Sir Thomas Cotton, of Connington.	Alice, fole dau. and heirefs, (2d wife.)	Edmond Anderfon, of Ey-worth, Bedfordfhire, Efq. † (fecond hufband).

Frances. Sir Tho. Proby.	Alice. Sir Humph. Monax, 1. Thomas, S. P. 2. Robert. 3. Philip.

Two daughters	Sir John Cotton. Dorothy Anderfon fole daughter and heirefs.

† WITHIN the chancel of the church of Eyworth, Bedfordfhire,—" In the fepulchre of his father, &c.
" lyeth buried the body of Edmond Anderfon, Efq. eldeft fon and heir of Sir Francis Anderfon, Knt.
" grand-fonne of Sir Edmond Anderfon, fometime Lord Chief Juftice of the Common Pleas.　He mar-
" ried Alice, the fole daughter and heir of John Conftable, late of Dromonby, in the countie of York,
" Knight, by whom he had iffue only one daughter, named Dorothy.　Ob. 4th April, 1638, leaving his
" faid daughter 9 years old."　　　　(*Vide Collins's Baronetage, vol.* 4. *p.* 430. *Edit.* 1741.)

FROM which it appears that the land here was taxed for five carucates, befides three more that might be rendered arable; and was held
before the conqueft, as one manor by Norman; but in the Conqueror's
time, was in the hands of Nigel, who held under Robert, Earl of Mortain, and was then wafte. The manor, being two miles in length, and
one mile broad, was valued in the time of King Edward the confeffor
at twenty-five fhillings.

IN the reign of Edward I. according to Kirkby's Inqueft, Great
Broughton was held by Nicholas de Meinell, of Peter de Mauley, as of
the barony of Mulgrave. The lands appear to have been granted out
in parcels at an early period; in the reign of Queen Elizabeth, William
Lord Eure was lord of the manor of Broughton; and part of the lands
here and at Kirkby were then in the poffeffion of Michael Tempeft, who
was attainted for treafon. *

OF little Broughton, which lies at a fhort diftance towards the eaft,
we find nothing in ancient records worthy of particular notice. Here
is a neat modern manfion belonging to Mifs Grenfide, which is fheltered on the eaft by a rifing plantation; the grounds adjoining exhibit
marks of neatnefs and fimplicity; and from the numerous trees in
hedge-rows which feem here to have attained a more than ordinary fize,
the place wears a rich and woody appearance.

WITHIN this parifh, on the fummit of the mountain that overlooks
the villages of Kirkby and Broughton, there is a fingular monument,
called by the neighbouring people, the *Wain-Stones;* which, according

---

* THE following extract is in *Dodfw. MSS.* from a booke in the cuftody of Sir Thos. Fanfhaw,
the King's Remembrancer of the Exchequer, being a furvey of the lands of the rebels that toke part
with the Erles of Northumberland and Weftmorland.   *Dodfw.* 99. *fo.* 55.

TERRE Michaelis Tempeft attincti in Broughton, Kirkby, &c. Redd. tenent. in Broughton, 8l.os. 4d.
*Capital. maner. de Broughton, vocat. Great Broughton, qd. Will. dnus. Eure tenet, et Grenehow in C eve-
land, XXl. per ann. Redd. tenent. in Kirkby* 40s. *Dorothea, ux, dci. Michaelis,* 17. *Eliz.*

I i

to the moſt probable etymology of the word, † may denote the ſtones of lamentation, and are probably Daniſh, erected in memory of ſome Daniſh chieftain ſlain here.   It conſiſts of a rude collection of ſtones, ſome of them of an immenſe ſize, and all of them apparently in their natural poſition, except one which ſtands erect, and appears to have formed a part of ſome ancient cromlech.   Upon one of the ſtones, now laid flat upon the ground, but which like the former, ſtood upright, till about fifty years ago, when it was wantonly thrown down, there is the following inſcription :

ROJȢOJ2

TⱲOUJngTD

A *FAC-SIMILE* of the above inſcription (the letters of which are four inches in length, and about half an inch deep), we publiſhed in the Gentleman's Magazine for the year 1801, in hopes that ſome explanation of its probable meaning might be obtained through the medium of that uſeful miſcellany ; but our expectations have hitherto been fruſtrated ; and we are, with reluctance, compelled to leave the ſubject open to the conjectures of future viſitors.

Thᴇ *ſoil* and *produce* of the pariſh are the ſubjects that next demand the reader's attention ; and theſe will be found in general, greatly ſimilar to thoſe in the adjoining pariſh of Stokeſley.   In the ſouthern parts of the pariſh the lands have a gentle inclination from the ſkirts of the

† Fʀᴏᴍ the Anglo-Saxon word WA, *dolor* ; from whence cometh the verb *wanian*, which ſignifies to *lament* or *grieve*.

mountains, towards the north; and confift chiefly of a gravelly loam, tolerably fertile both in corn and grafs; though perhaps from the fituation near the mountains, better adapted to the produce of the latter; nearly one half of the land is in tillage; and potatoes of a fuperior quality are produced here, and are in general found a profitable crop.

As we have not, after the moft folicitous application, been able to obtain the neceffary extracts from the parifh regifters, we cannot ftate the probable increafe or decreafe of the inhabitants. The following return made to government in the year 1801, ‡ will however give the reader fome idea of its ftate of population; and from which it will be feen that there were then 138 houfes or families and 625 inhabitants, giving an average of 4½ nearly to each family: of thefe the males and females are nearly equal.

‡ STATE of population, 10th March, 1801.

	Inhabited houfes.	Families.	Uninhabited houfes.	Males.	Females.	Total.
Kirkby	37	37	3	83	82	165
Broughton	101	101	10	232	228	460
Totals	138	138	13	315	310	625

I i 2

THE PARISH OF INGLEBY.

FROM Kirkby we proceed eaftwards to the parifh of Ingleby; or as it is fometimes fignificantly called Ingleby-Greenhow, as defcriptive of its fituation in a remote corner, at the foot of the mountains. This parifh, which in its greateft extent from eaft to weft, is four miles, and about three miles broad, contains three diftinct townfhips and manors: viz. Ingleby, Batterfby, and Greenhow; and is bounded on the eaft, weft, and north by the feveral parifhes of Kildale, Stokefley, and Kirkby; with a range of naked mountains, dividing it from the chapelries of Branfdale and Bilfdale on the fouth.

THE village of Ingleby, with the parifh church, is fituated near the centre of the parifh, and confifts of a few houfes irregularly built upon rifing ground, with a profpect to the weft; and is about five miles diftant from the market town of Stokefley.

IT appears, on the authority of Domefday-book, that Ingleby, at the time of the Conqueror's furvey, was within the foke or liberty of Stokefley, and contained feven carucates of land rated *ad geldum*. The Baliols were ancient proprietors; from whom the eftate defcended to the Eures; and continued in the poffeffion of that family, until about the year 1609, when it was fold by Ralph Lord Eure to Sir David Foulis, Knight; and is now the property of Sir William Foulis, the prefent Baronet, who is a minor. *

---

* *The pedigree of* FOULIS, *of Ingleby-Manor.*

(From Coll. Arms, Englifh Baronetage, Parifh Regifters, &c.)

THOUGH this family inhabited for many ages in that part of Great-Britain, called Scotland, yet in all probability, it was originally Englifh, fince one of the name made a confiderable figure in Kent before the Norman invafion, as Taylor in his *Hiftory of Gavelkind*, tells us; and that he, together with feveral others who oppofed King William I. being treated with much rigour and feverity, fled into Scotland, with Margaret, the fifter of Edgar Atheling (afterwards married to Malcolm Conmore, King of Scotland,) and fettled there, where his defcendants flourifh to this day; for which he cites *Rofs's Hiftory of Scotland.* See alfo *Holinfhed's Chron. fol.* 254. After this removal, 'tis likely the family fettled in the north of Scotland, and gave denomination to a town of their name, which now belongs to the *Monroes;* it is certain that feveral thereof bore confiderable offices under the Kings of Scotland, before they fettled in Yorkfhire.

ARMS.—*Arg.* three laurel, or bay leaves erect, *proper.*
CREST.—On a wreathe, out of a crefcent, *arg.* a crofs formè, fichè, *fable.*

William Foulis, keeper of the privy feal to James I. King of Scotland, 1430.

William Foulis.—Eliz. dau. of Sir Walter Ogilby, Knt.

1. William, ob. S. P.   2. James Foulis.—Margaret, dau. of Sir Thomas Henderfon, Knt.

James Foulis, heir to William, his uncle purchafed the lands of Collington from William Mafter, of Glencarne, 1519. He was keeper of the regifter to James V. King of Scotland, 1530.—Barbara, dau. of . . . . Brown, of Fordee, Efq.

Henry Foulis, of Collington.—Mary, dau. of . . . . Hadden, of Glenargis, by . . . . ., daughter of the Earl of Marr.

James Foulis, (eldeft fon,) whofe defcendant Sir James Foulis, of Collington, a Bart. of Nova Scotia, was living 1801.

David Foulis came into England with James VI. King of Scotland, and I. of England; and was made Knight, 1603; created Bart. 1619. He was agent from King James, to Queen Elizabeth, and cofferer to Prince Henry and Prince Charles. He purchafed the manor and feat at Ingleby-Manor of the Lord Eure, where he moftly refided, and died there in 1642. *Buried at Ingleby.* †

Cordelia, dau. of Wm. Fleetwood, of Great Miffenden, co, Bucks, Efq. ferjeant at law, and recorder of London, in Queen Elizabeth's time. Died and buried at Ingleby, Aug. 24, 1631.

† SIR DAVID FOULIS, Knt. and Bart. (founder of the family of Ingleby-Manor) was a native of North Britain, and employed by James VI. of Scotland and I. of England, in feveral weighty commiffions to Queen Elizabeth. He received the honour of Knighthood in 1603, and attending his royal mafter to Oxford, had there the degree of Mafter of Arts conferred upon him. He was appointed cofferer (a prin-

At a little diftance from the village of Ingleby towards the fouth, we approached the manfion houfe, called *Ingleby-Manor*, the ancient re-

5. William. 4. Edward 3. John. 2. Robert 1. Sir Henry Foulis,—Mary, eldeft dau. of Sir Thos.
died unmar.   died un-   of Ingleby-Manor, in | Layton, of Sexhowe, Knight,
                                married.   Cleveland, Bart. | ob. 1657.

                                                                 Anne married G.   Elizabeth
                                                                 Purvis, M. D.   died unmar.

4. Thos. 3. Edw. 2. Henry Foulis, 1. Sir David Foulis,—Catherine, dau. 1. Cordelia died unmar.
                 Fellow of Lin-   Bart. M P. for the   of Sir David   2. Mary mar. R. Shaftoe,
                 coln Coll. Ox-   Borough of Northal-   Watkins, Knt.   of Benwell, Northum.
                 ford. ob. 1669.   lerton, 1. James II. died 1717.   3. Catherine mar. R. Cole,
                                   died 1694.   of Brancepth, Durham.
                                                                        4. Elizabeth died unmar.

6. John, 5. Charles 4. Thomas, 3. William Foulis,—Anne, dau. of John Lau- 2. Henry 1. David,
ob. S. P. died young. ob. S. P. Bart. died 1741. rence, of Weftmorland,   died young. ob. S. P.
                                                   widow of Sir Lumley
                                                   Robinfon, of Kent well-
                                                   Hall, Suffolk, Bart.

Sir Wm. Foulis,—Mildred, eldeft dau. of
Bart. died 1756. | Henry Lord Vifcount   1. Honora mar. William Chaloner, Efq. of Guifbro'.
Buried at Ingle- | Downe, died 1780.   2. Mary mar. William Turner, Efq. of Stainfby.
by. | Buried at Ingleby.   3. Catherine mar. John Rudd, Efq. of Durham.
                                          4. Ann mar. Sir Reg. Graham, Bart. Norton Conyers.

cipal officer of the houfehold next under the comptroller) to Henry Prince of Wales, King James's eldeft fon; and after his death to the fame office under his fucceffor Prince Charles, afterwards King Charles I. In confideration of the good, long and faithful fervices done by Sir David Foulis, the manors of Green-howe and Templehurft were granted to him by letters patent; and he was farther advanced to the dignity of a Baronet, on the 6th February, 1619. || In 1609 he purchafed of Ralph Lord Eure, lord prefident of the council in Wales, " the manors of Ingleby and Batterfby, the manor-houfes, the fallow-deer-park and " the red-deer-park, with the rectory and church of Ingleby, and lands in Ingleby, Batterfby, and Green-hough." § He refided chiefly at Ingleby Manor where he acted as one of his Majefty's council for the northern parts, cuftos rotulorum, deputy lieutenant, and juftice of the peace for the north-riding; ‡ but as he oppofed with fome zeal, the commiffion which was iffued to compel gentlemen to compound for not having taken the honour of Knighthood, and let fall fome expreffions, reflecting upon the Lord Went-worth, lord prefident of the council, for his proceedings therein, he, and his fon Henry, were cenfured in the court of Star Chamber in 1633. Sir David was declared incapable of all the offices and places which he held, was committed prifoner to the Fleet, during his Majefty's pleafure, fined 5000l. to the King, and 3000l. to Lord Wentworth; for the payment of which fines, he was forced to fell part of his eftate. His fon and heir, Henry, was alfo committed prifoner to the Fleet, during his Majefty's pleafure, and fined 500l. *

|| *Patents, penes Sir Wm. Foulis.*   § *Conveyance, penes ibid.*   ‡ *Baronetage,*
* *Baronetage, and Rufhworth's collections, part 2. p. 215.*

fidence of the Lords Eures. The houfe is a refpectable and commodious manfion, built round two courts, and is probably of the time of King Henry VIII. or of Queen Elizabeth; but fomewhat improved and modernized by the late poffeffors. It ftands in the bottom of a deep fecluded vale, with fome rifing plantations; but the fituation is difadvantageous and ill-chofen, being fhut in on the eaft, weft, and fouth by a range of barren and gloomy mountains. Since the manor and eftate here became the property of the Foulis family, Ingleby manor, notwithftanding its fecluded and retired fituation, has been their principal refidence; and here that eminent hiftorian and divine, *Henry Foulis*, the fecond fon of Sir Henry Foulis, Bart. (a lineal defcendant of Sir David Foulis, or *de Foliis*) was born. His younger years being partly fpent in Scotland, (from whence his family came,) and partly in Yorkfhire, he was afterwards fent to Queen's College, Oxford, where he continued till he took his mafter's degree, and was elected Fellow of Lincoln College, in the year 1659. He entered firft into holy orders; but his genius inclining to hiftory, he chiefly betook himfelf to that ftudy; and being much difgufted at the extremes, which then prevailed *(Prefbytery* and *Popery)* wrote two books highly refented by thofe parties: *viz. the hiftory of the wicked plots and confpiracies of our pretended Saints, the Prefbyterians, &c.*—printed in the year 1662, and dedicated † to his

Sir Wm. Foulis,—Hannah, dau. of	1. Mildred died unmarried.
Bart. died at	John Robinfon, of	2. Ann mar. William Prefton, of Moorby, Efq. S. P.
Ingleby, 1780.	Buckton, in co.	3. Catherine married Robert Jubb, Efq. S P.
	York, Efq.	4. Mary mar. Boynton Langley, Efq. of Wykeham Abbey.

Sir Wm. Foulis,—Mary Ann, dau. of Edmund   John Robinfon Foulis,—Decima Helen Beatrix,
Bart. died 5th | Turner, of Panton, co. Linc.   of Buckton, Efq. | dau. of Sir Chrif. Sykes,
Sept. 1802. | Efq. | of Sledmere, Bart.

1. Sir. William Foulis,   2. Henry.   1. Hannah,   2. Mary Anne,   John Robinfon   Hannah.
Bart. a minor, 1806.   3. Catherine, and 4. Sophia,   Foulis.
                                                  all in their minority.

† As the dedication is fhort, and difcovers, in fome degree, the fpirit of the writer, we readily fubmit it to the reader's attention.

brother, Sir David Foulis, Bart. and his virtuous confort, the Lady Catherine. This book, it feems, highly pleafed the churchmen; infomuch
that fome of them, it is faid, had it chained to the defks in their churches, and other public places, to be read by the vulgar; but fo difgufted the Prefbyterians, that *Molinæus*, and others of that party have fallen
foul upon him for it. He alfo wrote *an hiftory of the Romifh treafons and
ufurpations, &c.* printed after his death, *in folio,* 1671. Anthony Wood
fays, " The products of his writings fhew him to have been a true fon
" of the church of England; a hater of Popery, Prefbytery, and Secta-
" rifm; he was endowed with a happy memory; converfant in hiftories,
" efpecially thofe that were private and obfcure. He alfo underftood
" books, and the ordering of them fo well, that with a little induftry he
" might have gone beyond the great *Philobiblos* JAMESIUS. He had
" alfo in him a moft generous and noble fpirit, a careleffnefs of the
" world and things thereof (as moft bookifh men have,) a moft becom-
" ing honeftie in his dealings; a juft obfervance of collegiate difcipline;

" To his loving brother, SIR DAVID FOULIS, BARONET, *of Ingleby-Mannor in Cleveland,*
" *in the north riding of Yorkfhire;* and *his virtuous confort, the* LADY CATHERINE FOULIS,

" DEAR BROTHER,

            " and

      " MADAM,

            " *If it had not been the cuftome, to eeke out every pamphlet with fome* dedicatory
" *paper, I fhould have done as fome people do with their brats, let them lie to the* patronage *of any that
" would take them up. For I could never yet underftand the advantage of the common cry, viz. the crav-
" ing and defiring* protection; *fince a good book is its own patronage; and no man will have a better
" opinion of the bad, for a few* epiftolary *lines to a third perfon: efpecially of late times, when I have
" known fome* Prefbyterians *dedicate wickednefs itfelf to God Almighty, Treafon to the King, Sacriledge
" and Schifm to Bifhops, and the worft of villanies to good men.*

      " *THOUGH I love good company, yet me thinks there is no perfect enjoyment with thofe, whofe greatnefs
" is rather an awe than fociety to the reft: where flattery is an obligation, though the object merit nothing
" but pity or fcorn.*

      " *BUT here the cafe is altered, the neerenefs of relation, familiarity and acquaintance, making all com-
" mendations rediculous, and complements odious; which is the reafon, that at this time, your names are
" here prefixt.*   " *By your ever loving brother,*

Linc. Coll. Oxford, 23d April, 1662.   HEN. FOULIS."

" and a hatred to new fangles and the French foolries of his time. He
" died the 24th December, 1669, aged 33, or thereabouts; and was
" buried in the chancel of St. Michael's church, Oxon, under the north
" wall." *Wood's Athenæ Oxon. vol.* 2. *p.* 455.

THE church of Ingleby is a plain modern ſtruſture, rebuilt about
the year 1741, with the ancient tower remaining; there is a ſide aile
on the north; and the whole being neatly ſeated, is rendered comfortable and commodious. This church which is dedicated to St. Andrew,
was formerly reſtorial; and was given in the year 1151 by *Adam de
Aengelby, ſon of Veil*, together with the mill here, * to the Abbey of
Whitby, for a free and perpetual alms. It was afterwards appropriated
to the ſaid monaſtry by John Thoreſby, Archbiſhop of York; and at
the diſſolution thereof, reduced to a perpetual curacy, certified to the
governours of Queen Anne's bounty, at 13*l.* 13s. 4d.: it has ſince received ſome augmentations † laid out in lands at Weſt Rounton and
Stockton, in the county of Durham, which have increaſed the income
to about 65*l.* per ann. The reſtorial rights at the diſſolution of the
monaſtry, were granted to Sir Ralph Eure, Knight, and afterwards came
by purchaſe, with the manor and eſtate to the Foulis family. Sir William Foulis, Bart. is the preſent impropriator and patron, and nominates
the curate. ‡

* IT appears from the original grant that the mill here was given by Adam, ſon of Veil, free and
clear from every ſervice and exaſtion, with all the privileges and liberties, which it previouſly enjoyed from his hand: viz. that his homagers ſhould keep in repair the mill-dam and houſe, and bring
thereto the main timber and mill-ſtones. This donation was afterwards confirmed by the donor's
heirs, on condition that they were to pay no *moulter* for what was confumed in their own families,
ſo long as their homagers and other men repaired the houſe and mill-dam, and brought the main
timber and mill-ſtones; nor, were they to make any other mill than that.
Charlton's Hiſt. of Whitby, p. 116.

† IN the year 1720 augmented with 200*l.* by Sir William Foulis, Bart. and 200*l.* more from
Queen Anne's bounty.

‡ INGLEBY CURACY.
DED. St. Andrew. Certified val. 13*l.* 13s. 4d. Sir William Foulis, Bart. patron.

K k

IT appears from the parish register, which begins in the year 1539, that many of the family of Eure lie buried here; though the church at present, contains no monumental inscriptions of that family. In the church yard there is a curious stone, but greatly defaced, probably belonging to some of the Eures; and on the outside of the church, under the eastern window, there is the effigies of an Ecclesiastic cut in stone, with his hands elevated; and upon a fold of his habit, down the breast, in an ancient character, *(sans date)* the following inscription:

WILLS. DE WRELTON. CAPELLAN.

AT a little distance towards the south, lies the township of

GREENHOWE;

a part of which, significantly called *Greenhowe-Bottom*, is a narrow secluded vale, so deeply intrenched with mountains that here, (like some parts of Borrowdale in Cumberland,) *in the depth of winter the sun never shines.*

WE have no particular mention of the manor of Greenhowe in the Domesday survey. According to Kirkby's Inquest, it appears that the Meinills of Whorlton were ancient proprietors; from whom the estate descended by marriage to the D'arcies; in which family it continued till the reign of Henry VIII. when Thomas Lord D'arcy, being principally concerned in the insurrection raised in the north, upon the suppression of the lesser monastries, called the *Pilgrimage of Grace*, was beheaded on Tower-hill, and his estates became forfeited to the crown. Greenhowe, it seems, remained in the crown till the reign of James I.

CURATES.

——, —— Mason,
1703, George Spencer,
1715, Peter Moone,
1722, Samuel Haffell,

1758, William Spedding,
1784, William Pennyman Consett,
1797, John Dixon, nominated by Sir William Foulis, Bart.

WE acknowledge our obligations to the *Rev. John Dixon*, for his friendly communications relative to this parish.

when it was granted by letters patent to Sir David Foulis, Knt. whofe
defcendant Sir William Foulis, Bart. is the prefent proprietor.

ABOUT a mile diftant to the north-eaft, from the village of Ingleby,
lies the townfhip of

BATTERSBY,

another manor within the parifh. This was ancient demefne of the
crown; and according to Domefday furvey, was taxed for two carucates, with arable land fufficient for one plough.

" Terra Regis.

" Manerium in Badresbi. Hauuard II. ad geldum: Terra ad I.
" car."

BATTERSBY, according to Kirkby's Inqueft, was held of the Baliols,
and at an early period was the property of the Percies, lords of Kildale;
and from them came by defcent, in the reign of Henry VIII. to the
Percies, Earls of Northumberland; in which family it continued till the
death of Henry, the eighth Earl, who fhot himfelf, during his imprifonment in the tower of London, (27. *Elizabeth)*. We afterwards find it
the poffeffion of the Eures, and was fold, together with Ingleby, by
Ralph Lord Eure, to Sir David Foulis, Knight; whofe defcendants have
fince continued lords here.

THE SOIL within the parifh not being very fertile either in corn or
grafs; and the inclofed grounds confifting nearly of an equal quantity
of arable, meadow, and pafture land, we find little, under this head,
worthy of particular obfervation. The foil is chiefly of a fpongy, and
cold quality; and the rays of the fun being, in fome meafure, fhut out
by the furrounding mountains, the crops are light, and the harvefts in
general rather late.

There is a confiderable extent of uninclofed common, or moor-land
within the parifh; a part of which is covered with heath, and affords
pafturage for a few fmall fheep of an inferior breed. There were alfo
anciently two extenfive deer parks, called in the conveyance deed of the

K k 2

Lord Eure, ' *the red-deer park, and the fallow-deer park* ;' but the deer, which we conceive, were not numerous, have been deftroyed, and a confiderable part of the inclofed grounds is now laid open to the adjoining common.

WITH refpect to *natural productions,* we may remark that near the fkirts of the mountain, which forms the fouthern boundary of the parifh, *coal* has been difcovered ; and a colliery was attempted a few years ago; but from fome difficulty in working the feam, which was found fmall, and the coal being of a very inferior quality, the working has been difcontinued.

FROM the fecluded fituation of the parifh, and the inhabitants being chiefly occupied in hufbandry, the population, as may be expected, is but fmall. From the return made under the *act* of 41. *Geo. III.* * it appears there were then 62 houfes, occupied by 71 families and 376 inhabitants, giving upon an average, upwards of five to each family. The males and females are nearly equal. According to the parifh regifters, we find that within the laft twenty years, there have been 200 baptifms, 109 burials, and 44 marriages. On comparing the number of baptifms with that of burials, which is nearly as 2 to 1, we are led to conclude that the number of inhabitants muft be increafing. The average number of burials in one year is $5\frac{1}{2}$ nearly ; from which it will appear that out of a population of 376, one only out of every 69 of the inhabitants dies annually ; a circumftance that ftrongly indicates the air and climate to be falubrious.

* STATE of population, taken 10th March, 1801.

Townfhips.	Inhabited houfes.	Families.	Uninhabited houfes.	Males.	Females.	Total.
Ingleby	29	34	–	88	92	180
Greenhowe	20	20	–	59	59	118
Batterfby	13	17	–	38	40	78
Totals	62	71	–	185	191	376

THE PARISH OF KILDALE.

WE now enter a more mountainous and barren district; the vales of which are narrow, and hemmed in by low heathy moors of confiderable extent, of an uniform afpect, and not heightened by any fcenes of pleafing wildnefs to infpire an idea of fublimity.

THIS parifh is of no great extent, and is bounded by the feveral parifhes of Stokefley, Guifbrough, Ingleby and Ayton; and is about fix miles diftant from the market town of Stokefley.

THE moft probable derivation of the name is from the Britifh word *Kil*, and *Dale;* the firft fyllable of which, according to fome etymologifts, fignifies a *wood* or *grove;* but this, we conceive to be only the fecondary fenfe of the word; the firft is equivalent to our modern *cell*, and occurs frequently in the names of places, both in Ireland and Scotland, where it is ufed often very nearly as our aneeftors ufed *kirk* in the compofition of local names.

KILDALE, in the Domefday Survey, is entered under the title

Terra Tainorum Regis.

In Childale habebat Ligulf VI. carucatas ad geldum. terra ad III. car. ibi habet orme I. carucatam, et VII. bordarios cum II. car. ibi presbiter et ecclesia Duas Lucas long. et I. lat. T. R, E. valebat XVI. solid. modo XX. solid.

FROM the above extract, we find that before the Norman Conqueft, Ligulf held fix carucates, rated *ad geldum*, with arable land fufficient for three ploughs; and that Orme had one carucate and feven *bordars* with two ploughs; that there was a church and minifter here; and that the manor, which was two miles in length, and one mile

broad, was valued in the Confeffor's time, at fixteen fhillings, but at
the time of the Survey was worth twenty.

It appears, upon the authority of the appendix to Domefday Book,
that Ligulf, who was one of the independent Saxon Lords, was difplaced of his poffeffions here ; for we there find, that Kildale, by grant
of the Conqueror, became the fee of Robert de Brus, Lord of Skelton,
who held of the king *in capite ;* and by failure of iffue-male, defcended by marriage with Lucy, daughter of Peter de Brus, to Marmaduke
de Thweng ; of whofe heir, according to Kirkby's Inqueft,* William
de Percy held one Knight's fee in Kildale, &c. where twelve carucates
made one Knight's fee. The Percies of Kildale appear to have been
a branch of the Percies, Earls of Northumberland ; and the manor
here was probably firft granted in the reign of Henry III. to Henry
de Percy, fon of Joceline de Lovaine, on his marriage with Ifabella,
daughter of Adam de Brus ; whofe fon William was ftiled Lord of
Kildale ; and procured of that king, a charter for a market and fair
here ; as alfo a' grant of free-warren, and the privilege of trying and
punifhing felons within the manor.† To him defcended almoft all the
vaft poffeffions of the Percy family, which were inherited after his
death by his four fons ; of whom Walter the fecond had Kildale and
other manors in Cleveland ; and was fucceeded by his fon William,
who attended King Edward the firft, in his expedition againft the Welfh,
in the year 1282.

The defcendants of this family continued in poffeffion of this lordfhip for feveral generations, and had a caftle here, where they general-

---

* " Willus. de Percy de Kildale tenet in *Kildale,* Crathorne, Barwick et Thormanby unum feod.
unde XII. car. faciunt feod. unius milit." *Kirkby's Inqueft.*

† " Willus. de Percy clamat habere Mercat. et Feriam in *Kyldayll,* per cartam Domini Regis
" Henrici, et warrenam in *Kyldayll* per eandem cartam, et furcam in *Kildayll,* fcilicet qualiter et a
" quo tempore non poteft inquiri." *Kirkby's Inqueft.*

ly refided ;* but which is now fo totally decayed, that the fite thereof is with difficulty traced. Upon failure of iffue in the branch originally fettled here, the manor and eftate came by defcent to the Earls of Northumberland ; and were purchafed, in the reign of Charles I. by John Turner, Efq. ferjeant at law ; whofe defcendant, Sir Charles Turner, Bart. of Kirkleatham, is the prefent proprietor, and lord of the manor.

THE church of Kildale ftands in a low retired fituation, at a little diftance from the village towards the fouth, and not far from the fite of the ancient caftle already mentioned. There is nothing in the ftile of architecture of the prefent edifice that points out the æra of its foundation ; but, upon the authority of Domefday Book, where the church is mentioned, we may conclude it to be of great antiquity, and was probably founded at an early period of the Saxon Heptarchy.

THIS church, dedicated to St. Cuthbert, is rectorial, and was anciently under the patronage of the Percies, lords of Kildale. The advowfon and right of prefentation are ftill appendant to the manor. There is a fmall glebe, and the whole revenues of the church amount

---

* From the teftamentary burials in *Torr's MSS.* it appears that many of this family lie buried in the church of Kildale ; and in *Dodfworth's MSS.* we find the following extract from Archbifhop Scroop's Regifter, viz.—" Eliz. Percy de Kildale. quondam uxor Johis Percy de Kildale, fenioris, " facit teftament. 4 mar. 1438, legat corpus fepeliri in Ec'clie. po'chiali de Kildale. Legat Willo " Filio un. poculum argent. coopert. Henrico Filio, et Eliz. Filiæ cuique I erat. argenti. Johi Percy " Filio I erat. Henrico Percy *Filiolo* I crater. argent. Will'us et Henricus Filii executores. Probat. " 18. Octob. 1438." *Fol.* 597 *Reg'trii Archiep. Scroop.*

KILDALE RECTORY.

Dedication, St. Cuthbert.   Sir Charles Turner, Bart. Patron.
A difcharged Rectory. Clear Yearly Val. 36l. 18s. 4d.   Archd. pro Syn. 4s.   Prox. 7s. 6d.

RECTORS.

Thomas Tame, 1280, *pref. Will. de Percy.*	Steph. de Wyrfaukes, 1349, *pref. Maria quond uxor Roberti de Percy.*
Walter de Staveley, 1295, *pref. Arnald de Percy*	
John de Middlefburgh, 1323, *pref. John de Percy*	John Grenehowe, 1349, *pref. eadem*

to about 140l. per ann. ‡ Within the church, on the fouth fide
of the chancel, there is a plain mural monument, to the memory of
Maurice Lifle, Rector of this parifh ; the lines on which, as being defcriptive of a learned, pious, and refpectable character, we havet hought
worthy of tranfcription, and have given them in the notes.* A flat

Peter de Marfke, 1392, *pref. John de Percy.*
Richard Bennoks—— *pref. idem.*
Tho. Routh, cap. 1406, *pref. idem.*
Tho. Gawnton, pbr. 1407, *pref. idem.*
John Kighley, pbr. 1436, *pref. idem.*
Will. Fyfhbruke, cap. 1440, *pref. idem.*
Rich. Hedelam, cap. 1472, *pref. idem.*
Brian Young, pbr. 1508, *pref. Henry de Percy, comes. Northumb.*
Mark Strangwayes, 1520, *pref. idem.*
Percival Sympfon, 1542, *pref. affig. T. Percy ar.*
Will. Johnfon, 1556, *pref. Eleanor relict. T. Percy.*
Barthol. Harbottle, pbr.——*pref. eadem.*
Will. Rogers, cl. 1568, *pref. eadem.*
Geo. Stockdale, cl. 1598, *pref. Rob. Stapilton, gent.*

John Leake, B. A. 1618, *pref. Hen. comes. North.*
Thomas Wilfon, cl. 1624, *pref. idem.*
Rob. Henderfon, cl. 1637, *pref. Algernon com. North.*
Rich. Wakefeld, cl. — — — —
Tho. Clarke, 1667, *pref. J. Turner, Efq. Serjeant at Law.*
Maurice Lifle, 1708, *pref. Charles Turner, Efq.*
Henry Forder, 1719, *pref. Charles Turner, Efq.*
John Nicholfon, 1723, *pref. Marg. Turner, wid.*
Will. Hide, 1737, *pref. Chomley Turner, Efq.*
Will. Leigh Williamfon, 1767, *pref. Ch. Turner. Efq.*
Jofeph Smith, 1805, *pref. Sir Ch. Turner, Bart.*

‡ Upon an inclofure of the common under an act of parliament, it was provided that the Rector fhould receive the fum of 105l. *per ann.* in lieu and perpetual difcharge of all tithes within the parifh. Whatever objections may be urged againft tithes, as a bar to agricultural improvements, we conceive that no fettled annual payment, confidering the almoft daily decreafe in the value of money, can poffibly long continue an adequate compenfation.

* Hic fepultus jacet Mauricius Lifle,
Ecclefiæ Anglicanæ Prefbyter, A. M.
E domo fancti Petri, cant.
Parochiæ hujus Rector.
Vir pietate, probitate, et integritate fingulari ;
Erga pauperes pro facultatem liberalis ;
Erga omnes humanus ac benevolus ;
Bonus pater familias, ac preftans Sacrorum Minifter ;
Inter alia ftudia etiam muficæ peritiffimus.
In matrimonio habuit Eliz. Tonftall
Lectiffimam fæminam vetere et honefta familia ;
Ex qua duodecim liberos, fex mares, et fex fæminas tulit,
Natus eft Anno Dom. 1653.
Menfis Augufti 23.
Obiit Anno Dom. 1719. Ap. 6to. Die
Annum agens ætatis 66.
Prope jacet Eliz. prædicti defuncti pia vidua.
Obiit 8vo. Die Octobris, Annoque Dom. 1723.
Annum agens Ætatis 64.
In Jefu quiefcunt,
Refurgant!

tomb-ftone in the church-yard records the death of *Jofeph Dunn, A. D.*
1716. He left to the poor of Kildale, *twenty fhillings;* of Commondale, *twenty fhillings;* of Danby, *twenty fhillings;* of Wefterdale, *ten
fhillings;* and as a relic of very ancient ufage, he directed the faid feveral fums to be paid to the poor of thofe places refpectively, upon his
grave-ftone by equal portions on the firft day of May, and the eleventh
of November, yearly, for ever.

WE have not been able to trace any remains of the ancient chapel
of St. Kilda, formerly in this parifh; and which, as appears from a
charter printed in Dugdale's Monaft. Angl. (vol. II. p. 290.) was given
by William de Percy, to the Canons of St. John the Evangelift, of Helagh-Park, with divers lands and privileges here; for which the faid
Canons were to find two of their own houfe, or two fecular Priefts to
celebrate divine offices in the faid chapel for ever. The particulars of
this grant moft worthy of notice appear as follow; viz.—"Eight acres
" and one rood of land in a culture on the east and north fide of the
" chapel, and two acres on the fouth fide thereof; alfo, feven acres in
" a culture called *Symond Croft*, with a rent-charge of two marks *per
" annum*, out of his water corn mill; and common of pafture for two
" hundred fheep, with their young of two years old; for ten cows, one
" bull, three heifers, and their followers of three years old; and for
" eighteen hogs and two fows, with their litter of two years old, free
" from *pannage* ‖ in his wood here; and for ten oxen, and two heifers
" in the faid pafture; alfo, to grind at his mill *multure free*; and to
" have *houfebote* ‡ and *haybote*,† with ten cart loads of turves out of his
" turbary at Hindfcough." In the reign of Edward II. there was a
houfe of croffed, or crouched friars here, which is thus noticed by

‖ PANNAGE or *pafnage* is that food which fwine feed on in woods, as the maft of beech or acorns,
and freedom from Pannage is a privilege from paying any thing for the fame.
‡ AN allowance of timber for repairing of houfes. † A liberty to take wood for hedging.

L l

Tanner.—" In the park of Sir Arnold de Percy, within this parish, a-
" bout the year 1312, the friars of the order of the Holy Crofs began
" to build an oratory and other offices for their fettlement here; but
" the place was interdicted by Archbifhop Grenfield, till it fhould be
" made appear that this fort of mendicants were allowed by the Pope."

(*Tanner's Notitia.*)

It does not appear, whether the buildings here were ever finifhed; there are not, however, at prefent any traces of their foundation.—This, and one at York, were the only houfes of that order in
this county.

This parifh, which we have already remarked to be of no great
extent, contains only one fmall village, and a few farm-houfes; and
the inhabitants, which are about 200 in number, are wholly occupied
in hufbandry. According to the enumeration made in the year 1801,‡
by order of the legiflature, there were then 27 houfes and 37 families,
and the total number of inhabitants being 201, gives upwards of
$5\frac{1}{2}$ to each family. The males and females within the parifh, were
equal. On comparing the number of baptifms with that of burials
within a given period, it appears that the population muft be increafing,
the numbers, according to the following table, being nearly two to
one.

	Bap.	Bur.	Mar.
From the year 1720 to 1739, inclufive	46	40	12
1781 to 1800.	145	80	37
Increafe	99	40	25

The average number of burials in one year is four, which fhews that
only one out of 50 of the inhabitants dies annually.

The *foil* within the parifh is various, fome of the old inclofures
confift of a deep rich loam, while the higher grounds adjoining the
common, are of a moorifh quality. The moors, which occupy a con-

‡ STATE OF POPULATION, March 10th, 1801.

Kildale.	Houfes.	Families.	Uninhabi-tedhoufes.	Males.	Females.	Total.
	27	37	—	100	101	201

fiderable portion of the parifh, are, in general, black and dreary; the furface covered with ling, and the top foil a black peat earth, upon a loofe free-ftone rubble.

THERE is nothing, perhaps, more worthy of remark within this parifh, than the inclofure of a large tract of moor or wafte land, by the late Sir Charles Turner, Bart. The improvements commenced about

---

The following are the Obfervations of ARTHUR YOUNG, ESQ. *on the State of Agriculture in this Parifh from his Six Months' Tour through the North of England, A. D.* 1768.

AT Kildale, another eftate of *Mr. (Sir Charles) Turner's*, there are feveral variations which deferve minuting.—The foil is various; inclofures furrounded by moors; the latter a black peat earth 12 or 14 inches deep, under which is a loofe foil of channelly ftone; the furface is covered with ling; other moor land is white, a light fandy foil, and clear of rubbifh.

THE old inclofures let from 18s. to £os. an acre, and the new ones taken from the common, from 3s. to 5s.—Farms are from 10l. to 100l. but generally about 30l. or 40l.—Their courfes are

$$1 \text{ Fallow} ——2 \text{ Wheat.} ——3 \text{ Oats.}$$
$$\text{Another,—} 1 \text{ Fallow} ——2 \text{ Maflin} ——3 \text{ Oats.}$$
$$\text{A Third,} — 1 \text{ Turnips} ——2 \text{ Oats.} ——$$

THEY plough four times for wheat, fow two bufhels and reap 20.—They fow fcarce any barley; but for oats they ftir but once, fow four bufhels, and gain five quarters, four quarters they get in their inclofures taken in from the common.—For maflin, or for rye, they ftir four times, fow fix pecks, and gain on the moor land 27 bufhels, and 30 on the beft.—They plough four times for turnips; never hoe, but get them in value from 2l. to 3l. feed them with fheep.—Rape they fow on new land, pared and burned; never feed it. The crop of feed they reckoned about half a laft; fow maflin or oats after it.—Clover has been fown by no one but *Mr. Williamfon*, who has, in this culture, followed *Mr. Turner's* example.—They lime on every fallow, one chaldron *per* acre; it cofts 10s. and as much leading.—Good grafs land lets at 25s. an acre; they turn it chiefly to dairying; the beft land, a cow to an acre through fummer, but upon other grafs, it takes two acres. Sheep, they reckon feven to a cow.

THEY manure their grafs well.

THE product of a cow they reckon at 5l. a good one gives five gallons *per* day: and about two maintain a pig. In winter, while dry, they keep them on ftraw. They never fuckle their calves; thofe which are for the butcher have new milk given them; by good management they drink themfelves without trouble.

THE joift of a cow in fummer, 1l. 5s. in winter, 3l. They keep them chiefly in the houfe.

the year 1773, when upwards of 600 acres were inclofed and brought into tillage ; and about 200 acres more planted with Scotch firs, and other foreft trees, which are now (except in fome of the moft unfavourable fituations) in a flourifhing condition. The inclofures have been, of late, fomewhat neglected, but ftill fhew how far, under proper management, the moft barren waftes, though difadvantageoufly fituated, are capable of improvement. Mr. Tuke, in his Agricultural Survey of the North Riding (publifhed in the year 1800) remarks, that " on " one fide of the wall nothing is to be feen but ling ; on the other fide,

THEIR flocks of fheep rife from 50 to 500 ; the fort fo poor that both wool and lamb, do not together pay 5s. a-year. They keep them through winter on the commons, upon the points of the ling ; but in fharp weather give them fome hay. The wool does not come to above 10d. *per* head.

IN their tillage, they reckon three horfes neceffary for 20 acres of arable land ; ufe two or three in a plough, and do an acre in a day. The annual expence *per* horfe, 8*l.*—The price per acre of ploughing, 5s.—From two to four rents to ftock farms.

LAND fells at 35 years purchafe.—Tythes are compounded ; wheat 5s. fpring corn 3s. and for hay up to 3s.—Poor rates from 6d. to 1s. 6d. in the pound.—The only employment from manufactures the poor receive, is a little fpinning of flax.—Tea is drank among them, but not fo much as in other parts.

THEIR method of breaking up old fwarth is this ; they plough it up in the fpring, let it lie fo, till the latter end of the year, then fow rye or maflin ; after that oats, of which they get fine crops, they then let it lie for grafs, without fowing any feeds.

THE following particulars will fhew the œconomy of their farms :—

162 Acres in all.	10 Cows.
12 Arable.	20 Sheep.
100 Grafs.	6 Young Cattle.
50 Moorland.	2 Men.
60*l.* Rent.	1 Maid.
3 Horfes.	

Another.

86 Acres in all.	6 Cows.
10 Arable.	10 Young Cattle.
30 Grafs.	300 Sheep.
46 Moors.	1 Man.
34*l.* Rent.	1 Boy.
3 Horfes.	1 Maid.

" a neglected pasture of ten or twelve years ley, producing plenty of
" coarse grass, and very large rushes, here and there slightly inter-
" sperfed with ling.   Had this land been continued in a proper courfe
" of husbandry, it probably would have paid the occupier abundantly
" more than it can do in its prefent ftate."   " Some of the fields,
" whilft the ley was frefh, produced crops of hay, equal to thofe on
" land of far greater value."

IT has been confidently afferted that thefe improvements were attended with a wanton wafte of money ; which probably proceeded
from making the growth of corn too much the farmer's object, the expence of lime, &c. being too great for the produce of corn to repay it.
If green crops and grafs, for the fupport of cattle and fheep, had been
more the object, the land, it is conjectured, would have been much
more improved, and at an expence, perhaps, of not more than one
fixth part of what was laid out.

See Notes at p. 203. of Tuke's Agricultural Survey.

BASEDALE AND WESTERDALE.

IN our account of Stokeffey, we omitted to fpeak of *Bafedale* and *Wefterdale Chapelry*, which are confidered as detached parts of that parifh ;
the former of which is fituated about three miles to the fouth-eaft
from the village of Kildale, in a deep fequeftered vale, watered by a
fmall branch of the river Efk, and inclofed by heathy moors.

WE have already noticed (at p. 205.) the fmall *Ciftercian Nunnery*
that was founded firft at *Hutton* by Ralph de Neville about the year
1162, and afterwards removed to *Nunthorpe*; and towards the latter

part of the reign of King Henry II. it was fettled at *Basedale* within the parifh of Stokefley, by the benefaction of Guido de Bovincourt; who, as appears from his charter in the monafticon, gave thereunto fix oxgangs of land in Stokefley, except the tofts thereto belonging; and two oxgangs in Wefterdale, and in his woods there, fufficient *firebote* and *houfebote*; alfo the meadow at the head of the town on the fouth under *Refholes*, containing four acres; and pafture for twenty cows, one bull, with their followers of two years old; 200 fheep, eleven fwine and one boar, with their young of two years old; and for five mares and one ftallion, with their foals to the fame age; and ten oxen and carriages throughout the territory. This grant, with the grants of divers benefactors to this priory, was confirmed by King Henry III. whofe charter is to the following effect :—

" Henricus Dei Gratia Rex *Angliæ*, Dominus *Hiberniæ*, Dux *Norma-*
" *niæ* et *Aquitaniæ*, Comes *Andegaviæ*, Archiepifcopis, &c. Salutem,
" Sciatis nos conceffiffe, et hac noftra carta confirmaffe, &c. Deo et
" beatæ *Mariæ* et Monalibus de BASEDALE, omnes donationes fuper-
" fcriptas; videlicet, ex dono *Guidonis de Bovincourt* totum redditum
" fuum de *Baderefby*. Ex dono ejufdem Guidonis totam terram, quam
" habuit in *Newby*, cum pertinentiis, excepto tenemento *Willielmi* de
" *Tameton*. Ex dono ejufdem Guidonis totam terram inter *Redemire*
" et *Hawkefmire*, cum toto bofco et Cilio montis ufque in aquam, quæ
" dicitur *Bafedale-beck*, et ipfam prenominatam *Redemire*, fcilicet ficut
" *Haffokemire* cadit a Cilio montis in *Bafedale-beck*. Ex dono *Radolphi*
" *de Nevill* duas carucatas, et unam bovatam terræ, cum tanto terræ
" fpacio ad edificationem fuam faciendam, quanto funt manfa in *Thorp*
" adjacentiæ fupradictæ terræ, et unum molendinum cum pertinentiis
" in eadem villa. Ex dono predicti *Guidonis* fex bovatas terræ in
" *Stokefly*, cum pertinentiis fuis, exceptis toftis ad eas pertinentibus, pro
" quibus dedit eis duas acras de cultura fua fuper *Rubera*, et quoddam
" pratum ad caput villæ de *Wefterdale*, et pafturam ad viginti vaccas,

" et unum taurum cum fua fecta de duobus annis, et ad ducentos oves
" fine fecta, et ad duodecem porcos fine fecta. Ex dono *Willielmi* filii
" *Fulconis* duas bovatas terræ in *Kyldale.* Ex dono *Stephani de Roffel*
" duas bov. terræ cum toftis fuis in *Newton* cum tanto prato, quantum
" adjacet eifdem bovatis, et quandam partem terræ cultæ, latitudinis
" feptem perticarum, cujus longitudo extenditur ufque ad pratum ver-
" fus *Stapelhow,* et quoddam pratum de fuo proprio, latitudinis—perti-
" carum, et pafturam ad fexaginta oves. Quare volumus, &c. Hiis
" teftibus, venerabili patre W. *Karl.* epifcopo. W. comite *Albemarle.*
" *Petro de Malolacu* et aliis. Datum per manum venerabilis patris *R.*
" *Ciceftrenfis* episcopi, cancellarii noftri, apud dunelmum, decimo die
" Septembris, anno regni noftri viceffimo."

Dugdale's Mon. Angliæ. vol. I. p. 840, 141.

BESIDES the donations recited in the above confirmatory charter
of Henry III. it appears from a charter, which we have given in the
notes,* that Hugh de Eure, fon of John, fon of Robert, gave to this
priory a rent-charge of eight fhillings *per ann.* out of his mill at Stokefley, to be paid at the two ufual feafts of the year.

THIS priory, like moft of the Ciftercian order, which were generally fixed in folitary and retired fituations, was dedicated to the

---

* THE following charter, which is not printed in Dugdale's *Mon. Ang.* nor noticed by Burton
in his *Monaft. Ebor.* is extracted from a fmall MSS. book, now in the Dean and Chapter's library,
Durham; without title, and referred to, as *B. Fo.* 16. in the Dean and Chapter's catalogue.

OMNIBUS *xti* fidelibus hanc cartam vifuris velaudituris Hugo de Euer, filius Dni Johis filii Robti,
falutem in Dno. Noveritis me dediffe, &c. Aliciæ forori meæ moniali de *Bafedale* unum annum
redditum 8to. folidorum percipiend. de moleudin. meo de *Stokefly* ad duos anni terminos ufual. &c.
tenend. et habend. dictæ Aliciæ in tota vita fuà, et poft obitum Aliciæ pro falute animæ meæ et anteceffo-
rum et fuccefforum in liberam puram et ppetuam eleam convent de *Bafedale* quiete reman.inpptuam
in cujus rei teftimonium duo inftrumenta in modo Cyrograph. fuerunt inde confecto unius tenoris,
quorum unum refidet penes dictam Aliciam et conventum de *Bafedale* figillo mei predicti Hugonis figil-
lat. et altum remanebit pènes dictum Hugonem figillo dictæ Aliciæ et conventus de *Bafedale* fignat.
Hiis teftibus, dno *Willo Percy,* dno *Robto de Stutvilla,* dno *Willo de Mowbray, Rada Teys. Thoma
Talebot, Johna de Thornton, Robto de Scotterfkelf, Robto de Seymer, Willo de Stokefley, Clerico,* &c.

bleffed Virgin Mary, and had a priorefs, and nine or ten religious, whofe income at the diffolution, (26 Henry VIII.) was valued, according to Dugdale, at 20*l.* 1s. 4d. but at 21*l.* 19s. 4d. according to Speed.

THE fite of the priory, together with the feveral lands, was granted in the 36 Henry VIII. to Ralph Bulmer and John Thyn, to be held of the King *in Capite* ; and the eight daughters and co-heireffes of Sir Ralph Bulmer, Knt. held this manor or monaftry in the 5th and 6th of Philip and Mary, by the fame tenure :—After divers grants and alienations it became the property of the Fotherleys of Caftleton ; and about the year 1729, was purchafed by Ann, daughter of William Pierfon, Efq. of the Middle Temple, London ; but the faid Ann dying unmarried and inteftate, her brother Bradfhaw Pierfon, Efq. fucceeded to her eftates. James Bradfhaw Pierfon, Efq. is the prefent proprietor.

THE buildings of the priory are now converted into farm holds, and retain little of their monaftic appearance.

THE land in the vale admits of fome degree of cultivation, and is, at prefent, comprifed in one farm of about 200 acres, with an extenfive common,—for nothing, perhaps, more valued at prefent, than its breed of moor-game, which is found in great abundance within the limits of this, and the adjoining liberties of Ingleby and Kildale.

WESTERDALE

lies about two miles to the eaft from Bafedale, and was probably firft fo named from its comparatively *more weftern* fituation. Here is a chapel under Stokefley with parochial rights, and ferved by a ftipendiary curate ; but we have not been able to afcertain the curate's income ; nor whether the chapel was ever certified to the governours of Queen Anne's bounty : it was about ten miles diftant from the mother-church.

WE find no mention of Wefterdale in the record of Domefday Book ; nor have we any documents to fhew the fucceffion of later proprietors.

The Yowards were a family anciently refident here, and poffeffed confiderable property.*　Sir Charles Turner, Bart. is the prefent lord of the manor.

THE vale, which is pleafing and retired, runs in a direction nearly north and fouth; and being divided into a number of fmall farms, is numeroufly inhabited; there being, in the year 1801, according to the return made to Government, 47 families and 257 inhabitants, making 5½ nearly to each family.‖

THE foil is in general dry; and the arable lands produce light crops of Wheat; with a few turnips and potatoes; oats are the principal crop; but the produce of the inclofed lands is in general fo fmall, that, with the moft rigid œconomy the occupiers could not fupport their

---

The Pedigree of YOWARD, *of Wefterdale.*

Robert Yoward, of Stokefley,　Muriell, dau. of Hen. Warcopp,
in the county of York.　of Greenhow.

4. Charles.　3. John.　2. William.　Muriell, mar. Gower of Stainfby.
M. D.　Anne, mar. Sam. Brafs of Hilton.
Mary, mar.——Wandsford.

1. Hen. Yoward, of Wefterdale,　Anne, dau. of James Pennyman,
county of York, ob. 1626.　of Ormefby, co. York, Efq.

4. Hen.　3. Robert.　Ralph Yoward,　Sufan, dau. of ...　William,　Jane, wife of Rob.
ob. S. P.　of Wefterdale,　Willis of ... in co.　died unm.　Stope, of Tun-
ob. 1640.　of ...　ftall, co. York.

2. Henry,　Richard Yoward, of Wef-　Frances, d. of Josias Matthews,　Anne, wife Robt. Rofs,
died young.　terdale, ob. 1666.　of Kirkby-Uuderhill, in county　of Leeds, in
of York.　co. of York.

2. Matthew.　1. Ralph Yoward, aged　1. Anne.　5. Eleanor.
3. Richard.　17. Sept. 8. 1666.　2. Barbara.　6. Catherine.
4. Charles.　3. Sufannah.　7. Jane.
4. Frances.

‖ STATE OF POPULATION, 10th MARCH, 1801.

WESTERDALE.	Inhabited House.	Families,	Uninhabited Ho.	Males,	Females,	Total,
	6.	47.	4.	132.	125.	257.

M m

families without the profits arifing from their flocks of fheep, which are
of a fmall breed, and depaftured upon the adjoining commons.

WESTERDALE is a truly fequeftered valley; and the inhabitants, being
almoft fecluded from the world, retain much of their primitive fimplicity,—untainted by the vices and luxuries of the more polifhed parts of
the kingdom.

> " Oh peaceful vale ——   ——
> " May ftill thy hofpitable fwains be bleft
> " In rural innocence ; thy mountains ftill
> " Teem with the fleecy race ; thy tuneful woods
> " For ever flourifh ; and thy vales look gay !"
>
> *Armftrong on Health.*

THE PARISH OF DANBY.

PROCEEDING eaftwards over an extenfive barren moor, we enter
the parifh of Danby ; the vale of which is narrow, fituated about eight
miles fouth-eaft from the market-town of Guifbrough ; and the parifh,
including the chapelry of Glafedale, is in length from north to fouth
ten miles, and near eight miles broad. It is bounded by Egton and
Lythe on the eaft ; by the chapelry of Wefterdale, and part of Guifbrough, on the weft ; by the feveral parifhes of Guifbrough, Skelton,
Eafington and Lofthoufe, on the north ; and by the chapelry of Rof-
dale, in the wapontake of Ryedale on the fouth.

THE name of the parifh is probably derived from the Britifh word
Dan, which fignifies a low and deep vale, and the iflandic *by*, which, next
to *ham* and *ton*, is one of the moft common terminations of local names,
and fignifies a dwelling : Danby, according to this etymology, is a

name defcriptive of its fituation, (i. e.) *villa in profundo.** Another
conjecture is that it might be fo called, as being the habitation of fome
Dane ; *q. d. habitatio Daci.*

DANBY, which is not recorded in the Domefday-book under any
name fimilar to the prefent, was one of thofe lordfhips given by the
Conqueror to *Robert de Brus*, who held of the king *in capite ;* he built
the caftle here, and dying in the fixth year of the reign of King Stephen
(1141) left this, and his other eftates in Yorkfhire, to Adam his fon,
who appears to have enjoyed this caftle but a fhort time ; " for King
" Henry II. took it from him, together with the lordfhip and foreft
" thereto belonging, and gave him inftead thereof the grange of *Mickle-*
" *thwaite*, with the whole fee of *Collingham* and *Berdefey*, whereof by
" violence he had bereft the Monks of Kirkftall, out of difpleafure to
" Roger de Mowbray ;" but Peter his grandfon, " earneftly defiring to
" repoffefs the lordfhip and foreft of Danby, of his ancient inheritance,
" rendered and quit-claimed to King John, in the fecond year of his
" reign, all his intereft in the above lordfhips of *Berdefey, Collingham*,
" and *Rington ;* and moreover paying one thoufand pounds *fterling*, ob-
" tained them accordingly." ‖   This Peter died 13. John, and his defcendants continued Lords of Danby, till Peter, the fourth of that name,
dying without iffue (55. Henry III.) left his four fifters his heirs, when
this and other eftates fell to Lucy the fecond, wife of Marmaduke de
Thweng ; and afterwards paffed by marriage to William de Latimer ;
by a daughter of whofe defcendant, it went to John Neville, fon of
Ralph Lord Neville, of Raby, who in her right became Lord Latimer.
But John his fon, dying without iffue in the reign of Henry VI. divers
of thofe lordfhips, of which he died feized, were entailed upon Ralph,
Earl of Weftmorland, his elder brother, who fettled them by feoffment
upon George, his third fon, who was thereupon fummoned to Parlia-

* IF this derivation be admitted, we may remark, that the word *Dæn* in the Irifh language, fignifies *a deep valley ;* and upon that word, the Saxons formed their *Dæin ;* and the place, on its being
fift inhabited, would be called *Dæinby.*

‖ DUGD. Baron. vol. I. p. 448.

ment, as Lord Latimer; † in whofe pofterity this dignity and eftate continued till John Lord Latimer, who died without iffue male in Queen
Elizabeth's time; when his eftates were divided among his four daughters and coheirs; and Danby fell to the fhare of Elizabeth, the eldeft,
wife of Sir John Danvers, of Dauntfey, Knt.; whofe fon Henry was in
her right, created a Baron (1. James I.) and afterwards by letters pat-
tent, Earl of Danby (1 Charles I.) but dying without iffue, the title became extinct,* having in his life time fold this lordfhip to five freeholders inhabitants of the place; of whom the caftle, manor, and greateft
part of the eftate were purchafed by Sir John Dawney, of Cowick, Knt.
afterwards created Lord Vifcount Downe; whofe defcendants have
fince continued proprietors of Danby.

FROM Kirkby's Inqueft, it appears, that in the reign of Edw. I. the
heir of Marmaduke de Thweng, held Danby, as one Knight's fee, of
the King *in capite*, and paid to the fine of the wapontake the fum of
eleven fhillings, for this and other lands which defcended from Peter
de Brus. We afterwards find, that William Lord Latimer, held Danby
as one Knight's fee, where ten carucates made a Knight's fee. ‡

---

† CLAUS. 10. Henry VI.

* THE title of *Earl of Danby*, which became extinct upon the death of the above Henry, without
iffue, was revived in the year 1674 in Thomas Ofborne, fon of Sir Edward Ofborne, Bart. by Anne,
daughter of Eleanor, one of the coheirs of John Neville, of Dauntfey, Lord Latimer. Being an
able ftatefman in the reign of King Charles II. he was made Lord high Treafurer of England, Vifcount Dumblane, &c. and at length, Earl of Danby; and being a great inftrument in bringing about
the Revolution, was created by King William III. (1689) Marquifs of Carmarthen, and in 1694,
Duke of Leeds. He died in the year 1712, and was fucceeded by his younger fon Peregrine, who
was fucceeded in 1729 by his youngeft fon and name-sake; who was succeeded in 1731, by his
only fon Thomas the 4th Duke, whofe fon Francis Godolphin fucceeded in 1789. He married
Amelia, the only furviving child of the Earl of Holdernefs, by whom he had iffue, George William
Frederick, the prefent Duke; who, on the death of his mother, Baronefs Conyers, January 26. 1784,
fucceeded to her barony; and on the death of his father in 1800, as Duke of Leeds.

‡ HÆRES Marmad. de Thweng, qui eft in Cuftodia Dni. Regis, tenet VIII. Feod. milit. et Dim.
et *Danby* pro uno Feod. Domino Rege *in capitie*; et reddere tenetur Ballivo Dni. Regis proporcione
ejus terr. et tenement. Dni. Petri de Brus pro fine Wapentag. *ol.* 11s. od.

WILLUS. Latymer tenet ibid. (*Danby*, de Feod. Latimere Lucie Thweng) unum Feod unde. X
Carucatæ terræ Feodum faciunt.   *Kirkby's Inqueft.*

THE following pedigree will assist the reader in forming an idea of the ancient proprietors of Danby.

Robert de Brus came into England = Agnes, Daughter of Fulke Paynell, with the Conqueror; and had by with whom he had the Manor of the Conquest the Lordships of Carleton, in Balme. Skelton, Marske, Uplyum, Brotton, Danby, Leventon, Yarm, &c. (ob. 1141.)

Adam de Brus, Lord of Skelton, = Ivetta, Daughter of William de Arches, Danby, &c. ob. 1167. Widow of R. de Flamville.

Adam de Brus, the 2d. = ob. 1180.

Peter de Brus, the first = Agnes, Daughter of Stephen, Earl of Albemarle, | Isabella de Brus = Sir Henry de Percy from of that name. Widow of A. de Romara, Earl of Lincoln. | *whom descended the Percies, Earls of Northumberland.*

Peter de Brus, the se- = Helewife, Dau. of Gilbert de Lancaster, cond, ob. 1240. Baron of Kendal.

Peter de Brus, the third = Hillaria, Daughter of Lord Malo-lacu, or Mauley.

Peter de Brus, | Lucy de Brus, = Marmaduke de Thweng, in Right | 1. Agnes = Walter de Fauconberge, had Skelton, Marske, &c.
the fourth, di- | the 2d. Dau | of his Wife, Lord of Danby, &c. | 3. Margaret = Robert de Rosse, Ld. of Werke, had Kendall, &c.
ed unmarried | had Danby, | | 4. Ladrina = Sir John de Bella-aqua, or Bellew, had Carlton
1271, leaving | Brotton and | | in Balme, &c.
his Sisters his | Yarm.
Heirs.

Robert de Thweng = Matilda, Dau | 3. Galivanus. 6. Peter. | 1. Hillaria. 4. Johanna.
eldest Son, before | of Sir Robert | 4. Edmund. 7. William. | 2. Matilda. 5. Maria.
his Father. | Hanfard. | 5. Richard. 8. Roger. | 3. Alicia.

William Latimer, = Lucy de Thweng = Robert de Everingham = Bartholomew Fenacourt, summoned to Par. died 20. Edw. III. | 2d. Husband. 3d. Husband. from 28. Edw. I. (*) to 1. Edw. III. (ob. 1. Edw. III.)

Marmaduke, the = Isabella, 2d. Son succeeded Dau. of his Father, and William was the first Ld. de Rosse, Tweng. of Igmanthorpe.

(*) SHE was first married to William Lord Latimer, and afterwards to Robert de Everingham, and lastly to Bartholomew Fanacourt, an alien, who was a domestic in the family of Lord Latimer; and being charged with having led a dishonest life with

The Arms of Latimer; viz. *Gules*, a Cross Flurie, *or.*

William Lord Latimer,=Elizabeth, Dau. of —— Lord
Heir of Lucy, of the | Botetourt, Baron of Weslegh,
age of 16 ys. *Ing.* 20. | (*in Com. Wigborn.*)
E. III.

Robert, second Son.
John, third Son.

William Lord Latimer, summoned to Parliament,=Elizabeth, Daughter of Edmund
from 42. E. III. to 3. Rich. II. (ob. 1381.) | Earl of Arundel.

Matilda, Dau. of Henry=John Neville, Lord of Raby,
Lord Percy, *1st Wife.* | in Right of his Wife, 1 Lord
Latimer.

=Elizabeth, Dau. and Heir=Robert Lord Willough-
of William 1 d. Latimer, | by, of Eresby, 2d. Hus-
born 1357. *2d Wife.* | band.

Ralph Lord Neville,=Joan, Dau. of John Duke of
Earl of Wettnor- | Lancaster. *2d. Wife.*
land, ob. 4. Henry VI.

George Neville,=Elizabeth Dau.
Lord Latimer, | of Richard de
the 3d Son of | Beauchamp,
Ralph in his lat- | Earl of War-
ter days became | wick.
an Ideot. (*ob. 9.*
Edw IV.)

John Neville,=Maud, Dau.
d Latimer, | of T. Lord
ob. S. P. (9 | Clifford, Wid.
Henry VI.) | of Richard
Earl of Camb.

Elizabeth=Thomas Willoughby, 2d. Son
Neville. | of Robert Lord Willoughby.

John Willoughby=Anne, Dau. and Coheirefs of Sir Edward Chency,
of Brooke, Co. Wilts, Knt.

Robert Willoughby=Blanch, Dau. and Coh.
of Rob. hampernon, Esq

Henry Neville, Knight, slain at the bat-=...Dau. of
tle of Edgcot. q Edw. 4) *patrevieute.*) | Lord Berners.

Robert=Elizabeth, D. and Coh. of Sir Richard
fon&heir | Beauchamp, of Powick, Knight.

Richard Neville, Lord Latimer, (ob=Anne, Daughter of Humphrey
succeeded his Grand-lather. (ob | Stafford, of Grafton, (*Com.*
22. Hen. VIII.) | *Wigborn.*)
(†)

Thomas Neville.

Nicholas de Meinell, (by whom she had a son named Nicholas, who was father of Elizabeth wife of *John D'arcy,*) she was divorced from the Lord Latimer, by sentence from the Court of Rome pronounced in the Ecclesiastical Consistory of York (5. Edw II.) Afterwards to prevent her estates descending to her son by that Lord, and at the intreaty of Meinell she conveyed all her lands and tenements, which came to her by inheritance, to the Rector of Rudby and others *in trust* for her issue by Meinell. But, upon her marriage with Fanacourt, as her husband could not legally take her estates for life by *Courtesy,* he being *an alien,* he obtained a licence from the Crown, and settled her estates, with the moiety of the advowson of the Monastry of Guisbro' to the use of herself and husband, and the survivor of them for life, and after their deaths, to the use of the said *John D'arcy,* and his heirs in fee.

(†) In the time of Henry VII. there was a contest between Richard Lord Latimer, and Sir Robert Willoughby, Lord Brooke, for the Barony of Latimer. The said Lord Brooke challenged the Barony as cousin, and heir of Elizabeth, his great-grand-mo-

2. Christopher.
3. George.
4. Marmaduke.
5. Thomas.
6. William

Dorothy, Sister and Coh. of John Earl of Oxd. (1st Wife.)

John Ld. Latimer (died 1542.) = Catherine, Daughter of Thomas Parr, of Kendal, Knt. (the last Wife to King Henry VIII.)

1. Margaret married .... son and heir to ..... Willoughby, Lord brooke.

2. Elizabeth.
3. Dorothy.
4. Catherine.
5. Susan.
6. Joane.

John Lord Latimer = Lucy, Dau. of Henry Earl ob. 20. Eliz. 1577. of Worcester. (ob. 1582.)

Margaret.

Lucia married Sir. W. Cornwallis, Knt.

Dorothy married Thomas Earl of Exeter.

Catherine married Henry Earl of Northumberland.

Sir John Danvers = Elizabeth. of Dauntsey, Knt.

Eleanore = Thomas Walmesley, of Dunkenhalgh, Com. Lanc. Esq.

Henry Lord Danvers, Earl of Danby, *died without Issue.* His Arms; *Gules,* a Cheveron between 3 Mullets of 6 Points, *ar.*

Anne = Sir Edward Osborne, of Kiveton, Co. Ebor. Bart.

Thomas Osborne, Lord Treasurer of England; created Viscount Latimer, and afterwards Earl of Danby: Ancestor to the present Duke of Leeds; whose Arms are, Quarterly *Ermine* and *Sapphire,* a Cross, *Topaz.*

ther, who was sister and heir of John Neville, Lord Latimer, who died without issue; and hereupon exhibited a petition to King Hen. VII. in Parliament; to which the said Richard Lord Latimer did by his answer shew, that after the death of the said John Neville, Lord Latimer without issue, the said Elizabeth was his sister and next heir, and married unto Thomas Willoughby; but King Henry VI. upon the death of the said John Neville, Lord Latimer without issue, the next heir being female, did therefore call to the Parliament, George Neville, Knt. 3d son of Ralph Neville, Earl of Westmorland, to be Lord Latimer, as cousin and next heir male of the said John Neville, Lord Latimer; wch George was grand-father of the said Richard. In debate, it was adjudged by the King in Parliament to the said Richard Lord Latimer, coming out of the *special heir male* against the Lord Brooke, descended of the *general heir male.* In the writ of Henry VI. Sir George Neville, Knt. was summoned to Parliament as Lord Latimer, being the *heir male,* and not Thomas Willoughby, Knt. husband of the said Elizabeth, *heir female. See Blome's Analogia Honorum, p. 55.*

THE CASTLE, of which there are ſtill ſome conſiderable remains, ſtands on the brow of a naked hill, of no great elevation, at a little diſtance to the ſouth from the banks of the river Eſk. From the ruins, we are led to conjecture, that the building has been extenſive; but can form no juſt idea of its ſtrength and ancient grandeur; nor have we met with any documents to determine the preciſe period of its erection. It was probably built ſoon after the conqueſt, by Robert de Brus; and was afterwards the occaſional reſidence of the Lords of Danby; who, as appears from the foregoing pedigree, were perſons of conſiderable conſequence in the country. There is ſtill a tradition in the neighbourhood, that a Queen of England formerly reſided here; alluding, no doubt to Queen Catherine Parr, the ſixth wife of King Henry VIII. who was married to John, Lord Latimer.

NOT far from the Caſtle, on the northern brink of the river, ſtands *Danby-Lodge*, a neat modern built houſe, belonging to Lord Viſcount Downe, where he occaſionally reſides, for a ſhort time, during the ſhooting-ſeaſon. The houſe does not afford accommodation for a numerous retinue; but is calculated merely for a ſmall party, to enjoy the ſports of the field, or to explore the wild mountain ſcenery in the neighbourhood.

CASTLETON, a ſmall hamlet within the pariſh, is ſituated towards the weſtern extremity of the vale; and appears to have been ſo called, from an ancient Caſtle, which ſtood here; and of which there are ſtill ſome evident remains; but at what period this fortification, which ſeems to have been of a circular form, was erected, our accounts are ſilent.

THE church of Danby is a modern edifice, and ſtands in a retired ſituation. It was anciently rectorial; but being appropriated to the priory of Guiſbrough, to which it was given by Robert de Brus the founder, on the diſſolution of that monaſtry it was reduced to a perpetual curacy, and was certified to the governours of Queen Anne's bounty at 16*l.* 3s. od. In the year 1767 it received an augmentation of 200*l.* by lot, which was laid out in the purchase of lands; and the whole revenue at present amounts to about 40*l. per annum.* Lord Viscount Downe is the patron, and nominates the curate.

THE general appearance of the parish, which, notwithstanding its mountainous and sequestered situation, is populous and well inhabited, is rather barren; though much has been effected towards improvement. The vale called *Danby-Dale,* produces good crops of corn, and contains some rich meadow and pasture lands. The soil is particularly adapted to the growth of oats, which are the crops principally cultivated. Great improvements have been made in agriculture within the parish, by draining the wet lands, and sowing them down with grass-seeds; there is also another mode of improvement worthy of notice, which appears to have been of late very generally adopted: viz. the light lands are first sown with rape, which is depastured with sheep, and afterwards with wheat; which is a method that has been found to produce an abundant crop. There is an extensive common or moor within the limits of this parish, which affords pasture for numerous flocks of sheep, of an inferior breed, not weighing more than ten or twelve pounds *per quarter;* but the horses and cattle are nearly of an equal size with those in the more fertile parts of Cleveland.—The lands within the parish are chiefly freehold, and the whole tythe-free, the tythes being vested in the freeholders.

A CONSIDERABLE colliery has been carried on here, for some time, under Lord Downe, which employs about forty workmen; and though the coals are of an inferior quality, and the seam, at first, only small;

DANBY CURACY.

Certified value 16*l.* 3s. Lord Viscount Downe, patron.

CURATES.

John Scarre, Curate, 1715.	Robert Greenwood, 1769,	ibid.
James Turner, Curate, 1720.	Robert Greenwood, Jun. 1775.	ibid.
James Deason, 1750. nominated by Lord Downe.	Daniel Duck, 1781.	ibid.

N n

yet it has been found annually to increafe, fo as to afford a fupply fufficient for the general fuel of the inhabitants.

THE moft ftriking feature, and what forms the only picturefque
fcenery within the parifh, is the river Efk; which, after collecting its
ftream from the mountainous regions of Cleveland, enters Danby, and
runs in a ferpentine courfe eaftwards through the parifh. Rapidity, as
the name imports,‡ is the leading characteriftic of this mountain rivulet;
a quality which it, in fome degree, retains, during its defcent through
the rich and fertile vale of *Efkdale*, till it reaches the vicinity of Whitby,
where it empties itfelf into the fea.

LELAND's defcription of its origin and courfe is tolerably accurate;
" *Efka fluvius oritur in Efkdale, defluitque per Danbeium nemus, et tandem*
" *apud Strenfhale in Mare fe exonerat."*   *Leland's Collect. vol.* 3. *p.* 37.

THIS river, during its courfe through the townfhip of Danby, is
croffed by three ftone bridges, of one arch each, and of a fimilar conftruction; on the centre or key-ftone of each there is a fhield bearing
the arms of Neville, Lord Latimer; from which we are led to conclude,
that they were originally built or repaired by fome of that family, while
they continued proprietors of Danby.

THE townfhip and chapelry of

GLASEDALE

lies on the eaftern extremity of the parifh, and adjoins to the parifh of
Egton. It was anciently the property of Robert de Brus, Lord of Skelton; and with Danby defcended to the Thwengs, and afterwards to the
Latimers, Lords of Danby. It has been long parcelled out into a number of freeholds; but together with *Lealholm*, a hamlet within this townfhip, conftitutes a part of the manor of Danby.

---

‡ THE river *Efk* is fuppofed by fome to derive its name from *Ofca* or *Efke*, the favourite fon of
Hengift; while others confider the name to be of greater antiquity; and fuppofe it to be the *Ifca*,
or *Æfica* of the Romans, who gave it that name, on account of the *rapidity of its current. Efk* is
fynonymous with *Ifis* and *Oufe*, and is derived from the Gaelic word *üi, üis,* or *üifk,* which fignifies
water in general.

THE chapel here is stated in Archbishop Sharp's *MSS*. to be parochial,* and was certified to the governours of Queen Anne's bounty at 9*l.* 11s. 8d.   There is an annual payment of 4*l.* charged upon the houses of the inhabitants, and 20 nobles *per ann.* settled upon the chapel by ———, an Alderman of Hull.   This is a perpetual curacy under the patronage of the Archbishop of York; but the whole revenues of the chapel have not been stated to us. §

GLASEDALE is a fertile, cultivated, and well-inhabited valley, watered by the river Esk.   The name appears highly characteristic and descriptive, the component parts signifying literally *a green and verdant dale.*

ALTHOUGH there is not any particularly large village within the parish, nor any manufactory, except a paper-mill at Lealholm, which employs about twenty hands, the population, as we have already remarked, is considerable; owing chiefly to the division of the landed-property into numerous small freeholds, regularly intersperfed throughout the vales, and occupied, in general, by their proprietors; who, shut out from a frequent intercourse with the inhabitants of more refined districts, retain much of the rude simplicity and independence of their ancestors; but are friendly and hospitable to strangers.

As we have not been favoured with the necessary extracts from the parish register, we cannot state the probable increase or decrease of the inhabitants; but from the nature of their property and occupation, we

---

* THE inhabitants marry at Danby, but have the privilege of burying at Glasedale, on paying the customary fee to the Curate of Danby.

§ GLASEDALE CHAPEL.
Certified value 9*l.* 11s. 8d.   The Archbishop of York, patron.
CURATES.
John Smith, Curate, 1715.
Jonathan Robinson, Curate, 1717, *nominated by the A. Bp.*
Richard Robinson, A. M. 1778,   *ibid.*
Benj. Richardson, ——— 1806,   *ibid.*

conclude the number to be nearly ftationary. In the year 1801, when an actual enumeration was made by order of the Legiflature, the population of the parifh ftood as follows:

	Inhabited houfes.	Families.	Uninhabited houfes.	Males.	Females.	Total.	Agriculture.	Trade, &c.	Refidue.	Total.
Danby	162	211	15	480	510	990	217	105	668	990
Glafedale	151	156	1	375	388	763	150	77	536	763
	313	367	16	855	898	1753	367	182	1204	1753

FROM the above table it appears that there are 313 houfes, occupied by 367 families and 1753 inhabitants; giving on an average $5\frac{1}{2}$ nearly to each houfe, and upwards of $4\frac{1}{2}$ to each family. The males and females are nearly of an equal number.

THE PARISH OF EGTON;

OR, as it is fometimes thus varioufly written, *Oketun, Ayketon, Echetun,* and in Domefday-book, EGETUNE *(villa quercuum)* was probably fo called from the number of oak trees that it produced, and which ftill grow fpontaneoufly in different parts of the parifh. It was formerly a chapelry under Lythe, but being now connected with that parifh in nothing but the payment of every third penny towards the repairs of the mother church, it may be confidered as a diftinct parifh.

IT is bounded on the eaft by the parifh of Whitby, and by Danby on the weft; by the parifh of Lythe on the north, and by Pickering, in the Wapontake of Pickering Lythe on the fouth; and ftretches in extent from north to fouth about fix miles, and is upwards of four miles broad.

IT appears from Domefday-book, that before the conqueft, the manor of Egton was in the hands of *Suuen*; but at the time of the furvey was held by *Nigel*, under Robert Earl of Moreton, being thus entered in that ancient record, under the title

" **Terra Comitis Moretonensis.**

" **In Egetune ad geldum III. carucatae, et tot car. possunt esse ; ibi**
" **habebat Suuen I. manerium. Nunc habet Nigel de Comite. Silva**
" **past. III. leuc. longa, et II. lat. Totum maner. IIII. leuc. long. et**
" **II. lat. T. R. E. valebat XX. sol. modo wastum est.**"

FROM the above extract we find that there were three carucates of land here, rated *ad geldum*, and as many more that might be rendered arable ; that there was a wood with pasturage for cattle three miles in length and two in breadth ; and that the whole manor, which was four miles long and two broad, was valued in the Confeffor's time, at twenty shillings, but was then wafte.

EGTON, in the reign of Henry I. was in the hands of Nigel Foffard, fon of *Nigel* above-mentioned, who came into England with the Conqueror ; and, as appears from the general furvey, held this and other large poffeffions under Robert, Earl of Moreton, who was half-brother to the Conqueror. It continued in this family till the reign of Richard I. when by failure of male-iffue, it paffed by marriage with Joan, daughter of William Foffard, to Robert de Turnham, whofe daughter Ifabel, marrying Peter de Malo-lacu, or Mauley, brought their great eftates to that family. ‖ The Mauleys continued proprietors for feveral generations ; Peter de Mauley, the third of that name, obtained a charter of free-warren in all his demefne lands, (38. Henry III.) and afterwards in the 43d year of the fame King's reign, procured a charter for a weekly market at Egton upon the Wednefday ; and a fair yearly for eight days, begining on the eve of St. Hilda in Winter. † Egton continued thus

---

‖ DUGDALE fays, that the fortune of the Mauley Family was made by King John, who employed this Peter, (a Poictevin) his Efquire, to murder Prince Arthur, fon of Geffery Duke of Britanny, his elder brother ; for which execrable fact, he rewarded him with the heirefs of the Barony of Mulgrave, &c.

† CART. Antiq. II. n. 8.

priviledged in the hands of the Mauleys, till Peter the eight of that name, and the laft Baron Mauley, who died without iffue (3. Henry V.) when with other poffeffions it defcended by marriage with Elizabeth his aunt, and coheir; (viz. the fifter of Peter de Mauley the feventh,) to George Salvine, Efq. * from whofe defcendants it came to the Earl of Suffex, who fold the eftate here to Carey Elwes, Efq. the prefent pro-prietor and lord of the manor.

IN Kirkby's Inqueft † we find that Peter de Mauley, in the reign of Edw. I. held two carucates of land here, where ten made one knight's fee; and that the free tenants had two carucates, which they held of the faid Peter; who, as appears from the *pipe rolls*, (8. Edw. I.) on the pay-ment of one hundred pounds as his relief, had livery of all his lands, which he held of the King *in capite* by barony, of the inheritance of William Foffard.

THE town of Egton is fmall, but pleafantly fituated on the declivity of a hill, about fix miles to the weft from the market town of Whitby: it confifts of one ftreet, with the manfion and market-houfe in the centre. The market has been difcontinued for near a century, nor indeed is fuch a convenience now particularly wanted by reafon of its proximity to the port and town of Whitby, to which the roads are now commo-dious, and kept in good repair. Egton, as we have already remarked, had likewife the privilege of holding a fair annually, by a charter grant-ed in the time of Henry III. called *St. Hilda's fair*, which was reforted to as a kind of jubilee by the people from the adjacent country. ‡ This

* LELAND obferves, " Salwayne had for his part of Mauley's landes, the barony of Eggeftone " on Efk, not farre from Whitby."

† PETRUS DE MALO-LACU tenet II. carucatas in Egton, unde X. car. faciunt feodum ;

LIBERI tenentes de Egton tenent II. car. terræ in eadem, de dicto Petro, unde X. car faciunt feodum. *Kirkby's Inqueft.*

‡ IT has been remarked on a fimilar fubject by an ingenious writer (Dr. Whitaker) that the houfes, the habits, the refrefhments, the diverfions of our homely forefathers affembled on this occa-fion, could they pafs in review before us, would form a fingular fpectacle, of which the laft would

fair has been difcontinued for fome time; but there are four fairs,
which are ftill kept annually: viz. on the Tuefday before May-day;
upon St. Bartholomew's day; on the Tuefday before St. Martin's day,
and on the Tuefday before the Purification *(old ftyle)*; which are frequented by the inhabitants of an extenfive circumjacent country, and
bufinefs to a confiderable amount is tranfacted in the fale of fheep,
horfes, and cattle; as alfo in different kinds of merchandize, toys, &c.
for which there is much demand among the country people, for *fairings*
and *rural finery*.

THE church or chapel of Egton is an ancient and venerable ftructure,
with a fide-aile on the fouth formed by round pillars fupporting circular arches; the chancel is feparated from the nave by a pointed arch
of modern architecture. It is fituated about half a mile to the weft
from the town, upon the fummit of a gently rifing eminence; from
whence there is a pleafing and extenfive profpect, particularly into the
fertile, cultivated and well inhabited vale of Glafedale. This chapel
was anciently dependent on the church of Lythe; but it feems to have
enjoyed parochial rights, as early as the year 1349; when, as appears
from *Torr's MSS.* " the chapel, with the chapel-yard thereof, was de-
" dicated by the Bifhop of Damafcus, to the honour of St. Hilda."

THE revenues of the church were certified to the governours of
Queen Anne's bounty at 21*l.* ‖ and with augmentations laid out in lands,

---

refemble the manners of the prefent day in nothing but groffnefs and immorality; for under all the
changing fcenes of time and cuftom, human nature adheres with undeviating exactnefs, to its original
corruption; and we may add, the Lady Abbefs *Saint Hilda*, would probably be no more delighted
by the manner of celebrating her feftival in the 13th than in the 19th century.

‖ PAYABLE by the vicar of Lythe, out of Archbifhop Frewen's augmentation of that vicarage.
Archbifhop Sharpe's MSS.

EGTON CURACY.

DED. to St. Hilda. Certif. val. 21*l.* Archbifhop of York, patron.

CURATES.

1698, John Smith, M. A. admitted curate,
1717, Jonathan Robinfon, nominated by the Archbifhop of York.
1778, Richard Robinfon, M. A. ——— by the fame,
1806, Benjamin Richardfon, by the fame.

amount at prefent to about 40*l. per ann.*   The rectorial rights within
the parifh belong to the Archbifhop of York, who is alfo patron of the
church and nominates the curate.

MONUMENTAL INSCRIPTIONS.

WITHIN the church, on the north fide of the chancel, there is a plain mural monument with the
following infcription : viz.

Nere this place lyes interr'd the body of
Thos. Savnders, fon of John Savnders, Efq.
who was born at his father's houfe, at Alvefcott,
in Oxfordfhire, on Holy Thurfday, being May
eve, in the year of our Lord 1668 ; he married Elizabeth, eldeft daughter of Sir Edward Chaloner,
of Gifborow, and had by her 4 children, Edward,
D'oyley, David, and Elizabeth ; he departed this
life at his own houfe, at Cots–Bank, in Growmond,
the 5 day of March 1695, in the 28 yeare of his age.

He liv'd in love, and loved to die
That he might live eternally.

———

Beneath the above,
In memory of Mr. D'oyley Saunders
of Coat-Bank, who departed this life
June 6th, 1773, in the 48 year of his age.
Alfo Elizabeth his daughter died in
her infancy.

Beneath—this ftone,—(what few vain marbles can,—)
May juftly fay, here lies an honeft man.

UPON the north wall, at the weft end of the church is an elegant monument of veined marble,
with the following infcription :

Sacred to the memory of JOHN BURDETT, Efq.
One of his Majefty's Juftices of the Peace, for the North-Riding of
this county.
He was a gentleman, who in the two great effentials of life
Ever conducted himfelf with ftrict honour and integrity.
To the public he acted as a moft worthy magiftrate,
A fincere friend, and a benevolent neighbour.

SOIL and PRODUCE.—The foil within the parifh is naturally of an indifferent quality, but has, of late, been confiderably improved by draining, and manuring with lime, which is a practice very generally adopted, and attended with beneficial confequences. The farms are in general fmall, few exceeding 100*l. per ann.* Wheat, rye, barley, and oats are the principal crops, with fome few acres of beans, potatoes, and other articles of provifion; which being more than fufficient for the confumption of the inhabitants, are fent as a fupply to the weekly market of Whitby. The air and water are falubrious, and the parifh is generally confidered healthy.

THE POPULATION—notwithftanding the inhabitants are chiefly occupied in hufbandry, will be found to be confiderable. The parifh contains but one townfhip; and according to the return made under the population act in the year 1801, there were then 190 houfes or families, and 971 inhabitants: viz. 476 males and 495 females, giving, on an average, upwards of 5 to each family.

FROM the parifh regifters it appears that the annual number of baptifms within the parifh, on an average is 20, and that of burials 18; but we cannot, from this ftatement, form any accurate idea of the probable increafe or decreafe of its inhabitants; as this near equality of number is owing chiefly to the number of Roman Catholics within the parifh, whofe burials, but not baptifms, are entered in the parifh regifter. From the average number of burials in one year, it will be feen, however, that one out of $48\frac{1}{2}$ nearly dies annually.

In private life he was as a tender hufband to his widowed mother,
And as a kind father to his brothers and fifters,
To whom in his life time, he gave very confiderable fortunes;
And dying unmarried, bequeathed them a handfome eftate
Which he had acquired by induftry and good management,
And ever fupported with credit and reputation.
He died the 4th April, 1737, aged 63 years.

O o

ABOUT a mile to the fouth from the town ftands
EGTON BRIDGE,
the feat of Thomas Smith, Efq. defcended from an ancient family, which had its origin in this county with the conqueft. The vale here is beautiful, being divided by the river Efk, which winds, in a meandering courfe through an extenfive range of rich pafture, meadow, and corn fields. * The country down the vale as far as Whitby, wears a pleafing cultivated afpect, and the banks of the river are richly ornamented. Here is an excellent ftone-bridge of three arches over the river Efk, and two convenient Inns for the accommodation of vifitors, the place being much frequented, in the Summer feafon, by parties from Whitby, &c. the neatnefs and fimplicity of the whole has a very pleafing and picturefque appearance.

PURSUING the courfe of the river Efk for about a mile to the eaft from *Egton Bridge*, we approached the imperfect remains of

GRANDMONT, OR GROWMOND ABBEY,
fituated on the northern bank of the river, and not far from the foot of *Goadland·Beck*. The· moft rigid enthufiaft could not have made choice of a fituation more reclufe, or better fuited to the purpofes of devotion and retirement

THIS was an alien priory, and a cell to the Abbey of Grandimont, in Normandy, founded in the third year of the reign of King John, by Joan, daughter of William Foffard, wife of Robert de Turnham, who gave a parcel of land in the foreft of Egton, (fince called Efkdale,) to that convent; who thereupon fent Monks of their own order † to

---

* THE river Efk is well ftored with trout of the fineft quality; and, in their proper feafon, falmon were formerly fo plentiful, as to afford to the inhabitants a cheap article of food ; but owing to the great and unreafonable height of the mill-dams at Rufwarp, and in the vicinity of Whitby, they are now in a great meafure prevented from paffing fo far up the river.

† THE order of *Grandimont* was firft inftituted, in the mountain of *Muret*, about the year 1076, by Stephen, a gentleman of Auvergne, in France; whofe fucceffor being chafed from thence, pretended to have been directed by a voice in the air, to the place where he fhould carry his monks,

fettle here, and called it after their own Abbey, Grandmont. Afterwards, when by reafon of the wars with France, the Kings of England
bore hard upon the alien priories, the abbot of Grandimont got leave
to fell the Advowfon, and all their right in this cell, to John Hewitt,
alias Sergeant, ‡ when it feems to have become *prioratus indigena.* It
fubfifted till the general diffolution, when there were only four Monks
in it, whofe revenues were rated (26. Henry VIII.) at 12*l.* 2s. 8d. *per
ann.* according to Dugdale, and 14*l.* 2s. 8d. according to Speed.

THE above grant of Joan the foundrefs, to the prior and monks
here, was confirmed to them by Robert de Turnham, her hufband;
who alfo made an addition to them out of his lands, and thefe gifts
were afterwards confirmed by King John, in the 15th year of his reign.
Peter de Mauley the third, (grandfon of Peter who married Ifabel,
daughter of the above Joan), was alfo a benefactor to this houfe; who,
poffeffing the two extenfive manors of Egton and Mulgrave, refided
alternately at Mulgrave-Caftle, and at Julian's Park, (now corruptly
called *Gilly Park,)* within this parifh. He took the prior and brethern
under his protection, and confiderably increafed their revenues; as ap-

___

which was *Grandimont*; a ftory eafily believed in thofe times of fuperftition. This Stephen was fo
rigidly auftere, that, not contenting himfelf with the rules of *Saint Benedict* (from whence, and the
regular canons he had formed his order) he added the manner of life of the Hermits. He is faid to
have worn an *iron cuirafs* next his fkin, flept without a bed or litter of any kind, in a wooden coffin
funk fome feet deep into the ground,—to have made the fkin of his knees like that of a camel's, and
laftly to have caufed his nofe to be turned upwards, by his frequent kiffing the earth in token of hu-
miliation.

THIS rule was confirmed by feveral of the Popes; but afterwards moderated, on account of its
great aufterity. Thefe monks were firft introduced into England, in the reign of Henry I. and placed at Adderbury, in Shropfhire; they had but two other houfes in this country, viz this at Growmond, in Efkdale, and another at Creffwell, in Herefordfhire. Their habit was much like the Bene-
dictins, and they were confidered a branch of that order.

‡ " QUOD Abbas de Grandimont poffit feofare Johannem Hewitt, *alias* Sergeant, in feodo advo-
cat. Prioratûs de Efkdale, et omnium maneriorum eidem pertinentium."

Pat. 18. *Rich. II. p.* 1.

pears by his charter, granting them his mill at Egton with its pool, water, fisheries, with all suits, dues, customs, liberties, and easements, as a pure and perpetual alms. He also granted out of his forest at Egton, sufficient main timber, both oak and alder, for the necessary repairs of the said mill, &c. binding his homagers to perform all manner of services pertaining to the same, not only in carrying the stones and main timber, but also in every repair necessary from time to time to be made,—on condition that the *corrector* and brethren shall add two more chaplains to their former number, to celebrate divine service every day in the year, and to sing by note an obit of his father, and mother, of himself and Nicholaa his wife, in the church of St. Mary, belonging to his house. The charter is dated at St. Julian's *(apud sanctum Julianum)* on St. Bartholomew's feast-day, which was the old feast-day or wake, in the year of our Lord 1294.

THE site of this house, and premises, amounting to the clear yearly value of 9*l*. 8s. § were granted (35. Henry VIII.) to Edward Wright, Esq. for the sum of 184*l*. 13s. 2d. subject to the yearly payment of 18s. 10d. in the court of augmentation of the revenue, of the crown, at the feast of Saint Michael the Archangel. In the year following the King granted him licence to alienate these premises to Francis Spring, who soon afterwards sold them to Sir Richard Chomley, Knight, and his heirs; in whose possession they continued till the year 1668, when they passed by purchase to Sir John D'oyley; whose sister soon after marrying John Saunders, Esq. they came by an exchange for an estate at Alvescott in Oxfordshire, into the Saunders family; whose descendant, D'oyley Saunders, Esq. of Coatbank-Lodge, in this parish, now enjoys a considerable part of the demesne; but the cell and lands adjoining became the property of Richard and Matthew Agar, and Mr. John Linskill.

§ By a late valuation worth 536*l. per annum.*

From the ruins of the convent a fpacious farm houfe, with out-offices, has been erected at the weft end of the priory church; which, from the remains, appears to have been but fmall; it was dedicated to Saint Mary, the virgin. ‖

On the fouth fide of the river Efk, at a little diftance from the convent, there is a field, called the *Chapel-Hills*, where the foundation of buildings may be diftinctly traced; fuppofed from the name, to have been fome religious houfe or chapel.

NEWBIGGIN,

a fmall, dependent manor within this parifh, is fituated at a fhort diftance from the Abbey, on the northern bank of the river Efk. This was an ancient manor belonging to the Mauleys, Lords of Mulgrave; and with Egton, and other poffeffions, defcended to the Salvins, by marriage with the coheirefs of that family. * From the Salvins, who continued proprietors for many generations, the manor and eftate paf-

---

‖ Burton (in his *Mon. Ebor. p.* 275.) fays, " there are no ancient infcriptions or tomb-ftones " preferved; but a large ftone-crofs with the holy-lamb upon it, was dug up, at fome diftance from " the fouth-eaft corner of the church."

* SALVINE *of Newbiggin.*

(Extracted from the Herald's office, by WM. RADCLYFFE, *rouge croix, pourfurvant*).

Arms.—*Argent.* on a chief *fable* two mullets, *or.* Quartering *or,* a bend, *fable,* for the arms of Mauley.

George Salvyne, of North Duffield, in the county of York, Efq. (living 3. Hen. V.) = Elizabeth de Mauley, fecond daughter, and aunt and coheir of Peter de Mauley the 8th, had the barony of Egton, Newbiggin, Ifle-Park, Cuckwold Banks, Doncafter, Barfe Caftle, &c. (living 3. Hen. V.)

Sir John Salvyne, of Newbiggin, Knight, died circa 1471. = Ifabella, dau. of Sir Thomas Gray, of Heton, county of Northumberland.

Gerard Salvyne, (2d fon.)

Elizabeth Salvyne.

Thos. Salvyne, of Newbiggin, Lord of Doncafter, &c. (ob. 17. Edw. IV.) = Mary, dau. of Ralph, Lord Greyftock.

Robert Salvyne, (2d. fon).

Elizabeth, dau. of Sir Hugh Haftings, of Fenwick, *co. Ebor.* Knt. = Sir Ralph Salvyne, of Newbiggin, Knt. Lord of Doncafter, &c. (living 24. Hen. VII.)

......, daughter of ......, of ...... (2d. wife).

fed by purchafe to Mr. Duck, and afterwards to the late —— Yeoman,
Efq. of Whitby; whofe heir, (now a minor,) fucceeds to the eftate.

NEWBIGGIN-HALL, the ancient feat of the Salvins has been long
in ruins; on the fite of which, a more modern and commodious man-

---

Anne Salvyne, wife George Salvyne, of Newbiggin,＿Margeria, daughter of　John.　Margery.
of W. Daniel, of Efq living circa 19. Hen. VIII. | Sir Wm. Bulmer, Knt.
Befwick.

Margery, dau. of Sir＿Sir Francis Salvyne, of＿Urfula, dau. of ...　Matthew,　William,　John,
Ralph Eures, and | Newbiggin, Knt. (liv- | Ellerker, 2d wife).　2d fon.　3d fon.　4th fon.
fifter of Wm. Lord | ing 2. Edw. VI.)
Eures.　　　　　　　　　　　　　　Robert Salvine

Anne Salvyne, mar.　Frances, wife to Geo. 3d.　Mary, wife of F Cop-　Jane, dau. of Sir Rich.＿
J. Thornholme, of　fon of Nich. Fairfax, of　pendall, of Howfome.　Cholmondley, of Rox-
Afthorpe.　　　　　Walton.　　　　　　　　　　　　　　　by, co. Ebor. Knt.

Ralph Salvine,＿Dorothy, dau. of Rich. Tockets, of　William.　Joan.　Elizabeth.
of Newbiggin. | Tockets, Efq (2d wife)

Joan, married Dennis Bainbrigge.　　　Francis, 2d fon.

Mary, wife of　Anne, wife　Elizabeth, wife　Margaret, wife　Ralph Salvine,＿Eleanor, dau. of
Rich. Poulton.　of Thomas　of James Daw-　of Chriftopher　of Newbiggin, | Tho. Dutton of
　　　　　　　Cooke.　　　fon　　　　　Thackray.　　　Efq. (living | Sherburne in co.
　　　　　　　　　　　　　　　　　　　　　　　　1612.)　　 | Gloucefter Efq.

Anne Salvine.　Dorothy, dau. of＿William Salvine, of Newbig-＿Anna, dau. of Lan-　2. Ralph.
　　　　　　　John Girlington. | gin, Efq eldeft fon and heir, | celot Carneby, of　3. Thomas.
......　Salvine, aged　　　　　　　　(living 1612).　　　　 | Halton, Northumb.
one year, A. D. 1612.　William Salvine, of Newbiggin,＿Anne, dau. of Marmaduke Cholmley,
　　　　　　　　　Efq aged 40 years, 25th Aug. | of Bardfey, co. Ebor. Efq.
　　　　　　　　　1665.

1. Mary.　Francis Salvine, Efq.　Thomas. 2d.　3. William Salvine of＿Anna, dau of
2 Anne.　eldeft fon, and heir　fon, (living　Newbiggin, Efq buried | John Raynes, of
3 Urfula.　apparent; aged 11　1665.　at York, 26th March, | Eafingwold. co
4. Dorothy.　years, 25th Aug. 1665.　　　　1726.　　　　　 | Ebor. Efq.

Thomas Salvine, of Eafingwold, Efq.＿Mary, daughter and heir of Edward　4. Marmaduke.
died 22d Jan. 1756. Buried at York. | Talbot, of Hamftead, co. Middlefex.　5. John

Thomas Salvine, of Eafingwold, Efq.　Mary Salvine, ob 22d July,＿Sir John Webb, of Cranford-
fon and heir; living without iffue, 1784.　1782. Buried at Lovaine.　Magna, Hatherop, Worlaby,
　　　　　　　　　　　　　　　　　　　　　　　　&c. Bart. (hath iffue.)

fion has been erected, in a warm, fequeftered fituation, environed with rifing oaks, to the growth of which the foil is peculiarly favourable.

FROM Growmond bridge, we purfued the courfe of *Goadland-Beck*,† which, at its confluence here with the Efk, becomes the eaftern boundary of the diftrict. This is a black and rocky mountain-river, the banks of which are rudely ornamented with wood, and afford a great variety of wild and romantic fcenery : but, what appears particularly interefting, is a remarkable water-fall, formed by a rivulet, which empties itfelf into the Goadland, and known in the neighbourhood by the name of *Mal-lin Spout.*

THIS fingular cafcade is precipitated down the front of a perpendicular rock, upwards of one hundred feet in height. The ftream at firft glides gently down the fhelving rock in a zig-zag courfe, for about half way down the precipice ; when falling upon a point more prominent than the reft, it becomes broken, and falls in fmall ftreams, like threads in the form of a fhower-bath.

ABOUT half a mile diftant from this fingular curiofity, upon the weftern bank of Goadland Beck, ftand *July-Park Houfes;* " near which,"

---

† ON the banks of this river, and not far from its confluence with the Efk, on a narrow neck of land, there are the remains of buildings, which we conjecture to have been ufed in the procefs of cryftallizing allum, and probably at a period prior to the date generally affigned for the introduction of that manufacture into England. The place has been long known by the name of the *Allum-Garth ;* and though now covered with a grove of *aged* oaks, which appear to be the fucceffors of others ftill *more ancient*, the works may be diftinctly traced, confifting of two rows of circular pits, 20 in each row, three feet in diameter, and $2\frac{1}{2}$ feet diftant from each other. On the north fide of thefe, which are built with hewn ftones, there is a large cooler, one foot in depth, of the form of a parallelogram ; and on the fouth, a fquare ciftern, fimilar to thofe ufed in modern allum-works. The bricks which appear to have been ufed in placing the furnaces, &c. are ftrongly glazed, and bear evident marks of fire. An allum rock near at hand, which appears to have been wrought, and particularly pieces of the burnt *allum-fhale*, frequently found in the vicinity of the place, are circumftances that concur with its name, to ftrengthen the conjecture of its being an *allum-work ;* and if this be admitted, we leave it to the confideration of the reader, whether it might not probably have been wrought, fome time prior to the reign of Queen Elizabeth, when the manufactory of allum was firft eftablifhed in the neighbourhood of Guifbrough by Sir Thomas Chaloner.

as Burton obferves, " are the traces of an ancient large building, which
" had been moated round.   The adjoining field is called *Kirkfield*,
" where, as tradition fays, there formerly ftood a church.   This, in all
" probability was the *St. Julians*, where the charter of Peter de Mauley
" to the priory of Growmond was dated; and was the feat of Lord
" Mauley's, who had great poffeffions here, or fome religious houfe, or
" both."

On our vifit, in the year 1801, we carefully examined the places,
noted by the above author; when we found *July-Park Houfes* to confift of a few farm holds, fcattered on the edge of an extenfive naked
and barren common.   The " foundations of the ancient large building," though now overgrown with trees and brufh-wood, may be diftinctly traced; and the moat is ftill vifible.

About forty yards weft from *July-Park Houfes*, we traced the remains of an ancient Roman military road, called *Wade's-Caufeway*,
which runs in a fouthern direction through this parifh to the Roman
camp on the moors near Pickering.   The road appears to have been fo
called from the Saxon Duke *Wada*; who, as Camden fays, " lived at
" a caftle on thefe coafts, (now called Mulgrave,) which was probably
" the abandoned Roman fortrefs or ftation."   " It is believed," adds
he, " that this Saxon Prince was a giant;" but without entering into
a repetition of the ridiculous traditional ftory of *Wade's wife and her
cow*, as the reafon of making this road, the following extract from
Drake's *Eboracum* will be more interefting to the reader, and more applicable to the fubject.   After noticing the *Dunum Sinus* of Ptolemy,
which our antiquaries have fixed at Whitby, and the egregious miftake
of Mr. Horfley in placing it at the mouth of the river Tees, without
regarding *Dunfley*, now a fmall village on this bay, which bears fome
teftimony of the ancient name, Mr. Drake adds, " but what makes
" it more confiderable is a Roman road which runs from it for many
" miles over the vaft moors and moraffes towards York.   This extra-
" ordinary road, not now made much ufe of, is called by the country

" people, *Wade's causeway*;" he further proceeds thus:—" I had my
" first intelligence of this road, and a camp upon it, from Thomas Ro-
" binson, of Pickering, Esq. ‡ a gentleman well versed in this kind of
" learning. My curiosity led me to see it, and coming to the top of a
" steep hill, the vestiges of the camp were easily discernable; at the
" foot of the hill began the road or causeway very plain; and I had
" not gone a hundred paces on it before I met with a mile-stone of the
" grit kind, a sort not known in this country; it was placed in the
" midst of the causeway; but so miserably worn, either by sheep or
" cattle rubbing against it, or the weather, that I missed the inscription,
" which I own I ran with great eagerness to find. The causeway is

‡ Extract of a letter from Thomas Robinson, Esq. of Pickering, in Yorkshire, to Mr. R. Gale.
October 10, 1724.

(From Bib. Topog. Brit. vol. III. p. 132.)

Sir,

I hope the criticising on the learned Doctor's way of writing will be soon over. It is agreeable news that he has made so good a progress north of Trent, and designs also a review. We build
upon many visits of your's into these parts, country ones too in our phrase, when we shall not lose
you so soon; and then the Antonine roads to have new honours done them.

I have applied to my friend, and it is owned, that the road from York to *Sinus Dunus* does not
lead to any Antonine station; but as your curiosity continues, the following hints perhaps may not
be too tedious.

The most distinguishable of Mr. Warburton's military-roads here, that I have met with, is now
commonly called *Wade's Causeway*; and the tradition is, that Duke *Wada*, of whom the Britannia
is now silent, was the erector; but this seems not to need a confutation. I was surprised when I
first met with it, distant about two miles from any town or dwelling, of the common stone of the
country, fit enough for the purpose, in a black, springy, rotten moor, which continues about six miles
near the *sinus*.

The disposition of the stone is to the best advantage imaginable in it. In view of it are many
tumuli, probably the burying places of the great in the following ages. One in view is called
Blackay-Topping on this moor, commonly of that prænomen, which, according to the learned Doctor's description in his *Itin. Curios. p.* 128. may well be called King's Barrow here. Among many
traces of camps near this, remain very many for the compass of ground; one is near to its entrance
of the moor from York, called *Cauthorn-Burroughs*, not unlike the camp at Ardock, under the title,
Thule, in Camden's Britannia, &c.

THOS. ROBINSON.

" juſt twelve feet broad, paved with flint pebbles, ſome of them very
" large, and in many places it is as firm as it was the firſt day, a thing
" the more ſtrange, in that not only the diſtance of time may be con-
" ſidered, but the total neglect of repairs, and the boggy rotten moors
" it goes over. In ſome places the agger is above three feet raiſed from
" the ſurface. The country people curſe it often.; for being almoſt
" wholly hid in the ling, it frequently overturns their carts, laden with
" turf, as they happen to drive acroſs it.

    " IT was great pleaſure to me to trace this wonderful road,eſpecial-
" ly when I ſoon found out, that it pointed to the bay aforeſaid. I
" loſt it ſometimes by the interpoſition of valleys, rivulets, or the ex-
" ceeding great quantity of ling growing on theſe moors ; I had then
" nothing to do, but to obſerve the line, and riding croſs-wiſe my
" horſes feet through the ling, informed me when I was upon it. In
" ſhort, I traced it ſeveral miles, and could have been pleaſed to have
" gone on with it to the ſea-ſide, but my time would not allow me.
" However, I prevailed upon Mr. Robinſon to ſend his ſervant and a
" very intelligent perſon of Pickering along with him, and they not
" only made it fairly out to *Dunſley*, but brought me a ſketch of the
" country it went through, with them, from which I have pricked it
" out in the map, as the reader will find at the end of this account."

THE PARISH OF LYTHE.

THIS is the extreme parifh in the eaftern part of Cleveland, and is feparated from the divifion of Whitby-Strand, by a rivulet, called *East-Row-Beck,*which is here difcharged into the fea. It is diftant from the town and port of Whitby about four miles, and is bounded by that parifh on the eaft ; by Hilderwell and Egton on the weft, and north-weft ; by Egton on the fouth ; and on the north, and north-eaft by the fea. The parifh is of confiderable extent, ftretching from eaft to weft nearly feven miles, and upwards of five miles from north to fouth ; and contains the following townfhips ; viz. Lythe, Hutton-Mulgrave, Barneby, Ugthorpe, Mickleby, Ellerby, Borrowby, and Newton-Mulgrave.

THE village of Lythe, which gives name to the parifh, and near to which the Parifh Church ftands, is fituated towards the eaftern extremity of the parifh, about a mile diftant from the fea. We have no notice of Lythe, in the record of Domefday ; but it appears from authentic evidence, to have been an ancient Manor within the Barony of Mulgrave, and of which the Foffards were anciently proprietors. It afterwards defcended by marriage to Robert de Turnham ; by whofe daughter and heir it paffed to the Mauleys in the reign of King John. Peter de Mauley the third, in the 38. Henry III. obtained a charter of free-warren in all his demefne lands, and alfo a licence for a weekly market at his Manor of Lythe, and a fair yearly, beginning at the Eve of Saint Ofwald ; but both the market and fair have been long difcontinued. The Mauleys continued proprietors for feveral generations, till male iffue failing 3. Henry V. it paffed through feveral families, by the heirs general, and is now the property of the Earl of Mulgrave ; whofe elegant manfion ftands at a fhort diftance towards the fouth from the village, upon the brow of a gently rifing eminence, and commands a pleafingly variegated and extenfive profpeƈt.

It appears from Kirkby's Inqueft, that in the reign of Edward I. there were certain free tenants, * who held two carucates of land here, where ten carucates made one Knight's fee. The Lords of Mulgrave, amongft other ancient privileges, had the wreck of fea within this Manor; as appears by the following extraƈt from an chartulary or chronicle kept by a Monk of Durham, ‖ and now among the M. S. S. in the Dean and Chapter's Library : " *Ao.* 1431. *in Vigilia Nativitatis, noƈe* " *intempeftâ, maxima Balœna in littus ejicitur prope Lythe, quam Dominus de* " *Mongreve fibi clamavit, jure regalitatis fuœ.*"

About the diftance of a mile from the village, towards the fouth, upon a fteep hill, ftand the ruins of an ancient Caftle ; which, as Camden informs us, was the fortrefs of *Wada,* a Saxon Duke ; who, about the year 800, (in that confufed anarchy of the Northumbrians, fo fatal to the petty Princes) having combined with thofe that murdered King Ethelred, gave battle to King Ardulph, at Whalley, in Lancafhire ; but with fuch ill fuccefs, that his army was routed, and himfelf forced to fly ; whereupon he fortified his Caftle here. He afterwards fell into a diftemper, of which he died, and was interred on a hill here, between two folid ftones, about feven feet high, which being at twelve feet diftance from one another, occafions a current opinion that he was of a gigantic ftature. ‡ Leland's remark *(vol. I. p. 65.)* is to the follow-

---

* Liberi tenentes, de Lithe tenent ibidem duas carucatas terræ,unde X. faciunt feodum.

Kirkby's Inqueft.

‖ The name of the recording Monk is entirely loft.

‡ These ftones are conjeƈtured by later writers to be Roman *Tumuli,*fimilar to thofe at Boroughbridge ; and the Caftle was probably creƈted on the fite of an abandoned Roman fortrefs or ftation, from whence the Roman road, called *Wade's Caufeway,* which we have already noticed, may be diftinƈtly traced.

ing effect : " Mongrave Caftle ftondith on a craggy hill, and on eche
" fide of it is a hill, far higher than that whereon the Caftle ftondith.
" The north hill on the top of it hath certain ftones commonly called
" *Wada's Grave*, whom the people there fay to have been a gigant, and
" owner of Mongrave. There is by thefe ftones a Bek, y^n out of the
" mores by Mougrave cum doun by many fprings, 2 bekkes, one of
" eche fide of the Caftelle, and y^n the valleys of the 2 great hilles.
" The one is caullid Sandebek, the other Eft-Bek ; and fhortly after
" goith to the fe that is not far of."

THIS Caftle and Barony, with other large poffeffions of Duke *Wada*,
were granted after the Conqueft to Nigel Foffard, and defcended by
the heirefs of that family, in the reign of Richard I. to Robert de Turnham ; whofe daughter Ifabel his fole heirefs, was given by King John
in marriage to Peter de Malolacu, or Mauley, a native of Poictou, in
France, as a reward for that execrable deed in murdering Arthur, his
nephew, his elder brother's fon, in order to clear his title to the crown.
But it does not appear that this Peter came into poffeffion of this Barony, till the 16th year of the reign of King John, when he paid a fine
of feven thoufand marks to that King for the fame. He remained a
firm adherent to this Monarch upon all occafions, and being much in
his confidence during the infurrection of the Barons, divers of them
being made prifoners, were committed to his cuftody ; upon which he
rebuilt the Caftle here for his defence, which was become decayed and
ruinous ; and the fabric when finifhed, appeared to him fo beautiful,
that he named it *Moult-Grace ;* but being a grievous yoke to the neighbouring inhabitants, they, by the change of a fingle letter, called it
Moult-Grave,—a name which it retains to this day.

THIS Peter was fucceeded by Peter his fon, who left another Peter
his heir in his minority ; upon which *Gerard de Grice* on paying five
hundred marks to King Henry III. obtained the farm of his lands, and
cuftody of his Caftle of Mulgrave, till he came of age. The Mauleys
continued proprietors till the reign of Henry V. when Peter, the eighth

of that name, dying without issue, this Castle and Barony descended by marriage with Constance, sister of Peter de Mauley the seventh, to Sir John Bigod, Knight; whose descendants continued heirs till the 3d Edward VI. when issue male again failing, the inheritance passed by marriage to the Radcliffes.

A Pedigree of the families of MAULEY, BIGOD, and RATCLIFFE.

THE following Pedigree of *Bigod* and *Ratcliffe*, is extracted from the Herald's office, and was presented to the Editor, by *William Radclyffe, Esq. Rouge Croix Pourfourvant;* for which, and other valuable communications he gratefully acknowledges his obligations. The Pedigree of Malo-lacu, or Mauley, is from *Dugdale's Baronage*, vol. I. p. 733, &c.

Arms. *Or, a Bend, Sable.*

Peter de *Malo-lacu*, or *Mauley*, a Poictevin, one of the Esquires of John Earl of Moreton (afterwards King John) by whom, on the death of Richard I. he was employed to murder Prince Arthur; for which he gave him in marriage the heiress of the Barony of Mulgrave. = Isabel, daughter and heir of Robert de Turnham.

Peter de Mauley, the 2d he was godfather at the Font to Prince Edward, eldest son of Henry III. and attended William de Fortibus, Earl of Albemarle, to the Holy Land, 25. Henry III. and died 26. Henry III. = Joan, eldest daughter of Peter de Brus, of Skelton-Castle.

Peter de Mauley, the 3d. obtained a charter of free-warren in his demesne lands at Lythe, Sands-End, Great Barrowby, &c. 38. H. III. = Nichola, daughter of Gilbert de Gant, son of Gilbert de Gant, Earl of Lincoln.

Peter de Mauley, the 4th, died 3. Edward II. = Eleanora, daughter of Thomas Lord Furnival.

Peter de Mauley, the 5th, received the honour of Knighthood by bathing &c. with Prince Edward; (obiit 29. Edward III.) = Margaret, dau. of Robert Lord Clifford.

Elizabeth, daughter and heir of Nicholas de Meinell, and widow of John Lord D'arcy. (1st wife.) = Peter de Mauley, the 6th Lord of the Castles, &c. of Mulgrave and Doncaster; (ob. 6. Richard II. = Constance, dau. and coheir of Sir Thomas de Sutton, of Sutton, in Holderness. (2d. wife.)

Peter de Mauley, eldest son and heir apparent, died in his father's life time. = Margaret, daughter and coheir of Sir Thomas Sutton, Knight.

Sir John Mauley = ...

Anna, wife of J. Pannel.　　Mary, wife of J. Colvile, Knt.

Peter de Mauley, the 7th, Lord of Mulgrave and Doncaster; (ob. 2. H.IV.) = Jane, daughter of Sir Wm. Wyer of . . . . Knight.

Peter de Mauley, the 8th, Lord of Mulgrave and Doncaster; ob. 3. Hen. V without issue. = Matilda, dau. of Ralph Neville, Earl of Westmorland.

Constance Mauley, eldest dau. aunt and coheir of Peter de Mauley, the 8th, she had the castle of Mulgrave, as part of her share. = Sir John Bigod, of Settrington, Co. Ebor. Knt. ob. 29. Hen.VI.

Elizabeth Mauley, 2d. dau. aunt and coheir of Peter the 8th, had the Castle and Lordship of Doncaster. = G.Salvyne, of N. Duffield, Co. Ebor. Esq. (See p.289.)

Sir Ralph Bigod, of Mulgrave Castle, Knt. slain at Towton Field, (1. E. IV.) = Anna, dau. of . . . L. Greystock.

Sir Francis Bigod, eldest son and heir, died without issue.

Henry Bigot, held lands at Scakilthorpe, c.E. 34.H.VI.

5. Richard
6. Philip
7. Peter
8. Edward

Sir John Bigod, Knt. eldest son and heir apparent, was slain with his father at Towton Field, 1.Ed. IV. = Elizabeth, daughter of Henry Lord Scrope, of Bolton.

2. William
3. Ralph
4. George

Sir Ralph Bigod, of Mulgrave Castle, Knt. Escheater, 6 Henry VIII. = Margaret, dau. of Sir Robert Constable, Knt. cousin and heir of Sir Ralph Constable.

Henry Bigod.

Agnes.

Elizabeth.

John Bigod, Esq. eldest son and heir = Joan, dau of Sir J. Strangwaies.

Ralph Bigod.

Anna, wife of John Bulmer.

Sir Francis Bigod, of Mulgrave Castle, Knt. attainted 29. Hen. VIII. (died 18. Eliz.) = Catherine, dau. of William Lord Conyers. (died 5. Eliz.)

RATCLIFFE. ||

Henry Radcliffe, of Tunstall, Co. Pal. Durb. = Isabel, eldest d. and coh. of T. Fulthorpe Esq.

Ralph R. Esq. of Tunstall, Co. Durham. = . . . dau. of W. Hanfard, of Walworth.

William Rad-clyffe, 2d son. = . . . d. of J. Moresby in Co. Cumberland Esq.

|| This family universally wrote their name RADCLYFFE, as appears by several of their family deeds, as well as by there signatures in the visitation. A.D. 1575.

Arms; Argent, a Bend ingrailed, Sable; A Mullet, for differance.

Ralph Bigod, of Mulgrave Castle, Esq. restored in blood by Act of Parliament, 3. Edw. VI. died without issue.

Dorothy Bigod, = Roger Radclyffe, = Margaret, d. of only sister and h. of Mulgrave. Ca. John Ryder, Esq. to her brother; *Jure Uxoris*, liv- of Ryder, Co. E. (*died 5 E.* 1st w. ing 1575. Will Cofferer to Edw. dated 1588. 30E. VI. 2d. wife.

Francis Radclyffe, of = Fridſwide, dau. of ... Mulgrave, Eſq. ſon Saville, of Barrowby, and heir; æt. 23. Co. *Leic.* 1575. *ob.* 1. *Feb.* 34. *Eliz.*

Katherine Radclyffe, only dau. by the firſt marriage; ſhe had the manor of Ugthorpe, by deed from her fa-ther, 10. Dec. 28. E. which the gave by will to her half bro-ther W. Radclyffe.

Jane, living Iſabel, wife Margaret William = Ann.. Ralph 1603, wife of ... Red. living R.of Ug- living Roger of .. Red. man living 1588. thorpe. 1614. man. 1603. living 1614

William Rad- Matthew, Catherine, Mary, Anne clyffe, of Ug- 1614. 1614. 1614. 1614. thorpe Gent. liv. Jan. 31.1614.

Roger, ſon and heir, aged 5, 1584; 14 y. of age, at the time of his father's death.

2 Henry.   3 Thomas. Helen.

ABOUT the year 1625, Mulgrave came into the poffeffion of Edmund, Lord Sheffield, of Butterwick, Lord Prefident of the North, who was created Earl of Mulgrave, by King Charles I. * He was fucceeded by Edmund, fon of his fecond fon John, and he by his fon John, who being Lord Privy Seal, was by Queen Anne, in the year 1703, created

---

* SHEFFIELD, Earl of Mulgrave.

(From Dugdale, and other authorities.)

Arms: *Argent, a Cheveron, between 3 Garbes, Gu.*

Edmund Lord Sheffield, of Butterwick, Lord Prefident of the North ; created Earl of Mulgrave. 1. Charles I. (ob. 1646.) == Urfula, dau. of Sir Robert Terwhitt, of Ketelby. 1ft wife. == Marian, dau. of Sir Wm. Urwine. 2d. wife.

James == Jane, dau. of Wm. Cockayne. Robert. Thomas.

1. Charles died unm. 2. Sir John Sheffield drowned in croffing the Humber, *vitâ patris.* (‖) == Grifwald, dau. of Sir Edm. Anderfon, *Ch. Juftice Com. Pleas.* 3. Edmund. (‖) 4. William.(‖) 5. Philip. (‖) 6. George. (‖)

Edmund, Earl of Mulgrave fucceeded his grandfather; inftalled Knt. of the Garter, 1674. == Elizabeth, daughter of Lionel, Earl of Midlefex.

John, Earl of Mulgrave created Duke of Bucks, by Queen Anne, 1703. ob. 1720. 2d. hufband. Sir Charles Sheffield, had Normanby, in Lincolnfhire. == Catherine, natural daughter of King James II. by Catherine Sedley, Countefs of Dorchefter, his miftrefs. Divorced from her firft hufband for ill ufage. == James, Earl of Anglefea. 1ft hufband.

Catherine. Edmund, Duke of Bucks, died S. P. 1735. Catherine only dau. and heir. == William Phipps, fon of Conftantine Phipps, Lord Chancellor in Ireland, 1714.

Conftantine Phipps created a Peer, Aug. 15. 1767; anceftor to the prefent E. of Mulgrave. == Lepel, eldeft daughter of John Lord Harvey. (died 1780.)

(‖) THE following remarkable cafualties are recorded by *Dugdale*, and are worthy of particular notice ; viz. *Sir John Sheffield, Knt. Edmund* and *Philip* his brothers, were drowned in croffing the river Humber at *Whitgift-Ferry*, in the month of December, 1614, in their father's life time ; *William* was drowned in France ; and *George* broke his neck in a new Riding Houfe, which his father had made of an old confecrated Chapel. *See Dugd. Bar. vol. II. p.* 387.

alfo Duke of Buckingham and Normanby; he died in the year 1720, when the title defcended to Edmund his only fon, who dying a minor and unmarried in the year 1735, the title became extinct; but was revived in the perfon of Conftantine Phipps, a Captain in the Royal Navy, and defcendant of the Anglefey family, who was created Lord Mulgrave, in the year 1767; to whom a leafe of the Mulgrave eftate had been granted by King George II. and in the year 1774, was confirmed to him and his heirs for the fum of 30,000*l.* on agreeing to pay to Government, a yearly quit-rent of 1200*l.* He married Lepel, eldeft daughter of John Lord Harvey; by whom he had iffue Conftantine John, ‖

‖ *The Hon. Conftantine John,* late Earl of Mulgrave, was the eldeft fon of *Conftantine Phipps,* created Baron Mulgrave, of New-Rofs, in the county of Wexford, in the Kingdom of Ireland. Having at an early age profeffed an inclination for maritime purfuits, he was entered on board one of his Majefty's fhips of war, and ferved as a Midfhipman on board *the Dragon,* at an attack of Martinico, under his relative, *Capt. Harvey.* He does not appear to have diftinguifhed himfelf in any particular manner in a fubordinate fituation; nor do the naval annals record any thing material except the mere dates of his commiffions, till the beginning of the year 1773, when he was appointed to the *Racehorfe,* bombketch, as fenior in command on the projected expedition to the North Pole.

This veffel, and the *Carcafe,* Capt. Lutwidge, were felected, as the beft calculated, on account of their folidity, to refift thofe affaults they might encounter from the ice, and other unforefeen impediments. After every poffible attention had been paid by the Admiralty Board, to the neceffary fupplies and proper equipment of the veffels, *Capt. Phipps* proceeded to the Nore, where he was joined on the 30th of May by his confort. They failed on their voyage on the 4th of June, and on the 28th, made the land of Spitzbergen.

The *Racehorfe* and *Carcafe* continued in thofe frozen feas till the 10th of Aug. occupied either in coafting the fhore of Spitzbergen, the land adjacent, the immenfe fields of ice, which might be faid to inclofe them, or in endeavouring to fulfil more completely the object of their expedition, by forcing a paffage through every channel that appeared in any degree open.

On the 31ft July, the fhips were clofely furrounded by the ice, which became fo thick and impenetrable, that the greateft fears were entertained, they would be prevented from returning. Every attention was of courfe immediately paid to the fafety of the people; the launches were hauled over the ice; and in fhort, no meafure that bore any appearance of tending to their deliverance omitted. At length, when leaft expected, and much labour had been fruitleffley, though prudently thrown away in the attempt, the fhips drifted to the weftward with the ice, paffed the boats which were taken immediately on board, and on the 10th Aug. about noon, having got clear of their furrounding difficulties, ftood out to fea. On the following day they anchored in *Smeerenberg* harbour. After a

the late Lord, who was created a Peer of Great Britain, June 16, 1790. His Lordfhip was born 1744, and married Eliza-Anne, daughter of Nathaniel Cholmley, Efq. of Whitby, by whom he had iffue, a daughter, born Oct. 10th, 1788; but dying without male iffue, Oct. 10th, 1792,

---

few unimportant attempts to pufh to the northwards, the wind coming round brifkly to the north— this circumftance, together with the very advanced feafon of the year concurred to determine *Capt. Phipps* to make no further exertions, which experience had taught him, could not be fuccefsful, but to proceed immediately to the fouthward.

A WALL of impenetrable ice was found to extend more than twenty degrees between the latitudes 80 and 81, through which there did not appear to be the fmalleft opening to the northward. The aftronomers landed on feveral iflands, and made a number of curious obfervations; a circumftance which ftands as an incontrovertible proof that the expedition was not undertaken in vain.

ON the 7th of Sept. the fhips arrived off Shetland; and from that time till the 24th, when they reached *Orfordnefs*, encountered conftant and moft violent gales of wind, which proved the judgment in choofing the time for the commencement of the voyage; as well as for abandoning any farther attempt, which, if perfifted in, muft inevitably have proved fatal.

Capt. Phipps, on the death of his father in the year 1775, fucceeded to his honours in the title of Mulgrave, &c. and was, through the friendfhip of *Lord Sandwich*, returned as Member for the town of *Huntingdon*, in the year 1777; which place he continued to reprefent till the general Election in 1784. His abilities in Parliament were confpicuous as a public fpeaker, a fpecimen of which he had given prior to his perilous voyage, having been elected one of the Reprefentatives for the Borough of *Lincoln*, after a fevere conteft with *Mr. Vyner*, in the year 1768; but from 1774, till the period of his election for *Huntingdon*, he had ceafed being a Member of the Houfe of Commons. He was alfo appointed one of the Commiffioners for executing the office of Lord High Admiral; which fituation he held during four Commiffions, refigning it on the 30th May, 1782. Though it may be naturally fuppofed that the oftenfible poft he held, as well as his duty to his conftituents, muft occupy a confiderable portion of his time, yet he fo blended his civil labours with thofe of his nautical ones, that both received additional luftre by his obfervance of them.

SOON after the commencement of the American war, he was employed, (being Captain of the *Ardent*, of 64 guns) in cruifing in the *Bay of Bifcay*. He was alfo prefent at the engagement off *Ufhant*, on the 27th July, 1778, in which his fhip, the *Courageux*, of 74 guns, bore a very diftinguifhed fhare. From that period till the year 1781, he was employed in the Channel-fervice, under the progeffive commands of *Sir Charles Hardy, Admiral Geary*, and *Mr. Darby*.

ON the 4th of January, in the above-mentioned year, being on a feparate cruife with the *Valiant*, a fhip of his own force, they fell in with two French frigates; one of which was chafed by the *Valiant*, while his Lordfhip purfued the other, which proved to be the *Minerva*, of 30 guns and 316 men, taken from the Englifh, in the Weft Indies, at the commencement of the war. The fea ran very high

his Englifh title became extinct, but was revived in 1794, in the perfon of his brother, the Right Hon. Henry Phipps, the prefent Earl. The ancient Caftle, feated on a natural eminence, the fteep declivities of which are beautifully covered with wood ; and being ftrongly fortified by nature, according to the tafte of feudal times, was eligibly fituated for a baronial manfion ; but there is nothing left, from which we can form a perfect idea of the ftrength, or ancient beauty and magnificence of the buildings.

THIS Caftle, being garrifoned for the King during the civil wars, was difmantled by order of Parliament, as appears from the journals of the Houfe of Commons, 22. Charles I, when it was refolved " that the " feveral Caftles of Tickhill, Sheffield, Knaresbro', Cawood, Sandal,

at the time the *Courageux* got up with her chace ; which, though evidently inferior in point of ftrength to her opponent, was with a courage almoft bordering on frenzy, fo obftinately defended by her commander, the *Chevalier de Grimouard*, that fhe did not furrender till after the Captain himfelf together with twenty-one perfons were dangeroufly wounded, and one of his Lieutenants and forty-nine of the crew killed. Soon after his return into port, his fhip being refitted from the damage fhe had received in the preceding engagement, he was fent with a fmall force to make an attempt on *Flufhing* ; which, from previous information of the meditated attack, proved fruitlefs.

HIS Lordfhip was not particularly noticed during the remainder of the war, except in having led the van of the Commander-in-Chief's divifion, in the flight encounter which took place off *the Streights*, on the 20th October, 1782, in the relief of *Gibraltar*, by the fleet under the command of *Lord Howe*.

THE *Courageux* being paid off foon after the Peace was made, his Lordfhip never accepted any other naval command, but confined himfelf to the duties of his civil appointments.

AT the general Election, in 1784, he was chofen Reprefentative for the Town of *Newark-upon-Trent :* and in the month of April, in the fame year, was raifed to the high ftation of joint Paymafter-General of the Forces ; and on the 18th of the enfuing month, was made one of the Commiffioners for managing the affairs of the Eaft India Company. Thefe offices, together with that of a Lord of the Committee of Council for the confideration of matters relative to Trade and Foreign Plantations, he held till the year 1791. Previous to this period, viz. on the 16th June, 1790, he was ftill further ennobled, by being raifed to the rank of a Peer of Great Britain, by the fame title he had held his Irifh honours.

THIS advancement, however, he did not long furvive ; dying on the 10th of October, 1792, and leaving no male iffue, the Englifh title became extinct ; but was revived in the year 1794, in the perfon of his brother, Henry, the prefent Earl.

" Boulton, Middleham, Hornfey and Mulgrave, in the County of York,
" being inland Caftles, be made untenable, and no garrifon kept or
" maintained in them."

FROM the ruins of this ancient fortrefs, purfuing the courfe of a
fmall rivulet, which here becomes the boundary of the diftrict, we approach the village of *Eaft-Row*, which lies within the parifh of Whitby,
and was anciently called *Thordifa*, from an heathen Temple erected here
by the Saxons to their God *Thor*, whom they believed to be the fame,
and to poffefs the fame power, as *Jupiter* did among the Romans. Upon
the fuppofed fite of this Temple are the ruins of an ancient hermitage,
dedicated to *St. James the Apoftle;* which, as appears from a charter
printed in the *Monafticon* (vol. I. p. 988.) was granted about the year
1150, by William de Percy, Lord of Dunfley, to the Monks and Abbot
of Whitby.

AT a little diftance towards the north, and not far from *Sands-End*,
we vifited *Marfdale;* where, it is reported, that within the memory of
man, were found the remains of a Roman altar, fuppofed to be dedicated to the God *Mars*. On this fubject, Charlton, in his hiftory of
Whitby, makes the following obfervations.—" The facrifices that had
" been made, and the worfhip that was paid by the Romans at *Marfdale*,
" near *Sands-End*, were afterwards, on the arrival of the Saxons, tranf-
" ferred a little foutherly to the village of *Thordifa*, whence there is a
" more extenfive profpect of the fea, and particularly of Dunfley-Bay.
" Here the place of worfhip feems to have been fixed by the heathens, till
" chriftianity did prevail ; and even then, though this temple was con-
" verted into an hermitage, whofe ruins are yet to be feen, yet that vil-
" lage ftill continued to be known by the name of *Thordifa*, during the
" exiftence of the Monaftry at Whitby." It was afterwards called *Eaft-
Row*, from its eaftern fituation from an *Allum-work*, which was begun
here about the year 1620.

SAND'S-END, a hamlet within this townſhip, is ſituated on the face of a rocky cliff near the ſea. Here is an extenſive *Allum-work*, the property of the Earl of Mulgrave, which has been carried on for many years, with conſiderable ſucceſs.

THE allum-rock, from which the allum is extracted, is here and in other parts along this coaſt, dug from the high cliffs that border the ſea ; and the works in this neighbourhood, being more advantageouſly ſituated for exportation, have totally annihilated the *allum-trade* at Guiſbrough, and the weſtern part of Cleveland ; where the manufactory of that article has for ſome time been diſcontinued.

IN the rocks here, and other places along the coaſt, black amber, or jett, is frequently found, by ſome naturaliſts called *Gagates*, which Camden ſays, was valued by the ancients among the rareſt ſtones and jewels.

DRAYTON, in his Poly-olbion, has the following rhyme ;

" The rocks by Moultgrave too, my glories forth to ſet,
" Out of their crannied cliffs can give you perfect jett."

IT is generally found in detached lumps, within the chinks or cliffs of the rocks ; and is outwardly of a reddiſh ruſty colour, but inwardly and when poliſhed, anſwers the deſcription given by *Solinus ;* who ſays, " In Britain there is a great ſtore of gagates or jett, a very fine ſtone ; if " you aſk the colour, it is black and ſhining ; if the quality, it is exceed. " ing light ; if the nature, it burns in water, and is quenched with oil ; " if the virtue, it has an attractive power when heated with rubbing."

MARBODŒUS, in his treatiſe on Jewels, alſo writes thus ;

Naſcitur in Libya lapis, et prope gemma gagates,
Sed genus eximium fœcunda Brittania mittit ;
Lucidus et niger eſt ; levis et lœviſſimus idem ;
Vicinas paleas trahit, attritu calefactus ;
Ardet aquâ lotus, reſtinguitur unctus olivo.

Jet-ſtone, almoſt a gem, the Libyans find ;
But fruitful Britain ſends a wond'rous kind ;
'Tis black and ſhining, ſmooth and ever light,
'Twill draw up ſtraws, if rubb'd till hot and bright ;
Oil makes it cold, but water gives it heat.

THIS ſtone was probably known to the ancient Britons, and was held by them in high eſtimation. Mr. Charlton, in his hiſtory of Whitby, has given us a drawing of an ear-ring, dug up ſometime ago, from one of the *Howes* or *Tumuli* which are found in conſiderable numbers upon the moors. The ring he deſcribes to be of jett, of the form of a heart, upwards of two inches broad, and about a quarter of an inch thick ; with a hole towards the upper end, by which it had been ſuſpended to the ear. It lay, he ſays, when found, in contact with the jawbone ; and his concluſion is, that it muſt have belonged to ſome Britiſh lady, who lived at, or before the time the Romans were in Britain, when ornaments of this ſort were univerſally uſed.

THE CHURCH of Lythe, dedicated to Saint Ofwald, the celebrated King and Martyr of Northumberland, ſtands at a little diſtance from the village towards the north-eaſt ; and is a neat modern edifice. It was given by Robert de Foſſard to the Priory of Saint Ofwald, at Noſtel in the Weſt Riding, together with ten oxgangs of land ; and the grant was confirmed by Pope Alexander III. out of which the canons had a penſion. It appears from *Torr's MS.* and other authorities, " that this church was an ancient rectory in the patronage of the Barons Mauleys, of Mulgrave ; from whom it came to the Bigods, Knights. Upon the attainder of Sir Francis Bigod, for high treaſon, in the reign of King Henry the eighth, this rectory came into the hands of the Crown, and was given to the Archbiſhoprick of York, to which it was appropriated by the King's licence, on the 8th of Auguſt, 1544, reſerving a competent portion for a Vicar. On the 20th of Sept. 1546, Robert Holgate, Archbiſhop of York, ordained that there be a perpetual Vicar in this pariſh-church (ſo appropriated to him and his ſucceſſors, and to his Archiepiſcopal Table) who on every vacation ſhall be collated by the Archbiſhop, and his ſucceſſors for ever ; and who ſhall have aſſigned him for his habitation a certain houſe and croft containing three roods, on the north ſide of the church ; and another croft and garden containing half an acre; and alfo fhall be paid in money 16*l*. † at Michaelmas and Lady Day, by the Archbifhop and his fucceffors, within forty days of each feaft, by equal portions : and that the charge of repairing the chancel fhall belong to the Archbifhop, excepting the repairs of the glafs in the windows of the chancel, which the Vicar fhall undergo." *Torr's MS.* ‖

THERE are many tomb ftones within the church yard, which, however, deferve no further notice than that while they blunder very innocently againft orthography and grammar, they imprefs this affurance upon the reader, that he who now compofes the duft beneath " *is not yet dead, but fleepeth.*"

---

† THIS payment was augmented by Archbifhop *Frewen,* to the fum of 60*l.* out of which the Curate of Egton was to be paid. *Archbifhop Sharpe's MS.*

‖ IT appears from this *MS.* that the Archbifhop and his fucceffors, are bound to diftribute 3*l. fterling p. ann.* among the poor of the parifh of Lythe, on the feaft of St. John Baptift's Nativity, or within 14 days next after for ever.

* LYTHE VICARAGE.

DEDICATED to Saint Ofwald. Archbifhop of York, patron. (Difcharged,) Pri. S. Ofwaldi ex-rectoria 24*l.* Archd. pro fyn & prox, ex-rectoria 16s. Clear yearly value 44*l.* Pri. Sti. Ofwaldi olim propr.

RECTORS.—1233. Hugo, *Clericus.* 1269. John de Toccotes. 1307. Will. de Wilton. 1318. Will. de Whitby. ——. Tho. Fox. 1319. Rich. de Milton. 1322. Adam de Hafelbeck. 1328. Francifcus Gaytanus, cl. 1330. Will. de Wardclowe. 1343. John de Bolton. 1370. Tho. de Myddleton, cl. 1372. John St. John, cap. 1372. John de Gafcoigne, cl. 1394. Tho. Kellowe. 1409 Will Gaunton. 1416. Rich. Yorke. 1417. John Semer. 1433. Richard Laugton. 1496. Chrift. Banks, M. A. cap. A. B. ——. Tho. Artas, cl. 1499. John Fifher, M. A. 1504. Hugo Afhton. 1511. John Froft, S. T. B. 1518. Hugo Afhton, *preb. Strenfall.* ——. Tho. Larke, *in Dec. bac.* 1523. James Cockerell, S. T. P. *prior Guifbro'.* 1537. Edw. Layton, prefented by King Henry VIII. on the attainder of Sir F. Tygod, Knt.

VICARS.———Henry Fletcher, cl. 1544. John Pykering, Cap. *pref. King Henry VIII.*——1707. Ralph Bateman, *pref. A. B.* 1737. Thomas Gawton, *pref. id.* 1739. Samuel Marfden, *pref. A. B.* 1760. Jonathan Robinfon, *pref. by the Archbifhop.* 1778. Wm. Harrifon, *pref. by the Archbifhop.* —— Porter the prefent incumbent.

* THE Rectory was charged at 34*l.* 4s. 2d; but fince the year 1544, appropriated to the fee of York.

WITHIN the church there are two elegant monuments ; the infcriptions on which we have given in the notes.

MONUMENTAL INSCRIPTIONS.

ON the north wall, an elegant marble monument bears the following infcription :

Near this place are depofited the remains of
ANNE ELIZABETH
Daughter of Nathaniel Cholmley Efq.
And Wife of Conftantine John, Lord Mulgrave.
She was born 7th Nov. 1769.
Died 22. May 1788.
Having in the Courfe of a few Years, by the Performance
of every Duty, and the practice of every Virtue, experienced
the greateft Happinefs human Nature is capable of.
She was removed from hence to receive the Reward
of eternal Life, promifed to thofe who believe in
The Word, fulfil the Commandments, and truft
in the Merits of Chrift.

NEAR to the above, an elegant marble, bearing the Infignia of his honour and profeffion, with
the following infcription :

In Memory of
Conftantine John, Baron Mulgrave
who was born the 9th of May 1744,
And died the 10th of Oct. 1792.
having paffed the period of an active Life
in the practice of every public and domeftic Virtue,
in the Service of his Country,
He was
a fkilful, gallant, and enterprizing Sea-Officer,
and a learned, upright and conftitutional Statefman.
In Society
an active and indefatigable Patron,
a fincere and unalterable Friend.
In his Family
a zealous, kind and liberal Brother
a Dutiful and affectionate Son
an indulgent, confiderate and tender Hufband.
He bore a tedious wafting Illnefs with the patient Firmnefs

GOLDSBOROUGH,

a fmall hamlet within this townfhip, lies about a mile diftant to the north-weft. Here was an ancient manor, which according to the Domefday Survey was taxed for two carucates, and contained two more that might be rendered arable, and fixteen acres of meadow. The whole manor, which was in the hands of *Suuen* before the Conqueft, was one mile in length, and half a mile broad; and in the Confeffor's time was valued at ten fhillings. At the time of the Survey it was held by *Nigel*, under Robert, Earl of Mortain, but was then wafte.

TERRA COMITIS MORITONIENSIS.

IN GOLBORG AD GELDUM II. CARUCATÆ, ET II. CAR. POSSUNT ESSF. IBI HABUIT SUUEN I. MANERIUM; NUNC HABET NIGEL DE COMITIE. SUNT PRATI ACR. XVI. TOTUM MANER. I. LEUCAM LONGAM, ET DIM. LAT. T. R. E. VALEBAT X. SOLID. MODO WASTUM EST.

Of a Philofopher
He faw the approach of Death, with the chearful
Refignation
of a Chriftian.
Having employed the concluding Hours of fuch a Life
in the active Exertion of his mental Faculties
in the placid Exercife of his humane affections,
he died
with the humble, but confident Hope
of
eternal Happinefs
through the Merits and Mercy
of his Saviour.

On a fquare plate of brafs in the wall, near the reading Defk, is the following fhort and modeft memorial of a late Vicar of this parifh:

Near this place
Lieth the Body of
The Rev. Mr. Marfden
late Minifter of Lyth, who
departed this Life, 22. Sept.
A. D. 1760. Aged 55 years.

WE find little in ancient records touching this place. According to Kirkby's Inqueft, ‖ Peter de Mauley held three carucates of land here, where ten made one Knight's fee. From the Mauleys, the manor and eftate defcended to the Bigods, and are now the property of Lord Mulgrave.

ABOUT two miles further northwards we approached *Kettleneffe*, which is a narrow point of land that runs into the fea, and forms the eaftern boundary of *Runfwick-Bay*. Here is an extenfive allum work, the property of Lord Mulgrave. The coaft, along the eaftern fide of the bay, is fteep and rocky ; and in the rocks are certain vaults, or large excavations, called *Kettles*, formed by the violence of the waves, which may be entered at low water, and afford curious and romantic retreats.

THE townfhip of

HUTTON MULGRAVE,

or, as it was anciently written, Hutton *Juxta* Mulgrave, lies in the fouth-ern extremity of the parifh, about three miles diftant from the parifh church. The manor here before the Conqueft, was in the hands of *Suuen*, but at the time of the Survey, was held by *Nigel*, under Robert, Earl of Mortain, and is entered under the title

TERRA COMITIS MORITONIENSIS.

IN HOTUNE AD GELDUM III. CARUCATÆ, ET III. POSSUNT ESSE. IBI HABUIT SUUEN I. MANERIUM. NUNC HABET NIGEL DE COM TE. WAST. EST. SILVA PAST. III. LEUCAS LONGAS, ET I. LAT. TOTUM MANERIUM IIII. LEUC. LONG ET I. LAT. T. R. E. VALEBAT XX. SOL.

FROM the above extract, it appears that this manor was taxed for three carucates, and contained three carucates more that might be ren-dered arable. There was a wood with pafturage for cattle three miles

---

‖ PETRUS DE MALOLACU tenet in Goldeburghe III. carucatas, unde X. car. terræ faciunt feodum.   *Kirkby's Inqueft.*

in length ; and the whole manor was four miles long and one broad ;
and was valued in the Confeffor's time, at twenty fhillings, but was
then wafte.

THIS is a fmall manor within the barony of Mulgrave ; and according to Kirkby's Inqueft, ‡ contained three carucates, where ten made
one Knight's fee, held by Peter de Mauley ; from whofe defcendants it
came to the Bigods, and is now the property of Lord Mulgrave.

THE village is fmall, and the whole townfhip contains about 90 inhabitants, oecupied chiefly in agricultural purfuits.

BARNEBY,

comprehending the two fmall villages of Eaft and Weft Barneby, lies
about two miles to the fouth-weft from the village of Lythe.   We find
no mention of Barneby in the Domefday Survey ; but, in Kirkby's Inqueft, * it appears to have contained four carucates of land, held by
the heir of Robert de Barneby, of Peter de Mauley, Lord of Mulgrave.

THE townfhip and manor of

UGTHORPE,

are fituated in the weftern part of the parifh.   This manor was ancient
demefne of the Crown, and, as appears from the Domefday Book, contained two carucates *ad geldum*, with lands fufficient for two ploughs ;
entered in the Survey under the title

"TERRA REGIS.

"MANERIUM IN UGHETORP, LIGULF II. CARUCAT. TERRÆ AD GELDUM.
"TERRA AD II. CAR. DUAS LEUCAS LONGAS, ET UNAM LAT. T. R. E. X.
"SOLID. INFRA HANC METAM GAME II. CARUCAT. AD GELDUM.   TERRA
"AD II. CAR."

---

‡ PETRUS DE MALOLACU tenet III. carucatas, in Hoton Juxta Mulgrave, unde X. car. terræ
faciunt feodum.   *Kirkby's Inqueft.*

* HÆRES — DE BARNEBY tenet ibidem (de feodo Petri de Malolacu) IV. carucatas terræ, unde X. caruc. faciunt feodum.   *Kirkby's Inqueft.*

FROM the above extract it appears that Ligulf held this manor before the Conqueft, which was two miles in length, and one broad, valued in the Confeffor's time at ten fhillings. Within the boundaries of this manor, *Game* held two carucates rated *ad geldum*, befides land fufficient for two ploughs.

THE Mauleys became Lords here at an early period, from whom the manor and eftate defcended by marriage to the Bigods, and afterwards to the Ratcliffes: by whom the eftate was fold in parcels, and the lands are now in the hands of different freeholders. The manorial rights are the property of Lord Mulgrave.

THE townfhip of

MICKLEBY,

lies at a little diftance from Ugthorpe towards the north. The manor here, before the Conqueft, was in the hands of *Suuen*, but, at the time of the Survey, was held by *Nigel*, under Robert, Earl of Mortain, and was taxed for four carucates, and contained two more that might be rendered arable, with fix acres of meadow, and under-wood. The whole manor was one mile long and half a mile broad; and was valued at the time of King Edward the Confeffor at twenty fhillings; but was laid wafte by the Conqueror.

" TERRA COMITIS MORITONIENSIS.
" IN MICHELBI AD GELDUM IIII. CARUCATÆ, ET II. CAR. POSSUNT ES-
" SE. IBI HABUIT SUUEN I. MANERIUM. NUNC HABET NIGEL DE CO-
" MITE. SUNT PRATI ACR. VI. ET SILVA MINUTA. TOT. I. LEUC. LONG.
" ET DIMID. LAT. T. R. E. VALEBAT XX. SOLID. MODO WAST. EST."

MICKLEBY was an ancient manor, which, in the reign of King John, came to the Mauleys, who held of the King *in capite*. The lands were granted out at an early period; for, in the reign of Edward I. according to Kirkby's Inqueft, † the free tenants had four carucates of land

---

† LIBERI Tenentes de *Mykelby* tenent IV. carucat. terræ in ead. *(de dicto Petro.)*
Kirkby's Inqueft.

here, which they held of Peter de Mauley, as of the Barony of Mulgrave.
Lord Mulgrave is, at prefent, the principal proprietor and Lord of the
manor.

PROCEEDING northwards we approach the townſhip and village of

ELLERBY,

anciently written ELVERDBY, and in Domeſday Book ELWORDEBI.
The manor here in the Conqueror's time was taxed for ſix carucates,
and contained three more that might be rendered arable, with ſix acres
of meadow, held by *Nigel* under Robert, Earl of Mortain ; but was then
waſte.   The whole manor was one mile long, and half a mile broad ;
and in the time of King Edward the Confeſſor was valued at forty
ſhillings.

" TERRA COMITIS MORITONIENSIS.

" IN ELWORDEBIE AD GELDUM VI. CARUCATÆ, ET III. CARUC. POS-
" SUNT ESSE. IBI SIUUARD I. MANER. HABUERUNT.   NUNC HABET NIGEL
" DE COMITE. SUNT IBI PRATI ACRÆ VI. TOTUM MANER. I. LEUC, LONG.
" ET DIMID. LAT. T. R. E. VALEBAT XL. SOLID. MODO WAST. EST."

ELLERBY was part of the great poſſeſſions of the Barons Mauleys,
of Mulgrave ; of whom, in the reign of Edward I. according to Kirby's Inqueſt, ‡ *Radulpus de Mennell* held certain lands here,where ten
carucates made one Knight's fee.

THE lands have been long parcelled out.   Lord Mulgrave is the
principal proprietor, and Lord of the manor.

THE townſhip of

BORROWBY,

forms a part of the weſtern boundary of the pariſh, and adjoins to the
chapelry of Roufeby.   We find little in ancient records touching
this place, except what is mentioned in the Domeſday Survey ; where,
like other manors within the pariſh, it is entered under the title

---

‡ RADULPHUS DE MENNEL tenet in Wilton, Lakenby, Laſingby, *Ellerdby*, &c. *(de dicto Petro in*
mediatate) unum feodum, unde X. caruc. faciunt feodum.

                                                        Kirkby's Inqueſt.

TERRA COMITIS MORITONIENSIS.

IN BERGEBI ET ROSCEBI AD GELDUM VI. CARUCATÆ, ET IIII. CAR.
POSS. ESSE. IBI HABEBAT SUUEN I. MANERIUM. NUNC HABET NIGEL DE
COMITE. SUNT IBI VIII. ACR. PRATI. SILVA NON PAST. DIMID. LEUC
LONGA ET I. QUARENT. LATA. TOTUM MANERIUM II. LEUC. LONGUM
ET I. LATUM. T. R. E. XXI. SOLID. MODA. EST.

AD HOC MANERIUM JACET SOCA IN NEUUETUNE AD GELDUM III.
CARUCAT. ET III. CAR. POSSUNT ESSE. WAST. EST.

FROM the above extract it appears that Borrowby and a part of
Roufby, (a chapelry within the parifh of Hilderwell,) were anciently
comprifed in one manor, which was taxed for fix carucates, with four
more that might be rendered arable, held before the Conqueft by *Suuen*,
and afterwards was in the hands of *Nigel*, who held under Robert,
Earl of Mortain ; that, there were eight acres of meadow, and a wood
not fit for feeding cattle, half a mile long, and one *quarenten* broad;
that the whole manor was two miles long and one broad, valued in
the Confeffor's time at twenty-one fhillings ; but, at the time of the
furvey, was laid wafte. It alfo appears, that to this manor there was a
foke or liberty within the townfhip of Newton (now called Newton
Mulgrave) containing three carucates of land rated *ad geldum*, and three
more that might be rendered arable, but were then wafte.

THIS manor, with thofe within the parifh already noticed, came to
the Mauleys, and defcended with the Barony of Mulgrave to the prefent Lord, who is alfo principal proprietor. The village is fmall, and
the whole townfhip does not contain more than about eighty inhabitants.

THE village and townfhip of

NEWTON, or NEWTON MULGRAVE,

fometimes written Newton *Juxta* Ellerby, as defcriptive of its fituation
near that village, lie toward the north, and adjoin to the parifh of
Hilderwell.

FROM the Domefday Book it appears, that the lands here at the
time of the Conqueror's furvey, were within the foke of Borrowby,

and confifted of three carucates rated *ad geldum ;* and three more that might be rendered arable ; but were then wafte. The Mauleys were ancient Lords here ; of whom according to Kirkby's Inqueft, ‖ Richard de Thweng, and Robert de Acklam held four carucates, as of the Barony of Mulgrave, where ten carucates made one Knight's fee. Lord Mulgrave is the principal proprietor.

AFTER this tedious, uninterefting detail of the feveral townfhips within this parifh, the CLIMATE, SOIL, and PRODUCE, are the fubjects that next demand the readers attention.

FROM the cliffs of the coaft, the lands rife rapidly to a great height, for a confiderable diftance into the country, on which the rays of the fun fall fo obliquely, that the *climate* is cold and fevere ; and the harvefts in general later, than in other parts of the diftrict lefs expofed to the chilling blafts from the fea. The *foil* confifts chiefly of a red ftiff clay, with a mixture of clayey loam. Towards Mulgrave there is fome of a light fandy quality ; and in fome of the vales a deep rich loam. The ground, at a certain diftance below the furface, abounds with *allum-mine ;* above which in many places excellent quarries of free-ftone are to be met with ; and in feveral places, *iron-ftones* are alfo found. In the cliffs along the coaft, *pyrites,* or fire-ftones, are not unfrequently found ; which, being rubbed with fteel, emit fire in a furprifing manner.

THE crops principally cultivated, are wheat, oats, and beans, with fome turnips ; the culture of which, from the example and encouragement given by Lord Mulgrave, * who is the principal proprietor of lands within the parifh, has, of late years, confiderably increafed.

‖ RICHARDUS DE THWENG et Rob. de Aclam tenent ibidem IV. caruc. terræ, unde X. faciunt feodum.   *Kirkby's Inqueft.*

* To excite a fpirit for improvement in the different branches of agriculture his Lordfhip diftributes annually rewards of induftry and merit amongft his tenants and cottagers. 'n the year 1802, the following premiums were given ; viz. a *filver tankard* to him whofe farm was in the beft condi-

POPULATION. We have again to regret, that we cannot ftate the probable increafe or decreafe of the inhabitants, as we have not been able to procure the neceffary extracts from the parifh regifters: the population is however confiderable, owing probably to the eftablifhment of two extenfive allum-works within the parifh; but the exact number of hands employed therein, have not been ftated to us. In the year 1801, when an accurate enumeration was made, by order of the legiflature, the total number of inhabitants, including the feveral townfhips within the parifh, was 2093. On a review of the table, ‡

tion, and a *filver cup* for the beft crop of turnips; premiums were alfo given for the beft breed of cattle and fheep.

On delivering the prizes, which were adjudged with the ftricteft impartiality, his Lordfhip made fuitable addreffes to the different fucceffful candidates, and concluded an appropriate and energetic fpeech, with exhibiting in a ftriking point of view, the important character of the *Englifh Farmer*, and the great dependence the nation had on his induftry and good management.

To the cottagers the following rewards were diftributed; viz. a *cow* to him who had brought up the greateft number of children born in wedlock, by his own induftry, and with the leaft parochial relief; to the next moft deferving *a new fuit of clothes;* to the third, *a fat pig*, &c. &c. Rewards were alfo given to thofe cottagers, who had their gardens in the beft condition; and it is worthy of particular remark, that fcarcely any of the candidates, notwithftanding their numerous families, had ever received any parifh allowance,—a circumftance that ftrongly evinces, how much may be effected by induftry and ftrict economy.

Such inftitutions are of the greateft national importance, as they create a fpirit of emulation, and give encouragement to the different branches of agriculture and farming, on which the wealth, the ftrength, and the very exiftence of the country depend: and if fimilar attention to cottagers, and the labouring part of the community could become general, it would be the beft means to beget induftry and good management,—and alfo nourifh that pride of independence fo neceffary in the prefent ftate of fociety.

‡ STATE OF POPULATION, 10th March, 1801.

Townships.	Inhab. houfes.	Fam-ilies.	Unhab. houses.	Males.	Fe-males.	To-tal.	Agri-culture	Trade. &c.	Refi-due.	To-tal.
Lythe,	201	223	3	512	525	1037	197	550	290	1037
Hutton Mulgrave,	17	17		46	47	93	93			93
Barneby,	47	48	4	119	135	254	109	109	36	254
Ugthorpe,	54	56	1	121	124	245	118	32	95	245
Mickelby,	40	41	1	90	86	176	119	28	29	176
Ellerby,	15	15		37	37	74	64	4	6	74
Borrowby,	16	17		35	46	81	71	1	9	81
Newton Mulgrave.	28	28	1	69	64	133	37	2	94	133
Totals.	418	445	10	1029	1064	2093	808	726	559	2093

S s

it will appear, that there were 418 inhabited houfes, and 445 families, which will give upwards of $4\frac{1}{2}$ to each family ; that the males and females are nearly equal ; and alfo, that the number of perfons employed in trade and manufactures, is nearly equal to that of thofe occupied in hufbandry.

THE PARISH OF HILDERWELL,

OR, as it is corruptly written, *Hinderwell*, feems to derive its name from *Saint Hilda*, ‖ Lady Abbefs of Whitby, to whom the church here is dedicated.   In the church yard, there is a well, or fpring of pure water, called *St. Hilda's well* (near which it is conjectured fhe had an occafional retreat) which not only ftill retains her name ; but communicates the fame to the parifh.   Rowland, in his *Mona Antiqua*

‖ SAINT HILDA was neice of Edwin, King of the Northumbrians, and with him was converted to Chriftianity and baptized by *Paulinus*, the firft Archbifhop of York.   Having devoted herfelf to a religious life, fhe firft went into a monaftry in France, where fhe continued about a year ; but was prevailed upon by *Aidan*, Bifhop of the Northumbrians, to return to her own country, where fhe became a Nun in a fmall monaftry on the banks of the river *Were ;* and foon afterwards was appointed to prefide over a fmall community of Nuns at *Hertefie* (Hartlepool) founded according to Tanner, about the year 640, on the firft converfion of the Northumbrians to Chriftianity, by a religious woman named *Hieu*, or as fome writers have it, *St. Bega*.   Being highly efteemed for her piety and wifdom, fhe was appointed by King Ofway, to prefide over the monaftry at Strenefhall, *(Whitby)* which on his fignal victory over *Penda*, King of Mercia, in confequence of his folemn vow to God, he built and endowed.   She continued Abbefs here during the remainder of her life, having conducted the fame with regularity of government and difcipline for feveral years.   She died in the year 680.   A convention was held at Whitby, in the year 664, before the Abbefs Hilda, who with Colman, Bifhop of Lindiffarne, withftood to the utmoft of her power, the tonfure of the clergy, and the celebration of Eafter after the Romifh manner ; but being oppofed by Wilfred, a man of great eloquence and knowledge of difputation, it was determined in favour of the cuftom of the Romifh church.

Reſtaurata, thinks it probable, that in very diſtant ages, churches were dwelling-houſes for the prieſts, as well as places of worſhip for the people ; and that therefore they were generally built near a well of clear water.

THE village of Hilderwell ſtands upon gently riſing ground, about a mile diſtant from the ſea ; and eight miles diſtant from the town of Whitby, towards the north-weſt.   The pariſh, including the chapelry of Rouſby, is of conſiderable extent, ſtretching from eaſt to weſt ſix miles, and about three miles from north to ſouth.   It is bounded on the eaſt and ſouth by the pariſh of Lythe ; by Eaſington on the weſt, and is waſhed on the north and north-eaſt by the ſea.

IT appears from the Domeſday book, that the manor here was taxed for four carucates and ſix bovates ; ‡ and contained two carucates and a half more that might be rendered arable ; with thirteen acres of meadow. It was held by Norman before the Conqueſt ; but was afterwards granted by the Conqueror to William de Percy, and was then waſte ; valued in the Confeſſor's time at twenty ſhillings.

"TERRA WILLIELMI DE PERCI.
"MANERIUM IN HILLDREUUELLE HABUIT NORMAN IIII. CARUCATAS
"TERRÆ ET VI. BOVATAS AD GELDUM ; UBI POSSUNT ESSE II. CAR. ET
"DIMIDIUM. WILLIELMUS HABET, ET WASTUM EST. PRATI ACR. XIII.
"T. R. E. VALEBAT XX. SOLID."

THERE were alſo ten carucates here within the ſoke of the manor of *Lofthouſe*, held at the time of the Conqueror's ſurvey by Hugh, Earl of Cheſter, but were then waſte.

THIS lordſhip, at an early period, became the property of the Thwengs of Kilton-Caſtle, who were powerful Barons in the north ; in which family it continued for ſeveral generations, till the laſt male

---

‡ A BOVATE or oxgang is ſaid to be as much as one, or a pair of oxen could plough or keep in huſbandry tilth in a year ; by ſome accounted 24 and 18 acres, by others but 10, 12, 15, or 13 ; but like carucates and other portions of land, was uncertain, according to the ſoil, which was harder, or eaſier to plough.   *Reg. Hon. Richm. II.   Brad. Hiſt.* 141.

heirs, Robert and Thomas, being clergymen, died without iffue, when
their large eftates defcended, in the reign of Richard II. to their fifters,
as coheireffes ; and Hilderwell,and other lands, came by marriage with
Lucia the eldeft to Sir Robert de Lumley, Knight, His defcendants
continued Lords here till the reign of Henry VIII. when John, Lord
Lumley, engaging in the northern infurrection called the *Pilgrimage of
Grace*, was attainted for high treafon ; and this, and all his other eftates became forfeited to the Crown.

WE have no evidence of the fucceeding proprietors of this manor
till the beginning of the reign of Charles I. when the Sheffields became
owners thereof ; from whom it defcended, and is now part of the great
poffeffions of Lord Mulgrave.

THE church here, (dedicated to St. Hilda) is rectorial. * " It was
" anciently under the patronage of the Lords Mauleys and Thwengs,
" who prefented by turns. The Thwengs' part defcended to the Lum-
" leys, Knights ; and the Mauleys' came to the houfe of Salvins, who
" alfo prefented by turns."   *Torr's M. S.*

* HILDERWELL RECTORY.

DEDICATED to St. Hilda. Sir Francis Boynton, Bart. patron. Firft fruits 12*l.* 13s. 6¼d.
Tenths 1*l.* 5s. 4¼d. Proc. 7s. 6d. Sub. 1*l.* 2s.
INCUMBENTS. 1307. Rob. Fil. Thomæ, *pres. Peter de Mauley.* 1309. John de Kilton;
pres. Marmad. de Tweng. 1328. Rad. de Hoton, *pres. P. de Mauley.* 1344. Will. de Rydelyerg-
ton, *pres. Rob. de Thweng.* 1365. John de Brathwell, cap. *pres. P. de Mauley.* 1379. Leo. de He-
don, *pres. Rex. ut Tutor Hæred. de Thweng.* 1407. Will. Gaunton, *pres. P. de Mauley.* 1409.
John Waftell, *pres. John de Lumley.* 1416. John de Kilvington, *J. Ellerker & alii.* 1439. John
Kighley, *pres. Tho. Lumley.* 1452. John Smallwood, *pres. J. Salvine.* 1457. J. Gibfon, *p. Tho.
Lumley.* 1489. John Jackfon, cap. *p. Affig. Tutor. Salvine.* 1506. Richard Lumley, *p. Geo. Lumley.* 1515. Rob. Keclyn, *p. Rad. Salvine.* 1519. Will. Highyngton, *p. John Lumley, Miles.* 1544.
Ric. Salvine, M. A. *p. Gerard Salvine Ar.* 1561. Fr. Scarthe.—1601. Ph. Weath, cl. *p. Rad. Salvine.* 1633. James Talbot, M. A. *p. Tho. Talbot. hac vice.* 1670. W. Middleton, B. A. *p. Rob.
Crompton, Gent.* 1714. Rich. Ofbaldefton, Dean of York; and afterwards Bifhop of Carlifle and London, *p. the Archbifhop ratione lapfus.* 1747. Matt. Dutton, *by the King on the promotion of Dr. Ofbaldefton.* 1763. Nich. Howlet, *by Boynton Langley, Efq.* 1781. J. Gilby, *by the Archbifhop, by lapfe.*
1790. Gilbert Ainfley, *by Mountain Lind, Efq.* 1793. William Smith, *by Dame Marg. Boynton, and
John George Parkhurft, Efq.*

Drawn by J.B.

A View of Brunswick Bay

Eng.d by R.Scott

The advowfon and right of prefentation paffed by purchafe to different families, and came to the Boyntons, of Burton Agnes, in the county of York, who prefented in the year 1792.

THE rectory, according to Torr, is valued in the King's books at 12*l*. 13s. 6½d; and is endowed with all manner of tithes within the parifh, which contains the following divifions; viz. Hilderwell, Roufby, Dalehoufe, Staithes and Runfwick. There are alfo about forty acres of glebe; half an acre of which lies *open* in the middle of a field at a little diftance towards the north from the parifh church, and is called *the Chapel-Hill*, where it is reported that there was formerly an oratory or chapel, probably the place of St. Hilda's retreat above noticed.

THERE was a plague, which broke out in this village, in the year 1603, and raged about fix weeks, carrying off a number of the inhabitants; but fortunately did not extend its baneful influence to any of the neighbouring villages. This dreadful malady arofe from a *Turkey-fhip* that was ftranded on this coaft; from which the infection was conveyed by fome of the paffengers into the village. In the parifh regifter for that year we find the following memorandum; " *Mortui* " *per peftilentiam in villâ Hilderwell, a primo die Septembris in decimum diem* " *Novembris, ut fequitur, et illic fepulti funt:*" then follow the names of thofe who died of the plague alluded to, amounting to forty-nine in number.

ON the eaftern part of the parifh, about a mile diftant from the village of Hilderwell, we vifited RUNSWICK; ‖ which is fituated near the fea, and confifts of a few fcattered huts, inhabited by fifhermen, and grouped irregularly together on the declivity of a fteep and rugged rock; the projecting top of which juts forward in an awful manner, and threatens at fome future period to overwhelm the inhabitants. The fituation of the place is fingular, and muft excite the curiofity of

---

‖ *RUNSWICK* feems to be derived from the Danifh word *Runs*, *Alveus*, which fignifies a *Channel*, and *Wick*, a village.

ftrangers; when in winding along the narrow paths between the houfes, they may on one fide enter the door of one dwelling, and from
thence look down the chimney of another in front. Pennant obferves, that " the houfes here make a grotefque appearance, fcattered
" over the face of a fteep cliff in a very ftrange manner, and fill every
" projecting ledge one above another, in the fame manner as thofe
" of the peafants in the rocky parts of China." The houfes are fheltered on the north and north-weft, and command a pleafing profpect
into the bay, which is upwards of a mile in extent,—with Kettlenefs
allum-works about a mile to the north-eaft. The lower part of the
town is almoft choaked with fand, which fills up every paffage; and
in wet weather is dirty and unpleafant.

    WE next vifited

STAITHES,

another fmall fifhing town, † about two miles to the north-weft from
Hilderwell, fingularly fituated in a narrow creek between two cliffs,
and fo near the fhore, that the fea reaches many of the houfes at high-
water. But this is not the only precarious tenure, to which the inhabitants are expofed. The ground, upon which the houfes are built, is
the property of Lord Mulgrave; to whom the occupiers pay only a trifling acknowledgment, which leaves his Lordfhip at liberty at any
time to difpoffefs them of their habitations; though we believe (and we
here record it to the honour of that family) it never yet entered nto
the mind of the noblePeer to affert his rights to the prejudice of individuals.

---

    † IN this obfcure place, the juftly celebrated circumnavigator, *Capt. Cook*, was firft apprenticed
to a refpectable fhop-keeper; and the following anecdote is related as the caufe of his relinquifhing
that occupation. It one day happened that a young woman, in payment for fome article purchafed
at the fhop, gave *Cook* a *fhining new fhilling*, which his mafter obferved; but not finding it afterwards
among the cafh in the till, accufed *young Cook* of purloining his property. *Cook* became indignant at
the charge, which he afferted to be falfe,—faying that the new fhilling was certainly in his pocket,but
had been duly replaced by another. Unable, however to brook the accufation, he abfconded the
next day, and went to fea; and from this fimple circumftance the world is indebted to his great difcoveries as a navigator.

THE inhabitants here, and at Runfwick, fubfift principally by fifh-ing. During the winter and fpring feafons, they go out to fea in fmall boats, called *cobles,* each carrying *three men,* flat bottomed, and fo conftructed as *to live* in very tempeftuous weather ; and they are generally fo fucceffful as to return fully loaden with the choiceft fifh, which are fold at very reafonable prices. In the fummer feafon, the fifhermen go out in large boats, of from ten to twenty tons burthen, called *five men boats :* they generally fail on the Monday, and continue at fea the whole week ; and on their return home, the fifh are cut up and falted by the women, which is not only a difagreeable, but labori-ous employment. After paffing through the *brine* or *pickle,* the fifh is fpread out upon the beach to dry, when the effluvia, during this pro-cefs, is offenfive in the higheft degree, particularly to ftrangers ; though to the inhabitants, to whom it is a fource of wealth and abundance, both the fight and fmell are, no doubt, highly gratifying.

ABOUT the month of September, thefe veffels go to the herring fifh-ery near Yarmouth. ‖ The fifhermen carry the produce of their labour thither; and the fifh are cured in the fmoaking-houfe there, by which pro-cefs they become what are termed *Red-herrings ;* thefe, with the dried fifh

---

‖ THE herring, *clupea harengus* (Lin. Syft. 1. p. 522. no. 1.) is a fifh of paffage, which fattens and impregnates in the north-feas, and comes fouthward to fpawn; but being a northern fifh it is feldom found farther fouth than the coaft of France.

THEY are fuppofed to fet out from the icy fea about the middle of winter, and in fuch numbers as to exceed all powers of imagination. At a certain latitude they feparate and become two grand divifions ; one of which moves weftward, and pours down the coafts of America ; while the other divifion takes a more eaftern direction, and in the beginning of March falls in with the great ifland of Iceland. At Shetland they again divide into two fhoals, and file off to the eaftern and weftern coafts of the Britifh ifles, where they become a valuable article of commerce, and of ineftimable bene-fit to the inhabitants near the coaft. It is now well afcertained, that the immediate caufe of their migration is their ftrong defire to remove to warmer feas for the fake of depofiting their fpawn, and not in queft of food ; as they are univerfally obferved to be fat and full of roe and milt upon their firft approach and lean and empty when they return.

before-mentioned, which confift chiefly of *Cod*, *Ling*, *Cole-fifh*, &c. are principally exported up the Mediterranean into moft of the Catholic-countries, where they find a ready market, particularly during Lent. *

BUT, befides fifhing, the inhabitants here, and along the coaft, during the fummer months, are occafionally occupied in making *Kelp*; which is a lixivial falt, obtained by the burning of fea-weeds; and confifts chiefly of the fixed vegetable alkali, ufed in the procefs of making allum, glafs, &c.   The fea weeds are cut at low water from the rocks; and when dry, are burnt in heaps, being conftantly ftirred with an iron-rake till it becomes condenfed and caked together in a large mafs; but if not ftirred it will burn to afhes.

KELP is a valuable manure for land; and the trade might be confiderably extended along the Cleveland coaft by particular attention to the cultivation of fea-weeds, for which premiums might be given. ‡

SEATON-HALL, WITHIN the townfhip of Hilderwell, lies about a mile from that village, nearer the fea.   There was an ancient manor here, which, according to the Domefday book, contained three carucates *ad geldum*, and two more that might be rendered arable, held by *Richard*, of Robert Earl of Moreton.   There was one carucate in demefne, and fix villeins with two ploughs.   The manor was one mile long, and half a mile broad, valued at ten fhillings.

TERRA COMITIS MORITONIENSIS.
IN SCETUN AD GELDUM III. CARUCATÆ, ET II. POSSUNT ESSE. IBI

---

* See *Rymer's Fæd.* (vol. 7. p. 788.) for the King's proclamation, in 1394, refpecting the herring fifheries; and a record (42. Edw. III.) mentions a duty on them in Ireland; which proves they had a method of curing them at leaft 50 years fooner than is generally thought.

‡ The following are the plants from which kelp is manufactured; viz. 1. *Fucus reficulofus*, Linn. the moft common fea-wrack, called alfo the fea-oak from the refemblance of its leaves to thofe of the oak-tree.   It is termed in the Orkneys, the *black tang*.

2. *F. nodosus*, Linn. the knotted fea-wrack, or bell-wrack, called in the Orkneys, *yellow tang*.

3. *F. serratus*, Linn. the jagged or ferrated fea-wrack, called in fome places, *ware*.

4. *F. digitatus*, Linn. the tangle.   *See the Highland Society Trans. for the year* 1800.

HABUIT UCTRED I. MAN. NUNC HABET RICARD DE COMITE. IN DOMIŅIO
I. CAR. ET VI. VILLANI CUM II. CAR. TOTUM MANERIUM I. LEU. LONG.
ET DIM. LAT. T. R. E. X. SOL. VALEBAT. MODO SIMILITER.
AD HOC MAN. JACET SOCA IN ROSCEBI II. CARUCATARUM AD GEL-
DUM ET II. CAR. POSS. ESSE. SILVA PAST. I. LEUC. LONG. ET III QUA-
RENT. LAT. TOTUM ROSCEBI II. LEUC, LONG. ET DIMID. LEUC. LAT. UC-
TRED TENET.

FROM the above extract it appears,that to this manor there was a *soke*
within certain lands at Roufby, confifting of two carucates *ad geldum*,
and two more that might be rendered arable, with a wood fit for pafturage, one mile long, and three *quarentens* broad, held by *Uctred*.

THIS place gave name to a refident family ; for in Kirkby's Inqueft*
we find that *Adam de Seaton* held four carucates of land here of the fee
of Marmaduke de Thweng, where ten carucates made one Knight's fee.
The Right Hon. Lord Mulgrave is the prefent proprietor.

THE townfhip or chapelry of

ROUSBY,

fometimes written *Roxby*, lies about three miles from the village of Hilderwell, and forms the weftern part of the parifh.   The village is fmall,
and the houfes, which are occupied chiefly by farmers, and labourers
in hufbandry, are fcattered on a gentle declivity, with an open northern
afpect.

BESIDES the lands above noticed, as within the *soke* of the manor of
Seaton, it appears from the Domefday book that there was one carucate,
which was demefne of the Crown, with land fufficient for one plough,
entered in the furvey, under the title,

TERRA REGIS.

MANERIUM IN ROZEBI NORMAN I. CAR. TERRÆ.   TERRA AD I. CAR.

---

* ADAM DE SETON tenet 4 carucatas terræ de dicta hæreditate *(Marmaduci de Thweng)* in Seton, unde 10 car. terræ faciunt feodum milit.

Kirkby's Inqueft.

T t

THE Boyntons, according to Kirkby's Inqueft, were proprietors of Roufby in the reign of Edw. I. and their defcendants continued Lords here, till the late Sir Griffith Boynton, Bart. who fold the manor and eftate to the late J. Turton, M. D.

There was an ancient manfion here belonging to the Boyntons ; but the buildings, which, from the foundations ftill vifible, appear to have been extenfive, have been long deftroyed.

ROUSBY is a chapelry dependent on the church of Hilderwell. The chapel, which is a fmall edifice, was founded and endowed by the Boynton family ‖ in the reign of Henry V. but neither the revenues thereof, nor its dedication have been ftated. It enjoys parochial rights of baptifms and burials ; and within the chapel we noticed the monumental infcriptions given in the notes. * In the centre divifion of the eaftern window, there are four effigies in painted glafs ; one of which bears the arms of Boynton : thefe are probably the effigies of benefactors, who contributed to the building or repairs of the chapel.

‖ On a brafs plate on the floor of the aile within the chancel, there is the following infcription:

pray for the foule of Choma Boynton of Roysby Efquier who caufed this churche fyrft to be hallowed ꝛ was y fyrft corfe that was beryed in yt ꝛ decefaed the rrɪr day of marche the yer of: lord god MIV ꝛ Twenty three on whofe foule ihu have mercy amen.

ON the fouth fide of the quire, an elegant marble monumental table, furrounded with iron rails, bears the following infcription :

FRANCES BOYNTON, SOMETIME
WIFE OF SIR MATTHEW BOYNTON OF
BARMSTON, KNIGHT AND BARONET,
DAUGHTER OF SIR HENRY GRIFFITH, OF
BURTON-AGNES KNIGHT. A FAMILIE
DESCENDED FROM ANCIENT
AND HONOURABLE
ANCESTORS.

THE SOIL within the parish is chiefly of a clayey quality, with a mixture of gravel and clayey loam, which is tolerably fertile; wheat, oats, and beans, are the principal crops; but from the situation of the lands near the sea, the climate is cold, and the harvests rather late.

Her Life much more remarkable for Graces, than for Days
yet in that more than ordinarilye abreviated Tyme, her exact
and holy Pilgrimage (the effects whereof in her prudent and
provident difpofing of all Things pertaining to the Duty of her Sex;
As alfo in her indefatigable Diligence in the faithful Education
of her Children,) was fo confpicuoufly manifefted, that befides
the good acceptance therefore, which God teftified in her, in a
numerous Pofteritie, fhe had alfo hereby ingraven foe deep an
Impreffion in the Hearts of all that knew her pious Converfation
(that were it not that Mortalitie doth deface the Memorie of Things)
fhee needed no other Monument.
She dyed about y^c. 3^d. of July, in y^e. Yeare
of her Age 36. Anno Dom. 1634.
The faid Sir Matthew Boynton, to manifeft
his Love to his fo well deferving Wife
hath, with his own Hands infcribed, and
caufed to be erected
THIS MARBLE.

On the north fide of the altar, upon a plain flat marble, there is the following infcription:
Vnder this Marble,
Refteth the Body of the religious
and honourable Lady Katherine,
Second Daughter of the Right
Honourable Thomas Lord Fairfax
of Gilling Caftle, Vifcount Emuly,
late Wife of Sir Arthur Ingram,
of Temple-Newfom in this County,
Knt. who departed this Life the 23d
of Feb. Anno Dni 1666.

T t 2

THE POPULATION of the parifh is confiderable; but not having received the neceffary documents from the parifh regifters, we can form no juft idea of the probable increafe of its inhabitants. From the enumeration taken in the year 1801, according to act of parliament, we find there were 362 houfes, 372 families, and 1414 inhabitants; on referring to the table fet forth in the notes, † it will be feen, that the number of females greatly exceeds that of the males, which is occafioned probably by a great majority of the latter being employed in the perilous and laborious occupation of fifhermen; and that the average number of perfons to each family hardly amounts to four, which is lefs than that of moft other parifhes within the diftrict.

† STATE of population, taken 10th March, 1801.

Townfhips.	Inhabited houfes.	Families.	Uninhabited houfes.	Males.	Females.	Total.	Agriculture.	Trade, &c.	Refidue.	Total.
Hilderwell,	329	339	10	471	753	1224	37	51	1136	1224
Roufby,	33	33	3	98	92	190	43	8	139	190
Totals.	362	372	13	569	845	1414	80	59	1275	1414

THE PARISH OF EASINGTON,

ADJOINS to Hilderwell on the weft; and with the Townfhip of Liverton, is of confiderable extent, ftretching from north to fouth upwards of fix miles, but not more than two miles broad. It is bounded on the eaft by the parifh of Hilderwell; by Lofthoufe and Skelton on the weft; by Danby on the fouth; and on the north by the fea. It comprehends the feveral manors of Eafington, Boulby, and Liverton; all which, as appears from the Domefday Survey, were anciently within the foke of the manor of Lofthoufe, held in the Conqueror's time by Hugh,

Earl of Chefter, and then wafte, except Eafington, in which there was one villein with one plough, a church without a Minifter, and a wood with pafturage for cattle, one mile long, and two quarentens broad. It alfo appears from another part of the general Survey, that there was one oxgang of land *ad geldum* at Eafington ; and one carucate at Boulby with land fufficient for one plough, valued at eight fhillings, which were ancient Demefne of the Crown, being entered under the title

" TERRA REGIS.
"IN ESTEINTUNE EST UNA BOVAT. TERRÆ AD GELDUM. VIII. SOLID.
" MANERIUM IN BOLEBI CHILUERT I. CAR. TERRÆ AD GELD. TERRA
" AD I. CAR. VIII. SOLID.

THESE manors were afterwards granted by the Conqueror to Robert de Brus, Lord of Skelton, By an Inquifition *poft Mortem*, taken 7. Edward I. it appears that Peter de Brus (55. Henry III.) died, feized of two Knight's Fees at Eafington, *et alibi*, which he held of the Conftable of the Caftle ; ‖ but dying without iffue, his four fifters became his heirs, when Margaret the third, who married Robert de Roos, Lord of Werke, had Eafington and other lands for her fhare ; of whom, according to Kirby's Inqueft, Gilbert de Camera, and Galfridus de Maucovenant held half a Knight's Fee here, where twelve Carucates made one Knight's Fee, and paid as a fine the fum of fix fhillings. ‡

‖ Inquifito de Feodis quondam Petri de Brus, &c. capta anno Regni Regis Edw. 7 mo. per Wilfiam de Munbody, &c. qui dicunt, quod idem Petrus tenuit de Conftabulario Caftri duo feoda, unde Ambrofius de Camera, et Galfridus Maucovenant tenuerunt unum feod. in Eafington et alibi.   *Ex Bund. Ecate.* 7 *Edw.* I. *n.* 32-

‡ Gilbertus de Camera, et Galfridus de Maucovenante tenent Dimid. Feod. in Eafington *(de dic- ta Margaret,)* unde XII. Carucatæ Terræ faciunt unum Feod. Et dictus Gilbertus, pro medietate sua illius feodi, reddit Ballio Dni. Regis pro fine III. S. Et dictus Galfridus pro fua medietate re ddit de fine III. S,   *Kirkby's Inqueft.*

THE eftate of Eafington and Boulby came to a branch of the ancient family of Conyers, who, for feveral generations, were feated at

Conyers of Boulby.

The former part of the following Pedigree is collected from *Dodfworth MSS.* (Vol. 99. fol. 58 &c)
and is the more worthy of notice as it carries the family farther back than the Vifitation in 1666.
The continuation was communicated by a particular friend.

CONYERS

Thomas Conyers, of = Alice　　　　　Chriftopher, =
Whitby, ob. 1449. |　　　　　　　Executor fratris |

2 Joan Tho. Conyers, = Alice, daughter　Ifabel = Rich. Wakelyne,　Thomas, 1449, on which his
3 Alice　ob. 1481. |　of . . . Danby.　　　　　　　　　uncle entailed his eftates on
　　　　　　　　　　　　　　　　　　　　　　the failure of his own iffue.

Chriftr. Conyers, = Barbara.　Tho. Conyers, = Anne. . . . = Thos.　　James, ob. = Ann.
of Scarbro, 1566. |　　ob. 1514.　　　　　　Lowther,　　1541. |

Richard.　　　　　　　　　　　　　　　Ann. Margery, = G. Mufgrave.

1 Gregory, fon = Ann, dau.　2 John. Eliz. = Wm. Cook, Ann = M. Wilfon　1 William. Elizabeth.
and heir. bailiff | of . . Read.　. . . = . . . Skelton.　　　　2 Leonard.
of Whitby 1540. |　ob. 1557.　　(*Dodfworth's MSS.*　　3 Francis.

Anthony = 1 George Conyers, = Jane, dau. of　3 William, = Lady Conway Margaret = Tho. Sutton.
2d fon. |　　　　　　Thos. Gower, 4 Henry,　5 Thomas, Elizabeth = Bryan Lacy.
Ann. 1557　　　　　of Stainfby. 6 Francis.　　　　　　　　Richard, 1557.

1 Nicholas = Ann, dau. of Am-　Leonard Conyers, of Whitby, = Ifabel, dau. of Ambrose
ob. S. P.　brofe Beckwith,　heir to his brother. 1612 | Beckwith, fifter to his bro-
　　　　　　　　　　　　　　　　ther's wife.

1 Nicholas Conyers of = Catherine, dau.　2 George of Iüingdale had iffue 1 Jane, = Chrift. Blincorne.
Boulby, Efq. ob. 1636. | of Rob. Trotter of 3 Robert of Guifbro, ｝　2 Eliz. = Henry Wills.
　　　　　　SkeltonCaftle, Efq. 4 James 5 Francis, ｝ ob. S. P. 3 Sufan = W. Serjeant of
　　　　　　　　6 Ralph.　　　　　　　　　　4 Marg. Guifbro.

Mary = W. Conyers, Margt. = W. 1 akin, of　1 R. Conyers = Anne, d of Sir 2 Nicholas = Grace,　3 Hen.
of Scarbro.'　　Yedington, in of Boulby, |　Ralph Con- of Cleafby,　d. of　and 4
　　　　Co. York, Efq. Efq. ob. 1640. |　yers, of Lay- Co. York. | ..Smith- Ant. d.
　　　　　　　　　　　　ton, in Co. | fon of unmar.
　　　　　　　　　　　　Durham. |　Moulton.

Boulby; and whofe capital manfion is now converted into a farm houfe; over the door of which, upon a fquare ftone, there is an efcutcheon bearing the arms of Conyers. This family continued fole proprietors till about the year 1664, when Nicholas Conyers, on his third marrriage

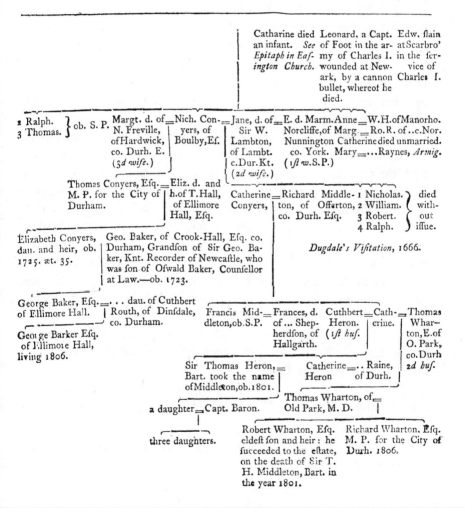

Catharine died an infant. *See Epitaph in Eaf-ington Church.*

Leonard, a Capt. of Foot in the ar-my of Charles I. wounded at New-ark, by a cannon bullet, whereof he died.

Edw. flain atScarbro' in the fer-vice of Charles I.

2 Ralph.
3 Thomas. } ob. S. P.

Margt. d. of N. Freville, ofHardwick, co. Durh. E. (3*d wife.*)

Nich. Con-yers, of Boulby,Ef.

Jane, d. of Sir W. Lambton, of Lambt. c.Dur.Kt. (2*d wife.*)

E. d. Marm. Norcliffe,of Nunnington co. York. (1*ſt w.*S.P.)

Anne, Marg. Catherine died unmarried. Mary ...Raynes, *Armig.*

W.H.ofManorho. Ro.R. of ..c.Nor.

Thomas Conyers, Efq. M. P. for the City of Durham.

Eliz. d. and h.of T.Hall, of Ellimore Hall, Efq.

Catherine Conyers,

Richard Middle-ton, of Offerton, co. Durh. Efq.

1 Nicholas. 2 William. 3 Robert. 4 Ralph. } died with-out iſſue.

Elizabeth Conyers, dau. and heir, ob. 1725. æt. 35.

Geo. Baker, of Crook-Hall, Efq. co. Durham, Grandfon of Sir Geo. Ba-ker, Knt. Recorder of Newcaftle, who was fon of Ofwald Baker, Counfellor at Law.—ob. 1723.

Dugdale's Vifitation, 1666.

George Baker, Efq. of Ellimore Hall.

.. dau. of Cuthbert Routh, of Dinfdale, co. Durham.

Francis Mid-dleton,ob.S.P.

Frances, d. of ... Shep-herdfon, of Hallgarth.

Cuthbert Heron. (1*ſt huf.*)

Cath-erine.

Thomas Wharton,E.of O. Park, co.Durh 2*d huf.*

George Barker Efq. of Ellimore Hall, living 1806.

Sir Thomas Heron, Bart. took the name ofMiddleton,ob.1801.

Catherine Heron

.. Raine, of Durh.

a daughter

Capt. Baron.

Thomas Wharton, of Old Park, M. D.

three daughters.

Robert Wharton, Efq. eldeft fon and heir: he fucceeded to the eftate, on the death of Sir T. H. Middleton, Bart. in the year 1801.

Richard Wharton, Efq. M. P. for the City of Durh. 1806.

with Margaret, daughter of N. Freville, Efq. of Hardwick, in the county of Durham, made over a great part of his eftates in truft for the ufe
of his children by his fecond wife; but his fons dying without iffue,
this part of the eftate came by marriage with Catherine his daughter, to
Richard Middleton, of Offerton, in the County of Durham, Efq. by
whofe daughter it paffed to the Herons; and was late the property of
Sir Thomas Heron, Bart. who took in addition the name of Middleton :
but, he dying without male iffue, and the eftate being entailed, it finally defcended to, and is now the property of Robert Wharton, Efq. the
next heir male, eldeft fon of the late Thomas Wharton, M. D. of Old
Park, in the county of Durham.

THE faid Nicholas Conyers, on this fettlement to his children by his
fecond marriage, kept to himfelf the allum works at Boulby; which,
with the remaining moiety of the eftate, defcended to his fon Thomas
by his third wife; three fourths of which came afterwards by marriage
with Elizabeth, his only daughter, to George Baker, of Crook-Hall,
Efq. whofe defcendant, George Baker, Efq. of Ellimore Hall in
the county of Durham, is the prefent proprietor. The other moiety
of the allum works, &c. being previoufly fold to John and William
Ward, brothers of Ralph Ward, Efq. of Guifbrough, came by marriage
to the Jackfons, and is now the property of William Ward Jackfon,
Efq. of Normanby-Hall.

THE village of Eafington is fmall and irregularly built; through
which there is a road, leading between Whitby and Guifbrough, in a
direction nearly eaft and weft.

THE church, which ftands nearly in the centre of the village, is a
plain and humble edifice; * and though originally founded before the

---

* WITHIN the church there is the effigy of an infant, fleeping in a cradle, and beneath upon a
common ftone, the following infcription :
> Here refteth Katherine, the
> youngeft Daughter of Nicholas
> Conyers of Boulby, Efqr.
> by Katherine his wife,—who

Co nqueft, retains nothing in its ftyle of architecture, that bears evidence of fo great antiquity.

THIS church, which is dedicated to All-Saints, is rectorial. It was given by Roger de Roffel, with one oxgang of land here, to the prior and convent of Guifbrough; and continued a rectory, (non-appropriate) in their patronage till the general diffolution, when it came to the Crown. ‖

THE townfhip and manor of

LIVERTON

are fituated on the fouth weftern part of the parifh. This is an ancient chapelry dependent on the church of Eafington. The chapel has parochial rights, but the inhabitants pay no acknowledgments to Eafington.

---

died in the Lord, July the firft, Anno
Domini 1621; of her age, one
Month
Corpus terra tenet;
parte tamen meliore mei,
fuper aftra ferar.

‖ EASINGTON RECTORY.

DEDICATION, All-Saints. The King, patron. Firft fruits 14*l.* 8s. 6$\frac{1}{4}$d. Tenths 1*l.* 8s. 10$\frac{1}{4}$d. Proc. 7s. 6d. Syn. 1*l.* 4s.

INCUMBENTS. 1304. John Reginald, pbr. *pres. prior and conv. Guifbrough.* 1305. Will. de Somerfett. 1317. Reginaldus de Stokefley. 1338. John de Wirkefall, cl. —— Will. de Wilton. 1340. Adam de Ebor, cl. *p. m.* Wilton. —— Tho. de Settrington. 1398. Will. Upfall, *p. m.* Settrington. 1410. Henry Bigging, *poft res.* Upfall. 1423. Walter de Erythorne, *poft res.* Bigging. 1443. Hugo Allerton, *p m.* Erythorne. —— Will. Tryndon. 1444. John Tryndon. 1455. John Leverfham, *poft res.* Tryndon. 1481. Robert Young. 1483. John Fawcone, cap. 1522. Richard Beyley, pbr. 1523. Will. Clarburgh, L. L. D. 1526. John Walls, *pbr. poft res.* Clarburgh. 1540. Oliver Grayfon, *poft res.* Walls. 1578. Rich. Stancliff, cl. *pres. Elizab. Regina.* 1594. John Bridges, M. A. p. m. Stancliffe. 1599. Zach. Steward, S. T. P. 1618. Abraham Jackfon, *p. m.* Steward. 1640. Rich Smelt. 1666. Samuel Tyerman, M. A. *p. m.* Smelt. 1679. James Lowd. 1699. George Wilfon. 1707. George Spencer. 1735. Jofeph Storr. *p. m.* Spencer. 1750. John Samuel Hill, D. D. *p. m.* Storr. 1757. Arthur Cayley, *p. m.* Hill. 1761. William Harper, *p. m.* Cayley. 1783. Walker King, D. D. *p. m.* Harper. 1799. Matthew Mapletoft, M. A. *poft res.* King.

U u

The advowſon of the chapel was given by Henry Fitz-Conan, to the priory of Guiſbrough ; and in the year 1219, the grant was recognized before Richard de Mariſco, Biſhop of Durham, then Lord Chancellor. The chapel is a ſmall modern built edifice, covered with ſlate ; but it does not appear either to have been certified to, or to have received any augmentation from the governours of Queen Anne's bounty.

THE village of Liverton conſiſts of about fifty houſes, ſcattered irregularly on the edge of a barren common. The manor here, as we have already noticed, was at the time of the Conqueror's ſurvey, within the ſoke of Lofthouſe, but was then waſte. It was afterwards granted to Robert de Brus, Lord of Skelton, to be held of the King *in capite ;* but, on failure of male iſſue in that family, in the reign of Henry the third, it came by marriage to Marmaduke de Thweng ; of whom, according to Kirkby's Inqueſt, Henry Fitz-Conan held half a Knight's fee, and paid as a fine the ſum of eight ſhillings. * From the Thwengs, the manor came by Lucia, daughter of Robert de Thweng, to William Lord Latimer ; in which family it continued till male iſſue failing in the laſt William (4 Richard II.) his daughter Elizabeth, then the wife of John Lord Neville, of Raby, was found his next heir, in whoſe right he was created Lord Latimer ; but iſſue male again failing, Elizabeth his daughter by marriage transferred it to the Willoughbies of Ereſby ; from whom it paſſed by Joan, the heir of Robert, Lord Willoughby, to Sir Richard Wells, Knight. Of the immediate ſucceeding proprietors we are uninformed. In the reign of Charles the firſt, we find Liverton in the poſſeſſion of Sir Thomas Dawney, Knight ; whoſe deſcendant, Lord Viſcount Downe, is the preſent proprietor and Lord of the manor.

THE POPULATION of this pariſh, which, as we have already noticed, contains the townſhips of Eaſington and Liverton, is conſiderable. In the year 1801, when an actual return was made, according to the act

---

* HENRICUS, filius Conani tenet dimid. feodi, de dicta hæreditate (Marmaduc de Thweng) in Leverton, unde X. carucat. terræ faciunt feodum et reddit. ballivo regis pro fine VIIIs.

Kirkby's Inqueſt.

of parliament, there were 154 houfes or families, and 730 inhabitants, giving an average of upwards of 4½ to each family. Of thefe one half are females ; and from the table given in the notes, † it will be feen that a majority of the males are occupied in manufactures, the allum-works at Boulby employing a great number of hands.

THE SOIL within the parifh is various ; in the northern part, towards the fea, a barren clay prevails ; which, as we proceed fouthwards, becomes of a moorifh quality. Wheat is lefs cultivated in this and the adjoining parifhes than in the more weftern part of the diftrict ; and the harvefts are rather late. Oats are the principal crop.

OF mineral productions, the allum-works at Boulby, the property of Meffrs. Baker and Jackfon, are worthy of particular notice. Thefe works are fituated on the verge of a ftupendous cliff ; and the rock, cut down by an almoft herculean labour, difcovers the different ftrata in the bowels of the earth, and affords a fpectacle at once pleafing, awful, and magnificent. As the allum rock lies at a confiderable depth below the furface of the ground, the labour of removing it is attended with much labour and expence ; but this part of the bufinefs is conducted with fuch order and regularity, as not only to equalize the labour to the ftrength of the different workmen, but alfo to enforce it in proportion to their wages. For this purpofe, they have wheel-barrows of various fizes, denominated *barrows*, *half barrows*, and *quarter barrows*; for which wages are paid in proportion to their fize. ‖ The workmen are divided

† STATE OF POPULATION, taken 10th MARCH, 1801.

TOWNSHIPS.	Inhab. houfes.	Fam-ilies	Unhab. houses.	Males.	Fe-males.	To-tal.	Agri-culture	Trade, &c.	Refi-due.	To-tal.
Eafington,	101	101	- - -	242	258	500	77	89	334	500
Liverton,	53	53	5	112	118	230	114	35	81	230
Totals,	154	154	5	354	376	730	191	124	415	730

‖ THE conftruction of the barrows ufed in the allum works, is the beft imaginable, and worthy of particular notice : for. although they contain a confiderable quantity of earth, the weight is fo judicioufly poifed upon the axle of the wheel or trundle, that little force is required to lift them ; and in wheeling, fo little weight refts upon the arms, that the labour is lefs fatiguing than what is required in *canal-work*, though the barrows do not contain half the quantity.

into two parties, with an overfeer, or *tally-man*, to fee that the affigned number of journeys is duly performed; and as they all run the fame diftance, whilft one party is out upon the journey, the other is employed each in filling his own barrow, which prevents all interruption and con-fufion.   By thus proportioning the fize of the barrows to the ftrength of the workmen, boys of twelve or fourteen years of age find employ-ment; and when a man, through age or infirmities, finds himfelf une-qual to a barrow of the largeft fize, he has an opportunity of making choice of a fmaller, his earnings being always in proportion.

As the procefs of making allum has been fully defcribed in Keir's Effay on Chemiftry, in Ray's Collection of Englifh words (p. 201.) in the Philofophical Tranfactions, (No. 842.) and other publications, we fhall not detain the reader with extracts from thefe authors, but briefly obferve, that the preparation confifts in rendering the ore, in the firft place aluminous, and afterwards in diffolving and purifying the falt. As moft of the allum ftone, (which, when dug from the rock is of the colour of flate,) is found to contain a mixture of clay and fulphur, the latter muft be converted into vitriolic acid, before it can form the aluminous combination; which is moft expeditioufly effected by actual combuftion.   After the ftone, which is thrown into large heaps, has been fufficiently burned, it is put into pits and fteeped in water, in or-der to extract the faline matter, where it remains till the ore is redu-ced to fuch a ftate, as that it may be made into pafte with the hand. The liquor is then run into other pits, where the vitriolic falts are pre-cipitated by the folution of *fal fodæ*, prepared from kelp, or the volatile alkali of ftale urine; and afterwards conveyed in wooden troughs to the *allum houfe*, where the fuperfluous water is evaporated by boiling, which is ufually performed in large leaden caldrons.

The lixivium, when fufficiently concentrated by evaporation, is conveyed through channels into coolers, where it is freed by depofition, from the groffer heterogenous particles.   In eight or ten days, the

lixivium, commonly called magiftral water, flows off into another veffel, leaving behind a number of fmall and impure cryftals, which in-
cruft the bottom and fides of the veffel. Thefe cryftals, when collected
and wafhed with cold water, are put into the boiler ufed for purifying
them, and diffolved in a fmall quantity of water, fo as barely to fuf-
pend the falt when boiling hot. The allum liquor is then poured into
large ftrong wooden cafks, in which the allum graduallly fhoots into
large cryftals about the fides : the liquor in the middle is then let out
by a cock in the bottom, and the veffel turned upfide down to drain
off more effectually the remaining fluid. The cryftals are afterwards
dried in a ftove, and finally packed up in cafks for fale. Mr. Gough,
in his additions to Camden's Britannia, obferves that, " when the feve-
" ral allum works, eftablifhed in this neighbourhood, were worked,
" near 6000 tons of allum were made annually, which was found to be
" almoft double the quantity that was ufed. At prefent, he fays, not
" more than 3000 tons are made annually, which coft the proprietors
" about 14*l*. per ton, and cannot be fold, with a living profit, for lefs
" than 16*l*: or 17*l*. per ton. Four or five hundred tons of allum are fent
" yearly to foreign markets, and the remainder coaft ways to London."

MANY of the allum works in Cleveland were formerly rented under
the Crown by Sir Paul Pindar; ‡ who employed 800 workmen, and
fold his allum at the rate of 26*l*. per ton; but on the death of Charles I.
this monopoly ceafed, and the right was reftored to the original proprietors. An extenfive plan for monoplizing this commodity was afterwards
laid by Meffrs. Gilbert and Company, about the year 1770; but the
high price of allum at that period, encouraging many of the proprietors
of allum works in England and foreign parts to increafe their quantity; and from not confidering that the quantity annually manufactured greatly exceeded the annual confumption, their plan failed; when

---

‡ THE rent paid to the Crown was 12,500*l*. per ann. with the further fum of 1640*l*. to the Earl
of Mulgrave, and 600*l*. to Sir William Pennyman.

a third monoply was attempted by Sir George Colebrooke ; but from the magnitude of the concern, and other caufes, he alfo was unfuccefsful in the attempt, which proved the ruin of his fortune, and procured him, among the directors of the Eaft India company, the appellation of *fhab-allum.*

THE price of allum, in the reign of Charles I. appears almoft incredible, particularly if we confider that wages, and every neceffary of life are now increafed four fold, and yet allum is fold at prefent at 20*l.* per ton ; but, although this monoply might enable the renters to charge their own high price for this commodity,and however they might be benefitted by the cheapness of labour, they were clogged with a heavy rent, which more than counterbalanced all their other advantages. Befides this, the prefent procefs of making allum is fo much improved in every refpect, as not only to equal the difference of the expence,but alfo to compenfate the difference of price ; an affertion that can hardly be doubted, when it is a known fact, that allum has been exported to the Venetian States ; and France, before the Revolution, was principally fupplied with that article from this country.

ON entering the vaft excavation, formed in the centre of the rock, by the hands of man, the fpectator is ftruck with pleafing aftonifhment, to behold the different ftrata of earth and rock, || arranged with fuch fymmetry and exactnefs, as can no where be found, but in the perfect works of the omnipotent. The petrifactions in the allum-rock are various, ‡ befides fhells of the *bivalve* kind, there are *trochitæ*, and pieces of petrified wood in various fhapes ; but the *ammonitæ,* or fnake ftones, which are found here, and in different parts along this coaft, in great abundance, are worthy of particular notice.

|| IN digging the allum rock, veins of metals, and foils of diverfe colours are found, particularly thofe of *ochre* and *murray*, from which coppera · was formerly extracted ; but, upon the difcovery of *pyrites* in the coal works in the counties of Durham and Northumberland, that manufacture is carried thither, and difcontinued here.

‡ IN the year 1800, the fkeleton of a fifh, 15 fee· in length, fuppofed to be of the cetaceous kind, was found petrified in the rock or fcar, upon the fea-fhore, not far from Staithes.

THE ftones, in which thefe fnakes are inclofed, are hard, and of an elliptical form; and if broken with care, difcover in the centre, a fubftance refembling a fnake in all its parts, except the head, which is always wanting. *

THE bodies of the fnakes, which are of a different mineral from the ftone that inclofes them, when firft difengaged from the bed or *Nidus*, are of a bright yellow colour; and are fometimes found powdered with fmall fhining fpecks; when broken, their fubftance greatly refembles faltpetre. The fnakes are of two kinds; viz. round-bodied and fluted,—or flat-bodied, ridged on the back, and pitted in the fides; the former are the more beautiful; but the latter are larger, the fpiral convolutions in fome fpecimens being fix or feven inches in diameter.

CAMDEN obferves, that there are certain ftones found here refembling the wreathes and foldings of a ferpent, the ftrange frolics of nature, which, (as one fays) fhe forms for her diverfion, after a toilfome application to bunfiefs; for one would believe that they had been ferpents crufted over with a cover of ftone. Fame afcribes them to the power of *Saint Hilda's* prayers, as if fhe had transformed them. † To

---

* OF thefe ftones, Drayton, in his Poly-olbion, gives the following defcription:

" And upon Huntcliffe-Nab, you every where may find,
(As though nice Nature lov'd to vary in her kind)
Stones of a fpheric form of fundry mickles fram'd,
That well they globes of ftone, or bullets might be nam'd,
For any ordnance fit, which broke with hammer's blows,
Do headlefs fnakes of ftone, within their rounds enclofe."

† THE monkifh tradition is, that in the time of *Saint Hilda*, Whitby and the neighbouring coafts were greatly infefted by ferpents; and that thefe, by the prayers of *St. Hilda*, were driven headlong down the cliffs, and converted into ftones, called to this day by the country people, *Saint Hilda's* ftones. Leland, (in his *Collectanea*, vol. 3. *p.* 36.) says, " Mira res eft videre ferpentes *(apud Stren-*"*fhale)* in orbes giratos, et in clementia cæli, vel ut monachi ferunt, precibus *D. Hildæ* in lapides concretos."

THE following lines of *Saint Hilda*, recording this pretended miracle, are said to have been carved on a pillar of the abbey:

this, his learned editor adds, that Bishop Nicholson, who made large observations on the natural rarities of these parts, affirms them to be the same with those, which the modern naturalists call *cornua ammonis*. Whether they be original productions of Nature, or petrified shell fishes of the *nautilus* kind, has been very much controverted by several learned men on both sides; but, he is of opinion, that they are rather spiral petrifactions produced in the earth by a sort of fermentation peculiar to the allum-mine. Hence they are plentifully found in the allum pits at Rome, Rochelle, and Lunenburgh, as well as those of this country; and perhaps Keinsham and other parts of England, where these stones are found, would likewise afford good store of allum.

> " An ancient building which you see, ⎫
> Upon the hill, close by the sea,   ⎬
> Was Strenshall-Abbey named by me. ⎭
> I above mentioned was the dame
> When I was living in the same,
> Great wonders did, as you shall hear,
> Having my God in constant fear.
> When Whitby town with snakes was fill'd
> I to my God pray'd, and them kill'd;
> And for commemoration sake,
> Upon the scar you may them take,
> All turn'd to stone, with the same shape,
> As they from me did make escape;
> But as for heads, none can be seen,
> Unless the've artificial been."

THE PARISH OF LOFTHOUSE.

PROCEEDING weftwards, about two miles from Eafington, we entered the village of Lofthoufe, on an elevated fituation, from which we conjecture the name to be derived. The village contains fome well-built houfes, forming a regular ftreet, which runs in a direction nearly eaft and weft, with a good road leading between Guifbrough and Whitby; from the former of which it is about eight miles diftant. A weekly market on Thurfdays has been lately eftablifhed here, which has been found of great convenience to the labourers in the allum-works; and during the fummer months, is much frequented by the farmers and inhabitants of the neighbouring villages.

THE parifh, which is in extent from north to fouth about four miles, but little more than one mile broad, is bounded on the eaft, weft, and fouth by the feveral parifhes of Eafington, Danby, and Skelton, and is wafhed by the fea on the north.

LOFTHOUSE, in Domefday book written *Loctufbum*, was an ancient manor, granted by the Conqueror, to Hugh de Abrincis, furnamed Lupus, Earl of Chefter, his nephew, who foon after beftowed this, and other large territories in this neighbourhood, on William de Percy, a Norman Baron, who, as his affociate, accompanied the Conqueror in his expedition into England. This manor, according to the Domefday furvey, was taxed for four carucates; and contained four more, that might be rendered arable; with underwood, and eight acres of meadow, held before the Conqueft by Siward, the magnanimous Earl of Northumberland. The whole manor, which was three miles long,

X X

and one broad, was valued in the time of King Edward the Confeſſor,
at forty eight pounds ; but at the time of the ſurvey, was of no value,
having been laid waſte by the Conqueror, after the ſiege of York, in
the year 1069.

"TERRA HUGONIS COMITIS.

IN LOCTUSHUM AD GELDUM IIII. CARUCATÆ, ET IIII. CAR. POSS. ESSE.
H. TENUIT COM. SIUUARD PRO I. MANER. NUNC HABET COM. HUGO, SED
WAST. EST. SILVA MUTIL. ET VIII. ACR. PRATI. TOTUM MANERIUM III.
LEUC. LONG. ET I. LAT. T. R. E. XLVIII. LIB. VAL. NUNC NICHIL.

AD HOC MANER. PERTINET SOCA HÆC. ROSCHELTORP (I. CARUC.)
HILDERUUELLE (X. CAR.) BOLLEBI (II. CAR.) ESINGTON (VIII. CAR.) LIU-
ERTUN (VI. CAR.) GIGHESBORC VI. BOV.) ROUDECLIF (II. CAR.) VPELIDER
(X. CARUC.) MERSC (II. CAR.) WESTLIDUM (II. GAR.) LEISINGBI (DIM. CAR.)
LACHEBI (I. CAR. ET VI. BOV.) INTER OMNES AD GELDUM XLVI. CAR. ET
DIMID. ET XXX. CAR. POSS. ESSE. OMNIA WASTA SUNT, PRÆTER ESING-
ETUN, IN QUA EST UNUS VILLANUS CUM I. CAR. ÆCCLESIA SINC PRES-
BYTRO. SILVA PAST. I. LEUC. LONG. ET II. QUARENTA LAT. TOTUM
IIII. LEUC. LONG. ET. DIMID. LAT."

FROM the above extract it appears, that to this manor, there was a
ſoke or liberty within the following places ; viz. *Roſcheltorp*, Hilderwell,
Boulby, Eaſington, Liverton, Guiſbrough, Rowcliff, Upleatham, Marſk,
Weſtleatham, Laſingby, and Lackenby ; containing in the whole forty-
ſix carucates and a half *ad geldum*, and thirty more that might be rendered
arable ; but were then all waſte and uncultivated except Eaſington.

THE Percies continued Lords of Lofthouſe for ſeveral generations,
of whom in the reign of Edward I. according to Kirkby's Inqueſt, ||
the prior of Guiſbrough, ‡ and other free tenants held half a Knight's

---

|| PRIOR DE GISBURNE, Will. Humet liberi Tenentes de Lofthouſe tenent dimid. Feod. in ea-
dem, unde XII. Carucatæ terræ faciunt feod. milit. Et dictus Will. de Humet reddit Ballivo Domini Regis 2s. 4d.   Prior de Guiſburne pro fine reddit 3s.   *Kirkby's Inqueſt.*

‡ THE following poſſeſſions within this pariſh were given to this priory ; viz : *Petronilla*, daughter of Alan de Percy, of Dunſley, relict of William de Giſeburne, quit-claimed one toft, croft, and
one oxgang of land here.   *John de Fauconberge*, Lord of Skelton, gave licence to John de Wirkeſale,
parſon of Eaſington, Walter de Giſeburne, vicar of Stranton, and Rob. de Brocton, late Maſter of
the Hoſpital at Lowcrofs, to give eight oxgangs, with eight tofts in this towaſhip, which John de

fee, where twelve carucates made one Knight's fee. We have no evidence on record, of the fucceeding proprietor of the lands here, which
feem to have been granted out at an early period. Lord Dundas is the
principal proprietor, and Lord of the manor; whofe anceftor purchafed of the late Zachary Moore, Efq. of fquandering memory; and
whofe father is worthy of notice, as being the founder of the Lofthoufe
allum-works.

THE church of Lofthoufe, dedicated to St. Leonard, is rectorial.*
It was given by William de Saucey, to the prior and convent of Guifbrough, and continued a rectory in their patronage till by the diffolution of that monaftry, it came to the Crown.

THE church ftands near the centre of the village towards the fouth,
and is a mean and humble edifice. The neglected condition of this
and feveral other churches within the diftrict, when compared with

---

Everingham had given to them. *William del Fehus,* of North Lofthoufe, fon and heir of Robert,
brother of Simon de Brus, gave one oxgang of land here in *Boythorp Land.* *Thos. fon of Eudo de
Humet,* gave a capital manfe here; which William de Humet, confirmed. *Petronilla,* daughter of
Robert, *the plaifterer,* gave two oxgangs of land. *William de Gifeburne* confirmed the oxgang of
land, and a toft and croft in this territory, which Thos. de Brotton gave with his corpfe. *Hillaria,*
relict of Robert de Furneys, gave two tofts and crofts, and one oxgang here.

Burton's Mon. p. 348.

---

* LOFTHOUSE RECTORY.

DEDICATION. Saint Leonard. The King patron. Firft fruits 10*l.* 11s. 0½d. Tenths 1*l.* 1s.
1¼d. Archd. pro fyn. 7s. 6d. Sub. 18s. od.

INCUMBENTS. 1294. John de Lefyngby. 1297. Will. de Wirkefall. 1314. Thos. de Myd-
delfburgh. — Roger Skyring. 1380. John de Foucotes. 1418. Rich. Driffeld. 1438. Robert
Kirkby. 1468. John Raghton, cl. 1513. Rob. Norham. 1521. Thomas Franke. 1573. Will.
Crofthwayte, cl. *pres. Eliz. Regina.* 1618. Will. Crofthwayte, B. A. *pres. King James.* 1663. Jo-
feph Wood, cl. *pres. King Charles II.* 1676. John Gee, *ly the King.* 1684. Will. Burton, *by the
King.* 1699. Thos. Burton, *by the King.* 1712. Adam Glafs, *by the Queen.* 1713. Edward Haw-
kins, *by the Queen.* 1732. Thos. Murgatroyd, *by the King.* 1780. George Johnfon, B. D. *by the
King.* 1788. William Alfton, M. A. *by the King.* 1799. Charles Baillie, M. A. *by the King;* 1801.
—— Murray, M. A. *by the King.*

X X 2

the convenience and external appearance of the houfes in general of the inhabitants, brought to our recollection the juftly merited reproof of an ingenious writer in the following reflection:

" How loft to piety, to virtue loft
Who with fuperfluous pageantry and pomp
Adorn their manfions, and negleĉt their God!
Their own a palace ;—his, the Lord of all,
Damp, fœtid, loathfome, a fepulchral cave !"

ABOUT two miles to the fouth from Lofthoufe, are the remains of

HANDALE OR GRENDALE ABBEY.

THIS was a fmall priory for Benedictine nuns, dedicated to the bleffed Virgin Mary, and founded in the year 1133, by Richard de Percy; who gave thereunto two tofts, ten acres of demefne land, and common of pafture for two hundred fheep in the town and fields of Dunfley and Grendale. It appears from a charter, printed in the monafticon, that Engram de Bovington gave certain lands at Marton, to this priory, which were afterwards granted by Avicia, priorefs here, in fee-farm, to Ralph, prior and convent of Guifbrough, to hold at the yearly rent of four quarters of Wheat, one half of which to be paid at the feaft of Saint Martin in winter, and the other half at Whitfuntide.

(Dugd. Mon. vol. I. p. 427.)

THE Advowfon of this priory was granted, in the time of King John, by Richard de Percy to Richard de Malbiffe and his heirs for ever, yielding in lieu of all fervices, one pound of incenfe yearly at the feaft of Pentecoft; which by the faid deeds, he affigned to be paid to the faid priory. At the time of the diffolution there were eight nuns, whofe revenues were valued only at 20*l*. 7s. 8d. *per ann.* according to Speed; and at 13*l*. 19s. according to Dugdale. ‡ After

---

‡ ANNE LUTTON was the laft priorefs; and at the diffolution, had an annual penfion of 6*l*. 13s. 4d. affigned her, which fhe enjoyed in the year 1553; at which time there remained in charge thefe penfions; viz. to Alice Brumpton and Mary Lodgame, each 1*l*. 13s. 4d.; to Ifabel Norman, and Cecily Watfon, each 1*l*. 6s. 8d.　　　　　　*Willis's Hift. Abbies, vol. II. p. 278,*

the reformation the fite of the priory was granted (35. Henry VIII.) to Ambrofe Beckwith, a defcendant from the faid Richard Malbiffe; to whom, in the year following, the King gave licence to alienate the fame to William de Percy and others, for the ufe of the faid Ambrofe Beckwith; || in whofe defcendants * it continued for feveral generations, till Roger Beckwith, the laft male defcendant, fold the fame to the late Mr. Sanderfon, of Staithes; by whofe daughter it paffed by marriage to Thomas Richardfon, and has been fince fold to Thomas Stephenfon, Efq. the prefent proprietor.

THERE is little of the monaftic buildings remaining, except the weft end of the chapel; from which it appears to have been of confiderable extent. A cotton manufactory was eftablifhed a few years ago by Mr. Richardfon, on the fite of the priory, for the fpinning and

---

|| REX conceffit licentiam Ambrofio Beckwith alienandi totum illud fcitum Prioratus de Handale in comitatu Ebor. cum omnibus tenuris, dominicalibus prioratus dicti; et diverfas terras in Rowfeby in dict. comitat. Wmo. Perci et aliis ad ufum dicti Ambrofii. *Anno Regni, Hen. VIII. 36to.*

Ex Mfs. W. Conftable, Arm.

* BECKWITH, *of Handale-Abbey.*

Roger Beckwith, of Handale Abbey=. . . . daughter of Peter Newark, in the county of York, Efq.	of Aikham, in co. York, Efq.	

1 Newark Beckwith, of=Mary, dau. of ... Handale Abbey, Efq. | Fifh, of Lexfield, *died* 1656. *ætat.* 66. | in co. Suffolk.	2 Philip.	Mary.	Anne,

Theophania, dau. of=Leonard Beckwith,=Ann, dau. of Thomas .. Grimfton, of Grimfton Garth, in Holdernefs, (1ft wife.)	of Handale Abbey, Efq. ætat. 47. 1666.	Thweng, of Heworth, in co. York, Efq. (2d. wife.)	Mary	Elizabeth, wife of Rob. Lafcelles, of Aireholme, in co. York, Efq.

Roger, fon and heir, æt. 18, 1666.	William died young.	Newark, æt. 16. 1666.	Marmaduke, æt. 9.	Ann.	Mary wife of Philip Garnett, of Delefmill, co. York.

Alben, æt. 1. Ann. 1666.	Helen, æt. 3. Ann. 1666.

Dugdale's Vifitation, A. D. 1666.

weaving of dimities, thickfets, corduroys, &c. but the demand, during the late war was fo much reduced, as to occafion the difcharge of many of the workmen; and the works are now at a ftand.

HANDALE is fituated towards the extremity of the parifh, and commands a pleafing profpect of the fea, from which it is about three miles diftant. The lands here, particularly the old inclofures, are of a fuperior quality, ornamented and fheltered with woods of an ancient growth, befides fome modern plantations in a thriving condition. ‡

ABOUT two miles from the village of Lofthoufe towards the north, we vifited the allum-works here, the property of Lord Dundas; which are carried on in the front of a fteep perpendicular cliff, wafhed by the fea; and feparated from the Boulby works by a narrow ridge of rock, left as a boundary line by the workmen of the refpective proprietors. It would be uninterefting to the reader to enter into a defcription of the works, or to repeat the mode of preparing and chryftallizing the allum, being greatly fimilar to that already noticed in our account of Boulby. We may however remark, that on our approach to the works, we were highly gratified, not only with a view of the vaft excavations, which ftrike the fpectator with a pleafing aftonifhment; but alfo with the profpect from the fummit of the cliffs, which, with the ocean beneath, forms a fpectacle truly interefting and fublime.

THE wide expanfe of water rolling at our feet, with its calm uninterrupted furface covered with innumerable fifhing boats, and veffels of different kinds,—the promontories and head-lands jutting forward at a diftance, as far as the eye can reach, were objects highly pleafing, and peculiarly ftriking:—thefe, with the numerous birds, that have their habitation in the clefts of the rocks beneath, fkimming over the deep in airy evolutions, brought to our recollection, Shakefpeare's

---

‡ FORTY acres of land were planted by Mr. Richardfon in the year 1791, with mixed timber trees, which thrive well; and for which a premium was granted to him by the Society of Arts; an account of which was publifhed in the 14th vol. of their tranfactions, for the year 1796.

beautiful defcription of the cliffs of Dover; which, with a trifling variation, may be applied to the rocks upon this part of the Cleveland.
coaft:

> " How fearful,
> And dizzy 'tis, to caft one's eyes below !
> The crows and choughs that wing the midway air
> Scarce feem fo grofs as beetles ; — halfway down
> Hangs one that gathers famphire ; dreadful trade !
> Methinks he feems no bigger than his head.
> The fifhermen, that walk upon the beach,
> Appear like mice ; and yon tall anchoring bark
> Diminifh'd to her cock ;—her cock a buoy;
> Almoft too fmall for fight.   The murmuring furge,
> That on th' unnumber'd pebbles idly chafes,
> Cannot be heard fo high ;—I'll look no more,
> Left my brain turn, and the deficient fight
> Topple down headlong."   *King Lear.*

WHEN we vifited this fcene, the fea was perfectly calm and tran-
quil ; but, could we have feen it in the wild workings of nature,
when the tempftuous uproar of the waves was agitated by a ftorm ;
and could we, at the fame time, have divefted ourfelves of the horror
that muft arife at the idea of the fufferings and diftrefs of thofe, who
might be expofed to the fury of the elements, what a fublime and awful effect would have been excited in the mind, by the contemplation
of fuch a tremendous fcene !

POPULATION.   This parifh confifts only of one townfhip ; the
population of which, however, owing to the number of workmen employed in the allum-works, is confiderable.   In the year 1801, when an
enumeration was made by order of the legiflature, it appears from the
return † then made, that there were 261 houfes or families, and 1186

† STATE of population, 10th March, 1801.

	Inhabited houfes.	Families.	Uninhabited houfes.	Males.	Females.	Total.	Agriculture.	Trade, and Manu.	Refidue.	Total.
Lofthoufe.	261	261	8	569	617	1186	77	311	798	1186

inhabitants, giving an average of 4½ nearly to each family. As we have not been favoured with the neceſſary extracts from the pariſh regiſters, in order to compare the number of births or baptiſms with that of burials, we are unable to form any idea of the probable increaſe of its inhabitants within any given period.

SOIL, PRODUCE, &c. This and the adjoining pariſh of Eaſington, being ſituated at an equal diſtance from the ſea, their ſoil and produce are greatly ſimilar. The lands towards the north are rather high and naked, declining gradually from the cliffs of the coaſt to the village; from whence they riſe gently, and aſſume a northern aſpect with an extenſive view of the ſea. This pariſh is watered by two ſmall brooks, which form their junction below the village, when the banks, which become ſteep and rugged, are ornamented with wood, and preſent ſome pictureſque and romantic objects.

THE PARISH OF SKELTON.

THERE are few local names, the etymology of which has occasioned greater difference of opinion among our learned antiquaries, than that of Skelton. Camden derives it from *ſkell,* which ſignifies a fountain or rivulet ; and Skinner from the Saxon word Sceale, a balance ; but Mr. Thoreſby is of opinion that Denton's derivation is the moſt proper, who calls it SKALE-TOWN *(Villa ad Skalingas)* as being a village ſituated in that place, where the country people, of ancient time, had certain temporary huts, in the Highlands of Scotland ſtill called *Shields, (Skalingas)* where the ſhepherds, and others employed about cattle, found ſhelter during the Summer, whilſt they depaſtured their cattle on the hills and fertile ſpots at a diſtance from home. ‖

THIS pariſh, comprehending the ſeveral townſhips of Skelton, Brotton, Skinningrove, Kilton, Moreſham and Stanghow, is of conſiderable extent, ſtretching in length from north to ſouth upwards of eight miles ; and is about ſix miles broad. It is bounded by the pariſhes of Lofthouſe and Eaſington on the eaſt ; by Guiſbrough, Upleatham, and Marſk on the weſt ; by Danby on the ſouth ; while its northern limits border on the ſea.

THE village of Skelton ſtands high, ſcattered irregularly on the declivity of an elevated ridge ; and contains ſome neat and commodious buildings. At a little diſtance, towards the north-weſt, ſtands

SKELTON CASTLE,

the ſeat of John Wharton, Eſq. which, having ſuffered much by time,

---

‖ THERE are many of thoſe places called *ſcales,* in the northern counties of England ; and *ſcaling,* a hamlet in this neighbourhood, is ſome confirmation of the etymology we have adopted.

Y y

and ftill more perhaps from family feuds and violence, has, at different periods, undergone confiderable alterations and repairs ; in which tafte and a wifh to preferve the ancient character of the place, have been fo little confulted, that the prefent edifice, we prefume, affords a very inadequate reprefentation of its former grandeur and magnificence.

We are unable, at this remote period, to afcertain the original proprietors of this ancient Caftle ; which, notwithstanding the uncertainty as to the precife æra of its foundation, is undoubtedly of great antiquity ; at lcaft we have hiftorical evidence of its exiftence foon after the Conqueft, when it was granted to *Robert de Brus,* a Norman of confiderable rank and talents, who accompanied the Conqueror intoEngland, and for his great fervices, was rewarded by him with forty-three Lordfhips in the Eaft and Weft Ridings of Yorkfhire, and fifty-one in the North Riding ; whereof the manor and caftle of Skelton was the capital of his barony. This manor, as appears from the Domefday book, was held before the Conqueft by *Uctred ;* but at the time of the furvey, was in the hands of *Richard,* who held then under Robert Earl of Moreton, being thus entered under the title

TERRA COMITIS MORITONIENSIS.

IN SCHELTUN AD GELDUM XIII. CARUCATÆ, ET VII. CAR. POSSUNT ESSE. IBI UCTRED HABUIT I. MANER. NUNC HABET RIC. DE COM. IN DOMINIO I. CAR. ET XII. VILL. CUM III. CAR. ET PRATI ACR. XX. SILVA PAST. II. LEUC. LONG. ET II. QUARENT. LAT. TOT. V. LEUC. LONG. ET II. LAT. T. R. E. XL. SOL. MODO XVI. SOL."

From the above extract it appears that Skelton was taxed for thirteen carucates, and contained feven more that might be rendered arable. There was one carucate in demefne, and twelve villeins with three ploughs, twenty acres of meadow, and a wood with pafturage for deer, two miles long, and two quarentens broad. The whole manor, which was five miles in length, and two miles in breadth, was valued in the Confeffor's time at forty fhillings ; but at the time of the furvey, was worth o ly fixteen fhillings.

It does not appear that this manor continued long in the poffeffion of Robert, Earl of Moreton ; as we find it foon afterwards given by the

Conqueror, to Robert de Brus, to be held of the King *in capite ;* whofe fee within the North Riding, which was granted after the Survey was made, confifted chiefly of lands within the following places, entered under this title : viz.

" Hic eft feudum ROBERTI DE BRUIS, quod fuit datum poftquam LIBER DE WIN-TONIA fcript. fuit ; videlicet ; in NORT. REDING, tenet idem Robertus IN APELTO-NA VI. CAR. TERRÆ ; IN HORNEBI II. CAR. IN WERCHESHALA III. CAR. IN LEUETONA VI. CAR. IN ALIA LEUETONA IIII. CAR. IN BORDELIA II. CAR. IN ERNECLIVE II. CAR. IN ENGLEBI VI. CAR. IN BUSCHEBIA II. CAR. IN CRA-TORNA ET FOXTUN IX. CAR. IN HILTONA III. CAR. IN TORMOZBIA I. CAR. ET DIMID. IN MARTONA IIII. CAR. IN NIUEHAM II. CAR. ET II. BOV. IN TO-LESBI III. CAR. IN ACHELUM II. CAR. IN BERGOLBI I. CAR. IN TORP VI. CAR. IN MORTONA III. CAR. IN NIEUTONA IIII. CAR. ET VI. BOV. IN UPESALE III. CAR. IN CHILDALA VI. CAR. IN ORMESBIA XII. CAR. IN LASINBIA I. CAR. ET DIM. IN GUISEBURNE I. CAR. IN ESTEINTONA I. BOV. IN MORHUSUM DIMID CAR."

THE Bruces continued Lords of Skelton for divers fucceffions ; and making the caftle here their baronial refidence, we may conclude, that whoever might be its original founder, the buildings would receive many of their chief ornaments from that family. In the latter part of the reign of King John, Peter de Brus, then Lord of Skelton, is recorded to have " delighted foe much in the beauty of the chapelle, that he gave " certaine landes unto Henry Percye, upon condition that every chrift-" maffe daye he fhould come to that caftell, and leade his wife by the " arme from her chamber to the chappell." *Cott. Mfs. Julius F. C. fol. 455.*

FROM the Bruces, in the 55th year of the reign of Henry III. Skelton defcended by marriage with Agnes, eldeft daughter of Peter de Brus the third of that name, to Walter de Fauconberge, Lord of Rife ; * who

---

* Ex rotulo claus. de anno regni Regis Edwardi primi primo. *Mem. II.*

PRO Waltero de Fauconberge ⎱ Rex, Johanni de Ryegate, efcatori ultra Trent. *falutem.* Sciatis
et Agnete uxore &c. ⎰ quod cepimus fidelitatem Walteri de Fauconberge qui Agnetem, unam de Sororibus, & Hæredibus Petri de Brus defuncti, qui de nobis tenuit *in capite,* duxit in ux-orem,—de Caftro de Skelton, cum parco citra caftrum, et cum proficuis batalorum *de Cotum* et *Red-*

in the 8th of Edward I. obtained of that prince, a charter of free-warren
in all his demefne lands here. It appears from the claim of the faid
Walter, made in the time of Edward I. in the plea of *quo warranto*, that
the Lords of Skelton enjoyed many liberties ; ‖ and had the privilege
of a market ; which, however fingular it may now appear, was held
weekly on Sunday ; when the people, according to the cuftom of that
age, generally affembled in the morning to attend divine worfhip, and
in the afternoon tranfacted their bufinefs, and regaled themfelves with

ker cum Dominicis de Skelton, pratis, vallibus, et reditibus villæ de Skelton, tam liberorum hominum, quam aliorum, et cum omnibus molendinis et tolneto et manerio *de Marfke* cum omnibus pertinentiis, et cum *Redkere*, et cum villa de *Stanghow*, et cum villa de *Grenrigg* cum pertinent. et cum
forefta de Skelton ; viz. cum Haya, et cum magno parco, et cum *Afdale*, et cum chacea de
Weftwiks cum forr. ficut iter altum extendit fe inter *Stanghow*, at KATERIDING ; et ita ficut
altum iter fe extendit ufque *Lardegate*, et ita per *Skeytebecks* ufque ad *Larthorne*, et ita a divifa
forefta de *Danby* ufque *Colmandale*, *Lokwite*, *Wernelfco*, *Hardale* et *Hale* ; et cum herbagio *de la
Greene* ; et cum herbagio *de la Dinant* ; falva predictis Waltero et Agnete, et fuis villatis communi
paftura ad pecudes et animalia fua, ficut prefatus Petrus et Villata predicta eam habere confueverunt. Quod quidem caftrum et terra predicta eifdem Waltero et Agneti affignavimus in partem ipfi Agneti jure hereditario contingentem de terris tenementis quæ fuerunt predicti Petri, fratris fui, et
ea fibi reddimus tenend. *de nobis in capite* per fervitium quarto partis fervitii, quod idem Petrus nobis
debuit de heriditate fua : Ita quod predictus Walterus coram nobis in adventu noftro in Anglia veniat,
nobis inde homagium fuum facturus. Et ideo vobis mandamus, quod accepta fecuritate a prefatis
Waltero et Agnete de rationabili relevio fuo ad nos inde pertinente nobis reddendo ad fcaccarium
noftrum eifdem Waltero et agneti de predictis caftro, terris et tenementis plenam Seifinam fine dilacione habere fac, tenend. ficut predictum eft.

DAT. per manum W. de Merton cancellarii noftri apud Weftminft. XVIto. die Decemb.

‖ IN clamea *de quo warranto* in com. Ebor. et alibi tempore Regis Edwardi primi,—inter alia fic
continetur, ut fequitur.

WALTERUS DE FAUCONBERGE clamat habere libertates fubfcriptas ; viz quoddam mercatum in
Villa *de Skelton*, qualibet Septimana per diem dominicum, et Emendationem Panis et Cerviciæ in eadem Villa. Et *Soke* et *Saka*, *Infangthief*, *Tol*, et *Team*, *Furcas*, *Pillory* et *Tumbercle* in eadem Villa
de *Skelton* in wapentag. de Langberge de Hereditate Agnetis uxoris fuæ una heredum Petri de Brus,
nuper defuncti. Et clamat liberam chaceam et warrenam per omnes diverfas terras fuas in wapentag. de Langberge ; fcilicet in *Skelton*, *Marfk. Grenrigg*, *Redker* et *Stanghow*. Idem clamat medietatem wrecci maris per Cofteram maris de *Blakescore* ufque *Runefwick*. Idem clamat medietatem
balliæ wapentag. de Langberge de hereditate Agnetis uxoris. Item, clamat habere &c. &c.

oat-ale, the homely beverage of our anceftors. † This market continued to be thus held, till the 13th Edward II. when John, Lord Fauconberge, obtained a licence from the King for changing it from Sunday
to Saturday; and alfo for a fair yearly upon the Monday, in Whitfun-
week, and two days following; but the market and fair have been
both long difcontinued.

The family of Fauconberge flourifhed here for many generations;
and at different periods may be fuppofed to have added feveral works
to the caftle, and greatly to have ftrengthened and ornamented the
whole. ‡

At length male iffue failing in Sir Thomas Fauconberge, Knight,
Skelton, with other lands, paffed by marriage with Joan his daughter,
to Sir William Neville, Knight, who foon after had livery of her eftates;
and in the feventh year of the reign of Henry the fixth, was created in
her right, Lord Fauconberge, and afterwards honoured by King Edward the fourth, with the title of Earl of Kent. He died 3. Edw. IV.
and left three daughters coheireffes: Alicia the youngeft married John
Conyers, afterwards Lord Conyers; who, upon the partition of the eftate, had the caftle and manor of Skelton, &c. which remained in this
family till the 3d and 4th of Philip and Mary; when John Lord Conyers dying without male-iffue, his three daughters became his heirs: *
Anne, the youngeft, married Anthony Kempe, Efq. whofe undivided
third part was purchafed *(20 Elizabeth)* by Robert Trotter, Efq. under
the defcription of all that undivided third part of the Lord Conyers'
lands, which fell to him in right of Anne his wife, in Skelton, Brotton,

† This cuftom continued without alteration till the reign of Edw. 4. when, in order to prevent
the irreligious profanation of the Lord's day, it was abolifhed by Act of Parliament; and the feveral Lords of manors, where fuch markets were kept, were empowered to appoint them to be held on
fome other day of the week.

‡ John, Lord Fauconberge, in the year 1330, rebuilt the chapel within the caftle; and alfo the
hall and other buildings there.

* See the pedigree, at pages 47, 48, 49.

Marſke, Eſton, Redcar, Upleatham, Stanghow, and Girrick. The remaining two thirds continued in the deſcendants of the other two daughters of the Lord Conyers, (who married Thomas Darcy, and John Atherton, Eſqrs.) till the year 1656; when by exchange or purchaſe, ‡ the whole became ſolely veſted in the deſcendants of the ſaid Robert Trotter; and continued in that family till the year 1727, when Lawſon Trotter, Eſq. the laſt male deſcendant, who died old and unmarried, ſold the ſame to Joſeph Hall, Eſq. of the city of Durham, who had married his ſiſter Catherine, anceſtor to the preſent proprietor.

TROTTER, of SKELTON CASTLE;
(With the connecting branches of HALL and STEVENSON.)

Robert Trotter, of — Iſabel, daughter of
Pickering, Eſq. | - - - Forcer, Eſq.

ARMS. *Arg.* a lion rampant *ſable*; a chief, *ermine.*

Robert Trotter, of — Margaret, daughter
Skelton Caſtle, Eſq. | of - - - Pudſey.
ob. 1611.

Sir Henry Trotter, of — Catherine, daughter of Anthony
Skelton Caſtle, Knt. | Witham, of Cliffe, *co. Ebor.* Eſq.
ob. 1625.

Urſula, daughter of Sir = George Trotter of — Mary, dau. of Sir   Robert   Dorothy.   Eliz. wife
Richard Chomley, of | SkeltonCaſtle,Eſq. | EdwardBoyce, of   died   of George
Whitby, Knt.(1ſt wife.) | ob. 1647. | Fredvil, co. Kent.   young   Nevill, of
                                           | (2d. wife)   - - co. Kt.

Henry died
unmarried.   Edward Trotter, of Skelton — Mary, daughter of   Hugh   Mary, wife of John
              Caſtle, co. York, Eſq. (ob. | Sir John Lowther,   Fulthorpe, of Tun-
              1708. *æt.* 71.) | of Lowther, in W.   George.   ſtall, co. Durham.
                                          | Knight and Bart.
                                          | ob. 1681.(1ſt wife.

John Trotter, — Elizabeth, daughter of   Mary.   Catherine. — W. Bower, Eſq.   Anne
ob. vita patris | Godfrey Lawſon, mer-   Elizabeth.   Margaret. — Geo.Lawſon, Eſq.   d. un-
1701.*ætat.*42. | chant at Leeds.   (ob. vita patris.)   Hannah. — CharlesPerrot. Eſq.   mar.

‡ THE heirs of Robert Trotter, in the year 1654, exchanged one third of Eſton, with Henry Stapylton, Eſq. for one third of Skelton, which had been purchaſed of the heirs of Lord Conyers by the ſaid Henry Stapylton's anceſtors; and afterwards in the year 1656, purchaſed the remaining third of Skelton of the heirs of Lord Conyers.

6 Robert,   5 Henry,   4 George,   3 John,   2 Edward   1 Lawfon | 2 Elizabeth,   3 Mary.   4 Mar-
d. unmar.   d.unmar.   d. unmar.   d.unmar.   d. unmar.   Trotter,Ef. | ob.unmarried   garet,
                                      fold Skelton | ob. in-

HALL.   to J. Hall, | fans.
                                        E. and died
                                        unmarried.

Jofeph Hall, of the City of Durham,__Catherine Trotter, eldeft daughter   **STEVENSON.**
Efq. purchafed Skelton, of Lawfon | of John Trotter, of Skelton Caftle,
Trotter; he was buried in Croffgate | Efq. (*ob.* 1740. *æt.* 46.)   John Stevenfon,__... dau.
Church, in the faid city, 1733.   of Byerftede,co. | of . . .
                                                           Durh.

Frances married Wal-   George Hall__... dau.   Thomas Hall__..... d.
ter Hawkefworth of   colonel in the | of Lord   a General. | of .....   Ambrofe Ste-__Anne, el-
Hawkefworth,c.Ebor.   army. | W. Man- | Carter   venfon, of Ma- | deft dau.of
Efq. whofe fon Walter | ners. | of ...c.   nor Houfe, in | An.Whar-
took the furname of   A daughter. | Camb.   the parifh of | ton, of Gil-
Fawkes to him and his   Lanchefter, | ling-wood,
iffue.   John.   Elizabeth.   co. Durham. | Efq.

John Hall, of Skelton Caftle, Efq.__Anne Stevenfon,   Frances, wife of William
took the name of Stevenfon in ad- | ob. 1790; buried   Farquarfon, of . . . .
dition. Died 25 March 1785. ætat. | at Skelton.   living 1795,a widow.S.P.
67. buried at Skelton.

John Hall,   Jofeph-William Hall-Stevenfon, of__Anne, daughter and heir of James Forfter,
eldeft fon   Skelton Caftle, Efq. and of Drum- | of Drumgoon, co. Fermanagh, in the King-
died unm.   goon, in the Kingdom of Ireland, | dom of Ireland, Efq. living 1806.
           2d fon; (ob. 1786. ætat. 45. buri-
           ed at Skelton.)

John Hall Stevenfon, of Skelton Caftle, Efq. M. P. for Be-__Sufan Mary Anne, 2d daughter of
ver ey, in the County of York. By Royal Sign Manual | General John Lambton, of Lamb-
dated May 3d (28. G. III.) he and the heirs of his body | ton, in the County of Durham;
were authorifed to affume the furname of WHARTON, and | married at Lambton, Oct. 1790.
no other; and alfo to bear the Arms of WHARTON only,
which were exemplified accordingly by patent, dated 5.
June following.

Margaret, 2d daughter.   Sufan, eldeft daughter.

John Rawdon,__Fanny Hall.   Margaret Hall,   3. William Hall,   2. James Hall, Ma
the next bro- | unmarried.   M. A. Vicar of   jor General of th
ther to Francis | Gilling, &c.   21ft Reg. of Light
Earl of Moira, | Dragoons.
married Dec. |
1793.

In an ancient MS. in the *Cotton library*, containing a defcription of the Lordfhip of Guifbrough, and the adjacent coaft, we find the following notice of Skelton Caftle.

" On the right Hande an antyent Caftle all rente and torne, and yt
" feemed rather by the Wit and Wyolence of Man, than by the envye
" of Tyme, fhewed ytfelf on the Syde of a broken Banke. I demanded
" of my Guide how the Caftle was named, and what Misfortune had
" foe miferablye depraved yt.

" S* quoth he, yt is *Skelton Caftle*, the ancyent inheritance of the Lord
" Bruce, and dignifyed with the Title of an Honnor, which by Marri-
" age came to the Lord Falconbridge, and fucceffively to the Lord Con-
" yers, who leaving three Daughters, Copartners of his Eftate, much
" Varyance fell betwixt the Hufbands for the Divifion of their Shares,
" that neither Partye being inclyned to yeld unto other, evry one for
" Defpite ruyned that parte of the Caftle whereof he was in poffeffion,
" left afterwards by Suyte of Lawe the Lott fhould fall to another, in-
" fomuch that the goodlye Chappell, one of the Jewells of this King-
" dome, rudely went to the Grounde, with the fayre Hall and large
" Towers : fo that now fcarcelye are the Ruynes of a Chappell to be
" feene, fuche Barbarifme rafeth out the Glorye of noble Familyes, when
" an entyre Right of Inheritance is not invefted in the Perfon of one
" Man."   *Cott. MS. Julius, F. C. Fol.* 455.

In the prefent manfion, which underwent a complete repair in the year 1794, when confiderable additions and improvements were made to the buildings and grounds adjoining, we find few traces of the ancient edifice, except in the back part, now converted into kitchen offices.

The caftle prefents a long extended front to the weft, fituated on the brink of a fmall ftream ; which, by being collected into a refervoir, forming an extenfive fheet of water, with floping banks, adds greatly to the natural beauties and furrounding ornaments of the place.

Drawn by J. Bird.

Engd by R. Scott.

SKELTON   CASTLE
The Seat of John Wharton Esqr M.P.
To whom this plate is most respectfully Dedicated by The Editor.

THE interior part of the manfion is elegant and commodious, with an excellent modern ftair cafe, and a fuit of genteel apartments. There are fome armorial bearings in painted glafs ftill preferved ; and in one of the windows in the front of the caftle, there is a fhield, bearing the arms of Trotter ; viz. *arg.* a lion rampant, *fable* ; a chief, *ermine* ; empaling the arms of Forcer, Pudfey, Witham, Chomley, Boyce, and Lowther ; which point out the intermarriages of that family after they became proprietors.

WE cannot conclude our account of this celebrated feat, without noticing, that while it was in the poffeffion of John Hall, Efq. § author of the *Crazy-Tales*, &c. its feftive board was attended by many of the *literati* of the age ; among whom, *Sterne* was of the number of its frequent vifitants. Where genius and talent were blended in fuch clofe union, we cannot but imagine that " *the feaft of reafon, and the flow of foul*," were happily realized.

§ THE following brief memoir of *John Hall*, of Skelton Caftle, Efq. author of *Crazy-Tales*, and other pieces of fingular merit, is extracted from the laft improved edition of his works, publifhed by J. Debrett, in the year 1795.

THIS gentleman was a native of the county of York, where he inherited a confiderable paternal eftate, of which *Skelton Caftle*, near Guifbrough, was the family feat. He was born in 1718, and died March 1785. Where he was inftructed in the firft rudiments of learning we have no information ; but it is well known that he completed his claffical education at Jefus' College in the Univerfity of Cambridge. Here it has been generally fuppofed that the friendfhip commenced between him and *Mr. Sterne*, who was of the fame College, which continued without interruption, while they were both fpared to enjoy it : though, as they were both educated in Yorkfhire, it is not improbable that their acquaintance might have commenced at a more early period. *Mr. Hall* afterwards made the tour of Europe ; and that he had made it with the beft effect, was evident in his converfations upon the fubjects connected with it. He was an excellent claffic-fcholar, and perfectly acquainted with the *Belles Lettres* of Europe. He could engage in the grave difcuffions of criticifm and literature with fuperior power, while he was qualified to enliven general fociety with the fmile of *Horace*, the laughter of *Cervantes* ; or he could fit in *Fontaine's* eafy chair, and unbofom his humour to his chofen friends. When he refided in London, he lived as other men of the world do, whofe philofophy partakes more

Z z

Pedigree of WHARTON.

(Extracted from the records of the College of Arms, London ; by ISAAC HEARD, Garter.)

ARMS.   *Sable*, a maunch, *argt.*
CREST.   On a wreath, a bull's head erafed, proper, *argt.* horns, *or*.
MOTTO.   *Generofus nafcitur,non fit.*

Henry Wharton, of Wharton, on the banks of the river Eden, in Parifh of Kirkby Stephen, in the co. Weftmorland, living 10. H. V. = Elizabeth, daughter of Sir Thos. Mufgrave, of Harcla Caftle, in co. Weftmorland, Knight.

Thomas Wharton, of Wharton Caftle, co. Weftmorland ; from whom the LORD WHARTONS defcended. = . . . daughter of . . . Lowther of Lowther, co. Weftmorland.

Gilbert Wharton, 2d fon. ob. 1436. = Joan, d. and fole heir of . . . Kirkby, of Kirkby Thore, co. Weft.

John Wharton, of Kirkby Thore. = Ifabella, d. of John Lancafter, of Brampton, (married 18. Hen. VI.)

Henry Wharton, Rector of Kirkby Thore, co. Weftmorland.

John Wharton, of Kirkby Thore, Council to Lord Clifford, 21 Henry VII. = . . . d. and coheir of . . . Fenwick of Wallington, co. North.

Chriftopher Wharton 2d fon, anceftor of the Whartons of Old Park, county Durham. =

Margaret married to William, fon of Thos. Wyllorg, of Clifton, co. Weft. Efq.

Katherine, daughter of John Machell, of Crackenthorpe, co. Weftmor. Efq. (1*ft wife*.) = Gilbert Wharton, of Kirkby Thore, in 4. H. VIII. fettles that eftate and others to the ufe of Katharine his wife during the minority of John his fon and heir. (ob. 1552.) = Elizabeth, dau. of . . . Crackenthorpe, of Newbiggin, co. Weft. Efq. 2. Edw. VI. (2d. *wife*.)

John Wharton. =
John Wharton, of Winfton. (ob. 1628.)

John Wharton, of Kirkby Thore, Efq. fon and heir. (ob. 6. James I. = Cecily, daughter of Sir John Thornborough, of Selfide, co. Weft. Knt. 14. *Eliz*.

Anthony Wharton, of Regell-Grange, co. Weftmorland. = Mary, daughter of John Beane, Alderman of York, and Lord Mayor thereof, 1568.

---

of *Epicurus* than the *porch ;* and in the country, when Skelton Caftle was without company, and he was threatened with the fpleen, to which he was occafionally liable, he had recourfe to a very fine library, and a playful mufe.

THAT he was a man of fingular genius, and a peculiar caft of thought, muft be acknowledged by all who read his works ; * that, while he caught the ridicule of life, he felt for its misfortunes, will be equally evident to thofe who read the page that contains the epitaph on *Zachary Moore ;* and nothing furely can be wanting to confirm the latter opinion, when we have added that he was the *Eugenius* of Mr. Sterne.

* As an apology for his performances, the author has obferved, that " outcries againft writings, compo-
" fed with no worfe intention than to promote good humour and chearfulnefs, by fighting againft the *Te-*
" *dium Vitæ*, were referved for an age of refined hypocrify. There ought to be a great diftinction between
" obfcenity evidently defigned to inflame the paffions, and a ludicrous liberty, which is frequently neceffary
" to fhew the true ridicule of hypocritical characters ; which can give offence to none, but fuch as are
" afraid of every thing that has a tendency to *unmafking*."

Humphrey Wharton, of ⎯ Agnes, daughter of Richard
Gilling-Wood, near Rich- | Cleburne. of Cleburne, co.
mond, co. Ebor. ob. 1635. | Weftmorland.

Sir Anthony Whar- Several Eliz. dau. and ⎯ Thomas Whar- ⎯ Sufannah d. of Philadel- ⎯ R. Mit-
ton. Knt. Lieut.Col. other heir of B.Lam- | ton, of Gilling- Sir T. Hayes, phia. | ford, of
to Henry Lord Per- children. bert, of Calton, | Wood, eldeft Lord Mayor of | Mitford
cy, and Dep. Gov. co. Ebor. | fon. ob. 1641. London. | Caftle,
of Oxford, Temp. | granted
King Ch. I. Humphrey Wharton, of ⎯ Mary d. of Chrift. by K. C.
Gilling-Wood, and of | Byerley, of Mid- I.
Kirkby Thore, Efq. (a- | ridge Grange, co.
ged 41, 1669.) | Durham. Geo. Reveley, ⎯ Barbara.
of Tropple, or |
Margaret, d. of Sir Wm. ⎯ Anthony Wharton, 1 Humphrey. Newton Under- |
Hicks, of Beverfton Caf- | of Gilling-Wood, E. 2 Robert. wood, co. Northd. |
tle, co Glou. Bart. and | (4. fon.) 3 Chriftopher
of Ruckholts, co. Effex. | W. Revely, of ⎯ . . . dau. and heir
Newby-Wifk, | of Simon Welby,
co. Ebor. | of Newby-Wifk.

Langdale Smithfon, 2d ⎯ Philadelphia.
fon of Sir Hugh Smith- |
fon. Bart. |

Hugh Smithfon, Duke of Northumberland, &c. took the name and Arms of
Percy, ob. 1786. ætat. 74.

Mary Wharton, of the parifh of St. Mi- William Margaret Wharton, Ann, eldeft ⎯ Ambrofe
chael's, York, youngeft child, died unmar- died of York, Spinfter, dau. bapt. Stevenfon,
ried 1776. ætat. 70. buried in York Minf- unmarried bapt. at Low Lay- at LowLay- of Manor-
ter. Names in remainder after the iffue 1746. ton, co. Effex, 24. Ap. ton, 10. Au. houfe, in co.
of her Neice ANN HALL, *Henry Reve-* 1697. died 1788. 1695. Durham.
ley of Newby-Wifk for life, remainder to
his fons, to take the name and arms of Ann Stevenfon, ⎯ John Hall, of Skelton
Wharton, or forfeit ; remainder to *Thomas* ob. 1790. buri- | Caftle, Efq. who took the
Wharton of Old-Park, co. Durham, Efq. ed at Skelton. | name of *Stevenfon* in ad-
and his heirs. dition. ob. 1785. ætat. 67.

See *Trotter's Pedigree*.

THE church of Skelton is a neat modern edifice, and ftands in a retired fituation at a fmall diftance from the village towards the north-
weft. It was anciently endowed with rectorial rights ; and was given
by Robert de Brus to the priory of Guifbrough ; but being appropriated
thereto, without any ordination of a vicarage, it was reduced to a per-

petual curacy, and at the diffolution of the priory, was given by King
Henry VIII. to the Archbifhop of York, who is the patron and nominates the curate. †

THIS church, dedicated to All-Saints, was certified to the governours of Queen Anne's bounty at 29*l*. 3s. 4d. and in the year 1715, was
augmented by a benefaction of 200*l*. procured by the intereft of Mrs.
Trotter, which, with a like fum obtained from the governours of the
bounty of Queen Anne, has been fince laid out in the purchafe of a freehold eftate within the parifh.

THERE was a chantry within the church, called Skelton-chantry;
founded according to Torr, in the year 1325, by Adam de Skeiton,
" who (having obtained the licence of John Lord Fauconberge, Lord of
" Skelton, and the King's licence alfo, 18. Edward I.) gave to the prior
" and convent of Drax, one meffuage and one carucate and a half of
" land in *Hylton*, in Cleveland; for which donation they granted to him
" for ever, that they would find one perpetual chaplain every day in
" the year to celebrate divine offices in the church of Skelton in Cleve-
" land, for the fouls of him the faid Adam and Margaret his wife; of
" Peter his father and Alicia his mother &c. And to allow the faid
" chaplain and his fucceffors *five marks* per ann. ftipend; who, within
" two months after every vacation, fhall be prefentable by him the faid
" Adam during his life; and after his deceafe, by the prior and convent
" of Drax, and their fucceffors."

---

† SKELTON CURACY.

DEDICATION, All-Saints.　Cert. val. 29*l*. 3s. 4d.　Archbifhop of York, patron.

CURATES.

1715　Matthew Walters, Curate.
1723　John Foulis, Curate.
1727　George Flower.
1730　Thomas Tancred.
1733　Thomas Caftley.
1760　Thomas Kitching.
1770　John Parrington

" THE ordination of this chantry was, according to the tenor of
" the premises, made by William, Archbishop of York *(apud Cawood)*
" on the 2d non. Septemb. 1327." *   *Torr's MS.*

MONUMENTAL INSCRIPTIONS.

ON a marble monument, within the church, is the following inscription :

To the
Memory of
JOHN TROTTER, Esqr.
who departed
this Life
Decemr. 23d. 1701.
in the 42d. Year
of his Age.
He married
ELIZABETH
Daughter of
GODFREY LAWSON, Esqr.
a Merchant of Leeds,
by whom she had six Sons
LAWSON, EDWARD, Rector
of Legstone. JOHN, Grocer &
Citizen of London. GEORGE,
an Officer in the army.
HENRY, Fellow of Jesus
College, Cambridge, and
Rector of Gravely in that
County ; and ROBERT who died
an Infant ; their daughters were
ELIZABETH, who died unmarried,
MARY, wife of THOMAS PURCHAS Esqr.
of Blaithwaite. Margaret, who died
in her Infancy, and CATHERINE,

Wife of JOSEPH HALL Esqr. who died
Septr. 29th. 1740, and was buried near her
Husband at Crossgate-Church, in the
City of Durham, having survived
him seven years. in the 46th year
of her age.
The said ELIZABETH TROTTER
gave, June 2d. 1715, one Hundred Pounds
and procured the like sum from her Relations
with which, and two hundred pounds given
by the Governors of Queen Anne's Bounty
this Curacy was augmented,
and the Money since laid out
in the purchase of Freehold Lands
in this parish.
She also gave by her Will fifty pounds
to the Charity School at Leeds, the place of her birth.
She died at Durham, Sep 23d, 1726, aged 63 years,
and was buried at the Church of St. Mary-le-Bow
in that City She passed through life with the general
Esteem of all Ranks and Degrees & was indeed a
woman of true and unaffected piety ; and died as
she had lived, without an Enemy.
JOHN TROTTER her Husband, died of that
painful distemper the Gout, with which he had
been many years afflicted, and which he
always bore with remarkable Patience and
Resignation, being a person of true piety.

---

* CATALOGUE OF CANTARISTS.

5. Non. Oct. 1327.	John de Malton,	Cap.	(pres. Adam de Skelton)
——	John de Driffield,	Cap.	ibid.
24. Oct. 1349.	Robert de Newland,	Cap.	(prior and convent, Drax.)

THE townfhip of

BROTTON

lies about two miles diftant from the village of Skelton towards the north-eaft. This was an ancient manor, taxed in the Conqueror's fur-vey for twelve carucates, and contained fix more that might be render-ed arable, entered under the title

"TERRA COMITIS MORITONIENSIS.

" IN BROCTUNE AD GELDUM XII. CARUCATÆ; ET VI. CAR. POSSUNT " E SE. IBI UCTRED HABUIT I. MANERIUM. NUNC HANC HABET RIC. DE " COMITE. IN DOMINIO I. CAR. ET VIII. VILLANI CUM III. CAR. IBI XII. " AC. PRATI. TOTUM MANERIUM I. LEUC. ET DIMID. LONGUM. ET I. LA-" TUM. T. R. E. VALEBAT XX. SOLID. MODO XIII. SOLID. ET IIII. DENAR."

" D HOC MANERIUM JACET SOCA IN MERSC. X CARUCAT. AD GEL-" DUM ET V. CAR. AD ARAND. IBI EST I. VILLANUS ARANS CUM II. BO-" BUS ET X. AC. PRATI."

On the north-wall, within the Church, there is a monument, with the following infcription :

EDVARDUS TROTTER Arm.ger
Ad boreale Latus adftantis Altaris
Exuvias mortales depofuit ;
Vir vere pius
Qui Conclavis, Templi, Altaris juge Sacrificium
Affiduo Cultu decoravit;
Cujus etiam

Gratiffima   Amicos Amænitas
Prodiga   Egenas Erogatio
Eximia erga Proximos Charitas
Spectata   Omnes Probitas
Mores denique Suavitate fingulari imbuti
Nomen pofteritati cogunt inclarefcere :
Natus Martii 19º 1637º
Denatus Februarii 8. 1708º
Viridi vegetaque Senectute in Domino obdormivit.
Duas duxit Uxores ; Priorem
MARIAM
JOHANNIS LOWTHER, DE LOWTHER

in Comitatu Weftmorl. Baronetti, Filiam,
Ex qua tres Filios, at undecim Filias fufcepit ;
Alteram ANNAM
EDWARDI CHALLONER de Gifbrough Equitis
Aurati, viduam,
Ex qua nulla proles.
Quumque tantum Filias fuperftites reliquit
Quarum Quatuor, (viz.)
KATHARINA, Relicta GUIL. BOWER de
Bridlington, Arm. MARGARETTA Uxor
GEORGII LAWSON de Harlfey, Arm. HAN-
NAH Uxor Honorabilis admodum CAROLI
PARROTT, Arm.
Civitatis Ebor. nunc Prætoris ;
ANNA cælebs, quas Teftamento noviffimo
Executrices infcripferat,
Monumentum hoc P. M. S.
Mæfte pofuere
Anno 1710º

FROM which it appears that there was one carucate in demefne, and eight villeins with four ploughs, and twelve acres of meadow ; that the manor was one mile and a half long, and one mile broad, valued in the Confeffor's time, at twenty fhillings ; but at the time of the furvey was only worth thirteen fhillings and four pence. There was alfo a foke of ten carucates *ad geldum* belonging to this manor, at Marfk, where there was one villein ploughing with two oxen, and ten acres of meadow.

BROTTON, before the conqueft, was in the hands of *Uctred ;* but when the furvey was made, was held by *Richard,* of Robert Earl of Moreton. It was afterwards granted to Robert de Brus, Lord of Skelton ; and defcended by marriage with Lucia, fifter and coheir of Peter de Brus the fourth, to Marmaduke de Thweng ; whofe pofterity enjoyed it till Thomas, a clergyman fucceeding to the inheritance, died without iffue (48. Edw. III.) and left his lands to the defcendants of his three fifters. Lucia the eldeft married Robert de Lumley ; and had this and other eftates affigned to her upon the partition ; of which, his defcendants continued proprietors till the reign of Henry VIII. when by attainder of John Lord Lumley, they came to the crown. The lands have been fince fold out in parcels ; a confiderable part of which is now the property of John Wharton, Efq. which was purchafed of the Pennymans, in the reign of Queen Elizabeth, by Robert Trotter, of Skelton Caftle.

BROTTON is an ancient chapelry, dependant on the church, and ferved by the curate of Skelton ; but the certified value has not been ftated, nor does it appear to what faint the chapel is dedicated. It enjoys parochial rights, and was augmented in the year 1718, by a donation of 200*l.* given by Mrs. Trotter ; which procured a like fum from the governours of Queen Anne's bounty. *

---

* AT the caft end of the chapel there is a large mural monument, with the following infcription.
Sacred to the Memory of WILLIAM TULLIE of Kilton
in this County, Efqr. who departed this Life XXVI. of May
MDCCXLI, aged LXXII, and is interred underneath this Monument.

THE chapel is a fmall edifice, but commands an extenfive profpect, and is an object that prefents itfelf to the view of the traveller at a confiderable diftance from the eaft, being fituated on the fummit of an elevated ridge, running north and fouth; the northern extremity of which is wafhed by the fea, and terminates in a fteep and lofty eminence, called *Huntcliff-Nab;* where, as Camden obferves, " the fhore, " which for a long way together has lain open, now rifes into high " rocks; and here and there at the bottom of the rocks, lie great ftones " of feveral fizes, fo exactly formed round by nature, that one would " think them bullets caft by fome artift for the great guns : if you " break them, you find within ftony ferpents wreathed up in circles, but " generally without heads."·‡

SALTBURN, a fmall hamlet within this chapelry, ftands about two miles to the north-weft, and confifts of a few houfes fcattered irregularly upon the fea-fhore, inhabited chiefly by fifhermen. The *Cott,*

He married ANN, fole Daughter and Heirefs of Thomas Thweng of Kilton Caftle in this County Efqr. by whom he left no Iffue: fhe died VII. of September MDCCXIX, and is buried in the fame Vault as her Hufband. He was univerfally efteemed for the Goodnefs of his Temper, the Candour of his Manners, and the Integrity of his Conduct; his Honour was ever unimpeached, his Generofity was diffufive and unaffected,—The exquifite Gratification of a mind naturally benevolent and fufceptible, a gratefulˉreturn for general efteem, which. tho' his Merit claimed, he was too humble to think he deferved : in Sweetnefs of Difpofition few have equalled,—none furpaffed him : no adverfe accident made him morofe or paffionate : no profperous Gale of Fortune fwelled him with Haughtinefs : thofe who lived conftantly with him, never faw him but equal, placid, engaging. JOSEPH TULLIE, his Nephew, now of Kilton Efqr. impreffed with a due Senfe of his many amiable Qualities, caufed this Marble to be erected—to perpetuate the Memory of one whom he affectionately loved, and whom all fhould imitate.

‡ *See notes at page* 339.

MS. which we have occafionally quoted in the progrefs of this work, affords the following defcription of this part of the Cleveland coaft. " At Saltburne Mouth a fmale Brooke difchargeth ytfelf into the Sea, " wch lyeinge lowe under the Banks, ferveth as a Trunke or Conduite " to convey the Rumor of the Sea into the neighbour Fieldes ; for when " all Wyndes are whifte, and the Sea restes unmoved as a ftanding " Poole, fometymes there is such a horrible Groninge heard from that " Creake at the leaft fix Myles in the mayne Lande, that the fifhermen " dare not put forth, thoughe Thyrfte of Gaine drive them on, hould- " ing an opinion that the Sea, as a greedy Beafte raginge for Hunger, " defyers to be fatiffyed wth Mens Carcafes."

" TOWARDS *Huntfcliffe* and *Bullfleet-Gate*, there are certain Rockes " that at lowe water are left difcovered, whereupon Seales in greate " Heardes like Swine ufe to fleepe and bafke themfelves againft the " Sunne ; for their better fecuritye they put in ufe a kind of military " Difcipline, warily preparing againft a foddaine Surprize, for on the " outermoft Rocke one great Seale or more keepes Sentinell, which " upon the firft inklinge of any Danger, giveth the Allarme to " the reft by throweing of Stones, or making a Noife in the water, " when he tumbles down from the Rocke, the reft immediately doe " the like, infomuch that yt is very hard to overtake them by Cun- " ning : yf yt fortune that any unawares hath chofen his fleepinge " forthe fo far from the Sea, that he is in Hazard to become a Praye to " the purfuer, he then betaketh himfelfe to his Armes, flynginge the " Pebbles and Sand from his hinder Feete with fuche a tempefte and " force, that a man had neede be well advifed before he approache too " neere ; they flye the fight of Men as of thofe from whom they have " received many fhrewde Turnes : where the poore Women that ga- " ther Cockles and Muffels on the Sandes, by often ufe, are in better

" Credyte with them.   Therefore whoe foe intends to kill any of them
" muft craftely put on the Habyte of a woman,. to gayne Grounde
" within the ßeache of his peece. ‖

 " It was ftreange to me and hard to be believed, that you had a
" yonge Seale taken upon the Seye Sande, w.ᶜʰ for the Space of a Moneth
" was kepte in your parloure, feedinge him with Milke and Breade
" which yt fucked greedily, and that in a few Dayes he knew his
" Keeper foe well that he woulde crawle after him lowinge aloud, from
" the Parlour to the Kitchen ; when upon the Hearthe, after his Belly
" was well fyled, he ufed to turn up his Syde to the Greate of the
" Fyre. He dyed as yt was tolde me by the Mifhappe of one that
" unawares treade on his Head. After that he had been a Weeke in
" the Houfe, and felte the Refrefhinge of the Fyre, he could never en-
" dure the Water, thoughe you threwe him often tymes into yt, and
" was willinge to let him efcape, but he ever returned to the Lande,
" and with a mournful Crye, as it were bemoaning himfelf to the Com-
" panie, would creep to the next he fawe and nible about their Feet,

---

‖ Olaus Magnus, Archbifhop of Upfall, fays " the Sea-calf, which alfo in latine is called Hel-
" cus, has it name from the likenefs of a land-calf, and it hath a hard flefhy body, and therefore is
" hard to be killed, but by breaking the temples of the head. It hath a voice like a bull, four feet,
" but not his ears, becaufe the manner and manfion of its life is in the waters.—She bringeth forth
" her young on the land, as cattle do, and fuckleth them at her dugs, but never more than two at
" once. She doth not bring her young from the land into the fea before it be 12 days old, and by
" degrees ufeth it to it." He further adds, " as a man and horfe, fo doth the fea calf grow grey ;
" and the young ones always reverence the elder ; for where 30 or 40 lye on the rocks afleep, as
" flocks of fheep, it hath been faithfully obferved, that the young ones and the old ones fleep afun-
" der ; and when one of the old ones goes down into the waters, not one of them will ftay behind
" on the mountain, rock, nor plain, or any part of the ice, unlefse it be to bring forth. If the fea
" be boyfterous and rife, fo doth the fea-calf's hair ; if the fea be calm, the hair is fmooth ; and thus
" may you know the ftate of the fea in a dead fkin. The Bothnick mariners conjecture by their
" own cloaths, that are mode of thefe fkins, whether the fea fhall be calm and their voyage profper-
" ous, or they fhall be in danger of fhipwrack."

                                                                    Book xx. Chap. 4: 5,

" not ceafing till fome one had taken him up in their Armes to carry
" him back again ; he was white, as having his Pigges hair yet on him,
" and not paft three Quarters of a Yeare longe."

THE townfhip of

SKINNENGRAVE,

or, as it is fometimes written *Skengrave*, and *Skynnergrefe*, lies to the
eaft. The village, which is fituated at the foot of a low creek near the
fea, is fmall; and the whole townfhip does not contain more than
about feventy inhabitants.

THIS was an ancient manor belonging to the Bruces, Lords of
Skelton, and came by marriage to the Thwengs of Kilton. Lucia, the
daughter and heir of Robert de Thweng, was firft married to William
Lord Latimer, afterwards to Robert de Everingham, and thirdly to
Bartholomew Fanacourt, to whom fhe conveyed the manor of Skinnengrave, with a fourth part of the wreck of Sea, between Runfwick
and Yarm ; of which he died feized 26. Edward III. but being a ftranger, and dying without iffue, the fame came to the Crown. The faid
manor of Skinnengrave, and all the lands and tenements which belonged to the faid Bartholomew Fanacourt, were afterwards granted by
King Edward the third, in the 33d year of his reign, to Peter de Routh,
to be held of the King *in capite ;* and in the forty-firft year of the faid
King's reign, he granted the fame to Sir William de Everingham,
Knight, and his heirs. † By an inquifition *poft mortem,* taken 45. Edw.
III. it appears that William de Everingham died feized in his de-

---

† (41 Edw. III.) *Inquifitio ad quod Damnum,* Juratores dicunt quod non eft damnum vel pre-
judicium Domini Regis, nec aliorum, fi idem Dominus Rex concedat *Petro de Routhe,* quod ipfud
Mañerium de *Skinergreive* cum pertinent. (quod de Dno. Rege tenetur *in Capite*) dare poffit et con-
cedere. Willo. de Everingham Chiv. habend. et tenend. eidem Willo. et Heredibus fuis una cum
Wrecco Maris inter Runfwyke et Yarum, et Sale *de Bruyffe* et omnibus aliis ad predict. Manerium
pertinent. &c. Et dicunt, quod predict. Manerium cum pertinent. una cum Wrecco et Sale predict. tenentur de Rege in Capite per Servitium militare.

mefne,*as of the fee of the manor of Skinnengrave, with the appurtenances, held of the King *in capite* by military fervice, confifting of twenty-four tofts, with divers effarts, ‡ worth fixty fhillings *per ann.* and a fourth part of the wreck of fea between Runfwick and Yarm, valued at three fhillings and four pence *per ann.* This William de Everingham died without male iffue; and leaving two daughters his coheireffes, the eftate became divided, and paffed into different families, but of the immediate fucceffions we are uninformed.

Richard Seton, Efq. held certain lands here in the reign of Charles the firft, which came afterwards to Brian Layton, by marriage with Alice, his widow, the daughter of John Turner of Kirkleatham, Efq. After divers alienations, the greateft part of the eftate came to Sir Laurence Dundas, Bart. anceftor to the Right Hon. Lord Dundas, who is the principal proprietor, and Lord of the manor.

The village of Skinnengrave ftands clofe upon the fea fhore, and was anciently a fifhing town of fome importance; which as Camden obierves, " *thrives by the great variety of fifh which it takes;*" but where, as the author of the *Cott. MS.* remarks, " the old Proverb is veryfied, " that abundance maketh them poore, for albeyt they take fuch abun- " dance of Fyfh, that often they are forced to throwe greate parte of " theire purchafe overboarde, or make their greater Sort of Fifh of light- " er Carriage, and fhorter by the Head, nevertheleffe for the mofte " part, what they have they drinke, and howfoever they reckon with

---

* *Inquifitio* 45 Edw. III.) *poft Mortem Willi. de Everingham.* Qui dicunt quod Willus. de Everingham tenuit in Dominico fuo, ut de feodo, die quo obiit, Manerium *de Skynnergrefe* cum pertinent. de Rege *in Capite* per fervitium militare; Quod quidem Manerium continet viginti quatuor Tofta cum diverfis affartis ibid. quæ valent per ann. fexaginta Solidos, &c.—Et dicunt quod eft ibid. pertinens dictis Toftis, quarta pars cujufdam Wrecci Maris inter Runnefwyke et Yarum, quæ valent per ann. cum accederit 3r. 4d. Et quod Johanna Ætatis 8 ann. et Katherina Ætatis 5 Annorum funt Filiæ et Heredes ipfius Willn.i. Propinquiores.

‡ *Affart,* or *Effart,* which feems fyncnymous with *Rode Land,* was ground reclaimed and brought into cultivation by grubbing up, and clearing away the wood; and is fuppofed by *Spelman* to be corrupted from *exfe·ere;* or ràther perhaps, according to *Skinner,* from the French *effarter,* which is derived from the Latin *exertum,* (i. e.) *evulfum, eradicatum.*

" God, yt is a familiar Maner to them to make even with the Worlde
" at Night, that pennileffe and careleffe they maye go lightly to their
" Labour, on the Morrow Morninge. It was my fortune to bee at the
" Cominge in of a five man Cobble, w.ᶜʰ in one Night had taken above
" 21 Score of greate fifh a Yearde or an Ell in Length. Happie were
" that Countrye yf a generall fifhinge were enterteined, by buildinge
" Buffes and Store of Fifh Boats."

CAMDEN mentions the report of a *fea-man* being caught by the fifhermen here; and the fame fabulous ftory is thus more particularly related in the ancient MS. above quoted:—" Old Men that would be
" loath to have their Credyt crackt by a Tale of a ftale Date, report con-
" fidently that fixty Yeares fince, or perhaps 80 or more, a *fea-man* ‖ was
" taken by the Fifhers of that place, where duringe many weeks they
" kepte in an oulde Houfe, giving him rawe Fifhe to eate, for all other
" fare he refufed; infteade of Voyce he fkreaked, and fhewed him-
" felf courteous to fuch as flocked farre and neare to vifit him;—fayre
" Maydes were wellcomeft Guefts to his Harbour, whome he woulde
" beholde with a very earnefte Countenaynce, as if his phlegmaticke
" Breafte had been touched wᵗʰ a Sparke of Love.—One Day, when the
" good Demeanour of this newe Guefte had made his Hofts fecure of
" his Abode wᵗʰ them, he prively ftoale out of Doores, and ere he
" coulde be overtaken recovered the Sea, whereinto he plounged him-
" felf;—yet as one that woulde not unmannerly depart without taking
" of his Leave, from the mydle upwardes he rayfed his Shoulders often
" above the Waves, and makinge fignes of acknowledgeing his good

‖ MANY centuries have elapfed fince authors firft wrote about the *Marmenill*, or *Sea-Man*. *Tor-faeus*, in his Hiftory of Norway fays, that it is met with in Iceland; and Bifhop *Pontoppidan* affures us, in his natural Hiftory of Norway, (vol. II. p. 302) that there are feveral fpecies of it.—*M. Stroem*, in his *Sundmoefchen*, p. 287) is very angry with thofe who will not believe in its exiftence; and *Childrey* afferts it as a fact, that fome fifhermen caught one on the coaft of Suffolk, in the year 1187; and that another was taken in Yorkfhire in 1535, being that above-mentioned.

" Enterteinment to fuch as beheld him on the Shore, as they interpre-
" ted yt;—after a pretty while he dived downe and appeared no
" more '

THE townſhip and village of

KILTON

lie to the eaſt. The name ſeems to be derived from the Britiſh word
Kil, which ſignifies a wood or grove, and the common termination *ton* ;
q. d. *Villa ad Lucum*,—a derivation highly charaċteriſtic of the ſituation
of the village, which conſiſts of a few farm houſes, ſeated in a deep ſecluded vale, ſheltered with trees of an ancient growth naturally diſpo-
ſed, and exhibiting a variety of ſylvan ſcenes by no means unintereſt-
ing.

WITHIN this townſhip there are two ancient manors, viz. *Kilton*,
and *Th rp* now called Kilton-Thorp, or Thorp *juxta* Kilton ; which, as
appears from the doomſday ſurvey, were held by *Torchil*, and were
ancient demeſne of the Crown, being entered in the ſurvey under the
title

TERRA REGIS.

" MANERIUM IN CHILTUNE, TORCHIL III. CARUCAT. TERRÆ AD GEL-
" DUM. TERRA AD II. CAR. IBI VIII. ACR. PRATI."

" MANERIUM IN TORP, TORCHIL II. CARUCAT. TERRÆ ET DIMID. AD
" GELDUM. TERRA AD I. CAR."

THESE manors were granted by the Conqueror to Robert
de Brus, nd deſcended by marriage to the Thwengs, many of
whom were ſummoned to parliament among the Barons : and
having a caſtle here, were called Lords of Kilton. William de
Thweng, having married Catherine, daughter of Thomas Lord
Furnival of Hallamſhire, died 15. Edward III. without iſſue, leaving his
brother Robert a clergyman, his heir ; from whom the inheritance
deſcended to Thomas his brother, who was alſo a clergyman, and
rector of Kirkleatham.—Thomas died at a great age without iſſue, 48,
Edw. III. and left his eſtate to the deſcendants of his three ſiſters ; upon
the partition of which, Kilton, with ſome other eſtates in Cleveland,
was aſſigned to Robert, the ſon of Marmaduke de Lumley, ſon of Lucia,

wife of Sir Robert de Lumley, knight. Robert died under age on the
12th Dec. 1374, as appears from an inquifition, taken at Guifbrough
in the 49. Edw. III. when it was proved, that Ralph de Lumley, his
brother, was his heir, then 13 years of age. This Ralph had fummons
to parliament among the Barons from the 8. Richard II. to the 1. Henry IV. when he joined with Thomas Holland, Earl of Kent, and others,
in the infurrection made for the reftoration of King Richard, who was
then depofed : and dying in battle, his lands were adjudged by parliament to be forfeited.—In the fixth year of the reign of King Henry IV.
his fecond fon, Sir John de Lumley, on the death of his brother Thomas, doing his homage, had livery of all lands, &c. which his father
was feized of, at the time of his attainder, and was afterwards reftored
in blood. In the firft year of Edward IV. on the petition of Thomas,
fon of John, the attainder of Ralph Lord Lumley, his grandfather, was
reverfed, and he had fummons to parliament accordingly. ‖

THIS family continued in poffeffion of Kilton for many fuccefiions,
till George, fon of John Lord Lumley, being one of the chief of thofe
northern Barons who joined in the infurrection, called the *pilgrimage of
grace*, his eftates came by attainder to the Crown. Kilton, we find, was
afterwards again the property of a branch of the Thwengs, and paffed
by marriage with Ann, fole daughter and heirefs of Thomas Thweng,
to William Tullie, Efq. who died without iffue 1741, leaving Jofeph
Tullie, Efq. his nephew his heir; from whom the eftate defcended to
the Rev. Dr. Waugh, Chancellor of Carlifle, whofe daughters and coheireffes fold the fame to J. Wharton, Efq. the prefent proprietor.

AT a little diftance from the village towards the fouth, on the brink
of a natural precipice wafhed by a fmall mountain rivulet, ftand the
remains of

KILTON CASTLE,

the baronial refidence of the ancient family of Thwengs : but the
edifice is now in fo ruinous a ftate, as to render it impoffible to form

‖ RYMER'S Fædera. vol. VIII. p. 429.

any idea of its former ftrength and magnificence.—From thefounda-
tions of the outer walls, it feems to have been in the form of a parallelogram, inacceffible on the eaft, weft, and fouth, and fortified by a deep
foffe or ditch on the north, where the only entrance was probably kept
by a draw-bridge.—The fituation of the caftle is romantic and retired ;
—the ruins of which are feen on the point of a rugged fteep, wafhed
by a mountain ftream, brawling among fragments of rock, at a great
depth beneath. The banks of the river rife fwiftly, and being wooded on either hand, encompafs the point on which the caftle ftands, and
form a picturefque foreground ;—while at a diftancé towards the fouth
a vaft range of mountains, with *Freebrough Hill*, detached and of a conical form, terminates the profpect, and adds beauty and grandeur to
the fcene.

FROM *Kilton*, purfuing the courfe of this mountain rivulet towards
its fource, which winds over a rocky channel, through a variety of
deep and wooded dells, we approach the townfhip of

MOORSHAM, OR MORESHAM ;

which comprehending Moorfham *magna* and Moorfham *parva*, forms
the fouthern extremity of the parifh. The former of thefe, (fometimes
called *Morefdon*,) was anciently a large town ; and the name feems evidently to have been given, as defcriptive of its fituation on the border
of an extenfive heathy moor or common ; over which the road between
Guifbrough and Whitby runs at no great diftance towards the fouth.

MOORSHAM *magna* and Moorfham *parva* were anciently two diftinct manors ; which, in the time of the Conqueror, were held by
Richard under Robert Earl of Moreton, being entered in the domefday furvey under the title

TERRA COMITIS MORITONIENSIS.

IN MOREHUSUM AD GELDUM III. CARUCATÆ, EΓ II. CAR. POSSUNT ES-
SE. IBI VCTRED HABUIT I. MANERIUM. NUNC HABET R CARD. DE COM.
ET WAST. EST. IN ALIA MOREHUSUM AD GELD. I. CARUCATA ET DIM-
ID. CAR. POFEST ARARI. IBI VCTRED HABUIT I. MANERIUM. NUNC HA-
BET RIC. DE COMITE, ET WAST. EST. TOTUM DIMID. LEUC. LONG. ET IF.
QUARENT. LAT.

THESE manors were afterwards granted by the Conqueror to Robert de Brus, Lord of Skelton; from which family, on failure of male iffue, they paffed by marriage to the Thwengs, and afterwards to the Lumlies; and in the reign of Henry VIII. on the attainder of George, fon of John Lord Lumley, they became forfeited to the Crown. John Wharton, Efq. is the prefent proprietor.

ABOUT a mile to the fouth from the village of Great Moorfham, ftands FREEBURG-HILL, a detached mountain of a conical form, called by Pennant, " *a vaft artificial mount or tumulus ;*" but it is evident, he obferved it only at a diftance; as there is a natural rock on its top, now wrought as a quarry, which is a decifive proof that it was not conftructed merely by the hand of art. It is conjectured by fome to have been a Druidical work, on the fame model as *Silbury-Hill*, in Wiltfhire; but confidering its altitude, fituation, and ftupendous dimenfions, has a much greater folemnity attached to it. Druidical remains confift of natural, as well as artificial eminences; and though *Freeburg* is evidently natural, much labour and art feem to have been employed in adjufting its fymmetry and proportions. As to the etymology of the name, it is undoubtedly of Saxon origin; ‡ and from whence derived, we have an explicit detail, on each fide of Speed's map of Huntingdonfhire, given by the mafterly hand of Sir Robert Cotton. Speaking of Huntingdon, at fection 4th of that learned work, he fays, " This coun-" ty, in decifion of tithes, and adminiftration of juftice, did at the firft, " as the Germans our anceftors, *jura per pagos et vicos reddere.* Every " townfhip, by their *friburgi*, or tenmentall, as triers : and the Baron,

---

‡ IT has been fuggefted to us, as a very probab'e conjecture, that the name of *Freeburg* might be derived from the Saxon Goddefs *Friga*, or *Frea* ; and in fupport of this etymology, it has been obferved, that the mountain *Rofebury*, which in ancient records we find frequently written *Othenburgh*, was certainly fo called by the Saxons from their God *Othan*, or *Odin*—the fame as *Woden* ; efteemed by them as their *God of Battle.*

B b b

" Thain, or head Lord there, or the *decanus* (a good freeholder) his de-
" puty as judge, determining all civil caufes ; a reprefentation of which
" ftill remaineth in our courts leet ; above this, and held twelve times
" a year, was our hundred, or wapentake court, *quæ fuper decem deca-*
" *nos, et centum friburgos judicabat,*" &c.

SPELMAN fays, " touching the King's peace, every hundred was
divided into many *freeburgs*, or tithings, confifting of ten men, who
ftood all bound one for the other, and did amongft themfelves punifh
fmall matters in their court, for that purpofe, called the *lite*, which was
fometimes granted over to the Lords of manors, and fometimes exercifed by peculiar officers.   But the greater things were alfo carried from
thence into the *hundred courts*.   Edward the Confeffor faith, there were
juftices over every ten *freeburgs* called *deans*, (that is, head of ten men)
which among their neighbours in towns compounded matters of trefpaffes done in paftures, meadows, corn, and other ftrifes rifing among
them.   But the greater matters were referred to fuperior juftices appointed over every *ten of them*, whom we call centurions, centenaries,
or hundradors ; becaufe they judged over every hundred *freeburgs*."

Spelman's Reliquiæ.

WE mean not, from the above obfervations, to infer, that *Freeburg-
Hill;* (though the name appears evidently to be of Saxon etymology,
and the place might be appropriated to the civil purpofes of that people,) was merely Saxon ; it has every appearance of a Britifh original,
and was probably defigned for popular conventions, fuch as the inau-
guration of princes, (like the hill *Tarah,* in Ireland) and the affemblage
of noblefs, &c. on occafions of great importance ; as well as religious
feftivals.   But when the Saxons gained a fettlement in the Brigantian
territory, they adopted the Roman ftations, Britifh faftneffes, and
Druidical remains, which they found prepared to their hands ; and
appropriating them to their own purpofes, they defended them with
ardour, fenfible of their confequence and importance.

ABOUT a mile to north-weſt from the village of *Moorſham magna*, lies the townſhip of

STANGHOW ;

of which, in ancient records, we find little worthy of particular notice. It was the lordſhip of Robert de Brus ; and in the reign of King Henry III. came by marriage with Agnes, one of the daughters of Peter de Brus, to Walter de Faʋconberge ; and afterwards, on failure of male-iſſue, to Sir William Neville, Knight ; who, in right of Joan his wife, daughter of Sir Thomas Fauconberge, was created Lord Fauconberge, and afterwards Earl of Kent : but dying without male-iſſue, his three daughters became his heirs, when this and other lands paſſed by marriage with Alicia, the youngeſt, to John Lord Conyers ; of whoſe deſcendants in the reign of Charles II. they were purchaſed by the Trotters of Skelton Caſtle ; and were afterwards ſold to Joſeph Hall, Eſq. anceſtor to the preſent proprietor.

SOIL, PRODUCE, and GENERAL APPEARANCE. In a pariſh of ſuch conſiderable extent, and with ſo great a variety of ſurface, the ſoil, as muſt be expected, will be various. In the ſouthern extremity of the pariſh, there is an extenſive moor or common, which being chiefly a barren heath, has a black and dreary appearance : the incloſed lands are chiefly a clayey loam, and in ſome ſituations a mixture of gravel ; which, under the improved modes of huſbandry, are rendered fertile, and produce good crops of wheat, oats and turnips : the grounds near the villages are more generally laid down to graſs. The pariſh is watered by a number of ſmall brooks, the banks of which are cloathed with wood ; and the vales, being ſcattered over irregularly with coppices and ſome modern plantations, afford a variety of pleaſing and intereſting proſpects.

POPULATION. The table given in the notes, from the return for the ſeveral townſhips within the pariſh, made to Government in the year 1801, ‡ will give the reader fome idea of the prefent number of inhabitants; and on a review of which it will appear that there were then 364 houfes, inhabited by 378 families, and containing in the whole 1689 inhabitants, giving 4½ nearly to each family. The number of baptifms &c. according to the parifh regifters, from the year 1781 to 1800 inclufive, will be feen from the following table; viz.

	Bapt.	Bur.	Mar.
Skelton	612	399	168
Brotton	328	161	57
Total	940	560	225

THE average number of baptifms within the parifh, for one year, according to the above ftatement, is 47, and that of burials, 28; from which it appears that of the total number of inhabitants one only out of every 60 dies annually.

‡ STATE OF POPULATION, 10th MARCH, 1801.

TOWNSHIPS.	Inhab. houfes.	Families.	Unhab. houfes.	Males.	Females.	Total.	Agriculture.	Trade, &c.	Refidue.	Total.
Skelton,	167	180	6	317	383	700	171	279	250	700
Brotton,	77	77	2	172	201	373	66	33	274	373
Skinningrove,	15	15	2	38	29	67	1	16	50	67
Kilton,	21	21	1	68	61	129	34	- - -	95	129
Moorfham,	65	65	4	142	160	302	117	39	146	302
Stanghow,	19	20	3	56	60	118	30	3	85	118
Totals.	364	378	18	795	894	1689	419	370	900	1689

THE PARISH OF UPLEATHAM;

O R, as it is fometimes written in ancient records, *Uplium*, and in
Domefday book, *Upelider*, adjoins to Skelton on the weft, and is
about three miles diftant from the market-town of Guifbrough.   The
village is fmall, confifting of a few houfes fcattered irregularly on the
fouthern declivity of a hill, and commands a pleafing view of Skelton
Caftle on the eaft; while the vale beneath prefents a profpect of
unrivalled beauty ; where fome fylvan god

" Waves the woods,
" Lifts the proud hills; and clears the filver ftream."

At a little diftance from the village towards the weft, ftands

UPLEATHAM HALL,

the feat of the Right Hon. Lord Dundas.   This is a neat modern manfion, facing to the fouth and weft, and fheltered on the eaft with thriving plantations ; the rifing grounds on the north are ornamented with
clumps of trees, and the furrounding fcenery prefents on the whole, an
afpect of tranquility and retirement.

The manor here, as appears from the Domefday book was anciently within the foke of Lofthoufe, ‖ and contained ten carucates of land,
held before the Conqueft by Siward, Earl of Northumberland, but granted by the Conqueror to Hugh, Earl of Chefter.   It was afterwards the
fee of Robert de Brus, and defcended to the Lords Fauconberge, and
from them to the Lords Conyers ; on the death of John Lord Conyers,
without male iffue, 3d and 4th Philip and Mary, it paffed by marriage
with Catherine his daughter and coheirefs, to John Atherton, Efq.

‖ See page 342.

whofe daughter Ann married Sir William Pennyman, of Marfk, Bart.
and died without iffue. Upleatham was afterwards the poffeffion of
the Lowthers of Marfk, who fold the fame to the anceftor of the Right
Hon. Lord Dundas, the prefent proprietor and Lord of the manor.

THE family of Colthurft § was anciently refident here, and poffeffed
confiderable property; which, on failure of male iffue, defcended by
marriage to the Smallwoods, || of Egton, who afterwards fettled here.

§ COLTHURST, of Upleatham.

Henry Colthurft of Upleatham, a branch—Elizabeth, daughter
of the family of Colthurft of . . . . . in | of . . . . Rudd, of
co. Lancafter. | . . . .

George Colthurft,   Robert Colthurft, of Upleatham.—Dorothy, daughter of William Craw,
died *fans iffue*. | of Upleatham.

3. William Colthurft—   2. George—   Elizabeth married John Turner, of Kirkleatham
Rob. and feveral daughters.   Rob.   Edmund.   Anne married Richard Wynne, of Guifbro.'
                                               Dorothy married George Powell, of Stokefley.

Robert Colthurft, of Upleatham —Elizabeth, daughter of Edw. Cayley, of Bromp-
ætat. 68. Sept. 8. 1666. | ton, in co. York, Efq.

Anne, wife of Robt.   Dorothy, wife of George Smallwood, of   Elizabeth, wife of Hen-
Cooke, of Upleatham.   Upleatham.   ry Roufby, of Crome, co.
                                                             York.
                                            Dugdale's Vifitation, 1666.

|| SMALLWOOD, of Upleatham.

Alan Smallwood, of Egton, a younger—
branch of the Smallwoods of . . . . in |
co. Stafford. Died 1614. |

2. Richard,   Jane, dau. of Wm.— Thomas—Alice, dau. of   3. Ralph.   4. James 5. George.
ob. S. P.   Garnett, of the Hee, | Smallwood | Rob. Watfon,
             co Weft. (1ft wife) | of Egton. | of Rofedale,
                                            | co. York, (2d
1. Alan Small- 1. Mary—R.Purfglove,of Glafedale. | wife.)
wood,D. D. v.   2. Jane—J. Twifley, of Danby
f Norton, co.   3. Eliz—S. Dickinfon,of Scarbro.'   2. George Smallwood,—Dorothy, dau. 3. Thos.
Durham; and   of Upleatham *ætat.* | of R Colthurft, of Nor-
fterwards rec-   39. 1666. | of Upleatham.   ton, in
torofGreyftock   co.Dur.
in Cumberland.   Dorothy, ætat. 8. 1666.   æt. 36.
ætat. 58. 1566.   1666.
                                                       Dugdale's Vifitation, 1666.

UPLEATHAM was an ancient chapelry within the parish of Guifbrough; and the chapel, which enjoyed parochial rights, was given by Robert de Brus, to the priory there; and remained dependent on the church of Guifbrough, till its augmentation by Queen Anne's bounty, when it became a perpetual curacy; and is now under the patronage of Lord Dundas, who nominates the curate. The Rev. Jofeph Wilkinfon is the prefent incumbent.

THE chapel ftands at a little diftance from the village towards the fouth, and is a fmall but ancient edifice; but having at different periods undergone fome alterations and repairs, much of its antiquity is deftroyed. The tower was rebuilt in the year 1684.

UPON the floor beneath the ftalls, on the north fide of the chapel, there is an ancient-effigy, much mutilated; and the arms on the wall above are fo much defaced, as to leave no room even to conjecture to what family this monument might belong. *

WITH refpect to the SOIL, PRODUCE, &c. of the parifh, we have only to remark, that the foil is chiefly a fertile clay, with fome clayey and gravelly loam; and from the modern, improved modes of hufban-

---

* MONUMENTAL INSCRIPTION.

IN the fouth wall of the chancel, there is a marble monument, with the arms of Smallwood; (viz. *parted per pale 1ft a lion rampant. 2d. a fefs between two zebras*) and the following infcription :

Memoriæ facrum
Georgii Smallwood de Vpleatham
In Agro Ebor. Jurifperiti; qui poftquam Vitam,
Pietate in Deum eximia, Amore in Uxorem
Singulari, et Charitate erga proximum
Admodum benefica et utili egiffet, unica
Solum Filia fuperftite, decimo tertio Die
Octobris, fummo omnium Mærore et Luctu
Vitam cum Morte commutavit,
Anno { ÆEtatis suæ 52 ;
{ Salutis humanæ 1680.
Cujus Corpus,
In antiqua hac Ecclefia parochiali,
reptl.........

dry recommended by Lord Dundas, who has been indefatigable in
pointing out to his tenants the moft approved fyftems and rotation of
crops, the lands are in a fuperior ftate of cultivation, and produce
wheat and other grain in great perfection: where the foil is fuitable,
turnips and clover are cultivated with fuccefs. Among other agricultural improvements, his Lordfhip was among the firft, who introduced
into Cleveland, an improved breed of fheep, by croffing his Lincolnfhire ewes with rams of the Difhley blood; which has rendered his
ftock very valuable, and fimilar modes of improvement are now very
generally adopted by the more opulent and beft informed farmers in
the diftrict.

POPULATION. In a parifh of fo fmall extent, we find little under this head, worthy of particular remark. From the return † made
in the year 1801, by order of the Legiflature, it appears that there were
then 61 inhabited houfes, 64 families, and 237 inhabitants, giving an
average of only 3¾ nearly to each family. The number of baptifms,
&c. from the year 1781, to the year 1800 inclufive, will appear from
the following table; viz,

	Males	Females	Total
Baptifms	77	71	148
Burials	51	34	85
Increafe	26	37	63

The number of marriages within the above period 33

It appears from the above ftatement, that the average number of
baptifms to that of burials in one year for the above period, is nearly in
proportion of two to one; from which we conclude, that while the
births within the parifh are as 1 to 32, the deaths will be found nearly

† STATE of population, 10th March, 1801.

	Inhabited houfes.	Families.	Uninhabited houfes.	Males.	Females.	Total.	Agriculture.	Trade, &c.	Refidue.	Total.
Upleatham..	61	64	1	106	131	237	35	21	181	237

as 1 to 56 annually; a circumftance that points out an apparent increafe of inhabitants, and indicates the air to be falubrious, and the fituation healthy.

THE PARISH OF MARSK,

LIES to the north, and extends along the fea coaft; the name of
which is very probably derived from the Anglo-Saxon word Mepꞃc,
a pool or marfh; or rather perhaps from the Latin *marifcus*, which according to Pliny, *juncum marinum unde fegetus texuntur fignat.* It is bounded on the eaft by the parifh of Skelton, from which it is divided by
a rivulet called *Saltburn-beck;* by Kirkleatham on the weft, and by
Skelton and Upleatham on the fouth.

THE manor of Marfk, in the time of the Conqueror's furvey, was
taxed for eight carucates, and contained four more that might be rendered arable. There were alfo fixteen villeins, who had five ploughs,
and eight acres of meadow; the whole being valued in the confeffor's
time at ten fhillings; but at the time of the furvey, worth twenty.

TERRA WILLIELMI DE PERCI.

MANERIUM IN MERSCHE HABEAT NORMAN VIII. CAR. TERRÆ AD GEL-
DUM: UBI POSSUNT ESSE IIII. CAR. NUNC HABET WILLS. IBI XVI. VILL.
CUM V. CAR. PRATI ACR. VIII. T. R. E. VALEB. X. SOL. MODO XX. SOL.

THERE were alfo two carucates *ad geldum,* within the foke of Lofthoufe, held by Hugh Earl of Chefter, but then wafte; and ten carucates
ad geldum within the foke of the manor of Brotton.

C C C

THE manor of Marſk was one of thoſe lordſhips granted by the Conqueror to Robert de Brus to be held of the king *in capite ;* but male iſſue failing in Peter de Brus, the inheritance became divided among his four ſiſters ; of whom Agnes the eldeſt, wife of Walter de Fauconberge, had this and other large eſtates for her ſhare in the diviſion ; whoſe deſcendants inherited for ſeveral ſucceſſions, till male iſſue failing in Thomas de Fauconberge, his eſtates came to Iſabel and Joan, his daughters and coheireſſes ; but Marſk came not immediately into the diviſion, becauſe Iſabel, the ſecond wife of the ſaid Thomas, ſurviving, had this and ſome other eſtates aſſigned for her dowery ; which however, at her death, returning to the heirs, were carried by marriage with Joan to Sir William Neville, Knight, who was created Lord Fauconberge, and afterwards Earl of Kent ; but he, dying without male iſſue, left three daughters coheireſſes ; when Marſk, by marriage, paſſed to the Conyers, and from them to John Atherton, Eſq. whoſe ſole daughter Anne married Sir William Pennyman, Bart. but leaving no iſſue, the eſtate came to the Lowthers, who afterwards ſold to the anceſtors of the right Hon. Lord Dundas, the preſent proprietor.

WE have no documents to ſhew at what period the lands here, which appear to have been anciently held in parcels, firſt came into unity of poſſeſſion. † In the reign of Edward the firſt, according to

---

† THERE were divers grants of lands here, and other privileges made by dfferent benefactors to the priory of Guiſbrough ; viz. Walter de Fauconberge gave two acres and one rood, in exchange for the ſame quantity of land at Skelton, which Peter de Brus the 3d had incloſed with his meadow ; and alſo granted for himſelf, Agnes his wife and their heirs, that all *rituals,* or cuſtomary tenants, inhabiting the premiſes which belonged to this priory at the date hereof (A. D. 1275) ſhall be exempt from the payment of tolls, in the towns and lands, which deſcended to him from Peter de Brus, as well in the market of Skelton, as elſewhere.—William, ſon of Reginald de Marſk, gave nine acres of land in theſe fields, viz. ſeven in the culture called *Ratteflat,* and two in *Heſelgrive ;*—and two oxgangs here, and in *Uplium* of the fee of *Uplium ;* and three tofts and crofts, and fourteen acres of land ; five of them in *Ratteflat,* and four and a half in *Rabec ;*—Umfrid, ſon of John de Tocottes, gave four acres and a half in this territory, near the prior's grange ; which grant was confirmed by Peter, ſon of Peter de Brus ; and William de Tocottes reſtored the tithes of his mill, ſituated in this pariſh.　　　　　*See Burton's Mon. Ebor. p.* 349, *&c.*

Kirkby's Inqueft, befides one knight's fee in the hands of Walter de Fauconberge, there were eight carucates held by Henry de Percy, probably the fame as mentioned in the general furvey ; and one carucate held by John de Tocottes, of the fee of the faid Walter, where twelve carucates made one knight's fee. ||

THE village of Marſk is of confiderable extent, and contains fome neat and well-built houfes, ſtretching from the fea coaſt in a direction nearly north and fouth ; with an ancient crofs in the centre, which according to tradition was erected nearly two hundred years ago, when the plague having nearly depopulated the town of Guifbrough, the market was, in confequence, removed hither. Near the centre of the village, towards the weſt, ſtands

MARSK HALL,

the prefent refidence of the Hon. L. Dundas ; a neat and commodious manfion, built by Sir William Pennyman, Bart. in the reign and according to the taſte, which prevailed about the time of Charles the firſt. On the front there are two ſhields ; one bearing the arms of Pennyman and Atherton, the latter of which with the motto cannot be well diſtinguiſhed ; the other the arms of Pennyman alone ; viz. a *cheveron*, between *three arrow heads ;* but the creſt appears to be different from that granted to the Pennymans of Ormefby.

THE church of Marſk ſtands at a little diſtance from the village towards the north-eaſt, and within a few yards of the brink of the fea-cliff ; the ſpire of which affords a confpicuous land-mark to the fiſhermen and mariners that frequent the coaſt. This is an ancient edifice, and confiſts of a middle and two fide ailes, divided by round pillars fupporting circular arches. The chancel is feparated from the nave by a pointed arch ; but the alterations occafioned by fome modern repairs

---

|| WALTERUS DE FAUCONBERGE tenet unum Feodum (in Marſke) unde 12 Carucatæ Terræ ciunt Feodum.

HENRICUS DE PERCY tenet VIII. Carucatas Terræ ibidem, unde 12 faciunt Feodum.

JOHN DE TOCOTTES tenet unam Carucatam Terræ in Marſke, de Feod. Faconberge, unde 12 Car. Terræ faciunt Feodum milit. et reddit Ballivo Domini Regis pro fine 2s.

Kirkby's Inqueſt.

in the windows, have deſtroyed the antiquity, and greatly injured the uniformity of the building, which is ſtill ſo ruinous, as to render a more complete repair immediately neceſſary.

THIS church is undoubtedly of great antiquity; at leaſt we have hiſtorical evidence of its foundation before the Norman conqueſt. ‡ It was dedicated to Saint Germain, by Egelric, Biſhop of Durham; and was given, together with the vill of Marſk, and the lands adjoining, to the convent of Durham; but it does not appear to have continued long in the poſſeſſion of that church; for ſoon after the conqueſt, on the foundation of the priory of Guiſbrough, it was given by Robert de Brus, the founder, to that monaſtry; and being appropriated thereto, and a vicarage ordained, " Ralph, prior and convent of Guiſbrough, " confirmed to Sir Suan, the chaplain, their clerk for life, in free and " perpetual alms, the chapellrie of Marſke; the tythe of one carucate of " their land; and the tythe of half a carucate of *Ralph de Redcar's,* and " of another half curacate of *Aſtinus de Merſc*; and the half part of the " tythe wool and lamb; and half part of the parſonage: and the half " part of line, and of al. piggs, and all other minute tythes, oblations, " and obventions pertaining to the church, except the tythe of fiſh: he " alſo acquitted the church towards the Archbiſhop of York, and his " officials, in all things belonging to them.

Torr's MSS.

THE rectorial rights and patronage of the church remained in the priory, till its diſſolution, when they came to the crown; and were granted afterwards to Sir William Pennyman—and from him came to

‡ HUTCHINSON, in his hiſtory of Durham, on the authority of *Leland* and *Symeon Dunelmenſis,* ſays, that " Copſi, whilſt deputy to Toſti, gave to the Church of Saint Cuthbert, and thoſe who ſer- " ved at his ſhrine, for ever, his Church of Marſk, dedicated to St. Germain by Biſhop Egelric; to- " gether with the vill of Marſk, and lands thereto adjoining; ten carucates and a half of land in " Marſk; two carucates in Thornton; ten oxgangs in Tocottes; half a carucate in Redcar—and " one carucate in Guiſbro'; and as a perpetual teſtimony of ſuch his grant, he gave therewith a " large ſilver bowl or cup, to be preſerved in the Church as a laſting memorial."

Anthony Lowther, Efq. whofe defcendants fold to the anceftor of the Right Hon. Lord Dundas, the prefent patron ; who has not only rebuilt the vicarage houfe, but augmented the vicarage with the fum of 200*l.* which, with the like fum procured from the governours of Queen Anne's bounty, has been laid out in the purchafe of lands at Great Broughton near Stokefley.

ABOUT two miles to the north-weft, over firm and fine fands, we approach the village of

REDCAR ;

which is a confiderable fifhing town, fituated clofe upon the beach ; and confifted formerly of a few miferable huts only, inhabited by fifhermen and their families : but is now a place of fafhionable refort for fea-bathing—and is much frequented during the fummer feafon by many genteel families from the country adjacent.—The lodging-houfes, which are annually increafing, are many of them neat and commodious ; with bathing machines, and every other accommodation ; which, in addition to a falubrious air, and the many delightful

---

MARSK VICARAGE.

DEDIC. St. Germain. The Right Hon. Lord Dundas, patron.

A difcharged living. Clear yearly value 25*l.* 15s. 0d. Archd. pro. Syn. 4s. proc. 7s. 6d.

VICARS.—1295. Stephen de North Alverton. 1300. Alan de Ormfbey.—Johannes. 1350. William Mody. 1351. Robert Lyon. 1392. Roger de Hill. 1394. William de Thorpe. 1400. John de Ingleby.—John Kent. 1406. William Thorlaye. 1406. Will. de Hurworth. 1410. Robert de Dalton. 1424. Will. de Helmeflay. 1460. Chriftopher Brown. 1464. Thomas Wright. 1488. Thomas Whiteby. 1517. George Davy, *Can. Mon. de Gyfburgh.* 1568. John Trenholme, *Pres. Eliza. Regin.* 1575. Chrift. Roger, *Pres. eadem.* 1623. Gervaife Thorpe, M. A. *Pres. Will. Pennyman, Efq.* 1638. Alan Smalwood, M. A. *Pres. Sir Wm. Pennyman, Bart.* 1662. John Kidd, B. A. *Pres. Anth. Lowther, Efq.* 1685. William Dixon, *Pres. idem.* 1717. John Langftaffe, *Pres. Sir Thomas Lowther, Bart.* 1749. Thomas Langftaffe, *Pres. Sir Wm. Lowther, Bart.* 1790. Jofeph Harrifon, *Pres. Sir Thomas Dundas, Bart.*

profpects in the neighbourhood, muft contribute to render it a defirable fummer retreat. ‡

THE following obfervations, made a few years ago, by a friend on
his firft vifit to Redcar, will be found not unworthy of the reader s attention.

THE ride from Saltburn to Redcar, for fix miles, over firm fands,
was very pleafant. When we arrived at this little village, (which was
formerly only a few huts, but now is greatly reforted to in the feafon
for the purpofe of bathing,) we noticed at our entrance, large heaps of
fand, nearly as high as the cottages ; which, on enquiry, we found were
driven up by the wind and tide in the winter.—The inhabitants of the
villages under the Glaciers of Savoy live in continual dread of being
overwhelmed by the *avalanches* of *Mount Blanc*, and the traveller, who
paffes over the deferts of Arabia, is apprehenfive of being buried be
neath the moving fands—but the inhabitants who occupy thefe cot
tages at Redcar live very compofedly, without any apprehenfions o
the kind. Upon our enquiry of a man, whom we faw ftanding at his
door, how he extricated himfelf from the mountain of fand, which had
blocked up his door and windows, he replied with *fang froid*—" *Why*,
I removes it with a fhovel."—This, our friend obferves, may be literally
called a refurrection.

REDCAR, though not recorded in the doomfday book, is a fmall
dependent manor ; which, with the principal part of the village, wa
purchafed, together with the manor and eftate at Marfk, by Lord Dun
das's anceftor.

SOIL, PRODUCE, and GENERAL STATE of AGRICULTURE
A confiderable portion of the land within the parifh is of a fine fandy
foil, with fome rich clayey loam ; the other parts are more incline
to a ftrong but fertile clay ; and is confidered to be equal to any par

‡ THE village is irregularly built ; and is a place, where the pleafures of fociety are requifite to
render it comfortable and agreeable ; and was it not for the civility of the hofpitable landlady Mrs.
C—, it would fail in one of its chief attractions. The amufements here confift chiefly in going out
in parties to fea,—in walking on the fands, which are extenfive,—or in riding to vifit the picturefque
fcenery in the neighbourhood of Guifbrough, Skelton, &c.

of Cleveland for the produce of wheat : other grain is cultivated with fuccefs.—It was an opinion formerly entertained by the farmers here, and in the neighbourhood, that the tillage land fhould not have more than two crops for a fallow ; but this feems now to be quite an exploded notion, and a more beneficial mode of cropping has been introduced by Lord Dundas, * who has been indefatigable in recommending

---

* THe following fyftem or rotation of crops has been fubmitted to the tenants for the management of the Marfk Eftate by the Right Hon. Lord Dundas.

Rotation of crops, when the land is a light turnip foil.
1. Oats.
2. Turnips, with manure.
3. Barley, fown down with feeds.
4. Meadow, the after-grafs eaten by fheep.
5. Pafture.
6. Do.
7. Break up for Oats.

Firft rotation for ftrong land.
1. Oats.
2. Fallow, with lime.
3. Wheat.
4. Beans, with manure, drilled at 27 inches.
5. Barley, fown down with red clover.
6. Clover.
7. Break up for Oats.

Second rotation for ftrong land.
1. Oats.
2. Fallow.
3. Barley, with compoft, fown down with red clover.
4. Clover.
5. Wheat.
6. Beans, drilled at 27 inches afunder.
7. Oats.

Third rotation for ftrong land.
1. Fallow, with lime and dung.
2. Wheat.
3. Beans, drilled at 27 inches afunder.
4. Barley, with 12lbs. of red clover, & compoft.
5. Clover.
6. Oats.

Fourth rotation for ftrong land.
1. Fallow, with lime and dung.
2. Wheat.
3. Beans, drilled at 27 inches afunder.
4. Barley, with red clover, and well-mixed compoft.
5. Clover.
6. Wheat.

Fifth rotation for a ftrong loam.
1. Oats.
2. Turnips with dung.
3. Barley, with 10 or 12lb. red clover.
4. Clover.
5. Wheat.
6. Beans.

N. B.—In all the above-mentioned rotations, if the tenant lays on fix chaldrons of lime, either before breaking up from grafs, or on the fallow, no more is expected to be laid on for 8 or 9 years ; a certain proportion of lime is however to be ufed, in making up compoft dunghills.

to his tenants, a fcale of cultivation, formed according to the modern improvements in agriculture, which is likely to become highly beneficial to the public.

POPULATION. This parifh, comprehending the Townfhips of Redcar and Marfk, both of which are confiderable villages, contained according to the enumeration made in the year 1801, by order of the legiflature, 217 houfes, 227 families, and 934 inhabitants. From the table given in the notes, it appears that the number of females greatly exceeds that of males; and within the townfhip of Redcar nearly in the proportion of two to one; which is a remarkable circumftance, and can be accounted for only perhaps by a great majority of the latter emigrating in fearch of employment as feamen to the different ports in the kingdom.

WE have no data, on which we can form any idea of the probable increafe of the inhabitants; and the neceffary extracts from the parifh regifters being withheld, we can form no ftatement of the mortality within the parifh. The number of inhabitants however, we believe, has for the laft twenty years continued nearly ftationary.

STATE OF POPULATION, 10th March, 1801.

	Inhabit. Houfes.	Families.	Males.	Females.	Total.	Agricul.	Trade, &c.	Refidue.	Total.
Marfk,	102	102	229	274	503	75	40	388	503
Redcar,	115	125	170	261	431	56	334	41	431
Totals,	217	227	399	535	934	131	374	429	934

THE PARISH OF KIRKLEATHAM;

CALLED in the old records *Lythum*, or according to our ancient hiftorians *Luthunum*, lies to the weft from the parifh of Marfk, and
is fituated about four miles to the north from the market town of Guifbrough; being bounded on the eaft by the parifh of Marfk; by Wilton on the weft; Guifbrough on the fouth; and is wafhed on the north
by the German ocean.

THE manor here, under the name of *Weftlidum*, was taxed in the
Domefday furvey, for four carucates, with two carucates that might be
rendered arable, held by *Norman* before the Conqueft; but at the time
of the furvey by William de Percy, who had one *fokeman* and feven
bordars with one plough. There was then a minifter and church within the manor, and fix acres of meadow; the whole being valued in the
Confeffor's time at ten fhillings; but at the time of the furvey at five
fhillings and four pence.

"TERRA WILLIELMI DE PERCI.
"MANERIUM IN WESTLIDUN HABEBAT NORMAN IIII. CAR. TERRÆ AD GEL-
"DUM UBI POSSUNT ESSE II. CAR. NUNC HABET WILLIELMUS IBI I. SOCH-
"MANUM ET VII. BORDARIOS CUM I. CAR. IBI PRESBITER ET ECCLESIA ET
"VI. ACR. PRATI. T. R. E. VALEBAT X. SOLID. ET IIII. DENAR."

THERE were alfo two carucates within the foke of the manor of
Lofthoufe; and from another part of the furvey, it appears that there
were nine carucates *ad geldum*, with five more that might be rendered
arable, and fourteen acres of meadow, held before the Conqueft by
Uɛtred, and afterwards in the hands of Robert, Earl of Mortain, but
then wafte, valued in the Confeffor's time at fixteen fhillings.

D d d

" TERRA COMITIS MORITONIENSIS.
" IN WESTLIDUN AD GELDUM IX. CARUCATÆ, ET V. CAR. POSSUNT ESSE.
" IBI HABEBAT UCTRED I MANER. NUNC HABET COMES, ET WAST. EST. IBI·
" XIIII. ACR. PRATI. T. R. E. VALEBAT XVI. SOLID."

KIRKLEATHAM, in the Conqueror's time, was granted to the Bruces of Skelton; and from that family defcended to the Thwengs of Kilton Caſtle; ‖ from whom it came by marriage to the noble family of Lumley, † and continued in their poſſeſſion till the reign of Henry VIII. when George, ſon of John Lord Lumley, becoming a partizan with the Lord Darcy, in that rebellious inſurrection called the pilgrimage of grace, was apprehended and committed to the Tower, and ſoon after ſuffered death; upon whoſe attainder, this eſtate came to the Crown, and in the 28th Elizabeth, was granted to Sir William Bellaſis, Knight; by whom it was conveyed, in the year 1623, to John Turner, Eſq. anceſtor to Sir Charles Turner, Bart. the preſent proprietor, Richard Bellaſis, Eſq. father of Sir William, having (30 Eliz.) obtained a previous conveyance thereof from the vendees of the laſt Lord Lumley.

KIRKLEATHAM HALL,

the ſeat of Sir Charles Turner, Bart. is pleaſantly ſituated in a rich and extenſive vale; and the building, which is in the Gothic ſtyle, and does great honour to the abilities of the late Mr. Carr, has a venerable and pleaſing appearance. Conſiderable improvements have of late years been made in this place and neighbourhood; and there are few ſituations in the north, which command the attention of the traveller

---

‖ EGO MARMADUCUS DE THWENG, Dominus de Danby, &c. dedi Marmaduco filio meo, Caſtellum de Kilton, et Manerium de Kilton, et Maneria de Lithum et Cotum.—Teſtibus Dominis Waltero de Fauconberg, Nicholas de Mennell, Johanne de Bulmer, Adamo de Seton, Willº. de Perci, & multis aliis.   Sine Dat.   Dodſw. 68. p. 10.

† 48. Edw. III. Hæredes Thomæ Thweng ſunt Robertus de Lumley, Johannes Hothum, Miles; Iſabel, Ux. Walteri Pedwarden, & Eliz. Ux. W. Botreaux.   Ex. Coll. Coſſinger.

more than Kirkleatham; its various natural beauties, and the many decorations art has furnished it with, render it a delightful retreat, and give an air of princely grandeur to the whole.

THE front of the house is 132 feet in length, and 65 feet in depth; and the cornice of the door cafe, which is supported by Corinthian pillars, is light and elegant. The dining and drawing rooms, as also the other apartments, are lofty and spacious, and are handsomely finished; the chimney pieces are of the best *Siena* marble, executed by *Wilton*; and the furniture of the whole modern and elegant. ‡

THE gardens are extensive, and laid out with much taste; and in the pleasure grounds there is a beautiful temple of an octagonal form, adorned with paintings, and carved and gilded in a superb style; from which there is a pleasing prospect over a fine extensive vale interfected with rich inclofures, and bounded by the fea and the river *Tees*; while the higher lands in the county of Durham fill the distant view.

NEAR this mansion stands

TURNER'S HOSPITAL,

a large and handsome building, incloiing three sides of a square, the fourth being ornamented with elegant iron-gates and palisadoes; the outer and inner courts are neatly laid out, in the latter of which, on a pedestal, is a statue representing JUSTICE, with the sword and balance.

---

‡ " THE dining room is 46 feet by 26, and 22 feet high; the ceiling coved in stucco, the cen-
" tral part in compartments describing an oval, in which is a blazed wreath of branches, furround-
" ing a horn pierced with arrows; around it compartments ornamented with scrolls and feftoons
" the cove decorated in the fame manner, and with *bafs reliefs*.

" The breakfast-room   27 by 20.
" The first bed-chamber 25 by 21; the dreffing-room 20 by 18.
" The fecond do.   18 by 18; the dreffing-room 24 by 21.
" The third do.   18 by 18.
" The fourth do.   24 by 18.
" there are ten bed chambers in the attic story;—in the bafement floor five, one dreffing-room, a
" hall and a billiard-room. Thefe apartments are all fitted up for company."

From a fix months tour through the North of England,

This truly chriftian and benevolent charity was founded and endowed
with a valuable eftate by Sir William Turner, Knight, in the year
1676,* and was the fame year eftablifhed by *letters patent* under the
great feal of Great Britain, and afterwards by Act of Parliament, in
the 30th year of the reign of King Charles II. for the maintenance of
forty poor people; viz. ten old men, and as many old women; ten
boys and ten girls; ‡ who are provided in a comfortable manner,
with all the neceffaries of life; and the children, after receiving a liberal and ufeful education, are bound out apprentices. The time of
admittance for the old people is at the age of fixty-three; and the children are admitted between the ages of eight and eleven, and leave at
fixteen.—A fum of money was bequeathed by John Turner, Efq. ferjeant at law, for cloathing each of the children on leaving the hofpital,
the expence of which, at that time, was eftimated at 3*l*. 6*s*. 8*d*. and after the expiration of their apprenticefhip, which has in general been
feven years, on producing proper certificates of their good behaviour
during that time, a benefaction of 6*l*. 13*s*. 4*d*. was given to each;—

---

* Over the entrance of the hofpital is the following infcription :—

"This Hofpital was founded and endowed 1676 by Sir William Turner, Knight, Lord Mayor
"of the City of London, whofe care, fufficiency, and integrity in that magiftracy and other public
"offices, in the moft difficult times, the unufual prefents and grateful acknowledgments of feveral
"companies of the city declare;—whofe charity and love for his native country, let this founda-
"tion teftify. The chapel, and two fchool-houfes were erected, and the mafter and miftrefs's houfes
"improved and enlarged 1742, by the orders and direction of Chomley Turner, Efq. the prefent
"Governour."

‡ Gough, in his additions to Camden, fays, "near the mouth of the Tees is Kirkleatham,
"where Sir William Turner, Lord Mayor of London, 1669, was born; and built and endowed a
"handfome hofpital for 40 poor aged perfons and children, with a chaplain, mafter, and miftrefs;
"to which, at his death, he bequeathed 5000*l*. for founding a free-fchool, with falaries of 100*l. per
ann.* to the mafter, and 50*l*. to the ufher."

The fchool is a large, handfome quadrangular building, erected by Chomley Turner, Efq. in the
year 1709;—and the lands, with which the fchool and hofpital are endowed, confift of nine farms,
containing 1810 acres, which upwards of thirty years ago were let for the fum of 773*l*. with an annuity of 50*l*. paid out of other lands; the income of thefe foundations is now confiderably increafed,

which has for many years been difcontinued, as the expence of cloathing, which is ftill continued, far exceeds the fum fet apart for that purpofe.—The hofpital is under the direction of Sir Charles Turner, Bart.
who is fole governour ; which office defcends to the poffeffor of Kirkleatham eftate for ever.   The management is committed to the care of
a chaplain, a mafter, and miftrefs, who have handfome falaries.

In the centre of the front, there is a fmall chapel, 35 feet in length
and 33 feet broad, finifhed in a ftyle of fuperior elegance ; the roof of
which is arched in compartments, and fupported by four light and
handfome columns of the Ionic order ; from the centre hangs a large
chandelier of burnifhed gold ; and over the altar is a beautiful window
of painted glafs, efteemed one of the fineft in the world, reprefenting
the offerings of the *Magi* at the birth of our Saviour.   On one fide, a
full figure of John Turner, Efq. ferjeant at law, in a fcarlet robe ; and
on the other, one of Sir William Turner, the founder, in his robes, as
Lord Mayor of London ; to which high office he was feveral times
elected ; and in the year 1669, during his mayoralty, he was alfo chofen prefident of the Bridewell and Bethlehem hofpitals.

In a large and commodious room within the hofpital is the LIBRA-
RY, furnifhed with many fcarce and valuable books, and feveral natural and artificial curiofities ; among the latter is a fingular piece of carved work, reprefenting *St. George and the Dragon*, cut out of one piece
of box-wood with a knife, and executed with a degree of delicate nice-
ty, fcarcely ever equalled.   In a handfome cafe, is a ftriking likenefs
of Sir William Turner, in wax, with the identical wig and band worn
by him in his lifetime.   Every thing that reminds us of this great and
good man, cannot fail of being contemplated with pleafure ; as the extenfive charity, of which he was the author, and the noble foundation
eftablifhed here, which is juftly accounted one of the greateft private
charities in Europe, bear ample teftimony.

AT a fhort diftance from the hofpital, is the PARISH CHURCH, a light and elegant building of ftone. The area within is 90 feet by 42 ; and the roof is fupported by fix neat columns of the Tufcan-order. At the weft end is a gallery, in which there is a fmall, but remarkably fweet-toned organ, both of which are the property of the hofpital, where the children are placed during the time of divine fervice, and fing feveral parts thereof in a folemn and harmonious manner. The pulpit and reading defk are of handfome workmanfhip.

IN the chancel is the monument of Sir William Turner, near which he was buried by his own defire, amongft the poor of his hofpital, the witnelles of his piety, liberality and humility. Adjoining to the eaft end of the church, is a fuperb maufoleum of a circular form, and co-vered with a dome, built by Chomley Turner, Efq. in the year 1740, under which is the family vault. ‖ Among other monumental ftatues are thofe of that gentleman and *William Turner*, Efq. executed by the famous *Schemacher*.

THE church of Kirkleatham, dedicated to Saint Cuthbert, was an ancient rectory belonging to the patronage of the Thwengs of Kilton Caftle ; † and from them, according to *Torr*, to the Lords Neville, of Raby, till fuch time as Ralph Neville, Earl of Weftmorland, founded the collegiate church of Staindrop, in the county of Durham, when he

---

‖ ON a fillet round the outfide of the maufoléum is the following infcription ; viz.
THIS MAUSOLEUM WAS ERECTED 1740, TO THE MEMORY OF MAR-WOOD WILLIAM TURNER, ESQ.

†IN the reign of Henry III. Cardinal *Otho*,being fent as legate from Pope Gregory,into England, took upon him to beftow benefices without the confent of fuch patrons as were laymen, though the churches were founded and endowed by their anceftors, and were of their own fee. This injurious ufurpation excited confiderable alarm among the Barons, who found their right of patronage in dan-ger, and was moft ftrenuoufly oppofed by *Sir Robert Thweng*, Knight, patron of the church of *Kirk-leatham*, who made his complaint firft to the Archbifhop of York ; but finding no remedy from him, took a journey to Rome, with letters from feveral nobles, reprefenting to his holinefs the great injury they fuftained in being deprived of the rights of their patronage By thefe letters, *Sir Robert Thweng*

gave this church thereunto : and on the 18. Dec. 1412,Henry Bowett, Archbifhop of York, appropriated it unto the mafter and brethren of the faid collegiate church ; and in recompence of the damage done to the cathedral church thereby, referved an annual penfion of 33s. 4d. to himfelf and fucceffors, and 20 fhillings to his dean and chapter, payable by the faid college out of the fruits of this church of Lethom, at Pentecoft and Martinmas, by equal portions ; and befides ordained that they fhould diftribute 6s. 8d. *fterling* yearly amongft the poor of the parifh.

FURTHERMORE he decreed and ordained, that there be in the faid church of *Lethom*, one perpetual fecular vicar, nominated by the faid Earl of Weftmorland and his heirs, to the mafter and brethren of the college, who fhall be by them prefented thereunto for ever ; whofe vicarage fhall confift in thefe following portions ; viz. in one competent manfion, with houfes fufficiently built for the vicar's habitation at the coft of the faid mafter and brethren, the firft time, either within the manfion of the rectory, or in any other place near the church. Alfo the vicar fhall receive 13*l.* 6s. 8d. *fterling* in money, of the faid college quarterly and annually, payable by equal portions. And fhall have befides twelve acres of land, with pafture to the fame belonging ; and that the faid mafter and brethren fhall for ever bear all burthens ordinary and extraordinary incumbent on the church of *Lethom* whatfoever."
                                                              Torr's MSS.

THIS church continued a vicarage under the patronage of the mafter and brethren of the collegiate church of Staindrop, till the general

---

found the eafier accefs to the Pope ; to whom he declared his title to the patronage of this church ; and as fuch, claimed the prefentation to the rectory upon every vacancy ; but complained that he was not permitted to enjoy it, by reafon of the papal prohibitions, which the legate pretended to execute. Upon the hearing of this title, thus pleaded in the Pope's confiftory, he obtained letters from the Pope, to be reftored to his rights, with further inftructions to the legate and Archbifhop of York, that for the future, they fhould not difturb the laity in their prefentations, nor inftitute any perfons, where they were patrons, without their confent, unlefs there were reafonable objections againft the perfon prefented.

diffolution, when it came to the Crown, and in the reign of Queen
Elizabeth, was granted to Richard Bellafife, Knight; and was after-
wards fold, together with the manor and eftate, to John Turner, Efq.
Serjeant at law.   Sir Charles Turner, Bart. is the prefent patron.

THERE was an ancient chantry here, called Thweng's chantry or
college, founded 22d Edward III. by Thomas de Thweng, Rector of
this church, and patron thereof; which was ordained to confift of
twelve chaplains and four clerks, to be under the government of the
rector, and to minifter continually in divine offices &c. and to comme-

---

KIRKLEATHAM VICARAGE.

A difcharged living, dedicated to Saint Cuthbert; clear yearly value 20*l.* 13s. 4d. *Colleg. de
Staindrop in Dunelm.* propr. Sir Charles Turner, Bart. patron.

RECTORS.—John de Fraunceys, pbr. ob. 25. Dec. 1267. 1267. Robert de Thweng, cl. *pres.
Marmad. de Thweng.* 1288. Gawen de Thweng *pres. W. de Thweng, mil.* 1292. Thomas de
Thweng, pbr. *himfelf patron.* 1374. William Kalefby, *pres. Edw. III. Rex, ut fator Robti. de Lum-
ley.*—Adam de . . . .—John Bernard, pbr. 1404. John Sandon. 1414. John Bernard, pbr.

VICARS.—John Wirkworth. 1476. John Gefeby, cap. 1485. Tho. Greyftock, cap. *pres.
dom. rad. E. Weftmorland.* 1500. John Brown, *pres. cuftos & fratres Coll. de Stayndrop.* 1506. Will.
Frothyngham, *pres. iidem.* 1515. Rob. Frothyngham, *pres. iidem.* 1519. Marmad. Waldeby, S. T. P.
pres. iidem. 1520. John Wilbour, *pres. iidem.* 1531. Peter Marfhall, *pres. iidem.* 1558. William
Watfon, cl. 1570. John Garthe, cl. 1574. John Fetlowe, cl. *pres. Eliz. regina.* 1578. Chriftopher Wyley, cl. *pres. eadem.* 1588. Bernardinus Meaburne, cl. *pres. Ric. Bellafife, ar.* 1613. Robert Wemys, M. A. *pres. W. Bellafife.* 1622. James Werays, cl. *pres. W. Bellafife, Knt.*—Geo. Em-
mott, cl. *pres. idem.* 1670. John Pattyfon, B. A. *pres. John Turner, Efq.* 1675. Tho. Nicholfon,
pres. idem.—Tho. Nicholfon, M. A. *pres. idem.* 1721.Tho. Beckett, A. B. *pres. Chomley Turner, Efq.*
1723. John Payley, A. M. *pres. idem.* 1732. Edward Nelfon, *pres. idem.* 1779. Richard Shuttle-
worth, *pres. Charles Turner, Efq.* 1796. James Stanley, *pres. Sir Charles Turner, Bart.* 1801.
William Hall, M. A. *pres. idem.* 1802. Thomas Simpfon, cl. *pres. idem.*

THWENG's chantry, }   *Apud Cawood, ult. Maii* 1348.
or college.   }

ORDINATION. } AT the requeft of Thomas de Thweng, Rector of the church of Lythum, and
                      } patron thereof, while he lived, William, Archbifhop of York, decreed and or-
dained, that there fhould be in the church of Lythum for the future, one Rector, at the prefentation
of the patron thereof, inftituted and inducted, who fhall prefide therein, and fhall exercife by himfelf
and others, the full cure and government of the church, in which he fhall perfonally refide.

CHANTRY. } Alfo, that there be in the fame church, a perpetual chantry, confifting of 12
            } chaplains and 4 clerks, continually miniftering in divine offices; which faid

morate in their maſſes and other prayers the healthful eſtate of the ſaid *Thomas de Thweng*, of the King and Queen of England, and of Lord Henry de Percy, &c.

THIS college of chantry prieſts did not long continue, but was diſſolved, on the appropriation of the rectory here to the collegiate church of Staindrop.

---

prieſts or chaplains ſhall be preſented by the patron of the church for the time being to the Archbiſhop, to be admitted in any one of their vacations : who, ſo conſtituted and inducted, ſhall obey the rector of the church ſubmiſſively in all things :

AND ſhall uſe garments ſuitable to their order, and black ſhoes : and ſix of theſe prieſts ſhall be on each ſide of the quire :

AND, at table, he ſhall ſit firſt, who firſt is come thither : and in all things, as well in the church as table, each one ſhall ſerve by turns, as *ebdomary*, according to the rector's ordination ; and they ſhall be preſent in the church in celebration of mattins, high maſſes, and other canonical hours, every day ; as ſhall alſo the 4 clerks, who ſhall aſſiſt the ſaid prieſts in divine offices.

AND every day one of the ſaid prieſts ſhall celebrate the maſs of *St. Trinity;* another the maſs of *St. Croſs ;* a third, of the *Holy Croſs ;* a fourth, of the *Bleſſed Virgin ;* a fifth, of the *Holy Angels ;* and a ſixth, of *All-Saints,* &c.

AND the other ſix prieſts ſhall every day celebrate thrice a day, whereof one ſhall celebrate the parochial maſs, &c. And the other two ſhall perform the office of the dead, and celebrate for the defunct, excepting on double feſtivals, and *feaſts of nine lections.*

ALSO, the ſix prieſts ſhall celebrate the maſs of *St. Mary Magdalen* or *St. Martha.*

AND on every ſabbath day, the ſaid rector and chaplains ſhall cauſe ſolemnly to be celebrated with note, the maſs of *the Virgin Mary* in the ſaid church, unleſs a double feſtival, or *feaſt of nine lections* do hinder.

AND every of theſe prieſts ſhall in their maſſes and other prayers, eſpecially commemorate the healthful eſtate of the ſaid Thomas de Thweng, of the King and Queen of England, and of Lord Henry de Percy ; and for the ſouls of their anceſtors, and of all rectors of the church of *Lythum,* and of the patrons thereof ; of Robert de Thweng, and Maud his wife ; Marmaduke de Thweng, and Lucia his wife ; and of Marmaduke, William, Robert, John, and Nicholas, brothers of the ſaid Thomas ; of Marmaduke Lumley, his father, mother, and heirs ; and of Robert de Hilton, and Margaret his wife, &c. for whom they ſhall ſay the office of the dead, and *placebo* (viz. of *dirige* and *commendation,* as well diſtinctly as devoutly every day, unleſs a greater feaſt do hinder ; and this after dinner, before the veſpers, in the ſaid church, according to the uſe thereof.

FURTHERMORE he ordained, that the ſaid 12 prieſts ſhall cohabit in one houſe, within the manſion of the rectory, and alſo lodge there ;

AT the diſtance of about two miles from Kirkleatham towards the north, ſtands the village of EAST COATHAM, an ancient hamlet within this pariſh, belonging to the Bruces, Lords of Skelton, and afterwards to the Thwengs of Kilton-Caſtle ; which, with the manor of Kirkleatham, came by purchaſe to the Turners, and is now the proper-

AND the rector ſhall have them all at his table, and cauſe them to be ſufficiently ſerved with meat and drink ;

AND, that the rector ſhall pay to every one of theſe 12 prieſts, 20 ſhillings per ann. ſterling ; and a robe yearly at Martinmas of one ſort, containing ſix ells of cloth &c. price one mark at leaſt.

AND alſo provide them all yearly on the vigil of *All-Saints*, 12 quarters of *ſea-ſoal*, and 20lb. of *candle of Paris*, for lights and fire, to be divided amongſt them : alſo two flaggons of the beſt ale, for to drink in their chambers every night, from the vigil of *All-Saints*, until the morrow of *the purification of St. Mary* yearly.

CLERKS. } Furthermore he ordained that there be in the ſaid church, four poor clerks, at bed and ſinging, who ſhall daily miniſter in the ſaid church in ſurplices and black capes, continually aſſiſting the ſaid prieſts in their celebrations ; to every one of which, the rector ſhall allow 20 ſhillings *per annum*.

MOREOVER, the ſaid rector and chaplains ſhall have one common ſeal kept in one cheſt, whereon ſhall be three locks, the rector having one key thereunto, and the two ſenior prieſts keeping the other two keys.

BESIDES he ordained that the Rector of the church for the time being, do every year, on the feaſt of *All-Saints*, give to 13 poor people of the pariſh 6 pence, and a gown of 20d. price at leaſt : alſo do yearly diſtribute among the poor of the pariſh, nine quarters of bread-corn, and as many quarters of peaſe. All which was confirmed by the chapter of York, on the 9th day of January, 1348.

CATALOGUE OF CHAPLAINS.

	1348 John de Barrowe, de Hackthorne. cap.	*pres. rector eccl.*
1ſt chap. { 1348 Symon de Kernetby, cap.	*pres. idem.*
1375 John de Oſton, pbr.	*pres. archiepiſcopacy.*
2d chap.—1348 William Arnald de Lythum ;	*pres. rector pro temp.*
3d chap.—1348 Henry de Keron ;	*pres. rector eccleſiæ pro temp.*
4th chap.—1348 Galfrid de Langton, cap.	*pres. rector eccleſiæ.*
5th chap. { 1348 John de Lund, cap.	*pres. idem.*
1349 Thomas de Beeford, cap.	*pres. idem.*
6th chap.—1348 William de Coryngham, cap.	*pres. idem.*
7th chap.—1348 John de Wilberfoſſe, cap.	*pres. idem.*
8th chap.—1348 Robert de Eleſham, cap.	*pres. idem.*
9th chap.—1348 John de Kyllom, cap.	*pres. idem.*
10th chap.—1348 Anſelmi de Thyrnum, cap.	*pres. idem.*
11th chap.—1348 Robert de Hunkelby, cap.	*pres. idem.*
12th chap.—1348 Thomas de Hunkelby, cap.	*pres. idem.* *Torr's MSS.*

ty of Sir Charles Turner, Bart. This was formerly a fishing town of some importance, and with Redcar, contributed towards the supply of different monastries, with the necessary article of fish. *

THE following extract from the *Cott. MS.* as it contains a description of the ancient state of this part of the coast, and of the customs peculiar to the inhabitants thereof, will not, we presume, be unacceptable to the reader.

" NEERE unto *Dobham* (the Porte of the Mouth of the Teefe) the
" Shore lyes flatt, where a Shelf of Sand raised above the highe water
" Marke, entertaines an infynite Number of Sea-fowle, which laye
" theyr Egges heere and there fcatteringlie in fuch Sorte, that in Tyme
" of Breedinge one can hardly fett his Foote fo warylye, that he fpoyle
" not many of theyr Nefts. Thefe curious Buylders may furnifh them-
" felves with choice of fhells and particoloured Stones fytt for the ma-
" kinge of artifyciall Works ; and as the Tyde comes in, yt bringethe
" a fmall wafh *Sea-cole,* which is imployed to the makinge of Salte, and
" the Fuell of the poore fifher Townes adjoininge : the oylie Sulphu-
" roufnefs beinge mixed with the Salte of the Sea as yt floweth, and

---

* LIBERTAS *Abbati de Fontibus* emendi pifces et alecia in *Redker* et *Cottum.*

UNIVERSIS Chriftianis fidelibus prefens fcrlptum vifuris et audituris, Petrus de Brus, tertius, falu-tem eternam in domino: fciatis me conceffiffe Deo et monachis ecclefiæ fanctæ Mariæ *de Fontibus* ut habeant facultatem et libertatem emendi pifces et alecia, et alia neceffaria apud *Cottum* et *Redker* in feodo meo : ita quod poft . . . . . a fervientibus meis ad opus meum proprium, fint cum pinnis fine impedimento vel aliqua contradictione. Et fi aliquis ipfis impedimentum intulerit, volo ut conftabu-larius meus de Skelton, qui pro tempore fuerit, eis fine dilacione faciat emendari. In cujus rei tefti-monio prefenti fcripto meo, pro me et hæredibus meis figillum meum appofui ; hiis teftibus, dno. Johe de Burton, dno. Ambrofio de Camera, dno. Rogero de Burton, Johe de Thocotes, Robto de Afelby, Willo Capun, et aliis ; *milliffimo ducentiffimo fexagiffimo fexto.*   *Dodfworth's MSS.*

THE monks of *Byland* were exempted by Adam de Brus, from the payment of tolls for their fifh bought here ; and the canons of *Guifbrough,* befides poffeffing confiderable *falt-works* upon this coaft, had the privilege, by the grant of Peter de Brus, of claiming 100lb. weight of fifh annually from each fifhing boat ; and the fhips and boats carrying the goods of the convent to that part of the Tees, or to the fhore of Coatham, as well as their own proper veffels, were free from tolls and cuftoms.

Vide Burton's Mon. Ebor.

" confequently hard to take fyre, or to keepe in longe without quench-
" inge, they have a Meanes, by making fmall Vaults to paffe under the
" Hearthes, into which, by fore-fetting the Wynde with a Board, they
" force yt to enter, and foe to ferve infteede of a pair of Bellowes, which
" they call, in a proper word of Art, *a Blowcole.*

" THE Shells, Sand, and Sea-Rock ferve inftead of Marle to enrich
" the Land, which is fruitfull of itfelf, but much bettered by the neigh-
" bourhood of the Sea, makinge the goode Hufbandes of the lowe
" Towns fatt in the purfe and merry in the Hearte. Within the Sea-
" marke on oone fyde lyeth a Rocke of excellent Plaifter, cankered by
" the Salte water ; but if it were fearched from Sande, yt is probable
" that yt would prove pure alabafter.

" FROM the paffage alonge the Sandes, by Reafon of the Fyrmeneffe
" and Smoothneffe frequented by fuch as delight in fwifte Horfes, you
" nexte come to R*edcarre*, a poor fyfher Towne, where at a lowe water
" you may difcover many Rockes within halfe a mile diftante from the
" Shore, fome in front and fome on either Hande lyein circle wife, ha-
" vinge certaine Inletts for the Boates called *Cobbles* to paffe in and out.
" Truly yt may be fayde of thefe poor Men, that they are lavifh of
" theyr Lives, who will hazard 20 or 40 Myles into the Seas in a fmall
" *Troughe*, foe thinne that the Glimfe of the Sunne may be feene
" through ytt ; yet at 10 or 11 of the Clocke in the Morninge, when
" they come from Sea, they fell theire whole Boatys ladinge for 4s. or
" if they doe gett a Crowne, they fuppofe to have chaffered fayre.
" Three commonly come in one Boate, each of them havinge twoe
" oares, which they governe by drawinge the one Hande over the
" other. The Boate ytfelf is built of Wainfcott, for fhape exceedinge
" all Modeles for fhippinge ; twoe Men will eafily carrye ytt on Lande
" betweene them, yett are they fo fecure in them at Sea, that fome in a
" Storme have lyved aboarde three Dayes. Their greatefte Danger is
" neareft Home, where the waves breake dangeroufly, but they ac-
" quainted with thefe Seas efpieyne a broken wave ready to overtake

" them, fuddenly oppofe the prowe or fharpe ende of theyre Boat unto
" yt, and mountinge to the Tope, defcende down as yt were unto a val-
" ley, hoveringe untill they efpye a whole wave come rowlinge, which
" they obferve commonly to be an odde one ; whereupon mountinge
" with their Cobble, as yt were upon a greate furious Horfe, they rowe
" with Might and Mayne, and together with that Wave drive them-
" felves on Lande. But many tymes it happeneth, that when their
" wives and children or Friends are readye to give them theyre Hands,
" the wave fodainely recoylinge backe, has wheelmed them topfye tr .-
" vey. But of Cortefeye they prevente their firfte Chapman with a
" fifhe, and if any byd money and be refufed, yet thoughe another
" outbyde him, it is in his Choife to be halfe in the Bargaine. They
" have a cuftome everye Yeare to change their Fellows for Luck fake,
" as they efteem yt; and upon St. Peter's Daye, they invite their Friends
" and Kinsfolk to a Feftyvall, kept after their Fafhion, with a free
" Hearte, and noe fhew of Nigardneffe : that Daye their Boates are
" dreffed curioufly for the Shewe, their Maftes are painted,and certaine
" Rytes obferved amongfte them, with fprinklinge their prows with
" good Liquor, fold with them at a Groate the Quarte ; which Cuftome
" or Superftition fuckt from their Anceftors even contynueth down
" unto this prefent Tyme. If the Sea growe proude by the ftyrringe
" of the Wyndes, yt is a worthye Spectacle to behoulde the fury of that
" vigorous Element, which with a hideous Roaringe befpeweth all the
" Rocks, and foameth, as a Pott boylinge over the Brymme. Many
" poore women get a fory Livinge by pullinge Crabbs and Lobfters
" out of the Rocks with hooks faftened to long poales. There are
" plenty of Cockles, Muffels and Lympetts, wherewith to bayte their
" Hookes, and for Oyfters fome fewe are taken by chance cleaving to
" theyre Lines."

THE village of Eaft Coatham is pleafantly fituated upon the fea-
fhore ; and being much frequented during the Seafon for the purpofe
of fea-bathing, contains fome neat and convenient lodging-houfes. A

large and commodious inn was erected here a few years ago by the
late Sir Charles Turner, Bart. and having the advantage of firm and
extensive sands, with bathing machines and other accommodations.
Coatham is in many respects superior to Redcar, as a seat of seclusion
for the invalid. †

THE SOIL within the parish is, in general, a strong clay, with a
mixture of rich black loam ; and towards the sea, the lands are of a
light marly loam. From the great exertions of the late Sir Charles
Turner, Bart. in the general improvement of his estate, by introducing
the turnip and clover culture, an improved breed of cattle, and ma-

---

† THE following description of *Coatham*, and its sister village *Redcar*, was published in a London newspaper, and dated at " *Coatham, Sept. 7th, 1795.*"

" NATURE seems to have designed this romantic spot in her most lovely mood. The delightful
scenery and extensive prospects, with which it is surrounded, conspire to attract the admiration of all,
who visit and contemplate its beauties. The small, though elegant circle, which at present enliven
the hemisphere of *Coatham*, proclaim it an infant watering-place, which, in its maturity, may vie with
the most fashionable resorts of the age. Its purlieus being, however, as yet somewhat confined, the
numerous assemblage of rank, beauty, and fortune, who would otherwise grace the hourly increasing
attractions of this charming village, is necessarily compressed into a select and polished few, who unite
in that harmony of sentiment, which can alone render a public rendezvous a pleasurable vehicle of
health. The air is remarkably salubrious, the sands extensive and peculiarly fine, and the machines
for bathing commodious. In a word, nothing remains to form this into a most favourite summer
residence, but an increase of accommodation for strangers.

THE sister village, *Redcar*, agreeably situated on the shore, is rather larger, though inferior in many qualities, which complete the interest of *Coatham*. A very respectable company of comedians
perform at the former village with considerable applause. The advantages of a genteel neighbourhood are added to enhance the native charms of these engaging and picturesque resorts; the social
unanimity with which their parties, balls, and other amusements are conducted, shed the most delightful influence over every breast. Much were it to be wished, that the innocent enjoyments of *Coatham*
might take place of the more fashionable dissipation of public watering-places ; and that the fair, in
lieu of ceding to the frantic infatuation of the gaming-table, might, as in the simple retirement of
Coatham, repose in the bosom of ease and tranquility.   Your's &c."

THE improvements at Kirkleatham by the late *Sir Charles Turner, Bart.* are worthy of the reader's particular attention. Besides the erection of an elegant mansion, he exerted himself with spirit
in the repair of the public roads throughout Cleveland, by promoting a subscription to defray the expence, without the assistance of tolls.

king a variety of experiments in different branches of agriculture, the farms here are in a fuperior ftate of cultivation, and produce abundant crops of corn and grafs.   About one half of the land is in tillage ; and the improved modes of management are generally adopted.

His farms lay generally in fcattered fields unconnected with each other, and fome of them at a diftance from the farm houfes, which were moftly in bad repair; thefe defects he remedied by building new farm houfes, with convenient barns and other offices in the moft eligible fituations, and throwing to each the lands that lay contiguous thereto.   The cottages upon his eftate were equally inconvenient, being wretched hovels placed in improper fituations.   This evil was remedied by erecting new ones, round an open fpace, *by way of green*, which has greatly ornamented the country ; and at the fame time, by building new houfes and fhops for a blackfmith, cartwright, fhopkeeper and butcher, he provided the neceffary tradefmen for the neighbourhood.   Inftead of paltry ale-houfes, which were the conftant receptacle of fmugglers that frequent the coaft, and an encouragement to idlenefs and drunkennefs, he built two commodious inns with good apartments, one in the new village above-mentioned, and the other at *Coatham*, a part of his eftate upon the coaft; to each of which a fmall farm was annexed ; and by fixing upon them creditable tenants, the pernicious practices of the former ale-houfes have been deftroyed, and numerous conveniences to the country eftablifhed in their ftead.   Befides thefe works, he erected a houfe near the fea with fpacious granaries &c. in order to fix a trade here : or at leaft to provide a proper place for the farmers to lodge their corn &c. ready for fhipping, and to enable the merchant to fpeculate in the corn trade ; a defign of a moft enlarged nature, and which promifes to be attended with the moft beneficial confequences. Thefe, it muft be acknowledged, were fpirited undertakings, but will appear ftill more extraordinary, when it is known, that the whole were planned and executed in the fhort fpace of three years.

Six month's tour through the North of England.

The common breed of horned cattle in Cleveland is the fhort-horned, called the *Tees-water* or Holdernefs breed, which feed to a great weight, but are confidered lefs profitable for the dairy and grazier, than the *Lancafhire* long-horned kind, which the late *Sir Charles Turner* procured at a confiderable expence, and brought to the greateft perfection.   His cattle of the fhort-horned breed were alfo perfect in their kind ; and an ox, feven years old, (bred from a Scotch kiloe of Lord *Caffillis'* breed, by a Cleveland bull) was killed at *Kirkleatham, October* 28th, 1767, which weighed as follows:

			Stone	lb
Four quarters	-	-	129	9
Head	-	-	3	5
Tongue	-	-	0	12
Feet	-	-	2	$12\frac{1}{2}$
Tallow	-	-	21	8
			158	$4\frac{1}{4}$

POPULATION. In the agricultural improvements at Kirkleatham, it was a point principally aimed at by the late Sir Charles Turner, Bart. to increafe the population of the parifh, not only by giving encouragement to labourers to fettle there, for whom he took care to procure conftant employment; but alfo by taking annually a certain number of boys from the foundling hofpital at *Ackworth*, in this county, whom he bound apprentices to his tenants, to be inftructed in the different branches of agriculture. By this liberal and enlightened conduct the number of inhabitants fince that period, have confiderably increafed, and without any additional burthen of poor rates upon the parifh. This increafe of population will more particularly appear from a comparative ftatement in the following table of baptifms &c. extracted from the parifh regifters; viz.

	Bap.	Bur.	Mar.
From the year, 1681 to 1700 inclufive,	227	141	57
1781 to 1800,	369	293	121
Increafe,	142	152	64

WHEN an accurate enumeration was made in the year 1801, † by order of the Legiflature, there were then 159 inhabited houfes, contain-

---

† STATE of population, 10th March, 1801.

	Inha-bited houfes.	Fami-lies.	Uninha-bited houfes.	Males.	Females.	Total.	Agri-cul-ture.	Trade &c.	Refi-du.	Total.
Kirkleatham.	159	165	5	314	366	680	95	61	524	680

Thomas Brown, a native of this parifh, is intitled to fome notice in the biography of the diftrict, for his brave conduct at the battle of *Dettingeu*, June 16th, 1743.

HE was born at *Kirkleatham* about the year 1712, of obfcure but honeft parents; and in the early part of life, inlifted as a private foldier into *Brigadier Bland's* dragoons; in which fituation we do not find that he he had any opportunity of particularly diftinguifhing himfelf, till that memorable day, when he difplayed the greateft intrepidity.

IN the early part of the engagement he had two horfes killed under him, and two fingers of his left hand were cut off; notwithstanding which, upon the lofs of their ftandard, occafioned by the cornet's receiving a wound in the wrift, *Brown* was determined to regain it, which he accomplifhed by firft fhooting the *gens d'armes* who was in poffeffion of it, through the head, and afterwards fighting his way back through the ranks of the enemy.

ing 680 inhabitants, occupied chiefly in agriculture, except a few fishermen and their families at Coatham. The average number of burials
in one year, within a given period, is 15, from which it will appear
that out of a population of 680, one out of 45½ dies annually.

THE PARISH OF WILTON

LIES to the fouth from Kirkleatham, and about three miles diftant
from the market-town of Guifbrough. It confifts only of one
townfhip, comprehending the manors of Lazenby and Lackenby, the

IN the execution of this exploit, he received eight cuts in the face, head and neck ; two balls lodged in his back, and three went through his hat ; and in this mangled condition, he rejoined his regiment with the ftandard he had retaken, and was received by his fellow-foldiers with the moft tri-
umphant acclamations.

AFTER the recovery of his wounds, he ferved a fhort time, as a private, in the horfe-guards;
and his undaunted courage would certainly have been rewarded with a commiffion ; but wanting
the advantage of education, and befides, having contracted a habit of drinking, which, we believe, was in a great meafure brought on by the pains he frequently experienced from the balls in
his back which could never be extracted, he was confidered totally unfit for fervice, and retired to the
town of Yarm, on a penfion of 30l. per ann. which, however, he did not long enjoy ; but died, and
was buried there on the 18. January, 1746.

WE have not been able to collect any anecdotes of *Brown* worthy of notice, after his difcharge;
but have to remark, that as a compliment to, and in fome degree to perpetuate the remembrance of
his heroifm, there was *a fign* erected foon after his death, in the town of Yarm, which remains to this
day, reprefenting him on horfeback, covered with wounds, and bearing the ftandard he had retaken
from the enemy.

THERE is alfo a fcarce portrait of *Brown*, with the fcars on his face and neck, engraved *ad vivum*,
by *L. P. Boitard*.

F f f

latter of which forms the western boundary of the parish, and adjoins
to the chapelry of Eston, within the parish of Ormesby, stretching
northwards to the sea, and the mouth of the river Tees.

It appears from the Domesday-book, that the manors of Wilton
and Lackenby were in the possession of *Norman*, before the Conquest;
but at the period of the survey, were held by *Nigel*, under Robert Earl
of Moreton, being entered under the title,

TERRA COMITIS MORITONIENSIS.

"IN WILTUNE AD GELDUM IIII. CARUCATÆ, ET II. CAR. POSSUNT ES-
"SE. IBI HABEBAT NORMAN I. MANERIUM; NUNC HABET NIGEL DE COM-
"ITE. IBI II. BORDARII SUNT, ET VI. ACRI PRATI. T. R. E. VALEBAT XVI.
"SOLID. MODO XVI. DENAR. IN EAD. VILLA AD GELD. SUNT IIII. BOU-
"VATÆ. SOCA PERTINET AD TERRAM NIGEL."

"IN LACHENBI AD GELDUM II. CARUCATÆ, ET I. CAR. POTEST ESSE.
"IBI HABEBAT NORMAN I. MANERIUM. NUNC HABET NIGEL DE COMITE
"ET WAST. T. R. E. VALEBAT XIII. SOLID. ET IIII. DENAR."

Wilton, according to the above extract, was taxed for four carucates with two more that might be rendered arable. There were two
bordarii, and six acres of meadow; and the manor, in the Confessor's
time, was valued at sixteen shillings, but at the time of the survey only
at sixteen-pence. There were also four bovates of land *ad geldum* in
the said village; the soke of which pertained to the lands held by Nigel. Lackenby contained two carucates *ad geldum*, valued in the Confessor's time at thirteen shillings and four-pence, but was then waste.

From another part of the general survey, it appears, that there
were also at Wilton three carucates, and six bovates of land *ad geldum*,
with arable land for two ploughs, entered under the title

"TERRA TAINORUM REGIS.

"MANERIUM IN WILTUNE HABUIT ALTOR III. CAR. TERRÆ, ET VI.
"BOUVATÆ AD GELDUM. TERRA AD II. CAR. IBI HABET MALDRED f.
"CAR. ET VIII. VILLANI ET X. BORD. CUM III. CAR. ET VI. ACR. PRATI.
"T. R. E. VALEBAT XX. SOL. MODO SIMILITER."

These lands were held by *Altor*, who was one of those Saxon Lords
called *Thanes*, who, in the times of the Saxons, were equal to the Barons

of the Normans. Maldred alfo held one carucate here, with eight villeins and ten bordarii, who had three plough lands, and fix acres of meadow. The whole was valued at twenty fhillings.

LAZENBY was taxed for four carucates and a half, with one ploughland and three acres of meadow, held by Leuenoff, and valued in the time of King Edward the Confeffor at ten fhillings. This was ancient demefne of the Crown, and is entered under the title

"TERRA REGIS.

" MANERIUM IN LESINGEBI LIEUENOT IIII. CARUCATÆ TERRÆ ET " DIMID. AD GELDUM. TERRA AD I. CAR. IBI ACR. PRATI. T. R. E. X. " SOLID."

THE Bulmers became at an early period Lords of Wilton, with its dependent manors of Lackenby and Lazenby, and the hamlet of *Weſt Coatham;* one moiety of which lands, according to Kirkby's Inqueſt, ‖ was held by John de Bulmer, under Ranulphus de Mennel, as of the fee of Peter de Mauley; and another part of the eſtate was held by John de Percy, of the King *in capite;* of whom the faid John de Bulmer had half a Knight's fee in Wilton and Weſt Coatham, where ten carucates made one Knight's fee.

THE Bulmers * were an ancient family of great reputation, and had large poſſeſſions in Yorkſhire, and the county of Durham; but at

‖ RANULPHUS DE MENNEL tenet unum feod. de Petro Malolacu, in *medietate de Wilton,* et *inLakinby, Weſt-Cotum, Elerdby,* et *Thorpe* juxta *Kilton,* unde X. car. ter. faciunt feod. Et. Johannes de Bulmer tenet illud feod. de dicto Ranulpho. Et idem Johannes reddit ballio dni. regis pro fine 6s. 8d.   *Kirkby's Inqueſt.*

JOHANNES PERCY DE TOPCLIFFE tenet dimid. feod. in Wilton, de domino rege in capite. Et Johannes de Bulmer tenet illud dimid. de dicto Johanne Percy, et idem Johannes Bulmer reddit X. lib. . . . Nomine liberæ firmæ.   *Ibid.*

* *The Pedigree of* BULMERS.

THE following pedigree, which differs from the account given of this family in *Dugdale's Baronage,* is compiled from GYLL's MSS. *Glover's Viſitation,* and other authorities.

ARMS. Gules, billette or; and a lion rampant of the fecond.
CREST. A bull, paſſant.

Henry Bulmer,
Allen Bulmer, . . . daughter of John Powther, Knt.

what particular period they became firſt feated at Wilton, we have no
information. In the 4. Edw. II. Ralph de Bulmer obtained a charter
in all his demeſne lands here; and in 1. Edw. III. he had ſummons to
Parliament amongſt the Barons. In the 4. Edw. III. he had ſpecial licence to make a caſtle of his manor-houſe at Wilton, and was that ſame
year conſtituted ſheriff of Yorkſhire, and governour of the caſtle at
York.

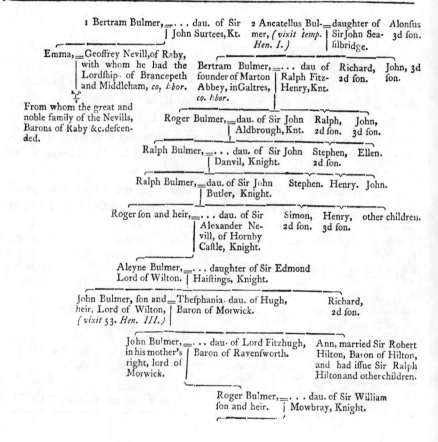

1 Bertram Bulmer,＿... dau. of Sir　2 Ancatellus Bul-＿daughter of　Alonſus
　　　　　| John Surtees, Kt.　　　mer, (vixit temp. | Sir John Sea-　3d ſon.
　　　　　　　　　　　　　　　　　　Hen. I.)　　| filbridge.

Emma,＿Geoffrey Nevill, of Raby,
　　| with whom he had the　Bertram Bulmer,＿... dau of　Richard,　John, 3d
　　| Lordſhip. of Brancepeth　founder of Marton | Ralph Fitz-　2d ſon.　ſon.
　　| and Middleham, co, Ebor.　Abbey, in Galtres, | Henry, Knt.
From whom the great and　co. Ebor.
noble family of the Nevills,
Barons of Raby &c. deſcen-　　　Roger Bulmer,＿dau. of Sir John　Ralph,　John,
ded.　　　　　　　　　　　　　| Aldbrough, Knt.　2d ſon.　3d ſon.

　　　　　Ralph Bulmer,＿... dau. of Sir John　Stephen,　Ellen.
　　　　　　　　　　　| Danvil, Knight.　　2d ſon.

　　　　　Ralph Bulmer,＿dau. of Sir John　Stephen. Henry. John.
　　　　　　　　　　　| Butler, Knight.

　Roger ſon and heir,＿... dau. of Sir　Simon,　Henry,　other children.
　　　　　　　　　　| Alexander Ne-　2d ſon.　3d ſon.
　　　　　　　　　　| vill, of Hornby
　　　　　　　　　　| Caſtle, Knight.

　　　Aleyne Bulmer,＿... daughter of Sir Edmond
　　　Lord of Wilton. | Haiſtings, Knight.

John Bulmer, ſon and＿Theſphania. dau. of Hugh,　　Richard,
heir, Lord of Wilton, | Baron of Morwick.　　　　2d ſon.
(vixit 53. Hen. III.)

　　　John Bulmer,＿... dau. of Lord Fitzhugh,　Ann, married Sir Robert
　　　in his mother's | Baron of Ravenſworth.　Hilton, Baron of Hilton,
　　　right, lord of　　　　　　　　　　　and had iſſue Sir Ralph
　　　Morwick.　　　　　　　　　　　　Hilton and other children.

　　　　　Roger Bulmer,＿... dau. of Sir William
　　　　　ſon and heir.　| Mowbray, Knight.

WILTON continued in this family for many generations till Sir John Bulmer, Knight, the last possessor of that family, engaging in the northern insurrection, called the *pilgrimage of grace,* was attainted for high treason, (28. Henry VIII.) when this and other estates were

Ralph Bulmer, = . . . dau. of William Fulthorpe,
obiit 40 *E. III.* | of Hathorpe, Esq.

Sir Ralph Bulmer, Knt. = . . . dau. of William Hilton,
(*vixit* 22. *Rich. II.* 1398.) | Knt. Baron of Hilton.

Sir William Bulmer, = Elizabeth, dau. | Ralph, | Jane.
Knt. | of Sir R. Eure, K. | 2d son.

Sir Ralph Bulmer, Kt. = Joane, dau. Robert, William, Anne &
(ob. 7. HenryVII.)* | of Sir Wil. 2d son. 3d son Ellen.
| Bowes, Kt.

Anne, married to
Marmaduke de
la Rivier.

Sir Wil. Bulmer, Knt. = Margery, dau. of Sir
John Conyers, Knt.
by Alicehis wife dau.
of . . . Falconbridge.

Sir William = Eliz. dau. and
Bulmer, Kt. | heir of Wil.
3d son. | Elmeden.

Margery married
to George, son &
heir of Sir Ralph
Salveyne, Knt.

Margaret, natural = Sir JohnBulmer, = Anne, dau. of
d. of E. Stafford, | Knt. eldest son; | Sir Ralph Bi-
Duke of Bucking- | attainted by King | got, Knight.
ham, & formerly | Henry VIII. and | (1st wife.)
concubine to the | his lands forfeited
fame Sir JohnBul-
mer, (2d wife.)

Francis Bulmer = Catharine, d.
| of R. Morton.

Ant. Henry, Francis,
2d son. 3d son.

Sir Bertram = Isabel, dau. of
Bulmer, Kt. | N. Tempest, of
| Stella, Knight.

Sir Ralph = Ann, dau. and
Bulmer, | coheir of Rog.
2d son. | Alke, of Alke,
| Knt. (1st wife.)

Dorothy d. = John Sayer of
and heir. | Worfall, Esq.

John Sayer, = . . . d. of
of Worfall, | G. Conyers,
son and heir. | ofSockbarn.

George Sayer, =
of Worfall, Esf.

W. Bulmer, = Joane, d.
of Leven- | and heir
nige, co. | of . . Wil-
Ebor. (2d | berfosse.
son.)

Sir R. Bul- = Anne, d.
mer, K. 1st | of Sir T.
son, was rest. | Tempest,
in blood. | Knight.

Anne = M. Boyton,
| of Acklam.
Eliz. = H. Newton.
Agnes = L. l ayton.
Mary = d. unmar.

* 7. HENRY VII. Radulphus Bulmer, miles, obiit in vigil. festi sancti Johannis Baptistæ: Willus. est filius et hæres plenæ ætatis; tenet in Wilton, Lakenby, West-Cotum, Lasingby, Bulmar et Foul-Sutton.

From Dodsworth's MSS, 98 *vol.*

forfeited to the Crown. Wilton was afterward granted, in the reign of Philip and Mary, to Sir Thomas Cornwallis, and his wife *in tail*, and confirmed, in the third year of King James I. to his son Sir William Cornwallis, *in fee*; whose descendant (Lord Cornwallis) sold the estate here to Mr. Fox (afterwards Lord Holland) of whom it was purchased by the trustees under the will of Robert Lowther, of Maul's Meburn, Esq. for the benefit of his son, the late Earl of Lonsdale, then an infant; who, dying without issue, was succeeded by John Lowther, Esq. the present proprietor, and Lord of the manor.

THE village of Wilton is small, and consists of a few houses, seated on the northern declivity of a hill; the summit of which being nearly level, has been brought into cultivation; while the sides, rising abruptly, are ornamented with young and thriving plantations. The grounds on the north from the village have an easy and gradual descent, and the prospect is extensive and pleasingly diversified: near at hand upon the right are seen the hospital and mansion, with the richly cultivated grounds of Kirkleatham, beyond which, tracing the circling line of shore to the left, the town of Hartlepool in a prominent position, with the bold

---

Pedigree:

Wil. Bulmer.=Dorothy, d. of J. G. Sayer, of Worsall, Esq.

Francis ca. d. & coh. mar. Constable, of Cliffe.

Mille, sente, d. & coh. mar. T Gray, of Borton, in Ryedale.

John Bulmer, of Pinchinthorpe in Cleveland.=Agnes, d. of James Crathorne, of Crathorne.

Anne, born after marriage, 1584.

Francis-ton Fenton, in the (*S. P.*)

Mary, after mar. ca, *Notha. Notha.*

Joane, d. & coh. mar Francis, son of Sir R Cholmley.

Dorothy, dau and coheir.=Wil. son of Sir Bertram Bulmer, Kt.

Robert Bulmer, son and heir=E dau. of .. Green, of Naborn

Anthony Bulmer, eldest son and heir. 1665.

Francis Bulmer, of Lennige.=Ann, d of M. Oglethorpe, of Thornton.

Henry Bulmer, ætat. 17. 1584.

Thomas, 2d son.

Eliz. mar. M. Nodell, of Howden.

Margaret mar. John Jackson, of Fenton, in the barony of Sherborne, in the W. R. of Yorkshire.

figure of its church, affords a ftriking object; while the ferpentine
courfe of the river Tees, which on its approach towards the fea, ex-
pands itfelf into a fine extenfive bay, is feen winding through a tract of
rich and fertile grounds beneath, adding greatly to the beauty and intereft of the general view.

AT the weftern extremity of the village ftand the remains of

WILTON CASTLE,

an ancient baronial feat of the Bulmers, which has gradually gone to
decay, and by the irrefiftible attacks of time, is now fo ruinous, as to
prefent little to the eye of the traveller, but its moulding tower,—a tot-
tering emblem of human greatnefs.

WILTON was an ancient chapelry within the parifh of Kirkleatham;
but the chapel feems not to have been dependent on that church. It
was dedicated to Saint Cuthbert, and being granted and appropriated to the priory of Guifbrough, at the diffolution of the monaftry,
became a perpetual curacy, endowed with fmall tithes, and certified to
the governours of Queen Anne's bounty at 19*l.* 9s. 6d. It has received
two augmentations by lot, laid out in the purchafe of lands at Great
Broughton, in the parifh of Kirkby. John Lowther, Efq. is the prefent patron, the right of nomination to the chapel being an appendage
to the manor.

UPON an inclofure of the open undivided fields, a few years ago,
under an Act of Parliament, an allotment was fet out to Sir Charles
Turner, Bart. as impropriator; and a portion of land, eftimated at one
hundred pounds *per ann.* to the curate, in lieu and perpetual difcharge
of all tithes, great and fmall, within the parifh.

NEAR the centre of the village, a little to the north-weft from the
mill, are the remains of St. Ellen's chapel, founded, according to *Torr,*
by Sir William Bulmer (23d Henry VIII.) for two priefts to fay mafs
for the fouls of him and his wife, with ftipends, one of 4*l.* 10s. and
the other 4*l. per ann.* to be paid by the church-wardens of Kirkleatham,

out of lands for that purpofe, and alfo for the fupport of four poor
men and four poor women.

THIS we conclude was a chantry chapel, which did not long continue; as thefe and fimilar foundations fhared the fame fate as the
greater religious houfes, being granted by Act of Parliament to King
Edward the Sixth, and foon afterwards deftroyed. ‖

POPULATION.   In a parifh of but fmall extent, and inhabited by
farmers and labourers in hufbandry, with a few ordinary mechanics,
we find little under this head worthy of particular obfervation.   When
an actual enumeration was made in the year 1801, by order of the Legiflature, there were then within the parifh, including the hamlets of
Lazenby and Lackenby, 67 houfes, 74 families, and 328 inhabitants,
giving $4\frac{1}{2}$ and upwards to each family. *

THE following table of baptifms, &c. extracted from the parifh regifters, from the year 1781 to the year 1800 inclufive, will give the reader fome idea of the increafe of its inhabitants.

	Males.	Females.	Total.
Baptifms	96	117	213
Burials	55	60	115
Increafe	41	47	98

Marriages within the above period 47.

WILTON CHAPEL.

DEDICATED to St. Cuthbert.   Priory of Guifbrough propr.
CERT. value 19l. 9s. 6d. augmented with 400l.   John Lowther, Efq. patron.

CURATES.

1699 William Jaques, curate.

1715 William Confett, *nom. Sir Stephen Fox.*

1721 John Langftaffe, curate.

1749 William Langftaffe.

1790 William Milner, *nom. Earl of Lonfdale.*

1797 Thomas Saul, A. B.   *idem.*

‖ OVER the entrance of the building is the figure of a man's head ; on one fide of which is a *bull,*
in an erect pofture ; and on the other, an animal now much defaced, which, it has been conjectured,
was probably a *mare,* forming a monkifh device of the name of *Bulmer.*

* STATE OF POPULATION, 10th March, 1801.

	Inhabit. Houfes.	Fami-lies.	Uninhab. Houfes.	Males.	Females.	Total.	Agri-cul.	Trade, &c.	Refi-due.	Total.
Wilton.	67	74	4	148	180	328	74	27	227	328.

FROM the above ſtatement it will appear that the number of baptiſms to that of burials is nearly as two to one ; and the average number of baptiſms in one year being 11 nearly, and that of burials $5\frac{3}{4}$, we
conclude that while for every 30 of the inhabitants a child is born, one
only out of 58 nearly dies annually.

SOIL, PRODUCE, &c. The lands within the pariſh conſiſt nearly
of an equal portion of arable, meadow, and paſture ; and the ſoil in
general a fertile clay ; which, notwithſtanding its northern aſpect, and
expoſure to ſevere blaſts from the ſea, produces crops of wheat and
other grain in great perfection, and the harveſts in general are as early
as in any of the more favoured parts of Cleveland.   The low grounds
near the river Tees are principally in graſs ; as was formerly an extenſive tract, which lay in common open fields, ſtretching from the village in a direction north and ſouth ; but, by the late incloſure, has been
brought into a more advantageous ſtate of cultivation.

WE cannot conclude our account of this pariſh without briefly
noticing the project of an embankment by the late Earl of Lonſdale,
in order to recover an extenſive tract of land and low grounds from the
influx of the ſea.   The works were begun in the year 1777 ; but being commenced within the boundaries of the manor of Kirkleatham ;
and from the conſideration that, if effected according to the propoſed
plan, they would not only obſtruct the navigation, and the ways and
paſſages thereto ; but alſo incloſe the limits within which the duties
of anchorage, &c. were claimed by the Turner family,—ſome objections were made by Mr. Turner to the further progreſs of the undertaking, unleſs conſidered as done without prejudice to his claim of
right to the ſoil and ground of that part of the embankment which
lay within the limits of his manor ; and of his other rights and privi-

G g g

leges. ‖ The embankment, however, was continued for fome time, in utter defiance of this claim; till meeting with fome unforefeen difficulty in the further profecution of the plan, and apprehenfive that the probable expence would greatly overbalance the advantages to be derived from it, after a fruitlefs expenditure of upwards of 60,000*l.* the works were abandoned, and the projeƈt given up.

¶ By a deed of conveyance, inrolled in the court of chancery, from Sir George Marwood, Bart. to John Turner, of Kirkleatham, Efq. bearing date April 14th, 1666, it appears that the *Turner family* became poffeffed of, and intitled to the *anchorage* and *groundage* of all manner of *fhips, keels, boats,* and other veffels, which fhould at any time land or come on fhore in any of the *harbours, ports, fhores, creeks,* and *places,* fituate or being weft or north-weft of *Redcar,* in the county of York, and from thence unto a river or place called *Caldcoat-fleet,* in the faid county; and alfo to all and every cuftomary *payment, duty, fum,* or *fums of money,* due and payable for, and in the name of *anchorage* or *groundage* for any *fhip,* &c. landing or coming on fhore in any of the *harbours,* &c. And, alfo to all *wreck* or *wrecks of fea, flotfam, jetfam,* and *legan, derelict, derelicts,* and *fifh royal,* which fhould at any time be wrecked, or caft upon any *fhore,* &c. And alfo to all *fea-weed, fea-ware, tangle,* and *kelp,* being or growing or which fhould be wrecked or caft upon any *rock, fcarr, fcawp,* or *fand,* within the *fhores,* &c. And to all benefits and advantages in getting *mufcles* or other *fhell-fifh;* with all and fingular privileges, profits, and appurtenances to them belonging, or therewith ufed, occupied, and enjoyed.

The duties payable are;
{
For a fhip with one or more mafts　　2s. 6d.
For a deck boat　　-　　-　　1s. 3d.
For a five man boat　　-　　-　　0s. 7½d.
}

By virtue of this grant, the *Turner family* from time to time received the anchorage and groundage duties, and enjoyed the other rights and privileges without interruption, till the year 1722, when a whale of confiderable value was left on fhore at a place called *Brans,* which introduced the firft difpute (Mr. Fox, the then owner of the lordfhips of *Wilton* and *Weft Coatham,* giving fome obftruction;) but Chomley Turner, Efq. took and carried away the faid whale, and after extracting the oil therefrom, placed the *jaw-bones* in the garden of the free-fchool at Kirkleatham, as an evidence of this exertion of his right.

THE PARISH OF GUISBROUGH.

THIS parish is of confiderable extent, ftretching from eaft to weft fix miles, and upwards of five miles from north to fouth. Befides fome fcattered hamlets, it contains the feveral townfhips of Guifbrough, Tockets, Hutton-Lowcrofs, Pinchinthorpe, and Commondale; and is bounded on the eaft by the parifhes of Skelton and Upleatham; by Ormefby and Newton, with a part of Ayton and Kildale, on the weft; by Wilton and Kirkleatham on the north; and by Danby, and the chapelry of Wefterdale, on the fouth.

IT appears from the Domefday furvey, that in the Conqueror's time there were three diftinct manors within the townfhip of Guifbrough; the firft of which was ancient demefne of the Crown, and taxed for one carucate, furveyed as follows, under the title

TERRA REGIS.

MANERIUM IN GHIGESBURG. VLCHEL I. CAR. TRÆ AD GLD. TRA AD DIM. CAR.

IN another part of the Survey we find that Guifbrough, together with Middleton and Hutton, which we conjecture to be Hutton-Low-crofs, was taxed for twenty-five carucates, held by *Uctred*, and entered under the title

TERRA COMITIS MORITONIENSIS.

IN GHIGESBURG ET MIDDLETON ET HOTUN AD GELDUM XXV. CAR-UCATÆ, ET XIIII. CAR. POSSUNT ESSE. IBI HABEBAT UCTRED III. MAN-ER. NUNC HABET COMES IN DOMINIO I. CAR. ET X. VILLANI CUM IIII CAR. PRESBITER ET ÆCCLESIA IBI EST, ET I. MOLD. IIII. SOLID. T. R. E. VALEBAT XL. SOLID. MODO XVI. SOL.

FROM the above extract, it appears that Robert, Earl of Moreton, had one carucate in demefne, and ten villeins, who had four ploughs; that there was a minifter, and a mill worth four fhillings. The whole in the Confeffor's time was valued at forty fhillings, but at the time of the furvey only at fixteen fhillings.

THE third notice of Guifbrough is under the title
" TERRA ROBERTI MALLET.
MANERIUM IN GHIGESBORG HABUIT LEISINC III. CAR. TERRÆ, ET
II. BOVAT. AD GELDUM, UBI II. CAR. POSSUNT ESSE. NUNC HABET RO-
BERTUS I. CAR. IBI ET III. VILLANOS CUM I. CAR. T. R. E. VALEBAT V.
SOLID. ET IIII. DENAR. MODO SIMILITER."

FROM which we find that *Lefing* had one manor here, containing
three carucates and two oxgangs of land *ad geldum*, with two carucates
more that might be rendered arable : that Robert Mallet held one carucate, with three villeins who had one plough.   The whole was valued
in the Confeffor's time at five fhillings and fourpence.   There were alfo
fix oxgangs of land *ad geldum* within the foke of the manor of Lofthoufe, held by Hugh Earl of Chefter, but then wafte.

THESE manors, at an early period after the Conqueft, became united under the fee of Robert de Brus, Lord of Skelton ; who, on the
foundation of the priory here, gave thereto all this territory, confifting
of twenty carucates and two oxgangs of land, together with the mill,
foc and multure ; and the Canons continued Lords here, till the diffolution of the monaftry, when the manor came to the Crown ; and in
the 5th and 6th of Philip and Mary, it was granted with feveral
parcels of the faid priory to Sir Thomas Chaloner, Knight, to be held
of the Queen by military fervice ; on whofe defcendants it has fince
continued, and is now the property of Robert Chaloner, Efq. the prefent Lord of the manor.

THE town of Guifbrough, which is of great antiquity, and, according to Baxter, was the *Urbs Caluvium* ‖ of the ancients, is pleafantly
fituated in a narrow but fertile vale ; and confifts chiefly of one principal ftreet, running eaft and weft, which is broad and fpacious, and
many of the houfes being built in a modern ftyle, the town has a neat

---

‖ " Videtur etiam Urbs Caluvium hodie dici GISBOROUGH, potius GHESTBOROUGH, quafi dicas
fpiritualis burgus.   Satis vetuftum hoc oppidum, et antiquo monafterio celebre ; unde et Saxonicum
nomen tractum videtur."   *Baxter's Glofi. p.* 61. *fub voce Caluvium.*

and pleafing appearance. There is a weekly market here on Monday, which is in general well fupplied with provifions; and five fairs annually for the fale of cattle and linen cloth, to which there is a confiderable refort from the circumjacent country.

IN Bifhop Gibfon's edition of Camden it is faid, " the place is real-" ly fine, and may in points of pleafantnefs, a grateful variety and other " advantages of nature, compare with Puteoli, in Italy; and in point " of healthfulnefs, it far furpaffes it. ‡ The inhabitants are obferved " by travellers to be civil and well-bred, cleanly in their diet, and neat " in their houfes. The coldnefs of the air which the fea occafions is " qualified by the hills between, and the foil is fruitful, and produces " grafs and fine flowers a great part of the year."

DRAYTON, in his Polyolbion, gives the following defcription :

" Mark Guifbrough's gay fcite, where nature feems fo nice,
" As in the fame fhe makes a fecond paradife,
" Whofe foil embroidered is with fo rare fundry flowers,
" Here large oaks fo long green, as Summer there her bowers
" Had fet up all the year—her air for health refin'd,
" Her earth with allum veins fo richly intermin'd."

To the above remarks of Camden and his editor, and the whimfical defcription of our old topographer, Drayton, we fubjoin the following extract from the *Cott. MS.* being a letter addreffed to Sir Thomas Chaloner, Knt. foon after he firft became proprietor of the Lordfhip of Guifbrough.

" SIR

" UNDERSTANDING by your Letter that you wifh to be informed of Rarertyes that lye in this Lordfhippe of yours called Gyfbrough in Cleveland, and in the Coafts neare at Hande, I thoughte, though in a confufed Manner to advertize you accordinglye; for the Seate of the

‡ Mr. PENNANT defcribes the town as pleafantly fituated in a vale furrounded at fome diftance by hills, and open on the eaft to the fea, which is about five miles diftant. It is, he fays, certainly a delightful fpot; but cannot fee the reafon why Camden compares it to Puteoli.

place being a Jorney remote out of all common Highwayes, I can lyken yt to noe place more than Puzzuolo, antiently called Puteoli, unto which it yeldes neither in Pleafantnefs nor Rarities but in holfomenefs of Ayre the fame."

* * * * * * * * * * * * * * *

" ALL above the Towne fouthwards and alonge Cleveland lyeth Blackamoore, antyently fuppofed to be called *Barton-Hyll*, which by the ploughed Land and Ruynes of Houfes in many places feeme to have been well inhabyted, but now in fix or feven Myles together you fhall fcarcely finde a Houfe excepte in a Dale, the refte is Heathe and a Roufte for Heathcocks; yet a Tenant of yours lately tryed that Grounde, being tylled for three or four yeares, wyll yeld good Oates or other Corne which Benefitt for want of induftrious People is utterly lofte, for in Truth the Skirts and Waftes of the Moore be in a Manner all defolate.   The Ayre at Guifbrough is fo temperate, that partly by Reafon of the Sea which is three Myles off, yet broken by Hylls lyinge betweene the Towne and yt, and the Happinefs of the Seate being a Valley mounted on fmall Hills compaffed about with very high Moun-taynes, the Sydes whereof are covered with fayre Trees, or beautifyed with green Bufhes or ftately Cliffs, intermingled with the Downfall of fmall Brooks, wch. with a trylling Murmur and variety of the often windings, makes the moft delightful Profpect I ever faw."

" THE Soyle in the Bottom is fruitfull both in Corne and Graffe ; the Graffe is not very long, but foe fweete and thicke platted, that an acre thereof fomereth as many Cattle as oure befte Groundes in the hart of England.   The Grounde mofte parte of the Yeare is covered with Flowers, whereby the Ayre is foe fweete, and the Earthe foe good a Sente, that Gentlemen commonly, when they will delight themfelves fay let us goe and pafs fome Dayes at Gifbroughe, and yet there is ne-ver a good Houfe in the Towne to recommende yt; and which is more, oulde Doctor Len of Yorke, a Phyfycian fecond or equall to Doctor Muffets (God of the Galenifts or Phyfycians) and Doctor

Howe, ufually fente his patyents to Gifbroughe to lye there to recover
their health. The people bread here live very longe, if they be a
while abfent they growe ficklye; they are all together given to pleafure, fcarce any good Hufband amongft them, Day and Nighte feaft-
inge, making Matches for Horfe Races, Dog runninge, or runninge on
Foote, which they ufe in a Field called Deere Clofe, where as if it were
in Campo Martio, you fhall fee from Morning to twelve of the Clocke
at Night Boyes and Men in their Shirtes exercifing themfelves. Their
Dyet is plentifull from the Sea, which yeilds fuch Store of Fifh, that
for ten Shillings you may keepe your Houfe heere with Conger, Burt,
Salmon, Troute, Soales, Turbett, Codde, Frefh-herrings and many
other forres of delicate Fifh three Dayes together; their Beefe and Mut-
ton is alfo very cheape and fweete in Tafte, that fuch as live there
of a long time can hardly brooke our Meate in this Country, foe is
their Venifon alfoe farre in Whiteneffe and Tafte furpaffing. I bought
at my laft beinge there eleven Crabbs and Lobfters for a penny, and
threefcore Herrings for as much. This maketh them content if they
have wherewith to live; for the refte they have a Saying, let thofe
that come after us fhifte for themfelves as we have done."

THE church of Guifbrough is dedicated to Saint Nicholas, and
ftands at the eaftern extremity of the town. It is a plain but neat
edifice, rather of a modern conftruction, and with fome late repairs, is
rendered commodious, and capable of containing a numerous congrega-
tion. It was given by Robert de Brus to the priory, which he founded
here; and being appropriated thereto, was afterwards reduced to a perpetual curacy. Upon the diffolution of the monaftry, the church,
with all the profits thereof, was granted to the fee of York, the rectorial
rights of which are now held by leafe under the Archbifhop of York,
who nominates the curate. The revenues of the curacy were not certified to the governours of the bounty of Queen Anne; but from Archbifhop Sharpe's MSS. it appears that there is a yearly ftipend or falary

of 46*l.* 13s. 4d. paid to the curate by the Archbifhop's farmer or tenant; which with fome late augmentations produces an income of about 100*l. per ann.* ||

AT a fmall diftance to the fouth from the parifh church are the remains of

GUISBROUGH PRIORY,

fituated in the bottom of a rich and fertile vale, which is divided into fine inclofures; and being furrounded by lofty hills, clad in the ver-

---

GUISBROUGH CURACY.

DEDICAT. St. Nicholas.   Not certified.   Priory of Guifbrough propr.   The Archbifhop of York, patron.

CURATES.

1694 John Hall.	1727 William Hide.
1722 John Hall.	1767 William Leigh Williamfon, M. A.
1722 Richard Cuthbert?	1798 Thomas Pym Williamfon, M. A.

|| THE following ftatement of the value of this curacy in the year 1767, is extracted from Archbifhop Sharpe's MSS.

Paid by the Archbifhop, at Lady day and Michaelmas, *per ann.*	46*l.* 13s. 4d.
Surplice fees, *communibus annis;*	5*l.* 10s. 0d.
Mr. Lumley's augmentation *	20*l.* 0s. 0d.
	72*l.* 3s. 4d.

* RICHARD LUMLEY, clerk, formerly curate of Guifbrough, and vicar of Stainton, by his will gave a farm at Carlton-Miniot, near Thirsk, (now [1767] let to John Aynfley at 20*l. per ann.)* to trustees in truft to pay the rent to the curate of Guifbrough, for reading prayers in the church every day.   *Sharpe's MSS.*

dant covering of their native woods, the fcene is at once folemn and majeftic.

We approached the ruins of this once fuperb and richly endowed monaftery on the eaft, which prefent nothing to the eye, but the magnificent arch of the eaft window of the priory church; which, as Mr. Grofe remarks, " exhibits a peculiar elegance of form, equal, if not fu- " perior, to moft buildings of this ftyle of architecture; and makes the " beholder lament that more of this fine ftructure has not been pre- " ferved."

The monaftic buildings which lay to the fouth of the priory church, have been fo totally deftroyed, that it is impoffible at prefent to trace out either the extent and arrangement of the apartments, or the fituation of any of the particular offices; and fuch has been the fate of this magnificent edifice, that no other part of the priory is now left, except a fmall gateway towards the weft end of the north wall; which, from its ftyle, is conjectured to be more ancient than the remains of the priory church, its outer arch being plain and femicircular, and the columns that fupport it remarkably thick; whereas the architecture of the window is peculiarly light.

Of the ancient ftate of the priory, the *Cott. manufcript* affords the following defcription: " Over a Doore in the Steeple are certaine auncy- " ent Letters circular wyfe written. Auncyent Men fometymes " broughte upp in the Monaftery told me that a Dutchman was Maif- " ter-workman of the abbey when it was builte, and yt feemeth to mee, " that the infcription is in Dutch. I remember that I had conference " once with you concerning the peopling of England. It is manifefte

---

The monaftic edifices appear to have fuffered the greateft havock under the reign of Queen Mary, on her attempt to reftore the monks to their poffeffions. *Fuller* says, " the edifices of abbeys, which were ftill entire, looked lovingly again on their ancient owners; in prevention whereof, fuch as poffeffed them for the prefent, plucked out their eyes by levelling them to the ground, and fhaving from them, as much as they could, all abbey characters."

H h h

" that that Parte of the Country called Cleveland hath been wonder-
" fully inhabyted more than yt is nowe; for within the length of a
" fewe Myles the Lordes following have had their Seates;—at Kyl-
" dale Caftle the Perceys, Earles of Northumberland; at Aton, Nevyll
" of Weftmorland; at Wharlton Caftle the Lord Menell; at Skelton
" Caftle, the Lord Sommers: at Danby Caftle the Lord Latymer; at
" Harlfey Caftle, Sr. James Strangwaies; at Wilton Caftle, Sr Ralf Bul-
" mer; at Mulgrave Caftle Sr. Ralf ——; at Ingleby, the Lord Eure;
" all thefe great Perfonages dwelte together in a fmall Cyrecuite, and
" in the mydefte of them the prior of Gyfbrough, who kepte a moft
" pompous Houfe, infomuch that the Towne confyftinge of 500
" Houfeholders, and had noe Lande, but lyved all on the Abbey; twoe
" Gatehoufes had Lodgings, and all Houfes of offyces appertayninge
" to a Dwellinge Houfe, whereof two of the Bulmers Knights within
" the Memory of me were refydent,havinge allowance when they came
" of a plentifull Dyet, at eyther to entertaine Strangers, and as many
" Horfe in Winter in the Stable as in Sommer at Graffe; the Number
" whereof and other particulars one Thompfone an Almefman there,
" and diverfe others have related to me; and alfoe of the State Pryor's
" Service by Yeomen, who broughte his Water to a rounde Hole in
" the great Chamber where it was receayved by Gentn. who ferved the
" Pryor only at his Table; one Thing I remember of this great Pro-
" vifion, that a Steward of theirs was put out of his offys becaufe he
" had aforehand but only 400 Quarters of Grayne to ferve their
" Houfe. But nowe all thefe Lodgings are gone, and the Countrye
" as a Wydowe remaynethe mournfull."

THIS priory, by the advice and admonition of Pope Calixtus II.
and Thurftan Archbifhop of York, was founded in the year 1129, ‡
by Robert de Brus, for canons regular of the order of Saint Auftin,

---

‡ CAMDEN fays that the monaftry at Guifbrough was founded in the year 1119; but Tanner,
from Brompton, fays in A. D. 1129. Brompton's words are as follow:—" Eodem anno (1129)
" fundata eft domus de Gyfeburna in Cleveland per Robertum de Brus de confenfu et confirmatione
" Papæ et Thurftini ebora cenfis archiepiscopi, ipfius etiam regis Henrici."

and dedicated to the honour of the bleffed Virgin Mary. The original donation confifted of all Guifbrough with its appurtenances; viz. twenty carucates and two oxgangs of land with the mill, foc and free multure, " with the privilege that none fhould fet up any mills in the " parifh without licence of thefe canons ;" and alfo the impropriation of the churches of Marfke, Brune, Skelton, Danby, Upleatham, Stainton, and Kirklevington, in the county of York; and of Hart and Stranton, in the county of Durham ; with permiffion to take from the foreft of Efkdale, timber and materials neceffary for building and repairs. There were diverfe benefactors to this priory, whofe grants were confirmed by the founder ; and the *monafticon* contains, (befides the foundation charter given in the notes,*) the charters of Peter de Brus, Robert, fon of William de Brus, and William, King of Scotland ; and alfo one of Richard Kellow, Bifhop of Durham ; all confirming different benefactions.

---

* CARTA FUNDATIONIS.

Regi Anglorum, et archiepifcopo eboracenfi, omnibufq. fanctæ matris ecclefiæ filiis, Robertus de Brus, falutem. Notum fit caritati veftræ, me concilio et admonitione Calixti Papæ fecundi, et Thurftini eboracenfis archiepifcopi, quoddam monafterium canonicæ religionis in *Gyfeburna* ad honorem Dei, et fanctæ Mariæ fundaffe, ibique cononicos regulares pro regis Angliæ et mei atq. uxoris meæ, liberorumq ; falute animarum, conftituiffe, et eidem ecclefiæ atq. Deo in eo fervituris, *totam Gyfeburnam* cum omnibus ad eam pertinentibus dediffe ; viz. XX. carucatas terræ, et duas bovatas, quas habeant in bofco et plano, pratis et pafcuis et aquis per eofdem terminos et metas ex omni parte villæ, per quas eas tenueram, excepta *Haia* et *Afadala,* quam retinui in manu mea ab orientali parte femitæ Ernaldi, quæ ducit ab *Holebec* ufq. in moram.

Reliquam vero partem Afadalæ in parte occidentis, et totam terram ufq. ad introitum nemoris de *Hellawath,* et inde totum nemus ab occidenti illius viæ quæ ducit ad *Hellawath,* ex utraque parte aquæ ; et totam moram a dextris ufq. ad introitum de *Schelderfcob* ; et inde totum nemus et moram a parte occidentis ficut aqua ducit ad *Colmanergas* ; et inde totum ficut aqua ducit ufq. in *Efc* ad *Dephil* ; et exinde totum, ficut via ducit a vado de fub *Dephil* in parte dextra ufq. ad hayam Ernaldi de *Hinderfcob* ; et inde totum a parte aquilonis, ficut vallis et aqua ducit ad viam, quæ defcendit verfus *Kildalam* ; et inde ficut magna via ducit ad femitam Ernaldi, quæ defcendit in *Golftandalam* ; et inde totum in parte dextra, ficut femita ducet ufq. ad aquam Golftandalæ ; et inde ad vallem et aquam quæ dividit territorium *Guifeburnæ* et *Atonæ* ; et inde per virulum ufq. ad magnam viam de *Henfberg,* et inde totum ficut via ducit ad femitam, eft defuper nemus Hotunæ, illis conceffi.

H h h 2

IT appears from the rolls of Parliament (18. Edward I.) that this monaftery having been burnt by accident, and all the books, relics, and goods, deftroyed, King Edward I. granted to the prior and convent on their petition, a licence to appropriate the churches of Efington, Berningham and Hefelerton, of which they had the avowfon; but it does not feem that the appropriation ever took effect. The priory was afterwards embattled or fortified by permiffion of King Edward II. and the privilege of frankpledge, waif, ftrays, return of writs, &c. was granted to the prior by King Henry IV. So amply indeed was this monaftery endowed, that at the furrender thereof (which was inrolled on the 22d Dec. 31. Hen. VIII.) its yearly revenues amounted, according to Speed, to 712l. 6s. 6d. and to 628l. 3s. 4d. as reported by Dugdale.

DEDI etiam præfatæ ecclefiæ molendina mea in *Gyfeburna* cum foca et molta, ficut ea habui; et ita ut nullus faciat molendina in parochia ejufdem villæ, abfque canonicorum licentia et conceffu. De terra autem *filii Gaufridi*, et de terra *Uctred de Clevelanda* liberum habeant fervicium, quod mihi debebatur.

DEDI etiam fupradictis fratribus *totam Iyum*, fcilicet, novem carucatas terræ cum illa parte de *Cotum*, quæ illi adjacet, et cæteris omnibus ad eam pertinentibus; et decimam dominii mei de *Lyum*; et ecclefiam de *Merfc*, et ecclefiam de *Burnus*, et ecclefiam de *Scheltona*, et ecclefiam de *Danby*, et ecclefiam de *Uplyum*, et ecclefiam de *Staintona*, et ecclefiam de *Levintona*, et ecclefiam de *Herts*, et ecclefiam de *Strantona* cum omnibus appendiciis et terris illarum. Et volo, ut decedentibus clericis, qui quafdam de prædictis ecclefiis tenent, habeant eas canonici præfati ad fuftentationem fuam ita libere et quiete, ficut aliqua abbatia liberius et melius tenet in toto archiepifcopatu eboracenfi. Dedi etiam illis materiam de *Efcadala* in perpetuum ad edificia fua et cætera omnia neceffaria domus fuæ.

HÆC omnia fupradicta dedimus et conceffimus, ego, videlicet, Robertus et Brus, et Agnes uxor mea &c. Ecclefiæ S. Mariæ de Gyfeburna, et fratribus ibid. fervituris, in liberam & quietam et perpetuam elemofinam cum omnibus libertalibus &c. quas in eis habuimus ex donatione & conceffione regis Angliæ.

QUOD fiquis violaverit, vel in deripiendo poffeffiones ecclefiæ, vel in diminuendo dignitates, Deum inde, ejufq. matrem fentiat vindicem. Confirmamus etiam donationes hominom noftrorum factas præfatæ ecclefiæ; viz. ecclefiam de *Ormefby* cum omnibus appendiciis fuis, et molendina de *Caldecotes* cum terra fibi adjacente, ex dono *Ernaldi de Percy*; et dimidium ecclefiæ de *Martona* cum omnibus fibi adjacentibus ex dono *Roberti Sturmy*; et ecclefiam de *Acclum* ex dono *Aluerdi*, et unam carucatam terræ in *Arufum* ex dono *Willielmi Engelram*. Et tres bovatas in *Lofius* ex dono *Theobaldi*; et unam bovatamin *Efingtun* de dono *Rogeri de Rofel*.   *Mon. Ang. vol. II. p.* 147.

A MOIETY of the patronage of this priory belonged to Marmaduke de Thweng, who married Lucia, daughter of Peter de Brus. In the 13. Henry IV. the advowfon belonged to the D'arcies of Temple Hurft;

A CATALOGUE OF PRIORS OF GUISBROUGH.

1132	William *		1393	Walter de Thorpe, a canon here
1145	Ranulph		1408	John de Hemefley
1184	Cuthbert		1436	Thomas de Thweng
1211	Roald.		——	Richard de Yrton
1211	Lawrence		1455	Thomas Darlington, a canon here
1218	Michael		1475	John Moreby, a canon here
1230	John		1491	John Whitby
——	Simon		1505	John Moreby, a canon here
1265	Ralph de Ireton †		1511	Benedict
1289	Adam de Newland		1511	William Spires, a canon here
1320	Robert de Wilton, a canon		1519	James Cockerill, S. T. P. ‡
1346	John de Derlington, do.		——	Robert Purfglove ‖
1391	John de Hurreworth, do.			

Out of the revenues of the priory, in the year 1553, there remained in charge the following penfions; viz-

	L.	S.	D.
To Robert Purfglove, the laft prior - - -	166	13	4
To Thomas Whitby . - - - -	3	0	0
To Henry Fletcher, Wm. Hinde, and Oliver Grayfon, each 6l. 13s. 4d.	20	0	0
To Chriftopher Thompfon - - - -	6	0	0
To Richard Sterne, Gilbert Harrifon, Edward Okerell, William Wyfedale, Chriftopher Mallow, Rob. Gregge, John Harrifon, John Leighton, Robert Watfon, George Hefiday, John Clarkfon, and Bartholomew Lilford, each 5l. 6s. 8d.	64	0	0
In annuities and corrodies - - - -	11	6	8
Total of annual out-payments - • -	271	0	0

* WILLIAM DE BRUS, brother to the founder, was the firft prior; he died 1145, and was buried in the chapter houfe at Guifbrough.

† HE was of a Cumberland family; and from this priory was advanced to the Bifhoprick of Carlisle. He died in the year 1292, being fuffocated in his fleep by the breaking of a blood-veffel.

‡ HE was firft a canon here, and afterwards prior and rector of Lythe; he was afterwards made abbot of Lillefhut, cov. dioc. and attainted for high treason.

‖ ROBERT PURSGLOVE, alias Sylvefter, was the laft prior, and held a penfion of 166l. 13s. 4d. per ann. which he enjoyed in A. D. 1553; he was alfo fuffragan Bifhop of Hull; and died May 2d, 1579.

Willis's Hift. Abbies, vol. II. p. 271.

but in the year 1421, the Fauconbergs, Lords of Skelton, were patrons thereof. The fite was granted (4. Edward VI.) to Francis Chaloner, and in 5. and 6. Philip and Mary, the Queen granted the manor of Guifbrough and feveral parcels of the faid priory to Sir Thomas Chaloner, to be held of the Queen by military fervice; whofe defcendants have fince continued proprietors.

ON the north fide of the church yard towards the eaft, ftand the ancient *hofpital* and *free-fchool of Jefus;* which were founded by letters patent of Queen Elizabeth, bearing date 5. June, 1561, by Robert Purfglove, the laft prior of Guifbrough; who endowed the fame with his lands, tenements, and fervices, at Bolam, in the parifh of Gainford, in the county of Durham.

THE hofpital is for twelve poor people; viz. fix men and fix women, to be of the age of threefcore years and upwards and unmarried; to have for their lodgings fix rooms within the faid alms-houfe; viz. two of them together in one chamber, having feveral beds for every one of them; and to receive for their weekly fuftenance and relief (according to the original ftatutes) the fum of twelve pence each, every Sunday at the faid alms-houfe; and every year at the nativity of St. John the Baptift, to have forty fhillings divided equally amongft them; firft in repairing and mending their beds, and then in fuch apparel as they have the moft need of.

TESTAMENTARY burials in this priory, from *Torr's MSS.*

Lucia, wife of Bartholomew Fanacourt, A. D. 1346.

Sir Walter de Fauconberge, knight, Nov. 9, 1372.

William Lord Latimer, 10th July, 4 Richard II. 1381.

Sir Roger Falconberge, knight, 10th Dec. 1391.

Sir Philip D'arcy, knight, 16th April, 1399.

Ifabella, relict of Sir Walter de Fauconberge, A. D. 1401.

Dame Conftantia Brus, lady of Skelton, A. D. 1402.

John Lord D'arcy and Menyll, 2d Auguft, 1411.

Dame Heleyn Gibfon of Gyfeburne, 28th June, 1451.

William Toccotes, of Gyfeburne, 5th April, 1526.

Roger Toccotes, of Toccotes, Efq. 27th May, 1536.

THE fchool-houfe adjoins to the hofpital on the eaft, and confifts of a fpacious fchool-room on the ground floor, and two chambers, with a garden and other offices, for the refidence of the fchool-mafter; who is bound by the ftatutes, " *to teach freely in the free fchool of Jefus, all fcho-* " *lars coming to learn in the fame, taking of every fcholar, only at his firft* " *admiffion, four-pence;*" and to have for his wages the fum of ten pounds *per ann.* paid at the four terms in the year, viz. at the feaft of the nativity of our Lord God; the annunciation of the bleffed virgin; the nativity of St. John the Baptift; and St. Michael the Archangel, by even portions for ever.

BY the original foundation deed, Roger Tockets, of Tockets, Efq. and George Conyers, of Pinchinthorpe, and their heirs, were appointed governours, and with two wardens to be elected annually, make a corporation for ever, who have a common feal, with power at every vacation to nominate a fchool-mafter, and appoint proper perfons to fuch rooms of the twelve poor people, as become void by death, deprivation or otherwife. The ftatutes and ordinances were made by the founder, and the fpirit of his regulations is admirable.

BY a late divifion of the common fields at Bolam, and fome future additional grants to this charity, its revenues have been greatly augmented, and thereby the fchool-mafter's falary, and the weekly allowance to the poor people, confiderably increafed.

GUISBROUGH is worthy of particular remark, as being the place where the firft allum works in England were attempted. The difcovery was firft made in the latter part of the reign of Queen Elizabeth, by the learned naturalift, Sir Thomas Chaloner, Knight; ‖ who, on his travels in Italy, examining the Pope's allum works near Rome, and obferving that the mineral there was greatly fimilar to one in the neigh-

---

‖ THE mineral is faid to have been firft difcovered here, by obferving that the leaves of the trees were of a pale green; that the foil was fpeckled with divers colours, and never froze; and in a clear night fhone and fparkled by the fide of the road like glafs.

bourhood of Guifbrough, became defirous to make the attempt; but, as he was a ftranger to the procefs, he found it neceffary to procure workmen from the Pope's allum works; whom, by fecret promifes of a large reward, he prevailed upon to accompany him privately into England; when he immediately erected an allum work upon his eftate at Guifbrough; which, in a fhort time, fo completely anfwered his expectations, as to reduce confiderably the price of allum, and brought him in yearly a large revenue. This circumftance fo exafperated the Pope, that he fulminated an anathema replete with curfes againft Mr. Chaloner, and the workmen whom he had feduced; the tenor of which being the fame as that of *Ernulphus*, quoted by Sterne, in his Triftram Shandy, and probably the form prefcribed by the church to be ufed againft notorious offenders, we forbear to repeat; but rather refer thofe who would not be fhocked at the impiety and abfurdity of the expreffions, to perufe it in that celebrated work. We have only to remark that the Pope's infallibility is in this refpect to be doubted; at leaft we do not find, that any of the curfes denounced by his holinefs, have fallen upon this heretic; as his defcendants have flourifhed here for many generations; and the procefs of making allum was carried on with fuch fuccefs, as to induce many of the neighbouring gentlemen to become adventurers in the trade; which, though difcontinued at Guifbrough, Ayton, &c. is now eftablifhed upon a folid foundation in the neighbouring parts of Cleveland contiguous to the coaft. *

ABOUT a mile to the north-eaft from Guifbrough, lies the townfhip of

TOCKETS;

which according to the Domefday book contained two carucates *ad*

---

* THE D'arcy family about the year 1600, began an allum work at Guifbrough, not far from Mr. Chaloner's; and a few years afterwards, another was erected at Sands End, in the parifh of Lythe, the produce of which was carried in veffels from Whitby to London. The following are the allum works now carried on in Yorkfhire; viz. Peak, Stoup-Brow, Little-Beck, Efkdale-Side, Sands-End, Kettlenefs, Boulby, and Lofthoufe: thofe at Guifbrough; Ayton, Carlton, Ofmotherley, and fome others, have been long difcontinued.

geldum ; held under Robert Earl of Moreton, and valued in the Confeffor's time, at five fhillings and four pence, but then wafte. It is
thus furveyed in Domefday under

TERRA COMITIS MORITONIENSIS.

IN TOSCUTUN AD GELD. II. CARUCATÆ, ET I. CAR. POTEST ARARI
IBI UCTRED HABEBAT I. MANERIUM. NUNC HABET RIC. DE COMITE, ET
WAST. EST. T. R. E. VALEBAT V. SOLID. ET IIII. DENAR.

FROM which it appears that *Uĉred* was the Saxon poffeffor of this
manor, which was firft granted by the Conqueror to Robert, Earl of
Moreton : it afterwards became part of the fee of Robert de Brus ;
from which family it defcended by marriage, with other large eftates,
to Marmaduke de Thweng. This place, at an early period, gave name
to the refident family ; many of whom were benefactors to the priory
of Guifbrough, ‡ and occur frequently as witneffes to fome of the
moft ancient charters relating to Cleveland. The Tocketts flourifhed
here, as mefne Lords, for feveral generations ; till the manor and eftate were alienated by the laft male heir, to William Chaloner, Efq.

‡ IT appears from the confirmatory charter of Peter, fon of Peter de Brus, given in the monafticon, that *William de Tockets* gave two oxgangs of land at Kirklevington to the priory of Guifbrough ; and *Roger,* fon of *William de Tockets,* one carucate of land at *Lyn* ; *William,* fon of *Roger
de Tockets,* one oxgang of land at Tockets, with toft and croft adjoining ; and *John,* fon of *Hum-
frey de Tockets,* one oxgang of land in the fame territory.

TOCKETTS, of Tocketts.

Roger de Tocketts,══Margaret, daughter of Robert Meynell,
of Tocketts, Efq. | fergeant at law.

2. Dorothy married to Raphe Salvayne, of Newbiggin, Efq.	1. Mary married W. Strangwaies, of Mid-dlefbro'.	1. George Tocketts,══Eliz. dau. of of Tocketts, Efq 1584. |... Hutton, of Hunwick, Durham.	2. Thomas. 3. Jofepha. 4. Margt.

4. Robert, died S. P.	2. James died unmarried.	1. Roger Tocketts,══Jane daughter of of Tocketts, Efq. |.... Cooke, of (died 1650. S. P.) Newcaftle.	Eliz. wife of F. Thomfon, of Scarbro'.
		1. William Tocketts,══Mary, daughter of Jofeph of Tocketts, Efq. di- | Conftable of *New Build- ed 1655. æt. 68. | ing, co. York, Efq.	

I i i

of Guifbrough ; who afterwards fold a moiety thereof to the late
General Hale, who erected a neat modern manfion, to which, probably from its being fheltered with rifing groves of oak, &c. he gave the
fignificant name of *Plantation.*

THERE was an ancient chapel here, dedicated to St. James, founded by the Tocketts family ; at which it appears, that the prior and
convent of Guifbrough agreed with William and John de Tocketts,
that the facrift of the priory every Monday, Wednefday, and Friday,
fhould find a chaplain to celebrate mafs in the faid chapel at Tocketts,
faving the rights of the mother church at Guifbrough ; but on Sundays and all feftivals, the faid William and John and their heirs, fhould
go to the mother church, and there give their oblations, &c. And the
faid William and John to fuftain the faid chapel at their own expence,
and alfo find a chalice, veftments, books, &c.

WE have no evidence that difcovers to us when this chapel was finally defecrated ; probably it continued till the diffolution of the monaftry, on which it was in fome meafure dependent. There is at prefent
no tradition, nor even the leaft veftige, to point out the fituation of this
facred edifice.

AT the foot of the hills, and about two miles fouth-weft of the
town of Guifbrough lie the townfhip and manor of

HUTTON ;

ore generally known by the name of *Hutton-Lowcrofs*, and not unfre-

---

5. Jofeph,—Cath. dau. of	3. George.	2. Thomas died	1. Elizabeth,—R.Ward, of Darlington.
... Eddon.	4. James.	an infant.	2. Catharine,—John Kirton.
			3. Bridget,—Mulgrave Ridley, of Fea-therftonhalgh.

1. Roger Tocketts, of Tocketts, Efq.—Cornelia, daughter of Marcus Van Val-
aged 46. Sept. 8. 1665.   kinburgh, in Holland.

| 2. Roger, di-ed young. | 1. George, fon and heir, ætat. 9, 8 Sep. 1665. | 1. Catharine, ætat. 3, 8 Sep. 1665. | 2. Margaret. 3. Cornelia. 4. Elizabeth, died young. | 5. Cornelia, died in her infancy. |

From Dugdale's Vifitation. 1666.

quently for the fake of diftinction, called in ancient records, *Hutton juxta Gifeburne.*

WE do not find the lands here particularly fpecified in the Domef-day-book; but furveyed with that part of Guifbrough, which was granted by the Conqueror to Robert Earl of Moreton, under the TER-RA COMITIS MORITONIENSIS. This manor afterwards became part of the fee of Robert de Brus, and defcended by marriage to the Thwengs ; of whom we find in Kirkby's Inqueft, that Hugh de Hoton, as mefne Lord, held fix carucates here and at Pinchinthorpe, whereof twelve made one Knight's fee. *

EXTENTA 7   * EXTENTA facta de terris et tenementis, quæ fuerunt Hugonis de Hoton,
18. Edward I. ∫   qui tenuit de hæredibus Roberti de Thwenge, (qui eft in cuftodia regis) die quo obiit, coram *Thomam Norvamville,* efcaft. domini regis ultra trent. apud Hoton, die Martis, in feptu-aginta pafchæ, anno regni Edw. 18° per *Ricardum* and focios fuos juratores ; qui dicunt fuper fa-cramentum fuum quod idem Hugo habuit in Hoton quoddam manerium, cum quadam alia camera et coquina ; II graing. unum bovar. &c.

SUNT ibidem infra claufurum et claufum dicti manerii, duas acras terræ, quæ jacent waftæ, et valent per annum cum claufa ejufdem manerii Vs.

ET funt ibidem CXXX acræ terræ arab. in dominico fuo pretium cujus libet acræ IVD. fum-ma XLIIIs. IVD. et XVI. acræ prati in dominico fuo, pretium cujus libet acræ IIs. fumma XXXIIs.

ET funt ibidem in bondagio XXII bovat. terræ ; et reddit per annum quælibet bovat. Vs. fum-ma CXs.

ET funt ibid. XXI toft. || pretium cujus libet per an. IIs, fumma XLIIs.

ET eft ibidem quoddam molendinum aquaticum ; et valet per annum XLs-

ET funt ibidem . . . . . de Hoton, fcilicet de Petro filio Yate pro una toft per annnm VID.

ET dicunt, quod tres carucatæ terræ in Pinchinthorpe tenentur de dicta Hugone per *forens fer-vicium;* quarum *Walterus de Thorpe* tenet XIV bovat. terræ pro homagio & fervicio, et reddit per annum unam libram cuminis, et unam libram *pepper,* ‡ et unum denarium ad natalem domini ; et

---

|| A toft was a meffuage inferior to a farm houfe, but fuperior to a mere cottage, fo called according to Skinner, from the fmall *tufts of trees,* with which dwelling-houfes were anciently furrounded ; a croft was a fmall portion of land annexed to it. Hence the *tofts and crofts* of our anceftors ; which were precifely what may now be obferved in many ancient villages, viz. cottages furrounded by their little garths.

‡ A pound of pepper, (now worth perhaps 2s. 6d.) was equivalent to about *twenty shillings,* which fhews how much the ancient feodal payments have been reduced by the gradual depreciation of money.

THIS family, who it seems affumed the local name, continued as
mefne Lords till the 9. Edward III. when John de Hoton, with the licence of Sir Bartholomew Fanacourt, Knight, and Lucia his wife, daughter of Robert de Thwenge, gave this manor to the prior and convent
of Guifbrough, who, the fame year, granted the faid manor to John,
fon of Hugh de Hoton, during his life for the annual penfion of 1*l*. 1s.

IN the year 1346, Nicholas, fon of John de Hoton, quit-claimed
all his right to this manor to the prior and convent; who continued
Lords of Hutton till the diffolution of the monaftery, when it came to
the Crown, and was held under leafe by the family of Yowards, from
whom it defcended to Mann Horfefield, Efq. whofe daughter, Mrs.
Robinfon, widow of the late ——Robinfon, Efq. now poffeffes the eftate.

WITHIN this manor there was an ancient hofpital, of which Tanner
makes the following mention: " Here was an houfe or hofpital for
" lepers, dedicated to St. Leonard, which was given to the priory of
" Guifbrough, by William de Bernaldby; and the donation was con-
" firmed by Peter, fon of Peter de Brus." ‡   *Tanner's Not. Mon.*

Johannes filius *Philippi de Thorpe*, tenet IV bovat. terræ in eadem pro homagio et fervicio; et *The-
mas Doyet* tenet unam bovat. terræ in croft. in eadem villa pro eod. fervicio. Et Hugo Doyet tenet
unam bovat. terræ in croft. in eadem villa, pro eodem fervicio. Et Richardus, filius Roberti, tenet
duas bovatas terræ in eadem villa pro homagio et fervicio. Et Johannes de Hoton tenet unam bovat. terræ in eadem villa pro homagio & fervicio. Et Johannes et Redmerfhall tenet duas bovatas
terræ in eadem villa pro homagio & fervicio. Et Ymana, quæ eft uxor Johannis de Mart, tenet duas acras terræ prat. in eadem villa, et reddit per annum III denaria ad natalem domini; et Richardus filius Julianæ tenet unum .... in eadem villa et reddit per annum IIIs. et libram cuminis ad
natalem domini.

ET idem Hugo quoddam toft vaftum tenet, et valet per annum IIs. Dicunt quod idem Hugo
tenet omnes terras fuas, et omnia tenementa fua et hereditamenta de Lucia, filia et hærede Roberti
de Thwenge, quæ eft in cuftodia domini regis. Et dicunt quod idem Hugo habet quendam fili-
um et hæredem, qui vocatur Johannes, et eft de ætate 15 ann. ad feftum Sti. Martini, in regni anno
reg. Edw. 18.
                                                    Ex MSS. Rawlinfon, vol. 448.

‡ IT is the opinion of Camden, that the leprofy (by fome called *elephantiafis*) was firft brought
into this ifland out of Egypt; and in the reign of Henry I. it ran by infection all over England.
Whatever might be the origin of the difeafe, it feems to have been fo prevalent, and confidered by

IT does not appear by whom this houfe was originally founded; the ancient refident family of Hoton, were confiderable benefactors; and we alfo find, that John, Lord of Hoton, and his anceftors, by an ancient cuftom, had a right to place one leprous perfon in this hofpital, which right he remitted to the prior of Guifbrough, and the keeper of the hofpital. ‖

A part of the buildings, which ftood in a folitary fituation, fhut in by rifing grounds overhung with deep and folemn woods, has been converted into a farm-houfe, with ftables and other out-offices, in which fome mutilated arches of doors and windows are ftill remaining.

PROCEEDING weftwards about three miles from the town of Guifbrough, we enter the townfhip of

PINCHINTHORPE.

THE village is fmall, fituated upon the road leading to Stokefley, and fhut in by a range of mountains on the eaft. We prefume not even to hazard a conjecture, as to the etymology of the name; but muft obferve, that the manor is entered in the Domefday-book under the name of *Thorpe* only, and is thus furveyed under

TERRA ROBERTI MALLET.

MANERIUM IN TORP. HABUIT EDMUND III. CAR. TERRÆ AD GELDUM; UBI II. CAR. POSSUNT ESSE. ROBERTUS HABET, ET WAST. EST. T. R. E. VALEBAT X. SOLID.

BY which it appears, that Edmund the Saxon Lord held three carucates *ad geldum*, with two more that might be rendered arable; which were afterwards granted by the Conqueror to Robert Mallet, and then wafte, but in the Confeffor's time valued at ten fhillings.

---

our anceftors fo loathfome and infectious, that the unhappy fubjects of it, (like the leprous perfons under the Mofaic law,) were excluded from all public commerce, and hofpitals for their reception were charitably erected in almoft every part of the kingdom.

‖ *Burton's Mon. Ebor. p. 357.*

THIS village feems alfo to have given name to a refident family, who were ancient proprietors of lands here; for we find in Kirkby's Inqueft, * that Adam de Thorpe, as mefne Lord, held two caiucates of the heirs of Marmaduke de Thwenge; and from the preceding record given in the notes, it appears that there were three carucates held of Hugo de Hoton by *foreign fervice;* of which Walter de Thorpe, John, fon of Philip de Thorpe, and others, held different portions of the faid Hugo de Hoton, by homage and fervice, &c.

IT does not appear who were the immediately fucceeding proprietors. A branch of the Conyers' family at an early period became Lords here; and in the 23. Henry VIII. we find that Sir William Bulmer, Knight, died feized of certain lands at Pinchinthorpe, leaving John his fon and heir, who was attainted by King Henry VIII. † From the Conyers, the manor and a confiderable eftate defcended by marriage to Gervafe Lee, * whofe defcendants have continued proprietors, and been refident here for feveral generations.

---

* " ADAM DE THORPE tenet in Pinchinthorpe, de hered. Marmaduci de Thwenge duas carucatas terræ, unde 12 car. terræ faciunt feodum milit." *Kirkby's Inqueft.*

† 23. Hen. VIII. Willus. Bulmer, miles, obiit 18. Octob. Johannes filius & hæres, ætat. 40 annor. et Anna Tempeft filia Thomæ Tempeft militis eft uxor dicti Johannis. Tenet terras in Wilton, Lafyngby, Weft-Cotum, Pinchinthorpe, Bulmer, Wilborne, &c. *Dodfworth's MSS. vol.* 98.

* LEE, of Pinchinthorpe.

Gervafe Lee,=... caughter of ... Conyers,
of Pinchinthorpe.

Roger Lee, of York, M. D.—Muriel, daughter of ... Gower,
of Stainfby, county of York.

William Lee, of Pin-—Eleanor, daughter of Cuthbert chinthorpe, died 1650. | Morley, of Normanby, co. York.

Dorothy married firft to ... Young, and after to Sir Philip Hungate, of Huddlefton, in co. York, Knight.

Roger Lee, of Pinchinthorpe,—Mary, daughter of John Turner, Efq. ætat. 33. Aug. 25. 1665. | of Welham, in county of York.

2 Robert.   1 George, ætat. 6.   1 Eleanor.   2 Dorothy.   3 Mary.   4 Elizabeth,
25 Auguft, 1665.   5 Ifabel.

From Dugdale's Vifitation, 1665.

The townſhip of

COMMONDALE ;

Or more properly written *Colmandale*, forms the ſouthern boundary of the pariſh. This is a narrow, ſecluded vale, about ſix miles from the town of Guiſbrough, ſurrounded with high and healthy moors ; and was ſo called from the venerable prelate *Colman*, biſhop of Lindisferne, who had formerly an hermitage or place of reſidence here, to which, on his journeys to the abbey of Whitby, he ſometimes reſorted. ‖

WE find no mention of Commondale in the Domeſday ſurvey; nor have we met with any records relating to the lands here, except that being within the limits of the original donation, they were given to the priory of Guiſbrough by the founder, and on its diſſolution came to the Chaloners, who have ſince ſold out the eſtate in parcels to different freeholders.

SKELDERSKEW-GRANGE, a hamlet within this townſhip, ſtands in the northern part of the vale. It was probably ſo called from *ſkell* a rivulet, and *ſkew*, *ſkeugh*, *ſkaw*, *ſhaw*, which, though thus variouſly written, always imply the ſame thing, viz. wood-ground ſtanding on a hill ; the name is ſtrongly characteriſtic of the ſituation of this hamlet ; of which we find nothing in ancient records, except that it was given to the priory at Baſedale, together with ſome other meſſuages and lands within the ſaid vale.

SOIL, PRODUCE, &c. This pariſh, as we have already obſerved, being of conſiderable extent, with a large tract of heathy barren moor, the ſoil is found to vary according to ſituation. The incloſed lands within the townſhip of Guiſbrough are chiefly of a ſtrong loam, which extends with little variation along the vale, to the weſtern extremity of the pariſh. A few farms towards the north-eaſt are of a ſtrong clay ; and here, as in Commondale, and other vales in Cleve-

---

‖ COLMAN, together with Cedd, biſhop of the Eaſt Saxons, and a train of prieſts and monks from the monaſtries of Kolmkill, and Lindi ferne, aſſembled with lady Hilda, abbeſs of Whitby, at the convocation held at the nunnery there, in the year 664, to contend with the Romaniſts reſpecting the time of celebrating the feſtival of Eaſter.   *See note, p.* 318.

land, there are fome fmall patches of good gravelly foil, which are generally found running in a direction from eaft to weft. The inclofures on the fkirts of the hills are of a moorifh quality ; fome of which being cloathed with wood contribute, with the trees in hedge-rows, and the variegated hues of meadow, pafture, and corn-fields, to give the country a rich and pleafing appearance. About one half of the inclofed lands within the parifh is in tillage ; and the crops principally cultivated are wheat, oats, and beans, with a few turnips. The mode of management is in general two crops to a fallow ; but fince the introduction of artificial graffes, clover between the white crops fometimes intervenes.

WITH regard to the improved breed of ftock, the farmers here are not inferior to any in Cleveland, having introduced the new Leicefterfhire breed of fheep by hiring rams of that kind from the firft breeders. Confiderable attention is alfo paid by fome of the principal farmers to their breed of cattle, which are of the beft fhort-horned kind.

POPULATION. * We fhall conclude our account of this par-

* ABSTRACT OF GUISBROUGH REGISTER.

	BAPTISMS.				*BURIALS.*			*MARRIAGES.*
A. D.	Males.	Females.	Total.		Males.	Females.	Total.	
1781	32	36	68		24	14	38	14
1782	28	35	63		19	29	48	10
1783	32	31	63		23	26	49	15
1784	41	33	74		31	30	61	16
1785	29	28	57		27	25	52	16
1786	20	38	58		16	21	37	17
1787	32	38	70		18	34	52	18
1788	29	42	71		23	16	39	14
1789	46	31	77		25	19	44	16
1790	30	25	55		41	41	82	11
1791	27	36	63		18	9	27	11
1792	34	29	63		22	20	42	12
1793	30	23	53		22	28	50	7
1794	27	24	51		19	22	41	12
1795	34	24	58		30	31	61	17
1796	31	27	58		21	14	35	10
1797	28	31	59		22	18	40	13
1798	19	36	55		11	26	37	7
1799	28	34	62		12	20	32	11
1800	31	31	62		20	23	43	13
Totals	608	632	1240		444	466	910	260

ifh with fome brief remarks on its prefent ftate of population.—By the table given in the notes, beingan extract from the parifh regifters it will be feen that from the year 1781 to 1800 inclufive, there were 1240 baptifms, 910 burials, and 260 marriages. According to the returns made to government in the year 1801, ‖ there were then within the whole parifh 428 inhabited houfes, 453 families, and 2003 inhabitants, giving $4\frac{1}{2}$ nearly to each family ; with which, when we compare the average number of burials in a year, it will appear that one out of $44\frac{1}{4}$ dies annually.

‖ STATE OF POPULATION, 10th March, 1801.

Townships.	Inhab. houfes.	Families.	Uninhab-houfes.	Males.	Females.	Total.	Agriculture.	Trade, &c.	Refidue.	Total.
Guifbrough,	383	407	38	771	948	1719	161	273	1285	1719
Tockets,	8	8		29	36	65	13	5	47	65
Hutton Lowcrofs,	11	11		31	28	59	22		37	59
Pinchinthorpe,	15	15		44	48	92	24		68	92
Commondale.	12	12		36	32	68	24	3	41	68
Totals,	428	453	38	911	1092	2003	244	281	1478	2003

к к к

THE PARISH OF ORMESBY,

IS undoubtedly fo named, as having been the habitation of *Orme,* the Saxon poffeffor, who feated himfelf here before the Norman conqueft; and as the faid *Orme* firft gave name to this place, fo in procefs of time the place gave name to his fucceffors; for we find Robert, fon of Henry, and Richard, fon of Simon de Ormefby, in the lift of benefactors to the priory of Guifbrough.

THIS parifh, which confifts of the townfhips of Ormefby, Normanby, Efton, and Morton, adjoins to the parifhes of Wilton and Guifbrough, on the eaft; to Marton, and the chapelry of Middlefbrough, in the parifh of Acklam, on the weft; to Newton and Ayton, on the fouth; and is wafhed on the north by the river Tees. It ftretches in extent from north to fouth upwards of four miles, and is about three miles broad.

THE manor of Ormefby, with the foke of two carucates of land at Upfall (a hamlet within the parifh) appears from Domefday-book to have been part of the poffeffions of the King's thains in the north-riding, being thus furveyed under the title

TERRA TAINORUM REGIS.

MANERIUM IN ORMESBI IIII. TAINI HABUERUNT XII. CAR. TERRÆ AD GELDUM. TERRA AD VIII. CAR. IBI HABET ORME I. CAR. ET II. VILLANOS, ET XVI. BORD. CUM III. CAR. IBI PRESBITER ET ÆCCLESIA. UNA LEUCA LONGA, ET I. LAT. T. R. E. VAL. IIII. LIB. MODO XL. SOLID. SOCA IN UPESHALE II. CAR. TERRÆ AD GELDUM. SOCA PERTINET AD ORMESBI."

THIS manor, which in the Conqueror's furvey was taxed for twelve carucates, foon afterwards became part of the fee of Robert de Brus; and feems to have been granted out, at an early period, to the Percies of Kildale, as mefne lords: William de Percy, in the reign of Henry

III. obtained a grant of free-warren in his demefne lands here; and in Kirkby's Inqueft, (13. Edw. I.) we find that the faid William held one Knight's fee at Ormefby, Normanby and Lafingby, of the heirs of Marmaduke de Thweng, where twelve carucates made one Knight's fee, ‖

Percy of Kildale.　　1420 *Harl. MSS. vol.* 19. *Brit. Mufeum.*

Walter de Percy, Miles, Dominus de Kildale. ⹀

Dominus Nicholaus de Percy, ob. S. P.　　Willielmus, Dominus de Kildale. ⹀

Arnald de Percy de Kildale, *carta ejus fine dat.*　　Wills. habet Ormefby ex dono patris, & ex confirm. fratris Arnaldi. (23. Edw. I.)

Alexander Percy de Ormefby, fuperftes 28. Edw. III. ⹀

Willielmus Percy. 16. Edw. III. ⹀

Juliana, filia & hæres. ⹀ Robert Conyers, of Hornby.

John Coniers, of Ormefby, ⹀ (ob. 1438)　†

Robert Coniers. ⹀ Aleonora.　　John Coniers.

Ann, daughter and heir. ⹀ James Strangwayes. (ob. 1517.)

Isabella Stranwayes, of Ormefby.

FROM the Percies, as appears from the above pedigree, Ormefby defcended by marriage to a branch of the Coniers' family; and afterwards paffed with Ann, daughter and heir of Robert Coniers, to James Strangwayes, Knight, whofe defcendants continued proprietors till

---

‖ " WILLS. DE PERCI de Kildale tenet in Ormefby, Lafingby et Normanby unum feodum, unde XII· car. faciunt, feod. milit." 　　　　　　　　　　　　　　*Kirkby's Inqueft.*

† JOHANNES CONYERS de Ormefby, miles, 2 June 1438, facit teftamentum. Legat corpus fepeliri in ecclefia parochiali de Ormefby. Lego Robto. filio et hærede, omnem armaturam meam; Alionoræ uxi. predicti Robti, 4 vaccas mulforias; and a chaplain to pray for him eight years àt the altar of St. Mary, in the church of Ormefby; the reft of his goods, to his younger children, and Tho. Coniers his baftard. Chriftopher Conyers, of Hornby, and John Moubray, of Efeby, executors. Probat. 18. Jul. 1438. 　　　　　　*Ex. Regift. Arciepis. Ebor.*—Dodfworth.

the latter part of the reign of Queen Elizabeth, when we find it in the poffeffion of the Pennymans; in which family it continued for feveral generations; and the manor and a confiderable moiety of the eftate are ftill the property of Sir James Pennyman, Bart.

PENNYMAN, of Ormefby.

Thomas Pennyman, ⸺ Anne, daughter of . . . of Stokefley, Efq. | Gattonby, of . . .

ARM. *Gules*, a cheveron, *Erm.* between three arrow heads, *or.* pointed, *arg.* CREST. A lion'- head, erafed, and pierced through with an arrow, *or.* on a mural crown, *gules.*

Thomas, ob. S. P.

George, ob. S.P.

Ralph Pennyman, Efq. ⸺ Jane, daughter of . . . . Saltmarfh.

Robert Pennyman, ⸺ Margaret, daughter of of Ormefby, Efq. | . . . Sayer, of Worfall.

William Pennyman, ⸺ Anne, daughter of Thoof Ormefby, Efq | mas Stainfby.

⸺ James Pennyman, of Ormefby, Efq. unto ⸺ Anne, daughter of . . . . whom William ꞓegar, Efq Norroy King | Burnett, of Breakhoufe, in of Arms by his inftrument, under the | Cleveland. feal of his office, bearing date 1ft May, 1599, granted this creft to his coat of arms; viz. *a lion's head erafed, and pierced with an arrow, or; on a mural crown, gules.*

William Pennyman, ⸺ Ann, dau. of Ro-Efq. one of the fix | bert Afk, of Aughclerks in Chancery. | ton, county York.

William Pennyman, ⸺ Ann, dau. of J. Atherof Marfk, created a | ton, by his wife, dau. and Bart. 1628, gover- | coheirefs of Chriftopher nour of Oxford, 1645. | Lord Conyers, of Horn-(ob. S. P.) | by Caftle.

3. John 4. Reginald 5. Thomas 6. Gilbert 7. Robert (ob. S. P.)

1. William, ob. S. P.

1. Ellen ⸺ AlanCertaine, of Redcar. 2. Mary ⸺ T. Pilley, of Ske'derfkew. 3. Ann ⸺ H. Yoward, of Wefterdale. 4. Eliza ⸺ S. Bradfhaw, of Upfall, in Cleveland.

Catherine, daughter ⸺ James Pennyman, of ⸺ Joan, daughter of . . . Smith, of Wm. Kingley, of | Ormefby, Efq. died | a citizen of London. (2d wife.) Canterbury. 1ft wife. | on St. Luke's day, 1655.

Thomas Pen- ⸺ Sarah, dau. nyman, D.D. | of J. Turner, of Stokefley. | of Kirkleat-ꞏham.

Sir James Pen- ⸺ Elizabeth, nyman, of Or- | dau. and mefby, Kt. and | coheir of Bt. made Kt. | Stephen by K. Charles | Norcliff, E. I. and Bart. by | of York. K. Charles II. |

William ⸺ Joan, dau. of . . . . Tockets, of . . . in co. Kent.

John. Joan, wife of J. Gibfon, of Welburne, co. York.

Sir Thomas Pennyman, ⸺ Frances, daughter of Ormefby, Bart. | of Sir John Low-ther, of Lowther, co. Weftm. Bart.

WARTON, OF BEVERLEY.

Michael Warton, of Be- ⸺ Catherine, dau. verley, Efq. was flain by | of Chriftopher a cannon bullet at Scar- | Maltby, of Maltbro' Caftle, in the civil | by, in Cleveland. wars, it being then a garrifon for the King.

Michael Warton, of Beverley,—Sufan, daughter of John Lord Paulet, of Hinton St. George, in Somerfetfhire.
Efq died 1688, aged 65.

John. Sir James Pennyman of Ormefby,—Mary, daughter of Michael Warton, of Beverley Park, Efq.
and Thornton, in Cleveland, Bart. died 1745, and buried at Stainton, aged 84.

1. James—Dorothy, dau. of Archbishop Wake. Pennyman, ob. vivo patre, S. P.
2. Sir W. Pennyman, Bart. fucceeded his Father, died unmar. and buried at Stainton church.
3. T. Pennyman, ob. 1759 aged 60.
4. Sir Warton Pennyman, Bart. fucceeded his brother William.—Charlotta, dau. of Sir C. Hotham, of Scarbro,' Bart.
5. Ralph Pennyman.—. . . d. of Wm. Gee, Efq of Bifhop Burton, in co. York.

2. Charles ob. infans.
1. James Pennyman, a Major in the Queen's regiment of dragoons died unmarried.
1. Mary,—William Berry.
4. Margaret,—H. Maifter, of Winfted, Efq
5. Harriot,— Stapylton, of Weyhill Park, Efq.
6. Caroline,— Roger Gee, of Bifhop Burton, Efq.
8. Diana,—George Hotham, of Scarbro' Efq.
2. Philippa.
3. Dorothy.
7. Gertrude. } died unmarried.

Elizabeth, daughter of—Sir James Pennyman, Bart.—- - - - - ...—W. Bethell, of Rife, Efq.
Sir Henry Grey, of | fucceeded his uncle, Sir Warton Pennyman, living in - - - - - - Dorothy—Rev. James Worfley, Stonegrave.
Howick, co. Northumberland, Bart. 1806.
(1ft wife)
- - - - - - Mary, died unmarried.

William Pennyman, Efq. eldeft—. . . . daughter of Bethell Robinfon, Efq.
fon and heir; living 1806.
3 fons died unmarried.
Three daughters living and unmarried 1806.

A part of the eftate was fold in the reign of King Charles I. by James Pennyman, Efq. and after divers alienations, was repurchafed in the year 1770 by Sir James Pennyman, the prefent Baronet; who has fince fold the fame to John Brown, Efq. the prefent proprietor.

James Pennyman, Efq. was a loyalift in the time of King Charles I. and raifed a troop of horfe; in fupport of which, and to defray the fum of 700l. levied upon him for his loyalty by the fequeftrators in the civil wars, he was obliged to difpofe of a part of his eftate at Ormefby, which was fold to Mr. Elwes, for the fum of 3500l. As an inftance of the rapid improvement, and advance in the value of landed property fince that period, we may remark, that this part of the eftate was purchafed, about the year 1720, by Ralph Robinfon, Efq. for the fum of 7500, and in the year 1770, was fold by his nephew, Marfhall Robinfon, Efq. to the prefent Sir James Pennyman, Bart. for the advanced fum of 47,500l.

ORMESBY-HALL, the feat of Sir James Pennyman, Bart. is a neat modern manfion, built by Mrs. Pennyman, daughter of Archbifhop Wake: it is fituated upon a gently rifing eminence at a little diftance from the village towards the fouth, and commands a pleafing profpect of the mouth and winding courfe of the river Tees, with a view of the fea, and the fouthern part of the county of Durham. The grounds adjoining are excellent, and ornamented with extenfive plantations.

THE church of Ormefby, dedicated to Saint Cuthbert, ftands near the manfion, and is a fmall but ancient ftructure. We have no evidence of the era of its original foundation, but from Domefday-book it appears that there was a church here before the Conqueft, although no part of the prefent edifice can lay claim to fo great antiquity. This was an ancient rectory, which, together with one carucate of land, was given by Arnald de Percy to the priory of Guifbrough; and upon the appropriation thereof to the faid priory, a vicarage was therein ordained; which confifts of all tithes, oblations and obventions of the town and parifh of Ormefby, excepting the tithe corn of Ormefby, and the tithes and whole alterage of the towns of Efton and Normanby, which were referved to the priory. This rectory, with the advowfon of the

---

ORMESBY VICARAGE.

DED DATED to Saint Cuthbert. King's books 6l. 18s. 6½d. Tenths 13s. 10¼d. Archd. pro fyn. 4s. Proc. 7s. 6d. Pri. Guifbro', propr. The Archbifhop of York, patron.

VICARS —1310 Stephen de Parum, *pres. prior & convent de Gyfburgh.* 1349 Walter de Wyr-kefdall, *id.* 1351 John Kyng, cap *id.* 1361 John Barker —— John de Stokefley. 1387 John de Kirkham. —— John de Karleolf. 1391 John de Wath, cap. 1402 Thomas Storr, *phr.* 1416 Thomas Todd, *phr.* 1434 Cuthbert Cunton. —— John de Stitname, *phr.* 1475 Richard Elme-don, *cap.* 1507 Richard Bayley, *phr.* 1407 Thomas Matthew, *phr.* 1546 Chriftopher Wylde, *phr. affig. pri. & conv. Guifbrugh.* 1554 Olyver Watfon. 1582 Richard Stapilton, *cl.* —— William Lawfon, *prefented by the Archbifhop of York.* 1635 Thomas Aftell, STB. *by the fame.* 1662 John Carter, *cl. by the fame.* 1673 Thomas Smallwood, BA. *by the fame.* 1676 William Perkins, *by the fame.* 1719 Thomas Sharpe, *by the fame.* 1719 Jofephus Milner, *by the fame.* 1720 William Confett, *collated by the Archbifhop.* 1762 John Tanch, MA. *collated by the Archbifhop, and appointed and licenfed to the chapel at Efton.*

vicarage remained in the priory, till the diffolution thereof; when they were granted to the Archbifhop of York and his fucceffors by the King and authority of Parliament. Upon the reftoration there was an augmentation of 20*l. per ann.* made to this vicarage, to be paid to the vicar by the Archbifhop's tenant, who holds the rectorial rights by leafe under the Archbifhop.

AT a little diftance from the village of Ormefby, towards the eaft, and within the chapelry of Efton lies the townfhip of

NORMANBY;

of which, in the Domefday furvey, we find that two carucates were then in the hands of the King, being thus entered under the title

TERRA REGIS.

MANERIUM IN NORMANBI HABUIT LIGULF II. CAR. TERRÆ. TERRA AD II. CAR. UNA LEUCA LONGA, ET DIM. LAT. T. R. E. VALEBAT XVI. SOLID.

FROM the fame record of Domefday it alfo appears that there were feven carutates *ad geld.* furveyed under the head

TERRA COMITIS MORITONIENSIS.

IN NORMANBI AD GELD. VII. CARUCATÆ, ET IIII. CAR. POSSUNT ESSE. IBI HABUIT UCTRED I. MANERIUM. NUNC HABET COMES, ET WAST. EST. T. R. E. VALEBAT XX. SOLID.

BY which it appears that thefe were held before the Conqueft by Uctred as one manor, which, at the time of the Survey, was in hands of Robert Earl of Moreton, and then wafte. In the Confeffor's time it was valued at twenty fhillings.

BESIDES the above there was alfo half a carucate, entered in the furvey under the title

TERRA ROBERTI MALLET.

MANERIUM IN NORMANBI HABUIT LEISINC DIM. CAR. TERRÆ AD GELD. ROBERTUS HABET, ET WAST. EST. T. R. E. VAL. V. SOL. ET IIII. DENAR.

THESE lands became part of the fee of Robert de Brus, and in the reign of Henry III. defcended by marriage to the Thwengs; of whom in Kirkby's Inqueft we find that William de Percy, of Kildale, held one Knight's fee at Ormefby, Lafingby, and Normanby; and that

Adam de Northmanby, or, as he is elfewhere called, Adam de Leventhorpe, held fix carucates of land here of the fame inheritance, where
twelve carucates made one Knight's fee, and paid as a fine the fum of
fix fhillings.

WE have no documents to fhew the regular defcent of proprietors.
In the reign of Henry VI. the Morley's poffeffed a part of the eftate,
which remained in that family, who were refident here, till the reign
of Charles the fecond. ‖ We afterwards find the Pennymans proprie-

---

‖ *MORLEY, of NORMANBY.*

THE following pedigree is chiefly from a copy of the Yorkfhire vifitation in the year 1584; with
fome additions from the *Harlean MSS. Brit. Mus.* 1118. made by Randal Holmes, about the year
1630. and continued from Dugdale's vifitation 1665.

. . . . Morley,⹀

ARMS. *Sable*, a griffin's
head, *arg.* jeffant a fleur
de lis, *or.*

John Morley, of Normanby,
in Cleveland; *ut per cart.
dat.* 12. *Hen. VI.*

Nicholas Morley,⹀Joan, daughter
of Normanby. | of John Hedlam,
(24. Hen. VI.) | Efq.(24.H.VI.

Chriftopher Morley, of⹀
Normanby, in Cleve-
land, Efq.

Ifabel, daughter of⹀Robert Morley of⹀Elizabeth, daughter of . . . Symonds,
Wil. Maltby, of | Normanby; he | of Kirklington : (2d wife.)
Maltby, (1ft wife.) | dwelt at Maltby. |

James Morley, of⹀Phillis, daughter
Maltby. 1584. | of C. Thornaby,
              | of Thornaby, E.
              |

Ann. daughter of⹀Cuthbert Mor-⹀Ifabel, dau. 1. Phillis.
Chrift. Thornaby, | ley,of Norman- | of . . . Wil- 2. Elizabeth
of Thornaby, Efq. | by, in Cleve- | fon, of . : . 3. Ann.
(1ft wife.) | land. | N. 2d wife.

John Morley⹀Ifabel, dau.   1. Jane.   1.JamesMor- 2. Thomas. Robert Morley⹀Elizabeth, Eleanor
eldeft fon ; | of N. Gow-   2.Phillis. ley, of Nor- 3. Chrift. of the city of | dau. of Sir wife of
æt. 10.1584. | er, of Thor- 3.Sufan. manby, æt.   York; an utter | John Sco- . . . . of
             | naby.   8; 1584,one   barrifter, Inner | rey, of . . . . . .
                                       of the fix   Temple; died | co. of He-
1. James. 2. Thomas 1. Joan.   clerks in   1651. | reford, Kt.
                    2. Phillis.   chancery,1636. |
                    3. Ann.
                    4. Mary.   ──
                    5. Jane.   Cuthbert Morley,⹀   2 James Morley⹀Cordelia, dau. Ifabel
                                       eldeft fon   of Newton upon of Tho. Dods-   &
                                                            Oufe,in co.York, worth, of . . . Ann.
                                                            æt. 38. 14. Sept. co. York; and
                                                            1665.   widow of . .
                                                                             Higginbottom.

tors; but how, or at what period that family came into poffeffion, we are not informed. William Pennyman, Efq. of Normanby, a defcendant, we prefume, of the Pennymans of Ormefby, died in the year 1719, leaving two daughters, coheireffes; who marrying two brothers, fons of —— Confett, Efq. of Linthorpe, a partition of the eftate was made in the year 1723, when the eaftern part thereof fell to the fhare of the Rev. William Confett, who erected the manfion, (now the refidence of Mifs Lambton) which, with a fmall eftate, is ftill in the poffeffion of that family. The other moiety, together with the ancient manfion, came by purchafe in the year 1764 to the late —— Jackfon, Efq. whofe fon, William Ward Jackfon, Efq. now poffeffes the eftate. The manfion has received confiderable improvements, and the grounds are greatly ornamented with thriving plantations.

PROCEEDING eaftwards we enter the townfhip of

ESTON,

which was certainly fo called, (quafi Eaft-Town,) from its fituation to the eaft of Ormefby and Normanby, which were probably firft inhabited. In the Domefday-book Efton is furveyed as follows, under the head

TERRA COMITIS MORITONIENSIS.

IN ASTUNE AD GELDUM VIIII. CARUCATÆ, ET V. CAR. POSSUNT ESSE. IBI HABUIT WALTEOF I. MANERIUM. NUNC HABET ROB. COMES, ET WASTUM EST. RICARDUS DE COMITE. T. R. E. VAL. XL. SOLID.

ESTON was one of those manors, which, at an early period, were granted to the Meinills, of Whorlton caftle; and was held of the Archbifhop of Canterbury, by performing the fervice of Pantler on the day of his confecration. From the Meinills, it paffed by marriage to the D'arcies, and from them to the Conyers; in which family it continued till the 3d and 4th of Philip and Mary, when John Lord Conyers, dying without male iffue, left three daughters, coheireffes; from whofe defcendants two thirds of the eftate here came by exchange and purchafe to Henry Stapylton, Efq. anceftor of Sir Martin Stapylton, Bart.

the prefent proprietor and Lord of the manor. The remaining third was the property of Lady Hewlay, who devifed the fame to pious purpofes ; and is now in the hands of truftees.

It appears from Burton and other authorities, that fundry parcels of land here were granted to the prior and convent of Guifbrough, and the following is a charter from Stephen de Meinill, of fixty acres of land, with a toft given to that monaftery : " Ego Stephanus de Mey" nill dedi et confirmavi ecclefiæ S. Mariæ de Gifburne 60 acras terræ " in campis villæ de Efton, et illud toftum quod habent multis retroac" tis temporibus de dono anteceſſorum meorum. Teſtibus D̃no. Wul. " de Percy, D̃no. Robto. de Stutville ; D̃no. Willo. de Mowbray, L̃no. Nich. " de Perier, Robto. de Hilton, Johe. de Meynill." ‖

The abbot and convent of Fountains had alfo two acres of land in Efton-Field by the grant of Stephen, fon of Robert de Meinill ; who alfo about the year 1230 gave all his land, as far as where the fea afcends to the Tees, to make fifheries thereon ; and Peter de Brus, as chief Lord, agreed before the juftices in Weftminfter-Hall (13. Henry III.) that neither he nor his fucceſſors would erect any fifheries within a league, faving the rights of the fifhermen of Coatham and others, who ufed to fifh there. Thefe monks had alfo free paffage over the lands of the faid Peter de Brus, where neither corn or meadow grew, for their fervants, horfes, and carriages, going and returning from buying of fifh.

There is an ancient chapel here, fituated at a little diftance from the village towards the north ; but neither the dedication thereof, nor the date of its foundation is now known. The chapel is a fmall but

---

‖ This deed, with the feal appendant bearing this infcription, viz. S GILLVℭ STⱻꝐⱭNI Ꝺⱻ ℭⱸYNILL, was tranfcribed from the original in St. Mary's tower at York, by *Mr. Ra. Dodfworth,* 1640.

ancient edifice, confifting of a nave and a chancel, with a ftrong fquare tower; which, as well as the chancel, appears to be of a more modern conftruction than the body of the chapel. The chancel is feparated by a circular arch; and the entrance by the door on the fouth is partly walled up, and the upper part converted into a fmall window; the zig-zag mouldings of the arch, which is circular, rifing from a capital, and round pillars, difcover this part of the building to be of great antiqui-ty. *

IT is probable that this chapel, though not mentioned, was granted together with the church of Ormefby, to the priory of Guifbrough; as the advowfon thereof is particularly named among thofe other ad-vowfons granted by King Henry VIII. to the Archbifhop of York, who is the patron of the chapel, and nominates the curate. It was certified

---

* IN the chapel-yard, amongft a variety of obliterated grave-ftones, there is a table monument with the following infcription :

Beneath this Stone,
in a Vault, built by her kind,
her difconfolate Hufband,
lies the Body of
ANN, Wife of WILLIAM MEWBURN;
Miftrefs of a great many Virtues
moral and religious,
which adorned a fingle Life,
and would have bleffed a matrimonial one;
But fhe was called
to a higher and better Sphere,
Augt. ye· 16th 1757.
in the 34 year of her age;
having been married 7 Months and 5 Days.
Reader from hence this ufeful Leffon fcan,
This Life's uncertain, and in Length a fpan.

L l l2

to the governours of Queen Anne's bounty at 17*l*. 10s. 4d. and having
since been augmented by two allotments, the revenues amount to about
40*l*. per annum.

THE village of Efton is fmall, and irregularly built, and ftands on
the fkirts of a detached hill of confiderable elevation, called Barnaby
or Efton Moor; the fummit of which runs out into a bold point or
promontory called

ESTON NAB ; †

where a telegraphic beacon, or watch houfe, has been lately erected,
commanding a profpect both of fea and land, which, for beauty, variety, and extent, is feldom equalled.   In front is the mouth of the river
Tees, the winding courfe of which may be traced for many miles towards its fource in the weft ; beyond which, the hills above Richmond,
and fome of the moft elevated mountains in Lancafhire, Weftmorland,
and Cumberland, with the Cheviot hills in Scotland, are vifible ; while
nearer at hand a great extent of coaft to the eaft and the north, and the
principal part of the county of Durham, with villages and farm-houfes
interfperfed, may be diftinctly feen.   Rofeberry-Topping, with the
range of Cleveland hills, and the heights of Black-Hambleton, appear
on the fouth.

ON the fummit of this promontory, which fpreads out to the fouthwards into an extenfive plain, there is an ancient encampment, conjectured to be of Saxon origin, confifting of a double circle of rough loofe
ftones ; the inner rampart or entrenchment being 150 paces in circumference; and the whole ftill perfect, except on the north, where a fmall
portion of the circle is cut off by the abruptnefs of the rock, which on
that fide is nearly perpendicular.   This, as we have already obferved,
was probably conftructed by the Saxons, about the year 492, when

---

† The *nab*, or rather *knap* of a hill, is fo called from the Saxon word Cnæþ, which, according to
Skinner, fignifies *jugum feu fupercilium montis.*

they were overthrown by the Britons at the battle of *Badon-Hill* ; which, according to Holinſhed, and other hiſtorians, was fought in this neighbourhood about that period.

THE townſhip of

MORTON,

lies in the ſouthern extremity of the pariſh, and was ſo called, (*quaſi*, Moor-Town, *villa ad ericetum*) from its ſituation on the ſkirts of Barnaldby, or Barnaby Moor.   We find little in ancient records worthy of particular notice touching the lands here ; which, from the appendix to the Domeſday-book, conſiſted of three carucates *ad geldum*, part of the fee of Robert de Brus.   The townſhip is ſmall and contains only three farm-houſes, and about 27 inhabitants. Lord Rookby, and Richard Garbutt, are the preſent proprietors.

EAST and *WEST-UPSALL*, which are hamlets within the townſhip of Ormeſby, adjoin to Morton, on the eaſt.   According to the Domeſday ſurvey, there were two carucates here within the ſoke of Ormeſby, and one carucate, which was ancient demeſne of the Crown, entered under the title

TERRA REGIS.

IN UPESALE NORMAN I. CAR. AD GELD. TERRA AD DIMID. CAR.

THESE lands were part of the fee of Robert de Brus ; and were afterwards granted to the Percies, as meſne Lords ; from whom they deſcended by marriage to the families of Conyers, Strangwayes, and Bradſhaw ; from the Bradſhaws a part of the eſtate came to the Pierſons, and has been lately ſold to William Ward Jackſon, Eſq. of Normanby Hall, who by purchaſe of the different proprietors, now poſſeſſes the whole eſtate, which he is greatly improving by extenſive plantations, particularly on the waſte grounds, incapable of cultivation.

THE SOIL, PRODUCE, and GENERAL APPEARANCE of the pariſh are ſubjects that next demand the reader's attention ; upon which we may briefly remark, that the lands here, two thirds of which are now in tillage, and in a complete ſtate of cultivation, are as favourable to the different branches of agriculture, as any within the diftrict; having, befides a foil in general fertile, the advantage of an excellent port upon the river Tees, called *Cargo-Fleet*, or *Cleveland-Port*, where extenfive and commodious granaries have been erected, and from whence at leaft two thirds of the whole produce of Cleveland are fhipped, and fent coaftwife to London, Newcaftle, and other markets. *

In the northern extremity of the parifh, which is wafhed by the river Tees, the lands are nearly level; and the foil a rich and fertile clay, remarkable for its produce of wheat and beans. From the village of Ormefby the grounds rife gradually towards the fouth, where the foil is a mixture of gravelly and clayey loam, and the furface is rendered uneven by a variety of gentle fwells, terminating in a ridge called *Hameldon*, † which commands a profpect of the furrounding country, and exhibits fome home and diftant views highly interefting.

There are no confiderable grazing or dairy farms within the parifh; the produce of grain, fince its great advance in price, being more an object of the farmer's attention, than the breeds of horfes, cattle, and fheep, for which, about thirty or forty years ago, this parifh and neighbourhood were particularly noted. The lands, however, are in an improved ftate of cultivation, and we may add, that the annual value thereof has been increafed, within the laft eighty years in nearly a feven fold proportion.

POPULATION. In the year 1781, the townfhips of Ormefby and Morton contained 73 families and 372 inhabitants; and thofe of Ef-

* The goods exported are corn, butter, cheefe, pork, and bacon; and the imports timber, hemp, flax and iron, with coals and lime from the north. To give the reader fome idea of the importance of this comparatively fmall *out port*, we may remark, that the trade carried on here, according to the ftatement we have received, amounts upon an average to about 1000*l.* a day, throughout the year.

† The etymology of the word *Hameldon* is of Britifh origin, compofed of *Am ael don*, *ad fupremium mentis*.

ton and Normanby 88 families, and 443 inhabitants, making in the whole 161 families, and 815 inhabitants, which is upwards of 5 to each family. In 1801, when an actual enumeration was made, by order of the Legislature, there were within the several townships 168 families, and 771 inhabitants; so that within a period of twenty years there is an increase of families, but a considerable decrease of inhabitants, which is not easily to be accounted for. ‖

It appears by the extract from the parish registers § which we subjoin to this account, that the total number of births or baptisms from the year 1781 to 1800 inclusive, is 482, and that of burials 311, giving an average of 24 baptisms and 15 burials in one year. From these data we are led to infer, that to every 32⅛ inhabitants a child is born, while one out of 51 dies annually.

‖ STATE OF POPULATION, 10th MARCH 1801.

Townships	Inhab-Houses	Fam-ilies	Uninhab-Houses	Males.	Females.	Total.	Agri-culture.	Trade, &c.	Resi-due.	To-tal.
Ormesby,	74	76	1	174	183	357	132	51	174	357
Morton,	3	3		15	12	27	16		11	27
Eston,	61	67	2	130	158	288	170	31	87	288
Normanby,	22	22	1	45	54	99	69		30	99
Totals,	160	168	4	364	407	771	387	82	302	771

§ ABSTRACT OF THE REGISTER BOOKS FOR THE PARISH OF ORMESBY, AND CHAPELRY OF ESTON.

Ormesby and Morton.

	Bap.	Bur.	Incr.	Mar.
From the year 1701 to 1720 inclusive,	141	100	41	43
1781 to 1800,	208	129	79	55
Difference,	67	29		12

Eston and Normanby.

	Bap.	Bur.	Incr.	Mar.
From the year 1701 to 1720 inclusive,	136	90	46	37
1781 to 1800,	274	182	92	54
Difference,	38	92		17

THE PARISH OF MARTON.

MARTON, comprifing the ancient hamlets of *Tolefby* and *Newham*, is the next adjoining parifh to the weft, ftretching in a direction from north to fouth five miles, and about two miles broad. * The village is fmall, fituated about a quarter of a mile to the fouth from the road leading from Stockton to Guifbrough ; and confifts chiefly of a few farm houfes and cottages, ranged irregularly on the fummit of a gentle elevation, and divided into eaft and Weft Marton ; with the manfion houfe of the Lord of the manor to the north. The grounds adjoining confift of rich and fertile paftures which feem never to have been in tillage ; but from the appearance of numerous foundations of houfes, were probably the fite of a town of much greater magnitude and importance than the prefent village. ‖ Thefe evident traces of buildings concur with the compofition of the local name to ftrengthen the conjecture, that the place was originally called Marton, *(qu. Mart*, or *Market-Town)* as having formerly the privilege of a market; at leaft we may conclude that the fertility of the foil had in early times attracted attention, and made it one of the parts of the country that was firft inhabited and cultivated.

---

* MARTON is 5 miles diftant from Stockton, 7 miles from Guifbrough and Stokefley, and 8 from Yarm ; and the parifh is bounded by Ormefby on the eaft ; Acklam and Stainton on the weft ; the chapelry of Middlefbro' on the north ; and by Nunthorpe, in the parifh of Ayton, on the fouth.

‖ IN digging into the grounds near the village, *paved roads* have been found covered with *vegetable foil*, at leaft three feet in depth, on which were growing trees and hawthorn hedges of great antiquity; and in fome of the old foundations, a quantity of *charred wood*, which appeared to have been ufed in the roofs &c. of houfes, and probably occafioned by the great conflagration when this part of the country was laid wafte by the Conqueror

THE church of Marton, situated on rather elevated ground at the western extremity of the village, is a small but ancient edifice, consisting of a nave, chancel, and square tower; but contains nothing remarkable in its style of architecture, nor any monumental inscriptions worthy of particular notice. This church, dedicated to St. Cuthbert, was anciently rectorial, and " was given by Robert de Sturmey, together " with divers parcels of land here and at Tolesby, to the priory of Guis-" brough; and the grant was confirmed by Peter, son of Peter de Brus. " It was afterwards appropriated to the priory, and a vicarage ordained " therein by Walter Gray, Archbishop of York; who, at the presenta-" tion of the prior and convent, having admitted William de Boleby to " the vicarage thereof, taxed the same to consist of the whole altarage " of the church, reserving the residue of the church to the proper use " of the said priory, according to the form of Pope Urban's Indulgence." Upon the dissolution of the priory, this rectory, with the advowson of the vicarage was given to the Archbishop of York, who is patron. The vicarage, is valued in the King's books at 4*l.* 18s. 9d. and the rectorial rights are held by lease under the Archbishop, by the Lord of the manor, who pays an augmentation of 20*l. per ann.* to the vicar.

THE lands within this parish are surveyed in Domesday as follow:
TERRA REGIS.
MANERIUM INMARTUNE VLCHIL I. CAR. AD GELD. TERRA AD DIMID. CAR.

MARTON VICARAGE.
DEDICAT. St. Cuthbert. Archd. pro syn. 4s. Prox. 7s. 6d. King's books 4*l.* 18s. 9d. Tenths 9l. 9s. 10¼d. Mon. Guisb. propr. Archbishop of York, patron.

VICARS.—Will. de Boleby. 1292 Roger de Bilmond. 1303 Galfr. de Yarum. 1315 Robert de Eston. —— Rob. de Lakenby. 1349 John Dand, *cap.* —— John de Kirkham. 1377 John Barker de Stokesley. 1380 John de Bedall. —— Tho. Wylde. 1391 Rob. Dalton. 1410 John de Burton. 1416 John Todd. 1423 Rob. Betherd. 1430 John Mayson. 1454 Rad. Walker. 1461 John Cornay. 1486 John Gill. 1516 Tho. Clarke. —— 1566 Christ. Watson, *cl. pres. Archbishop of York.* 1572 Will. Reynaldson, cl. *id.* 1588 Rich. Phare, cl. 1604 Mich. Sturdy. 1622 Hen. Hitchman, M. A. —— Richard Gibson. 1631 Christ. Graundige, cl. 1642 Tho. Wray, M. A. 1666 John Mawman. 1701 Henry Alain, *pres. Archb.* 1728 Philip Kitchin, 1749 John Grenside, *pres. id.* 1798 Daniel Duck, *p. m.* Grenside, *pres. Archbishop.*

M m m

MANERIUM IN NEUUEHAM LESING II. CAR. ET II. BOV. AD GELD. TER-
RA AD I. CAR. X. SOLID.
 MANERIUM IN TOLLESBI LESINC II. CAR. AD GELD. TERRA AD I. CAR.

But a more confiderable portion of the lands here are furveyed un-
der the title
                    TERRA ROBERTI MALLET.
MANERIUM IN MARTUNE HABUIT EDMUND V. CAR. TERRÆ AD GELDUM,
UBI POSSUNT ESSE III. CAR. ROBERTUS HABET NUNC, ET WAST. EST.
T. R. E. VALEB. XX. SOLID,
 MANERIUM IN NEUUEHAM HABUIT EDMUND X. BOV. TERRÆ AD GEL-
DUM, UBI POTEST ESSE I. CAR. ROB. HABET, ET WAST. T. R. E. VAL. X.
SOLID.
 B. IN TOLLESBI SUNT III. CAR. TERRÆ AD GELDUM, QUÆ PERTI-
NENT AD MARTUNE. WAST. SUNT.

The Remainder of Marton, and its dependent *Berewick* of Tolefby,
we find thus entered under the title
                  " TERRA TAINORUM REGIS.
" MANERIUM IN MARTUNE ARCHIL III. CAR. TERRÆ AD GELD. TERRA
" AD II. CAR. IDEM IPSE HABET IBI I. CAR. ET XIIII. VILLANOS, ET VI.
" BORDARIOS, CUM III. CAR. T. R. E. VALEB. XL. SOLID. MODO XX. SOL.
 " B. IN TOLLESBI IIII. CAR. AD GELDUM, PERTINENS AD MARTUNE.
" TERRA AD II. CAR. WAST. EST."

Of the above lands, as appears from the appendix to the Domefday
book, there were four carucates at Marton, two carucates and two oxgangs at Newham, and three carucates at Tolefby, which were part of
the fee of Robert de Brus ; " *quod fuit datum poftquam Liber de Wintonia*
" *fcript. fuit.*"

By the Bruces, who were chief Lords, and held of the King *in capite*,
the lands appear to have been granted out, at an early period, to different proprietors ; for in Kirkby's Inqueft, taken 13. Edw. I. we find
that William de Bovington held three parts of one Knight's fee at
Marton, Tolefby, and Acklam, of the heirs of Marmaduke de Thweng ;
and Roger de Sturmey, Robert de Skoterfkelf, and Robert Gower, had
two Knight's fees at Marton *et alibi*, which they held of Margaret de
Roos, where ten carucates made one Knight's fee.

WE have no information of the immediately fucceeding proprietors ; but by the grant of King Henry VIII. to Ralph Bulmer, and John Thynn, it feems that the nuns of Bafedale had the manor of Marton, with five cottages, and fome meadows in Weft-Marton, and three ox-gangs of land in Marton fields ; with one meffuage and fix oxgangs, and the tithes at Tolefby.

A confiderable portion of land here was alfo given to the cell of Middlefburgh, by William Malbiffe ; who, by his charter in the *Monafticon Anglicanum*, gave all the lands and paftures in his freehold at *Brackenhoe*, in Marton, included within the following boundaries ; "*fcilicet*, ficut forera *Radulfi Longi* vadit in fletum de *Caldcotes*, et inde " per medium fletum, ufque in fletum molendinum verfus *Felebrige*, uf-" que proximam metam terræ *Thomæ de Marton*, et inde furfum ufque " foreram predicti *Radulfi Longi*."

THE manor and eftate came afterwards to the Lowthers of Ack-worth Park, and appear to have continued a long time in the poffeffion of that family.　John Lowther, Efq. of Ackworth Park, died without

---

THIS humble village is in nothing more worthy of notice than in claiming the honour of giving birth to the immortal *Captain James Cook*, who was one of nine children, born of honeft and induf-trious parents, in the loweft walks of fociety, on the 27th of October, 1728. * His father is fuppo-fed from his dialect to have been a native of Northumberland ; but his mother, a plain, illiterate, la-borious woman, like her hufband, was probably from this part of the country ; a circumftance that ac-counts for their return to, and finally fettling in it.　This fon, as well as the reft of the younger part of the family, was taught to read by the fchool-miftrefs of the village, at an expence, which we, who know the country, the ftate of manners, and the circumftances of the times, can eafily fuppofe did not exceed one fhilling *per quarter*.　But the father, being in confequence of his merit, promoted to the place of *hind*, or *head-fervant* to Thomas Skottowe, Efq. of Ayton, near Stokefley, this fon was, by the liberality, and at the expence of Mr. Skottowe, fent to the day fchool in that village, an obfcure feminary ; the mafter a decent man, who taught reading, writing, and arithmetic, according to *ancient practice*.

WE truft we fhall be pardoned by our readers, if we here introduce fome particulars refpecting the illuftrious fubject of this memoir ; which, although they may by fome be confidered as *nugæ*, not

---

*　" James, fon of James Cook, day labourer, was baptifed Nov. 3d, 1728." 　　 *Marton parifh reg.*

iffue, and by his will, dated 3d Feb. 1728, left one moiety of the manor and eftate in *fee fimple*, to his three nieces; viz. Elizabeth, wife of Samuel Saville, of Thribergh, in the county of York, Efq. Catherine, wife

worthy of notice, will, neverthelefs, we flatter ourfelves, prove acceptable to thofe who admire the man. The mind involuntarily confers importance upon trifles which bear affinity to fuch a character; by a fpecies of alchemy, as it were, it changes drofs into gold, and dwells with fecret complaifance on thofe minute indications of character, which mark with a bold outline the mental features of mankind.

DURING young Cook's continuance at this village feminary, it appears that he was never much regarded by the other boys of the fchool, and was generally left behind in their juvenile excurfions; a circumftance, which can only be attributed to his fteady adherence to his own plans and fchemes, never giving way to the *contre-projets* of his affociates. This, inftead of conciliating their regard, naturally rendered them averfe from his company. It has been afferted by thofe who knew him at this early period of his life, that he had fuch an obftinate and fturdy way of his own, as made him fometimes appear in an unpleafant light; notwithftanding which, *there was a fomething* in his manners and deportment, which attracted the reverence and refpect of his companions.

THE feeds of that undaunted refolution and perfeverence which afterwards accelerated his progrefs to immortality, were confpicuous, even in his boyifh days. Frequently, on an evening, when affembled together in the village, to fet out in fearch of bird's-nefts, Cook might be feen in the midft of his comrades, ftrenuoufly contending that they fhould proceed to fome particular fpot: This he would fometimes do, with fuch inflexible earneftnefs, as to be deferted by the greater part of his companions.

As to his attainments in the fchool, they could not be confiderable, had his opportunities been greater than they were; but we believe there was nothing which diftinguifhed him from other boys. He did not prognofticate his future greatnefs, like Hercules in his cradle; nor had he any keen or experienced obferver to fay of him, as *Sylla* did of *Cæfar*, that " in that boy, he perceived many *Marius's*." But, notwithftanding this, at the age of thirteen years, his proficiency in writing and the common rules of arithmetic was fuch, as was thought fufficient to qualify him for a *countryfhopkeeper*. He was accordingly bound apprentice to Mr. William Sanderfon, a fhopkeeper at *Staithes*, a fmall fifhing town in the parifh of *Hilderwell*, about ten miles north of Whitby.

WITHOUT giving at all into the idea, that there is any thing like deftiny in the fates of men, it cannot well be denied to have been providential, that *Cook* fhould have conceived a diflike to a courfe of life for which he was but ill qualified,—to make a fecond choice, and then to chufe one, to which his talents were eminently well adapted. He quitted *Staithes*, and the retail of *Inkles* and *Tapes*, and was a fecond time bound apprentice for feven years to *Meffrs. John and Henry Walker*, of Whitby, who were of the religious perfuafion called Quakers, and confiderable owners of fhips in the *coaltrade*. This apprenticefhip he ferved out with fidelity, and continued for feveral years a *fore-maft man*, in veffels chiefly engaged in that trade, without having fhewn any thing at all peculiar either in his abilities or his conduct.

of John Smith, and Margaret Frank, fpinfter; and the other moiety thereof to his two nieces, Margaret and Dorothy Norton, daughters of William Norton, of Sawley, in the faid county, Efq. by his fifter Mar-

---

At length, in the year 1755, being in the courfe of his bufinefs in the river Thames; and there being at that time, preparatory to the impending war, an hot prefs, he refolved voluntarily to enter into the fervice of his king and country, and did accordingly enter with an officer of the *Eagle man of war*, a fhip of fixty guns. Here being in the element fo fuited to his nature, his genius and worth were firft difplayed fo as to command and gain very general efteem; and it was foon difcovered that he was an able, active, and intelligent feaman.

We fuppofe it to have been through the intereft of Mr. Skottowe, to whom *Cook's* father had ftill more ftrongly recommended himfelf by his fkill, care, induftry, and integrity, that *Mr. Ofbaldefton*, then Member of Parliament for Scarbrough, was prevailed upon to write to *Captain*, afterwards *Sir Hugh Pallifer*, then the commander of the *Eagle*, in favour of *Cook*. But it was ftill more fortunate for *Cook's* future fame, that he was placed under a commander, not only able to difcern, and habitually prone to patronize merit; but, who himfelf poffeffing no ordinary fhare of naval fcience, and feeking or hoping for diftinction in fervice only from fuperiority of fkill, naturally animated all thofe who were emulous of great examples, with a fimilar fpirit. A large portion of it fell to the lot of *Cook:* feldom has there been fo able a mafter; and perhaps feldomer a pupil, whofe proficiency was fo great. Thus patronized, and thus qualified to do credit to any patronage, in 1759, he obtained a mafter's warrant, and failed to America, in the Mercury, to the fiege of Quebec, under the immortal *Wolfe*. It was here, on the recommendation of *Sir Hugh Pallifer*, who could now appreciate fairly the fagacity and refolution of this rifing feaman, that he was employed in an important, but difficult and dangerous fervice—that of taking foundings in the channel of the river of *St. Lawrence*, which, for feveral nights together, he performed in the night-time, in the front of the French fortified camp at *Montmorency*.

It is not known, that he had ever before ufed a pencil, or that he was at all acquainted with drawing: his being able, therefore, now to render this effential fervice to his country, fo much to the fatisfaction of his employers, proves a point which we believe to be true, and which can hardly fail to be of great ufe to all thofe who, like Cook, are doomed to begin life with few acquirements, that generally fpeaking, whatever a man refolves he *will do*, that he *can do*.

Cook now became known in the navy, not only as a man of courage and conduct, but as one, who poffeffed real and great abilities; and he was, very foon after, employed to take a furvey of the river below *Quebec*, in thofe parts where the navigation was thought to be peculiarly difficult and dangerous. This alfo he accomplifhed, and drew a chart of the foundings and bearings with fuch fkill and accuracy, that it is ftill in great repute, and no other has ever fince been thought neceffary.

Cook next became mafter of the *Northumberland*, and, with Lord Colville, wintered at Halifax; where in his few hours of leifure he firft read Euclid, and applied himfelf to the ftudy of aftronomy and other fciences. Like many other felf-taught men, of whom we have read or heard, his dili-

garet. Dorothy Norton died under age and unmarried ; when one entire moiety accrued to her fifter Margaret ; who, in the year 1741, purchafed the other moiety of her coufins, the above-mentioned Elizabeth,

gence and intenfe application compenfated for the flendernefs of his opportunities, and the fcantinefs
of his libraiy ; and his attainments in theoretical knowledge now far exceeded his former ftores, derived folely from practice and obfervation.

AT *Newfoundland* he was fortunate enough to arreſt the notice and approbation of the Governour,
Admiral Graves, by his ſkill and diligence in furveying the harbour and heights of the iſland.

RETURNING to England, in 1762, he married at Barking, in Effex, *Mifs Elizabeth Batts ;* and
in 1763, returned with *Admiral praves* to Newfoundland, where he furveyed the iflands of *Miguelon*
and *St. Pierre ;* and in 1764, when Sir Hugh Pallifon was Governour, Cook was made Marine
Surveyor of *Newfoundland* and *Labradore*, a ſtation which he held with increafing reputation till
1767. The feveral furveys he made during this period, and the charts of them which he publifhed,
reflected additional luftre on his character ; and a paper, which was printed from his communications, in the Philofophical Tranfactions, on the fubject of an eclipfe of the fun, likewife fecured to
him the character of an able mathematician.

EARLY in 1768, the *Royal Society*, anxious to promote that fpirit of difcovery which was then
as it were but in its dawn, but which has fince fhone forth with fuch unexampled fp'endour, as will
give to the prefent reign a diftinguifhed honour in the page of the hiftorian ; and no lefs anxious to
promote any fcheme which tended to the advancement of any branch of philofophical fcience, prefented a memorial to the King, praying that a veffel might be ordered, at the expence of Government, to convey fuitable perfons to the *South Sea*, there to make an obfervation of the tranfit of Venus over the fun's difk, which was expected to take place in 1769. This petition was inftantly complied with ; it being one of the moft prominent features in the character of George III. that he has
always been ready and eager to encourage whatever feemed likely to advance the arts and fciences.
Mr. Alexander Dalrymple, an eminent member of the Royal Society, and deemed one of the firſt naval
geographers of his age, was the perfon pitched upon to direct this important expedition. But *Mr.
Dalrymple* not belonging to the royal navy, which was regarded as an effential requifite, and *Sir Edward Hawke*, then firſt Lord of the Admira'y, refufing to fign a commiffion for any perfon who
was not a naval-officer, the difpute was terminated by the appointment of *Cook*, who was then promoted to the rank of a Lieutenant in the royal navy.

ALTHOUGH we profefs not, in this brief biographical fketch, to write panegyric, it is but juftice
to this great man, to notice the following anecdote, which feems to have been unnoticed by his preceding biographer ; as it places him in the moft amiable point of view, and ftrongly pourtrays the
native goodnefs of his difpofition.

AFTER his appointment to this fcientific expedition, which was to be undertaken in a fhip of ten
guns, and twelve fwivels, called the *Endeavour*,—at the time the fhip was fitting out in the river, the
mafter of a fmall floop, which traded between *Stockton* and *London*, as he was going up the river, la-
en with goods, accidentally run athwart the bow of the *Endeavour*, when fhe was dropping down,

Catherine and Margaret Frank; and thereby became poffeffed of the entire *fee fimple* of the manor and eftate of Marton. Margaret Norton was twice married, firft to Thomas Bright, of Badfworth, in the county

and did her confiderable damage. Upon this, he was immediately ordered on board, to explain his conduct to the commander; and on entering the cabin, *Cook*, with a frown of difpleafure, fharply reproved him for his negligence. The mafter of the floop, who had been his *quondam* friend, fchoolfellow and companion, without attempting to excufe himfelf, faid with a feaman-like bluntnefs, " he hoped he would deal kindly with an *old acquaintance."* *Cook's* curiofity now induced him to requeft an explanation, which his friend accordingly gave him, by fimply reciting the adventures of their youthful years. The furprife and pleafure which he teftified on this occafion was very great; and he liftened to the anecdotes of his *native village* with emotion: they founded in his ears, in the fituation he then was, as " *tales of other times;* and the prefence of the companion of his infancy recalled to his remembrance the almoft obliterated fcenes of early life. On his departure, *Cook* fhewed him every mark of kindnefs and refpect, and made him prefents of wine and other articles, as a token of his friendfhip and regard. When we confider the relative fituation of the parties,—the one appointed the conductor of an undertaking of the greateft national importance, the other toiling in an employment the moft humble and laborious, we cannot fufficiently admire *him*, who forgot the fuperiority of his ftation in the ardour of friendfhip; and, rejecting the dictates of pride, generoufly recognized his old companion with affection and efteem.

As it is far beyond the compafs of this fketch to give any thing like a detailed account of the many important events, which occurred to this firft of circumnavigators, in his different voyages, which, (befides the hiftories of thofe voyages) have already been no lefs than thrice prefented to the world with great advantage: viz. by *Dr. Kippis*; the *Biographia Brittanica*, and the *Scotch Encyclopædia*; an epitomized chronological feries of fuch circumftances as perfonally moft effected our countryman will, we truft, be as much as can reafonably be expected from us.

LATE in Auguft 1768, he fet fail in the *Endeavour*, accompanied by *Sir Jofeph Banks*, now prefident of the Royal Society; *Dr. Solander*, an eminent naturalift; and *Mr. Charles Green*, a no lefs eminent aftronomer; befides a fhip's company, confifting of 84 perfons. In April 1769, he arrived at *Otaheite*, which, on the recommendation of *Capt. Wallis*, had been pitched upon as the proper fpot for making the propofed obfervation; and on the 3d of June it was made in a ferene and cloudlefs fky, with all poffible advantage. In the November following, at another ifland, they made a fimilar obfervation on the tranfit of Mercury; and here alfo the day proved fo favourable, that not a cloud intervened during the whole tranfit.

SPENDING nearly fix months in the examination of *New-Zealand* (referring our readers to the hiftory of the voyage for the particulars of his obfervations and difcoveries) we content ourfelves with remarking, that very large additions to the knowledge of navigation and geography were here made; and the manner in which he had performed this arduous enterprize was fo entirely to the fatisfaction of his king and country, that almoft immediately after his return he was promoted to be a commander in his Majefty's navy; and would have been made a poft-captain, if the etiquette of the fer-

of York, Efq. by whom fhe had one daughter, Mary, who married the
Marquis of Rockingham ; and fecondly, to Sir John Ramfden, of By-
rom, Bart. by whom fhe had iffue one fon, Sir John Ramfden, the pre-

vice would have permitted it.   A much admired account of the voyage was, in due time, communicated to the public by *Dr. Hawkefworth ;* it was written by authority, and drawn up from *Captain
Cook's* journal, and from the papers of Sir Jofeph Banks.

ANOTHER expedition being refolved on to profecute ftill farther difcoveries, two veffels were now
deftined to the fervice, the *Refolution* of about 462 tons burthen ; and the *Adventure* of 363 tons.
To the command of the former *Captain Cook* was appointed ; and *Mr. Tobias Furneaux* to the latter ; the *Refolution* being to be navigated by 112 men ; and the *Adventure* by 81.   *Mr. William
Hodges,* an eminent landfcape painter ; *Mr. John Reinhold Fofter,* and his fon, well known for their
fkill in natural hiftory ; and *Mr. Wales* and *Mr. Bailey,* both of them eminent aftronomers, were
affociated with *Cook* in this voyage : and in July 1772, he fet fail a fecond time to circumnavigate the
globe, with inftructions to refolve, if poffible, the much agitated queftion about the exiftence of a
fouthern continent, and on a more enlarged plan of difcovery than, till then, had been known in the
hiftory of navigation.   In the courfe of their voyage, the two fhips were feparated early in February ; and did not meet again till about the middle of May, in *Queen Charlotte's Sound,* in New
Zealand ; but in November parted again, and met no more during the voyage.

FROM the time of their leaving the *Cape of Good Hope,* to their return to it, the *Refolution* had
failed no lefs than twenty thoufand leagues ; an extent of voyage nearly equal to three times the
equatorial circumference of the earth, and which has never before been accomplifhed by any fhip, in
the fame fpace of time.   And now the great purpofe for which this voyage was undertaken being
obtained, as far as there appeared to be a poffibility of attaining it, *Captain Cook* once more began
to turn his thoughts towards England.   And, on the 30th day of July, 1775, he landed at Portf-
mouth, having been abfent from Great Britain, three years and eighteen days ; in which time, and
under all changes of climate, he had loft but four men, and only one of them by ficknefs.   All future
plans of fearching for, or hopes of finding a fouthern continent, which had occafionally engroffed the
attention of fome of the principal maritime powers, and had, in different ages, been urged with great
ardour by philofophers and geographers, were now for ever abandoned.

ON his return, he was received by all ranks of people with a refpect almoft bordering on enthu-
fiafm ; our nation being juftly proud of having among her natives a man, whom all Europe now regarded, not only as one of extraordinary fagacity and courage, but alfo one of the ableft and moft fci-
entifical navigators then living.   As a proof of the high eftimation in which he was held, he was
now raifed to the rank of a Poft-Captain, and alfo made a Captain in *Greenwich Hofpital ;* an appointment which, no doubt, was intended as an honourable and comfortable fupport for the remainder of his life.   Soon after he was unanimoufly elected a fellow of the Royal Society, and had alfo
the honour to receive a golden medal for the beft experimental paper of the year.

CONSIDERED as a national work, and one, in which the character of the nation at large was not
a little interefted, it had been thought proper that the compiling, digefting, and arranging the ma-

sent Baronet; to whom, by her will, dated April 14th, 1774, she devised the manor and estate of Marton, and who, in the year 1786, sold and conveyed the same to Bartholomew Rudd, Esq. of Marsk, the present

---

terials, collected from the several journals of his first voyage, should be committed to the care of a professed literary man. But as to this second voyage, *Captain Cook* himself was justly regarded as perfectly competent to the relation of his own story. His journal only required to be divided into chapters: and perhaps to be amended by a few verbal corrections. Nor is there any extravagance in the assertion, that in point of composition, this history of this voyage reflects on the writer no small degree of credit. His stile is modest, natural, clear, and manly; and particularly well suited both to the subject, and to the *Captain's* own character; so that it has been questioned on a comparison of the two narrations, whether the former did not lose as much in simplicity and interest, as it gained in elegance.

In July 1776, *Captain Cook* in the *Refolution*, with *Mr. King*, a scientific man of high reputation, as well as an active and able seaman, as his second Lieutenant, accompanied by *Capt. Clark*, in the *Difcovery*, set sail on a *third* voyage; the object of which was, not now as before, to explore the *terra auftralis incognita*, but to discover, if possible, whether there was or was not a possibility of shortening the passage to the East Indies, by sailing round the northern parts of the continents of Europe and Asia. To do all that could be done towards effecting this object, he resolved to reverse the usual plan of discovery; and instead of a passage from the Atlantic into the Pacific, to try if he could not find one from the latter into the former. Accordingly, he was ordered to proceed to the Pacific ocean, through the chain of the *new iflands*, which he had lately visited in the southern tropic; and after he should have crossed the equator into the northern parts of that ocean, he was then to hold such a course, as might probably fix many interesting points in geography, and produce intermediate discoveries in his progress northward to the principal scene of his operations. But, as it is the avowed intention of this epitome, not to attempt a detail of every circumstance, in which *Capt. Cook*, as a navigator, was concerned, we again refer our readers to his history at large of the voyage, and content ourselves with observing, that after having passed some time in the *Society* and *Friendly Iflands*, employed entirely in promoting the great purposes of their voyage, they sailed to the northward, to prosecute the more immediate object of the expedition; and at length, in March 1778, arrived at *New-Albion*, in 44° 33″ of N. latitude, and 235° 20″ of E. longitude. Here they carefully explored *Nootka*, or *King George's Sound*; the grand features of the country, its animals, and vegetable productions, appearing very much to resemble those of *Hudfon's Bay* and *Canada*. Soon after they arrived at *Oonalafhka*, and next at *Cape Prince of Wales*, the most western extremity of America, yet explored.

This extremity is distant from the eastern cape of *Siberia*, not more than thirteen leagues; and thus the vicinity of the two continents was ascertained; and from the affinity which was found to

N n n

proprietor and Lord of the manor, who has erected a convenient manfion in the centre of his eftate, in an open fituation, on the fummit of a
gentle flope; from whence the fea, generally crowded with fhips em-

---

fubfift between the dialects of the *Greenlanders* and the *Efquimaux*, and thofe of the inhabitants of
Norton's Sound, in lat. 64° 55' and *Oonalafhka*, there is ftrong reafon to believe, that all thefe nations
are of the fame extraction; and if that be the cafe, the exiftence of a northern communication of
fome kind by water, between the weft fide of America, and the eaft fide, through *Baffin's Bay*, can
fcarcely be doubted; which communication, neverthelefs, may effectually be fhut up againft fhips, by
ice and other impediments.

AIMING to direct his courfe to *Kamfchatka* in his way thither, he ftopped for the fake of provifions at *Owhyhee*, one of the group of the *Sandwich Iflands*. This purpofe it completely anfwered,
and after having victualled their veffels far beyond what could have been hoped for in an uncivilized
country, they left the bay of *Karakakooa*, where it had been effected; to which, however, a violent
ftorm obliged them to return in a few days. This return, alas! was fatal to our diftinguifhed countryman; for, endeavouring with his cuftomary humanity and courage, to refcue fome of his crew
from the mifchiefs and danger of an unfortunate quarrel with the Indians, he was fhockingly murdered by fome of the barbarians, on the 14th of February, 1779; who, however, little knew of how
much injuftice they were guilty, or what irreparable injury they did to the whole civilized world.
His death was univerfally regretted, not only in Great Britain, but alfo in other parts of Europe, by
thofe, to whom his merits and public fervices were known.

IT now remains only, that we clofe this biographical fketch of this truly extraordinary man
with fomething like a fummary of his character, deduced from a comprehenfive view of the whole
of his hiftory. In drawing up this brief fummary, fo copious and rich are the materials, from which
our extracts are made, our greateft difficulty will be to determine, not what we are to felect, but
what we muft omit; for we may, and can truly affert, with a late celebrated compiler of hiftory,
that we fhall not omit a fingle paffage, without a painful confcioufnefs, that from the nature of our
work, we muft forbear to infert many, highly worthy of infertion.

IN his perfon, *Captain Cook* was tall, being upwards of fix feet high, ftout and robuft, rather than
elegant, but well adapted to the courfe of life which providence deftined him to lead; for, he was inured to labour and toil, and capable of bearing almoft any hardfhips. In all bodily gratifications he
was not only habitually temperate; but, when neceffary, abftemious. Owing to the manner in
which he had been brought up in early life, his ftomach bore, without difficulty, the coarfeft and
leaft palatable food; as little loathing the *train-oil* of *Nootka Sound*, as he was regaled with the richeft and moft poignant fauces of the moft luxurious table in London.

THE qualities of his mind, like thofe of his body, were hardy and vigorous; and he was as capable of intenfe thought, as he was of fevere labour. His underftanding was ftrong and perfpicacious;
and his judgment, efpecially in every thing that related to the fervices in which he was engaged,
quick, clear and fure. Cool and deliberate in forming his plans and purpofes, fagacious in determi-

ployed in the coal-trade, prefents an interefting object on the eaft, with a view to the weft, north, and fouth, which is extenfive and pleafingly attractive.

THE hamlet of TOLESBY is fituated at a fhort diftance from the village of Marton, towards the weft. The eftate appears to have been long in the poffeffion of the family of Forfters, who were formerly refi-

---

ning, active in executing, vigilant, cautious, and perfevering; unfubdued by labour, difficulties, and difappointments; fertile in expedients; never wanting prefence of mind; always poffeffing himfelf and the full ufe of a found underftanding, he poffeffed, in an eminent degree, the qualifications requifite for his profeffion, and thofe arduous undertakings to which he was called by the unanimous voice of his king and country.

SUCH were the outlines of *Captain Cook's* character; but its moft diftinguifhing feature was that unremitting perfeverance in the purfuit of his object, which was not only fuperior to the oppofition of dangers, and the preffure of hardfhips, but even exempt from either any occafion for, or any defire of thofe ordinary relaxations, which, like the unbending of a bent bow, have, in moft other inftances, been found neceffary to reftore and preferve the fpring and vigour of the mind.

IF any country may be proud of having produced a man, who, in various ways, enlarged the bounds of human knowledge, that pride is the fair boaft of *this diftrict* of the kingdom; and his hiftory, from the conviction it fo forcibly brings, that even ordinary talents, when animated by a prevailing defire to excel, and a laudable ambition to obtain diftinction and eminence by perfevering and unwearied efforts to deferve well of mankind, will be ultimately crowned with fuccefs, may animate *us all*, as far as our feveral peculiar capacities, ftations, and attainments will permit us, to " *go and do likewife.*" There is hardly a corner of the earth, whither the fame of *Cook* has not reached; nor have we yet heard of any people fo blind to, or fo regardlefs of great worth, as not willingly to have paid the tribute of applaufe to his virtues. Europe, at leaft, has been unanimous in contemplating, admiring, revering, and emulating this great mafter in his profeffion, whofe fkill and labours have extended nautical fcience, enlarged natural philofophy, and difclofed the long-concealed, but admirable arrangements of the almighty in the formation of this globe; and, at the fame time, the arrogance of mortals for prefuming to account by their fpeculations, for the laws, by which he was pleafed to create it. It is now difcovered, beyond all doubt, that the fame great being, who created the univerfe by his *fiat*, by the fame ordained our earth to keep a juft poife without a correfponding fouthern continent; and it does fo. " *He ftretches out the north over the empty place, and* " *hangeth the earth upon nothing.*"—JOB. xxvi. 7.

IF the arduous but exact refearches of this extraordinary man have not difcovered a *new world*, they have difcovered feas unnavigated and unknown before. They have made us acquainted with iflands, people, and productions, of which we had no conception. And, if he has not been fo

dent here; and was fold by a defcendant of that family, to the late
Earl of Lonfdale, who devifed the fame to the prefent Earl, then Sir
William Lowther, Bart. by whom, in the year 1803, it was fold to
Bartholomew Rudd, Efq. the prefent poffeffor. *Tolefby-Hall*, the ancient refidence of the Forfters, is now gone to decay; the materials of
which have been lately removed by the prefent proprietor, who is
erecting a more modern manfion upon a larger fcale, and in an open
and more eligible fituation.

NEWHAM lies in the weftern extremity of the parifh, adjoining
to Stainton; and, as appears from the Domefday furvey already ftated, contained two carucates and two oxgangs of land *ad geldum;*
which afterwards became part of the fee of Robert de Brus, who, in
the reign of Henry I. gave the fame, together with the chapel of *St.
Hilda*, at Middlefburgh, to the abbot and convent of Whitby. Newham continued in the poffeffion of that monaftery, till the diffolution,
when it came to the crown; but of the firft grantees, and their fucceffors, we are equally uninformed. It was late the property of ——
Cookfon, Efq. of Norton, in the county of Durham, with whofe niece

---

fortunate as *Americus* to give his name to a Continent, his pretenfions to fuch a diftinction remains
unrivalled; and he will be revered, while there remains a page of his own modeft account of his voyages; and as long as mariners and geographers fhall be inftructed by his new map of the fouthern
hemifphere, to trace the various courfes and difcoveries he has made. If public fervices merit public
acknowledgments; if the man who adorned and raifed the fame of his country, is deferving of honours, then CAPTAIN JAMES COOK, a native of the *diftrict*, which is the fubject of this hiftory,
deferves to have a monument raifed to his memory by a generous and grateful nation. * " *Virtutis
uberrimum alimentum eft honos."*   VALERIUS MAXIMUS, LIB. 2. CAP. 6.

---

* IT is much to be regretted, that a plan, which was formed fome years ago, of erecting a pyramid or
obelifk on the fummit of *Rofeberry*, to the memory of this indefatigable and fcientific navigator, has not yet
been executed. A better fituation cannot be chofen than the peaked fummit of that conical mountain, fo
bold and towering, and happily in unifon with the genius of the *immortal Cook*. We flatter ourfelves, that
at no very diftant period, we may have the fatisfaction of feeing his memory handed down to pofterity in
a manner worthy of his name.

it paſſed by marriage to Thomas Simpſon, Eſq. who ſtill poſſeſſes part of the eſtate; the other moiety of which was lately purchaſed by, and is now the property of, George Brown, Eſq. of Stockton.

Of the SOIL and PRODUCE of this pariſh, which contains about 4000 acres, one half of which is in tillage, we may remark that the lands conſiſt chiefly of a clayey loam, which is fertile, and produces abundant crops of wheat. The ſoil, in the ſouthern and weſtern parts of the pariſh, is clay, upon a cold bottom; but near the village of Marton, the lands are fertile, and, as we have before obſerved, remarkable for a great extent of rich old paſtures, producing herbage of the fineſt quality. The following rotation of crops is now generally adopted; viz. fallow, wheat, clover, beans.

The improved breed of ſheep, known by the name of the *Diſhley*, or *New-Leiceſter*, has been lately introduced; and likewiſe the ſhort-horned breed of cattle, both of which, having a great propenſity to fatten, and coming much earlier to maturity than the old breeds, are conſequently found more profitable to the farmer.

ASPECT and GENERAL APPEARANCE. The lands in the northern extremity of the pariſh are nearly level, from whence there is a regular and eaſy aſcent towards the ſouth, where the ſurface becomes varied and uneven, riſing into ſome gentle ſwells. There are no plantations within the pariſh except thoſe lately made by Mr. Rudd, who has planted upwards of one hundred acres of waſte grounds in different parts of his eſtate, chiefly with oak and larch, which are in a thriving condition; but the hedges being in general good, with a number of trees in the hedge-rows, the country has a pleaſing and chearful aſpect.

POPULATION. The following tables ſubjoined in the notes, will ſhew the population of the pariſh. * In the year 1801, when an

	Inhab. Houſes	Fam-ilies	Uninhab. Houſes.	Males.	Fe-males.	Total.	Agri-culture.	Trade, &c.	Refi-due.	To-tal.
	‖ STATE OF POPULATION, 10th MARCH 1801.									
Marton,	80	80	5	170	172	342	180	26	136	342

accurate furvey was made according to Act of Parliament, there were
80 houfes or families, and 342 inhabitants, giving 4¼ to each family.
The average number of baptifms and burials annually being nearly
equal, we may conclude that there has been little or no increafe or decreafe of inhabitants for the laft century.

ABSTRACT OF MARTON PARISH REGISTER.

Years.	BAPTISMS. Males.	Females.	BURIALS. Males.	Females.
1700	5	1	4	6
1710	8	5	7	4
1720	8	3	3	3
1730	5	4	4	2
1740	4	3	0	5
1750	3	4	5	5
1760	5	3	5	5
1770	11	8	2	2
1780	9	6	6	3
Totals	58	37	36	35

	M.	Fe.	Tot.
Baptifms from 1781 to 1800,	101	92	193
Burials from do. to do.	72	94	166
Marrriages from do. to do.			59

THE PARISH OF ACKLAM;

CONSISTING of the townfhips of Acklam, Linthorpe, and the chapelry of Middlefbrough, adjoins to Marton on the eaft ; and is bounded in the fouth and weft by the parifh of Stainton, and wafh-ed on the north by the navigable river Tees.

IT is no improbable conjecture that this place was originally cal-led Acklam (qu. Oaklam, *villa quercuum*) from its fituation in the time of the Britons, as being a town or dwelling furrounded with a foreft of oaks : or, it might be fo named (qu. *villa lutofa*) from its clayey foil.

THE village is fmall, fituated upon the road leading from Stock-ton ; from which it is about three miles diftant, and feven from the market town of Stokefley.

THE lands here, at a very early period, were in the hands of differ-ent proprietors. According to the Domefday furvey there were three carucates, which were ancient demefne of the Crown, entered under the title

TERRA REGIS,

MANERIUM IN ACLUN LESING III. CAR. AD GELDUM. TERRA AD. II. CAR. XX. SOLID.

FROM another part of this ancient record it appears that Hugh, Earl of Chefter, held lands here, which before the Conqueft were in the poffeffion of Siward, Earl of Northumberland. This part of Ack-lam is furveyed with Ingleby Berwick, as follows ;

TERRA COMITIS HUGONIS.

BER.

IN ACLUN ET ENGLEBI AD GELDUM XI. CARUCATÆ; ET VII. CAR.

COM.

POSS. ESSE. HOC TENUIT SIWARD PRO I. MANERIO. NUNC HUGO CO-MES HABET; ET HUGO, FILIUS NORMANNI SUB EO. IN DOMINIO III.

CARUCATÆ, ET XII. VILLANI, CUM III. CAR. ECCLESIA ET PRESBITER.
TOTUM MANERIUM II. LEUC. LONG, ET I. LAT. T. R. E. VALEBAT XLVIII.
LIB. MODO XL. SOLID.

(II. CAR.)   (III. CAR.)
AD HOC MANERIUM PERTINET SOCA HÆC; COLEBI. HEMELINGETUN ;
(II. CAR.)   (III. CAR.)   (III. CAR.)   (IV. CAR.)   (III. CAR.)   (III. CAR.)
STEINTUN. TORNETUN. MALLEBI. ENGLEBI. TORMOTBY. STEINSBI. IN-
TER TOTUM AD GELDUM XXV. CARUCATÆ, ET XV. CAR. POSSUNT ESSE.
OMNIA WASTA PRÆTER ENGLEBI, UBI SUNT III. CAR.

BESIDES the above, there was one carucate, entered in the Domefday book under the title

TERRA ROBERTI MALLET.

MANER. IN ACLUN HABEBAT EDMUND I. CAR. AD GLD. ROBT. HABET
ET WAST. EST. TERRA. AD. DIM. CAR.

THE manor of Acklam, comprehending the lands of Linthorpe,
Airfholme, and Middlefbrough, became at an early period part of the
fee of Robert de Brus; by whom, or his immediate fucceffors, who
held of the king *in capite*, it was granted out to the ancient family
of Bovington, or Boynton. By an inquifition *poſt mortem*, (taken 7.
Edward I.) it was found that William de Bovington held of Peter de
Brus, at the time of his death, one knight's fee at Acklam ; and that the
faid William and others *(fui participes)* held half a knight's fee at Leventhorpe, where ten carucates made one knight's fee.

ACKLAM continued in the family of the Boyntons, for feveral generations, till the reign of Charles I. when it was fold by Sir Matthew
Boynton, Knight and Baronet, to William Huftler of Bridlington, Efq.
grandfather to Sir William Huftler, Knight ; in whofe immediate
defcendants it continued till the year 1784, when Evereld, the daughter of Sir William Huftler, Knight, dying unmarried, devifed the eftate to her nephew, Thomas Peirfe, Efq, who took the name of Huftler ; and whofe fon, Thomas Huftler, Efq. is the prefent proprietor.

ACKLAM HALL,

the feat of Thomas Huftler, Efq. ftands a little to the eaft of the village, about half a mile from the road leading to Stockton ; the ap-

proach to which is through an extenfive avenue of ancient firs and lime trees. The manfion, which was chiefly erected by Sir William Huftler, Knight, § is a handfome fquare building, fronting to the fouth and weft, and fheltered on the eaft and north with plantations ; which, from the road at a diftance, have a good effect upon the landfcape. As the fituation is rather low, the profpect is not greatly varied, nor very extenfive, but the grounds in front, which are fmooth and level, having been opened and improved by the prefent owner, prefent a verdant foreground, and give to the whole a foft and plea-fing afpect.

THE church of Acklam ftands near the manfion on the north, and is a fmall modern ftructure, confifting of a nave ‖ and chancel ; lately rebuilt of hewn ftone, and covered with flate ; and being well lighted, and feated in a regular and uniform manner, is a neat and commodi-ous place of worfhip. This being one of the few Cleveland churches mentioned in Domefday, may certainly claim an high antiquity ; al-

§ ON the front of the manfion over the door, are the arms of Huftler; viz. *arg.* on a fefs, *az.* three fleur de lis, *or.* between two martlets, *fable.*

‖ IN the fouth wall, there is a neat marble monument, with the following infcription :
Sacred to the memory of EVERELD HUSTLER
the youngeft and only furviving Daughter
Of SIR WM HUSTLER of this place, KNIGHT,
by Dame ANNE, Relict of *Sir Matthew Wentworth*
of *Bretton,* in the County of York *Bart.*
She was born the 18. of Auguft, 1698,
and died the 11th January 1784.
Her *Life* was an Example of moft extenfive Benevolence,
united with the Practice of every religious and focial Duty ;
Her *Death* a Leffon of that Compofure and Refignation,
which the Hope of Immortality, grounded on a well-fpent Life,
Could alone infpire.
THOMAS HUSTLER ESQR. (late PEIRSE) her *Nephew*
dedicated this flender Tribute of Gratitude and Affection
to his kind *Benefactrefs.*

O O O

though the æra of its foundation is not known.   It was given by *Al-vereaus* to the priory of Guifbrough ; and the grant thereof, with fome others, was confirmed by Peter de Brus.

IT appears from Ecton, and other authorities, that this was anciently a chapel to Stainton ; and with that church, on the diffolution of monafteries, was given to the Archbifhop of York, who is the patron and nominates the curate.   The dedication of the church is not known.   It was certified to the Governours of Queen Anne's Bounty at 17*l*. 3s. 4d. *per annum*, and having received two augmentations b⸱⸱ lot, laid out in lands at Ofmotherley and Eaft-Harlfey, the revenues amount to about 60*l. per ann.*

THE townfhip of

LINTHORPE, or LEVENTHORPE,

including the hamlet of *Airfholme*, and the modern village of *Newport*, lies to the north, and conftitutes a part of the manor of Acklam.   As the lands here are not mentioned in Domefday, they may be prefumed to have been included under the furvey of Acklam.   Linthorpe, in the reign of Edward I. was in poffeffion of the Boyntons ; while Airf-holme (anciently written *A·fum*, and fometimes *Harhufum*) appears to have been held in parcels ; for in Kirkby's Inqueft, we find that Arnald de Percy, of Kildale, held one Knight's fee at Nunthorpe, Upfall, and Arfum, of the heirs of Marmaduke de Thweng, where ten carucates made one Knight's fee : but the Ingelrams appear to have been the principal proprietors ; ‡ whofe inheritance, after feveral defcents,

---

ACKLAM CURACY, OR CHAPEL.
DEDICATION unknown.   Certified value 17*l*. 3s. 4d.   The Archbifhop of York, patron.
CURATES.
1699 Robert Burrel.
1725 Philip Kitchin, afterwards vicar of Marton.
1729 Nicholas Richards, *poft refig.* Kitchin.
1739 John Grenfide, afterwards vicar of Marton.
1769 William Moore, *poft refig.* Grenfide.
‡ JOHN DE INGELRAM gave one carucate of land here ; with a place for a fifhery on the river

came to the Boyntons, though, by what means, or at what period, we have no information ; and by them, together with Acklam, was alienated to the Huftlers.

NEWPORT is a modern village, fituate upon the banks of the river Tees, and being an out-port belonging to Stockton, contains a commodious quay and granaries, for the reception of corn and other articles, which are fhipped coaftwife to London, Newcaftle, &c.

IN the northern extremity of the parifh, lies the townfhip or chapelry of

MIDDLESBROUGH ;

which confifts only of four farm-houfes, fituated on the fouthern banks of the river Tees. The lands here are not noticed in Domefday ; but appear to have been of the fee of Robert de Brus : and at an early period, were held in parcels ; but we have no information of the principal proprietors, till the reign of Charles I. when the Huftlers became owners thereof, and continued in the fole poffeffion till the year 1730, when, on the death of Sir William Huftler, Knight, one fourth of his Acklam and Middlefbrough eftates defcended with Anne, his eldeft daughter, to Thomas Peirfe, of Hutton-Bonville, Efq. whofe defcendant, upon the divifion by Act of Parliament, became poffeffed of a part of Middlefbrough, as his fhare ; which has fince been fold to different purchafers. Thomas Huftler, Efq. of Acklam-Hall, is the principal proprietor.

Tees, to the canons of Guifbrough, as appears from the following charter in Dodfworth's MS. *(vol. 3. p. 5.)* copied from the original in Saint Marie's tower at York :

" Ego Johannes Engelram, filius Willi. Engelram, concilio uxoris meæ et confenfu Adalinæ, filiæ et heredis mei, dedi unam carucatam terræ in *Harhufum,* ecclefiæ fanctæ Mariæ de Gifburgh, cum locis ad faciendas pifcarias in Teifia. Teftes, *Will. Fil. Rogeri,* cum fratribus fuis *Ricard.* et *Ada. Robertus Scarbota ; Umfridus de Hoton,* et *Robertus Frater* ejus. Teftes conceffionis autem uxoris et filiæ meæ, ifti funt, *Robertus de Bruis, Ofbertus de Setima, Johannes,* filius ejus &c. *B.* 155.

THERE was an ancient chapel here, dedicated to *St. Hilda*, which, with its appurtenances, and two carucates and two oxgangs of land at Newham, was given, in the latter part of the reign of King Henry I. by Robert de Brus, and Agnes his wife, to the abbot and convent of Whitby; * on condition, that they fhould caufe fome Benedictine monks of their houfe, to refide and perform divine fervices here; fo that this chapel became a ceil to that monaftery, and continued till the general diffolution by King Henry VIII. when there were only two or three monks refident here. By the valuation taken 26 Henry VIII. its revenues amounted to 21*l*. 3s. 8d. *per ann.* and its fite was granted (6 Elizabeth, 1546) to Thomas Reeve.

THIS chapel was anciently dependent on the church of Stainton; ‖ but on the grant thereof to the abbey of Whitby, which was

---

* " ROBERTUS DE BRUS, de MIDLESBURG.

ROBERTUS DE BRUS, omnibus fanctæ matris ecclefiæ fidelibus, falutem. Scitote, quod ego et *Agnes* uxor mea, filiufque nofter *Adamus* de *Brus*, pro falute domini noftri *Henrici* regis *Angliæ*, animarumque noftrarum, et heredum noftrorum remedio, ecclefiam fanctæ *Hyldæ* de *Midlefburg*, cum omnibus rebus, quæ ad eandem ecclefiam pertinet, et duas carucatas, et duas bovatas terræ in *Nchuham*, in perpetuam elemofinam, ecclefiæ et fratribus fancti *Petri*, et fanctæ *Hyldæ* de *Whiteby* dedimus, conceffimus et confirmamus, ea conventione, ut in prefata ecclefia de *Midlefburg*, quidam monachi fint, qui deo et fanctæ Hildæ de *Whitebi* deferviant, et qui de ftipendiis præfatæ ecclefiæ largè et fufficienter vivere valeant, et ut mater ecclefia de *Whiteby* de ea femper valeat habere proficuum. Hii funt teftes, *Willielmus* Capellanus; *Arnaldus* de *Percy*; *Umfridus* de *Elthot*; *Willielmus* de *Fugeris*, et multi alii." *Dugd. Mon. Ang. vol. I. p.* 413.

‖ IT appears from the regifter of Whitby abbey *(Fo.* 8. *Appen. No.* 177.*)* that there was a difpute between the canons of *Guifbrough*, who were impropriators of the mother church of *Stainton*, and the monks of *Whitby*, owners of the chapel of *Middlefbro*,' touching the tithes, parochial dues mortuaries, &c. of twelve carucates of land, which the canons of Guifbrough claimed, as belonging to their mother church, and the monks, as to their chapel of *Middlefbrough*: but the matter was thus fettled between them, by the interpofition of *Robert de Brus* their common patron; viz. that the canons of *Guifbrough* fhould have the tithes, &c. of fix carucates, as belonging to their church at *Stainton*; and the monks of *Whitby*, the tithes, &c. of the other fix carucates, as belonging to their chapel of *Middlefbrough*, which, for the future, was to be *emancipated from Stainton, and deemed a mother church*. And, in order to prevent difputes in future, it was directed and agreed, that the monks of *Whitby* were to have the tithes, &c. of four carucates of the fee of *John Ingelram* in *Arfum*; of a fifth of the fee of *Mallet*, who was a vaffal of *Roger de Mowbray*, in *Leventhorpe*; and of a fixth, being their own land at *Middlefburgh*. And the canons of *Guifbro*' were to have thofe of three carucates of the fee confirmed by King Henry I. and by Thurſtan, Archbiſhop of York, (who alſo exempted it from archiepiſcopal juriſdiction or cuſtoms) it was ſevered from the mother church, and made parochial. It was certified to the governours of the bounty of Queen Anne, at 6*l*. os. *per ann.* and has ſince received three augmentations by lot, laid out in lands, which produce an income of about forty pounds a year. Thomas Huſtler, of Acklam Hall, Eſq. is the patron, and nominates the curate. The chapel has been long in ruins, and nothing of the ſacred edifice now remains; the ſite of which, together with the chapel-yard, which is ſtill uſed occaſionally as a burying-place by the inhabitants, lies open, and uncloſed from the adjoining grounds.

THERE are ſome faint traces here of an ancient entrenchment or fortification, which probably gave name to the place, and is conjectured to be of Roman origin; but there is no hiſtorical evidence, nor have we met with any diſtinguiſhing marks of that people to ſupport the conjecture.

AGRICULTURE, SOIL, PRODUCE, &c. This pariſh is worthy of particular notice for the ſpirit of huſbandry which prevails here; and we have to remark, that the value of the eſtate has been greatly increaſed within the laſt ten years by the preſent proprietor; whoſe at-

---

of *Robert de Brus*, in *Acklam*; of a fourth of the fee of *Robert de Sturmey*, in the ſame townſhip; of a fifth of *Mallet*, held of *Robert de Brus*; and of a ſixth, being their own land at *Arſum*. This circumſtance only ſhews, how very tenacious thoſe religious houſes were of their particular rights and privileges, and with what difficulty it was that they ſubmitted to the claims of each other.

MIDDLESBROUGH CHAPEL.

DEDIC. Saint *Hilda.* Certif. val. 6*l*. os. Thomas Huſtler, Eſq. patron.

CURATES.

1699 Robert Burrell, admitted curate.
1725 Philip Kitchen, nominated by Sir William Huſtler, Knight.
1729 Nicholas Richards,   by the ſame.
1739 John Grenſide,   by ———— Huſtler, Eſq.
1769 William Moore,   by Mrs. Evereld Huſtler.

tention to agricultural improvements is indefatigable; particularly in
the encouragement which he gives to his tenants to promote the introduction of the improved breeds of cattle and sheep. *

THE lands are nearly level, except in the southern part of the parish, where they have a gentlei nclination towards the north. The soil
in the level lands near the river is chiefly clay, with a mixture of rich
loam; and near the village of Acklam, and Acklam Hall, a sandy loam
prevails. Wheat and beans are the principal crops, but the cultivation of turnips and clover has been introduced upon the loamy soil.
The buildings and fences are kept in excellent repair; and the grounds
near the mansion are sheltered by plantations, which, with trees scattered in the hedge rows, contribute to give the whole a richly cultivated
appearance.

POPULATION. This parish being small, and the inhabitants occupied chiefly in agricultural pursuits, we find little under this head
worthy of particular observation. From the enumeration of the inha-

---

* To promote improvements, and excite a spirit of industry and emulation amongst his tenants
and cottagers, Mr. Hustler distributes annually the following premiums and rewards; viz.

I. FOR the *farm* which shall be in the best condition and most skilful state of cultivation, and on
which the greatest and most permanent improvements shall have been effected.—A SILVER CUP,
value FIVE GUINEAS.

II. FOR the *best cow*, in milk, and in calf, bred by the owner.—TWO GUINEAS.

III. FOR the *best two-year old heifer* in calf, bred by the owner.—TWO GUINEAS.

IV. FOR the best *pen of three one-shear gimmers*, bred by the owner.—TWO GUINEAS.

V. FOR the best *pen of three one-shear wethers*, bred by the owner.—TWO GUINEAS.

VI. FOR the *best sow* in pig.—ONE GUINEA.

VII. To the *cottager* or *day-labourer* (having a settlement in the parish of *Acklam*, or in the
township of *Linthorpe*) who shall have brought up and educated in habits of industry, the greatest
number of legitimate children, with the least parochial relief; a PIG, value THREE GUINEAS.

IN adjudging the several premiums, every allowance is made for soil and situation, so as to place
the several candidates on an equal footing.

bitants within the feveral townfhips taken the year 1801, † we find that there were 64 houfes or families, and 337 inhabitants, giving an average of $5\frac{1}{2}$ nearly to each family ; the males and females are nearly equal.

The number of baptifms, burials, and marriages, according to the parifh regifters, will appear from the following table ; *

	Males.	Females.	Total.
Baptifms from 1781 to 1800 inclufive,	105	91	196
Burials from do. to do.	49	44	93
Increafe	56	47	103
Marriages within the above period	-	-	79

From the average number of baptifms and burials in one year, according to the above table, it will appear that to every $37\frac{1}{2}$ nearly of the inhabitants a child is born, while one only out of 84 dies annually.

† STATE OF POPULATION 10th MARCH, 1801.

Townships.	Houfes.	Fam ilies.	Uninhab. Houfes.	Males.	Fe- males.	Total.	Agricul- ture.	Trade &c.	Refi- due.	To- tal.
Acklam.	21	21		51	47	98	47	12	39	98
Linthorpe.	39	39	2	101	113	214	88	11	115	214
Middlefbro.'	4	4		13	12	25	25			25
Totals.	64	64	2	165	172	337	160	23	154	337

* The above ftatement of baptifms &c. includes thofe within the chapelry of Middlefbrough ; as no diftinct regifter is kept of the entries within that chapelry.

THE PARISH OF STAINTON

ADJOINS to Acklam and Marton on the eaft, and confifts of the feveral townfhips of Stainton, Hemlington, Maltby, Thornaby and
Berwick. It is bounded by Hilton and Seamer on the fouth; on the
weft by the river Leven, which divides it from the parifh of Yarm;
and on the north and north-weft by the river Tees. Its greateft extent
from eaft to weft is fix miles, and about five miles from north to fouth.

THE village of Stainton, which gives name to the parifh, is fituated
on rather elevated ground, about five miles from the market-town of
Yarm, and four from Stokefley; and was probably fo called (qu. *villa
faxofa*) from its fite being anciently covered with ftones; which, when
the place was firft inhabited, and before the improved ftate of the country, might perhaps be found here in great abundance. ‖

THE townfhip of Stainton, which is the moft confiderable divifion
of the parifh, comprifes the feveral manors of Stainton, Thornton, and
Stainfby; and the lands here, befides thofe already mentioned under
the furvey of Acklam, as being within the foke of that manor, are
thus noticed in Domefday; where we find Thornton furveyed under
the title

TERRA REGIS.

MANERIUM IN TORNETUN VLCHIL II. CAR. TERRÆ AD GELDUM. TERRA
AD I. CAR. DIMID. LEUC. LONG. ET DIMID. LAT.

STAINTON, with the foke of one carucate at Thornton, is entered
as follows, under the head

‖ IN confirmation of this conjecture, we may remark, that at a little diftance from the village of
Stainton, there is a large quarry of blue *whinftone*, or *granite*, fimilar to that already noticed within
the parifh of Ayton, being a continuation of the great blue *ftone dyke*, which appears in different parts
of the county of Durham, and has been traced running from thence in a line eaftwards, through
Cleveland, to the fea below Whitby.

TERRA ROBERTI MALLET.

MANER. IN STEINTUN HABEBAT EDMUND II. CAR. TERRÆ AD GELDUM.
SOCA IN TORNETUN EST. I. CAR. TERRÆ AD GELD. SOCA PERTINENS AD
STEIN. WAST. EST.

THESE lands became part of the fee of Robert de Brus, which he
held of the King *in capite*; and defcended by marriage with Lucia,
daughter of Peter de Brus, to Marmaduke de Thweng; of whom, according to Kirkby's Inqueft (13. Edw. I.) the prior of Guifbrough held
certain lands at Stainton; and Ingelram de Bovington held three parts
of one knight's fee at Thornton *et alibi*, where ten carucates made one
knight's fee. ‡

WE find little worthy of notice in ancient records touching thefe
places. The lands have been long held in parcels, and are now in the
hands of different freeholders; but we have not been able to trace the
fucceffion of the proprietors of the manors; as the manerial rights
have not for many years been exercifed; nor does it clearly appear to
whom they now belong. The Pennymans of Ormefby have been long
in poffeffion of a confiderable eftate at Thornton, where they had an
ancient refidence; but the houfe and gardens, which appear to have
been extenfive, are gone to decay, and the materials of the buildings
have been lately removed.

WITHIN this townfhip, about a mile to the north from the village
of Stainton, lies the ancient hamlet, or manor of *Stainfby*; which, befides three carucates, as within the foke of the manor of Acklam, contained, in the Conqueror's time, two carucates ad geldum, thus entered
in the Domefday furvey under the title,

TERRA TAINORUM REGIS.

IN STEMANESBI II. CAR. TERRÆ AD GELDUM. TERRA AD I. CARUCAT.
UCTRED HABET, ET WAST. EST.

---

‡ PRIOR de Gifburne tenet unum feodum in Thormonby, Staynton, Leventhorpe, &c. (de hereditate Marmaduci de Thweng) unde 10 carucatæ faciunt unum feod. milit. et reddit pro finibus 6s.

INGELRAMUS DE BOVINGTON tenet tres partes unius feodi de dicta hereditate Marmaduc. de
Thweng, in *Aclum*, Thornton, &c. unde 10 car. terræ faciunt feodum milit. et reddit ballivo domini
regis pro fine 3s.   *Kirkby's Inqueft.*

P P P

STAINSBY was afterwards granted by the Conqueror to Robert de Brus, as chief Lord, who held of the King *in capite ;* and at an early period, the place gave name to the refident family ; for in Kirkby's Inqueft, we find that Walter de Stainfby held four carucates of land here of the fee of Marmaduke de Thweng, where fourteen carucates made one knight's fee. ‖

THE Gowers afterwards became proprietors, whofe defcendants, as appears from the annexed pedigree, * continued in poffeffion for feveral generations ; and from whom the eftate came to the Turners, of Kirkleatham, and has fince been purchafed by the anceftor of Lord Harewood, the prefent proprietor, and Lord of the manor.

THE church of Stainton ftands on elevated ground, at the weftern extremity of the village ; with the vicarage-houfe adjoining to the church yard on the fouth, which is a large and fpacious manfion, lately rebuilt by the Rev. Archdeacon Baillie, the prefent incumbent, and finifhed in an elegant ftyle.

‖ WALTERUS DE STAINSBY tenet ibidem 4 carucatas terræ, unde 14 car. faciunt feodum, et reddit ballivo dom. regis pro fine 3s.

* GOWER, of STAINSBY.

EXTRACTED from the Herald's office, by W. Radclyffe, *rouge croix.*

ARMS. *Azure,* a cheveron between three hounds courant, *argent.*

Nicholas Gower,—- - - - daughter of - - - -

———✓ Mauleverer, of Arneclifffe.

Thomas Gower,—- - - daughter of Ralph Crathorne, of Stainfby. | of Crathorne, Efq.

Thomas Gower,—- - - daughter of Sir of Stainfby. | Nicholas Forfter.

Ralph Gower, of—- - - daughter of - - - a daughter. Pickton, 2d fon. | Wray, *2d wife.*

Nicholas Gower,—- - - - daughter of of Stainfby. Conyers, of Laton.

Roger Gower, of—Mary, daughter of F. Melfonby ; *vixit* | Norton, eldeft fon to *A. D.* 1612. | Richard Norton, *attainted.* 2d wife.

John Gower, *attinctus.*

Edward Gower, of—Margery, daughter of Melfonby, living | - - - Wither, of Copgrove, in co. York. D. 1612. | grove, in co. York.

John Gower, fon and heir, ætat. 7. 1612.

Henry Gower, *2d fon.*

two daughters.

The church is an ancient edifice, which, with some modern repairs, is rendered neat and commodious. It consists of a nave and a chancel, with a cross aile to the north, separated by a flat pointed arch': the nave is 15 paces in length, and six paces wide, uniformly and neatly seated with oak. The chancel, which is of equal dimensions with the body of the church, is separated by a pointed arch, and contains some elegant mural monuments, erected in memory of some of the Penny-man family buried here.

This church, dedicated to Saint Peter, was an ancient rectory, which, with five oxgangs of land, was given by Robert de Brus to the priory of Guisbrough; and being appropriated thereto about the year 1247, a vicarage was ordained therein; which, according to the parlia-

STAINTON VICARAGE.

Dedic. St. Peter. Priory of Guisbro' propr. Archbishop of York, patron. King's book's 5l. 14s. 2d. Yearly tenths 11s. 5d. Archd. pro syn. 4s. Proc. 7s. 6d.

VICARS.

—— Will. de Bolteby, cl. *pri. & con. of Guisbro'*.
1247 Roger de Chesterton,	*iidem.*
1269 Roger de Morton,	*iidem.*
1270 Thomas de Gysburne,	*iidem.*
1289 John de Mydelburghe,	*iidem.*
1309 Roger de Belmand, pbr.	*iidem.*
1311 Galfr. de Yarum,	*iidem.*
1324 Alan de Alverstan, pbr.	*iidem.*
—— John de Newton, pbr.	*iidem.*
1362 Will. de Birdsall, cap.	*iidem.*
1366 Thomas Castleford,	*iidem.*
1370 John de Wyneston, pbr.	*iidem.*
1373 John Bartlemew, pbr.	*iidem.*
1390 Robert de Bageby,	*iidem.*
1395 John Flemyngs, pbr.	*iidem.*
1410 John de Britby, pbr.	*iidem.*
1435 Thomas Todde, pbr.	*iidem.*
1450 Will. Adyngham, pbr. *pri.&con.of Guisbro.'*

1467 Will. Hutton, vel Leeton, cap.	*iidem.*
1478 Milv. Mershden, pbr.	*iid.*
1490 John Getour, vel Shetour,	*iid.*
1493 Will. Braunch, pbr.	*iid.*
1515 Robert Blakeston, pbr.	*iid.*
1529 Cuthbert Foxe, pbr.	*iidem.*
1549 Christ. Jackson, cl. *assig. p. & conv.*
1582 Henry Mann, cl. *archiep. ebor.*
1622 Will. Lawson, B. A.	*idem.*
1663 John Gillyott, cl.	*idem.*
1667 Richard Lumley, cl. *by the Archbishop.*
1689 Francis Nicholson,	*by the same.*
1731 Thoph. Garencieres, M. A.	*idem.*
1750 William Cayley, M. A.	*idem.*
1760 Francis Cleator, M. A.	*idem.*
1801 Charles Baillie, M. A. Archdeacon of Cleveland, *pres. by the Archbishop.*

mentary furvey (26 Henry VIII.) was found to be of the yearly value
of 5*l.* 14s. 2d.   Upon the diffolution of the priory, the rectory, with
the advowfon of the vicarage, was granted (36 Henry VIII.) to the
Archbifhop of York, and his fucceffors ; by whom the rectorial rights
are leafed out to Sir Charles Turner, Baronet.

HEMLINGTON

is a fmall townfhip, fituated to the eaft from Stainton ; and, with the
hamlet of Coleby, contains only about fixty inhabitants, occupied folely in hufbandry.   The lands here, according to the Domefday furvey,
were within the foke of the manor of Acklam ; and being a part of the
fee of Robert de Brus, were granted at a very early period to Robert de
Stoteville ; whofe defcendants continued proprietors till male iffue failing in the reign of Henry III. the eftate came by marriage to Hugh de
Wake ; in which family it remained till the reign of Edw. III. when
by failure of iffue in Thomas, fon of Baldwine de Wake, it defcended
to Margaret his fifter, widow of Edmund de Woodftock, Earl of Kent ;
whofe fons Edmund and John dying *fans* iffue, it was carried by their
fifter Joan, (for her beauty called " the fair maid of Kent") to Sir Thomas Holland, Knight; who in right of his wife, without creation, was
ftiled Earl of Kent.   Hemlington continued in the poffeffion of this
family till the 9 Henry IV. when Edmund, dying without iffue, his
five fifters became his heirs ; of whom Elizabeth, the youngeft, had
this and other eftates in this county affigned as her purparty ; which
by marriage with Sir John Neville, Knight, became the property of
the Nevilles, Earls of Weftmorland, who continued proprietors here till
the 13 year of the reign of Queen Elizabeth, when by attainder it
came to the Crown.

WE have no documents to fhew, to whom the eftate here was firft
granted out by the Crown.   The lands have been long held in parcels,
and are now in the hands of different freeholders.   *Hemlington-Hall,*
with a confiderable eftate, was the property of the family of Killing-

halls; of whom it was purchafed by General Hall, the prefent proprietor.

MALTBY,

another townfhip within this parifh lies about a mile to the weft from Stainton. The village is fmall, confifting of a few farm houfes and cottages, fituated on the fummit of a gently elevated ridge, from whence the grounds have an eafy defcent northwards.

MALTBY, according to the Domefday book, confifted of three carucates *ad geldum;* and is furveyed as a foke within the manor of Acklam. We find little in ancient records touching this place, except that at an early period, it gave name to a refident family; for, in the reign of Edward I. according to Kirkby's Inqueft, we find, that John de Maltby held fix carucates of land here, of the fee of Walter de Fauconberge, where ten made one Knight's fee. ‡ This family continued in poffeffion for feveral generations, till, by failure of male iffue, a part of their eftate here paffed by marriage to the Morleys, of Normanby; which being afterwards alienated to the Pennymans of Ormefby, is now the property of Sir James Pennyman, Baronet. The other moiety of their eftate in the reign of Charles the firft, came to Sir George Wentworth, of Wolley, Knight, by marriage with Averall, daughter of Chriftopher Maltby, Efq. Alderman of York. It has been fince fold out in parcels, and is now in the hands of different proprietors.

IN the northern extremity of the parifh, which is bounded by the river Tees, lies the townfhip or chapelry of

THORNABY;

or, as it is anciently written, *Thornaldby;* which, as well as Thornton already noticed, might be fo called, qu. *villa fpinofa,* vel *juxta locum fpinis confitum;* although by fome etymologifts it may be fuppofed to de-

---

‡ JOHANNES DE MALTEBY tenet ibidem fex carucatas terræ, unde 10 carucatæ teiræ faciunt feodum unius militis; et reddit ballivo domini regis de fine wapentag. 6s.   *Kirkby's Inqueft,*

rive its name, as ſtanding on the ſite of a Roman ſtation, *—*Thorn-ald-by*, ſignifying, according to the Saxon, a dwelling in the great camp.

THORNABY, which, according to the orthography of Domeſday, is written TORMOZBI, beſides three carucates within the ſoke of Ack-lam, contained one carucate and a half, which was ancient demeſne of the Crown, ſurveyed under the title

TERRA REGIS.

MANER. IN TORMOZBI VLCHIL I. CAR. ET DIMID. AD GELD. TERRA AD I. CAR.

AND in another part of the ſurvey, we alſo find the following no-tice of lands here, under the head

TERRA ROBERTI MALLET.

MANER. IN TORMOZBI HABEBAT EDMUND II. CAR. TERRÆ, ET DIMID. AD GELDUM.

H HABET ROBERTUS MALLET, ET WAST. SUNT.

THESE lands were of the fee of Robert de Brus, who held of the King *in capite;* and, as appears from Kirkby's Inqueſt, and other authorities, were granted out at an early period to different propri-etors. William de Boyville was the Lord here; and the manor was afterwards given to the prior and convent of Guiſbrough; wherein King Edward the third granted them free-warren. The abbot of By-land alſo had conſiderable poſſeſſions in this territory, which were given by Robert de Hilton and Emma his wife, daughter of William de Boyville; whoſe ſon and heir William de Hilton, Lord of Thor-modby, confirmed and quitted claim to the ſame; his charter, (ex-tracted from a ſmall MSS. book in the Dean and Chapter's library, Durham, *(marked B. Fo.* 16.) is to the following effect—" Omnibus ſanctæ matris eccleſiæ filiis preſens ſcriptum viſuris vel audituris, Willus, filius et hæres Robti de Hilton de Thormodby, et Emmæ uxo-ris ejus, ſalutem in Deo. Noveritis me conceſſiſſe, confirmâſſe, et qui-

---

* IT was an obſervation made by that eminent antiquary, *Roger Gale*, that whenever the appel-lation *thorn* occurs in a local name, a Roman ſtation was always near at hand, if not at the place.

ete clamâſſe Deo, et Beatæ Mariæ et abbati et conventui de *Bella landiâ*
pro me et hæredibus meis, omnes terras et tenementa quæ habent ex
dono dictorum patris et matris meæ in territorio de *Thormodeby* in
Cleveland; et totum jus et clameum, quod in dictis terris et tenementis unquam habui, vel aliquo modo habere potui, nomine hæreditatis
predictæ tenendis &c. Hiis teſtibus, dominis Willo. de Bovington,
Willo. de Hilton, Willo. Mowbray de Tameton, militibus. Willo. de
Staynesby, Robto. Fil. Walteri de Thormandeby et aliis."—*Sans Dat.*

THE Gowers, of Sexhow, alſo poſſeſſed lands here in the reign of
Edward the third; ‖ and a branch of this family continued proprietors, and were reſident here for ſeveral generations : † but of their
immediate ſucceſſors we are uninformed. The lands have been long
held in parcels ; and the manor, with a conſiderable eſtate, after divers alienations, is now the property of George Brown, Eſq. of Stockton.

‖ SCIANT preſentes et futuri, quod ego Johannes Gower de Sexhowe dedi &c. Johannæ uxori
meæ, et Nicholæ filio meo et hæredibus ipſius Nicholai homagium et ſervitium Roberti de Thor-
modby, quod mihi debet pro terris, quas prædictus Robertus clamat tenere de me in territorio de
Thormodby. Teſtibus Johanne Percye de Kildale, Johanne Gower de Stanesby. Dat. anno 46.
Edw. III. *From the Herald's office.*

† THE following teſtamentary burials of the Gower family, are extracted from Dodſworth's
MSS. *Ex Regiſt. Archiep. Ebor.*

17. *Dec.* 1548. Thomas Gower de Staynſby Ar. l. c. s. *(legat corpus ſepeliri)* in Eccleſia de
Staynton; my Daughter Conſtance; my Sons Thomas, James Cuthbert and Philip ; to my Son
Ralph Graye my beſt Horſe ; to Jane Conyers my *Dtr* my ſecond Sylver Colte. to the Wieff of
Thoˢ. Gower decᵈ. Son of Nicholas Gower, two Kye. Thoˢ. Gower, Son of Nicholas, my Exor.
Ralph Gower my Brother, Chriſtʳ. Layton, Geo. Conyers Eſqʳ. Superviſors. *Probat.* 2 *Maii* 1548.

2. *Eliz.* Cuthbert Gower of Thormonbie in Cleveland Gen. l. c. s. in Eccleſia de Stainton ; my
Wieff Felicie ; my Son Nicholas ; my Brothers in Law, John and Reynold Anderſon to rule my
Children ; to my *Dtr.* Joyce Gower 10£. to my Son Marmaduke 10£. to my Brother in Law John
Anderſon, my little ambling blake Nagg; my gray Gowne to my Broʳ. John Anderſon .—to my
Bro. Thoˢ. Gower a bay Nagge. to my Nephew Thoˢ. Gower all my Hawkes, Hounds and
Grehounds ; to my Nephew Thomas Gower of Stayneſby one young dun Horſe : my Wieff Felicie,
and my Daughters Muriel and Elinor, Executors. My Nephew Thomas Gower of Staynesby, and
my Bro. Geo. Conyers, Superviſors. *Probat.* 21. *Julii* 1560.

THE village of Thornaby, which is fmall and irregularly built, ftands on the fouthern banks of the river Tees, and about two miles diftant from the market town of Stockton; the road to which leads over a handfome ftone bridge of five arches, built by Act of Parliament, and finifhed in the year 1771.

THERE is a chapel here, dependent on the church of Stainton, with which it was given to the priory of Guifbrough; but not having been certified to the Governours of Queen Anne's bounty, it has received no augmentation. The chapel, which does not enjoy parochial rights of baptifms, &c. is fmall, and ftands near the centre of the village; but the dedication thereof is not known.

PURSUING the courfe of the river Tees from Thornaby fouthwards, we enter the townfhip and manor of

BERWICK,

called in ancient records *Berewyke juxta Tees*, from its fituation on the banks of that river. The lands here are furveyed in Domefday, together with Acklam; being, as the word *Berewick* there implies, * a hamlet or village pertaining to that manor.

BERWICK, by grant of the Conqueror, became part of the fee of Robert de Brus; and at an early period, was granted out to the Percies of Kildale, as *mefne* Lords. Alice, the daughter of William de Percy, of Kildale, married Adam de Stavely, and for her dower in marriage had the village and lordfhip of Berwick upon Tees: they had iffue Alice their daughter and heir, who married Randolph Fitz-Henry, and left two fons Adam and Henry. Adam died without iffue, and was fucceeded by his brother, who had two fons; viz. Randolph, who died without iffue, and Hugh his brother and heir, who

---

* WE adopt this etymology of *Ingulphus* in preference to that of *Leland,* who derives it from *Aberwick* (i. e.) *urbs ad oftium fluminis.* Somner, in his Anglo-Saxon dictionary, fuppofes it to have the fame fignification as Beneⱦun, (i. e.) *villa frumentaria.*

died at Berwick upon Tees (32. Edw. I.) leaving Henry his fon and heir; who, being called Henry Fitz-Hugh, his defcendants affumed that furname, and continued proprietors till the 4 Henry VIII. when Sir George Fitz-Hugh, Knight, dying without iffue, Alice, the wife of Sir John Fines, Knight, eldeft daughter of Henry Lord Fitz-Hugh, and Thomas Parr, Knight, fon of Elizabeth, another daughter of the faid Henry, were found his next heirs.

WE have no evidence of the fucceeding proprietors; the family of *Fetherftonhalgh* poffeffed lands here in the reign of James the firft; and the principal part of the eftate, with the manerial rights, coming afterwards by purchafe to the Turners of Kirkleatham, is now a part of thofe lands, of which the endowment of the hofpital and fchool at Kirkleatham confifts.

THAT part of the townfhip, called in ancient records, *Ingleby-Loringe*, and fometimes *Cold-Ingleby*, lies to the fouth, and is bounded on the weft by the river Leven; the banks of which are naked and rife abruptly to a confiderable height. There were fix carucates of land here, entered in the Domefday furvey, as within the foke of Acklam; which, from the Bruces as chief Lords, defcended by marriage to Walter de Fauconberge; of whom, according to Kirkby's Inqueft, Stephen Gower, and Lucia his wife, held half a Knight's fee, where twelve carucates made one Knight's fee, and paid as a fine the fum of eight fhillings.

THE lands have been long parcelled out into farm-holds, and are now in the poffeffion of different freeholders.

SOIL, AGRICULTURE, and PRODUCE. On thefe fubjects we find little worthy of particular notice; the foil, like that of the adjoining parifhes, being chiefly a ftrong but fertile clay, producing wheat, oats, and beans, in great perfection. The lands near the river Tees, at Thornaby and Berwick, are of a rich loamy foil, and chiefly in grafs; but where brought into tillage, well adapted to the culture of barley and turnips. The cattle and fheep here are of the improved breeds, but

not numerous ; horfes are in general good ; and the modes of hufbandry greatly fimilar to thofe practifed in the beft cultivated parts of Cleveland.

POPULATION. The parifh, which is of confiderable extent, including the feveral townfhips already noted, contained, in the year
1801, when an actual enumeration was made by order of Parliament,
185 families, and 800 inhabitants ; of whom one half are females. ||

FROM the annexed table of baptifms and burials in the three following periods, extracted from the parifh regifters, it appears that the population of the parifh has continued nearly the fame fince the revolution.

THE average number of baptifms in one year is 22, and that of burials 16 ; from which it will be feen that out of the total number of inhabitants, the births within the parifh annually are as one to 36 nearly, and the burials exactly in the proportion of one to 50.

|| STATE OF POPULATION, 10th MARCH, 1801.

	Inhab. Houfes.	Fam-ilies.	Uninhab. Houfes.	Males.	Fe-males.	Total.	Far-mers.	Trade, &c.	Refi-due.	To-tal.
Stainton,	65	66	5	128	144	272	102	99	71	272
Hemlington	12	12		30	28	58	43		15	58
Maltby,	37	39	2	70	71	141	111	30		141
Thornaby,	30	37	3	83	84	167	49	5	113	167
Berwick,	30	31	1	78	84	162	33	17	112	162
Totals,	174	185	11	389	411	800	338	151	311	800

ABSTRACT OF STAINTON PARISH REGISTERS.

Years.	Bap.	Bur.	Years.	Bap.	Bur.	Years.	Bap.	Bur.
1666	26	25	1741	13	24	1798	26	18
1667	21	21	1742	13	23	1799	21	11
1668	24	20	1743	20	12	1800	24	19
1669	23	29	1744	23	16	1801	15	12
1670	23	35	1745	18	14	1802	20	17
1671	17	21	1746	16	28	1803	26	21
1672	22	20	1747	22	18	1804	27	15
1673	21	13	1748	29	21	1805	21	21
1674	21	19	1749	19	12	1806	22	18
1675	18	24	1750	24	20	1807	25	12
	216	227		197	188		227	164

Marriages within the laft period 65.

APPENDIX.

———◦◦•×•◦◦———

No. I.

Since our account of the *new caſt iron bridge* over the river Tees at Yarm was printed off; (an accurate view of which accompanies our deſcription at page 68,) we are concerned to ſtate, that this elegant and novel piece of architecture fell, about midnight, January 12th, 1806.

We pretend not to enter into a minute detail of the progreſs of the failure of this beautiful arch, and its conſequent total deſtruction; but from the report of four experienced and diſintereſted archi-tects, who were called in by the magiſtrates of the North Riding of the county of York, and of the county of Durham, to aſcertain the probable cauſe of its fall, it appears that on a minute examina-tion into the internal maſonry of the abutments, they were found ſo very inſufficient to reſiſt the great lateral preſſure of the arch, as to be conſidered clearly to occaſion its fall. A complaint, it appears, was made by the ſurveyor to the magiſtrates, of the inſufficiency of the ſouth abutment; and after ſuch a repreſentation, it is a matter of equal ſurprize and regret that the work ſhould be ſuffered to proceed, without a further and more minute inveſtigation.

The manner of placing the ribs of the iron arch upon the abutments was not generally approved of, " as not being calculated to make an equal preſſure, or bearing upon them; a circumſtance eſ-" ſentially and fundamentally requiſite in the conſtruction of all arches;" but this, however, was not conſidered to have any immediate effect, or to contribute in the preſent inſtance, to the failure of the bridge; which, as has been already ſtated, muſt be attributed to the abutments not being adequate to ſupport its weight.

The cirumſtance, however, of its failure, from whatever cauſe it might proceed, is a proof that ſomething is yet wanting in the conſtruction of *iron-arches* to enſure that permanence and durability, which the experience of ages affords in favour of *ſtone-bridges*; and from this conſideration the ma-giſtrates have been induced to adopt the plan of widening and repairing the *old bridge*; which, fortu-nately for the public, was not yet taken down, although the *new iron bridge* was then finiſhed, and had been open to foot-paſſengers for ſome time.

APPENDIX.

No. II.

Ex Rotulis et Escaet. in a small MS. book, in the Dean and Chapter's library, Durham, marked B. Fo. 16. *(without title.)*

(CASTLE LEVINGTON, PAGE 91.)

27. Edw. I.	Manerium de Castlevington tenetur p. Nich. Meinill.
5. Edw. II.	Idem tenetur per Johannem Meinill.
11. Edw. III.	Idem tenetur p. Johannem; et quod Johes. est fil. et hæres.
11. Ric. II.	Idem tenetur p. Aliciam, uxorem Waltri Bointon in feod. talliat. et quod Walt. Bointon est fil. et hæres.
12. Ric. II.	Idem tenetur p. Waltr. Bointon in feod. talliat. et quod Willus. Percy est hæres propinquior ejusd. Waltri.
21. Ric. II.	Idem tenetur p. Willum Percy in Christiana uxore, quodq; Will. Percy est filius & hæres Will. & Christianæ.
1. Hen. IV.	Idem in manu regis post mortem Will. Percy. fil. Willi.
5. Hen. V.	Tertia pars ejusdem tenetur p. Christianam, quæ fuit uxor Johis. Banke in dotem de donatione Willi. Percy de Castle-Leventon, quondam viri sui, reversione inde Margaretæ uxori Thomæ Blanfront, sorori et hæredi dicti Willi. Percy; et quod Eliz. Heringe est filia et hæres Christianæ.
30. Hen. VI.	*Castle-Newton*, alias idem Castle Leventon, tenetur per Christopherum Boynton. Willus. fil. et hæres. *See the pedigree of the Meinills of WhorltonCastle, p. 139.*

No. III.

Ex Scriptis Magistri J. Coffinger, in an old MS. in the Dean and Chapter's Library, Durham, *sans num. et sans dat.*

(MOUNT-GRACE PRIORY, p. 129.)

Omnibus Christi fidelibus, salutem. Sciatis me Willum. Eure, milit. relaxavisse, et in perpetuum pro me et hæredibus meis quietum clamasse domui *de le Mount Grace*, et monachis ibid. Deo, beatæ Mariæ et beato Nicholao servientibus, et successoribus eorum omne jus et clameum; quod habeo, habui, vel habere potero in sex acris terræ in *Arncliffe*, quondam Katerinæ matris meæ, vel Willi. Aton, mil.   Hiis testibus, dno. *Henrico Fitzhugh*, dno. *Johe. Percy*, dno. *Robto. Constable*, dno. *Thoma Surtays*, militibus. *Jacobo Eure, Nich. Tempest, Johe. Pudsay*, Rado. Surtays, et Alexand. Surtays, clericis. Dat. die hinc prox. post fest. sancti Petri apost. Ao. 14.   *Seal utterly effaced.*

No. IV.

(STOKESLEY, page 224.)

Inquisitio }
35. Hen. III } Juratores dicunt, quod dominus Hugo de Baliol dedit manerium de *Stokesley* et pertinent. Adæ filiæ suæ in liberum Maritagium; et quod dicta Ada post

APPENDIX.

mortem viri fui feoffavit Hugonem et Robertum, filios fuos, de predicto manerio die dominica prox. ante feftum fancti Barnab. anno 34. Hen. III. et dicta domina Ada obiit apud Stokefley, die fabbati prox. ante feft. fancti Jacobi apoft. anno 35. Hen. III. poft cujus mortem attornat. predicti Hugonis et Roberti pofuit fe in nomine fuo et Roberti fratris fui, et obtinuit per vim ———— donec expulfus fuit per literas domini regis, et per totam patriam, quæ ibi venit per vicecomit. et efcaet.

Ex MSS. in the Dean and Chapter's library, Durham. B. fol. 16.

No V.
(BASEDALE, page 266.)

OMNIBUS &c. Johannes de Eure miles. Sciatis me dediffe, conceffiffe, et hac carta mea confir maffe Johannæ prioreffæ de *Bafedale* et monalibus ibid. et fucceffioribus in perpetuum tres libras piperis, et quatuor modios frumenti autumpno in tempore meffis annuatim percipiend. de omnibus terris meis in *Stokefley, Ingilby* et *Kirkby.* Hiis teftibus, *Stephano Eure* de Axholme, *Hugone Eure, Petro Lounde* milite. *Waltro de Kirkby, Ricardo Hanfard* milit. *Johanne Gifors, Willo. Normanno,* et aljis. Dat. apud Stokefley in craftino purific. beatæ Mariæ Virginis, 1338.

Ex MSS in the Dean and Chapter's library, Durham ; but not expreffed whence taken.

No. VI.
(KIRKLEATHAM, page 393.)

THE following lines, by a late ingenious poet, * who " poffeffed from nature a fertile imagination, and heart of ftrong feeling and quick fenfibility," owe their birth to a fubject fo far connected with our diftrict, as to induce us to add them as an embellifhment to our hiftory. The following note, fubjoined to the poem explains to the reader the hint, on which the production is founded

" IN the hofpital, endowed by an anceftor of *Sir Charles Turner, Bart.* at Kirkleatham, amongft " other natural and artificial curiofities, is a very fingular tree. It had been cut down (in Kirk- " leatham-Park) and divided into lengths for the purpofe of converting it into fire-wood : but upon " its being fplit by the woodman's wedge, the heart of the tree turned out round and entire ; the " outward part which inclofed it being about the thicknefs of four inches. Round the inner bole or " heart, which is about a foot in diameter, are feveral letters carved in a rude and feemingly irregular " manner ; but, upon a clofer obfervation are found to wind in a *fpiral* form, and the following cou- " plet is plainly legible :

" This tree long time witnefs bear
" Two true lovers did walk here."

* THE late Rev. Thomas Brown, of Kingfton upon Hull. *See his poems p. 78.*

APPENDIX.

"There are likewife other letters, which feem to be the initials of the lovers' names, who appear to "have frequented the folitary fpot, where the tree has grown, to vent the effufions of their mutual "paffion, and to enjoy the pleafure of each other's converfation, fequeftered and unobferved."

The Lovers to their favourite Tree.

Long the wintry tempefts braving
 Still this fhort infcription keep;
Still preferve this rude engraving,
 On thy bark imprinted deep;
" This tree long time witnefs bear,
" Two true lovers did walk here."

By the fofteft ties united,
 Love has bound our fouls in one;
And by mutual promife plighted,
 Waits the nuptial rite alone.—
Thou a faithful witnefs bear
Of our plighted promife here.

Tho' our fires would gladly fever
 Thofe firm ties they difallow;
Yet they cannot part us ever—
 We will keep our faithful vow.
And in fpite of threats fevere,
Still will meet each other here.

While the dufky fhade concealing,
 Veils the faultlefs fraud of love;
We, from fleeplefs pillows ftealing,
 Nightly feek the filent grove;
And efcap'd from eyes fevere,
Dare to meet each other here.

Wealth and titles difregarding,
 (Idols of the fordid mind)
Calm content true love rewarding,
 Is the blifs we wifh to find.—
Thou tree, long time witnefs bear
Two fuch lovers did walk here.

To our faithful love confenting
 (Love unchang'd by time or tide)
Should our haughty fires relenting
 Give the fanction yet deny'd;
Midft the fcenes to mem'ry dear
Still we oft will wander here.

Then our ev'ry wifh compleated,
 Crown'd by kinder fates at laft,
All beneath thy fhadow feated,
 We will talk of feafons paft;
When by night, in filent fear
We did meet each other here.

On thy yielding bark, engraving,
 Now in fhort our tender tale;
Long, time's rougheft tempeft braving,
 Spread thy branches to the gale;
And for ages witnefs bear,
Two true lovers did walk here.

No. VII.

LE NORTHE-RIDINGE; Libertas de *Langbarghe.* A. D. 1584. Liberi tenentes infra wapetagium.

Robertus Rookfby, de Marfk, ar. *juftic. pacis.*
Thomas Layton, de Hutton Rudby, ar. *juftic.*
Thomas Gower, de Stainfby, ar.
Jacobus Strangwaies, de Ormefby, ar.
Raphe Salvyne, de Newbiggine, ar.
Rogerus Mennel, de Burford, ar.
Rogerus Tocketts, de Langbarghe, ar.

Rogerus Ratcliffe, de Moulgrave, ar. *juft.*
John Conftable, de Dromondby, ar. *juft. pac.*
Radus. Craythorne, de Craythorne, ar.
Thomas Fulthorpe, gen. } *mortuus.*
Francifcus Fulthorpe, gen. } *attinctus.*
Chrift. fil. Thomæ Fulthorpe, *nothus.*
Radulphus Yoward, de Bafdale, gen.

APPENDIX.

Will. Welberry, de Lazenby, gen.

Franciscus Whitley, de Gilly-Park, gen.

Robertus Trotter, de Horneby, gen.

Will. Bate, de West-leys, gen.

T. Sorthwayte, alias Milner, de Scoterskelfe, gen.

Thomas Warcopp, de Greenhowe.

Thomas Addyson, de Normanby.

Johes. Bulmer, de Pinchinthorpe, gen.

Johes. Hewardine, de Broughton, gen.

Jacobus Pennyman, de Moreton, gen.

Willus. Robinson, de Stokesley, gen.

Thomas Pylley, de Eseby, gen.

Jacobus Gower, de Borrowby, gen. *mort.*

Jacobus Bradshaw, de Guisbrough, gent.

Henricus Strongwaies, de Slathenbank, gen.

Robertus Yoward, de Stokesley, gen.

Cuthbertus Morley, de Normanby, gen.

Georgius Carlisle, de Pinchinthorpe, gen.

Cuthbertus Lockwood, de Eston, gen.

Willus. Crawe, de Uplythum, gen.

Carolus Layton, de Sexhowe, gen. *fil. Thomæ.*

Will. Maleverer, ar. *justi. fil. & hæres Edmundi.*

Lucas Blackburn, de Marton.

Franciscus Lasenbie, de Marton.

Ricardus Gascoyne, de Ingleby-*Lovell.*

Glover's Visit. 1584.

No. VIII.

THE following list of the names of those gentlemen in CLEVELAND who contributed to the defence of this country at the time of the threatened *Spanish Invasion* in 1588 ; contains a large proportion of the contributors in Yorkshire, probably because CLEVELAND being on the coast, produced more alarm and interest than the interior parts of the county. Taken from a book printed in 1798, by *Leigh* and *Sotheby*, York-street, Covent-Garden, London; with a brief account of the spirited conduct of the English nation, &c. at that period.

NAMES OF CONTRIBUTORS.		Day of Contribution.	Sum Contributed.
Thomas Milner	(*Scoterskelfe*)	May 13th	£ 25
Katherine Ratcliffe	(*Ugthorpe*)	May 14th	25
William Bates	(*Easby*)	May 14th	50
Robert Trotter	(*Skelton*)	May 15th	25
Robert Rokeby	(*Marske*)	May 16th	25
George Tocketts	(*Tocketts*)	May 16th	25
John Sayer, Esq.	(*Worsall*)	May 16th	100
John Constable	(*Dromondby*)	May 16th	25
George Consett	- - - -	May 17th	25
Thomas Gower	(*Stainsby*)	May 20th	25
Ralphe Salvyne	(*Newbiggin*)	May 21st	25
John Thornholme	- - - -	May 23d	25
Thomas Conyers	- - - -	May 25th	25
James Strangwaies	(*Ormesby*)	May 25th	25
Francis Ratcliffe	- - - -	May 29th	25
Christopher Consett	- - - -	May 30th	52
Leonard Conyers	- - - -	June 2d	25
Christopher Conyers	- - - -	June 4th	100

APPENDIX.

No. IX.

A table of pariſhes and townſhips within the wapontake of Langbergh, with the ſum paid by the ſaid wapontake on an order of Seſſions for a general rate upon the North-Riding; and alſo the proportion paid by each townſhip.

	£	S.	D.	£	S.	D.	£	S.	D.
Upon an order of Seſſions, for - -	100	0	0	500	0	0	1000	0	0
Langbargh Wapontake pays - -	16	15	5	83	7	1	167	14	2

Pariſhes.	*Townſhips.*	£	S.	D.	£	S.	D.	£	S.	D.
Acklam	Acklam	0	2	11¼	0	14	9	1	9	5¾
	Linthorpe	0	2	11¼	0	14	9	1	9	5¾
	Middleſbrough	0	2	11¼	0	14	9	1	7	5¾
Appleton	Appleton on Wiſk	0	5	3¾	1	6	6¼	2	13	0½
Arnecliffe	Arnecliffe	0	2	9½	0	13	11½	1	7	11
Ayton	Ayton Great	0	6	3¾	1	11	7	3	3	2
	Ayton Little	0	2	4½	0	11	9¼	1	3	6¾
	Nunthorpe	0	4	6½	1	2	9¼	2	5	6½
Carleton	Carleton	0	3	6½	0	17	8	1	15	4¼
Crathorne	Crathorne	0	5	1½	1	5	8	2	11	4
Danby	Danby	0	9	9¼	2	8	10¼	4	17	8½
	Glazedale	0	9	9¼	2	8	10¼	4	17	8½
Eaſington	Eaſington	0	5	8	1	8	4½	2	16	9
	Liverton	0	3	0	0	15	0½	1	10	1
Egton	Egton	0	19	5¼	4	17	1¾	9	4	3½
Faceby	Faceby	0	2	5¾	0	12	4¼	1	4	8¾
Guiſbrough	Guiſbrough	0	11	1¾	2	15	9½	5	11	7¼
	Tocketts									
	Hutton Lowcroſs	0	2	3	0	11	3½	1	2	6¾
	Pinchinthorpe	0	2	5¼	0	12	2¼	1	4	4¼
	Commondale	0	1	4¼	0	6	9¾	0	13	7½
Hilton	Hilton	0	3	8¾	0	18	8	1	17	4
Hilderwell	Hilderwell	0	5	8¼	1	8	5	2	16	10
	Rouſby	0	3	0	0	15	0½	1	10	1
Ingleby	Ingleby	0	2	9¼	0	13	11	1	7	10
	Greenhowe	0	3	7¾	0	18	3½	1	16	6¾
	Ballerſby	0	2	3	0	11	3½	1	2	6¾
Kildale	Kildale	0	3	9½	0	18	11½	1	17	10¾
Kirkby	Kirky	0	3	11½	0	19	8½	1	19	5
	Broughton	0	6	1½	1	10	7¾	3	1	3½
Kirkleatham	Kirkleatham	0	5	10¼	1	9	3	2	18	6
Kirklevington	Kirklevington	0	5	5½	1	7	3	2	14	6
	Caſtle Levington	0	4	3½	1	1	5¼	2	2	10½
	Worſall	0	4	10¾	1	4	6½	2	9	1
	Pickton	0	2	11	0	14	7¾	1	9	3½
Lofthouſe	Lofthouſe	0	5	4½	1	16	10½	2	13	8¾
Lythe	Lythe	0	5	4¾	1	16	11¼	2	13	10¾
	Hutton Mulgrave	0	2	2	0	10	10½	1	1	9¼
	Barneby	0	4	0¾	1	0	3½	2	0	7
	Ugthorpe	0	3	0	0	15	0½	1	10	1
	Mickleby	0	2	6½	0	12	8½	1	5	4¾
	Ellerby	0	2	2	0	10	10¼	1	1	8½
	Borrowby	0	2	2¾	0	11	1½	1	2	3
	Newton Mulgrave	0	3	0	0	15	0½	1	10	1

APPENDIX.

Pariſhes.	*Townſhips.*	£	S.	D.	£	S.	D.	£	S.	D.
Marſke	Marſke, Redcar	0	10	3¼	2	11	4¼	5	2	8½
Marton	Marton	0	5	11½	1	9	8¾	2	19	5½
Newton	Newton	0	2	4¼	0	11	9¼	1	3	6½
Ormeſby	Ormeſby	0	6	4¾	1	12	0	3	4	0
	Morton	0	1	8¾	0	8	7	0	17	2¼
	Eſton	0	4	3	1	1	2¼	2	2	4½
	Normanby	0	3	3¾	0	16	6¼	1	13	0½
Rudby	Rudby	0	3	3½	0	16	5½	1	12	11
	Hutton	0	4	2½	1	1	1	2	2	2¼
	Sexhowe	0	1	4½	0	6	10¼	0	13	8¾
	Eaſt Rounton	0	4	4¾	1	1	11½	2	3	11¼
	Middleton	0	2	7	0	12	11	1	5	10¼
	Skutterſkelfe	0	1	7¼	0	7	10¾	0	15	9¼
Seamer	Seamer	0	6	10½	1	14	3¾	3	8	7½
	Newby	0	2	5¼	0	12	2½	1	4	5
Skelton	Skelton	0	5	1¼	1	5	5¾	2	10	11½
	Brotton	0	7	6¼	1	17	7½	3	15	3¼
	Skinningrove									
	Kilton									
	Moorſham	0	5	1¼	1	5	5¾	2	10	11½
	Stanghow									
Stainton	Stainton	0	4	3	1	1	2¼	2	2	4½
	Hemlington	0	2	5¼	0	12	2	1	4	3¾
	Maltby	0	2	5¼	0	12	2½	1	4	5
	Thornaby	0	3	9½	0	18	11½	1	17	10¾
	Berwick	0	3	10½	0	19	4	1	18	7¾
Stokeſley	Stokeſley	0	5	10½	1	9	4¼	2	18	8½
	Buſhby	0	4	7¾	1	3	2½	2	6	5
	Eaſby	0	2	6	0	12	6	1	5	0
	Weſterdale	0	4	3	1	1	2¼	2	2	4½
Upleatham	Upleatham									
Whorlton	Whorlton	0	9	4¾	2	7	0½	4	14	1
	Pottowe	0	3	6¾	0	17	10	1	15	8
Wilton	Wilton	0	6	8¾	1	13	7¾	3	7	3½
Yarm	Yarm	0	5	5½	1	7	3½	2	14	7

No. X.

POPULATION OF CLEVELAND.

Pariſhes.	*Townſhips.*	*Houſes.*	*Families.*	*Males.*	*Females.*	*Total.*
Acklam	Acklam	21	21	51	47	
	Linthorpe	39	39	101	113	
	Middleſbrough	4	4	13	12	
		64	64	165	172	337
Appleton	Appleton	96	100	242	209	451
Arnecliffe	Arnecliffe	58	58	124	129	253

APPENDIX.

Parifhes.	Townfhips.	Houfes.	Families.	Males.	Females.	Total.
Ayton	Ayton Great	201	206	409	456	
	Ayton Little	13	13	34	35	
	Nunthorpe	17	17	75	57	
		231	236	518	548	1066
Carleton	Carleton	66	66	127	148	275
Crathorne	Crathorne	59	65	160	147	307
Danby	Danby	162	211	480	510	
	Glazedale	151	156	375	388	
		313	367	855	898	1753
Eafington	Eafington	101	101	242	258	
	Liverton	53	53	112	118	
		154	154	354	376	730
Egton	Egton	190	190	476	495	971
Faceby	Faceby	26	30	54	73	127
Guifbro'	Guifbrough	383	407	771	948	
	Tocketts	8	8	29	36	
	Hutton Lowcrofs	11	11	31	28	
	Pinchinthorpe	15	15	44	48	
	Commondale	12	12	36	32	
		429	453	911	1092	2003
Hilton	Hilton	27	28	67	69	136
Hilderwell	Hilderwell	329	339	471	753	
	Roufby	33	33	98	98	
		362	372	569	845	1414
Ingleby	Ingleby	29	34	88	92	
	Greenhow	20	20	59	59	
	Batterfby	13	17	38	40	
		62	71	185	191	376
Kildale	Kildale	27	37	100	101	201
Kirkby	Kirkby	37	37	83	82	
	Broughton	101	101	232	228	
		138	138	315	310	625
Kirkleatham	Kirkleatham	159	165	314	366	680
Kirklevington	Kirklevington	49	49	117	122	
	Caftlevington	9	9	27	20	
	Low Worfall	40	40	76	89	
	Pickton	18	18	42	49	
		116	116	262	280	542
Lofthoufe	Lofthoufe	261	261	569	617	1186
Lythe	Lythe	201	223	512	525	
	Hutton Mulgrave	17	17	46	47	
	Barneby	47	48	119	135	
	Ugthorpe	54	56	121	124	
	Mickleby	40	41	90	86	
	Ellerby	15	15	37	37	
	Borrowby	16	17	35	46	
	Newton Mulgrave	28	28	69	64	
		418	445	1029	1064	2093

APPENDIX.

Parishes.	Townships.	Houses.	Families.	Males.	Females.	Total.
Marſke	{ Marſke	102	102	229	274	
	Redcarr	115	125	170	261	
		217	227	399	535	934
Marton	Marton	80	80	170	172	342
Newton	Newton	38	38	68	81	149
Ormeſby	{ Ormeſby	74	76	174	183	
	Morton	3	3	15	12	
	Eſton	61	67	130	158	
	Normanby	22	22	45	54	
		160	168	364	407	771
Rudby	{ Rudby	13	15	42	38	
	Hutton	161	161	359	348	
	Sexhowe	6	6	21	23	
	Eaſt Rounton	20	20	53	56	
	Middleton	20	20	61	49	
	Skutterſkelfe	6	6	21	21	
		226	226	557	535	1092
Seamer	{ Seamer	49	52	122	127	
	Newby	30	30	63	64	
		79	82	185	191	376
Skelton	{ Skelton	167	180	317	383	
	Brotton	77	77	172	201	
	Skinningrove	15	15	38	29	
	Kilton	21	21	68	61	
	Moorſham	65	65	142	160	
	Stanghowe	19	20	58	60	
		364	378	795	894	1689
Stainton	{ Stainton	65	65	128	144	
	Hemlington	12	12	30	28	
	Maltby	37	39	70	71	
	Thornaby	30	37	83	84	
	Berwick	30	31	78	84	
		174	184	389	411	800
Stokeſley	{ Stokeſley	334	351	60	759	
	Buſhby	17	17	60	61	
	Eaſby	21	26	61	77	
		372	394	731	897	1628
Upleatham	Upleatham	61	64	106	131	237
Whorlton	{ Whorlton	121	124	273	271	
	Pottowe	36	36	92	82	
		157	160	365	353	718
Weſterdale	Weſterdale	46	47	132	125	257
Wilton	Wilton	67	74	148	186	328
Yarm	Yarm	347	360	607	693	1300

APPENDIX.

No. XI.

A CATALOGUE OF

CLEVELAND ANIMALS.

For a definition of each *genus*, and the defcription of the different *fpecies* in the following catalogue, we refer the reader to *Pennant's Zoology, Bewick's Hiftory of Britifh Birds and Quadrupeds*,
and other works of natural hiftory.

Class I.

Quadrupeds.

Div. I. *Hoofed.*
Sec. I. *Whole Hoofed.*
Genus I. *Horfe.*

1. Horse. *Equus caballus.* Lin. Pen. Zool. 1.
2. Ass. *Equus afinus.* Lin. Pen. Zool. 2.
3. Mule. *Equus Mulus.* Lin. Pen. Zool. 2.
   Sec. II. *Cloven hoofed.*
   Genus II. *Ox.*
4. Bull, Cow, and Ox. *Bos taurus.* Lin. Pen. Zool. 3.
   Genus III. *Sheep.*
5. Sheep. *Ovis aries.* Lin. Pen. Zool. 4.
   Genus IV. *Goat.*
6. Goat. *Capra hircus,* Lin. Pen. Zool. 4.
   Genus V. *Hog.*
7. Hog. *Sus fcrofa.* Lin. Pen. Zool. 9.

Div. II. Sec. I.

Digitated Quadrupeds.

Genus VI. *Dog.*
8. Dog. *Canis familiaris.* Lin. Pen. Zool. 10.
9. Fox. *Canis vulpes.* Lin. Pen. Zool. 11.
   Genus VII. *Cat.*
10. Wild Cat. *Felis catus.* Lin. Pen. Zool. 12.
11. Domestic Cat. *Felis Catus.* Lin.
    Genus VIII. *Badger.*
12. Common Badger. *Urfus meles.* Lin. Pen. Zool. 13.
    Genus IX. *Weafel.*
13. Foulmart. *Muftela putorius,* Lin. Pen. Zool. 14.

APPENDIX.

14. MARTIN. *Muſtela martes.* Lin. Pen. Zool. 15.
15. FERRET. *Muſtela furo.* Lin.
16. STOAT, or ERMINE. *Muſtela erminea.* Lin. Pen. Zool. 18.
17. COMMON WEASEL. *Muſtela nivalis.* Lin. Pen. Zool. 17.
    GENUS X. *Otter.*
18. OTTER. *Muſtela lutra.* Lin. Pen. Zool. 19.

SEC. II.

Herbivorus, Frugivorous.

GENUS XI. *Hare.*
19. HARE. *Lepus timidus.* Lin. Pen. Zool. 20.
20. RABBIT. *Lepus cuniculus.* Lin. Pen. Zool. 22.
    GENUS XII. *Squirrel.*
21. SQUIRREL. *Sciurus vulgaris.* Lin. Pen. Zool. 23.
    GENUS XIII. *Dormouſe.*
22. DORMOUSE. *Mus avellanarius.* Lin. Pen. Zool. 24.
    GENUS XIV. *Rat.*
23. BLACK RAT. *Mus rattus.* Lin. Pen. Zool.
24. BROWN RAT. Pen. Zool. 26.
25. WATER RAT. *Mus amphibius.* Lin. Pen. Zool. 27.
26. FIELD MOUSE. *Mus ſylvaticus.* Lin. Pen. Zool. 28.
27. COMMON MOUSE. *Mus muſculus.* Lin. Pen. Zool. 30.
28. SHORT TAILED MOUSE. *Mus terreſtris.* Lin. Pen. Zool. 31.
    GENUS XV. *Shrew.*
29. FETID SHREW. *Sorex arancus.* Lin. Pen. Zool. 32.
30. WATER SHREW. *Sorex aquaticus.* Lin. Pen. Zool. 33.
    GENUS XVI. *Cavy.*
31. GUINEA PIG. *Mus porcellus.* Lin.
    GENUS XVII. *Mole.*
32. MOLE. *Talpa europæa.* Lin. Pen. Zool. 34.
    GENUS XVIII. *Urchin.*
33. HEDGE HOG. *Erinaceus europæa.* Lin. Pen. Zool. 35.

DIV. III.

Pennated Quadrupeds.

GENUS XIX. *Seal.*
34. GREAT SEAL, or SEA CALF. Pen. Zool. 36.
35. COMMON SEAL. *Phoco vitulina.* Lin. Pen. Zool. 37.

APPENDIX.

Div. IV.
Winged Quadrupeds.

GENUS XX. *Bat.*

36. LONG EARED BAT. *Vespertilio auritus.* Lin. Pen. Zool. 40.
37. COMMON BAT. *Vespertilio murinus.* Lin. Pen. Zool. 41.

CLASS II.

BIRDS.

Div. I. *Land Birds.*

ORDER I. *Accipitres.*

GENUS I. *Falco.*

1. KITE, or GLEAD. *Falco milvus.* Lin. Lath. Synop. 43. Pen. Zool. 53.
2. COMMON BUZZZARD. *Falco buteo.* Lin. Lath. Synop. 28. Pen. Zool. 54.
3. MOOR BUZZARD. *Falco druginosus.* Lin. Lath. Synop, 34. Pen. Zool. 57.
4. HEN-HARRIER, *male. Falco cyaneus.* Lin. Lath. Synop. 74. Pen. Zool. 58.
5. RINGTAIL, *female. Falco pygargus.* Lin. Lath. Synop. 75. Pen. Zool. 59.
6. KESTRILL. *Falco tinnunculus.* Lin. Lath. Synop. 79. Pen. Zool. 60.
7. HOBBY. ‖ *Falco subbuteo.* Lin. Lath. Synop. 90. Pen. Zool. 61.
8. SPARROW HAWK. *Falco nisus.* Lin. Lath. Synop. 85. Pen. Zool. 62.

GENUS II. *Strix.*

* 9. LONG EARED OWL. *Strix otus.* Lin. Lath. Synop. 5. Pen. Zool. 65.
* 10. SHORT EARED OWL. *Strix crachyotus.* Lin. Lath. Synop. 9. Pen. Zool. 66.
11. BARN, or WHITE OWL. *Strix flammea.* Lin. Lath. Synop. 26. Pen. Zool. 67.
12. BROWN, or WOOD OWL. *Strix stridula.* Lin. Lath. Synop. 28. Pen. Zool. 69.

Order II. Picæ.

GENUS III. *Corvus.*

13. RAVEN. *Corvus corax.* Lin. Lath. Synop. 1. Fen. Zool. 74.
14. CARRION CROW. *Corvus corone.* Lin. Lath. Synop. 3. Pen. Zool. 75.
15. ROOK. *Corvus frugilegus.* Lin. Lath. Synop. 4. Pen. Zool. 76.
16. ROYSTON CROW. *Corvus cornix.* Lin. Lath. Synop. 5. Pen. Zool. 77.
17. JACKDAW. *Corvus monedula.* Lin. Lath. Synop. 9. Pen. Zool. 81.
18. MAGPIE. *Corvus pica.* Lin. Lath. Synop. 29. Pen. Zool. 78.
19. JAY. *Corvus glandarius.* Lin. Lath. Synop. 19. Pen. Zool. 79.

GENUS IV. *Cuculus.*

¶ 20. CUCKOO. *Cuculus canorus.* Lin. Lath. Synop. 1. Pen. Zool. 82.

‖ BIRDS marked thus ¶ are those which migrate at particular seasons of the year; and this mark *
denotes those which are not common in Cleveland.

APPENDIX.

Genus V. *Jynx.*
21. Wryneck. *Jynx torquilla.* Lin. Lath. Synop. 1. Pen. Zool. 83.
　　Genus VI. *Picus.*
22. Green Woodpecker. *Picus viridis.* Lin. Lath. Synop. 25. Pen. Zool. 84.
23. Greater spotted Woodpecker. *Picus major.* Lin. Lath. Synop. 12. Pen. Zool. 85.
　　Genus VII. *Sitta.*
24. European Nuthatch. *Sitta europæa.* Lin. Lath. Synop. 1. Pen. Zool. 89.
　　Genus VIII. *Certhia.*
25. Common Creeper. *Certhia familiaris.* Lin. Lath. Synop. 1. Pen. Zool. 91.
　　Genus IX. *Alcedo.*
26. King Fisher. *Alcedo ispida.* Lin. Lath. Synop. 16. Pen. Zool. 88.

Order III. Passeres.

　　Genus X. *Sturnus.*
27. Common Starling. *Sturnus vulgaris.* Lin. Lath. Synop. 1. Pen. Zool. 104.
　　Genus XI. *Turdus.*
28. Thrush, or Throstle. *Turdus musicus.* Lin. Lath. Synop. 2. Pen. Zool. 107.
29. Missel Thrush. *Turdus viscivorus.* Lin. Lath. Synop. 1. Pen. Zool. 105.
¶ 30. Fieldfare. *Turdus pilaris.* Lin. Lath. Synop. 11. Pen. Zool. 106.
¶ 31. Redwing. *Turdus iliacus.* Lin. Lath. Synop. 7. Pen. Zool. 108.
32. Blackbird. *Turdus merula.* Lin. Lath. Synop. 46. Pen. Zool. 109.
¶ 33. Ring-Ouzel. *Turdus torquatus.* Lin. Lath. Synop. 49. Pen. Zool. 110.
　　Genus XII. *Loxia.*
34. Bulfinch. *Loxia pyrrhula.* Lin. Lath. Synop. 51. Pen. Zool. 115.
35. Greenfinch. *Loxia chloris.* Lin. Lath. Synop. 35. Pen. Zool. 117.
　　Genus XIII. *Emberiza.*
36. Common Bunting. *Emberiza miliaria.* Lin. Lath. Synop. 8. Pen. Zool. 118.
37. Yellow-Hammer. *Emberiza citrinella.* Lin. Lath. Synop. 7. Pen. Zool. 119.
38. Reed Sparrow, or Bunting. *Emberiza schæniculus.* Lin. Pen. Zool. 120.
　　Genus XIV. *Fringilla.*
39. Chaffinch. *Fringilla cælebs.* Lin. Lath. Synop. 10. Pen. Zool. 124.
40. Goldfinch. *Fringilla carduelis.* Lin. Lath. Synop. 51. Pen. Zool. 125.
41. House Sparrow. *Fringilla domestica.* Lin. Lath. Synop. 1. Pen. Zool. 127.
* 42. Siskin. *Fringilla spinus.* Lin.
43. Red headed Linnet. *Fringilla linaria.* Lin. Lath. Synop. 75.
44. Canary Bird. *Fringilla canaria.* Lin. Lath. Synop. 62. Pen. Zool. 347.
　　Genus XV. *Muscicapa.*
45. Pied Flycatcher. *Muscicapa atricapilla.* Lin. Lath. Synop. 2.
　　Genus XVI. *Alauda.*
46. Sky Lark. *Alauda arvensis.* Lin. Lath. Synop. 1. Pen. Zool. 136.
47. Wood Lark. *Alauda arborea.* Lin. Lath. Synop. 3. Pen. Zool. 137.

APPENDIX.

48. TITLARK. *Alauda pratensis.* Lin. Lath. Synop. 5. Pen. Zool. 138.

* 49. FIELD LARK. Lath. Synop. 6. Pen. Zool. 139.

GENUS XVII. *Motacilla.*

¶ 50. BLACK AND WHITE WAGTAIL. *Motacilla alba.* Lin. Pen. Zool. 142.

¶ 51. YELLOW WAGTAIL. *Motacilla flava.* Lin. Lath. Synop. 6. Pen. Zool. 143.

¶ 52. GREY WAGTAIL. *Motacilla boarula.* Lin. Lath. Synop. 4. Pen. Zool. 144.

GENUS XVIII. *Warbler.*

¶53. RED-TAIL. *Motacilla phænicurus.* Lin. Lath. Synop. 11. Pen. Zool. 146.

54. ROBIN RED BREAST. *Motacilla rubicola.* Lin. Lath. Synop. 38.

¶ 55. BLACK-CAP. *Motacilla atricapilla.* Lin. Lath. Synop. 5.

¶ 56. PETTY-CHAPS. *Motacilla hippolais.* Lin. Lath. Synop. 3. Pen. Zool. 149.

57. HEDGE SPARROW. *Motacilla modularis.* Lin. Lath. Synop. 9.

¶ 58. YELLOW, or WILLOW WREN. *Motacilla trochilus.* Lin. Lath. Synop. 147.

* 59. GOLDEN-CRESTED WREN. *Motacilla regulus.* Lin. Lath. Synop. 145.

60. COMMON WREN. *Motacilla troglodytes.* Lin. Lath. Synop. 143.

¶ 61. SEDGE BIRD. *Motacilla salicaria.* Lin. Lath. Synop. 21. Pen. Zool. 155.

¶ 62. WHIN-CHAT. *Motacilla rubetra.* Lin. Lath. Synop. 54. Pen. Zool. 158.

¶ 63. STONE-CHAT. *Motacilla rubicola.* Lin. Lath. Synop. 46. Pen. Zool. 159.

¶ 64. WHITE THROAT. *Motacilla sylvia.* Lin. Lath. Synop. 19. Pen. Zool. 160.

GENUS XIX. *Parus.*

65. OX-EYED TITMOUSE. *Parus major.* Lin. Lath. Synop. 1. Pen. Zool. 162.

66. BLUE TITMOUSE. *Parus cæruleus.* Lin. Lath. Synop. 10. Pen. Zool. 163.

67. COLE TITMOUSE. *Parus ater.* Lin. Lath. Synop. 10. Pen. Zool. 164.

68. MARSH TITMOUSE. *Parus palustris.* Lin. Lath. Synop. 8. Pen. Zool. 165.

69. LONG TAILED TITMOUSE. *Parus caudatus.* Lin. Lath. Synop. 18.

GENUS XX. *Hirundo.*

¶ 70. HOUSE SWALLOW. *Hirundo rustica.* Lin. Lath. Synop. 1. Pen. Zool. 168.

¶ 71. MARTIN. *Hirundo urbica.* Lin. Lath. Synop. 3. Pen. Zool. 169.

¶ 72. SAND SWALLOW. *Hirundo riparia.* Lin. Lath. Synop. 10. Pen. Zool. 170.

¶ 73. SWIFT, or BLACK MARTIN. *Hirundo apus.* Lin. Lath. Synop. 34. Pen. Zool. 171.

GENUS XXI. *Caprimulgus.*

¶ 74. GOATSUCKER. *Caprimulgus europæus.* Lin. Pen. Zool. 172.

ORDER IV. *Columba.*

GENUS XXII. *Columba.*

75. STOCK-DOVE. *Columba ænas.* Lin. Lath. Synop. 5. Pen. Zool. 101.

76. RING DOVE. *Columba palumbus.* Lin. Lath. Synop. 29. Pen. Zool. 102.

ORDER V. *Gallinæ.*

GENUS XXIII. *Pavo.*

77. PEACOCK. *Pavo cristatus.* Lin. Lath. Synop. 1.

GENUS XXIV. *Meleagris.*

78. TURKEY. *Meleagris gallopavo.* Lin. Lath. Synop. 1.

APPENDIX.

GENUS XXV. *Pintado.*

79. GUINEA-HEN. *Numida meleagris.* Lin. Lath. Synop. 1.
GENUS XXVI. *Phasianus.*

80. DOMESTIC COCK. *Phasianus gallus.* Lin. Lath. Synop. 1.

81. COMMON PHEASANT. *Phasianus cholchicus.* Lin. Lath. Synop. 4.
GENUS XXVII. *Tetrao.*

82. RED-GROUS. *Tetrao scoticus.* Lin. Lath. Synop. 13. Pen. Zool. 94.

83. COMMON PARTRIDGE. *Tetrao perdix.* Lin. Lath. Synop. 8. Pen. Zool. 96.

¶ 84. QUAIL. *Tetrao coturnix.* Lin. Lath. Synop. 24. Pen. Zool. 97.
GENUS XXVIII. *Rallus.*

¶ 85. LAND RAIL, or CORN CRAKE. *Rallus crex.* Lin. Lath. Synop. 1. Pen. Zool. 216.
GENUS XXIX. *Charadrius.*

86. YELLOW PLOVER. *Charadrius pluvialis.* Lin. Lath. Synop. 1. Pen. Zool. 208,

87. SEA-LARK. *Charadrius hiaticula.* Lin.

Div. II. *Water Birds.*

ORDER VI. *Grallæ.*

GENUS XXX. *Ardea.*

88. COMMON HERON. *Ardea cinerea.* Lin. Lath. Synop. 50.

* 89. BITTERN, or MIRE DRUM. *Ardea stellaris.* Lin. Pen. Zool. 174.
GENUS XXXI. *Scolopax.*

90. CURLEW. *Scolopax arquata.* Lin. Lath. Synop. 1. Pen. Zool. 176.

91. WHIMBREL. *Scolopax phæopus.* Lin. Lath Synop. 6. Pen. Zool. 177.

¶ 92. WOODCOCK. *Scolopax rusticola.* Lin. Lath. Synop. 1. Pen. Zool. 178

¶ 93. GREENSHANK. *Scolopax glottis.* Lin. Lath. Synop. 18. Pen. Zool. 183.

94. COMMON SNIPE. *Scolopax gallinago.* Lin. Lath. Synop. 6. Pen. Zool. 187.

95. JACK-SNIPE. *Scolopax gallinula.* Lin. Lath. Synop. 8. Pen. Zool. 189.
GENUS XXXII. *Tringa.*

¶ 96. LAPWING, or PEE-WIT. *Tringa vanellus.* Lin. Pen. Zool. 190.

97. GREY PLOVER, *Tringa squatarolla.* Lin. Pen. Zool. 191.

¶ 98. COMMON SANDPIPER. *Tringa hypoleucos.* Lin Pen. Zool. 204.

¶ 99. DUNLIN. *Tringa alpina.* Lin. Lath. Synop. 33. Pen. Zool. 205.

¶ 100. STINT, or PURRE. *Tringa cinclus.* Lin. Pen. Zool. 206.
GENUS XXXIII. *Hæmatopus.*

101. OYSTER CATCHER, or SEA-PIE. *Hæmatopus ostralegus.* Lin.
GENUS XXXIV. *Fulica.*

102. WATER-HEN. *Fulica chloropus.* Lin. Lath. Synop. 12.

¶ 103. WATER RAIL. *Rallus aquaticus.* Lin. Pen. Zool. 214.

104. WATER-OUZEL. *Sturnus cinclus.* Lin.

105, COMMON COOT. *Fulica atra.* Lin. Lath. Synop. 1. Pen. Zool. 220.

APPENDIX.

ORDER VII. *Anferes.*

GENUS XXXV. *Anas.*

* 106 WILD SWAN. *Anas cygnus.* Lin. Lath. Synop. 1. Pen. Zool. 264.

107. TAME SWAN. *Anas cygnus manfuetus.* Lin. Pen. Zool. 265.

108. WILD GOOSE. *Anas anfer.* Lin. Lath. Synop. 21. Pen. Zool. 266.

109. TAME GOOSE. *Anas anfer domefticus.* Lin. Lath. Synop. 21.

¶ 110. SCOTER, or BLACK DUCK. *Anas nigra.* Lin. Pen. Zool. 273.

111. SHELDRAKE. *Anas tadornea.* Lin. Lath. Synop. 51. Pen. Zool. 278.

¶ 112. WILD DUCK, or MALLARD. *Anas bofchas.* Lin. Pen. Zool. 279.

¶ 113. WIGEON. *Anas penelope.* Lin. Lath. Synop. 63. Pen. Zool. 286.

¶ 114. TEAL. *Anas crecca.* Lin. Lath. Synop. 88. Pen. Zool. 290.

* 115. TUFTED DUCK. *Anas fuligula.* Lin.

GENUS XXXVI. *Alca.*

¶ 116. AWK, or RAZOR-BILL. *Alca torda.* Lin. Lath. Synop. 5.

¶ 117. PUFFIN, or SEA PARROT. *Alca arctica.* Lin. Pen. Zool. 232.

GENUS XXXVII. *Colymbus.*

¶ 118. GUILLEMOT. *Colymbus troile.* Lin. Lath. Synop. 1. Pen. Zool. 234.

¶ 119. BLACK GUILLEMOT. *Colymbus grylle.* Lin. Lath. Synop. 3. Pen. Zool. 236.

* 120. SPECKLED DIVER, or LOON. *Colymbus ftellatus.* Lin.

121. DOBCHICK, or LITTLE GREBE. *Colymbus minutus.* Lin. Pen. Zool. 226.

GENUS XXXVIII. *Sterna.*

¶ 122. GREATER TERN. *Sterna hirundo.* Lin. Lath. Synop. 14. Pen. Zool. 254.

¶ 123. LESSER TERN, or SEA SWALLOW. *Sterna minuta.* Lin. Pen. Zool. 255.

GENUS XXXIX. *Larus.*

124. BLACK BACKED GULL. *Larus marinus.* Lin.

125. HERRING GULL. *Larus fufcus.* Lin. Pen. Zool. 246.

126. WAGEL, or GREY GULL. *Larus nævius.* Lin. Pen. Zool. 247.

127. COMMON GULL. *Larus canus.* Lin. Lath. Synop. 8. Pen. Zool. 249.

128. BLACK HEADED, or PEWIT GULL. *Larus ridibundus.* Lin. Pen. Zool. 252.

129. KITTIWAKE, or ANNETT. *Larus riffa.* Linnæus.

¶ 130. TARROCK. *Larus tridactylus.* Lin. Bewick, vol. 2, p. 231.

* 131. BROWN GULL. *Larus catarractes.* Lin. Do. p. 233.

GENUS XL. *Procellaria.*

* 132. STORMY PETREL. *Procellaria pelegica.* Lin.

GENUS XLI. *Pelecanus.*

¶ 133. BLACK CORMORANT. *Pelicanus carbo.* Lin. Pen. Zool. 291.

* 134. SHAG. *Pelicanus graculus.* Lin. Lath. Synop. 14.

N. B. WE have omitted fome birds which are feen in this diftrict only occafionally, during their migratory excurfions. Since the above catalogue was drawn up for the prefs, an eagle of the follow-

APPENDIX.

ing remarkable dimenfions was fhot, in December 1807, at *Staingate*, near Danby-Lodge, (the fporting feat of the Right Hon. Lord Vifcount Downe) viz.

	F.	I.
Breadth between the tips of the wings,	6	10
Length from the beak to the tip of the tail,	3	10
Extreme breadth of the tail,	2	3
Height, in an erect pofture,	2	7
Weight, fixteen pounds, two ounces.		

The colour, a mixed brown and white; the back nearly white. This extraordinary bird, which
we conjecture to be the SEA EAGLE, *falco offifragus* of Linnæus, has been put into a ftate of prefervation by Mr. Frank, at Danby-Lodge.

INDEX.

A

INDEX.

INDEX.

Subscribers Names.

—∘∘∘∘∘—

A

The Right Hon. Dowager Lady Amherst, *large paper.*

John Arden, Esq. Pepper-Hall, Yorkshire, *large paper*

Geo. Allan, Esq. Blackwell-grange, Durham.

John Allison, Esq. Stockton.

The Rev. Christ. Anstey, M. A. Norton, *large paper.*

The Rev. R. M. Atkinson, M. A. Croft, Yorkshire.

The Rev. John Atkinson, Hartforth, Yorkshire.

The Rev. Daniel Addison, Vicar of Leek, Yorkshire.

Miss Ambler, Bishop-Middleham, Durham, *large paper.*

Mr. Watson Alcock, Surgeon, Stockton.

Mr. R. Appleton, Surgeon, Stokesley.

Mr. Aiskill, Newport, Yorkshire.

Mr. R. C. Alderson, Richmond, Yorkshire.

Mr. John Andrew, Saltburn, Yorkshire.

B

The Rt. Rev. the Lord Bishop of Bangor, *large paper.*

Sir George Bowyer, Bart. Christ Ch. Oxford, *large paper.*

The Honourable George.Bowes, *large paper.*

The Honourable Thomas Bowes, *large paper.*

Sir Wastel Brisco, Bart. Crofton-place, Cumberland, *large paper.*

The Rev. Jonathan Boucher, M. A. Epsom, Surry.

The Rev. Charles Baillie, M. A. Archdeacon of Cleveland.

The Rev. F. Blackburn, M. A. Vicar of Brignal, Yorkshire.

The Rev. John Brewster, M. A. Greatham, Durham.

The Rev. J. Brownfield, Whitby, Yorkshire.

William Bethell, Esq. Langton Hall, Yorkshire.

Mrs. Bethell, ditto, *large paper.*

Thomas Bland, Esq, Kippax-Park, Yorkshire, *large paper.*

William Burgh, Esq. York.

John Brown, Esq. Ormesby, Yorkshire.

William Bray, Esq. Great Russel-street, London.

Matthew Butterwick, Esq. Thirsk.

John Bell, Esq. Thirsk.

Humphrey Bowles, Esq. Merton Coll. Oxford, *large paper.*

Henry Barton, Esq. Carleton, Yorkshire.

Henry Butterfield, Esq. Durham.

George Brown, Esq. Stockton.

Rowland Burdon, Esq. Castle-Eden, *large paper.*

Admiral Brunton, Stockton.

John Boulby, Esq. Aislaby, near Whitby, *large paper.*

Richard Bell, Esq. Sellaby, Durham.

Mrs. Bramwell, Yarm, *large paper.*

Mr. John Benson, Whitby.

Mr. John Boulton, Chester-le-street, Durham.

Mr. Joseph Bulmer, South Shields.

Mr. Timothy Bulmer, junior, ditto.

Mr. George Bell, Newport, Yorkshire.

Mr. Ralph Boville, Swainsby, do.

Mr. George Brigham, Rudby, do.

Mr. John Beardshaw, Marsk, do.

Mr. John Bird, Landscape Painter, Whitby.

Mr. Miles Brown, Surgeon, Stokesley,

C

The Rev. Robert Croft, M. A. Residentiary, York.

The Rev. Richard Chapman, Easington, Yorkshire.

Robert Crowe, Esq. Kipling, ditto.

Thomas Crathorne, Esq. Crathorne, 2 *copies large paper.*

Robert Chaloner, Esq. Guisbrough.

Mrs. Chaloner, Guisbrough.

John Chaloner, Esq. Guisbrough.

John Colpits, Esq. Streatham, Durham.

Robert Clarke, Esq. Attorney at Law, Stockton.

Mr. William Clarke, Bookseller, London, *large paper.*

Mr. A. H. Colling, Hurworth, Durham.

Mr. James Crowe, Stockton.

Mr. Robert Christopher, Stockton, *large paper.*

Mr. John Christopher, Bishop-Auckland.

Messrs. Christopher & Jennett, Booksellers, Stockton.

Messrs. Cooke, Booksellers, Oxford, 2 *copies large paper.*

SUBSCRIBERS' NAMES.

Mr. Chilton, Billingham, Durham, *large paper*.
Mr. John Chipchase, Stockton.
Mr. Matthew Crowe, Stockton.
J. C. Coates, Esq. Whitby.
Mr. Joseph Claxton, Yarm.
Mr. Benjamin Claxton, Stokesley.
Mr. Coates, Attorney at Law, Stokesley.
Mr. Thomas Claxton, York.

D

The Right Hon. Lord Dundas, Upleatham-Hall.
The Right Hon. Lord Duncannon, Christ Church, Oxford, *large paper*.
The Right Hon. Lord Viscount Downe, *large paper*.
William Danby, Esq. Swinton, Yorkshire, *large paper*.
Peter Denys, Esq. Fremington, ditto, *large paper*.
Henry John Dickens, Esq. Barrister at Law, *large paper*.
Richard Dixon, Esq. Middleham, Yorkshire.
Rev. ―― Davison, M. A. Brancepeth, Durham.
Rev. Joseph Dawson, Sedgefield, ditto.
Rev. Thomas Dockray, Vicar of Well, Yorkshire.
Mr. John Dales, Druggist, York.
Mr. Geo. Perrott D'uxelle, Yarm.
Mr. Daniel Duck, Stokesley.
Mr. Richard Dickson, Stockton.
Mr. Geo. Dodds, Boulby-Allum-Works, Yorkshire.
Mr. Robert Davison, Topcliffe, Yorkshire.
Mr. Duck, Druggist, Stokesley.

E

The Rev. John Eyre, M. A. Residentiary, York.
The Rev. W. Elstob, L. L. B. Trinity-Hall, Cambridge.
The Rev. Thomas Ewbank, M. A. Stockton.
The Rev. ―― Ella, M. A. Fell, of Pembroke Hall, Cambridge.
Mr. Thomas Ewbank, Attorney at Law, Malton.

F

Sir William Foulis, Bart. Ingleby Manor, 2 *copies large paper*,
David Burton Fowler, Esq. Yarm, *large paper*.
F. T. Foster, Esq. Christ Church, Oxford, *large paper*.
Walter Fawkes, Esq. Farnley-Hall, Yorkshire.
The Rev. Isaac Fearon, Whitby.
The Rev. R. Frankland, Guisbrough.
The Rev. Robert Fawcitt, West Rounton, Yorkshire.
Mr. Thomas Fawell, Yarm.
Mr. Benjamin Flounders, Yarm.
Mr. Michael Friar, Reeth, Yorkshire.
Mr. J. A. Fletcher, Surgeon, Guisbrough.

Mr. Flounders, Liverpool, 2 *copies large paper*.
Mr. Favell, Faceby, Yorkshire.
Mr. Jos. Frank, Attorney at Law, Stockton.
Mr. Richardson Ferrand, Druggist, Stockton.
Mr. Christopher Fowler, Yarm.
Mr. Robert Fairbridge, Surgeon, Yarm.

G

Sir Henry Goodrick, Bart. Ribston.
R. Gough, Esq. F. A. S. Director.
Francis Gibson, Esq. F. A. S. Whitby.
Robert Greenhill, Esq. M. P. for Thirsk.
John Grenside, Esq. London.
The Rev. Ralph Grenside, M. A. Rector of Crathorne.
The Rev. Jeremiah Grice, M. A. Vicar of Rudby.
Mr. Grey, Stockton.
Mr. William Grenside, Surgeon, Whitby.
Mr. Daniel Graves, Threlkeld, Cumberland.
Mr. Thomas Graves, London.

H

The Right Hon. Lord Harewood, Harewood House, *large paper*.
The Right Hon. Lady Harewood, do. *large paper*.
Sir Robert D'arcy Hildyard, Bart. Sedbury.
W. H. H. Hartley, Esq. Belvedere, Bath, *large paper*.
George W. Hartley, Esq. York.
Michael Hardcastle, Esq. Haughton, Durham.
G. Hutton, Esq. Thornaby Grange, 2 *copies large paper*.
Thomas Hustler, Esq. Acklam-Hall, Yorkshire.
G. L. Hollingsworth, Esq. Darlington.
John Hogg, Esq. Norton, Durham.
Shaftoe J. Hedley, Esq. Shaftoe House, Durham.
George Hubback, Esq. Cowpan, Durham, *large paper*.
George Hartley, Esq. York.
Fowler Hicks, Esq. London, *large paper*.
Miss Hall, York.
Mrs. Hale, Plantation, Yorkshire.
Miss Harrison, Guisbrough.
The Rev. James Hewgill, M. A. Smeaton, *large paper*.
The Rev. N. Hollingsworth, M. A. Hartlepool.
The Rev. J. Harrison, Vicar of Marske, Yorkshire.
The Rev. J. Harriman, Gainford, Durham.
The Rev. H. Hildyard, Stokesley, *large paper*.
Mr. Henry Hirst, Attorney at Law, Northallerton,
Mr. Thomas E. Hixon, Attorney at Law, Darlington.
Mr. Edward Heelis, Manchester.
Mr. John Hixon, Billingham, Durham.
Mr. John Hutchinson, Stockton.
George Hutchinson, Esq. Stockton.

SUBSCRIBERS' NAMES.

Mr. Henry Hutchinson, jun. Stockton, *large. paper.*

Mr. William Hutchinson, Newsham, Yorkshire.

Mr. Joseph Hickson, Guisbrough.

Messrs. Hanwell and Parker, Oxford, 2 *copies large paper.*

Mr. Jon. Hornby, Schoolmaster, Danby, Yorkshire.

Mr. Thomas Haw, Stockton.

Mr. David Hobkirk, Preston-Hall, Durham.

J.

The Rev. C. Jackson, D. D. Dean of Ch. Ch. Oxford.

The Hon. C. Jenkinson. Christ Church, Oxford, *large paper.*

Sir Alexander Ramsay Irvine, Bart. Harlsey-Hall.

W. Ward Jackson, Esq. Normanby-Hall, *large paper.*

W. Raper Janson, Esq. Stockton, *large paper.*

Mr. Andrew Irwine, Skelton, Yorkshire.

Mr. William Jackson, Whitby.

Mr. Richard Jackson, Northallerton.

Mr. Anthony Jameson, Surgeon, Yarm.

Messrs. F. Jollie & Sons, Booksellers, Carlisle, 6 *copies.*

K.

Mr. Thomas Kirton, Stockton.

Mr. Richard Kingston, Arncliffe, Yorkshire.

L

The Hon. W. H. Lyttleton, Ch. Ch. Oxford, *large paper.*

W. Lygon, Esq. St. James's Square, London, *large paper.*

R. J. Lambton, Esq. M. P. Lambton, Durham.

Miss Lambton, Normanby, Yorkshire.

Mrs. Lewin, Ridgeway, Hampshire.

Sir John Lawson, Bart. Brough-Hall, *large paper.*

John Lowther, Esq. Swillington, Yorkshire.

T. F. Lewis, Esq. Harpton Court, *large paper.*

George Lynn, Esq. Southwick, Northamptonshire.

The Rev. W. Lipscombe, M. A. Rector of Welbury.

Mr. J. Liddell, Durham.

Mr. Langdale, Bookseller, Northallerton.

Mr. John Lincoln, Easby, Yorkshire.

F. Lumley, Esq. Stockton.

M

The Right Hon. Earl of Mansfield, *large paper.*

The Right Hon. Lord Mulgrave, *large paper.*

The Hon., Lady Milbank, Halnaby, *large paper*

The Hon. and Rev. Thomas Monson, Bedale, *large paper.*

The Rev. M. Marsh, M. A. Christ Church, Oxford, *large paper.*

The Rev. W. Meynell, Ellingham, Northumberland, *large paper.*

The Rev. W. Moore, Acklam, Yorkshire.

The Rev. James Mewburne, M. A Acomb, near Hexham.

William Marwood, Esq. Busby Hall, 2 *copies.*

Mrs. Mauleverer, Arncliffe-Hall, Yorkshire.

Edward Meynell, Esq. Friarage, Yarm, *large paper.*

Thomas Meynell, Esq. Friarage, Yarm, *large paper;*

Henry Maire, Esq. Lartington-Hall, *large paper.*

Charles Mitchell, Esq. Forcett, Yorkshire, *large paper.*

John Matthews, Esq. Tynemouth.

J. Masterman, Esq. Stokesley.

William Markham, Esq. Becca Lodge, *large paper.*

Mr. W. Middleton, Whitby, *large paper.*

Mr. Mowbray, Kirkleatham, Yorkshire.

Mr. Richard Myles, Yarm, *large paper.*

Mr. Thomas Myers, Scarbrough.

N

The Hon. Mr. Nassau, London, *large paper.*

The Honourable R. Neville, Ch. Ch. Oxford, *large paper.*

Mr. Joseph Neville, Crathorne, Yorkshire.

Mr. Thomas Neasham, Stokesley.

O

Mr. Oldfield, Attorney at Law, Stockton.

P

The Rev. Matthew Parrington, Rector of Birkby, Yorkshire.

The Rev. John Parrington, Marton, ditto.

The Rev. —— Peacock, Thornton Hall, Durham.

Miss Pemberton, Low Middleton Hall, *large paper.*

John Parker, Esq. Trinity College, Oxford, *large paper.*

Fotherley Pannell, M. D. Ayton, Yorkshire

William Prissick, Esq. Shrewsbury.

John Peacock, Esq. Norton, Durham, *large paper.*

Mr. W. Powell, Attorney at Law, Stokesley, *large paper.*

Mr. James Proctor, Yarm.

Mr. Joseph Proctor, South Shields, *large paper.*

Mr. William Phillips, Seamer, Yorkshire.

Mr. Thomas Prest, Bedale.

Mr. William Perkins, Stockton.

R.

Sir John Russell, Bart. Checkers, *large paper.*

G. Russell, Esq. Leven Grove, 2 *copies large paper.*

The Rev. Matthew Raine, D. D. Charter House, London.

SUBSCRIBERS' NAMES.

Jonathan Raine, Esq. M. P. London.
Bart. Rudd, Esq. Marton Lodge, 2 copies large paper.
Thomas Rudd, Esq. Tolesby, Yorkshire, large paper.
Mr. Thomas Rayner, Armin-Hall, Yorkshire.
Mr. W. Rayner, Edward-Street, Portman-Square, London.
Mr. John Rayner, Druggist, Thirsk.
Mr. Aaron Richardson, Stockton.
Mr. Richard Richardson, Carlisle.
Mr. Ridley, Richmond, Yorkshire.
Mr. Reeve, London, large paper.
Leo. Raisbeck, Esq. Attorney at Law, Stockton.
Mr. John Richardson, Stockton, 2 copies.
Mr. Rigg, Attorney at Law, Northallerton.
J. Russell Rowntree, Esq. Stockton, large paper.

S

The Right Honourable Earl Spencer, large paper.
Sir Mark Masterman Sykes, Bart. large paper.
Sir Martin Stapylton, Bart. Myton, large paper.
The Rev. Geo. Sayer, M. A. Egglescliffe, Durham.
The Rev. W. Smith, M. A. Rector of Hilderwell, Yorkshire.
The Rev. John Starkey, M. A. Lecturer, of Stockton.
The Rev. Thomas Saul, M. A. Lancaster.
George Sutton, Esq. Stockton, large paper.
William Sleigh, Esq. Stockton, large paper.
Robert Surtees, Esq. Durham, large paper.
Charles Spearman, Esq. Thornley, Durham.
Thomas Simon Scroope, Esq. Danby, large paper.
Robert Surtees, Esq. F. A. S. Mainsforth, large paper.
Grenville Smith, Esq. Jervaux Abbey.
Richard Strangwayes, Esq. Well, Yorkshire.
Mrs. Selby, Biddlestone, large paper.
Mrs. Scurfield, Stockton.
Robert Stephenson, Esq. Brotton, Yorkshire.
Mr. Jonathan Ward Sanders, Whitby.
Mr. Thomas Spence, London.
Mr. Sanderson, Manchester.
Mr. Geo: Sanderson, Handale Abbey, Yorkshire.
Mr. Thomas Simpson, Leven Bridge, ditto.
Mr. Richard Smith, Egton Bridge, ditto.
Mr. Isaac Spencer, Druggist, York.
Mr. George Smith, Piersbridge, Durham.
Mr. Mark Stainsby, Yarm.
William Strickland, Esq. York.
Gordon Skelly, Esq. Hurworth, Durham, large paper.
Thomas Simpson, Esq: Newham, Yorkshire.
Michael Scarth, Esq. Castle-Eden, Durham.

Mr. W. L. Sanderson, Guisbrough.
Mr Christopher Stonehouse, Yarm.
Stockton Book-club.

T

Sir Charles Turner, Bart. Kirkleatham, 2 copies large paper.
Sir H. V. Tempest, Bart. M. P. Winyard, large paper.
J. Townley, Esq. F. R. S. F. A. S. Devonshire Place, London.
The Rev. J. Thornhill, M. A. Ainderby-Steeple, large paper.
Thomas Tunstall, Esq. Stockton.
Captain Thrush.
The Rev. Henry Taylorson, Stokesley.
Mr. Todd, Bookseller, York, 2 copies.
Mr. Tesseyman, Bookseller, York.
Mrs. Thompson, Welton, near Hull.
Mr. John Tennant, Stockton.
Mr. Leonard Tinkler, Stockton.

W

Sir George Warrender, Bart. Ch. Ch. Oxford, large paper.
The Rev. C. Wyvill, Burton-Hall, large paper.
The Rev. F. Wilkinson, M. A. Vicar of Bardsey, Yorkshire.
The Rev. —— Wastell, M. A. Fellow of Clare-Hall, Cambridge.
The Rev. W: Wharton, M. A. Gilling, large paper.
The Rev. T. Pym Williamson, M. A. Guisbrough.
Miss Williamson, Guisbrough.
John Wharton, Esq. M. P. Skelton Castle, 2 copies large paper.
Major General Wharton, 21st Light Dragoons, large paper.
Thomas Wilkinson, Esq. Mildenhall-place, Suffolk.
William Wilson, Esq. Ayton, Yorkshire.
John Wilkinson, Esq. Stockton.
John Waldy, Esq. Yarm.
Rowland Webster, Esq. jun. Stockton.
Edward Wolley, Esq. York, large paper.
Robert Wilkinson, Esq. Stockton.
N. Waterhouse, Esq. Liverpool, large paper.
W. Wilson, Esq. Berwick upon Tees, large paper.
William Welbanke, Esq. Newcastle, large paper.
William Whytehead, Esq. York.
Mr. James Wilkinson, Stockton.
Mr. John Wilson, Stockton.

SUBSCRIBERS' NAMES.

Mr W. Walker, Attorney at Law, Thirsk.
Mr. W. Wilson, jun. Surgeon, Guisbrough.
Miss Wilson, Rotherham, Yorkshire.
Mrs. Walters, Yarm.
Mrs. Wood, Coedriglian, Glamorganshire.
Mr. W. Wright, Baldersby Brooms, Yorkshire.
Mr. Thomas Wright, Richmond.
Mr. W. Wells, Booth-Ferry, Yorkshire.
Mr. Peter Wells, Hull.
Mr. Cuthbert Wigham, Yarm.

Mr. Wardell, Attorney at Law, Guisbrough.
Mr. Wilson, Architect, Sunderland.
Mr. Matthew Wadeson, Stockton.
Mr. William Wetherill, Stockton
Mr. William Watson, Stockton.

Y

The Hon. and Most Rev. Dr. Vernon, Lord Archbishop of York, *large paper.*
The very Rev. the Dean of York, *large paper.*
York Minster Library, *large paper.*

ERRATA.

PAGE 32, line 9 from bottom, *for* Rolte Cross, *read* Ralph's Cross—P. 33, l. 21, *for* Καλευξον, *read* Καλευιον—P. 33, l. 4 from bottom. *for* Calai-iii, *read* Calai-ui—P. 39, l. 8 from bottom, *for* circumstances, *read* circumstance—P. 63, l. 12, *for* toll-both, *read* toll-booth—P. 79, l. 3, et alibi, *for* monastry, *read* monastery—P. 82, l. 4, *for* Charles I. *read* Charles II.—P. 204, l. 13, *for* by, *read* of—P. 210. l. 2. *for* considerably, *read* considerable—P. 219 l. 9, from bottom, *for* moss thown, *read* mass thrown—P. 268, l. 4 from bottom, *for* was, *read* lies.—P. 302, l. 1 of the biographical note, *for* Earl of Mulgrave, *read* Baron Mulgrave—P. 306, et alibi, *for* Earl of Mulgrave, *read* Lord Mulgrave—P. 345, l. 8, *for* Thomas Stephenson, Esq. *read* Stephenson Thomas, Esq.—P. 381, l. 8, *for* segetus taxunter, *read* segetes texuntur—P. 401, l; 10, *for* prevente, *read* presente—P. 408, l. 3, *for* charter, *read* charter of free warren—P. 411, l. 10, *for* meulding, *read* mouldering—P. 430, bottom line, *for* ore, *read* more.

ERRATA IN THE APPENDIX.

No. 3, *for* falco druginosus, *read* falco æruginosus.—No. 10. *for* strix crachyotus, *read* strix brachyotus —No. 24. *for* Silla europæa, *read* sitta europæa—Genus X. *for* starnus, *read* sturnus.

FINIS.

Printed by F. Jollie & Sons, Carlisle.